THE ATHENIAN TRIBUTE LISTS

THE
ATHENIAN TRIBUTE LISTS

BY

BENJAMIN DEAN MERITT
Institute for Advanced Study

H. T. WADE-GERY
New College, Oxford

MALCOLM FRANCIS McGREGOR
University of Cincinnati

VOLUME III

THE AMERICAN SCHOOL OF CLASSICAL STUDIES AT ATHENS
PRINCETON, NEW JERSEY
1950

To

WILLIAM TUNSTALL SEMPLE

AND

LOUISE TAFT SEMPLE

*who have fostered
these studies for
more than twenty years*

CONTENTS

PREFACE

The second and third volumes of *The Athenian Tribute Lists* were prepared concurrently during the year 1947-1948, when the authors were able to be together once again at the Institute for Advanced Study in Princeton. The first two volumes are, it is obvious, directed primarily towards the specialist; this third volume, we hope, will have a wider appeal.

Our chief purpose has been to present a history of the Athenian Empire in narrative form, and to accomplish this we have deliberately divided the book into three parts. Thus we have endeavoured to remove, to an extent, the discussion of special and technical problems from the narrative section. In Part I we have placed the additional commentary on the tribute and assessment lists, and it is here, for the most part, that we explain the changes which we have made in the texts of Volume I and printed in Volume II. Part II embraces those problems which arise from evidence outside the tribute records, and which, it seemed, might interrupt the story in Part III. A strict division is of course impossible, and Part III will be found to contain its share of argument.

In the composition of Part III we have tried to keep in mind the needs of readers who have little or no Greek; it is our hope that the book will not be restricted to classical scholars and students, but will prove informative to laymen as well. We have therefore, in Part III, resorted freely to translations and have relegated passages of Greek to parentheses and footnotes. Our guiding principle has been that a knowledge of Greek should not be a prerequisite for an intelligent reading of at least the first nine chapters of Part III. Although we cannot claim that the reading is always easy, we are confident that one who wishes to do so will have no real difficulty in understanding what we have to say.

The Athenian Empire has been a fertile field to historians and others, and the literary yield is indeed rich. In acknowledging our debts to our predecessors we have not attempted to be exhaustive; in general, we cite the latest and the fundamental discussions of a given problem. The more complete bibliography, however, is reserved for Volume IV, where it will accompany the detailed index to the first three volumes. This work is already in progress and its publication, we trust, will not be long delayed.

Yet there is one book which merits particular mention here. A. W. Gomme's *Commentary on Thucydides*, Volume I, has been before us continuously and we could scarcely acknowledge in footnotes the great contribution which it has made to the study of fifth-century history. Even when we disagree with his conclusions, Gomme has set out the evidence and stated the problem so clearly that our own path has been made relatively firm.

ix

It is pleasant to have another opportunity of expressing our gratitude to those benefactors who, by material and intellectual aid, contributed to the writing of Volumes II and III. Meritt recalls his debt to the Master and Fellows of Balliol, to the Electors of the George Eastman Professorship, and to the President and Board of Directors of the Association of American Rhodes Scholars who administer the Eastman Fund. Wade-Gery extends his thanks to the Visitatorial Board of Oxford University, to the Warden and Fellows of New College, and to the Institute for Advanced Study. McGregor acknowledges his indebtedness to the University of Cincinnati, to the John Simon Guggenheim Memorial Foundation, to Professor and Mrs. William T. Semple, to the Charles Phelps Taft Memorial Fund, and to Mrs. John L. Caskey and Cedric G. Boulter.

That we have been able to complete the writing within a comparatively brief period of time is a tribute to the skill and loyalty of Mrs. Wesley Dauncey and Miss Virginia Spurrier, who prepared the difficult manuscript, Greek and English, for the printer. The J. H. Furst Company of Baltimore has again given its constantly expert attention to the presswork of the volume. As we said in the Preface of Volume II, it is always a privilege to submit a manuscript to them, and we are especially grateful to Mr. Fred Furst, their skilled compositor. In reading the proofs and verifying the references we have been greatly aided by Ruth Allen, of the University of Cincinnati, Donald W. Bradeen, of Washington and Jefferson College, and Daphne Hereward, of the Institute for Advanced Study. The publication has been sponsored by the American School of Classical Studies at Athens and has been under the general supervision of Paul Clement, Managing Editor of its Publications. To him and to the School we remain under a deep sense of obligation.

Benjamin D. Meritt
H. T. Wade-Gery
Malcolm F. McGregor

Institute for Advanced Study
Princeton, New Jersey
October 1, 1948

ADDENDA ET CORRIGENDA

1. On I viii read F. N. Pryce instead of H. N. Pryce.

2. On I xxxii read Ianell instead of Iannell as the editor of Vergil.

3. On I 34 read Fig. 42 for the photograph of No. 64.

4. On I 187 the reference to *Cl. Phil.* in the bibliography of List 20 should be XXI (1926).

5. On I 483, Col. II, read Θετταλὸς instead of Θέτταλος.

6. On I 523, Col. I, *s. v.* Μυριναῖοι παρὰ Κύμην read Smyrna instead of Sardis.

7. On I 529, Col. II, *s. v.* Ὀλύνθιοι read Ἐπετηρὶς instead of Ἐπιτηρὶς.

8. On I 548, Col. I, read Mytilene and Mytilenaean instead of Mitylene and Mitylenaean.

9. On II 29 (25 III 64) read ἀπὸ instead of ἀπό.

10. On II 40 (A9, line 9) read ἐς instead of ἐς.

11. On II 42 (A9 II 115) read [Ὀ]ρανι[έται] and identify with the Ouranion in the Karic Chersonese; cf. II 87.

12. On II 83, Col. II, read Χε[ρρονεσῖται] instead of Χε[ρρονησῖται].

13. On II 86, *s. v.* Κολοφώνιοι, add a reference to Leicester B. Holland, " Colophon," *Hesperia*, XIII (1944), pp. 91-171.

14. On II 87, Col. II, add the lemma Στυρῆς with a note that William Wallace has shown good reason not to emend the names Αἰγίλεα of Herodotos, VI, 101, and Αἰγλείη of Herodotos, VI, 107. Cf. *Hesperia*, XVI (1947), pp. 130-133.

15. On II 88 the second testimonium under Aischines should be T3 and the first line should read as follows: T3 (II, 175): πάλιν δὲ εἰς πόλεμον διὰ Μεγαρέας πεισθέντες καταστῆναι, καὶ τὴν χώραν τμηθῆναι.

16. On II 103 add to T76 line 3 of *I. G.*, I², 97: [τ]ὸν ἐπιφορὸν, and date the inscription in 430/29 or earlier. The text has nothing to do with Melos, but is concerned solely with Athenian tribute and with the organization of an expedition to make the collection of it effective. The selection of soldiers ἐκ τὸν ἐλεχότον for this expedition recalls Aristotle, Ἀθ. Πολ., 24, 3: ἄλλαι δὲ νῆες αἱ τοὺς φόρους ἄγουσαι τοὺς ἀπὸ τοῦ κυάμου δισχιλίους ἄνδρας. It is tempting to associate these texts, if the reading φόρους in the papyrus can be retained. In that case we should include Aristotle, Ἀθ. Πολ., 24, 3, among our testimonia.

17. On I 549, *s.v.* Σκαβλαῖοι, we equated tributary Skabla with the Skabala of Theopompos. In a dissertation entitled *A History of Chalkis to 338 B. C.*, presented to the faculty of the University of Cincinnati in 1947, D. W. Bradeen has argued that Skabla was a Chalkidian colony and that Skabala was an Eretrian dependency in Euboia, not to be identified with the tributary Σκαβλαῖοι.

18. On II 56 (line 45) read [δέ]κα instead of [δέ]κα.

19. On II 58 (lines 6-7) read [αἰσυμνέτει] instead of [αἰσυμνέτοι].

20. On II 60 (line 86) read ἐπιτ[ελê]ται instead of ἐπιτ[έλε]ται.

21. On II 65 (V, line 3) read [ἀναγράψαντας] instead of [ἀναγράψαντες].

22. Adolf Wilhelm has proposed different restorations in D2 and D19 in *J. H. S.*, LXVIII (1948), pp. 124-129.

23. On II 67 (D14, § 4) read ἀτ[ιμίας] instead of [ἀτιμίας].

24. On I 580 and II 103 (T77) we now question whether lines 47-49 and 54-55 of *I. G.*, I², 108 have anything to do with the ἀπαρχή from the tribute. This has been the traditional opinion (cf. also I 525-526), but the evidence must be discussed at length elsewhere. All the restorations in the latter part of this inscription have been made with too long a line.

TABLE OF ABBREVIATIONS

This table is supplementary to the Table of Abbreviations printed in *A. T. L.*, I, pp. xxi-xxxii. It contains (1) expansions of those abbreviations which we have employed in Vols. II and III but not in I, (2) bibliographical information concerning editions of those ancient authors cited in Vols. II and III but not in I, and (3) bibliographical information concerning ancient authorities cited in Vol. I, but for whom we have used different texts in Vols. II and III.

A. T. L. = Benjamin Dean Meritt, H. T. Wade-Gery, Malcolm Francis McGregor, The Athenian Tribute Lists, Vol. I (Cambridge, Mass., 1939), Vols. II-III (Princeton, New Jersey, 1949 and 1950)

Abh. Gött. = Abhandlungen der historisch-philologischen Klasse der königlichen Gesellschaft der Wissenschaften zu Göttingen

Aevum = Aevum, Rassegna di scienze storiche linguistiche e filologiche, pubblicata per cura della facoltà di lettere dell' università cattolica del sacro cuore (Milan)

Ἀθήναιον = Ἀθήναιον, σύγγραμμα περιοδικόν, Vols. I-X, 1872-1881, published at Athens

Aischylos = Aeschyli septem quae supersunt Tragoediae, recensuit Gilbertus Murray (Oxford, Clarendon Press, 1937)

Androtion — Edited by Müller, *F. H. G.*, I (Paris, 1885), pp. 371-377

Apollodoros = Sir James George Fraser, Apollodorus, the Library, with an English translation (2 vols., The Loeb Classical Library, London and New York, 1921)

Arch. Anz. = Archäologischer Anzeiger, Beiblatt zum Jahrbuch des deutschen archäologischen Instituts

Aristophanes — We cite fragment 220 (T38h) from Kock, *Comicorum Atticorum Fragmenta*, I (Leipzig, 1880), p. 447

Aristotle, Pol. = H. Rackham, Aristotle, the Politics, with an English translation (The Loeb Classical Library, London and New York, 1932)

Ast = Lexicon Platonicum sive Vocum Platonicarum Index, condidit D. Fridericus Astius (3 vols., Leipzig, 1835-1838)

Athenaeum = Athenaeum, Studii periodici di Letteratura e Storia dell' Antichità . . . pubblicati sotto gli auspicii della R. Università di Pavia

Austin, Stoichedon Style = R. P. Austin, The Stoichedon Style in Greek Inscriptions (London, 1938)

Barber, Ephorus = G. L. Barber, The Historian Ephorus (Cambridge University Press, 1935)

Bauer, Themistokles = Adolf Bauer, Themistokles, Studien und Beiträge zur griechischen Historiographie und Quellenkunde (Merseburg, 1881)

Bechtel = Friedrich Bechtel, Die historischen Personennamen des Griechischen bis zur Kaiserzeit (Halle, 1917)

Beloch, Attische Politik = Julius Beloch, Die attische Politik seit Perikles (Leipzig, 1884)

Bericht über die . . . Verhandlungen der . . . Akademie der Wissenschaften zu Berlin = Bericht über die zur Bekanntmachung geeigneten Verhandlungen der königl. preuss. Akademie der Wissenschaften zu Berlin (sometimes catalogued as Monatsberichte der Akademie)

Berve, Das Alexanderreich = Helmut Berve, Das Alexanderreich auf prosopographischer Grundlage (2 vols., Munich, 1926)

Berve, Miltiades = Helmut Berve, " Miltiades, Studien zur Geschichte des Mannes und seiner Zeit," Hermes, Einzelschriften, II (Berlin, 1937)

Bétant, Lexicon = E.-A. Bétant, Lexicon Thucydideum (2 vols., Geneva, 1843-1847)

Binneboessel, Urkundenreliefs = Rosemarie Binneboessel, Studien zu den attischen Urkundenreliefs des 5. und 4. Jahrhunderts (Diss., Leipzig, 1932)

Capps Studies = Classical Studies Presented to Edward Capps on his Seventieth Birthday (Princeton University Press, December 21, 1936)

Casson, Cat. Acrop. Museum = Stanley Casson, Catalogue of the Acropolis Museum, Vol. II (Cambridge University Press, 1921)

Cavaignac, Histoire de l'antiquité = Eugène Cavaignac, Histoire de l'antiquité (4 vols., Vol. I in two parts, Paris, 1913-1920)

Charon — Edited by Jacoby, Frag. Gr. Hist., IIIA (Leyden, 1940), no. 262, pp. 1-8

Cicero, de Officiis = M. Tulli Ciceronis Scripta quae manserunt omnia, Fasc. 48, de Officiis, iterum recognovit C. Atzert; de Virtutibus, recognovit O. Plasberg (Leipzig, Teubner, 1932)

Classen = Thukydides, erklärt von J. Classen (8 vols., Berlin, 1875-1885); Vols. I and II in the third edition, Vols. III-VIII in the second

Classen-Steup = Thukydides, erklärt von J. Classen, bearbeitet von J. Steup (8 vols., Berlin, 1892-1922); Vols. I and II in the fifth edition, Vols. III-VIII in the third

Collart, Philippes = Paul Collart, Philippes ville de Macédoine depuis ses origines jusqu' à la fin de l'époque romaine (Paris, 1937); Vol. V of Travaux et Mémoires, publiés par les professeurs de l'Institut supérieur d'études françaises et les membres étrangers de l'École française d'Athènes

Crawley = The Complete Writings of Thucydides, The Peloponnesian War. The unabridged [Richard] Crawley Translation with an Introduction by Joseph Gavorse (The Modern Library, New York, 1934); the Crawley translation was first published in 1874 (London)

De Sanctis, Storia dei Greci = Gaetano De Sanctis, Storia dei Greci dalle origini alla fine del secolo V (2 vols., Florence, 1939)

Deutsche Literaturzeitung = Deutsche Literaturzeitung, Wochenschrift für Kritik der internationalen Wissenschaft

Dionysios, Anaplus Bospori = Dionysii Byzantii Anaplus Bospori, . . . edidit . . .
    Rudolf Güngerich (Berlin, 1927)

Échos d'Orient = Échos d'Orient, revue trimestrielle d'Histoire de Géographie et de
    Liturgie orientales

Ehrenberg, Aspects of the Ancient World = Victor Ehrenberg, Aspects of the Ancient
    World, Essays and Reviews (New York, 1946)

Eng. Hist. Rev. = The English Historical Review

Epigraphica = Epigraphica, Rivista italiana di epigrafia (Milan, from 1939)

Essen = Index Thucydideus, ex Bekkeri editione stereotypa, confectus a M. H. N.
    von Essen (Berlin, 1887)

Eunomia = Eunomia, Studia Graeca et Romana eduntur a societate Graecoromana
    Pragensi; Vol. I, Fasc. 1 (not seen by us) seems to have appeared in 1939,
    after which publication ceased

Fischer, de Atheniensium sociis = Paul Fischer, Quaestiones de Atheniensium sociis
    historicae (Diss., Bonn, 1887)

Forbes = Thucydides Book I, edited with introduction and notes by W. H. Forbes
    (2 parts, Oxford, Clarendon Press, 1895)

Francotte, Finances = Henri Francotte, Les finances des cités grecques (Liège and
    Paris, 1909)

Friedel, Der Tyrannenmord = Hans Friedel, Der Tyrannenmord in Gesetzgebung
    und Volksmeinung der Griechen (Stuttgart, 1937); Vol. XI of *Würzburger*
    Studien zur Altertumswissenschaft

Gaebler, Münzen von Makedonia = Hugo Gaebler, Die antiken Münzen von Make-
    donia und Paionia (2 vols., Berlin, 1906-1935); Vol. III of *Die antiken Münzen*
    Nord-Griechenlands, published under the general editorship of F. Imhoof-
    Blumer and, for III, 2, Theodor Wiegand

Glotz-Cohen, Histoire grecque = Gustave Glotz and Robert Cohen, Histoire grecque
    (4 vols., Paris, 1925-1938), Pierre Roussel co-author of Vol. IV; Part II of
    Histoire ancienne, the whole a part of *Histoire générale*, publiée sous la
    direction de Gustave Glotz

Gomme, Commentary = A. W. Gomme, A Historical Commentary on Thucydides,
    Vol. I, Introduction and Commentary on Book I (Oxford, 1945)

Gomme, Essays = A. W. Gomme, Essays in Greek History and Literature (Oxford,
    1937)

Gött. Nachrichten = Nachrichten von der Gesellschaft der Wissenschaften zu Göt-
    tingen, philologisch-historische Klasse

Haggard, Secretaries = Patience Haggard, The Secretaries of the Athenian Boule
    in the Fifth Century B. C. (Diss., University of Missouri, 1930)

Hampl, Staatsverträge = Franz Hampl, Die griechischen Staatsverträge des 4. Jahr-
    hunderts v. Christi Geb. (Leipzig, 1938); Vol. LIV of *Fürstlich Jablonow-*
    skischen Gesellschaft zu Leipzig, Preisschriften

Hellenika of Oxyrhynchos — See *A. T. L.*, I, p. xxv, *s. v.* Hell. Oxy.; edited also by Jacoby, *Frag. Gr. Hist.*, IIA (Berlin, 1926), no. 66, pp. 17-35

Hercher, Epistolographi Graeci = Rudolph Hercher, Epistolographi Graeci (Paris, Didot, 1873)

Hermathena = Hermathena, A Series of Papers on Literature, Science, and Philosophy by Members of Trinity College, Dublin

[Herodes], περὶ πολιτείας = Engelbert Drerup, [Ἡρώδου] περὶ πολιτείας. Ein politisches Pamphlet aus Athen 404 vor Chr. (Paderborn, 1908); Vol. II, 1 of *Studien zur Geschichte und Kultur des Altertums*, edited by E. Drerup, H. Grimme, and J. P. Kirsch

Herodotos = Herodoti Historiae, recognovit . . . Carolus Hude (2 vols., third edition, Oxford, Clarendon Press, 1926)

Heuss, Klio, Beiheft XXXIX = Alfred Heuss, " Stadt und Herrscher des Hellenismus in ihren staats- und völkerrechtlichen Beziehungen," *Klio*, Beiheft XXXIX (Leipzig, 1937)

Highby, Klio, Beiheft XXXVI = Leo Ingemann Highby, " The Erythrae Decree, Contributions to the Early History of the Delian League and the Peloponnesian Confederacy," *Klio*, Beiheft XXXVI (Leipzig, 1936)

I. G., XII, Suppl. = Inscriptiones Graecae, Vol. XII (Berlin, from 1895), Supplementum (1939), edited by F. Hiller von Gaertringen

Isokrates — For VIII, 82 (T79c) we use George Norlin, Isocrates, with an English translation, Vol. II (The Loeb Classical Library, London and New York, 1929)

Istros — Edited by Müller, *F. H. G.*, I (Paris, 1885), pp. 418-427

Kahrstedt, Staatsgebiet = Ulrich Kahrstedt, Staatsgebiet und Staatsangehörige in Athen, Studien zum öffentlichen Recht Athens, Vol. I (Stuttgart and Berlin, 1934); Vol. IV of *Göttinger Forschungen*

Kahrstedt, Untersuchungen = Ulrich Kahrstedt, Untersuchungen zur Magistratur in Athen, Studien zum öffentlichen Recht Athens, Vol. II (Stuttgart, 1936); Vol. X of *Geisteswissenschaftliche Forschungen*

Kallisthenes — Edited by Jacoby, *Frag. Gr. Hist.*, IIB (Berlin, 1929), no. 124, pp. 631-657

Kratinos — Edited by Kock, *Comicorum Atticorum Fragmenta*, I (Leipzig, 1880), pp. 11-130; see also D. L. Page, Greek Literary Papyri, with texts, translations, and notes, Vol. I (The Loeb Classical Library, London and Cambridge, Mass., 1942), no. 38, pp. 196-201

Ktesias = Ctesiae Cnidii operum Reliquiae. Fragmenta collegit, . . . recognovit . . . Joannes Christianus Felix Baehr (Frankfurt, 1824)

Liddell-Scott-Jones, Lexicon = A Greek-English Lexicon, compiled by Henry George Liddell . . . and Robert Scott, a new edition . . . by Henry Stuart Jones . . . with the assistance of Roderick McKenzie (Oxford, Clarendon Press, 1925-1940)

Lipsius, Das attische Recht und Rechtsverfahren = Das attische Recht und Rechts-
    verfahren mit Benutzung des attischen Processes, von M. H. E. Meier und
    G. F. Schömann, dargestellt von Justus Hermann Lipsius (3 vols., Vol. II in
    two parts, Leipzig, 1905-1915) ; the title varies slightly

Loeschcke, de tit. aliquot att. = Georg Loeschcke, de titulis aliquot Atticis quaestiones
    historicae (Diss., Bonn, 1876)

Meineke = August Meineke, Fragmenta Comicorum Graecorum (5 vols., Vols. II
    and V in two parts, Berlin, 1839-1857) ; Vol. V, Comicae Dictionis Index,
    is by Heinrich Jacobi

Meisterhans, Grammatik = K. Meisterhans, Grammatik der attischen Inschriften
    (third edition, revised by Eduard Schwyzer, Berlin, 1900)

Mélanges Glotz = Mélanges Gustave Glotz (2 vols., Paris, 1932)

Meritt, Epigraphica Attica = Benjamin Dean Meritt, Epigraphica Attica (Cambridge,
    Mass., 1940) ; Vol. IX of the Martin Classical Lectures

Meritt, The Greek Political Experience = B. D. Meritt, " Athens and the Delian
    League," in The Greek Political Experience, Studies in Honor of William Kelly
    Prentice (Princeton and London, 1941), Chapter IV

Nepos = Corneli Nepotis Vitae, recognovit . . . E. O. Winstedt (Oxford, Clarendon
    Press, 1904)

Nicole, Textes grecs inédits de Genève = Jules Nicole, Textes grecs inédits de la
    collection papyrologique de Genève (Geneva, 1909)

Olynthus = Excavations at Olynthus, . . . directed and edited by David M. Robinson;
    all volumes, by various authors, are parts of The Johns Hopkins University
    Studies in Archaeology (Baltimore and London, from 1929)

P. Oxy. = The Oxyrhynchus Papyri, edited with translations and notes by Bernard
    P. Grenfell and Arthur S. Hunt (Egyptian Exploration Fund, Graeco-Roman
    Branch, London, from 1898) ; A. S. Hunt was sole editor of Vols. VII-IX
    and XVII; H. I. Bell was co-editor of Vol. XVI; E. Lobel, C. H. Roberts,
    and E. P. Wegener edited Vol. XVIII; E. Lobel, E. P. Wegener, C. H.
    Roberts, and H. I. Bell edited Vol. XIX

P. Rylands = Catalogue of the Greek and Latin Papyri in the John Rylands Library
    Manchester, Vol. III, Theological and Literary Texts, edited by C. H. Roberts
    (Manchester, 1938)

P. W., R. E. = A seventh supplement has been published (1940), edited by Wilhelm
    Kroll and Karl Mittelhaus, in addition to Vols. XX, 1 (1941) and VII, 1
    (Zweite Reihe, 1939), by the same editors

Paton, The Erechtheum = James Morton Paton (editor), The Erechtheum, measured,
    drawn and restored by Gorham Phillips Stevens; text by Lacey Davis Caskey,
    Harold North Fowler, James Morton Paton, Gorham Phillips Stevens (Cam-
    bridge, Mass., 1927)

Perrin = Bernadotte Perrin, Plutarch's Lives, with an English translation (11 vols.,
    The Loeb Classical Library, London and New York, 1914-1926)

Philochoros — Edited by Müller, *F. H. G.*, I (Paris, 1885), pp. 384-417

Pindar = Pindari Carmina cum fragmentis, recognovit . . . C. M. Bowra (Oxford,
    Clarendon Press, 1935)

Plato, Rep. = Plato, Respublica; in Vol. IV of the Oxford edition

[Plutarch], Decem Orat. vit. = [Plutarch], Decem Oratorum vitae (no. 63 of the
    Moralia in the Planudean corpus; printed in Vol. V of Bernardakis' Teubner
    edition)

Plutarch, Moralia — For sections of the Moralia not yet included in the new Teubner
    edition (*A. T. L.*, I, p. xxx) see Plutarchi Chaeronensis Moralia, recognovit
    Gregorius N. Bernardakis (7 vols., Leipzig, Teubner, 1888-1896)

Poppo, Commentarii = Thucydidis de bello Peloponnesiaco libri octo, . . . [edidit]
    Ernestus Fridericus Poppo, Pars III, Commentarii (4 vols., Leipzig, 1831-
    1838)

Poseidippos — Edited by Kock, *Comicorum Atticorum Fragmenta*, III (Leipzig, 1888),
    pp. 335-348

Powell, Herodotus = J. Enoch Powell, The History of Herodotus (Cambridge Uni-
    versity Press, 1939); Vol. IV of *Cambridge Classical Studies*, edited by F. M.
    Cornford, D. S. Robertson, F. E. Adcock

Powell, Lexicon = J. Enoch Powell, A Lexicon to Herodotus (Cambridge University
    Press, 1938)

Pritchett and Neugebauer, Calendars of Athens = W. Kendrick Pritchett and O.
    Neugebauer, The Calendars of Athens (Cambridge, Mass., 1947)

Ravennas = Aristophanis Comoediae undecim cum scholiis, Codex Ravennas 137, 4,
    A, phototypice editus praefatus est J. van Leeuwen (Leyden, 1904); Vol. IX
    of *Codices Graeci et Latini photographice depicti*, duce Scatone De Vries

Robert, Études Épigraphiques et Philologiques = Louis Robert, Études Épigraphiques
    et Philologiques (Paris, 1938); Vol. CCLXXII of *Sciences historiques et
    philologiques*, published by the Bibliothèque de l'École des hautes études

Robert, Hellenica = Louis Robert, Hellenica, recueil d'épigraphie de numismatique et
    d'antiquités grecques (Limoges, from 1940)

Robinson, Ancient Sinope = David M. Robinson, Ancient Sinope, an Historical
    Account, with a Prosopographia Sinopensis and an Appendix of Inscriptions
    (Baltimore, 1906)

Robinson and Clement — See Olynthus

Rogers = Aristophanes, with the English translation of Benjamin Bickley Rogers
    (3 vols., The Loeb Classical Library, London and New York, 1924)

Rostovtzeff, Iranians and Greeks = M. Rostovtzeff, Iranians and Greeks in South
    Russia (Oxford, 1922)

Rutherford, Scholia Aristophanica = Scholia Aristophanica, being such Comments adscript to the Text of Aristophanes as have been preserved in the Codex Ravennas, arranged, emended, and translated by William G. Rutherford (2 vols., London, 1896); Vol. III, published in 1905, bears the title A Chapter in the History of Annotation

Schweizerische Numismatische Rundschau = Published (at Bern) as Revue Suisse de Numismatique 1891-1924, with the German title added 1910-1924; published under the German title with the French added 1926-1936, 1942

Seltman, Greek Coins = Charles Seltman, Greek Coins, a History of Metallic Currency and Coinage down to the Fall of the Hellenistic Kingdoms (London, 1933)

Sitzungsber. Ak. Heidelberg = Sitzungsberichte der Heidelberger Akademie der Wissenschaften (Stiftung Heinrich Lanz), philosophisch-historische Klasse

Steinwenter, Streitbeendigung = Artur Steinwenter, Die Streitbeendigung durch Urteil, Schiedsspruch und Vergleich nach griechischem Rechte (Munich, 1925); Vol. VIII of *Münchener Beiträge zur Papyrusforschung und antiken Rechtsgeschichte*

Steup — See Classen-Steup

Sturz = F. W. Sturz, Lexicon Xenophonteum (4 vols., Leipzig, 1801-1804)

Süsserott, Griechische Plastik = Hans Karl Süsserott, Griechische Plastik des 4. Jahrhunderts vor Christus, Untersuchungen zur Zeitbestimmung (Frankfurt, 1938)

Swoboda, Gr. Staatskunde = Georg Busolt, Griechische Staatskunde, Vol. II, Darstellung einzelner Staaten und der zwischenstaatlichen Beziehungen, by Heinrich Swoboda (Munich, 1926); Ivan von Müller's *Handbuch der Altertumswissenschaft*, IV, 1, 1 (third edition)

Thucydides = Thucydidis Historiae, recognovit . . . Henricus Stuart Jones, . . . correxit et auxit Johannes Enoch Powell (2 vols., Oxford, Clarendon Press, 1942)

Tod, Greek Hist. Inscr. = Marcus N. Tod, A Selection of Greek Historical Inscriptions to the End of the Fifth Century B. C. (second edition, Oxford, 1946), cited by us as I²; Vol. II, A Selection of Greek Historical Inscriptions from 403 to 323 B. C. (Oxford, 1948)

Venetus = Ἀριστοφάνους Κωμῳδίαι, Facsimile of the Codex Venetus Marcianus 474, with a preface by John Williams White and an introduction by Thomas W. Allen (London and Boston, 1902)

Wilamowitz, Aristoteles und Athen = Ulrich von Wilamowitz-Moellendorff, Aristoteles und Athen (2 vols., Berlin, 1893)

Wilamowitz, Coniectanea = U. von Wilamowitz-Moellendorff, Coniectanea, prefaced to *Index Scholarum publice et privatim in Academia Georgia Augusta per semestre aestivum a d. XV. m. Aprilis usque ad d. XV. m. Augusti a. MDCCCLXXXIV habendarum* (Göttingen, 1884)

Wilhelm, Attische Urkunden = Adolf Wilhelm, Attische Urkunden, Vol. IV (*Sitzungsber. Ak. Wien*, CCXVII, 5, 1939), Vol. V (*Sitzungsber. Ak. Wien*, CCXX, 5, 1942)

THE ATHENIAN TRIBUTE LISTS

VOLUME III

PART I

THE EVIDENCE OF THE TEXTS

CHAPTER I

THE TEXTS OF THE FIRST ASSESSMENT PERIOD
(454/3–451/0)

As printed in *A. T. L.*, II the texts of Lists 1-4 exhibit several minor changes from the form in which they appeared in *A. T. L.*, I.

The initial epsilon in 1, II, 8 cannot reasonably be taken as part of any name not already in List 1, and [Θερμαῖοι] ἐ[ν Ἰκάροι : Ⱶ] becomes, consequently, an almost certain candidate for the restoration of 1, II, 7-8. This reading has been added to the text.

The quota of Ἀργίλιοι in 1, IV, 22 is transcribed as ⟨H⟩Ⱶ. This appears on the stone as XⰔ; it is not a normal figure even when considered alone, nor does it fit well into the whole record of the tribute of Argilos. This city paid 1 talent a year, where the amount is preserved, beginning with List 9 in 446/5 and continuing down to the founding of Amphipolis in 437/6. After 437 the normal tribute was lowered to 1,000 drachmai a year, and the explanation for this reduction has been generally, and rightly, sought in the effect which the establishment of the new colony had upon the resources of its older neighbour.

But there is no similar explanation at hand for the reduction from 10½ talents to 1 talent of tribute between 454/3 and 446/5. Our own earlier suggestion (*A. T. L.*, I, p. 453) that the figure XⰔ should be rationalized to a normal X with an appended temporary increment of Ⱶ, perhaps representing a kind of ἐπιφορά, is inadequate. Even a tribute of 10 talents would be too high, especially in view of the provision of the Peace of Nikias (Thucydides, V, 18, 5 [T134]) that Argilos should be autonomous, paying to Athens only τὸν φόρον τὸν ἐπ' Ἀριστείδου. Gomme apparently thought that the reading should be X⟨Ⱶ⟩;[1] but this leaves the Thucydidean text, and the great reduction between 454/3 and 446/5, even more difficult to explain. Perdrizet put forward the suggestion that the reading should be HⰔ; he wished to change the first of the two figures rather than the second, and in so doing he obtained not only a normal figure, but one which allows an intelligible interpretation of Thucydides and an acceptable reduction in the amount of the tribute either in 450 or in 446. There are several examples of the same ratio in tribute-reduction in 450 and in 446, and in spite of the further great reduction after the founding of Amphipolis in 437 it is possible that adjustments of territory between Amphipolis and Argilos were contemplated in 421 which would have justified thereafter the payment of the original tribute of 1½ talents a year. If the assessment of Argilos in 425 was very severe (it is not known

---

[1] *Commentary*, I, p. 277 (unless his reference to the 15 talents is merely an error).

how high it was), the payment later of 1½ talents may have been considered a fair return to a pre-war normal figure.[2] We believe that the figure XℲ is in error and that our text should read ⟨H⟩Ⅎ.

The combined quota of Olynthos, Skabala, and Assera in 1, V, 8 is now restored as H[HℲΔΓ]HIIII rather than H[HHΔΓ]HIIII. When the first separate records appear, Olynthos has a quota of HH, Skabala of Ⅎ, and Assera of ΔΔΔΔ. The total of the three figures is less than the old restoration by 26⅔ drachmai and greater than the new by 23⅓. Admittedly there is not much to choose between them, but we believe that the less than full composite payment is slightly to be favoured.

In 1, V, 16 the restoration is Πίκρες Συαν[γελεύς: Ⅎ]. The tribute of Syangela was usually 1 talent when it included that of Amynanda (see the Register, *s. v.* Συαγγελῆς), but the appearance of Ἀμυνανδὲ[ς] in List 2 with its own separate quota shows that the two cities divided the payment between them in the first period. Hence the quota for Syangela in 1, V, 16 should be only half the later normal figure of H.

The *Postscript* of List 1, which was cut on the right lateral face of the stone, gives the totals for the year in silver and in gold. The figure for the staters of Kyzikene gold was largely restored in *A. T. L.*, I (p. 129): [στατêρ]ες Κυ[ζικενοὶ: hεχσέκοντ]α hὲχ[ς: hέκται τέτταρες]. But it might have been as little as 56 or as much as 96, and there is no assurance about the hektai. So we prefer to read the text of these lines as they now appear in *A. T. L.*, II, simply as [στατêρ]ες Κυ[ζικενοὶ: ....έκοντ]α hὲχ[ς ------]. The amount of silver was given as [ℲX]XXHHHΔΔ[.....¹¹.....]. This calculation was based rather largely on an analogy with List 7,[3] but our study of the first assessment period, and of List 1 in particular,[4] has shown that this amount is too low. One higher restoration is possible for the quota of silver: [ℲT]XXHHHΔΔ[---]. This represents a tribute of 383+ talents, which the increment of the gold (whatever the restoration) will raise to about 400 talents or more, and this higher figure must surely be restored in line 9 of the *Postscript*.

Only one change has been made in List 2 from the text as printed in *A. T. L.*, 1: the restoration Ἀ[ρισβαῖοι] replaces Ἀ[λινδες] in 2, IV, 15. Arisbe was very near Abydos and dropped out of the tribute lists in Periods V and VI when the tribute of Abydos was raised from 4 to 6 talents. We believe that it should be restored in List 2 when the tribute of Abydos was still probably assessed at 4 talents. The only recorded appearance of Alinda will now be that in 4, V, 21: HΔ -- Ἀλ[ινδες]. It appears there with other Karic names which probably paid only sporadically, or when coerced. If it appeared at all in List 2 it should be sought with its neighbouring Karic

---

[2] Perdrizet wished not merely to emend the text, but to change the reading (*B. C. H.*, XLVI [1922], p. 45), and he makes the following extraordinary declaration: " Je n'ai pas vérifié la pierre, et n'en ai pas d'estampage sous les yeux; mais je suis sûr qu'elle portait HℲ."

[3] Meritt, *D. A. T.*, pp. 61-65 and 96-97.

[4] See below, pp. 265-274.

towns in column I rather than with the regularly enrolled cities in column IV (see below, pp. 8-9).

The reading of the text in 3, I, 30 has now been deciphered as [καὶ Λ]ύκιοι. This line implies, of course, a preceding name, for which the evidence of 9, III, 33-34 strongly suggests Τελεμέσσιοι. But this name can also be spelled Τελμέσσιοι and as such it falls admirably into the Karic-Lykian group at the end of List 4, where we now restore [Τελμέσ]σιοι,[5] and where the concluding line of the list may be restored, on the analogy of List 3, as [καὶ Λύκιοι]. These two entries, in 3, I, 29-30 and in 4, V, 32-33, give mutual confirmation to the restorations proposed. The style of the lists suggests that the single quota should be spaced in bracket position before lines 29-30 in List 3 and entirely in line 32 of List 4.

In these early lists of Period I the order in which the names appear on the stone reflects largely the time sequence in which the various amounts of tribute were received, and at the end of List 4 it is thus possible to date the payments to the latter part of the year 451/0 and to bring them into connection with Kimon's campaign to Kypros in the summer of 450. His naval squadron collected tribute from remote or inland cities in Karia and Lykia, many of which do not normally appear in the quota lists.[6] The only comparable group of unusual names is at the beginning of List 2,[7] where the Karic entries again give evidence of the presence of an Athenian fleet engaged, though perhaps not primarily so engaged, in tribute collection. These names in the first column of List 2 all have odd amounts of quota before them. The figure ΔΓΗΗ obviously represents an assessment of 1000 drachmai, for which the normal quota was ΔΓΗΙΙΙ. Similarly, the unusual figure of ΡΔΓΗΗΙΙΙΙ for Ἐρινῆς probably represents a normal ΡΔΓΗΙΙΙ, the odd ΡΙΙΙΙΙ for Ἀμυνανδε[ς] a normal Ρ, and the odd ΗΔΗΗΗΙΙΙΙ for Πακτύες Ἰδυμ[εύς] possibly a normal Η. In every instance the fleet had collected a normal tribute plus an increment, the logical explanation being that the additional amount was a tax for late payment, or possibly a charge for the trouble of collection. But these Karic cities, being late in payment of their tribute and probably visited by an Athenian squadron returning to Athens from the east toward the close of summer, could only have appeared in the first column of List 2 if in fact their payments had been due in List 1. We have, therefore, in column I of List 2 a kind of appendix to List 1. The names and the tribute both belong to 454/3, rather than to 453/2, and the record shows them in the latter year only because the hellenotamiai of 454/3 had closed their books before the payments reached Athens with the fleet. No name in column I of List 2 appears in List 1; on the contrary, the Lepsimanioi,

---

[5] The reasons for abandoning an earlier restoration [Πτελεό]σιοι are given in A. T. L., I, p. 174, note on 4, V, 32.

[6] See below, pp. 211-212. Cf. also Nesselhauf, Klio, Beiheft XXX, pp. 24-25; Meritt, D. A. T., p. 92 with note 59.

[7] One city, Ouranion, does indeed appear in both groups, and helps to indicate their similar character.

whose late payment for 454/3 was booked in 2, I, 12, appear again in the same list (2, VIII, 13), making their payment for 453/2.[8]

The nature of the fleet which was operating in Karic waters in 453 is not known. Meritt once proposed that it was the relief squadron returning from Egypt after the great disaster,[9] but this was when the date of the disaster was assumed to be 453,[10] and the combination is no longer possible now that the traditional date 454 can be vindicated by the chronological study of the events of the Fifty Years.[11]

The names at the bottom of column I in List 2 must be supplemented by restorations in the lost lines 2-10 in order to give the complete record of late payments which belonged properly in 454/3. The second column, perhaps, initiated in its own right the record of 453/2. There is no doubt about the first name in this column ([Κο]δαπês), but its precise geographical location is unknown (it is surely Karic) and we cannot be certain (without the quota) whether the payment belonged to 454/3 or 453/2. The columns in List 2, however, were unusually short, and perhaps the change from one year to the next was the occasion for this brevity, being punctuated by the end of column I and the commencement of column II. We have no evidence to decide the issue, and even if the payment of Κοδαπῆς was normal and belonged to 453/2 it may still have been gathered in and brought back to Athens by the ships which brought back also the tribute of column I.

The names which should be restored in column I are undoubtedly to be sought among the rare entries at the end of List 4. For purposes of illustration we suggest here a tentative restoration, which we believe to be generally correct, though we did not think it precise enough in detail to justify its inclusion in the text as published in *A. T. L.*, II:

	[– – – –]	[Σ/. – – – – –]
	[ΗⱤΗΙΙΙΙ]	['Αλινδês]
	[ΔΓΗΗ]	[. σουρι – –]
5	[ΔΔΔΗΗΗΙΙ]	[Χαλκετορês]
	[ΓΗΗ]	[Κυδαιês]
	[ΔΓΗΗ]	[ℎυβλισês]
	[ΔΓΗΗ]	[Κιλλαρês]
	[ΔΓΗΗ]	[Θύδονος]
10	[ΔΔΓΙΙΙΙ]	[Σίλοι]

[8] The record of Lepsimandos in the first period was irregular, and it is possible that the payment of 2, VIII, 13 was complementary to that of 2, I, 12 (cf. Meritt, *D. A. T.*, p. 84, note 33), but this is not probable. It is also possible that some of the names represent double payments, covering both 454/3 and 453/2. Ouranion is a case in point. Its quota in List 4 is only ΓΗΗΙΙ; the quota in List 2 is approximately double this.

[9] *D. A. T.*, p. 92, note 59.

[10] See Gomme, *Commentary*, I, note 2 on pp. 412-413.

[11] See below, pp. 158-180.

	ΔΓͰͰ	Βο[λβαι]ês
	ΔΓͰͰ	Λεφσιμάνιο[ι]
	ΡΔΓͰͰͰΙΙΙΙ	Ἐρινês
	ΡΙΙΙΙ	Ἀμυνανδε[ς]
15	ΗΔͰͰͰΙΙΙΙ	Πακτύες Ἰδυμ[εύς]
	ΔΓͰͰ	Ὀρανιêτ[αι]
	ΔΓͰͰ	Ὀλα[ι]ês
	ΔΓͰͰ	Τ[α]ρβανês

The restorations of the quotas have been made with the slight increment which was characteristic of the late payments from 454/3 in this column.

The first assessment period (454/3–451/0) is represented also by A1 (*A. T. L.*, II, p. 40), the assessment decree of 454, which was copied by Krateros and quotations from which have been preserved by Stephanos of Byzantion. As a note on Δῶρος in his *Ethnica* Stephanos writes: ἔστι καὶ Καρίας Δῶρος πόλις, ἣν συγκαταλέγει ταῖς πόλεσιν ταῖς Καρικαῖς Κρατερὸς ἐν τῷ περὶ ψηφισμάτων τρίτῳ " Καρικὸς φόρος· Δῶρος, Φασηλῖται." This comes at the end of a long account of the Phoinikian Δῶρος and Stephanos thus betrays his belief that there was in Karia a separate Δῶρος, named in one of the Athenian decrees about tribute. This separate attribution to Karia has been favoured also by some modern scholars, Meineke, for example, in his edition of Stephanos, even suggesting as possible that the quotation from Krateros should be printed with a lacuna after the word Δῶρος in order to make room for other truly Karic cities to be associated with it and for an additional heading Παμφυλιακὸς φόρος to serve as a suitable introduction to Φασηλῖται.[12] We now know, of course, that Phaselis, though situated geographically in Lykia,[13] always appeared in the tribute lists under the heading Καρικὸς φόρος, or (when the Karic and Ionic panels were merged) under Ἰωνικὸς φόρος. Plainly Krateros and Stephanos were both correct, the one in his copy and the other in his quotation. Every city to the east of Karia in the tribute lists was Karian, whether it lay in Lykia, Pamphylia, Kilikia, or (for that matter) on the coast of Phoinike, and hence there is no more reason to deny the identity of Doros in A1 with the well-known Phoinikian city than there is to deny the identity of Phaselis with the Phaselis of Lykia.[14] Koehler long ago arrived at the correct equation,[15] observing that the only evidence for Doros being Karian

---

[12] August Meineke, *Stephani Byzantii Ethnicorum quae supersunt*, I (Berlin, 1849), p. 256: *mirum vero Phaselin accenseri urbibus Caricis. itaque nescio an post Δῶρος Caricarum urbium nomina omissa sint, ante Φασηλῖται autem exciderit Παμφυλιακὸς φόρος.*

[13] Not in Pamphylia, as Suidas and Aristodemos have it; cf. Wade-Gery, *Harv. Stud. Cl. Phil.*, Suppl. Vol. I (1940), p. 135.

[14] Yet the tendency persists. Kahrstedt, *Gött. gel. Anz.*, 1939, p. 413, still seems to believe that Doros was in Karia.

[15] *Urkunden und Untersuchungen*, p. 121, note 3: " Δῶρος war eine phönikische Stadt; dass

came from the heading of the Karic list of tribute which Krateros had before him, and suggesting that Athens temporarily had a foothold on the Palestinian coast below Mt. Carmel. These views have been set forth in *A. T. L.*, I (p. 483), and some of the reasons have been given for attributing the assessment list in question to 454 (*op. cit.*, pp. 203-204). The facts are that Krateros arranged his work in chronological order; that citations from the records of assessment in book IX belong to 410/09; and that the quotations from book III belong earlier at least than 451, for parts of a decree mentioning ναυτοδίκαι are cited in book IV and these quotations may with virtual certainty be attributed to Perikles' law of citizenship,[16] the date of which is known from Aristotle, 'Αθ. Πολ., 26, 3: – – – ἐπὶ 'Αντιδότου (451/0) διὰ τὸ πλῆθος τῶν πολιτῶν Περικλέους εἰπόντος ἔγνωσαν, μὴ μετέχειν τῆς πόλεως, ὃς ἂν μὴ ἐξ ἀμφοῖν ἀστοῖν ἦ γεγονώς. Körte [17] argues that the functions of the ξενοδίκαι in the general scrutiny of 445/4 B. C. (Plutarch, *Pericles*, 37) must date the law to which Krateros refers at least later than 443/2, when ξενοδίκαι (not ναυτοδίκαι) were still handling cases of ξενία,[18] and hence he does not believe that Krateros is quoting Perikles' law. But, as Gomme justly observes,[19] the ξενοδίκαι seem to have been created and to have functioned for a particular occasion *ca.* 445/4. Hence one may seek ναυτοδίκαι before as well as after, and Krateros' law may still be Perikles' law. Nor is it a contrary argument that the one speaks of penalizing a son who has both parents aliens, implying that it was legitimate to enroll in a phratry if one parent was alien, while the other demands that both parents be citizens. Our quotation from the law in Krateros is fragmentary, and no such fine distinction can be inferred for the whole law from the little that has been preserved. What is certain is that both laws deal with citizenship; that the date 451 B. C. suits admirably the schedule of Krateros' collection; and that the evidence of the ξενοδίκαι is entirely concerned with a quite different occasion.

But the telling argument for dating Krateros' fragments from book III to 454/3 is his mention of Doros and Phaselis. He was quoting from an Athenian decree, and "although assessments were no doubt made before this date, it was not until 454/3 that they became decrees of the Athenian state." [20] The assessment of Doros would have been inexplicable before the campaign to Egypt in 460. Yet for that campaign,

---

eine gleichnamige in Karien existirt habe, ist aus der Schätzungsliste geschlossen, in der der Name unter dem karischen Tribut stand. Sollte nicht doch die phönikische Stadt gemeint sein und die Athener dort vorübergehend festen Fuss gefasst haben?"

[16] Fragment 4 (Krech), from Harpokration, *s. v.* ναυτοδίκαι· Λυσίας ἐν τῷ πρὸς 'Αλκιβιάδην, εἰ γνήσιος ὁ λόγος. ἀρχή τις ἦν 'Αθήνησιν οἱ ναυτοδίκαι· Κρατερὸς γοῦν ἐν τῷ δ' τῶν ψηφισμάτων φησίν " ἐὰν δέ τις ἐξ ἀμφοῖν ξένοιν γεγονὼς φρατρίζῃ, διώκειν εἶναι τῷ βουλομένῳ 'Αθηναίων, οἷς δίκαι εἰσί, λαγχάνειν δὲ τῇ ἕνῃ καὶ νέᾳ πρὸς τοὺς ναυτοδίκας." Some further evidence about the nautodikai appears in new readings of *I. G.*, I², 68/69; Meritt, *Hesperia*, XIV (1945), pp. 114-115.

[17] *Hermes*, LXVIII (1933), pp. 238-242.

[18] Cf. *I. G.*, I², 342, lines 38-39, and 343, line 89.

[19] *Essays*, p. 80, note 2.

[20] *A. T. L.*, I, p. 203.

and thereafter until 454, the Athenians needed a way-station along the route by which they maintained communication with their forces of occupation, a route which led eastward by way of Phaselis, Aspendos, and Kelenderis (all doubtless assessed in 454), and then southward to Kypros, the main forward base, and on to Doros and the mouths of the Nile. One of the public funeral lists is mute epigraphic testimony to the fighting in Phoinike that attended the establishment of this base at Doros in 460.[21]

Athens still remained mistress of the sea, even after the Egyptian disaster,[22] and no doubt held, or tried to hold, Doros. So it was assessed in 454, the one assessment *par excellence* in which its name should have appeared. By 450 Athens was fighting again in Kypros, regaining lost ground, and we do not know the fate of Doros or Athenian aspirations concerning it. It may at that time have been completely lost, and Athens definitely could have held no hope of recovering it after the ratification of the Peace of Kallias.[23]

This fragment from Krateros serves therefore to define the extent of the Athenian Empire at the time of its greatest expansion. Incidentally it shows that in the assessment decree of 454 there was a geographical panel headed Καρικὸς φόρος. Presumably the other panels were also headed by their respective titles: Ἰωνικὸς φόρος, Ἑλλησπόντιος φόρος, ἀπὸ Θράκης φόρος, and Νησιωτικὸς φόρος. In this assessment the Karic and Ionic panels were not combined; when they were, the title Ἰωνικὸς φόρος served as heading for the composite list.[24] These geographical headings do not, of course, imply administrative districts; nor do the geographical divisions in the later assessment decrees and quota lists imply administrative districts.[25] There is no reason, in fact,

[21] *I. G.*, I², 929. For the date and interpretation see below, pp. 174-175.

[22] See also below, pp. 262-264.

[23] The years between 460 and 454 are the most appropriate for the reference which Lykourgos, κατὰ Λεωκράτους, 72 (T87), makes to Athenian prestige: Φοινίκην δὲ καὶ Κιλικίαν ἐπόρθησαν.

[24] Gomme (*Commentary*, I, p. 371, note 2) thinks that the evidence from Krateros for a separate heading " Καρικὸς φόρος " in the assessment of 454 is " remarkably thin." But what else was Krateros copying? The presence of Doros eliminates the alternative that it was the assessment of 443 (cf. Meritt, *A. J. A.*, XXIX [1925], p. 258).

[25] Schaefer, *Hermes*, LXXIV (1939), pp. 243-264, makes this abundantly clear, even though his argument has many irrelevancies and misuses much of the evidence. He misses completely the significance of the Decree of Klearchos (D14), which he persists in dating *ca.* 414 B. C. (*op. cit.*, p. 256), nor does he recognize the reflection of geographical divisions in the quota lists as early as 450/49. At about the same time Kahrstedt, in his review of *A. T. L.*, I, writes (*Gött. gel. Anz.*, 1939, p. 412): " die Verfasser sind der Ansicht, dass er [Krateros] die Tribute der Veranlegung von 454 und der von 410 genannt hat, der ersten und der letzten nach der Verlegung der Verwaltung nach Athen. Sehr plausibel, wenn wir auch daraus, dass er schon zum Jahre 454 von Καρικὸς φόρος usw. gesprochen zu haben scheint, nicht schliessen dürfen, dass diese Provinzeinteilung schon damals amtlich war." Administrative classification is here confused with clerical (and practical) convenience. Nor do we understand the implication of " gesprochen zu haben scheint." This is too vague. Krateros is giving a precise and direct quotation from the official record.

except that of orderly record and bookkeeping convenience, why the geographical districts should ever have appeared in the quota lists; in the assessment decrees they were probably useful primarily in defining the routes of the heralds who announced the assessments. The lists of the first four years show no order of names other than that of time of payment,[26] and such geographical grouping as there is probably means merely that envoys who were neighbours sometimes travelled together to Athens with their money. Beginning with the lists of the second period, one discerns the first fumbling efforts at systematization in the quota lists by an arrangement of names more or less by geographical panels.[27] Complete systematization was achieved later, but the convenient device of separating the Empire into geographical districts is now proved for the assessment decrees much earlier than it appears, even indirectly, in the quota lists.

Nesselhauf recalls Kirchhoff's thesis that the " Bezirkeinteilung " may be as early as the history of the Confederacy,[28] and concludes that it may date back to a time between 477 and 448. Krateros proves that the date must be at least as early as 454, and we believe that some grouping into lists that did not overlap, and that yet included all the names, was essential as soon as there was a general alert or any occasion for the despatch of heralds.[29]

We assume, therefore, that a valid copy of each current assessment was kept in Athens, and that after the treasury had been moved from Delos this copy was used as a control whenever the envoys of a tributary city brought in their payment of phoros. The formality of payment was not complete until the money had been delivered to the apodektai and to the hellenotamiai in the presence of the Council. In writing of the early days of the Confederacy Thucydides says that the hellenotamiai were the magistrates who received the money and that the treasury was Delos.[30] The apodektai and the Council, of course, could have had no part in the transaction there. Pollux, on the other hand, is authority for the rôle played by the apodektai.[31] It was the opinion of Schwahn[32] that the evidence of Pollux carries little weight and must

---

[26] This observation is of long standing: Beloch, *Rh. Mus.*, XLIII (1888), p. 106; Busolt, *Gr. Gesch.*, III, 1, note 1 on pp. 74-76; Nesselhauf, *Klio*, Beiheft XXX, p. 41.

[27] Segre, *Clara Rhodos*, IX (1938), p. 168.

[28] *Klio*, Beiheft XXX, p. 41; cf. Kirchhoff, *Hermes*, XI (1876), pp. 13-48.

[29] Reference is sometimes made to the rejection of Kirchhoff's thesis by Meyer, *Forschungen*, II, pp. 82-87. The fallacy both in thesis and in refutation is the exaltation into " administrative provinces " of these early visiting lists of the Confederacy.

[30] I, 96, 2 (T109) : καὶ Ἑλληνοταμίαι τότε πρῶτον Ἀθηναίοις κατέστη ἀρχή, οἳ ἐδέχοντο τὸν φόρον. — — — ταμιεῖόν τε Δῆλος ἦν αὐτοῖς.

[31] VIII, 97 (T98a) : ἀποδέκται δὲ ἦσαν δέκα, οἳ τούς τε φόρους καὶ τὰς εἰσφορὰς καὶ τὰ τέλη ὑπεδέχοντο — — —.

[32] Schwahn, P. W., *R. E., s. v.* φόροι, p. 633-634: " Entscheidend ist, dass Thuk. I 96, 2 ausdrücklich sagt, dass die Hellenotamiai die φ. annahmen. Das gilt zwar zunächst für die delische Zeit; wenn aber später darin eine Änderung eintrat, hätte es vermerkt werden müssen. Überdies

yield to the superior authority of Thucydides, but we interpret his evidence as applicable to the years after 454, meaning that the apodektai as agents of the Council received the money which they then handed over to the hellenotamiai as its permanent stewards. The apodektai were not themselves a custodial board, and, though they received funds, they had to distribute them again to the responsible magistrates who enjoyed the duties of public stewardship. The Council is also said to have numbered among its obligations that of receiving the tribute from the allies.[33] This ultimate responsibility of the Council has been generally recognized,[34] and is now assured by the discovery of the new fragments of D7 which describe the process of bringing in the tribute and of reading off the amount of each contribution before the Council. The procedure as outlined in D7 is evidently much more rigorous than it had been before the passage of this decree (448/7), for one of the purposes of the decree was to tighten the control of the Athenian Demos over the collection of money from the Empire. The institution of tokens ($\xi \acute{\nu} \mu \beta o \lambda a$) was probably new, for the decree expressly states that these tokens were to prevent any malpractice on the part of the couriers who brought the tribute to Athens. After 448/7, at least, the envoys from each city came bringing not only the tribute entrusted to them but also a tablet on which the amount of the tribute was written and which was sealed with the city's own individual token. These tablets were produced on the floor of the Council chamber, and in the presence of the Council the token was matched by the half of it that was kept on file in Athens, the seal on the tablet was broken, and the amount of the tribute read out aloud. If the tribute actually produced did not tally with the amount thus read out the couriers were held to an accounting. This new evidence from D7 gives more detail than we have ever had about the actual booking of the money. There must have been an immediate record made, presumably upon a tablet of wax, with the name of the city and the amount of its payment duly entered. Presumably also this record was made with a reference of verification to the current assessment list in which the names of the cities were arranged in geographical panels. The keeping of this record, and of the money, as Swoboda rightly notes, was the primary business of the hellenotamiai.[35] In the years of the first assessment period they evidently made no attempt to perpetuate in their records of the tribute received the subdivision into geographical panels which

hätten sonst die Hellenotamiai seit der Überführung der Reichskasse nach Athen gar keine eigene Tätigkeit mehr ausgeübt, sondern nur eine Übermittlerrolle gespielt."

[33] [Xenophon], 'Αθ. Πολ., III, 2 (T154): τὴν δὲ βουλὴν βουλεύεσθαι πολλὰ μὲν περὶ τοῦ πολέμου, πολλὰ δὲ περὶ πόρου χρημάτων, πολλὰ δὲ περὶ νόμων θέσεως, πολλὰ δὲ περὶ τῶν κατὰ πόλιν ἀεὶ γιγνομένων, πολλὰ δὲ καὶ ⟨περὶ τῶν ἐν⟩ τοῖς συμμάχοις, καὶ φόρον δέξασθαι καὶ νεωρίων ἐπιμεληθῆναι καὶ ἱερῶν.

[34] Though recently questioned by Schwahn, op. cit., p. 634.

[35] Swoboda, Gr. Staatskunde, p. 1133: "Die Hauptaufgabe der Hellenotamiai blieb die Verwaltung der Reichskasse. Sie empfingen aber die Phoroi nicht mehr unmittelbar von den Abgesandten der Bündner, sondern durch Vermittelung der Apodektai. Die Hellenotamiai hatten jedoch über die Einzahlungen fortlaufend Buch zu führen."

existed in the assessment. They wrote down the names and the amounts of tribute in chronological order. When one wax tablet had been filled with names, they presumably went on to a second, and a third, and a fourth tablet until the record could be closed at the time of the Dionysiac festival.[36] If any payments came in after this date, they could still be added, but the record was finally closed at the end of the year when the quotas to the Goddess were reckoned, the entire record submitted to the logistai, and the so-called quota list inscribed on stone and set up on the Akropolis.[37] Meritt has already commented upon the reflection in these copied records of the spelling of the names from the assessment.[38] There was an intermediary stage between this purely chronological method and the systematic grouping by geographical districts which was perfected in 443/2. The imperfect grouping of List 5 (450/49) suggests that there was an attempt to keep on one wax tablet the receipts from Ionia and Karia, on another the receipts from Thrace, and so on, but determination to hold the records separate was not thoroughgoing and one may suppose that the irregularities in the list show the intrusion of names from one panel into the tablet belonging to another panel. We can only surmise what the reasons may have been, but one simple explanation could be that when the scribe had filled one tablet with names he put down the next names in whatever space was available to him whether or not it happened to be in the tablet that belonged to the district pertinent to the name. There was greater systematization in 446, and, as we have noted, the clerical staff had developed its keeping of the books to such a degree of efficiency that one may well believe that in 443/2 the quota lists were a fair reflection even of the assessment list itself.

The Dionysia have long been known as the date when the payments of tribute were due. To the literary evidence afforded by Aristophanes and Eupolis [39] may now be added the epigraphical evidence of the rubric M[ετὰ Διονύσια] in 7, IV, 30 (A. T. L., I, p. 453; cf. also Meritt and West, A. J. A., XXXII [1928], p. 291), which names nine cities that paid later than the others and that were subsequently inscribed, and

---

[36] Except for late payments.

[37] See Swoboda, op. cit., p. 1133. The hellenotamiai showed their record (and the calculation of the sixtieth) to the logistai, who verified it; then the hellenotamiai turned the sixtieth over to the ταμίαι τῶν τῆς θεοῦ.

[38] Meritt, A. J. A., XXIX (1925), p. 259 (= Studies in the Athenian Tribute Lists, p. 259).

[39] Acharnians, 504-506 (T26):

> αὐτοὶ γάρ ἐσμεν οὑπὶ Ληναίῳ τ' ἀγών,
> κοὔπω ξένοι πάρεισιν· οὔτε γὰρ φόροι
> ἥκουσιν οὔτ' ἐκ τῶν πόλεων οἱ ξύμμαχοι.

Schol. Acharnians, 504 (T27): χειμῶνος γὰρ λοιπὸν ὄντος εἰς τὰ Λήναια καθῆκε τὸ δρᾶμα. εἰς δὲ τὰ Διονύσια ἐτέτακτο Ἀθήναζε κομίζειν τὰς πόλεις τοὺς φόρους, ὡς Εὔπολίς φησιν ἐν Πόλεσιν. Cf. also the scholion (T27) on οὑπὶ Ληναίῳ τ' ἀγών in the same line: ὁ τῶν Διονυσίων ἀγὼν ἐτελεῖτο δὶς τοῦ ἔτους, τὸ μὲν πρῶτον ἔαρος ἐν ἄστει, ὅτε καὶ οἱ φόροι Ἀθήνησιν ἐφέροντο, τὸ δὲ δεύτερον ———; and the scholion (T25) on line 378, which reads in part: εἶπε γὰρ δρᾶμα τοὺς Βαβυλωνίους τῇ τῶν Διονυσίων ἑορτῇ, ἥτις ἐν τῷ ἔαρι ἐπιτελεῖται, ἐν ᾧ ἔφερον τοὺς φόρους οἱ σύμμαχοι.

the evidence of D7 and D8. These two decrees, the one from 448/7 and the other from 426/5, must be studied together, for some of their provisions are remarkably alike. Both provide for calling a meeting of the ekklesia soon after the Dionysia;[40] both provide for publishing the names of the cities which paid and of those which did not pay; and both authorize the despatch of collectors to exact the tribute still due. The wording differs, and D7 speaks of giving receipts to those which paid, of which D8 says nothing (448/7, perhaps, as against 426/5); but the important item of similarity is the publishing of the lists of cities that paid and of cities that were in default. The best preserved statement is in D7 (lines 20-22): [ἀ]ποδεῖχσαι Ἀθεναίοις τὸμ πόλεον τὰς ἀποδόσα[ς τὸμ φόρον ἐ]ντελê καὶ τὰς ἐλλιπόσας χορίς, ἡόσαι [ἄν τινες ὀσιν]. Those which paid in full were contrasted with those which were either wholly or in part in arrears, and this meaning of ἐλλιπόσας reappears with the same force in D8 (lines 18-20): ἀναγ[ραφόντον δὲ ℎοι ἐλλ]ενοτα[μ]ίαι ἐς σανίδι τὰς [πόλες τὰς ἐλλιπό]σας τô φό[ρ]ο καὶ τὸν ἀπαγόντ[ον τὰ ὀνόματα κα]ὶ τιθέναι – – –. The similarity between the two decrees requires that τὸν ἀπαγόντ[ον τὰ ὀνόματα] must mean " the names of those who paid in full."[41] The ἀπάγοντες were the paying cities, as argued by Meritt in D. A. T. (p. 34),[42] but the word so obviously also means couriers—especially in the early lines of D7—that it must be taken to be the cities as represented in their couriers. The personal consideration was clear, but when the names came to be written on the panel, they were corporate names like Ἀφυταῖοι, Ἐφέσιοι, etc., rather than *nomina* and *nomina patrum*.[43]

We do not know whether this formality of inscribing the names of payers and defaulters in each year after the Dionysia began earlier than D7. But at least from 448/7 there must have been a growing archive of these complete records of tribute collection. We have suggested in D8 (line 21, restored) that the tablets were set up in front of the speaker's rostrum. They were more detailed than the quota lists, and they gave the amounts of tribute, not merely the ἀπαρχαί. If they began in 454/3 there must have been as many of them as there were of the quota lists. Yet of the quota lists, which were carved on stone, we have almost a continuous sequence; of these still more valuable records, which were on wood, no single trace has been preserved. These are the records to which reference is made in D3 (lines 13-16): ἐὰν [κοινὸν] φσέφισμά τι περὶ τôν ὀφειλεμάτον τôν ἐν τê[ισι σανί]σι γίγνεται μεδὲν προσℎεκέτο

---

[40] Schwahn's attempt in P. W., R. E., s. v. φόροι, p. 633, to restore [ἐν τôι ℎιερôι τôι τô] Διονύσ[ο τô ἐκ Λιμ]νôν ἀ[ναγραφόντον τὰς πό]λες in D8, lines 13-14, needs to be mentioned only to be rejected.

[41] Hill and Meritt should not have changed this rendering (*Hesperia*, XIII [1944], p. 11) to read " and the names of the couriers." There are factual difficulties involved here, for if a city defaulted entirely there could have been no couriers and hence no names to inscribe.

[42] The same is probably the meaning in D7, lines 58-59 (cf. also lines 43-46).

[43] The delegates at an American political convention are known by the names of their states, and in the convention hall carry placards announcing that they are, in fact, Alabama, Arkansas, etc., as the case may be.

Μεθοναίο[ις ἐὰμ μὲ χ]ορὶς γίγνεται φσέφισμα περὶ Μεθοναίον. The earlier restoration here (cf. *A. T. L.*, I, p. 162) has been ἐν τε̑[σι στέλε]σι, but this is made improbable not only by the fact that a στήλη implies marble, of which nothing has survived, but by the facts also that there must have been many of them, making the absence of survival still more remarkable, and that D7 and D8 call them σανίδες or πινάκια.[44]

We had assumed earlier that these tablets were to be set up in front of the Metroön, and the text of D8 was so restored in *A. T. L.*, I. Dow had already raised certain objections to this, on the ground, partly, that the space before the Metroön was probably never used for general notices of such secular character, but he made no alternative suggestion.[45] Our present restoration, which places the tablets in front of the bema of the council chamber, has been made largely because of our belief that " whitened tablets " must have been posted indoors where they would have been at least protected from the weather. Obviously these records were meant to last for a number of years, and we hold that such protection would have been essential. Moreover, even the assessments cut in stone were set up inside the Bouleuterion (A9, lines 24-25). We do not know where, inside the chamber, they were, but a precise location for the σανίδες can be given by the restoration in D8 of πρόσθε[ν το̑ βέματος]. We conceive that the tablets need not have been unduly high, but in the prominent position thus suggested they would have been a constant reminder to the Council of the source of Athenian wealth and of the obligations of the allies.[46]

Mention of the Dionysia in connection with tribute, though not with certainty to be referred to the payment of it, has been rescued from a passage in Isokrates by Norlin and explained at length by Raubitschek.[47] There was an Athenian decree which authorized the display, talent by talent, of the " surplus of the funds derived from the tributes of the allies," [48] the money being brought by hirelings into the orchestra during the festival of Dionysos. The phrase τὸ περιγιγνόμενον ἐκ τῶν φόρων ἀργύριον cannot mean the annual surplus from current tribute, for the decree belongs to the period

---

[44] D7, lines 44-45: πινάκιον λελ[ευκομένον]; D8, line 19: σανίδι. The reading δρ[αχμεῖσ]ιν in D4, lines 38-39, seems to us preferable to δρ[αχμαῖσ]ιν (so also Meisterhans, *Grammatik*³, p. 121, note 1105), and it makes easier the orthography assumed above in the reading ἐν τε̑[ισι σανί]σι (D3, lines 14-15). Kirchhoff, *Abh. Ak. Berlin*, 1861, p. 561, note 1, rejected the reading τε̑[ισι] because later in D4 the spelling τε̑σι appears.

[45] Dow, *A. J. A.*, XLII (1938), pp. 602-603.

[46] Antiphon (περὶ τοῦ χορευτοῦ, 40) is the *locus classicus* for the bema in the fifth century: Φιλοκράτης αὐτὸς οὑτοσὶ ἐν τῷ βουλευτηρίῳ ἐναντίον τῆς βουλῆς, ἑστὼς μετ᾽ ἐμοῦ ἐπὶ τοῦ βήματος, ἁπτόμενος ἐμοῦ διελέγετο.

[47] See Raubitschek, *T. A. P. A.*, LXXII (1941), pp. 356-362, and George Norlin, *Isocrates with an English Translation*, II (*The Loeb Classical Library*, London and New York, 1929), pp. 56-57. Part of Norlin's text of the *de Pace* (VIII, 82 [T79c]) reads as follows: οὕτω γὰρ ἀκριβῶς εὕρισκον ἐξ ὧν ἄνθρωποι μάλιστ᾽ ἂν μισηθεῖεν, ὥστ᾽ ἐψηφίσαντο τὸ περιγιγνόμενον ἐκ τῶν φόρων ἀργύριον, διελόντες κατὰ τάλαντον, εἰς τὴν ὀρχήστραν τοῖς Διονυσίοις εἰσφέρειν ἐπειδὰν πλῆρες ᾖ τὸ θέατρον· καὶ τοῦτ᾽ ἐποίουν − − − ἐπιδεικνύοντες τοῖς μὲν συμμάχοις τὰς τιμὰς τῆς οὐσίας αὐτῶν ὑπὸ μισθωτῶν εἰσφερομένης − − −.

[48] The translation is Norlin's.

of the early Archidamian War, and in the Archidamian War there was never an annual surplus.[49] Nor do we believe that the phrase can mean " the annually incoming tribute money." [50] The verb περιγιγνόμενον, being present in tense, refers to the ever changing amount of the total surplus. This was suitable for display, and it always included the untouchable reserve of 1000 talents, though in fact the free balance declined in amount regularly throughout the Archidamian War.[51]

This accumulated reserve (Thucydides, II, 13, 3 [T117]) belonged to Athena and to the Other Gods, and drafts against it for the expenses of the war were charged as loans, on which the Athenian state paid interest.[52]

But most of the money had in fact come from the φόροι, and there is no need to assume that Isokrates implies the existence of any different fund. There was none. Raubitschek uses an indication in the *Knights* of Aristophanes [53] to suggest that Kleon was the author of the decree and that it was probably passed soon after the death of Perikles.

One other detail of bookkeeping should here be mentioned. Schwahn has described how enormous would be the task of merely counting all the tribute if it were to come in on the festival day, and he concludes that it would in fact have been impossible even if the receiving officers and the Council had sat all day doing it, which in itself was hardly to be expected of them during the holiday season.[54] One has no need to imagine so strenuous a scene. In the first place, the Dionysiac festival was a *terminus post quem non*. Any city could pay earlier, some at least undoubtedly did, and in later years we have the evidence of Thucydides that collections were made by Athenian ships during the year.[55] Even so, the allies were present in Athens in large numbers for the Dionysia and most of the tribute must have been, as a rule, collected at that time. But the collections could be made on working days before the festival, and we believe the process of collection to have been very easy: the appearance before the

[49] See below, pp. 341-344.

[50] So Raubitschek.

[51] See below, pp. 341-344. One may object that the exhibit of decreasing reserves could hardly have been good for morale; but the fund could still provide a pageant of over 2000 porters, each carrying a talent, in any year before 425 B. C. This spectacle could be counted upon to allay anxiety among the allies and stop any rumour that may have spread abroad that Athens was short of money.

[52] *I. G.*, I², 324. Cf. Meritt, *A. F. D.*, pp. 136-143; Tod, *Greek Hist. Inscr.*, I², no. 64; Broneer, *Hesperia*, IV (1935), pp. 158-159; Oguse, *B. C. H.*, LIX (1935), pp. 416-420; Pritchett and Neugebauer, *Calendars of Athens*, pp. 95-105; Meritt, *Cl. Quart.*, XL (1946), pp. 60-64.

[53] Line 313 (T37b): Kleon is described as ἀπὸ τῶν πετρῶν ἄνωθεν τοὺς φόρους θυννοσκοπῶν; the scholiast comments (T37c): οὐ λανθάνουσι τὸν Κλέωνα τῆς πόλεως ἐπιβαίνοντες οἱ τοὺς φόρους φέροντες.

[54] Schwahn, in P. W., R. E., s. v. φόροι, p. 632: " Das ist alles praktisch unmöglich. Dass der gesamte Rat und die Finanzbehörde an einem der höchsten Feste von früh bis spät dienstlich tätig waren, ist ausgeschlossen. Eine Summe von 400 bis 500 t in über 150 verschiedenen Posten konnte an einem Tage von einem Finanzkollegium in keinem Falle angenommen, nachgezählt (1 t hat 1500 Stücke zu 4 d) oder nachgerechnet und verbucht werden."

[55] T119, T125, T130, T133; cf. Meritt, *A. F. D.*, pp. 19-20.

Council, the matching of the tallies, the reading of the tablet, and the transfer of the jars or bags of coin to the apodektai. The record was made, just as one makes a deposit in a bank today; small payments could be checked at once, and the verification of larger sums looked to later. We suggest this as one of the duties which occupied the hellenotamiai on days when there was no other pressing business. If the envoys who brought the money had departed, their proxenos could guarantee them against a miscount and otherwise represent their interests when the seals on the jars were broken. But there was evidently no long delay. The heralds who set forth to demand arrears also carried receipts for those who had paid.

CHAPTER II

THE ASSESSMENT OF 454/3 B.C.

There is evidence enough from the original membership of the Delian Confederacy[1] and from the tribute-quota lists to show what the nature of the first assessment (478/7) must have been. Prerequisite is a determination of the assessment list of 454 (A1); the evidence of the quota lists will therefore be set forth in detail in order that the general conclusions derived from them may be employed later in our study of the assessment of 478/7.[2]

Gomme has proposed certain principles for the calculation of tribute assessed during the first six periods after the treasury of the Confederacy was moved from Delos to Athens. He makes two assumptions:[3] "(1) that a city which is known to have paid at least once within an assessment period paid the same tribute in every year of that period, and (2) that a city which is known to have paid regularly in, say, four or even three of the first six periods --- paid also in the other two or three periods, unless we have evidence to the contrary."

In general these principles are good, but in searching for the amount of the original tribute it is unnecessary to develop the calculation for each of the first six periods. The important period is the first, before Kimon's last campaign. Our own opinion, as will appear, is that when the Confederacy first began to function the payments in cash ($\chi\rho\acute{\eta}\mu\alpha\tau\alpha$) were relatively few; so we favour, for the sake of the argument, including in the assessment of 454 not merely cities that have appeared three or four times in the first six periods, but cities that have appeared even once, unless (as Gomme observes) there is evidence to the contrary, or unless the cities under consideration obviously joined the Confederacy later than 454/3–451/0. Our resulting list will therefore represent a maximum. Every critical reader will wish to control the tabulation and to know more than the total for the period, which is of little use unless he knows how it was reached. Consequently, we put down the list of cities, name by name,[4] with a serial number and an amount of tribute attached to all whom we are prepared at this stage to include in the assessment of 454; if, in our opinion, a city was not assessed in A1, serial numbers and amounts will be withheld. Each city will bear a geographic label. When the evidence from the quotas gives odd (*i. e.*,

[1] See Chapter III of Part III below; for the individual districts see especially pp. 198-199 (Islands), 204 (Ionia), 206-207 (Hellespont), 213 (Karia), 223 (Thrace).

[2] See Chapter V of Part III below, pp. 234-243.

[3] *Commentary*, I, pp. 274-275.

[4] In general, the roster of names passed in review is that of the Register of *A. T. L.*, I, with the adjustments noted in *A. T. L.*, II, Chapter III; a few broken entries, which do not merit space in the Register, have been added.

irregular) amounts of tribute, whether this is caused by increments or partial payments or something else, our practice will be to compute what we conceive to have been the assessed sums and to use those figures.

The reader will find notes where we feel enquiry is likely to arise, but certain categories of cities which we exclude from the assessment of 454 B. C. can be named more compendiously here:

(1) Cities whose first appearances in the records, generally but not always in the special rubrics or in A9 and A10, are caused by apotaxis.[5]

(2) Cities whose lateness in entering the records shows that they were not previously members of the Confederacy; many of these were peripheral and are found in the special rubrics.[6]

(3) Euxine cities (not assessed before 425/4) and Aktaian cities of the Lesbian peraia (not assessed separately before the reduction of Mytilene, 428/7).[7]

THE ASSESSMENT OF 454/3

		T.	Dr.
1.	Ἀβδηρῖται (Th.)	15	——
2.	Ἀβυδηνοί (Hel.)	4	——

The figure in 1, II, 29 with which this name is restored is HHHHΔΔΔΓⱵⱵIIII. We take the nearest round figure as the assessment, especially in view of the odd quota HHHHΓⱵIC in 10, II, 3 and the consistent quota of HHHH in 13, II, 8; 14, II, 29; 15, I, 31.

		T.	Dr.
3.	Ἄζειοί (Hel.)	——	400
4.	Ἀθῆναι Διάδες (Ins.)	——	2000
5.	Αἰγάντιοι (Th.)	——	3000
6.	Αἰγινῆται (Ins.)	30	——
7.	Αἰνειᾶται (Th.)	3	——
8.	Αἴνιοι (Th.)	12	——
	Αἰολῖται (Th.)		

First in the πόλεις αὐταί rubric of List 21.

		T.	Dr.
9.	Αἱραῖοι (Ion.)	3	——
	Αἶσα (Th.)		

First in the ἰδιῶται rubric of List 21.

		T.	Dr.
10.	Αἰσώνιοι (Th.)	——	1500
11.	Ἀκάνθιοι (Th.)	5	——

The figure is restored in 5, III, 34, but there is not space for the smaller quota of HHH which commences in 446/5.

Ἀκρόθῳοι (Th.)
Only in A10.

		T.	Dr.
12.	Ἁλικαρνάσσιοι (Kar.)	1	4000
13.	Ἀλινδῆς (Kar.)	1	3000

The quota in 4, V, 21 is HΔ ———; our estimate is a maximum.

Ἀλωνήσιοι (Hel.)
Only in A9.

		T.	Dr.
14.	Ἀλωποκοννήσιοι (Hel.)	1	——

The figure in 5, V, 14 is ⱵHⱵⱵⱵ. It is irregular and may be complementary (see below, p. 33 and note 55 on pp. 59-60). On this assumption we conjecture that the assessment was 1 talent. Later quotas show a tribute of 1000 or 2000 drachmai, normal variants.

Ἀμαξιτός (Akt.)

Ἄμιοι (Kar.)
Only in List 27 (Karic Chersonese syntely).

[5] For ἀπόταξις see below, pp. 195-196.
[6] See below, p. 195.
[7] See below, pp. 223-224.

		T.	Dr.

'Αμόργιοι (Kar.)

First in the πόλεις αὐταί rubric of List 21.

15. 'Αμυνανδῆς (Kar.)   ——   3000

The quota of Amynanda appears as ⊢IIIII in 2, I, 14.

'Αναφαῖοι (Ins.)

First in List 27; Anaphe was not in the Empire until after the conquest of Thera (see below, p. 198 with note 24).

16. "Ανδριοι (Ins.)   12   ——

"Αντανδρος (Akt.)

'Απολλωνία (Eux.)

17. 'Αργίλιοι (Th.)   1   3000

18. 'Αρισβαῖοι (Hel.)   2   ——

19. 'Αρκέσσεια (Kar.)   ——   1000

First in List 5, and a doubtful candidate for A1; see Βρυκούντιοι.

'Αρλισσός (Kar.)

Only in List 10.

20. 'Αρπαγιανοί (Hel.)   ——   300

First in List 7; see below, note 58 on p. 207.

'Αρταιοτειχῖται (Hel.)

First in List 27.

21. 'Αρτακηνοί (Hel.)   ——   2000

22. "Ασπενδος (Kar.)   (amount unknown)

This city was assessed in 425/4 (A9, II, 156-157), and, since the only excuse for the appearance of the name there was probably that it had been assessed at some time when Athens controlled the coast east of Phaselis, it was in all likelihood included in the assessment of 454. See 'Ιτύρα.

23. 'Ασσηρῖται (Th.)   ——   2400

We give the figure from 4, III, 22. With Skabala and Olynthos the total amounts to a tribute of 2 T. 5400 Dr. This differs from the total represented by the quota of 1, V, 6-8, where we now restore Η[ΗⲘΔΓ]⊢IIII, but is reasonably close to it.

24. 'Αστακηνοί (Hel.)   1   3000

25. 'Αστυπαλαιῆς (Kar.)   2   ——

"Αστυρα Τρωϊκά (Hel.)

Only in A9.

26. 'Αστυρηνοὶ Μυσοί (Ion.)   ——   500

27. Αὐλιᾶται (Kar.)   ——   500

28. 'Αφυταῖοι (Th.)   3   ——

'Αχίλλειον (Akt.)

29. Βαργυλιῆς (Kar.)   ——   1000

Βέλβινα (Ins.)

Only in A9.

30. Βεργαῖοι (Th.)   ——   3000

The normal figures for the quota are ΔΔΔΔΓ⊢⊢⊢ and ⲘⲎ⊢. It is still a question whether the quota of 8, I, 93 ought not to be restored [ΔΔΔΔΓ]⊢⊢⊢.

31. Βηρύσιοι (Hel.)   ——   1000

Βισάνθη (Hel.)

Only in A9, A10, and A13.

32. Βολβαιῆς (Kar.)   ——   1000

The quota of Bolbai in 2, I, 11 is ΔΓ⊢⊢I, which represents a normal quota of ΔΓ⊢IIII, plus an increment.

Βορμίσκος (Th.)

Only in A9 and A10.

Βουθειῆς (Ion.)

This is a special case. Boutheia may not have been separately assessed, but while Erythrai (q. v.) was in revolt the loyal Erythraians on the peninsula paid a tribute of 3 talents. This was booked under the name Βουθειῆς. Erythrai was not recovered until early summer of 452; see D10 and below, pp. 252-255. In the actual collection of 454/3, Boutheia should be included (with 3 talents), but Erythrai, which was assessed, should be omitted; see below, p. 266.

Βρικινδάριοι (Kar.)

First in List 26.

Βρυκούντιοι (Kar.)

These allies were probably not assessed simultaneously with Καρπάθιοι until the definitive apotaxis of 434. The name appears in Period II, and Karpathos

T. Dr.

alone may represent the assessment in Period I, as it did in Periods III (probably) and IV. But no Karpathian name has actually survived in Period I and the assessment may be regarded as doubtful.

Βρυλλειανοί (Hel.)
First in List 22.

33. Βυζάντιοι (Hel.)   15 ——
Βύσβικος (Hel.).
First in the ἰδιῶται rubric of List 21.

Γαλαῖοι (Th.)
First in List 19 (ἄτακτοι, see below, pp. 86-87, and note 109 on p. 218).

34. Γαλήψιοι (Th.)   1   3000
35. Γαργαρῆς (Ion.)   —— 4500
36. Γεντίνιοι (Hel.)   —— 500
Γίγωνος (Th.)
First in the ἰδιῶται rubric of List 21.

37. Γρυνειῆς (Ion.)   —— 1000
38. Γρυγχῆς (Ins.)   —— 1000
Δανδάκη (Eux.)
39. Δαρδανῆς (Hel.)   1   3000
Δαρεῖον (Hel.)
Only in A9.

40. Δασκύλειον (Hel.)   —— 500
41. Δαυνιοτειχῖται (Hel.)   —— 1000
Δειραῖοι (Th. ?)
We now assign this name from Krateros to A13.
Διακρῆς ἀπὸ Χαλκιδέων (Ins.)
First in the ἰδιῶται rubric of List 21.
Διάκριοι ἐν Εὐβοίᾳ (Ins.)
First in List 26.
Διάκριοι ἐν Ῥόδῳ (Kar.)
First in List 25.

42. Διδυμοτειχῖται (Hel.)   —— 1000
43. Διῆς ἀπὸ Κηναίου (Ins.)   —— 1000
44. Διῆς ἀπὸ τοῦ Ἄθω (Th.)   1 ——
45. Δίκαια παρ' Ἄβδηρα (Th.)   —— 3000
46. Δικαιοπολῖται (Th.)   4 ——
47. Διοσερῖται (Ion.)   —— 1000
Δρῦς (Th.)
Only in A10.

48. Δῶρος (Kar.)   (amount unknown)

T. Dr.

The name is known for the Confederacy only from Krateros, but it belongs to the assessment of 454; see above, pp. 9-11.

Ἑδριῆς (Kar.)
Only in A9.

49. Ἐλαῖται (Ion.)   —— 1000
Ἐλαιούσιοι ἐν Χερρονήσῳ (Hel.)
In the Hellespontine Chersonese syntely.
Ἐλαιούσιοι Ἐρυθραίων (Ion.)
These were included in the assessment of Ἐρυθραῖοι in 454. See Ἐρυθραῖοι.

50. Ἐρετριῆς (Ins.)   6 ——
First in List 7.

51. Ἐρινῆς (Kar.)   —— 4000
The figure is based on 2, I, 13: ⲫΔΓΗΗΙΙΙΙΙ.

52. Ἐρυθραῖοι (Ion.)   9 ——
Erythrai was in revolt in 454, but even so was probably assessed. The estimated figure of 9 talents is deduced from the record of the second period. Cf. *A. T. L.*, I, p. 272. The loyal part of the peninsula paid under Βουθειῆς (*q. v.*).

53. Ἑστιαιῆς (Ins.)   —— 1000
First in List 5.
Ἐτεοκαρπάθιοι (Kar.)
First in the πόλεις αὐταί rubric of List 21.

54. Εὐρυμαχῖται (Hel. ?)   —— 1000
Only in Lists 7 and 8, a doubtful candidate for the assessment of 454.

55. Ἐφέσιοι (Ion.)   7   3000
The assessment included that of Isinda, Marathesion, Pygela.

Ζέλεια (Hel.)
Only in List 14 and A9.
Ζερεία (Th.)
Only in A10.
Ζώνη (Th.)
Only in A10.
Ἡράκλειον (Th.)
Only in A9 and A10.
Ἡρακλειῶται (Eux.)

T. Dr.

56. Ἥσσιοι (Ion.)   1 ——
    Ἡφαιστιῆς (Ins.)
    The name Λήμνιοι with a quota of 900 drachmai in 3, I, 3 shows that Lemnos was assessed as a unit. Apparently Ἡφαιστιῆς paid either simultaneously with Μυριναῖοι, for whom there is no evidence in the first period, or alone for Lemnos in 2, V, 14. Or Hephaistia may have made a partial payment on the Lemnian tribute, as Koresos did on that of Keos (see 4, I, 21 and V, 22). See Λήμνιοι.

57. Θασθαρῆς (Kar.)   —— 500
58. Θάσιοι (Ins.)   3 ——
59. Θερμαῖοι (Ion.)   —— 3000
    Θέστωρος (Th.)
    Only in A10.
    Θηραῖοι (Ins.)
    Thera did not become a member of the Empire until after 431; see note 24 on p. 198 below.

60. Θραμβαῖοι (Th.)
    Therambos was assessed in 454 with Skione. See Σκιωναῖοι.

61. Θύδονος (Kar.)   —— 1000
    Θύμβρα (Akt.)
62. Θύσσιοι (Th.)   —— 4000
63. Ἰασῆς (Kar.)   1 ——
    First in List 5.
64. Ἰᾶται (Ins.)   1 ——
65. Ἰδυμῆς (Kar.)   1 890
    This is surely a maximum figure; the posting in 2, I, 15 indicates a possible lower assessment.
    Ἱερά (Kar.)
    Only in A9.
66. Ἰηλύσιοι (Kar.)   10 ——
67. Ἴκιοι (Th.)   —— 1500
    Ἴλιον (Akt.)
    Ἴμβριοι (Ins.)
    In the Hellespontine Chersonese syntely.
    Ἰσίνδιοι (Ion.)
    First in List 10; see Ἐφέσιοι.

T. Dr.

Ἰτύρα (Kar.)
Only in A9. Ityra lies beyond Phaselis, and so beyond the limits to which the Athenian Empire extended after the Peace of Kallias. Its inclusion in the assessment of 425 shows that it had been assessed earlier, when the coast east of Phaselis was in Athenian control, possibly in 458, almost surely in 454, and possibly also in 450, though this is not equally sure. But so many names in older regions of the Empire were listed separately after the extensive apotaxis of the late 'thirties and of the early years of the war (including the assessment of 425/4) that we believe the region beyond Phaselis to have been represented in 454 by Aspendos and Kelenderis, and the coast of Phoinike by Doros. These three names we place in the assessment of 454, but we reverse the principle of apotaxis and assume that places like Ἰτύρα, Μιλύαι, Πέργη, and Σίλλυον (there were undoubtedly others) did not in the early years appear separately from the larger cities. The assessment of 425/4 included not only all the larger cities from regions of the Empire which Athens no longer controlled; it included all the names that could be derived by apotaxis. This is the most reasonable explanation also for many broken entries in the text of A9 that cannot be expanded to give the name of any known city, e.g., [.]λονε[--], [.]ρανι[--], [.]βυδα[--], [.]οκα[--] (A9, II, 112, 115-117).

Καλλιπολῖται (Hel.)
First in the πόλεις αὐταί rubric of List 21.

68. Καλύδνιοι (Kar.)   1 3000
    Καμακαί (Th.)
    Only in List 34.
69. Καμειρῆς (Kar.)   9 ——
70. Καρβασυανδῆς (Kar.)   —— 1000

T. Dr.

71. Κᾶρες ὧν Τύμνης ἄρχει — 3000
First in List 10, a doubtful candidate for the assessment of 454.

72. Καρηναῖοι (Ion.) (amount unknown)
Only in a citation from Krateros, belonging to A1.
Καρκινῖτις (Eux.)
Κάρουσα (Eux.)

73. Καρπάθιοι (Kar.) — 1000
First in List 10, a doubtful candidate for A1; see Βρυκούντιοι.

74. Καρυανδῆς (Kar.) — 1000
Καρνῆς (Kar.)
Only in A9.

75. Καρύστιοι (Ins.) 7 3000
Κάσιοι (Kar.)
First in the πόλεις αὐταί rubric of List 21.

76. Κασωλαβῆς (Kar.) — 2500

77. Καύνιοι (Kar.) — 3000

78. Κεβρήνιοι (Hel.) 3 —

79. Κεδριᾶται (Kar.) — 3000

80. Κεῖοι (Ins.) 4 —
Assessment includes Κορήσιοι; the full amount was probably not collected in 451/0.

81. Κελένδερις (Kar.) 1 —
Only in A9, with an assessment of 2 talents. It was assessed in 454, certainly on a lower scale; see Ἰτύρα.

82. Κεράμιοι (Kar.) 1 3000
Κερασοῦς (Eux.)
Κερία (Ins.)
Only in A9.

83. Κιανοί (Hel.) — 1000
Κίθας (Th.)
First in the ἰδιῶται rubric of List 21.

84. Κιλλαρῆς (Kar.) — 1000
Κιμ[μερι — —] (Eux.)
Κίμωλος (Ins.)
Only in A9 and List 39, not tributary before the reduction of Melos.

85. Κινδῆς (Kar.) 1 —

86. Κλαζομένιοι (Ion.) 1 3000

87. Κλαννδῆς (Kar.) 1 —
First in List 11, a doubtful candidate for A1.

T. Dr.

Κλεωναί (Th.)
First in the ἰδιῶται rubric of List 21.

88. Κνίδιοι (Kar.) 3 —

89. Κοδαπῆς (Kar.) — 1000

90. Κολοφώνιοι (Ion.) 3 —
Κολώνη (Akt.)
Κολωνῆς (Hel.)
Only in A9.
Κορήσιοι (Ins.)
See Κεῖοι.
Κοσσαῖοι (Th.)
Only in A9.
Κρουσῆς (Kar.)
Only in A9.

91. Κρυῆς (Kar.) — 2000

92. Κυδαιῆς (Kar.) — 400

93. Κυζικηνοί (Hel.) 9 —
The figure is very uncertain, for the record begins consistently only in 443/2. Perhaps it is by chance that the name is lost from Period III; but it may be that the proximity of the Persian provincial capital at Daskyleion (just south of Kyzikos) prevented Kyzikos from making more than scattered and uncertain payments earlier than 443.
Κύθηρα (Ins.)
Kythera was not a member of the Empire until 424/3 (cf. Thucydides, IV, 57, 4 [T132]).

94. Κύθνιοι (Ins.) 3 —
First in List 5.

95. Κυλλάνδιοι (Kar.) 2 —

96. Κυμαῖοι (Ion.) 12 —

97. Κυρβισσός (Kar.) — 2000
Κυστίριοι (Th.)
Only in List 21, as an ἄτακτος πόλις.

98. Κῷοι (Kar.) 5 —

99. Λαμπώνεια (Hel.) — 1000

100. Λαμψακηνοί (Hel.) 12 —
Λάρισα (Akt.)

101. Λάτμιοι (Kar.) 1 —

102. Λεβέδιοι (Ion.) 3 —
Λέρος (Ion.)
See Μιλήσιοι. Leros should not be placed

T. Dr.

in the assessment of 454, but paid tribute in 454/3, while Miletos was in revolt.

103. Λήμνιοι (Ins.)   9 ——
See Ἡφαιστιῆς.

Ληρισαῖοι (Ion.)
Only in A9.

Ληρ[....]ι (Kar.)
Only in List 27 (Karic Chersonese syntely).

104. Ληψιμάνιοι (Kar.)   —— 1500
This name appears in 2, I, 12 with a quota of ΔΓΗΙ, and again in 2, VIII, 13, making its proper payment (ΔΔΓ), we may conjecture, for 453/2. Apparently full arrears for 454/3 were not collected.

Λιμναῖοι (Hel.)
In the Hellespontine Chersonese syntely.

105. Λίνδιοι (Kar.)   8 2700
Later assessments included Οὔατοι.

106. Λύκιοι (Kar.)   12 ——
We estimate the assessment at slightly more than the combined tribute of the Lykian syntely in 446/5.

107. Μαδνασῆς (Kar.)   2 ——
Μαδύτιοι (Hel.)
In the Hellespontine Chersonese syntely.

108. Μαιάνδριοι (Ion.)   —— 4000
Μαραθήσιοι (Ion.)
See Ἐφέσιοι.

Μαρκαῖοι (Hel.)
This name is known only from a fragment of Krateros, probably attributable to A13 (410/09).

109. Μαρωνῖται (Th.)   1 3000
Μεθωναῖοι (Th.)
First in List 23.

110. Μενδαῖοι (Th.)   8 ——
111. Μηκυβερναῖοι (Th.)   1 ——
This city paid in 454/3 with Stolos and Polichne.

Μήλιοι (Ins.)
Melos was assessed first in 425/4 (A9, I, 65); it was captured and colonized

T. Dr.

in 416/5 (Thucydides, V, 116, 3-4) but was never tributary.

Μητρόπολις (Hel.)
Only in A9 and A10.

112. Μιλήσιοι (Ion.)   10 ——
Miletos was in revolt in 454/3; see D11 and below, pp. 255-256. Although the figure of 10 talents should be counted in the assessment, with nothing for Leros and Teichioussa, the record of actual collection in 454/3 must comprise only Leros and Teichioussa and omit Miletos.

Μιλητοτειχῖται (Hel.)
Only in A13.

Μιλτώριοι (Th.)
First in List 20 (ἄτακτοι).

Μιλύαι (Kar.)
Only in A9; see Ἰτύρα.

113. Μυδονῆς (Kar.)   —— 1500
114. Μνήσσιοι (Ion.)   1 3000
115. Μυκόνιοι (Ins.)   1 3000
116. Μυλασῆς (Kar.)   1 ——
First in List 5.

117. Μύνδιοι (Kar.)   —— 500
Μυριναῖοι ἐν Λήμνῳ (Ins.)
See Ἡφαιστιῆς.

118. Μυριναῖοι παρὰ Κύμην (Ion.) 1 ——
119. Μυσοί (Hel.)   —— 2000
120. Ναξιᾶται (Kar.)   —— 1000
121. Νάξιοι (Ins.)   9 ——
After the klerouchy was founded (450) Naxos paid 6⅔ talents. We estimate the early figure at 9 talents on the basis of the payments after the Peace of Nikias; see below, pp. 65-66, 287.

122. Ναρισβαρῆς (Kar.)   —— 1000
123. Νεάνδρεια (Hel.)   —— 2000
Νεάπολις ἀπ' Ἀθηνῶν (Hel.)
First in List 13; see below, p. 205.

124. Νεάπολις παρ' Ἀντισάραν (Th.)—— 1000
125. Νεοπολῖται (Th.)   —— 3000
Νῆσος (Akt.)
Νικωνία (Eux.)

126. Νισύριοι (Ion.)   1 3000

		T.	Dr.

Νίψα (Eux.)

127. Νοτιῆς (Ion.) — 2000

Νύμφαιον (Eux.)

128. Ὀθώριοι (Th.) — 500
First in List 7, a doubtful candidate for A1.

129. Οὖᾶται (Kar.) — 3300
See also Λίνδιοι.

130. Οἰναῖοι (Ion.) 1 2000

131. Ὀλοφύξιοι (Th.) — 2000

132. Ὀλύνθιοι (Th.) 2 —
See Ἀσσηρῖται.

Ὀτληνοί (Hel.)
First in A9.

133. Οὐλαιῆς (Kar.) — 1000
This name appears in 2, I, 17 with a quota of ΔΓΗΗΙ.

134. Οὐρανιῆται (Kar.) — 1000
This name appears in 2, I, 16 with a quota of ΔΓΗΗΙ.

Ὀφρύνειον (Akt.)

135. Παισηνοί (Hel.) — 1000

136. Παλαιπερκώσιοι (Hel.) — 500

Παλαμήδειον (Akt.)

137. Παργασῆς (Kar.) — 1000
First in List 5, a doubtful candidate for A1.

138. Παριανοί (Hel.) 1 —

139. Πάριοι (Ins.) 16 1200

140. Παρπαριῶται (Kar.) — 1000

141. Πασανδῆς (Kar.) — 3000

Πάτ[ρασυς] (Eux.)

142. Πεδιῆς ἐν Λίνδῳ (Kar.) — 2000
First in List 7, a doubtful candidate for A1.

143. Πελεᾶται (Kar.) — 4000

144. Πεπαρήθιοι (Th.) 3 —

Περγαμοτειχῖται (Th.)
Only in A9.

Πέργη (Kar.)
Only in A9, but probably assessed in A1 with Aspendos; see Ἰτύρα.

145. Περίνθιοι (Hel.) 10 —

146. Περκώσιοι (Hel.) — 1000

Πέτρα (Akt.)

		T.	Dr.

147. Πηδασῆς (" Milesian " Pedasa, Kar.) 2 —

Πηδασῆς (" Halikarnassian " Pedasa, Kar.)
Only in A9.

Πίερες παρὰ Πέργαμον (Th.)
Only in A9.

Πίλωρος (Th.)
Only in the ἰδιῶται rubric of List 21.

Πίστασος (Th.)
First in the ἰδιῶται rubric of List 21.

148. Πιταναῖοι (Ion.) — 1000

149. Πλαδασῆς (Kar.) — 2000
First in List 7, a doubtful candidate for A1.

Πλευμῆς (Th.)
First in the πόλεις αὐταί rubric of List 21.

Πολιχναῖοι Ἐρυθραίων (Ion.)
See Ἐρυθραῖοι.

150. Πολιχναῖοι Κᾶρες (Kar.) — 1000

Πολιχνῖται (Hel.)
Only in A9.

151. Πολιχνῖται παρὰ Στῶλον (Th.) — 2000
The quota is inferred from 1, V, 12.
See Στώλιοι.

Πορδοσελήνη (Akt.)

Ποσίδειον (Th.)
Only in A10.

Ποσίδειον ἐν Εὐβοίᾳ (Ins.)
Only in A9.

152. Ποτειδεᾶται (Th.) 6 —
First in List 9.

Πράσσιλος (Th.)
Only in List 34.

153. Πριανῆς (Ion.) 1 —

154. Πριαπῆς (Hel.) — 500

155. Προκοννήσιοι (Hel.) 3 —

Πτελεούσιοι Ἐρυθραίων (Ion.)
See Ἐρυθραῖοι.

Πυγελῆς (Ion.)
See Ἐφέσιοι.

Πυθοπολῖται (Hel.)
Only in A9 and A10.

156. Πύρνιοι (Kar.) — 1000

157. Ῥηναιῆς (Ins.) — 1000

Ῥοίτειον (Akt.)

　　　　　　　　　T.　Dr.

158. Σ/ --- (Kar.)　　(amount unknown)
　　　Only in 4, V, 20.
　　　Σάλη (Th.)
　　　Only in A10.
159. Σαμβακτύς (Kar.)　　　　　　1 ——
　　　The figure in 1, II, 27 is ΗΓΗΙΙΙΙ, but
　　　the round sum of 3, V, 12 must repre-
　　　sent the assessed tribute.
160. Σαμοθρᾷκες (Th.)　　　　　　6 ——
161. Σαναῖοι (Th.)　　　　　　　　1 ——
　　　Σάριοι (Kar.)
　　　First in List 27.
　　　Σαρταῖοι (Th.)
　　　First in the πόλεις αὐταί rubric of List 21.
　　　Σεριοτειχῖται (Hel.)
　　　First in List 27.
162. Σερίφιοι (Ins.)　　　　　　　2 ——
163. Σερμαῖοι (Th.)　　　　　　—— 500
　　　First in List 5.
164. Σερμυλιῆς (Th.)　　　　　　　6 ——
　　　The assessment is an estimate from the
　　　confusing figures of Period I.
165. Σηλυμβριανοί (Hel.)　　　　　6 ——
　　　Σήστιοι (Hel.)
　　　In the Hellespontine Chersonese syntely.
166. Σίγγιοι (Th.)　　　　　　　　4 ——
167. Σιγειῆς (Hel.)　　　　　　—— 1000
　　　First in List 5.
　　　Σιδούσιοι Ἐρυθραίων (Ion.)
　　　See Ἐρυθραῖοι.
　　　Σικινῆται (Ins.)
　　　First in A9.
　　　Σίλλυον (Kar.)
　　　Only in A9, but probably assessed in
　　　A1 with Aspendos; see Ἰτύρα.
168. Σίλοι (Kar.)　　　　　　　—— 1500
　　　Σίνος (Th.)
　　　First in the ἰδιῶται rubric of List 21.
169. Σίφνιοι (Ins.)　　　　　　　　3 ——
　　　First in List 5.
170. Σκαβλαῖοι (Th.)　　　　　　—— 3000
　　　See Ἀσσηρῖται.
171. Σκαψαῖοι (Th.)　　　　　　—— 1000
172. Σκάψιοι (Hel.)　　　　　　　　1 ——

　　　　　　　　　T.　Dr.

173. Σκιάθιοι (Th.)　　　　　　—— 1000
　　　First in List 5.
174. Σκιωναῖοι (Th.)　　　　　　6 ——
　　　Therambos was included in this assess-
　　　ment.
　　　Σμίλλα (Th.)
　　　First in the ἰδιῶται rubric of List 21.
　　　Σομβία (Hel.)
　　　First in List 27.
175. Σπαρτώλιοι (Th.)　　　　　　2 ——
176. Σταγιρῖται (Th.)　　　　　　—— 1000
177. Στρεψαῖοι (Th.)　　　　　　　1 ——
178. Στυρῆς (Ins.)　　　　　　　　1 ——
　　　First in List 5.
179. Στώλιοι (Th.)　　　　　　　　1 ——
　　　The quotas of Mekyberna, Stolos, and
　　　Polichne respectively were probably Η,
　　　Η, and ΔΔΔΗΗΙΙ. The complete total
　　　in 1, V, 12 was ΗΗΔ[Δ]ΔΗΙ.
180. Συαγγελῆς (Kar.)　　　　　—— 3000
　　　Σύμη (Kar.)
　　　First in the ἰδιῶται rubric of List 21.
181. Σύριοι (Ins.)　　　　　　　—— 1500
　　　Ταμυράκη (Eux.)
　　　Τάραμπτος (Kar.)
　　　Only in A9.
182. Ταρβανῆς (Kar.)　　　　　　—— 1000
　　　The quota in 2, I, 18 is ΔΓΗΗΙ.
　　　Τειχιοῦσσα (Ion.)
　　　See Μιλήσιοι. Although Teichioussa is
　　　not to be placed in the assessment of
　　　454, it does appear (while Miletos is
　　　absent) in the record of actual pay-
　　　ments in 454/3.
183. Τελεμήσσιοι (Kar.)
　　　Included in the assessment of Λύκιοι.
184. Τενέδιοι (Hel.)　　　　　　　4 3000
185. Τερμερῆς (Kar.)　　　　　　　2 3000
186. Τήϊοι (Ion.)　　　　　　　　　6 ——
187. Τηλάνδριοι (Kar.)　　　　　　1 ——
　　　Τήλιοι (Kar.)
　　　First in List 28.
188. Τήνιοι (Ins.)　　　　　　　　3 ——
　　　First in List 5.

T. Dr.

Τηρεία (Hel.)
Only in A9 and A10.

Τινδαῖοι (Th.)
First in the ἰδιῶται rubric of List 21.

189. Τορωναῖοι (Th.)   12 ——

Τράϊλος (Th.)
Only in A9 and A10.

Τριποαί (Th.)
Only in List 34.

Τυμνησσῆς (Kar.)
Only in A9.

Τύρας (Eux.)

190. Τυρόδιζα (Hel.)   —— 1000

191. Ὑβλισσῆς (Kar.)   —— 1000
The figure in 4, V, 26 is ΔΓΗΙΙΙΙ

Ὑδισσῆς (Kar.)
The name appears only in Period II.

Ὑλιμῆς (Kar.)
The name appears only in Period II.

192. Ὑμισσῆς (Kar.)   —— 1200

193. Ὑρωμῆς (Kar.)   —— 2500
First in List 5.

T. Dr.

194. Φαρβήλιοι (Th.)   —— 1000
195. Φασηλῖται (Kar.)   6 ——
196. Φηγήτιοι (Th.)   —— 1600

Φολεγάνδριοι (Ins.)
First in A9.

197. Φωκαιῆς (Ion.)   3 ——
198. Χαλκειᾶται (Kar.)   —— 3000
First in List 5.

199. Χαλκητορῆς (Kar.)   —— 2000
200. Χαλκιδῆς (Ins.)   5 ——
First in List 7.

201. Χαλχηδόνιοι (Hel.)   7 3000
202. Χεδρώλιοι (Th.)   —— 500
First in List 5 (as Ἐρόδιοι).

203. Χερρονήσιοι (Kar.)   3 ——
204. Χερρονῆῖται (Hel.)   18 ——
205. Χῖοι Κᾶρες (Kar.)   —— 2000
206. [.]σσυρι—— (Kar., 4, V, 23) —— 1000
207. [..⁵...]ῆται (1, I, 28)   —— 4000
208. An unknown name or group (3, II, 2-4)   1 ——

This is the over-all total for the assessment of 454. A maximum of 208 names yields a maximum tribute of 498 talents, 1390 drachmai.[8] The figure is given in cash, without regard to whether some cities other than Lesbos, Chios, and Samos were still furnishing ships. These were the states, and this the value of the assessment, at the time when the Athenian Empire had its widest extent.[9]

[8] Amounts have not been included for four cities: Aspendos, Doros, Karene, and S/. ———, which would probably raise this figure by a few talents, but we let the total stand because elsewhere maximum figures have been taken where there has been doubt.

[9] Diodoros, XI, 85, 2 (T55); see below, pp. 259-260. We do not believe that the actual assessment of 454/3, the document cut on stone and seen by Krateros (called by us A1), included the names of those cities which were to provide ships. In this respect our proposed assessment differs from A1; but we shall subtract these naval allies, and certain other cities, later (see below, Part III, Chapter VII, especially pp. 267-268).

CHAPTER III

THE TEXTS OF THE SECOND ASSESSMENT PERIOD

(450/49–447/6)

1. Complements and Arrears

Period II, from the assessment of 450 to that of 446, saw the conclusion of peace with Persia, and the most conspicuous symptom of this is the absence of a quota list for 449/8.[1] The period naturally falls into the two parts, List 5 before the peace, and Lists 7 and 8 after the peace. We have found no cogent evidence of any completely fresh assessment between 5 and 7-8,[2] and we believe the cities who paid tribute were of approximately the same number (just over 160) in all three years. But they were not the same cities: there are some dozen who pay in List 5 but not in 7 or 8, and about the same number who pay in 7 and 8 but not in 5. No new assessment was needed for the former names to drop out, but some revision of the assessment in 448 may account for the latter names coming in. The simpler explanation, that they were assessed in 450 but failed to pay immediately, is perhaps more likely, whether because they held that the prospect of peace released them from the obligation, or because those troubles in Thrace and the Hellespont which led ultimately to the operations based on Eion and Tenedos (8 I 105, II 108-109) were already pre-occupying them.

The other conspicuous feature is the recording of complementary payments and of arrears. In the task of tracking these items, to avoid ambiguity, we keep as strictly as possible to the following nomenclature. The most comprehensive term is " payment "; a " whole-payment " is the payment in one sum of the whole tribute due. By " partial payment " we denote a city's first payment for any given year if that payment is partial; the further payments, if made in the same year, we call " complementary payments " or " complements." But if the payment of the balance left by a " partial payment " is deferred (or its record is deferred) to the next year, we call that " arrears." Either arrears or complement may be paid in more than one instalment. We reserve the term " whole-arrears " for cases in which the whole sum due is paid after the end of the year in which it was due.

We note, at this stage, that the above distinctions refer (in strictness) to the

---

[1] For this date for the missing list see below, pp. 278-281, 299.

[2] That is to say, the figures, where comparable, seem to stay the same after the peace as they were before. The change of spelling from [Γ]ρυνχês in 5 IV 33 to Βρ[υ]νχειês in 7 IV 12 is remarkable; possibly we should write [Β]ρυνχês in 5 IV 33.

record rather than to the actual payment. The payment which was first entered in the record was not necessarily the first payment made by the city; a payment whose record is deferred to the next year need not have been actually made so late as that. We believe that some at least of these apparent " arrears " and " complements " are really moneys levied (*e.g.*, on cities near the Hellespont) by a military commander, most probably *before* the balance was sent to Athens; they were entered late in the record because the record waited for the commander to come home and report the transaction. The evidence for this view is presented in the course of this chapter and we shall not anticipate it here; but we are concerned to make clear that we use the terms defined above (" arrears," " complements," etc.) without prejudice to the real nature of the payment, and solely on the *prima facie* evidence of the record.

In citing the amounts of payments, we cite always the quota (not the tribute). Wherever feasible we use arabic numerals, giving no denomination; the denomination is to be understood always as drachmai. Obols are shown as fractions of a drachma. No city, until A9, pays a quota of as much as 1 talent.

2. List 5 as a Whole

List 5 is the first in which we find the names grouped according to the tribute districts. In Period I, we have seen, the assessment was made by the five districts (Karic, Ionic, Thrakian, Hellespontine, Insular)[3] but the order of the names in the quota lists of Period I was probably the order of payments, and certainly was quite irrespective of the districts. It is not till Period IV that the tribute districts are set out, in the quota lists as they had always been in the assessments, into separate panels; but the quota lists of Periods II and III show perceptible traces of this grouping. This is probably to be explained by the fact that the tribute of each district was received at Athens, and booked, in its own special register;[4] the quota lists from List 5 onwards are consolidated out of these separate district lists. No care was taken in this act of consolidation (until Period IV) to preserve the groups intact, but the effect is naturally not obliterated. We shall disentangle the groupings for List 5 only; in List 7 they are more confused, but the Ionic-Karic names are massed in columns I and II, Thrakian and Hellespontine come chiefly in III, and Insular in IV. List 8 (apart from its appendix) is copied from List 7.

List 5 has five columns of names, the first four of 40 lines each (*sc.* lines 2-41), the fifth of 39 lines (*sc.* lines 2-40; line 41 was not inscribed). That makes 199 lines

[3] We have no evidence for the order in which these five were put. For Period I see Chapter I above.

[4] See above, pp. 13-14.

[5] I 14-15, II 2-3, 11-12, 26-27, 36-37, III 10-11, 13-14, 19-20, 26-27, 28-29, IV 12-13. That is 11 cases, an average of about 1 in 10 lines of the extant parts of columns I-IV. In our computation

of names; but in columns I-IV two-line names are fairly frequent [5] and in column V there are several second entries. We may provisionally estimate the second entries in column V at 20 lines and the two-line names in the whole remainder at 16. This will leave (199-20-16 =) 163 names for the list.

There appear to be four tribute districts: first the Ionic-Karic in columns I-II; next the Thrakian in column III; the Hellespontine at the foot of III and in the first half of IV; the Insular in the second half of IV. The Karic and Ionic districts seem to be combined in one.[6] In the following analysis we tentatively assign the gaps to a district if names of that district immediately precede and follow the gap.[7]

First come the Ionic-Karic names: I 2-15, [16-41], II 2-17, [18-25], 26-32, 35-41. That is to say, in columns I and II (the first 80 lines) all but two of the extant names are Ionic-Karic, but there is one large gap of 26 lines and a smaller one of eight lines in which the names are lost. Detached Ionic-Karic names come in III 35-36, V 2,[8] 11, 13, 18-30,[9] 40.

The next group (after a gap of six lost lines, III 2-7) is Thrakian: III 8-27. Detached Thrakian names come in III 30-32, 34, 40-41, IV 9, 11, 14-15, 17-18, possibly V 2.[10]

The Hellespontine group is more interrupted but its nucleus is III 28–IV 16. The Hellespontine names (including this nucleus) occur as follows: II 33-34, III 28-29, 33, 37-39, IV 2-5, [6-7], 8, 10, 12-13, 16, 25, V 3, 10, 12, 14-17.

on p. 32 we propose to restore 30 Ionic-Karic names in the 34 blank lines of columns I and II (*sc.* 4 two-line names), and in the figures on p. 32 we allow 12 unassigned names for those 13 blank lines of columns III and V which we allot to unassigned whole-payments (*sc.* 1 two-line name): a total of five two-line names of which four must be Ionic-Karic. We have in mind such possibilities as Καρπάθο | Βρυκόντιοι, Κεδριᾶται | ἀπὸ Καρίας, Ναχσία | παρὰ Μυδόνα, Πακτύες | Ἰδυμεύς, Πεδιês | ἐλ Λίνδοι, Πριαπês | παρὰ Πάριον, perhaps Διês | hοι ἐχς Ἄθο or Ὀλοφύχσιοι | ἐχς Ἄθο. It will be noticed that List 5 habitually uses the fullest designations, noticeably fuller than 7 and 8; *e. g.*, Μύνδιοι | παρὰ Τέρμερα does not recur till List 25.

[6] This is not quite conclusive. All the 13 names extant in column I are Karic; column II starts with four Ionic names and the remainder of the column is pretty well mixed. This evidence would perhaps admit the possibility of the Karic names having come first, in the upper part of column I, and the Ionic next, in the remainder of column I (which is all lost) and the top of column II. The remainder of column II is not more mixed than parts of III and IV. But this possibility is due mainly to the fact of the 26-line gap in column I in which we are supposing that the two districts were kept separate. We believe that the right reading of the evidence is to assume a single Ionic-Karic district. This is perhaps confirmed by D7 (lines 25-28) and D14 (§ 9 in the composite text).

[7] *I. e.*, I 16-41 and II 18-25 to the Ionic-Karic, IV 6-7 to the Hellespontine, IV 36-38 to the Insular. III 2-7 we leave unassigned, since it is preceded by Ionic-Karic names and followed by Thrakian. We note that IV 26-35 is predominantly Euboic (Kythnos, Seriphos, and Naxos intrude), and we think it very probable that [Χαλκιδês] and [Ἐρετριês] should be restored in 36-37, with their pre-klerouchic figures of [Ϻ] and [ϺΗ] respectively. Line 38 will then be [Σύριοι] or [Μυκόνιοι].

[8] If we write [Πιτα]ναῖοι.

[9] For this large nucleus (the " southeastern group ") see below, pp. 35-36.

[10] If we write [Τορο]ναῖοι.

The Insular group is IV 19-24, 26-35, [36-38], 39-41. That is to say, in the lower half of column IV all but one of the extant names are Insular, but there is one small gap where the names are lost (see above, note 7). For the restorations in IV 40-41 see below, note 22. There are no detached Insular names extant.

We have then in columns I-IV the following numbers of names of the four districts (we allow for a proportion of two-line names in the Ionic-Karic gaps; see above, note 5).

> Ionic-Karic: 41 names in 46 lines extant; [30 names in 34 lines in the gaps]: total, 71 names in 80 lines.
> Thrakian: 28 names in 32 lines; [no gaps assigned]: total, 28 names in 32 lines.
> Hellespontine: 16 names in 18 lines extant; [two names in two lines in the gaps]: total, 18 names in 20 lines.
> Insular: 19 names in 19 lines extant; [three names in three lines in the gaps]: total, 22 names in 22 lines.
> Unassigned: six lines in III 2-7 (containing perhaps five names).

We have so far omitted column V. This column contains an appendix which we shall have to analyse; provisionally, we note that it consists of second entries (which for the count of names we may disregard), and whole-payments made probably late in the year. Of the 39 lines, 14 are wholly lost and unrestored; of the remaining 25, 11 (lines 10-15, 17, 24, 26, 39-40) are probably second entries, while 12 (lines 16, 18-23, 25, 27-30) are probably whole-payments; in lines 2-3 no determination is possible. Of the 12 whole-payments, all are Ionic-Karic except Byzantion, which is Hellespontine. In the remaining 16 (lines 2-3 indeterminate, lines 4-9 and 31-38 unrestored) we estimate that there were seven lines of whole-payments, but we do not attempt to assign these among the districts. Column V then may be estimated to contain (besides its 20 lines of second entries) the following: 11 Ionic-Karic names, 1 Hellespontine, 7 unassigned lines. We add these to our previous figures and obtain the following:

> Ionic-Karic: 82 names (71 in I-IV, 11 in V).
> Thrakian: 28 names.
> Hellespontine: 19 names (18 in I-IV, 1 in V).
> Insular: 22 names.
> Unassigned first payments: perhaps 12 names (in 13 lines: 6 in III, 7 in V).
> Second entries: 20 lines in V.

3. List 5, Column V

In the analysis of column V the first thing is to determine as nearly as possible the number of " complements," or second entries. In the following cases we have a partial payment recorded in columns I-IV, and the complement in column V:

Erythrai	pays	[45]	in	II 13-17	and	855	in	V 13:	total	900
Kos	"	356	"	I 7	"	144	"	V 40:	"	500
Pasanda	"	50	"	I 8	"	50	"	V 26:	"	100 [11]
Perinthos	"	[38]2⅙ [12]	"	III 37	"	617⅚	"	V 10:	"	1000
Tenedos	"	288	"	III 39	"	162	"	V 15:	"	450

In the following the partial payment is recorded in columns I-IV; the complement is to be presumed in column V:

Aigina	pays	2620	in	IV 39	leaving	380	due:	total	3000
Dardanos	"	46	"	III 33	"	54	" :	"	100
Ios	"	14	"	IV 23	"	86	" :	"	100
Kebrene	"	145	"	II 33	"	155	" :	"	300
Myrina	"	100	"	IV 41	"	50	" :	"	150
Singos	"	183⅓	"	IV 11	"	16⅔	" :	"	200
Stolos	"	66⅔	"	IV 17	"	16⅔	" :	"	83⅓

And there are probably two more partial payments in IV 6-7 where two unknown cities are credited with amounts which almost certainly are not whole-payments.

In the following a complement is recorded in column V and a partial payment is to be presumed in columns I-IV:

Alopekonnesos	pays	54	in	V 14	complementary	to	46	:	total	100 [13]
Bargylia	"	16⅔	"	V 24	"	"	50	:	"	66⅔ [14]
Chersonese	"	1380⅔	"	V 12	"	"	419⅓	:	"	1800
Erine	"	54	"	V 11	"	"	12⅔	:	"	66⅔ [15]
Kalchedon	"	300	"	V 17	"	"	600	:	"	900

[11] This is twice the normal amount, but we have probably to conclude that Pasanda's tribute was in fact doubled in this assessment period. See below, note 14.

[12] The figure is [ΗΗΗΡΔ]ΔΔΗΙ.

[13] See above, p. 20.

[14] In 8 II 41 Bargylia pays this amount, which is four times its normal. We suggested in *A.T.L.*, I, p. 474, that Bargylia's tribute was doubled in this period, that it demurred and paid only its old amount in Lists 5 and 7, but made up these arrears in List 8, the figure 66⅔ in 8 II 41 being composed of 33⅓ for 447/6, 16⅔ arrears for 448/7 and 16⅔ arrears for 450/49. If this were so, this figure of 66⅔ in 8 II 41 would be unique in two ways: it would be the only example we know of in List 8 where arrears and current payment are consolidated into a single sum, and it would be the only example of arrears going back further than one year. We believe therefore that the tribute was not doubled in Period II but quadrupled. The reasons for this increase we suggest below, in note 54; observe meanwhile the parallel case of Pasanda (note 11 above). Both names come right amongst a group of whole-payments, are geographically close to that group (Bargylia is closer), are absent from the group in List 8, and pay an amount which is normally a whole-payment.

[15] See above, p. 7.

There is probably another complement in V 39 where an unknown city pays 17½.

We have then five cases in which a second payment is reasonably certain, six in which the amount recorded in column V looks like a second payment, and nine in which the amount recorded in columns I-IV suggests that a second payment was due. If the collection this year was thorough, and partial payments were in fact mostly followed by complementary payments, we could add our three classes together and obtain 20 cases in which the evidence points to a partial followed by a complementary payment; no doubt the blank lines might conceal one or two more. And whether or no, we have at least evidence that 20 cities or more failed to pay the whole amount in their first payment.

We believe that the collection of complements was fairly thorough, and we estimate as follows. In columns I-IV there were probably 144 quotas altogether (160 lines minus 16 two-line names). For just over half that number the figures are extant sufficiently to determine whether they are for whole payments or for partial, and out of 73 payments 60 are whole, 13 partial.[16] For the remaining 71 quotas (lost or so damaged that we cannot reasonably judge), we may roughly estimate 61 whole-payments and 10 partial, making 23 partial payments altogether in columns I-IV. In column V we have 21 figures well preserved, of which 11 are probably complements (V 10-15, 17, 24, 26, 39-40; for Alopekonnesos see below, note 55); of the total of 39 figures we may roughly expect that about 20 would be complements. It looks from this as if the number of complements in column V was not materially fewer than the number of partial payments in I-IV.

There are many hazards in this computation; in particular, any estimate of what stood in the still unrestored lines of column V must be largely arbitrary. We can apply one more control. We are assuming that we have about 13 out of 23 partial payments extant in I-IV, about 11 out of 20 complements in V, that is, roughly two 50% lists. The two lists, when complete, of partial payers and of complementary payers, being of about the same number, should be virtually identical. If this were so we should expect two 50% lists to show about 25% coincidence, that is, five coincident names in twenty. We have in fact four coincident names (Kos, Pasanda, Perinthos, Tenedos) and may probably add as a fifth Erythrai.[17] We conclude, then,

---

[16] A partial payment can be recognized even when the figure is incomplete or the name missing, and consequently the proportion of partial payments may be above the true average; we have done our best to adjust this by recognizing as whole-payments some incomplete figures which may be reasonably so recognized, namely, II 10, 26, 38, III 13, 25, 30, 32, 34-36, 38, 40-41 (13 in all). The following are certainly whole-payments: I 2-6, 9-14, II 28-32, 34-36, III 15-19, 21-23, 31, IV 8-10, 12, 14-16, 18-22, 24-29, 40. These 47 certain, plus the 13 probable, make the 60 whole-payments. The 13 partial payments are: I 7-8, II 33, III 33, 37, 39, IV 6-7, 11, 17, 23, 39, 41.

[17] Erythrai's inclusion is questionable, since its figure is not extant and therefore was not one of the 13 partial payments, extant in columns I-IV, from which we started; we feel confident enough to restore [ΔΔΔΔΓ] for Erythrai in II, 15. Note, however, that two of these 13 partial payers are

that just over 20 cities made partial payments and that there were about 20 complementary payments, and that very nearly every city which made a partial payment in columns I-IV made a complementary payment in column V.

There are also whole-payments in column V. The certain and probable cases are:

V 16 Byzantion pays 1500		V 23 Kindye pays 100	
V 18 Miletos " 1000		V 25 Karyanda " 8⅓	
V 19 Latmos " 100		V 27 Madnasa " 100	
V 20 Myous " 100		V 28 Pelea " 50	
V 21 Iasos " 100		V 29 [Ephes]os " [750]	
V 22 Priene " 100		V 30 [Euromos] " [41⅔]	

The restorations of Ephesos and Euromos as making whole-payments in V 29-30 are due to the following consideration. In 8 I 108-113, II 103-107,[18] we have this sequence:

Miletos pays [1000]		Kindye pays 100	
Latmos " [100]		Madnasa " 100	
Myous " [100]		Pelea " 50	
Ephesos " [7]50		Mylasa " 100	
Iasos " 100		Euromos " 41⅔	
		Karyanda " 8⅓	

In both lists, this sequence of whole-payments interrupts an appendix which consists largely of complements. The names in the two sequences are mostly the same: Byzantion and Priene occur in 5 and not in 8, Mylasa and Euromos in 8 and not in 5. Byzantion may be removed from the group at once: it stands separate from the rest of the sequence in 5 and it is geographically unique. Of the other names which are not common to both versions of the group, Euromos can be restored in 5, since here the sequence ends in a lacuna, and we have so restored it in 5 V 30. But Mylasa made its whole-payment in 5 I 12 and therefore cannot be restored in 5 V; similarly Priene made some payment (and no doubt a whole-payment) in 8 I 75 and cannot in any case be restored in this part of the appendix of 8, since there is no lacuna.

We have evidently a group of cities, from the neighbourhood of Ephesos and Miletos, which habitually made their payments late in the year. We shall call them the "southeastern group." In List 5 they consequently come into the appendix of complements; they do not (with the exception of Priene) come into List 7 at all, and in List 8 they again come in an appendix. The group appears to be constant, except that in List 5 Mylasa paid (exceptionally) in good time, while in Lists 7 and 8 Priene

anonymous (IV 6-7) and so is one of the complementary payers (V 39). This reduces our two lists of named payers to just 50%, and from these we must expect no more than 25% coincidence.

[18] These names probably run in direct sequence: the cutter brought his columns level at line 102, then cut I 103-113, then II 103-113. See below, note 26.

did the same. They may perhaps be distinguished from their appendix-fellows in that their late payment was very likely due to distance.

There is one rather more certain inference which we may draw at once. This " southeastern group " did not appear in the main body of List 5, and we consequently find its whole-payments in the appendix. The group did not appear in List 7 nor in the main part of List 8 (this main part, so far as the list of names goes, is identical with List 7). We should therefore look, in the appendix of List 8, for the group's whole-payments twice over, once for 448/7 and once for 447/6. It is extant only once, and we must supply the second record in one of the lacunae. We believe that this second record came in 8 II 74-84. The question, which record is for 448/7 and which for 447/6, we shall discuss later.

We have then, in column V of List 5, the eleven names of the " southeastern group " making whole-payments, and besides them the isolated case of Byzantion. But there are seven lines in this column still unaccounted for and we have provisionally estimated that these too contained whole-payments. We have no evidence into which gaps these should be put, and (as we have already noted) we cannot even determine whether V 2-3 are complements or whole-payments; but, *exempli gratia*, we suggest the following schematic arrangement:

V 2-8	[whole-payments] 7	
V 9		[complement] 1
V 10-15		complements 6
V 16	whole-payment 1	
V 17		complement 1
V 18-23	whole-payments 6	
V 24		complement 1
V 25	whole-payment 1	
V 26		complement 1
V 27-30	whole-payments 4	
V 31-38		[complements] 8
V 39-40		complements 2
Totals:	whole-payments 19,	complements 20

4. List 7

List 7 is very much shorter than List 5; the columns are not so long, and there are only four instead of five. Because of the fact that the names in List 7 were repeated exactly (with some insignificant changes of order) in the upper part of List 8, we can reasonably restore all but five lines. We find that two-line entries are avoided: the only example is [Δικαιοπολῖται] | Ἐ[ρετριῶν ἄποικ]οι in 7 I 35-36 = 8 I 37-38.

There were exactly 150 names, the last 9 of them set off in List 7 by the rubric M[ετὰ Διονύσια].[19]

This difference in length does not mean that many fewer cities paid in 448/7 than in 450/49. The eleven names of the " southeastern group," whose habit of especially late payment has been already noticed, no doubt paid for this year and were listed as having paid in the appendix to List 8.[20] This brings the total up to 161. Our estimate of 163 for List 5 was not exact, and in fact the total number of cities paying in the two years was almost identical; but we can save ourselves any attempt to bring them quite even, by observing that while there are only five spare lines in List 7 there are 18 names in List 5 either extant or reasonably supplied (and no doubt others which have not been supplied) which do not appear in List 7 or the " southeastern group." These 18 names are:

Ionic-Karic (3): Erine, Pargasa, Pasanda.
Thrakian (3): Akanthos, Olynthos, Skiathos.
Hellespontine (9): Alopekonnesos, [Artake],[21] Astakos, Chersonese, Daskyleion, [Kyzikos], Neandreia, Perinthos, [Prokonnesos].
Insular (3): [Aigina], [Hephaistia], [Myrina].[22]

It is among these 18 names that we should look first for the five names still to be restored in List 7; and after them, among those names absent from Period II (but present in neighbouring periods) which are listed below on pp. 58-59. We take the five places one by one:

(1) 7 I 30 = 8 I 32: a name of seven letters ending in iota. None of the above 18 will answer to this, and of the second class of names only Ἐλαῖται, if the double iota be crowded as in 3 III 4 and 14 II 9. We therefore suggest [Λέμνιοι]; this will cover the two cities of Lemnos (Hephaistia and Myrina), which are found in the appendix to List 8, apparently paying both arrears (8 I 96) and complements (II 111, 113). The name Λέμνιοι appears, as well as that of Ἐφαιστιês, in Period I.

(2) 7 II 19 = 8 II 10: a name of 8 letters ending in iota, which in 8 II 10 is credited with a quota beginning with Δ. All the three Thrakian cities listed above will fit the space, but only Skiathos fits the quota, unless the payment was partial. Since partial payments are rare in List 8 proper, we suggest [Σκιάθιο]ι.

---

[19] In List 8 these 9 are distributed systematically among the other names; see A. T. L., I, p. 176.
[20] See above, p. 36. The eleven names are those in 8 I 108-113, II 103-107.
[21] For this supplement see A. T. L., I, p. 186 (note on 16 II 20).
[22] In A. T. L., I, p. 175, note on 5, IV, 39-41, we suggested [Ἐφαιστιês] and [Μυριναῖο]ι. " The first sure appearance of Μυριναῖοι, however, is in 8, II, 111," and so we refrained from restoration in the text. The record of the Lemnian cities in the first two periods seems to us now to eliminate this objection, nor are we reluctant, as we might have been earlier, to restore a partial payment in List 5. The Lemnian tribute was halved after the founding of the klerouchy in 450; see below, pp. 46, 289-293.

(3) 7 I 32 = 8 I 34: we have no data for the name, but the quota in 8 I 34 had probably Γ as its second sign. Of the cities listed above, Astakos, Pargasa, and Skiathos each pays normally 16⅔, ΔΓΗΙΙΙΙ. None of the others has Γ as the second sign of its normal quota (Myrina, which has ⊡, is already included under the name [Λέμνιοι]). Of the three named, Skiathos has been proposed for 7 II 19; between the other two, Astakos and Pargasa, choice is quite arbitrary. We suggest [Παργασῆς].

(4) and (5) 7 II 14-15 = 8 II 4-5: there are no data, and any name would fit. The appearance of Kyzikos in 8 I 95, paying what is probably arrears from 448/7, makes [Κυζικενοί] a plausible candidate for one place, and we suggest ['Αρτακενοί] for the other because these two names frequently stand together.

We do not include these tentative names in our text, since they go beyond any sort of strict evidence, but we list here the forms in which they would have to be restored:

7	I 30	[ΗΗΗΗΔΙΙΙ]	[Λέμνιοι]	8	I 32	[Η]ΗⒶ	[Λέμνιο]ι
7	I 32	[ΔΓΗΙΙΙΙ]	[Παργασῆς]	8	I 34	[Δ]Γ[ΗΙΙΙΙ]	[Παργασῆς]
7	II 14	[ⒺΗΗΗΗΔΔΓΙΙΙ]	[Κυζικενοί]	8	II 4	[ⒺΗΗΗΗ]	[Κυζικενοί]
7	II 15	[ΔΔΔΙΙΙΙΙ]	['Αρτακενοί]	8	II 5	[ΔΔΔΙΙΙΙΙ]	['Αρτακενοί]
7	II 19	[ΔΓΗΙΙΙΙ]	[Σκιάθιο]ι	8	II 10	Δ[ΓΗΙΙΙΙ]	[Σκιάθιοι]

The quota of Lemnos in 7 allows for the arrears in 8 I 96, that in 8 allows for the complements in 8 II 111, 113; the quota of Kyzikos in 7 allows for the arrears in 8 I 95. The remaining quotas are for whole-payments.

If we made these restorations, we should still be left with the following 12 names found in List 5 but not in List 7 (nor in that " southeastern group " which should be added to List 7; see below, p. 49):

Ionic-Karic (2): Erine, Pasanda.
Thrakian (2): Akanthos, Olynthos.
Hellespontine (7): Alopekonnesos, Astakos, Chersonese, Daskyleion, Nean-
    dreia, Perinthos, Prokonnesos.
Insular (1): Aigina.

It is evident that however we restored the five gaps in List 7, some names of the first importance which had been present in List 5 would be absent in List 7. We have included in our suggested restorations two important names, Lemnos and Kyzikos. We could just possibly restore Akanthos in 7 I 32 (taking the quota to have been the single sign Ⓕ), or, e. g., Perinthos either there or in 7 II 15. But it is very improbable that all the blank lines should have been of this exceptional importance; and even then we should be left with, e. g., Aigina, Chersonese, Prokonnesos (all very large payers) unaccounted for. Three possible reasons occur to us. Some cities may have refused to pay after the peace with Persia had been sworn; Aigina could have done this and have had Spartan backing. Some cities may have been in trouble with their barbarian neighbours: Astakos, for example (cf. the passage of Memnon quoted in the Gazetteer, *s. v.* Ἀστακηνοί), or the city Cherronesos in the Thrakian Chersonese (cf. Plutarch, *Pericles*, 19, 1 [T97a]). Some cities may have been otherwise involved in near-by military operations; this might account for Perinthos and Prokonnesos, since there were probably land operations in Thrace. All three causes may have contributed. The number of Hellespontine names among the cities absent in List 7 is remarkable, and we shall find an equally remarkable number of Hellespontine names among the partial payers of this year.[23] We think there is little doubt that some of the operations against the Thrakians mentioned by Plutarch (*Pericles*, 19, 1) took place during this year 448/7, and the presence of a fleet at Tenedos is indicated in List 8 by the entry ἐσς Τένεδον.[24]

5. LIST 8: THE SECTIONS i-x

We need not argue the fact that List 8 begins by repeating, in virtually identical order, all the names in List 7. It is sufficiently established and is now a mere matter of observation.[25] It will be well, however, to start by dividing List 8 into its sections. The mason did not cut the whole of column I before beginning column II, but cut first a length of I, then the same length of II, then a further length of I, then the same further length of II, and so forth. These sections are as follows (compare also Figs. 1 and 2):

(i)   I 4-55   (iii) I 56-73   (v)   I 74-86   (vii) I 87-102   (ix) I 103-113
(ii) II 4-55 (iv) II 56-73 (vi) II 74-86 (viii) II 87-102 (x) II 103-113

For sections i-v, in which the names of List 7 are repeated, it is sufficient to refer to *A. T. L.*, I, p. 176; that the mason cut those names in this order is likewise a simple

[23] We deal with these partial payments when analysing the appendix to List 8, and they are shown in italics in the tables on pp. 53-57. The most remarkable instance is Lampsakos, which in 7 IV 3 pays only 86⅔ out of 1200, and in 8 II 59 only 60. There seems a good case for supposing that Lampsakos made large contributions to the campaign in both years, the levying officer being careful first not to levy the whole, so that something might be left to send to Athens for the festival.

[24] II 108-109. Compare I 105, ἐς ['Ε]ιόνα ℎαβδερῖ(ται), which no doubt indicates operations which culminated in the establishment of the colony at Brea. But whereas for the money paid to the officer at Eion the payer is named, none is named for the two payments to the officer at Tenedos. It is just conceivable that the payer's name was written vertically downwards, along the margin of the stone; if (as seems much more likely) it was omitted, it is a striking example of how little the compiler is concerned to give a clear account of how the money came in. He is concerned about the quittance (see below, pp. 41, 44) and " the two sums turned in at Tenedos " was enough identification for his purpose.

[25] See Meritt and West, *A. J. A.*, XXXII (1928), pp. 281-297; *A. T. L.*, I, p. 176.

matter of observation. Sections vi-x form the appendix. To establish the order in which he cut the names of this appendix is more risky (especially with the large lacuna in lines 74-99) and we do not claim the same certainty. Our main guide has been the "southeastern group," whose names come in I 108-113 and II 103-107 in approximately the same sequence as in 5 V 18-30. We infer from this that II 103 follows immediately on I 113, i. e., that new sections start at line 103.[26] That the mason started the appendix with a new section at II 74, and did not continue the old section at I 87, seems to us likely;[27] this will mean that sections vii and viii start at line 87.

The divisions between these sections are presented to the eye in Figures 1 and 2 on pp. 42 and 43. The drawing here reproduced is not a facsimile but a diagram. It is not to scale; the breadth has been slightly exaggerated by plotting it on a square chequer.[28] And we have drawn vertical lines between the columns of names and figures, and horizontal lines between the "sections," neither of which are on the stone. Its purpose is primarily to show (by these horizontal lines) the "sections," which we have numbered in the margins from i to x. Next, it aims to present visually the system on which the columns, names, and figures were plotted. The whole available breadth is divided into 28 stoichoi, 14 for each of the two main columns; in each main column 4 stoichoi are reserved for figures, 10 for names. There is much overrunning of these limits, and, especially, the names of column I and the figures of column II are allowed to run into each other freely. The names of column I run over to the right into the space meant for the figures of column II (I 10, 12, 18, 37, 38, 42, 48; in Fig. 1, I 56, 57; in Fig. 2, I 90, 91) and the figures of column II run over to the left, and begin in the space meant for the names of column I (II 19, 32; in Fig. 1, II 53, 55; in Fig. 2, II 100, 101). Sometimes, but much more rarely, a name in column II encroaches in this way on the figure column to its left (II 39; in Fig. 1, II 53); sometimes the letters of a long name in column II are crowded (II 39; we have often to presume such crowding, e. g., in II 28, and in Fig. 1, II 53, 59).[29] In no case

[26] See above, note 18. An alternative inference would be that the sequence in 8 is II 103-107 followed by I 108-113, i. e., that new sections start at line 108. It will be seen that this practically inverts the two halves of the group as given in List 5 and is therefore much less probable.

[27] We believe that he started it with the names of the "southeastern group" and that three of these should be restored to fit the traces in II 74-76. This involves the "jog" which we suppose in section vi (II 74-86, see Fig. 1); the fact that this jog has been abandoned before II 100 may perhaps serve to confirm our view that the new sections began before line 100.

[28] The actual proportion of height to breadth of the chequer is about 7 to 6.5, but the vertical interval varies. See A. T. L., I, p. 178, note on 8 I 87.

[29] It is possible that, whether by systematic crowding or by a slight widening of the available surface, 11 stoichoi were obtained for the names of column II in the upper part of the list. Without measurements on the stone itself this would be hard to determine, but if it were true it would account for the fact that the name Δαμνιοτ[ειχῖται] in II 53 is written one stoichos to the right of [Διδυμοτ]ειχῖται in II 73 (i. e., the last extant letter of the former is in the same stoichos as the first extant letter of the latter; see Fig. 1). In the latter place (II 66-76 = fragment 83) the right-hand

do the figures of column I encroach directly upon the names, but sometimes a very long figure is split and part of it is put after the name (*e. g.*, I 5; in Fig. 2, I 103, 104, 106). In column II the figures do encroach on the names sometimes, when they are thrust forward by especially long names in column I, *e. g.*, II 37, 38; we must presume such encroachment in II 10. We have drawn vertical lines (with the necessary " jogs ") between these columns of figures and of names, so as to make clear to the eye where the vertical divisions came and how much they were overrun.

More particularly, the diagram presents visually the " jog " which we presume in section vi. We infer the existence of this " jog " from the traces in II 74-76; unless the column was here jogged to the left we should have an improbable series of exceptionally short names (one of five letters and two of six). Supposing it to exist, we account for it by two factors: first, the last name in the section above (II 73) had certainly been jogged 3 or 4 spaces leftwards; next, the names in the section to the left (section v) are all rather short. We have perhaps exaggerated this last factor by writing (in the diagram) Νεάπολις and Λαμπονῆς in I 81-82 instead of Νεοπολῖται and Λαμπόνεια; both of these shorter forms are indeed found, but it will be seen from the diagram that (owing to the shortness of most of the figures in section vi) there is plenty of room for the longer forms.

The diagram also shows, more clearly than either our facsimile or our transcript, the place in line 60 where the sentence about the Erythraian syntely runs across the whole breadth of both columns. Finally, we have incorporated in the diagram some tentative restorations which are too uncertain to be put into the transcript (see pp. 36, 46-47, 50): especially II 74-84, also I 88 and the quotas in I 79, 90, 91, II 111. The supplements on pp. 37-38, offered, *exempli gratia*, for filling the gaps in 7 and the corresponding gaps in 8, are not covered by the diagram; our further suggestion (note 45) that I 89 be restored either [Αἴνι]οι or ['Αζει]οί seemed too doubtful to be incorporated.

The content of this appendix of 67 lines is unique in the lists, in that it picks up arrears for the previous year as well as late and complementary payments for the current year.[30] The purpose of the list is to give the hellenotamiai quittance for their obligations to Athena's tamiai in respect of the quota (or " sixtieth "); it does not aim to give an intelligible account of how the money came in,[31] and consequently

edge of the stone is extant and it is quite clear that here stoichos 10 of this name-column (*i. e.*, stoichos 28 of the whole inscription) is the last stoichos on the stone. See *A. T. L.*, I, p. 41, Fig. 52; the facsimile in *A. T. L.*, I, Plate VIII, is in this respect inaccurate.

[30] A provisional analysis was given by Wade-Gery, *Hesperia*, XIV (1945), pp. 227-228. We have a column of arrears in 2 I, and isolated examples of arrears in 25 I 43, 46, 26 IV 45 (in these latter cases the fact is, conformably to the practice of the later lists, explicitly stated). We distinguish arrears from complements (see above, p. 29). For the treatment of arrears, which with the few exceptions named are disregarded in the extant lists, see D3, lines 9-16; D7, lines 18-28, 43-46, 57-77, and above pp. 14-16.

[31] This aim began to be felt in the later lists, which become increasingly explicit about such matters; see, *e. g.*, note 30 above.

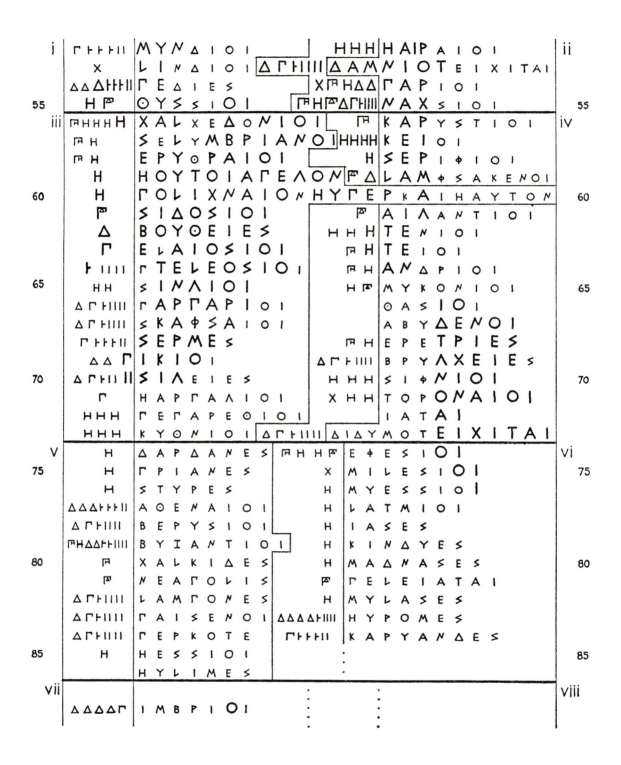

Fig. 1: List 8, sections i-vi (the smaller letters and figures are not extant)

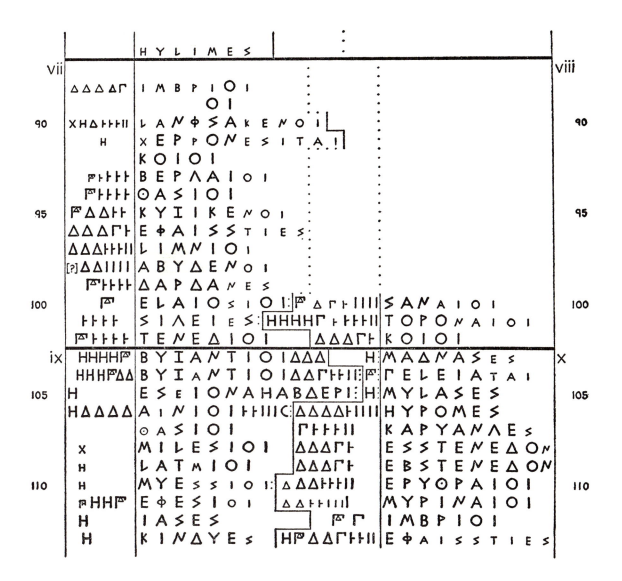

Fig. 2: List 8, sections vii-x (the smaller letters and figures are not extant)

no distinction is made among these various components, and they were probably not kept strictly separate.

6. THE APPENDIX TO LIST 8: ARREARS FOR 448/7

The first component which we shall try to pick out is the arrears due from the previous year (*sc.* 448/7), which can be recognized by the fact that when added to the figure preserved for the same name in List 7 they give a normal total.[32] We shall find that these arrears come in sections vii, viii, and one in the upper part of ix, and we shall presume that most of the other entries in this part of the appendix are also arrears.

For Thasos, we have in 7 IV 9 a payment which is certainly partial, [ΗΗΔΔΔ]ΔΓⱵ (246). The actual amount is uncertain but this supplement fits the space well.[33] In 8 I 94 we have for Thasos 54; the two add up to the normal Thasian quota of 300. We conclude *prima facie* that in 8 I 94 we have the arrears which complete the payment for 448/7. There are two more Thasian payments in 8: one in the main body, 8 II 66, one in the appendix, 8 I 107. The figure is lost in both places. We conclude again, *prima facie*, that in 8 II 66 we have a partial payment for 447/6, and in 8 I 107 the complement. And we note this indication that arrears for 448/7 stood in 8 I 94 (section vii) while complements for 447/6 stood in 8 I 107 (section ix). We believe this indication is sound, but there is a margin of doubt.[34]

For Dardanos we have in 7 IV 17 a payment of 46. In 8 I 99 we have for Dardanos 54; the two add up to what is later the normal Dardanian payment of 100. Again we conclude, *prima facie*, that in 8 I 99 we have the arrears from 448/7. There is the same slight margin of doubt. Dardanos' payment for 447/6 stood in 8 I 74, and is completely lost; she may there have made the same partial payment of 46 as in 7 IV 17 (and for that matter in 5 III 33).

For Sigeion we have in 7 III 36 a payment of 12⅔; the normal payment, made in List 5 and in Period III and later, is 16⅔. In 8 I 101 we have for Sigeion 4, and again we conclude that this is the arrears for 448/7.[35]

---

[32] The margin of doubt is this: if in each case we restore in List 8, sections i–v, the same partial figure which we have in List 7, these alleged arrears might then be regarded as complements. But see below, note 44.

[33] It was clearly a long figure, since it is very much crowded at the end; the Γ stands perceptibly more to the right than the Γ of Lampsakos' figure, six lines above. There are thus at least 4 signs certainly to be restored, and the restoration of 5 is better.

[34] See below, note 44. The payment in 8 II 66 was certainly partial; if it was the same as the partial payment in 7 IV 9, there would be no longer reason to call 8 I 94 arrears for 448/7 rather than complement for 447/6. It would not be easy to restore the 8 signs needed for this hypothesis between the names [Π]αρπάρι[οι] and [Θάσ]ιο[ι] in line 66 of List 8, but it is perhaps not impossible.

[35] The 447/6 payment for Sigeion stands in 8 I 70; the very end of the figure (2 obols) is extant. The crowding seen here (compare, *e. g.*, Πε[διᾶς] in 8 I 54) makes it more plausible, we think, to restore the normal whole-payment. But the same partial payment as in 448/7 is, again, not impossible.

For Sane, the evidence is more complex but perhaps firmer. In Periods III and IV Sane pays 66⅔, in Periods V and VI she pays 100. The short figure (H = 100) is most probably to be restored in 2 VIII 18, 5 III 12, 8 II 6.[36] In 8 II 100 we have 66⅔. Since no complement is required to the whole payment in 8 II 6, we assume that in 8 II 100 we have the arrears from 448/7, and we restore the figure of 33⅓ in 7 II 16.[37]

For Torone we have in 7 IV 16 the very long figure of 790⅔ (10 letter spaces). In 8 II 101 we have the almost equally long figure of 409⅓. The two add up to 1200, which is what Torone pays in Period VII (in III, IV, [V], and VI she pays 600). We assume that in 8 II 101 we have the arrears from 448/7. Torone's first payment for 447/6 stood in 8 II 71 and is lost, but it is virtually certain that the long figure of 790⅔ could not have stood in that place, and this makes it likely that 8 II 101 is not a complement.[38]

For Abdera we have in 7 II 27 the figure of 1400. The normal figure, in Periods I, III, and in List 5, is 1500. In 8 I 105 we have what we assume is the arrears, the figure 100 and the words ἐς ['E]ιόνα haβδερῖ:, "paid by Abdera to (the officer at) Eion." As usual, we cannot be certain that this is arrears,[39] rather than complementary to a similar partial payment in 447/6; the signs for 1400 would probably have left some trace on the stone at 8 II 17 but not certainly.

The upshot of the above is that we probably have arrears from 448/7 entered in the following places in the appendix of List 8:

in section vii,	in section viii,	in section ix,
I 94 Thasos	(upper part lost)	I 105 Abdera
I 99 Dardanos	II 100 Sane	
I 101 Sigeion	II 101 Torone	

There are, however, other elements in section vii (which is the only well preserved section in this part of the appendix). Elaious in I 100 makes a whole-payment of 50; Limnai in I 97 pays 33⅓, which is four times its normal whole-payment. Both these names appear here for the first time, and we believe they represent a break-up of the

[36] See *A. T. L.*, I, p. 177, note on 7 II 16.

[37] *Loc. cit.* (in note 36 above).

[38] Torone either made a whole-payment in 447/6 (and this seems to us the most likely) or else a partial payment to which the figure in 8 II 101 is not complementary.

[39] These payments to officers (cf. II 108-109) are perhaps wrongly designated as "arrears" or "complements." We imagine that the officer called for what he needed, at a time when the tribute was being assembled by the paying city before it was sent to Athens; after making such a payment to the officer the city would send the balance to Athens. If so, these payments to officers are "advances" rather than "arrears." The question whether a large number of what we have called "arrears" from 448/7 and "complements" for 447/6 may not in fact have been similar "advances," made to commanders in the field, is discussed below, pp. 59-61.

old Chersonese syntely consequent on the klerouchy of 447 (see below, p. 59). Madytos and Sestos, two cities which later belong to this group, do not appear here, and we believe that Limnai's payment covers them. The other two components of the old syntely are Cherronesitai and Imbros; Cherronesitai stands in I 91 and Imbros is tentatively restored in Fig. 2 at I 88. Neither of these last two has the quota preserved; in Fig. 2 we tentatively restore the whole-payment (100) for Cherronesitai, and a partial payment of 45 for Imbros (to which the 55 in II 112 will be the complement). Here then is a coherent group:

in section vii,

8 I 88	[ΔΔΔΔΓ]	[Ἴμβρι]ο[ι]
8 I 91	[Η]	[Χ]ερ[ρ]ον[εσῖται]
8 I 97	ΔΔΔΗΗΙ	Λιμν⟨α⟩ῖο[ι]
8 I 100	⊡	Ἐλαιό[σι]οι

in section x,

8 II 112	⊡Γ	Ἴμβριοι

If these entries are correct, they cover the obligations of the old Chersonese syntely as re-defined after the klerouchy was settled. They stand in the appendix and not in sections i-v, and this will probably mean that they did not pay in 448/7 but first in 447/6.

There is another name which probably did not stand in 7 or in sections i-v of 8, and which also probably makes a whole-payment in section vii:

8 I 93   [⊡Ͱ]ͰͰͰ   Βεργαῖ[οι]

Berge had appeared in Period I and may have been assessed for Period II; but we suspect that it had been detached from the Empire by the Thrakians, and was only recovered by that force at Eion which is mentioned in 8 I 105.

There is one more group that we must examine, the Lemnian cities. Hephaistia pays 36 in section vii and 177⅓ in section x. Myrina pays an uncertain sum in section x. It is just possible that we have a close analogy to the Chersonese group. We could regard the two Hephaistian payments as amounting to 200 plus a fine; for Myrina, we could read the broken figure as 100 (Ḥ); this keeps Hephaistia and Myrina in their normal proportions, and we could suppose that this was the total obligation as re-defined after Lemnos had received a klerouchy. The serious objection to this lies in our supplements in 5 IV 40-41, which we regard as better evidence (see above, note 22); these suggest very strongly that the Lemnian klerouchy was already established before 449 and that the total obligation in 450/49 was at least 400. Moreover the proposed fine is surprising, and so is the assumed whole-payment by Myrina in section x, and finally the supposition that the total obligation was 300 (instead of 450 as in later periods, or 900 as in Period I) is difficult. We therefore believe that the tribute situation in Lemnos was not analogous to that in the Chersonese. We have presumed that the Chersonese paid no tribute in 448/7 and so did not appear in 7 or in sections i-v of 8. Lemnos is not likely to have been in the same degree a theatre of actual operations, and we therefore posit that Lemnos paid in both years, and have therefore tentatively supplied the name for 7 I 30 ([Λέμνιοι]) and 8 I 32 ([Λέμνιο]ι). (The coexistence of the designations Λέμνιοι and Ἐφαισστιês is attested for Period I.) The Lemnian group will then appear as follows (*exempli gratia*):

448/7 main list (List 7),
    7 I 30   [ΗΗΗΗΔΗΗΗ]   [Λέμνιοι]

448/7 arrears (section vii),
    8 I 96   ΔΔΔΓΗ   Ἐφαισσ[τιês]

447/6 main list (sections i-v),
    8 I 32   [Η]ΗℙℷΗ   [Λέμνιο]ι

447/6 complements (section x),
    8 II 111   [ΔΔΗΙΙΙ]Ι   Μυριναῖοι
    8 II 113   ΗℙΔΔΓΗΗΙ   Ἐφ[αισστιês]

The remaining names in section vii are: Lampsakos, Kos, Kyzikos, Abydos, Tenedos. We presume all to be here credited with paying arrears for 448/7. With the three names already identified as such (Thasos, Dardanos, Sigeion), and perhaps I 89 (Ainos?), they make up the arrears component of section vii. The four names out of these five which are extant in List 7 all made partial payments there, but since those partial payments and these arrears do not (or cannot be shown to) add up to whole-payments we could not include them in our first identifications. The fifth name, Kyzikos, we have tentatively restored in one of the gaps, 7 II 14 = 8 II 4. We suggest below, in note 45, that possibly I 89 should be restored as [Αἴνι]οι. We have then the following table:

			Arrears				Main List
8 I 89	[– – –]	[Αἴνι]οι		7 I 37	[. . .]		Αἴ[νιοι]
8 I 90	[ΧΗΔΗΗΙΙ]	[Λα]νφσα[κενοί]		7 IV 3	ℙΔΔΔΓΗΙΙΙΙ		Λαμφ[σακενοί]
8 I 92	[– – –]	Κôιοι		7 III 10	[ΗΗΗℙℾ]Η		Κôιοι
8 I 94	ℙΗΗΗ	Θάσιοι		7 IV 9	[ΗΗΔΔΔ]ΔΓΗ		Θάσιοι
8 I 95	ℙΔΔΗ	Κυζικε[νοί]		7 II 14	[ℙΗΗΗΗΔΔΓΗΗ]		[Κυζικενοί]
8 I 96	ΔΔΔΓΗ	Ἐφαισσ[τιês]		7 I 30	[ΗΗΗΗΔΗΗΗ]		[Λέμνιοι]
8 I 98	?ΔΔΙΙΙΙ	Ἀβυδεν[οί]		7 IV 10	[– –]ΙΙΙΙ		Ἀβυδενοί
8 I 99	ℙΗΗΗΗ	Δαρδα[νês]		7 IV 17	Δ[Δ]ΔΔΓΗ		[Δαρδ]ανês
8 I 101	ΗΗΗ	Σιγει[έ]ς		7 III 36	ΔΗΙΙΙΙ		Σιγειέ[ς]
8 I 102	ℙΗΗΗΗ	Τενέδιοι		7 I 3	[. .᾽. .]ΗΗΙ		Τεν[έδι]οι

and in section viii,

8 II 100	𐅆[ΔΓⱵ]IIII	Σαν[αῖοι]	7 II 16 [ΔΔΔⱵⱵII]	[Σαναῖο]ι
8 II 101	ΗΗΗΗΓ[Ⱶ]ⱵⱵII	Τορο[ναῖοι]	7 IV 16 𐅆ΗΗ𐅆ΔΔΔΔIIII	[Τορο]ναῖοι

and in section ix,

8 I 105	Η	ἐς ['E]ιόνα haβδερῖ	7 II 27 ΧΗΗΗΗ	haβ[δερῖται]

In nine of these cases (Abdera, Dardanos, Hephaistia, Kyzikos, Lampsakos, Sane, Sigeion, Thasos, Torone) the two sums will add up to a whole-payment; for four of these, Hephaistia, Kyzikos, Lampsakos, and Sane, this depends on our supplements. The same may have been true of Ainos (see below, note 45), but since neither figure is extant any bi-partition of the payment would be arbitrary.

In three cases, however (Abydos, Kos, and Tenedos), the two payments cannot be restored so as to add up to a whole-payment. The record of Abydos is so irregular (see the Register) that it is hard to determine its normal whole-payment at this time; but it is unlikely that it was the sum of two figures, one ending in 20⅔, the other in ⅔. The figure 356 for Kos in 7 III 10, though largely restored, is very probable, since Kos makes this same first payment in both List 5 and List 8. The balance (as paid in 5 V 40) is ΗΔΔΔΔⱵⱵⱵ, and this figure is too long to restore in the figure column in 8 I 92. Had this been the figure, it would have been split and part put after the name, and we can see that this was not done. But all three cities, Abydos, Kos, and Tenedos, are known to have made partial payments in List 7, so that arrears are to be presumed; we have evidently to consider they were paid in two instalments, the other instalment standing in one or other of the lacunae.

So far, then, we have 13 partial payers of 448/7 whose arrears are noted in List 8. Of five (Abdera, Dardanos, Sigeion, Thasos, Torone) we have positive evidence that the entries in List 7 and 8 add up to the required total. Of four more (Abydos, Kos, Lampsakos, Tenedos) we know from List 7 that their payment there was partial. The names of two (Kyzikos, Lemnos) we have restored *ad hoc* in List 7 because their payments in List 8 look like arrears. For the other two (Ainos, Sane) we have no figure in List 7; the case for its having been a partial payment is strong for Sane (see p. 45) but for Ainos rather weak (see below, note 45). From the direct evidence of List 7 we can add two more for certain, Byzantion and Ios, and one doubtful, Bargylia. Byzantion in 7 IV 22 paid, instead of the normal 1500, some unknown figure ending in ⱵⱵⱵ. Ios, in 7 IV 15, paid 14 instead of the normal 100; the amount in 8 II 72 is not preserved, and the arrears for 448/7 should be sought in List 8, section viii. Bargylia's payment, as restored in 7 III 11, [ΔΓⱵII]II, is, we believe, partial (see above, note 14); the restoration of the extra initial sign (𐅆), which would make it a whole-payment, would mean more crowding than the two extant obol signs seem to warrant. If we add these three, we have 16 partial payers in 448/7; there were probably less than 20 altogether.[40]

For recording in List 8 the arrears of these 15 to 20 cities we have probably rather over 20 lines.[41] We have already supposed that three of our sixteen names paid their arrears in two instalments (which brings the lines accounted for to 19). This may have happened once or twice more, and there may have been two or three more partial payers; but there is not much space left unaccounted for, and we need not presume any large number of unidentified partial payers in 448/7.

These then are the arrears for 448/7. We have suggested above (pp. 35-36) that the names of the " southeastern group " must be restored in II 74-84. These did not appear in List 7 nor consequently in the main part of List 8. Their habit, we believe, was to pay late, but when they paid to make whole-payments; consequently we must expect them twice in this appendix, paying once for 448/7 (whole-arrears) and once for 447/6 (late payments). We have now found that the 448/7 arrears stand chiefly in sections vii and viii, and we shall likewise find that the 447/6 complements stand chiefly in sections ix and x; that is to say, the arrangement we first detected in the case of Thasos (p. 44 above) may probably be generalized. We therefore think it likely that it is their " whole-arrears " for 448/7 which we should restore in II 74-84 (section vi), and that the " southeastern group's " second appearance, in sections ix-x, very near the end of the whole list, is consequent on their having paid in their normal fashion in 447/6, whole-payments at the very end of the year.

7. THE APPENDIX TO LIST 8: COMPLEMENTS FOR 447/6

There remain, for complements and late payments of the current year, the 22 lines of sections ix-x: 11 of these are the " southeastern group," 11 are left for com-

---

[40] The kind of computation we made in note 16 above for List 5 will not help much here, since a high proportion of these partial payers are massed in the well-preserved upper part of column IV. Of the 145 payments (the Erythraian syntely here counts as one) perhaps 97 may be determined as whole or partial: certainly whole, I 15-22, II 2-11, 20-26, 28-34, III 4, 14, 19-22, 25-27, 33-34, 37, IV 2, 4-7, 14, 20-21, 23-28, 34-39; probably whole, I 5, 12-14, 25, III 2, 12-13, 15-18, 23, 35, 38, IV 11, 13, 18-19, 32-33; altogether 85 certain or probable. Partial: I 3, II 27, III 10-11, 36, IV 3, 9-10, 15-17, 22; altogether 12 (4 of our 16, i. e., Ainos, Kyzikos, Lemnos, Sane, cannot be recognized as partial payers from their extant quotas). The proportion 85 to 12 in the extant figures would give about 42 to 6 among the missing figures, altogether 18 partial payments or 2 more than the 16 identified. But if we leave out column IV, we shall get a smaller number: 59 to 5 determinable, giving 40-41 to 3-4 among the non-determinable; the 4 will be Ainos, Kyzikos, Lemnos, and Sane, and there would be no more to be presumed. The case for omitting column IV is that the area apparently most affected (Thrace and Hellespont) is especially well represented there.

[41] Besides the 13 lines in which we have recognized or restored them (I 89-90, 92, 94-96, 98-99, 101-102, 105, II 100-101), we have I 87, II 85-86 (since the " southeastern group " will end at II 84), and perhaps most of II 87-99 (the blank lines in section viii). Some of this last will be

plements. This is probably not far from the right number, and we believe that many of these 11 lines do in fact record such complements; if there are a few not recorded here which we should expect, we must remember that these categories are not kept apart on principle and a few displacements are to be expected. Most of the payments to which these complements are complementary were in sections i-v; we must therefore now try to estimate the number of partial payments in those sections.

Out of 145 entries [42] in sections i-v, we have (either complete or readily restorable) 81 figures extant; of these only five (Erythrai, Kos, Lampsakos, Tenedos, and probably Galepsos)[43] come under reasonable suspicion of being other than whole-payments. Among the 64 lost figures we should expect about 4 more partial payers, and we can perhaps name three of them: Ainos, Byzantion, Thasos. It is unlikely that there were many more.[44]

First we take the three whose figures are not extant in sections i-v: their complements are in section x. Ainos paid 142$\frac{7}{12}$ in the appendix to List 8 (I 106); the amount paid in List 7 is lost, but there is not room on the stone for the amount which we need if the figure in 8 I 106 is to be the arrears. We presume that Ainos paid some round sum [45] in List 7, as is required by the space in 7 I 37, and the partial payment of 1057$\frac{5}{12}$ in 8 I 39, and that the payment in 8 I 106 is complementary to this latter. Byzantion made a partial payment in 7 IV 22 (amount uncertain, but certainly partial) but the two payments in 8 I 103-104 cannot be, either separately or together, the arrears to complete that payment. Together they come to 877$\frac{1}{3}$, and we presume a partial payment of 622$\frac{2}{3}$ in 8 I 79. For Thasos see above, p. 44 with notes 33 and 34; the complement for 447/6 stood probably in 8 I 107.

taken by the stray complements (a second complement for Kos, one or two for Lampsakos, perhaps some for Galepsos, Tenedos [see below, notes 43, 46], etc., about 6 lines in all; see below, p. 51), but we should probably allow about 7 of these blank lines for the arrears.

[42] For this purpose we count the six names of the Erythraian syntely as one entry, since they had only one figure.

[43] Galepsos paid 120 in List 8 (II 40) but 150 in List 9 and in Period I; this drops to 50 by List 12 (10 and 11 are missing), which is perhaps due to the colony at Brea. The amount paid in List 5 was something over 100, in List 7 it is lost. It is possible that 120 is a whole-payment for Period II, but not likely, since 120 as a whole-payment would be a unique figure.

[44] The figures which we reckon as determinable are: I 4-25, 28-31, 33, 54-55, 69-70, II 6-9, 11-14, 19, 23-59, 61-63, and Erythrai's payment in I 58-64. The five partial payments are I 5, 58-64, II 37, 40, 59; that is, 1 partial in 16. This gives us a strong reason for believing that those payments in sections vii and viii which we have supposed arrears from 448/7 are really so; we can hardly assume, in the face of these figures, that partial payments were really as common in 447/6 as we have allowed for in notes 32, 34, and 35 above.

[45] Since (whatever the reason) partial payments were evidently much commoner in 448/7 than in 447/6, we should not infer that this must have been the whole-payment of 1200. We suspect, indeed, that Ainos paid arrears for 448/7 in 8 I 89, where we need a name of that unusual shortness. The only serious alternative there to [Αἶνι]οι is [Ἀζει]οί; this latter possibility prevents our inserting [Αἶνι]οι into Fig. 2.

Next we consider the 5 whose partial payments can be recognized in sections i-v. Erythrai pays her complement in 8 II 110 for the partial payment of 8 I 58-64. For Tenedos, it is tempting to suggest that the two payments of 36 each " to (the officer at) Tenedos " were made by the city of Tenedos, and that one of the two figures be corrected from 36 to 126;[46] between them they will then complete the partial payment in 8 I 5. These two entries are in II 108-109. For Lampsakos and Kos, who both made partial payments in both years, it is not easy to distinguish between arrears and complements, and certainly no complement for them stood in sections ix-x. We should probably regard 8 I 90, 92 (in section vii) as arrears, and look for their complements, and that of Galepsos, in the lacuna of section viii; in the last line of that section (II 102) we have probably the final complement for Kos.

So far, then, we find that the complements for 447/6, paid by Byzantion, Ainos, Thasos, Erythrai, and perhaps Tenedos, may be reasonably thought to stand in sections ix-x, and the final complement for Kos in the last line of section viii. There is one intruder, Abdera's arrears for 448/7 in I 105. Otherwise the rest of sections ix-x is occupied by the " southeastern group's " late payments for 447/6 and by the three entries in II 111-113, Myrina, Imbros, Hephaistia; these are also probably complements for 447/6 (see above, pp. 46-47). We then suggest that Myrina's and Hephaistia's payments complete a partial payment by [Λέμνιο]ι (to be restored in 8 I 32), while that of Imbros completes the partial payment which we propose to restore in 8 I 88 (see Fig. 2). The partial payments stood thus in separate sections, because Imbros had belonged financially to the Chersonese while Lemnos had not. The three complements stand together; the two islands are in fact neighbours and these three complements were evidently levied at one time.

We present the layout of List 8, sections vi-x (the appendix), in tabular form. We have entered, without brackets, all the tentative restorations given in Figs. 1 and 2 (and also Ainos, as paying arrears for 448/7 in I 89; see above, note 45). Brackets indicate the blank lines for which we have made no proposal beyond the numerical division into 6 complements and 10 arrears. A = arrears for 448/7; C = complement for 447/6; P = partial payment for 447/6; W = whole-payment for 447/6. The letters (CH) are added to the successors of the old Chersonese syntely, (SE) to the " southeastern group."

---

[46] That is, from ΔΔΔΓⱵ to ΗΔΔΓⱵ. In support, we note that the cutter began by omitting the second entry: he started to write Ἐρυθραῖοι from the line below. He may have been somehow influenced by the fact that Erythrai's figure began with ΔΔΔ. If this be so, then the 54 in 8 I 102 will be partial arrears for 448/7, as by position it should be; and we must expect that another payment of arrears stood in the lacuna. If the supposition of error be rejected, we ought probably to assume that a payment of 90 from Tenedos, for 447/6, stood likewise in the lacuna.

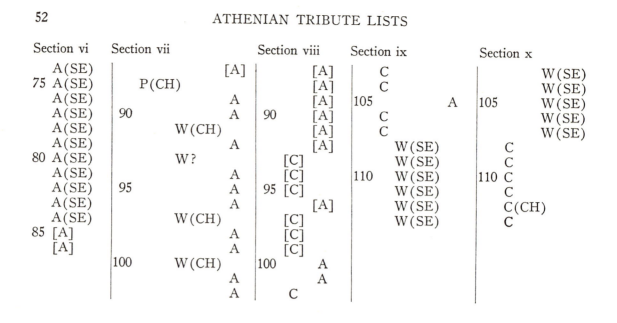

Section vi	Section vii	Section viii	Section ix	Section x
A(SE)	[A]	[A]	C	W(SE)
75 A(SE)	P(CH)	[A]	C	W(SE)
A(SE)	A	[A]	105 A	105 W(SE)
A(SE)	90 A	90 [A]	C	W(SE)
A(SE)	W(CH)	[A]	C	W(SE)
A(SE)	A	[A]	W(SE)	C
80 A(SE)	W?	[C]	W(SE)	C
A(SE)	A	[C]	110 W(SE)	110 C
A(SE)	95 A	95 [C]	W(SE)	C
A(SE)	A	[A]	W(SE)	C(CH)
A(SE)	W(CH)	[C]	W(SE)	C
85 [A]	A	[C]		
[A]	A	[C]		
	100 W(CH)	100 A		
	A	A		
	A	C		

8. THE ASSESSMENT OF 450 B. C.

The following four tables contain the names, in each of the four districts, which appear in any of the three quota lists. The following distinctions are made, on the basis of the foregoing determinations:[47] cities who made partial payments are in italics, cities who made whole-payments are in roman type without brackets, cities whose payments cannot be determined as whole or partial are in roman type with square brackets. The figures in the left-hand column give the whole-payment presumed due from cities which do not appear in List 7 or 8, those in the right-hand column give the presumed whole-payment for all the remainder (except that we can give no figure for Hylima). The figure changed within the period for the Thrakian Chersonese, and we therefore give figures for Cherronesitai in both columns.[48]

[47] Whole and partial payers in List 5 are given as in note 16 above, in List 7 as in note 40, in List 8 as in note 44. The 5 blank lines in Lists 7 and 8 are filled as on pp. 37-38 (for Lemnos see below, note 48). The " southeastern group " is reckoned as making whole-payments in Lists 7 and 8. For the Chersonese syntely, the Lemnian cities, and Berge, in List 8, see above, pp. 45-47. For Chedrolos (= Erodioi) and Othoros see below, p. 61. These determinations are not of course certain, and they may slightly exaggerate the whole-payments in all three lists. The names are given where possible in the form used on the map in A. T. L., I, and are arranged alphabetically.

[48] We have omitted Lemnos, since its payments in all three lists are more conveniently given under Hephaistia and Myrina. We have also omitted the 5 cities of the Erythraian syntely other than Erythrai. We have kept Pitane in 5 V 2, though Torone is a possible alternative, and though [Πιταναῖ]οι is the only likely Ionic-Karic name which would fit the gap in 5 I 27; the entry in 5 V 2 could be a second entry.

IONIC-KARIC

	List 5	List 7	List 8	
	Arkesseia	Arkesseia	Arkesseia	16⅔
	Assos	Assos	[Assos]	100
		[Astypalaia]	Astypalaia	200
	Auliatai	Auliatai	[Auliatai]	8⅓
	Bargylia	*Bargylia*	Bargylia	66⅔
		Brykous	Brykous	8⅓
	Chalke	[Chalke]	Chalke	50
	Chalketor	Chalketor	Chalketor	35
	Cherronesos	Cherronesos	Cherronesos	300
		Chios	Chios	33⅓
	Dioseritai	Dioseritai	Dioseritai	16⅔
	Ephesos	Ephesos	Ephesos	750
66⅔	*Erines*			
	Erythrai	[Erythrai]	*Erythrai*	900
	Euromos	Euromos	Euromos	41⅔
		Gargara	[Gargara]	75
		Gryneia	Gryneia	16⅔
	[Hairai]	Hairai	Hairai	300
	[Halikarnassos]	[Halikarnassos]	Halikarnassos	200
	[Hylima]	[Hylima]	[Hylima]	
	Ialysos	[Ialysos]	Ialysos	1000
	Iasos	Iasos	Iasos	100
		Idyma	[Idyma]	86⅔
	[Kalydnioi]	Kalydnioi	[Kalydnioi]	150
	Kameiros	[Kameiros]	Kameiros	900
	Karbasyanda	Karbasyanda	[Karbasyanda]	16⅔
	Karyanda	Karyanda	Karyanda	8⅓
	Kasolaba	Kasolaba	[Kasolaba]	41⅔
		[Kaunos]	[Kaunos]	50
		[Kedreai]	Kedreai	50
		[Keramos]	Keramos	150
	Kindye	Kindye	Kindye	100
	[Klazomenai]	Klazomenai	[Klazomenai]	150
	Knidos	Knidos	Knidos	500
		Kodapes	Kodapes	16⅔
	Kos	*Kos*	*Kos*	500
	Krya	Krya	[Krya]	33⅓
	[Kydai]	Kydai	Kydai	6⅔

List 5		List 7	List 8	
		Kyllandos	Kyllandos	200
		Kyme	Kyme	900
[Kyrbissos]		Kyrbissos	Kyrbissos	33⅓
Latmos		Latmos	Latmos	100
[Lebedos]		[Lebedos]	Lebedos	300
		[Lepsimandos]	[Lepsimandos]	25
		Lindos	[Lindos]	1000
Madnasa		Madnasa	Madnasa	100
Miletos		Miletos	Miletos	1000
		Mydones	[Mydones]	25
Mylasa		Mylasa	Mylasa	100
[Myndos]		Myndos	[Myndos]	8⅓
Myous		Myous	Myous	100
Myrina		[Myrina]	Myrina	100
		[Narisbara]	Narisbara	16⅔
		Naxia	[Naxia]	8⅓
Notion		Notion	Notion	33⅓
[Oine]		[Oine]	Oine	100
Pargasa		[Pargasa]	[Pargasa]	16⅔
[Parpariotai]		[Parpariotai]	[Parpariotai]	16⅔
100	*Pasanda*			
		Pedasa	Pedasa	100
		[Pedies]	Pedies	33⅓
Pelea		Pelea	Pelea	50
Phaselis		Phaselis	[Phaselis]	300
		[Phokaia]	Phokaia	300
[Pitane]		Pitane	Pitane	16⅔
		[Pladasa]	Pladasa	33⅓
Priene		Priene	[Priene]	100
Pyrnos		Pyrnos	Pyrnos	16⅔
Syangela		[Syangela]	Syangela	100
		Telandria	[Telandria]	50
Teos		Teos	Teos	600
Termera		[Termera]	[Termera]	250
		Thasthara	[Thasthara]	8⅓
Thermai		[Thermai]	Thermai	50
		Ydissos	Ydissos	100
		Ymissos	Ymissos	20

(166⅔)   Ionic-Karic total (less Hylima) 13290

THRAKIAN

	List 5	List 7	List 8	
	Abdera	*Abdera*	[Abdera]	1500
		Aige	Aige	50
	[Aineia]	[Aineia]	[Aineia]	300
	[Ainos]	*Ainos*	*Ainos*	1200
500	Akanthos			
		Aphytis	Aphytis	300
	Assera	Assera	Assera	40
			Berge	54
	Chedrolos	Chedrolos	Chedrolos	8⅓
	Dikaia (Abdera)	Dikaia (Abdera)	Dikaia (Abdera)	50
	[Dikaia (Eretria)]	[Dikaia (Eretria)]	[Dikaia (Eretria)]	100
		Dion	[Dion]	100
	[Galepsos]	[Galepsos]	*Galepsos*	150
	Haison	[Haison]	[Haison]	25
		Ikos	Ikos	25
	Maroneia	[Maroneia]	Maroneia	150
	Mekyberna	[Mekyberna]	Mekyberna	100
		Mende	Mende	1500
	Neapolis (Antisara)	Neapolis (Antisara)	Neapolis (Antisara)	16⅔
	[Neapolis (Mende)]	Neapolis (Mende)	[Neapolis (Mende)]	50
		Olophyxos	[Olophyxos]	25
200	Olynthos			
		[Othoros]	Othoros	8⅓
		Peparethos	[Peparethos]	300
	Pharbelos	Pharbelos	[Pharbelos]	16⅔
	Phegetos	Phegetos	[Phegetos]	26⅔
	Samothrake	Samothrake	Samothrake	600
	[Sane]	*Sane*	Sane	100
	Serme	Serme	[Serme]	8⅓
		Sermylia	Sermylia	300
	Singos	[Singos]	[Singos]	200
	Skabala	Skabala	Skabala	50
	Skapsa	Skapsa	[Skapsa]	16⅔
	Skiathos	[Skiathos]	[Skiathos]	16⅔
		Spartolos	Spartolos	200
	Stageira	Stageira	Stageira	16⅔
	Stolos	Stolos	Stolos	83⅓
	Strepsa	[Strepsa]	Strepsa	100
		Thasos	*Thasos*	300
	Thyssos	[Thyssos]	Thyssos	150
		Torone	[Torone]	1200

       Thrakian total   9437⅓

HELLESPONTINE

	List 5	List 7	List 8	
	[Abydos]	*Abydos*	[Abydos]	400
100	*Alopekonnesos*			
	[Artake]	[Artake]	[Artake]	33⅓
16⅔	Astakos			
	[Berytis]	Berytis	[Berytis]	16⅔
	Byzantion	*Byzantion*	*Byzantion*	1500
1800	*Cherronesitai*		Cherronesitai	100
	Dardanos	*Dardanos*	[Dardanos]	100
8⅓	Daskyleion			
	[D....oteichitai]	[Daunioteichitai]	Daunioteichitai	16⅔
		Didymoteichitai	[Didymoteichitai]	16⅔
			Elaious	50
		Eurymachitai	Eurymachitai	16⅔
	Gentinos	[Gentinos]	Gentinos	8⅓
		Harpagion	[Harpagion]	5
	Kalchedon	Kalchedon	[Kalchedon]	900
	Kebrene	Kebrene	Kebrene	300
		Kios	Kios	16⅔
	[Kyzikos]	*Kyzikos*	[Kyzikos]	900
		Lamponeia	[Lamponeia]	16⅔
	Lampsakos	*Lampsakos*	*Lampsakos*	1200
			Limnai	33⅓
33⅓	Neandreia			
		Paisos	[Paisos]	16⅔
		[Palaiperkote]	Palaiperkote	8⅓
1000	*Perinthos*			
		Perkote	[Perkote]	16⅔
		[Priapos]	Priapos	8⅓
300	[Prokonnesos]			
	Selymbria	Selymbria	[Selymbria]	600
	Sigeion	*Sigeion*	Sigeion	16⅔
	Tenedos	*Tenedos*	*Tenedos*	450

| (3258⅓) | | | Hellespontine total | 6746⅔ |

INSULAR

	LIST 5	LIST 7	LIST 8	
3000	*Aigina*			
	Andros	Andros	[Andros]	600
	[Athenai Diades]	Athenai Diades	[Athenai Diades]	33⅓
		Chalkis	[Chalkis]	500
	[Dion]	Dion	Dion	33⅓
		Eretria [49]	[Eretria]	600
	[Grynche]	[Grynche]	[Grynche]	16⅔
	Hephaistia	*Hephaistia*	*Hephaistia*	300
	[Hestiaia]	[Hestiaia]	Hestiaia	16⅔
			Imbros [50]	100
	Ios	*Ios*	[Ios]	100
	Karystos	Karystos	Karystos	500
	Keos	Keos	Keos	400
	Kythnos	Kythnos	[Kythnos]	300
		[Mykonos]	[Mykonos]	150
	Myrina	[Myrina]	*Myrina*	150
	[Naxos]	Naxos	Naxos	666⅔
	Paros	Paros	Paros	1620
	Rhenaia	Rhenaia	Rheneia	5
	[Seriphos]	Seriphos	Seriphos	100
	Siphnos	Siphnos	[Siphnos]	300
	Styra	Styra	[Styra]	100
		[Syros]	Syros	16⅔
	Tenos	Tenos	Tenos	300

(3000)		Insular total	6908⅓

The four totals amount to 36382⅓ drachmai quota, or 363 talents 4940 drachmai tribute; we may disregard Hylima whose tribute will hardly have been as much as a talent. This then will have been the total tribute paid in 447/6 if (as seems likely enough) all complements were collected. For 448/7 we should deduct the following quotas: 54 for Berge, 283⅓ for Elaious, Limnai, Cherronesitai, Imbros (*i. e.*, the members of the old Chersonese syntely); this leaves 36045 quota, or 360 talents 2700 drachmai tribute, in 448/7.

[49] For Eretria's figure see below, p. 294 with note 96.
[50] Imbros was included with the Thrakian Chersonese in Period I and in List 5, but from List 8 onwards it is in the Insular district.

For the assesment of 450 we have now to add the figures of the left-hand column, a sum of 7125 drachmai quota, 71 talents 1500 drachmai tribute. This is for the cities which paid in 450/49 but not in the two later years; these cities include the three very important names of Aigina, Cherronesitai (on the larger scale), and Perinthos, and were surely in the assessment. This brings the total of the assessment of 450 B. C. to 431 talents 4200 drachmai.

There are no doubt some small adjustments to be made. We have estimated for the following numbers of cities:

(a) the 150 names common to Lists 7 and 8,[51]

(b) the twelve names, not in (a), which come in List 5,[52]

(c) the eleven names of the " southeastern group," in 8 I 108-113, II 103-107.

We thus have 173 cities. About ten of these cannot have stood in List 5, where we have estimated about 163 names (above, pp. 30-31). If we compare the distribution into districts as shown for Lists 7 and 8 in our tables, and as estimated for List 5 (above, p. 32), it seems likely that List 5 had more Ionic-Karic names and fewer Thrakian; and though the members who paid in the Hellespontine district perhaps did not alter much, yet there were evidently some Hellespontine names present in 5 and absent in 7 and 8, and *vice versa*. This probably means that some Ionic-Karic names lapsed after List 5, while some Thrakian and Hellespontine names came in,[53] and these latter should not be counted in the assessment of 450. They were probably not names of the first or second magnitude; 10 minor names would not account for much more than 3 talents, and we shall probably be making due allowance if we reduce our assessment total to about 425 talents.

There are some names which are not extant in any of the three lists of the period but which may have been in one or other of them (most likely in 5). The most important, financially, are Poteidaia and Kolophon; Poteidaia is later assessed for 6 talents, Kolophon was assessed for 3 talents in 454 and the reduction to 1½ talents in 446 was due, we believe, to the founding of a colony. We think it likely that Poteidaia was not yet assessed for tribute but still provided ships. We consider that Kolophon also should be regarded as really absent from all three lists (and not merely lost by damage to the stone), and that the trouble dealt with in D15 began already in 450. But it is possible that it began after the assessment, and that Kolophon had been

---

[51] For this purpose we are counting separately the Erythraian syntely-members and the two Lemnian communities; we omit Hylima (for which no figure can be determined), Berge, and four members of the Chersonese syntely (Cherronesitai, Elaious, Imbros, Limnai).

[52] That is, all the names which have figures in the left-hand column of our tables given above.

[53] Some of the Hellespontine names present in 5 and absent in 7 and 8 (*e. g.*, Perinthos) perhaps did not lapse but rather commuted their payment for military service; see below, note 61. But the Karic names which we must presume in the big gaps in 5 I and 5 II were perhaps simply allowed to lapse.

assessed, at the Panathenaia of 450, for 3 talents. The other absentees worth noticing
are as follows (we add their quotas in the neighbouring periods) : [54]

Azeia (6⅔ in I)
Argilos (150 in I, 100 in III)
Maiandros (66⅔ in I and III)
Parion (100 in I, 33⅓ in IV)
Skepsis (100 in I and IV)
Tyrodiza (16⅔ in I, 8⅓ in III).

9. The Campaigns of 447

There are three entries in the appendix to List 8 which indicate that those payments were not sent to Athens in the normal way, but paid to officers stationed at Eion
(8 I 105, probably " arrears " for 448/7) and Tenedos (8 II 108-109, probably
" complements " for 447/6). The focus of operations of the latter was no doubt
the Thrakian Chersonese; apart from Plutarch, *Pericles*, 19, 1 (T97a), we see that,
whereas in List 5 the old Chersonese syntely is still a single unit paying something
like its old tribute of 18 talents, in List 7 the Chersonese seems to be wholly absent
and in List 8 it appears in the fragments familiar for the rest of the century, paying
not more than 3 talents altogether.[55]

A further symptom of these operations is probably the large number of partial
payments from this area. A glance at the Hellespontine table on p. 56 will show how
frequent partial payment was in 448/7 in this area especially. We note, from the
actual Dardanelles channel, the following: Abydos. Dardanos, Lampsakos, Sigeion;
and we may add Tenedos, which made a partial payment in 448/7 as well as in 447/6.
Lampsakos' partial payment is a very small fraction of her important tribute (less
than 1 talent out of 12), and in the next year, 447/6, she pays less again, only one
twentieth of the whole. Of the three reasons which suggest themselves, namely:

(1) that these cities are recalcitrant and refusing to pay,

(2) that they are being molested by the Thrakian enemy and unable to pay,

(3) that they are making direct contributions to the war and sending only the
balance to Athens,

[54] Some one or two may have been lost by the damage to the stone (*e. g.*, Azeioi from 8 I 89?
See above, note 45), but the chief interest of the list is its indications of incipient trouble (*e. g.*,
Argilos). We do not include some small Karic towns (Hyblissos, Killara, Oula, Ouranion, Polichne,
Sambaktys, Siloi, Tarbanes), of some of which Bargylia may have been taking care, with a tribute
increased from 1000 drachmai to 4000 drachmai.

[55] Alopekonnesos, which is situated in the Chersonese, seems always to have paid separately,
and it too seems to have had a drastic reduction of tribute. We have presumed that its old assessment was for 1 talent; in Period IV it pays 1000 drachmai tribute, and 2000 in Periods V and VI.

we think (3) by far the most likely; (1) is at variance with Plutarch, and (2) is intrinsically very improbable. We surmise therefore that the officer at Tenedos (this need not have been his permanent, or his only, base) levied contributions in the early part of 447 on tribute money which had been collected ready for sending to Athens,[56] and at least from Lampsakos and Tenedos did the same in the latter part of the year, levying what would be due to go to Athens in the following spring. We may no doubt include slightly more distant cities in this same category, Kyzikos, Ainos, Byzantion.[57]

The other focus seems to be the mouth of the Strymon, at Eion. Abdera's payment of 1 talent out of her 15 " to the officer at Eion " is surely not because the officer collected 1 talent as a residue but because he levied it as an advance. The partial payments by Thasos, Sane, and Torone in 448/7 and by Galepsos and Thasos in 447/6 are perhaps symptoms of the same thing. This Strymon campaign is not explicitly mentioned in our sources, but no doubt it was these operations which culminated in the settlement at Brea in 446.[58] This procedure, of levying advance contributions in the field, is exceptional, and it is of interest to recall that no tribute had been received in the spring of 448, and that the Papyrus Decree (D13) had virtually emptied the hellenotamiai's treasury.[59]

There are also some important absentees, Perinthos and Prokonnesos from the Hellespont, Akanthos and Argilos from Thrace. All these are most likely absent from Lists 7 and 8; Argilos is missing in List 5 also, but this may be the chance of survival.[60] It is possible that these cities handed their whole tributes to the military commanders; it is also possible that they commuted their payments, in this emergency, for personal military service.[61] If Argilos was really absent from List 5 also, this would

In Lists 7 and 8 it appears to be absent, and we think it may be covered by the unusually large payment of Limnai.

[56] We may compare, in the quite different circumstances, the Rhoiteion incident, Thucydides IV, 52, 2 (T131) ; see below, p. 88.

[57] For all statistics about partial payments we refer to the tables on pp. 53-57, in which the italics denote a partial payer, and square brackets indicate that the payment cannot be determined as whole or partial.

[58] Tod, *Greek Hist. Inscr.*, I², no. 44; cf. Plutarch, *Pericles*, 11, 5 (T96), χιλίους μὲν ἔστειλεν ἐς Χερρόνησον κληρούχους, --- εἰς δὲ Θρᾴκην χιλίους Βισάλταις συνοικήσοντας. For the date see below, pp. 287-288 with note 64.

[59] See below, pp. 281, 327.

[60] Absentees from Lists 7 and 8 can be readily recognized in the tables (pp. 53-57) : their figures stand in the left-hand margin. Their identity is not absolutely certain, because of the 5 blank lines in Lists 7 and 8; for this see above, pp. 37-38. The significant names which are absent in List 5 as well as Lists 7 and 8 are listed on pp. 58-59 above; some of them may have stood in List 5's large gaps. Olynthos was also probably absent from the Thrakian area in Lists 7 and 8, but this is perhaps due to other causes.

[61] If they had handed over their whole tributes, the hellenotamiai would owe the quota, but no such late whole-payments of quota are extant (they may of course have all stood in the lost portions of sections vi-viii). For the military levy compare Xenophon, *Hellenica*, I, 3, 10: Alkibiades

probably indicate that the crisis which called for the Strymon campaign and ultimately for the colony at Brea had begun already before the spring of 449.

There is one small group of Thrakian cities which still calls for mention (there is no reason to connect it especially with the Strymon operations): Othoros, Pharbelos, Chedrolos. We have now accepted West's equation of Ἐρόδιοι (Ἐρώδιοι) and ℎεδρόλιοι (Ἑδρώλιοι) as two variants for the later Chedrolos (Χεδρώλιοι; see A. T. L., I, p. 175, note on 5 IV 17-18). The two renderings of the name are indeed substantially different and one of them must have been false.[62] The equation enables us to restore Othoros in Lists 7 and 8. Ὀθώριοι and Ἐρώδιοι are, in their Greek forms, names of the same length (7 letters). A name whose length was determined in 7 II 18 as of this length or less, and whose quota was determined in 8 II 8 as 8⅓, was restored as [Ἐρόδιοι] in S. E. G., V, and A. T. L., I, because Erodioi paid this amount in List 5. But we now hold that Erodioi's payments in 7 and 8 appear under the name Hedrolioi (7 III 3, 8 II 33), so that in 7 II 18 and 8 II 8 we can restore [Ὀθόριοι]. We have now a group of three names whose fortunes are linked closely: Othoros, Chedrolos, Pharbelos. Miltoros also is closely linked, with the last two especially, in Periods V-VI (see the table on pp. 62-63, and Fig. 3 on p. 87 below). We have no doubt, then, that our tentative placing of Othoros in the Gazetteer was wrong; the four towns must have formed a group. Their rubric history in Periods V and VI is especially interesting.[63] All four appear in List 20 as ἄτακτοι; in List 21 Chedrolos, Pharbelos, and Miltoros pass into the πόλεις αὐταί rubric, Othoros into the ἰδιῶται rubric; they are probably all absent in List 23, certainly all in List 25. We understand this as follows:

(a) The four cities were not assessed in Period V, but tribute was collected from them in the last two years.[64] No doubt this was a consequence (in some way or other) of the founding of Amphipolis.

marches on Byzantion ἔχων Χερρονησίτας τε πανδημεί – – –. Military contingents of Hellespontines for Hellespontine service are further recorded in Thucydides, I, 89, 2 (479/8), and in the casualty list of 465 (I. G., I², 928; see below, pp. 108-109, 205-206 with note 55, and note 17 on p. 249). A similar obligation in emergencies for the Thrakian district was included in the syngraphai mentioned in I. G., I², 45, 13-17 (T78c); cf. Thucydides, IV, 7 (ξυλλέξας – – – τῶν ἐκείνῃ ξυμμάχων πλῆθος), 105, 1 (ξυμμαχικὸν – – – ἀγείραντα), 129, 2 (τῶν αὐτόθεν ξυμμάχων). But we do not know that military service excused a city from the payment of its tribute.

[62] No doubt Ἐρώδιοι is the false rendering, due perhaps to a false equation with the Greek name of a heron (ἐρῳδιός or ἐρωδιός). Their name was perhaps still unfamiliar in 450; they will have been assessed in 450 in this false form, but before List 7 the truer form was known. This may suggest that they were not known in Period I, and that therefore in 4 III 30 we should restore [Νεάπ]ολ[ις] and not [ℎεδρ]όλ[ιοι].

[63] We have not attempted to show this in the table on pp. 62-63; it can be conveniently followed in Fig. 3 on p. 87 below.

[64] That is to say, they were ἄτακτοι in List 19 as well as List 20, but the compiler of List 19 did not think the fact needed to be specified; see below, pp. 82, 84, and note 109 on p. 218.

(b) In the assessment of 434 Chedrolos, Pharbelos, and Miltoros entered the πόλεις αὐταί rubric; this means that they resumed their position (or Miltoros assumed her position) in the alliance under terms of some specific contract.[65]

(c) Othoros did not avail herself of this contract, and was consequently enrolled at the representation of some individual Athenian.

(d) Neither the contract nor Othoros' assessment survived the troubles in Chalkidike connected with Athens' quarrel with Perdikkas[66] and the revolt of Poteidaia.

In the following table we have added for comparison the records of Argilos and Berge, which reveal these two cities' different reactions to events round Amphipolis. Our figures here are figures of tribute, not of quota. We have entered without question-mark all data either extant or supplied in our texts;[67] to interpret these data we have often added the entry " absent? " where the circumstances seem to point to absence.[68] The entry [ ] indicates that the name is present but the figure unknown.

		Argilos	Othoros	Chedrolos	Pharbelos	Miltoros	Berge	
I	1	1T. 3000 Dr.	absent?	absent?	1000 Dr.	absent?	?	454/3
	2	?	absent?	absent?	?	absent?	?	453/2
	3	?	absent?	absent?	?	absent?	2880 Dr.	452/1
	4	?	absent?	absent?	?	absent?	[ ]	451/0
II	5	absent?	?	500 Dr.	1000 Dr.	absent?	absent?	450/9
	[6]							[449/8]
	7	absent	500 Dr.	500 Dr.	1000 Dr.	absent	absent	448/7
	8	absent	500 Dr.	500 Dr.	1000 Dr.	absent	3240 Dr.	447/6
III	9	1 T.	700 Dr.	?	1000 Dr.	absent?	?	446/5
	10	1 T.	?	?	1000 Dr.	absent?	?	445/4
	11	1 T.	?	?	1000 Dr.	absent?	?	444/3
IV	12	1 T.	700 Dr.	absent	1000 Dr.	absent	absent	443/2
	13	1 T.	700 Dr.	absent?	1000 Dr.	absent?	absent?	442/1
	14	1 T.	700 Dr.	absent?	1000 Dr.	absent?	absent?	441/0
	15	1 T.	?	absent?	?	absent?	absent?	440/39
	16	?	?	absent?	?	absent?	absent?	439/8
V	17	1 T.	absent?	absent?	absent?	absent?	absent?	438/7
	18	?	absent?	absent?	absent?	absent?	absent?	437/6
	19	absent?	700 Dr.	500 Dr.?	1000 Dr.	1000 Dr.?	?	436/5
	20	absent	700 Dr.	500 Dr.	1000 Dr.	1000 Dr.	3120 Dr.	435/4

[65] For this contract see below, pp. 82-85.

[66] Especially no doubt the settlement of seceding allies round Lake Bolbe; Thucydides I, 58, 2.

[67] The question-marks against Chedrolos and Miltoros in List 19 and Othoros in List 22 indicate that these are possible supplements; see A. T. L., I, p. 444 (foot of right-hand column), and below, p. 82. We have rejected the possible alternative of [ℎεδρ]όλ[ιοι] in List 4; see note 62 above.

[68] E. g., for Lists 17 and 18; the fact that the cities are ἄτακτοι in List 20 implies that they were not assessed in 438.

		Argilos	Othoros	Chedrolos	Pharbelos	Miltoros	Berge	
VI	21	?	500 Dr.	1000 Dr.	500 Dr.	3000 Dr.	?	434/3
	22	1000 Dr.	500 Dr. ?	1000 Dr.	500 Dr.	3000 Dr.	3120 Dr.	433/2
	23	absent	absent ?	absent	absent	absent	3120 Dr.	432/1
	24	?	?	?	?	?	?	431/0
VII	25	1000 Dr.	absent	absent	absent	absent	absent	430/29
	26	1000 Dr.	absent	absent	absent	absent	[ ]	429/8
VIII	27	?	?	?	?	?	?	428/7
	28	?	?	?	?	?	?	427/6
	29	?	?	?	?	?	?	426/5
IX	A9	[ ]	?	?	?	?	?	425
X	A10	?	1000 Dr.	?	500 Dr.	?	?	422/1

CHAPTER IV

THE TEXTS OF THE LATER ASSESSMENT PERIODS
(446/5–406/5)

In the texts of *A. T. L.*, I the restoration of the quota of Ὀθώριοι in 9, III, 3 and 13, III, 26 as [ΔΗΙΙΙΙ] was based upon the fact that this figure is preserved on the stone in 12, III, 27. We have, however, in 20, VI, 24 the numerals ΔΗΙΙΙΙ and the surface of the stone is such in 14, II, 55 that [Δ]ΗΙΙΙΙ is a certain reading. Both figures, ΔΗΙΙΙΙ and ΔΗΗΙΙΙΙ, are irregular but the odds seem to us to favour the first. We therefore restore [ΔΗΙΙΙΙ] in 9, III, 3 and 13, III, 26, and we assume that this should have been inscribed in 12, III, 27, the mason having cut the second drachma by error; in the latter entry we therefore print ΔΗ{Η}ΙΙΙΙ.

In 20, VI, 5-6 we have the following:

ΓΗ   Ποτειδεᾶται

ΧΓ   Σκιωναῖοι

The figures (especially the second) are sufficient to encourage an examination of the records of the two towns. In Periods III and IV Poteidaia unquestionably pays a tribute of 6 talents. On the basis of the ΓΗ in List 20 we have restored [ΓΗ] in 19, V, 20 and assumed that this is the assessed figure in Period V. In Period VI the assessment is 15 talents; the quota ΧΓ is preserved in 22, II, 70 and is restored in 21, V, 21. The striking increase is to be associated with the disaffection in Poteidaia and is in no way disturbing. The revolt of Poteidaia in 432/1 brings her payments to an abrupt stop.

In Period I Skione and Therambos pay a joint sum of 6 talents; in Period II their assessment is included in that of Mende (15 talents), which had previously paid 8 talents. In Periods III and IV Skione is separately assessed for 6 talents. Period V is represented only by the entry here under discussion (ΧΓ), and Period VI by the 4 talents of 23, II, 52. In Period VII Skione twice pays 9 talents; these are war years. The town was assessed in 425/4 but the amount is lost.

It requires no argument to demonstrate the anomalous character of a tribute of 15 talents for Skione in 435/4, where we might expect the normal 6; in any case, we should anticipate no startling increase, especially in view of the decrease in the next period. If we were confronted with a tribute of 15 talents for Poteidaia, however, in 435/4, our suspicions would not be aroused, for this, we believe, was the assessed amount in the subsequent year. The following hypothesis, then, which we do not consider secure enough to indicate in the texts of *A. T. L.*, II, must at least be presented for consideration: that in 435/4 Skione paid 6 talents, as she had for years past, and Poteidaia 15; that the mason transposed the figures by error. Acceptance of the hypothesis would lead to certain conclusions: the record of Skione becomes normal; the trouble in Poteidaia begins earlier than we have supposed, for Athens is adopting disciplinary measures at least as early as 435/4; the restoration [ᴾH] for the quota of Poteidaia in 19, V, 20 (436/5) becomes open to scepticism. Changes of tribute within assessment periods, however, are not without parallel, and the necessity of supposing such a change for Poteidaia in 435/4 is not an argument against the hypothesis;[1] Athens could adjust an assessment by special action at any time.

We have returned, in 20, V, 31, to the restoration [Γαλαῖ]οι ἄτακτοι. Our decision is based upon a fresh study of the πόλεις ἄτακτοι and involves the restoration of the quota [ΔⱵⱵΙΙ] opposite [Γαλ]αῖοι in 19, V, 26. For the argument we refer to p. 86 with note 41 below.

Also dependent upon fresh study is our completion, by restoration, of the βουλή rubric in List 25, III, 60-65, which we now print as follows:

τᾱῖσδε h[ε] βολὲ καὶ hοι πεντακόσιοι
καὶ χίλ[ιοι ἔτ]αχσαν

ᴳⱵⱵ[ⱵΙΙ]	[Κλεοναί]
[ΔΔΔ]	[Συμαῖοι]
[ΔⱵⱵΙΙ]	[Διακρὲς ἀπὸ Χαλκιδέον]
[ᴾ]	[Βυσβικενοί]

For the evidence and the conclusions we refer the reader to pp. 80-82 with note 30 below.

The document published as List 33 in *A. T. L.*, I, plus a new fragment,[2] we retain in 422/1, although Meritt once advocated placing it in 418/7 as List 37;[3] for the evidence which leads us to adhere to our original dating see below, pp. 351-352. For the later lists, however, we now follow Meritt (*loc. cit.*) without repeating his arguments.

In *A. T. L.*, I, List 36, line 4 we left the quota of Νάχσι[οι] unrestored as ᴾHH – – –. We have now assigned this fragment to List 38 (417/6) and have completed the quota of Naxos as ᴾHH[HH]. Similarly, in List 39, I, 27 we restore the quota of Νάχσιοι as [ᴾHHHH]. The first certain quota for Naxos is recorded in 7, III, 25, as ᴾHᴾΔᴳⱵΙΙΙΙ, and we have with confidence restored this figure in 5, IV, 35, the initial appearance (450/49) of Naxos in the lists. We believe, however, that the island was assessed in 454/3 and paid in the first period.[4] Our estimate of 9 talents

---

[1] Cf. the Register, *s. vv.* Σαμοθρᾶκες (Period IV), Σκαβλαῖοι (V, VI), Μενδαῖοι (IV), Συαγγελῆς (III); these variations do not seem to be due to partial payments.

[2] Meritt, *Hesperia*, XVII (1948), pp. 31-32.

[3] *A. J. P.*, LXII (1941), pp. 1-15.

[4] Cf. below, note 13 on p. 268.

for the assessment of Naxos in Period XI (418/7-415/4) is based upon two beliefs: (1) that the assessment of 6⅔ talents in Period II represents a decrease after the founding of the klerouchy in 450,[5] and (2) that the assessment of 421 was made on the Aristeidean scale and in many cases employed the Aristeidean figures.[6] We estimate the original assessment of Naxos at 9 talents,[7] and assume that, after the sharp increase to 15 in 425 (A9, I, 63), the " Aristeidean " assessment of 421 brought a return to 9 talents.[8]

[5] For the klerouchy see below, p. 287; cf. Meiggs, *J. H. S.*, LXIII (1943), pp. 32-33. For the assessment of 454/3 see above, p. 25.

[6] For the assessment of 421 see below, pp. 347-353.

[7] At the close of the sixth century, according to Herodotos (V, 28), Naxos was the most prosperous of the islands.

[8] The fragmentary ΓHH-- surviving in List 38 proves that Naxos paid at least more than 7 talents in 417/6.

CHAPTER V

ASSESSMENTS AND RUBRICS

[Xenophon] names amongst the duties of the Council the assessments of tribute (T155): τὸ δὲ μέγιστον εἴρηται πλὴν αἱ τάξεις τοῦ φόρου· τοῦτο δὲ γίγνεται ὡς τὰ πολλὰ δι' ἔτους πέμπτου. Whatever the exact date of his treatise on the *Constitution of the Athenians*, the epigraphical evidence supports his testimony that, as a rule, assessments were made every four years.[1] It also proves that these four-year periods were the span from one Great Panathenaia to the next (A9, lines 26-33), for severe penalties were voted in 425/4 for the prytaneis in office in the future if they failed to introduce and carry through the business of the new assessments at succeeding Great Panathenaia. One expects, therefore, that after 425 the reassessments of the tribute will take place at the Panathenaia of 422, 418, 414, 410, and 406.[2] Either these dates must be held valid, or good arguments must be advanced against them. The evidence for assessment years earlier than 425 indicates 454, 450, 446, 443,[3] 438, 434, 430, and 428: for the most part, but not exactly, every four years.[4]

The First Assessment: 454/3

The first year of administration of the tribute in Athens was 454/3 (List 1) and fragmentary quotations from the Athenian decree of assessment have been preserved in Krateros (A1).[5] List 34, according to its prescript, belongs in the archonship of Aristion, 421/0, which is specified as the thirty-fourth year of tribute payment in Athens; this proves that 454/3 was the era date.

The Second Assessment: 450/49

The fact of a new assessment in 450 B. C. finds threefold support in the quota lists:

1) There are numerous changes in quota between the lists which precede and those which follow this date.[6]

[1] Meritt, *D. A. T.*, pp. 41-42 with note 55, favoured a date for the treatise early in 424 B. C.; for a general discussion of the essay see Gomme, *Harv. Stud. Cl. Phil.*, Suppl. Vol. I (1940), pp. 211-245, who favours a later date (see, *e. g.*, pp. 244-245). The most recent treatment is by Hartvig Frisch, *The Constitution of the Athenians* (*Classica et Mediaevalia, Dissertationes*, II, Copenhagen, 1942), who dates it before the Chalkidic revolt of 432 B. C. (see especially pp. 47-62).

[2] Meritt, *A. F. D.*, p. 15.

[3] For the first four periods see Meritt, *A. J. A.*, XXIX (1925), pp. 247-273 (= *Studies in the Athenian Tribute Lists*, pp. 247-273).

[4] It does not seem necessary to discuss the dates of the assessments as given by Schwahn in *P. W., R. E., s. v.* φόροι, pp. 619-627.

[5] See above, pp. 9-11.

[6] See the Register in *A. T. L.*, I, and additions and corrections in *A. T. L.*, II, Chapter III.

2) The fifth list is cut off from the end of the fourth list on the stone by a considerable uninscribed area which seems to mark a significant major division.

3) The order of names in List 5 betrays a different geographical grouping from that which Krateros proves for the first assessment period. This new grouping is a reflection of the assessment decree of 450 B. C., in which the Ionic and Karic districts were merged; the evidence lies partly in the Decree of Klearchos (D14).[7] That the Karic district was listed separately in 454/3 is proved by Krateros' citation of Καρικὸς φόρος (frag. 1 Krech) from A1.

The Third Assessment: 446/5

In this period the original fivefold listing of the cities of the Empire is again discernible, and together with changes in the amounts of quota (see the Register) it testifies to the reassessment of 446.[8]

The Fourth Assessment: 443/2

The evidence for a reassessment in 443, the first time when a new assessment was made in a year other than that of the Great Panathenaia, lies principally in the new systematization of the lists which was effected when Sophokles was hellenotamias (List 12) and in the changed spelling of many of the names even when the quotas remained the same.[9]

The Fifth Assessment: 438/7

The disposition of the fragments on the obverse of the second stele proves that the listing of names in five districts persisted through 439/8 (List 16) and changed in 438/7 (List 17) to four districts, the Ionic and Karic panels henceforth being combined. The year 438 was a Panathenaic year, and the changes in the order of listing reflect the change in the new assessment decree. There are also differences in quotas and differences in the spelling of the names, but the precise year of the assessment is proved by the change in the districts.[10]

The Sixth Assessment: 434/3

The inception of a new assessment period in 434 is marked by the appearance in the lists for the first time of the special rubrics πόλεις αὐταὶ φόρον ταξάμεναι and πόλεις

This criterion has been recognized by all students of the quota lists, and does not need to be documented again.

[7] See Segre, *Clara Rhodos*, IX (1938), pp. 151-178.

[8] See especially Nesselhauf, *Klio*, Beiheft XXX, pp. 36-41.

[9] See especially Meritt, *Studies in the Athenian Tribute Lists*, *passim*.

[10] This is discussed by Meritt, *A. J. A.*, XXIX (1925), pp. 292-298 (= *Studies in the Athenian Tribute Lists*, pp. 292-298).

ἃς οἱ ἰδιῶται ἐνέγραψαν φόρον φέρειν. Moreover, certain cities from whom money was collected in 435/4, even though they were not assessed (notably Μιλτώριοι, Ὀθώριοι, Φαρβήλιοι, Χεδρώλιοι, and Γαλαῖοι), appear in List 21 as cities that have been assessed. The assessment was therefore that of 434.[11] There were also changes of tribute in 434/3 for Spartolos and, perhaps, Poteidaia.[12]

Methone must have been first assessed in 434, for the Methonaians petitioned in 430/29 for the privilege of paying only the quota assessed upon them in 430 (D3, lines 5-9). The privilege was granted (cf. D3, lines 29-32; List 26, II, 53), but at the time Methone owed arrears, which could only have been accumulated by virtue of an earlier assessment (D3, lines 9-16). Moreover, if these arrears belonged to more than one year (τὰ ὀφειλήματα, not τὸ ὀφείλημα), they offer the additional testimony that Methone could not have been first assessed at a hypothetical assessment in 431 even if one wishes to assume that she waited more than a year to protest against the levy.[13]

The Seventh Assessment: 430/29

No quota list has been preserved for 431/0, and some scholars have thought that the assessment may have been made in 431, a year earlier than the normal time. The evidence of the quota lists, however, places a reassessment in 428; and a subsequent reassessment in 425 is fixed by the assessment decree and list (A9) of that year. We hold that the dates 430, 428, and 425 are corroborated by Thucydides' mention of tribute-collecting expeditions which he sets in these very years.[14] " Though the *terminus ad quem* for the payment of tribute seems to have been the Dionysiac festival, the Athenians in war time probably needed tribute money as soon as they could get it, and made attempts to collect from the allies as soon as the amounts of tribute were known. --- In years of new assessments, the difficulty of making collections must have been increased by the unwillingness of subject states to pay heavier taxes. In these years the expeditions were powerful enough to engage in military enterprises worthy of the attention of the historian. There were doubtless tribute-collecting ships in every year during the period of the war, but in years of new assessment the forces sent out for this purpose must have been more than usually strong."[15] Nesselhauf's opinion that these tribute-collecting expeditions are not significant (*op. cit.*, p. 141)

[11] Cf. the contrary opinion of Nesselhauf, *Klio*, Beiheft XXX, p. 69, and Meritt's reply in *A. J. P.*, LV (1934), pp. 283-285.

[12] For Poteidaia see above, pp. 64-65.

[13] See Meritt, *A. F. D.*, p. 23. For Methone see below, pp. 133-137.

[14] Thucydides, II, 69 (T119), Melesandros, 430/29 winter; III, 19 (T125), Lysikles, 428/7 winter; IV, 50, 1 (T130), Aristeides, 425/4 winter; IV, 75 (T133), Demodokos, Aristeides, Lamachos, 424 early summer.

[15] Meritt, *A. F. D.*, pp. 17-25, especially pp. 19-20.

is answered briefly by Meritt (*A. J. P.*, LV [1934], p. 285) ; and Accame (*Riv. di Fil.*, LXIII [1935], p. 397), accepting the connection between assessments and tribute-collecting expeditions, regards the dates 430 and 428 for assessment years as certain.

List 25 (430/29) exhibits a marked increase in the assessment of the Hellespontine panel,[16] and other changes not to be associated with cities in revolt, particularly in the Islands. It also marks the end of the attempt to collect ἐπιφορά for late payments. We have already commented on the significance of Methone's record for the date.

The Eighth Assessment: 428/7

The evidence that a new assessment was made in 428, soon after the death of Perikles, is partly that Thucydides mentions tribute-collecting ships in the winter of 428/7,[17] partly the consideration that the only year to which the quota list now published as List 27 can be assigned is 428/7, with the consequence that its new names and changes in quota reflect the assessment,[18] and partly the consideration that Athens badly needed money for the siege of Lesbos.[19] The Aktaian cities were taken over by the Athenians at the time of the subjugation of Lesbos in the spring of 427 (Thucydides, III, 50, 3 [T128] ; IV, 52, 3 [T131]) and their assessment must have been supplementary to that of 428. We now hold that there is explicit reference to them in D22, which regulates not only the holding of the Lesbian kleroi but also the tributary status of the cities " on the mainland," that is, the Ἀκταῖαι πόλεις (D22, lines 13-15) :

$$[οἰκõντας πάντα] τ[ὰ] σφ[έτερα] αὐτõ[ν πλὲν]$$
$$[ἒ παραδό]ντας [σφõν τὰ κα]τ̣' ἔ[πειρον χορία hάπερ π]$$
$$[αραδõν]αι Ἀθεν[αῖο]ι κελεύοσ[ιν].$$

In the assessment of 428 the tribute of Aphytis (the only evidence for the Thrakian district) was raised from 3 to 5 talents and the city was granted the privilege of paying the quota only (cf. D21, lines 17-18).

The Ninth Assessment: 425/4

For the assessment of 425/4 we have the rich evidence of A9, the decree moved by Thoudippos governing the reassessment and future procedure, to which is added the list of the cities. We give first a translation of the decree.[20]

---

[16] See below, p. 352.

[17] Thucydides, III, 18, 5; III, 19 (T125) ; see above, note 14. Cf. Meritt, *A. F. D.*, p. 20.

[18] Meritt, *op. cit.*, pp. 17-18. See the Register.

[19] Meritt, *op. cit.*, p. 19.

[20] Modern study of this document is based on Meritt and West, *The Athenian Assessment of 425 B. C.* (University of Michigan Press, 1934). Our translation is of the text printed in *A. T. L.*, II ; it will be obvious that we have employed the translation of Meritt and West, *Ath. Ass.*, pp. 47-50, as a base.

Gods

Assessment of tribute

(FIRST DECREE)

Resolved by the Council and Demos, while Leontis was the tribe in prytany, [....]on was secretary, and [...⁷....] was the presiding officer. Thoudippos made the motion:

I (4-26): *The Current Assessment*

1. The Demos shall send heralds, to be elected by the Council from those who receive pay, to the cities, two to Ionia and Karia, two to Thrace, two to the Islands, and two to the Hellespont. These shall announce in the commune of each city that representatives are to come (to Athens) in the month of Maimakterion.

2. The Demos shall elect by lot 30 eisagogeis. These are to choose a secretary and an assistant secretary from the entire citizen body.

3. The Council shall select ten men (taktai) to assess the tribute. These shall enroll the cities within five days of the time they are selected and swear their oaths, or for each day each of them shall pay a fine of 1000 drachmai.

4. The administrators of the oath shall swear in the taktai on the very day of their selection, or each administrator shall be subject to the same fine.

5. The eisagogeis shall care for the adjudications concerning the tribute according as the Demos may vote. They and the archon and the polemarch shall hold preliminary interrogations of the cases in the Heliaia (building), as is done with the other cases, namely, those which come before the heliasts.

6. If the taktai do not assess tribute on the cities according to the adjudications, each one of them shall be subject at his euthyna according to the law to a fine of 10,000 drachmai.

7. The nomothetai shall establish a new court of one thousand jurors. Since the tribute has become too small, they (the jurors) shall join with the Council in making the current assessments, just as in the last administrative period, all in due proportion during the month of Posideion. They shall also deliberate daily from the first of the month in accordance with the same procedure in order that the tribute may be assessed in the month of Posideion.

8. The Council shall deliberate in full session and continuously in order that the assessments may be effected, unless the Demos votes otherwise. They shall not now assess a smaller amount of tribute on any city than it has been paying previously, unless because of impoverishment of the country there is a manifest lack of ability to pay more.

9. This recommendation of the Council and this decree, together with the amount

of tribute assessed on each city, shall be inscribed by the secretary of the Council on two stelai of stone, one of which he shall erect in the Bouleuterion, the other on the Akropolis. The poletai shall let the contract, the kolakretai shall provide the funds.

II (26-33): *Future Assessments*

1. In the future, announcements concerning the tribute shall be made to the cities before the Great Panathenaia.

2. The prytany which happens to be in office shall introduce the business of assessments at the time of the Panathenaia. If the prytaneis do not then introduce this to the Demos and if they do not vote a court concerning the tribute and if they do not deliberate in their own term of office, each one of the prytaneis shall be subject to a fine of 100 drachmai to be consecrated to Athena Nike and 100 to be paid to the public treasury, and each one shall be subject at his euthyna to a fine of 1000 drachmai; and if anyone else introduces a motion that the cities shall not be assessed at the time of the Great Panathenaia in the time of the prytany which holds office first in the year, he shall be deprived of civic rights and his property shall be confiscated and a tenth given to the goddess.

III (33-38): *Provision for Action*

1. These proposals shall of necessity be brought before the Demos by the prytany of Oineis as the first item on the agenda after the religious business on the second day after the expedition returns.

2. If the business is not finished on this day there shall be continuous deliberation about it beginning immediately on the following day until it is finished within the time of the prytany named.

3. If the prytaneis do not bring the matter before the Demos or do not complete the business during their own term of office, each one of them shall be subject at his euthyna to a fine of 10,000 drachmai on the ground of preventing the contribution of phoros to military expeditions.

IV (38-51): *Details of Assessment Procedure*

1. The heralds who are summoned are to be brought by the public summoners, in order that the Council may judge them if they do not seem to be performing their duties correctly. As for the routes of the heralds who are to travel, the taktai are to prescribe these, indicating how far they shall proceed, in order that they may not journey uninstructed. The heralds shall be compelled to announce the making of the assessments to the cities wherever the (local) archontes shall deem it best. The Demos shall vote on what must be said to the cities about the assessments and the decree, and on any other matter of urgency which the prytaneis may introduce.

2. As soon as the Council effects the assessment of the tribute, the generals shall see to it that the cities pay the tribute, in order that the Demos may have sufficient money for the war.

3. The generals shall give consideration to matters of tribute, each year, after investigating first, on land and sea, how much must be spent for military expeditions or for any other purpose. They shall regularly introduce suits which concern this subject at the first session of the Council without consulting the Heliaia and the other courts, unless the Demos votes that they shall introduce them after the dikastai have first made a decision.

4. The kolakretai shall provide the pay for the heralds who are to travel.

(RIDER)

[. . . .⁹. . . .] moved:

1. That the resolution of the Council be adopted with the following amendment: those assessments which may be determined for individual cities after appeal shall be laid by the prytaneis who then happen to be in office and by the secretary of the Council before the court when it deals with the assessments, in order that the dikastai may give their concurrence.

(SECOND DECREE)

Resolved by the Council and Demos, while Aigeis was the tribe in prytany, Philippos was secretary, and [. . .⁷. . . .]oros was presiding officer. Thoudippos made the motion:

1. All those cities assessed tribute in the year of the Council for which Pleistias was first secretary, in the archonship of Stratokles, shall bring to the Great Panathenaia a cow and a panoply of armour.

2. They shall take part in the festival procession in the same manner as colonists.

(THE RECORD OF ASSESSMENT)

Tribute was assessed upon the cities as follows by the Council for which Pleistias [. . . . .¹¹ ᵈᵉᵐᵒᵗⁱᶜ . . . .] was first secretary, in the archonship of Stratokles, in the term of office of the eisagogeis for whom Ka[. . .⁸ ᵒʳ ¹⁰ . .] [. .⁹ ᵒʳ ⁷ ᵈᵉᵐ. . . .] was secretary:

(Here follows the list of cities)

In some details our text differs from that of *A. T. L.*, I, and consequently our interpretation of the document is affected.[21] The text falls into sections according to

---

[21] See the commentary of Meritt and West, *Ath. Ass.*, pp. 50-63.

its content and these we have indicated in the translation and shall employ for ease of reference.[22]

I, 1: The heralds, we believe, could not have been chosen from the ranks of the Boule, in view of the language used of them in IV, 1 (especially lines 39-40: $[\dot{\epsilon}]\grave{\alpha}\mu$ $\mu\grave{\epsilon}$ $\dot{o}[\rho\theta\dot{o}s]$ $\delta o\kappa\hat{o}\sigma[\iota \, \delta\iota\alpha\kappa o]\nu\hat{\epsilon}[\nu]$, an expression scarcely applicable to a Councillor). We need a body to whom $\chi\epsilon\rho o[\tau o\nu\acute{\epsilon}\sigma\epsilon\iota]$ and $[\delta\iota\alpha\kappa o]\nu\hat{\epsilon}[\nu]$ will apply; the first is an objection to $[\delta\epsilon\mu o\sigma\acute{\iota}o\nu]$ since the $\delta\eta\mu\acute{o}\sigma\iota o\iota$ were slaves, the second to $[\beta o\lambda\epsilon\upsilon\tau\hat{o}\nu]$. We have also discarded $[\zeta\epsilon\upsilon\gamma\iota\tau\hat{o}\nu]$ as too general. In the text in *A. T. L.*, II we print $[\mu\iota\sigma\theta o\tau\hat{o}\nu]$, from $\mu\iota\sigma\theta\omega\tau\acute{o}s$. We understand these $\mu\iota\sigma\theta\omega\tau o\acute{\iota}$ as workers for hire, who were always at the disposal of the state and who were paid by the piece; they were citizens, as the verb $\chi\epsilon\rho o[\tau o\nu\acute{\epsilon}\sigma\epsilon\iota]$ requires. In Isokrates, VIII, 82 (T79c), the writer says that at the Dionysia the imperial funds were paraded through the theatre $\dot{\upsilon}\pi\grave{o}$ $\mu\iota\sigma\theta\omega\tau\hat{\omega}\nu$, "by hirelings," as Norlin renders it. We take it that these too were $\mu\iota\sigma\theta\omega\tau o\acute{\iota}$. The $\mu\iota\sigma\theta\omega\tau\acute{\eta}s$, on the other hand, was a contractor who paid out $\mu\iota\sigma\theta\acute{o}s$, and was not always, perhaps was seldom, a citizen; cf. *I. G.*, I², 374, lines 99-102. The orthography of the inscription would be better satisfied if the article preceding a noun beginning with mu were spelled $\tau\hat{o}\mu$. The surviving stroke of the third letter, however, is better read as nu, for the distinctive slope of mu is absent. But we note $[\pi\rho\hat{o}\tau]o\nu \, \mu\epsilon\tau[\acute{\alpha}]$ in line 35 and perhaps the mason was not wholly consistent. The orthographic difficulty could be avoided by reading $[\dot{\epsilon}\mu\mu\acute{\iota}\sigma\theta o\nu]$, on the analogy of the $\ddot{\epsilon}\mu\mu\iota\sigma\theta os$ $\pi\acute{o}\lambda\iota s$ of Plutarch, *Pericles*, 12, 4; yet the parallel of $[\mu\iota\sigma\theta o\tau\hat{o}\nu]$ with the passage of Isokrates is closer. Another possibility is $[h\alpha\iota\rho\epsilon\tau\hat{o}\nu]$, which would be the antecedent of $[{}^{h}\acute{o}s]$: "the Demos shall send heralds (whom it shall pick) from among those to be chosen by the Boule." We should thus have a prokrisis by the Council, and indeed, even with $[\mu\iota\sigma\theta o\tau\hat{o}\nu]$, this is conceivable. We read tentatively $[\mu\iota\sigma\theta o\tau\hat{o}\nu]$, *exempli gratia*, and we construe the passage with $[\kappa\acute{\epsilon}\rho\upsilon\kappa\alpha s]$ as the antecedent of $[{}^{h}\acute{o}s]$. This paragraph of the decree deals entirely with the election of the heralds and a general statement of their duties.

I, 2: There were to be eight heralds and ten taktai; we should expect the number of eisagogeis to be specified. In Aristotle's time there were five ('Αθ. Πολ., 52, 2); but these performed a quite different function and the number is unsuitable epigraphically in line 7. We posit 30, because considerable litigation must have been anticipated and because $[\tau\rho\iota\acute{\alpha}\kappa o\nu\tau\alpha]$ allows a credible restoration of the passage. The Demos must be understood as the subject of $[\kappa\nu\alpha\mu\epsilon\hat{\upsilon}\sigma\alpha\iota]$. The paragraph establishes a board of eisagogeis, with a secretary and an assistant secretary.

I, 3: We prefer $[\dot{\alpha}\nu\alpha\gamma\rho\alpha\phi\sigma\acute{\alpha}\nu\tau o\nu]$ to $[\dot{\epsilon}\gamma\gamma\rho\alpha\phi\sigma\acute{\alpha}\nu\tau o\nu]$, because the latter, on the analogy of the $\iota\delta\iota\hat{\omega}\tau\alpha\iota$ rubric (*A. T. L.*, I, p. 455), should mean "add names to an already existing list." The paragraph concerns the selection of taktai, their basic duty, and sanctions to be applied in case of failure.

---

[22] For the restoration of $[\Lambda\epsilon o\nu\tau\grave{\iota}s]$ in line 3 see Meritt, *Hesperia*, XIV (1945), pp. 118-119.

I, 4: This deals with the oaths of the taktai, to be administered by the ὁρκωταί.

I, 5: The time of the activity of the eisagogeis is already determined below (lines 16-19) and does not require a further decree. We therefore supply in line 12 [καθάπερ ἄν] rather than [ἐπειδάμ]. The other changes depend upon our understanding of the paragraph as a whole. It treats the diadikasiai, the adjudications upon appeal, and it is to handle these that the eisagogeis are created. They are additional archons, so to speak, to cope with the extra litigation. Their duty is to get the cases to court (εἰσάγειν), which normally implies ἀνάκρισις and then ἡγεμονία δικαστηρίου. The eisagogeis and the archon and the polemarch are to share out the ἀνακρίσεις. The ἀνακρίσεις are to be heard in the building called the Heliaia, in which other cases, i. e., those involving the regular heliastic jurors, are heard.

I, 6: We believe that these lines also deal with the διαδικασίαι, and their connection with the taktai. These officers represent the state at the appeals; the assessments thus determined in court, the " diadikastic " assessments, are to be binding on the taktai, under threat of penalties.

I, 7: The diadikasiai, which do not come before the regular heliastic jurors, demand a special court, which is here established as required by I, 5-6. This is not the first time that such a court has been created, however, as is proved by lines 17-18: [καθάπερ ἐπὶ τῆς τελευτ]αίας ἀρχῆς, and by the existence of the βουλή rubric (A. T. L., I, pp. 456-457) as early as 430/29. The establishing of such a special court in past assessment years and in the future is perhaps reflected in the tense of κα[θ]ιστάντον. It had become a recognized procedure. The thousand jurors form the subject of χσυντα[χσάντον] and can be said to coöperate with the βουλή in that they hear all appeals and refer their decisions to the Council through the taktai. Their work begins on the first of Posideion, lines 18-19, where we retain parallel construction by restoring χ[ρεματιζόντον] in place of χ[ρεματίζεν]. A further echo of the previous assessment period is found in [κα]τὰ τ[αὐτά], which means that the continuous session of the court enacted in 425 follows the model of 428/7.

I, 8: Just as the court is to sit continuously, so is the Council, in the absence of instructions from the Demos to the contrary. The subject of [ταχσάντ]ον is the Councillors, who are given a general guide for assessment. Despite its coöperation with the court, this is to be the Boule's assessment; cf. line 58: [κατὰ τάδε ἔτα]χσεν τὸμ φό[ρον τῆ]σι πόλεσιν hε βολ[έ].

I, 9: The paragraph concerns publication of the decree and the assessment list.

II, 1-2: The decree here looks forward to future assessments, which are to fall in Great Panathenaic years. In line 28 we have abandoned the restoration of A. T. L., I because it is not the business of the prytaneis to introduce assessments to the court, nor is the latter a permanent body; it is created in assessment years and it is dissolved when its work is done. It must be recreated in every Great Panathenaic (assessment) year. The prytaneis, then, must see that such a court is brought into existence: [ἐὰν δὲ ℎοι πρυτάνες μὲ τότε — — — φσεφίζονται δικαστ]έριον. We again direct attention to the tense of κα[θ]ιστάντον in line 16. The court is νέον in every Great Panathenaic year. Our change of text in line 30 brings the sanctions upon all the prytaneis rather than upon the secretary alone.

III, 1-3: These paragraphs prescribe speedy consideration of the probouleuma by the Demos.

IV, 1: Here we return to the immediate assessment. We understand lines 38-44 of the heralds and in lines 38-39 we restore τὸς δ[ὲ κέρυ]κας as a suitable introduction. Lines 38-40 are more applicable to the heralds than to private offenders or prytaneis. The taktai determine the routes of the heralds, who are thus not uninstructed ([ἄτακ-τοι]). The task of the heralds is to announce to the cities that a new assessment is under discussion and that envoys are to go to Athens. The words τὰς τά[χσ]ες (line 42) are to be taken in a general sense; no figures are to be revealed until the presbeis arrive in Athens. Indeed, the taktai will scarcely have had time to consider figures; their initial task is to draw up the list of cities and this must be done rapidly (in five days) in order that the taktai may speed the heralds on their way. The latter will choose where they should discharge their message on the advice of the archontes in the cities. These officials would be better informed on local matters than would the Demos; hence our change of restoration. The Demos, however, is to participate in the work of the heralds, for it is here instructed to provide them with a form of words which will not necessarily reveal to the tributary cities the extent of the increases contemplated by Athens.

IV, 2: Collection is to be the responsibility of the generals.

IV, 3: This paragraph deals with bye-assessments. When the generals consider additional assessments necessary, they are to submit the names and appeals direct to the Council without consulting the heliastic or any other court; this is to be the pro-cedure unless the Demos votes that the dikasts must first pass on these cases before the generals bring them to the Council. We have eliminated [ἄλλοθί πο] πρὸ[τον δικά]σα[ντας] in line 50 in favour of [δικαστὸν] πρὸ[τον δικα]σά[ντον] because the verb δικάζειν is inappropriate to the generals; it should be used only of δικασταί. It is in order in line 39 ([ℎ]ε βολ[ὲ δικά]σε[ι]) because the Council is to serve as a court.

IV, 4: The clause provides for the pay of the heralds.

Rider: The objection to the restoration of A. T. L., I is that ἐφιέναι needs as its subject a litigating party; an organ of government would be unique. Furthermore, if the assessments are drawn up jointly by the Council and the court (as [χσυντάττον-ται] would have to mean), it is difficult to understand why appeals to the court would be necessary. Our present interpretation is that assessments which have been decided after appeal and which the Boule includes in its final list must be reported back to the court. Previously (lines 14-16) the taktai have been ordered to make such assessments in accordance with the decisions of the court. The rider now gives to the court the opportunity to see that its decisions have been carried out by the taktai.

The second decree governs the religious obligations of the allies, and is followed by the record of assessment. We set out here our conception of the procedure envisaged by the document as a whole.

Immediately after ratification of the probouleuma by the Demos, the Council elects eight heralds and chooses ten taktai; the horkotai at once administer the oath to the taktai. The month is Metageitnion.[23]

Within five days the taktai enroll the cities which are to be assessed. With their list of cities they prescribe the routes which the heralds are to take. The heralds draw their funds from the kolakretai.

The Demos decides what the heralds are to announce to the cities; this may perhaps include something about the scale of the assessment. The Demos then officially despatches the heralds. The Demos elects by lot a board of 30 eisagogeis to deal with appeals, which are expected in large numbers; the eisagogeis select a secretary and an assistant secretary from the citizen body.

During the absence of the heralds the taktai add the amounts of assessment to the names on their list.

The nomothetai establish the special court of 1000 to hear appeals.

In the meantime the heralds visit every city on the list and, under the direction of the local archontes (Athenian or native), disclose their rescript.

In Maimakterion the presbeis from the cities arrive in Athens. They are notified of the amount of their respective assessments by the taktai.

Some of the cities demur and take advantage of their right of appeal. Preliminary hearings come before the eisagogeis, the archon, and the polemarch, who place the cases on the docket of the special court.

Beginning on the first day of Posideion the court hears appeals, sitting daily until the docket is cleared. The taktai represent the Athenian state and are compelled to abide by the court's judgments. The 1000 jurors, we imagine, are divided into panels, to which the cases have been assigned by the eisagogeis, archon, and polemarch.

The taktai add the adjudicated figures to their list. They then submit their revised list to the Boule.

The Council now ratifies (or adjusts) the figures, both the original assessments made by the taktai and the adjudicated assessments which come from the court through the taktai; the latter are not subject to change. The Council compares the figures with previous assessments to make sure that no city is paying less than before (except as special local conditions justify exceptions), and then has the final list in its hand. The figures in this list which are entered against cities which have appealed are

---

[23] Towards the end of the month; Wade-Gery and Meritt, *A.J.P.*, LVII (1936), p. 393.

reported to the court, which confirms them. If any figure disagrees with the court's original decision, the taktai are liable to penalty. The assessment is now complete and the month is Posideion.

The decree and the list of cities with their assessed tributes are published on marble.

Payment is due by the time of the Dionysiac festival. The generals are entrusted with collection. This means that they encourage early payment or provide convoys where necessary for cities which pay promptly, and apply persuasion to recalcitrants. Prompt action, necessitated by the financial strain of the war, is reflected in the winter of 425/4 by the presence of Aristeides, εἷς τῶν ἀργυρολόγων νεῶν Ἀθηναίων στρατηγός, at Eion (Thucydides, IV, 50, 1 [T130]). Action against recalcitrants may perhaps be seen in the summer of 424, when Lamachos commands a tribute-collecting squadron in Hellespontine waters and himself goes as far as Herakleia in the Pontos (Thucydides, IV, 75, 1-2 [T133]).

During the assessment period (i. e., in the years before the next assessment) the generals may decide that extra levies are necessary, either from cities already assessed or from cities not included in the list of 425/4. These cases, which will probably involve appeals, are to be introduced direct to the Boule by the generals, without reference to any court. This provision was originally subject to amendment by the Demos; but, so far as we know, no action was taken (the rider in lines 51-54 concerns current procedure and refers to the special court).

Future assessments are to be made in Great Panathenaic years. The cities will be notified before the festival, will participate in the festival, and will then be available to accept assessment or to appeal the proposed amounts. At the time of the Great Panathenaia the prytaneis are to be responsible for placing the business of assessment on the agenda of the ekklesia and for seeing that the special court is established on the pattern of the court of 425/4.

That the court of 425/4 is not an innovation is shown not only by the words [ἐπὶ τὲς τελευτ]αίας ἀρχὲς (lines 17-18) and [κα]τὰ τ[αὐτά] (line 19), but by the known existence of a similar body as early as 430 B. C. In 25, III, 60-65 we meet:

ταῖσδε h[ε] βολὲ καὶ hοι πεντακόσιοι	
καὶ χίλ[ιοι ἔτ]αχσαν	
ΓΗΗ[ΗΙΙ]	[Κλεοναί]
[ΔΔΔ]	[Συμαῖοι]
[ΔΗΗΗΙΙ]	[Διακρὲς ἀπὸ Χαλκιδέον]
[Ͱ]	[Βυσβικενοί]

This rubric finds its mate in the following year (26, II, 43-49), although the wording is slightly changed:[24]

---

[24] For the omission of the article with [βο]λέ cf. D17, line 13: πρὸς βολὲν καὶ δὲμον.

[ταῖσδε βο]λὲ [σὺν τ]ôι
[δικαστερί]ο[ι ἔ]τ[α]χ[σεν]
[ΔΔΔ]   Συμαῖοι
[ΔΗΗΙΙ]   Διακρ[ὲς ἀ]πὸ
           Χαλκι[δέον]
[Ⅎ]   B[υσβ]ι[κε]νο[ί]
[ΓΗΗΙΙ]   Κ[λε]ον[αί]

In 430 the court is a body of 1500, whereas in 425 its size is limited to 1000; the number of jurors, of course, is no indication of the amount of litigation anticipated. In 430/29 at least four cities appealed and later paid; some may have appealed and defaulted. The court which sat in 430, then, is well attested. But we can also be sure, from the phrase [ἐπὶ τὲς τελευτ]αίας ἀρχὲς, that a court was established in the assessment year 428. The decree of 425, we believe, looks forward to considerable litigation: the court is to sit continuously and [30] eisagogeis are appointed to see the cases through. If our restoration [κα]τὰ τ[αὐτά] is right, the court of 428 also sat continuously and we may conjecture that then, too, much litigation was expected. The assessment of 428 was the first assessment since the death of Perikles, and it is our view that in this year the scale of the assessment was raised; an increase of litigation would not be surprising, for more cities than usual would appeal.

The function of the special court in A9 is not to review all assessments, as Kahrstedt believes,[25] but to hear the appeals and to adjudicate them; the διαδικασίαι are the "hearings to adjudicate assessments upon appeal." We may safely assume that the courts of 430 and 428 existed for the same purpose. The allies had always had the privilege of appeal, we think, even though specific evidence is lacking. The testimony of D3, however, shows that Methone had appealed to the Demos, although not, to be sure, to arbitrate a specific assessment, but to question whether she should pay the whole tribute or the quota alone. In D7 the allies are allowed to defend themselves against a charge of defaulting. In A9 we note that in non-assessment years the generals may levy tribute upon additional cities (or increase the assessment of members), and that appeals in these cases are (unless the Demos votes otherwise) to go straight to the Boule without reference to the heliastic or other courts. We may perhaps infer that in the past appeals had been heard by heliastic courts. The special court, which must not be included in [τ]ὸν ἄλλον δικαστερίον, would not be sitting in off-years; its work fell wholly during the year of the assessment. But before 430, we suggest, allied appeals came before a heliastic court.

The special court, whose sole function was to adjudicate appeals and whose span of existence lasted scarcely a month, was an innovation of 430. This method of dealing with appeals was continued in 428 and again in 425; but that it was also to play a

---

[25] *A. J. P.*, LVII (1936), p. 419.

part in the machinery of future assessments seems to us logical, as we indicate by our restoration of A9, line 28: [ἐὰν δὲ hοι πρυτάνες μὲ τότε – – – φσεφίζονται δικαστ]έριον. A well-established procedure may be recognized in the tense of κα[θ]ιστάντον (line 16): the nomothetai are to institute, as they regularly do and as they will in the future, a new court. The court is new in every assessment year.

The assessment of 425/4 is essentially that of the Boule (see line 58). Yet the court can be said to coöperate in that it hears appealing cities, whose adjudicated assessments are incorporated in the list presented to the Boule by the taktai. This coöperation is reflected in the decree by the use of the compound verb ξυντάττειν in lines 17 and 45. The procedure in 425 embodies new features, however, for the list of assessed cities shows no special rubrics. These are to be abolished and the final roster of names (in geographic panels) approved by the Boule is authoritative, with no public distinction made among various classes, or between cities which appeal and cities which do not. This is a return to the practice of the early assessment periods.

The rubrics of Periods VI and VII, we believe, reflect the character of the assessment lists of 434/3 and 430/29. The categories of assessed cities were carefully distinguished and as a result we have in the quota lists of these two periods the πόλεις αὐταί, ἰδιῶται, βουλή, τάκται, and ἀπαρχήν rubrics.[26] These were eliminated in 425 and some confirmation of this statement may be found in the complete absence of the rubrics named from the fragments of the later lists. List 33 is based upon A9 and we should scarcely expect to see traces of rubrics in its meagre remains, chiefly from the tops of the columns; List 34, however, although very fragmentary and based upon the assessment of 421, gives us a wider sampling of the original stone. Similarly, the fragments of Lists 35, 38, 39 and 40 fail to preserve any trace of these rubrics, although some of the cities which were once catalogued under them continue to pay tribute.

In the early days there was probably little appeal of assessments and no special arrangements were felt desirable. The tribute was levied, down to the outbreak of the Peloponnesian War, on the scale of Aristeides' assessment, and even in 430/29 we know of only four cities which appealed; these are duly entered in the βουλή rubric of Lists 25 and 26. We may conjecture that litigation increased in 428, when the scale of assessment was raised and the court was ordered to sit continuously.

The special categories which appear in Periods V, VI, and VII require some further examination. The names in the βουλή rubric are: Syme, Kleonai, Bysbikos, and Diakres. It is significant that all four are found in the ἰδιῶται rubric of Period VI. As in A. T. L., I (p. 455), we hold that the ἰδιῶται, who in 434/3 added names to the list of those cities assessed tribute by the taktai, were members of the Athenian citizen

---

[26] The separate rubrics recording money paid in the field or to magistrates, on the other hand, represent the circumstances of payment rather than conditions of assessment.

body; their action was taken at a meeting of the ekklesia.[27] During Period VI we can identify thirteen cities whose names were added to the assessment list by ἰδιῶται; the total was at least fourteen.[28] Some of these states had been separated from larger neighbours by apotaxis, some had no previous connection with the Empire, thanks to isolated or peripheral locations. Only one has a previous tributary history, and this city, Othoros, we shall consider shortly; some disappear in 430.[29]

The course of events now seems clear and we recapitulate. In 434 Athenian citizens in the ekklesia added new names to the assessment list presented by the taktai; this caused the amended list to show a special class of cities and this clerical procedure is reflected in the quota records of the period. In 430, however, we may assume that the cities of this group were included in the list of names drawn up by the taktai; some of them took advantage of the new court and appealed their assessments. Whether they appealed the amounts or their liability to assessment at all we cannot say; it may be that no such opportunity had presented itself in 434/3. The adjudicated figures went from the court to the Council (perhaps through the taktai), and in this sense the cities were assessed by the βουλή and the πεντακόσιοι καὶ χίλιοι (or δικαστήριον). Final authority, as in 425/4, rested with the Council, which ratified the adjudicated figures. It will be noted that in 425 certainly and in 430 probably the taktai assess the cities to the extent that they add the figures to the list of names, which (after adjustment upon appeals) is then submitted to the Council.

Our restoration of the complete βουλή rubric of List 25 to include Syme, Diakres, and Bysbikos is based upon the considerations already advanced;[30] the quotas are

[27] This is the interpretation of Kahrstedt, *A. J. P.*, LVII (1936), pp. 420-421, and Schaefer, *Hermes*, LXXIV (1939), pp. 240-241, in refutation of Nesselhauf, *Klio*, Beiheft XXX, p. 61, who thought the ἰδιῶται were private persons in the cities who on their own initiative bound their communities to pay tribute.

[28] Thirteen, including the five πόλεις Κροσσίδος making a joint payment, occur in List 21; the category is incomplete in List 22, which we know contained one name absent from List 21, for the quota ΔΔΔΗΗΗΙ[Ι] is new to the group. The rubric is also incomplete in List 23.

[29] Piloros does not occur again, Pistasos only in A10, the πόλεις Κροσσίδος only in A9 and A10. They may have been affected by the revolt in Thrace, although they may very well have been assessed, some of them, perhaps, under the βουλή rubric. We note that all three non-Thrakian cities in the rubric are listed in the βουλή rubric of the next period. Syme and Diakres are in all three extant lists of Period VI, Kleonai is in Lists 21 and 22, Bysbikos only in List 21. Since all four continue in Period VII we may suggest that [Βύσβικος] should perhaps be restored at the bottom of the extant names of the rubric in Lists 22 and 23, and [Κλεοναί] in the same position in List 23. The defaulting area is Thrakian (but Kleonai remained loyal). That there was defaulting is proved by the fact that the lines missing in Lists 22 and 23 could scarcely accommodate all the cities known to have been in this class.

[30] I. e., we expect the non-Thrakian rather than the Thrakian names of the ἰδιῶται rubric to survive in Period VII; the Thrakians have apparently begun to fall away by List 22 (433/2). In the βουλή rubric of List 26 we have four names occupying five lines; in the same rubric of List 25 we have only four lines. We had therefore restored in *A. T. L.*, I only [Κλεοναί], on the basis of the quota. But we now draw attention to the fact that no name in List 25 occupies two lines; entries

less sure, but since Kleonai's remains the same as in the previous period we have restored them all on the same principle, although without absolute certainty.

We have seen how four of the cities nominated for assessment by ἰδιῶται in 434 pass into the βουλή rubric in 430. There is one name in the ἰδιῶται rubric which has a previous tributary history. Othoros pays in Periods II, III, and IV, but was not assessed in Period V, for the Ὀθόριοι are entered as ἄ[τακτοι] in List 20, VI, 24. They are not unique, for in the same list we find similarly described Φαρβέλιοι, Χεδρόλιοι, Μιλτόριοι and (as printed in *A. T. L.*, I) [--ᶜᵃ˙ ⁶--]οι. In List 19 we have Pharbelos and Othoros, and since it belongs to the same period as List 20 we may safely conclude that the two cities were unassessed, although that designation was not recorded on the stone. Now all these names (Othoros, Pharbelos, Chedrolos, Miltoros) are Thrakian and they all lie in the same area in the interior of the Chalkidic peninsula.[31] We think that these payments by unassessed cities must be associated with an Athenian force or delegation in the field, whose commanders or leaders annexed the states to the Empire, perhaps by agreement, and levied money. Both Pharbelos and Othoros had been members of the Empire, but for some reason were not assessed in 438/7.

We can go further by stipulating that Miltoros and Chedrolos, neighbours of Pharbelos and Othoros and unassessed in List 20, were brought into the Empire by the same agency and at the same time as Pharbelos and Othoros. We therefore posit that both Miltoros and Chedrolos were entered in List 19. That this is compatible epigraphically with the fragments of List 19 is shown by the fact that [Μιλτόρ]ιοι, with a quota of [ΔΓΗΙΙΙ], could be restored in 19, V, 19, and [Χεδρόλιοι], opposite the quota ΓΗΗΗΙΙ, in 19, VI, 22. In the table on p. 87 (Fig. 3) we show them thus, although we have not placed them in the text printed in *A T. L.*, II, because there are other possibilities for these two lines and Miltoros and Chedrolos could have stood elsewhere in the list.[32]

That there is some relationship between the ἄτακτοι of Period V and the πόλεις αὑταί rubric of Period VI is proved by the fact that all (except Othoros) of those whom we have identified as ἄτακτοι pass into the πόλεις αὑταί rubric. This we show graphically in Figure 3 (p. 87). An attempt to define this relationship must also take into account the personnel of the τάκται rubric of Period VII; it is composed wholly of names drawn from the πόλεις αὑταί rubric of the previous period, and this too we indicate in Figure 3.

which are normally cut in two lines are here inscribed in one. Διακρῆς ἀπὸ Χαλκιδέον would therefore have required a single line and the number of names in the βουλή rubric was the same in each of the two lists. The restoration allows us to state that the following were absent from the full panel and rubric of List 25: Othoros, Piloros, Pistasos, Sinos, and the πόλεις Κροσσίδος.

[31] See above, p. 61.

[32] Nor are the quotas certain; we use the figures of the next period, when the tributes of some of the ἄτακτοι have changed.

The full form of the πόλεις αὐταί rubric is: πόλεις αὐταὶ φόρον ταξάμεναι. In *A. T. L.*, I (p. 456) we translated: "Cities assessed tribute separately." Our comment was: "These cities represent cases of apotaxis and as such are similar to the towns in the ἰδιῶται rubric." The translation and interpretation have long been disputed and our own renderings have been criticized, especially by Gomme and Meiggs.[33] We have now reached the conclusion that we were mistaken in restricting the cities of this class to cases of apotaxis. Pharbelos, for example, pays tribute in the first four periods and is not assessed in 438/7; why, we cannot say, but the town was surely not annexed by a neighbour for a few years only, to be separated in 434/3 after contributing unassessed sums in 436/5 and 435/4. We therefore believe that the cities of the πόλεις αὐταί rubric are in part communities separated by apotaxis from neighbours and in part isolated or peripheral communities, some of whom had not been members of the Empire. This interpretation demands a change in our translation of the rubric heading, for αὐταί can no longer be rendered "separately." On the other hand, we hold that any form of self-assessment is impossible. We cannot believe that Athens would have tolerated self-assessment and our conviction is strengthened by Thucydides' use of the middle of τάττειν. The best example is in I, 101, 3 (T110), where he describes the end of the Thasian revolt: Θάσιοι δὲ --- ὡμολόγησαν Ἀθηναίοις τεῖχός τε καθελόντες καὶ ναῦς παραδόντες, χρήματά τε ὅσα ἔδει ἀποδοῦναι αὐτίκα ταξάμενοι καὶ τὸ λοιπὸν φέρειν ---. Did the Thasians, after their unsuccessful revolt, themselves determine the amount of their immediate indemnity and future tribute? Did they voluntarily tear down their walls and surrender their ships and their rich peraia? Rather, "they accepted assessment of what they *had* (ἔδει) to pay immediately and to contribute regularly in the future."

We are aided in our search for the meaning of πόλεις αὐταὶ φόρον ταξάμεναι by the τάκται rubric, of which we give the full form: ταῖσδε ἔταξαν οἱ τάκται ἐπὶ Κρ[...]ου γραμματεύοντος ("the taktai assessed tribute on these cities in the year when Kr[....]s was their secretary"). In *A. T. L.*, I (p. 456) we identified Kr[....]s as secretary of the taktai in 434/3, when the πόλεις αὐταί rubric was first used and included all the names of the later τάκται rubric; we thought that the two prescripts were essentially the same in meaning, the second more formal than the first. This view has been challenged by Gomme:[34] "Clearly not. If they had been assessed by the regular τάκται in 434-3 ---, they would have needed no special rubric—they would have appeared in the general list. The assessors to whom Kr. was secretary must have been a special

---

[33] For our translation see E. B. Couch, *A. J. A.*, XXXIII (1929), pp. 502-514; for other interpretations see Nesselhauf, *Klio*, Beiheft XXX, pp. 59-62; Schaefer, *Hermes*, LXXIV (1939), pp. 241-242; Meiggs, *Eng. Hist. Rev.*, LV (1940), p. 106; Gomme, *Cl. Rev.*, LIV (1940), pp. 67-68. Nesselhauf and Schaefer think the cities assessed themselves; so, apparently, does Gomme (cf. *Commentary*, I, p. 283, on Thucydides, I, 99, 3).

[34] *Cl. Rev.*, LIV (1940), pp. 68-69.

board, probably of the previous year, who officially adopted the assessments originally proposed by the states themselves—what is the value of words if οἱ τάκται ἔταξαν αὐτοῖς is to mean the same as αὐτοὶ ἐτάξαντο?"

In the first place we do not believe in a special board of taktai of the previous year. This would have been 431/0, for the rubric appears in 430/29, an assessment year. The taktai were established as a board in every assessment year to carry out a specific task; in off-years the taktai did not exist. We are loth to suppose a special board in 431/0 in the absence of any evidence. As a matter of fact, the evidence points the other way, for when cities that had not been assessed paid tribute, no taktai were appointed to regularize procedure; rather, such cities could be entered in the quota records, with (see List 20) or without (List 19) the designation ἄτακτοι. If we happened not to possess List 20, we should never know that Pharbelos, which pays in List 19, was unassessed in Period V. In the year 431/0, whose quota list is lost, we may be sure that the rubrics (πόλεις αὐταί and ἰδιῶται) typical of Period VI had their usual places on the stone; no taktai were necessary in the fourth year of the period officially to adopt what had been the practice for three years.

Kr[....]s, then, was secretary of the taktai either in 430/29 or in 434/3, the previous assessment year.[35] The year 430/29 is manifestly out of the question and we are therefore sure of 434/3. The only excuse for the presence of the rubric in Period VII is that the cities listed in it were not assessed by the taktai of 430/29; that is, the taktai of 430/29 took over the previous assessments without giving thought to adjustment. We may put it in yet another way: the cities were immune from adjustment (i. e., increase) in 430/29. So some guarantee must have been vouchsafed by Athens to this group, and, no doubt, to all the cities of the πόλεις αὐταί rubric, some of whom fail to appear in 430/29. Here then we have the explanation of the πόλεις αὐταί rubric. It sets off in Period VI a class of cities with whom Athens had made specific agreements regarding the scale of assessment now and in the future.

Some of these (Miltoros, Chedrolos, Pharbelos, and, as we shall urge later, Gale) had been ἄτακτοι in Period V, before passing into the πόλεις αὐταί rubric in Period VI. We now present a reconstruction of the procedure which led to the appearance of these rubrics in the quota lists. During Period V the Athenians incorporated into the Empire certain states whose names had not been entered in the assessment list of 438/7; some had been Athenian tributaries in the past (Pharbelos, Othoros, Chedrolos), some had not (Miltoros, Gale). How this was done, whether through military persuasion or (more likely) through agreement with Athenian representatives, we do not venture to say. At the time of the assessment of 434/3 these cities were written in the taktai's list, their tributes were determined, and by special agreement they were

---

[35] No earlier year comes into question, for the cities which occur in the τάκται rubric were not assessed before 434/3.

guaranteed against future increases; they were joined by other cities, from all parts of the Empire, who were new to the records but who had made similar agreements. This is not to say that the cities assessed themselves; apart from the *prima facie* improbability of such a procedure, there is the fact that the tribute of Miltoros was increased from 1000 to 3000 drachmai and that of Chedrolos was doubled (500 to 1000 drachmai). Negotiation, however, was probably countenanced by Athens. We now translate the rubric heading as follows: " Cities which accepted assessment by special arrangement." [36] The names remained on the taktai's list and perhaps the taktai represented Athens in the negotiations. In a general sense, at all events, the taktai assessed them, and they belonged in the list of the taktai of 434/3. Nor does this interpretation contradict the rubric heading: the taktai entered the figures (ἔταξαν), the cities accepted them (ἐτάξαντο). At the assessment of 430/29 Athens remained true to her pledge; the new board of taktai set aside the cities in this class,[37] for their assessments had been already determined by the previous board, whose secretary was Kr[. . . .]s, and could not be changed.

The cities who accepted assessment by special arrangement, then, form in a sense a favoured group. But Athens could grant concessions when she felt it necessary, as is shown by her willingness to accept the quota alone from Methone, Haison, and Dikaia in 430/29. This, to be sure, was after the war had begun; yet signs of unrest were visible in Thrace some years earlier [38] and perhaps Athens was already taking steps to secure her position in Thrace and to maintain loyalty. That her concessions were unavailing is proved by the absence of the Thrakian names (except Sarte) from the πόλεις αὐταί rubric of 432/1 (List 23).[39]

Othoros, ἄτακτος in Lists 19 and 20, is exceptional in that it moves, in List 21, not into the πόλεις αὐταί rubric but into the group of cities nominated by ἰδιῶται. For some reason Othoros, although it was adjacent geographically to Pharbelos, Miltoros,

[36] This is not quite the same as an adjudicated assessment after appeal, for these cities were given guarantees for the future. Our translation of αὐταί is a logical extension of the meaning given in Liddell-Scott-Jones, *Lexicon*, s. v. αὐτός, I, 2: " of oneself," " of one's own accord." The cities concurred in the assessment.

[37] Eteokarpathioi is the only non-Thrakian name of the πόλεις αὐταί rubric which does not pass into the τάκται rubric. The rubric heading reflects the assessment list, while the names that appear under it record only the cities that paid; defaulters (and there were certainly some in 430/29) would have been entered in the assessment, but are absent from the quota lists. In Period VII we expect defection in Thrace. Aioleion and Pleume are absent from List 25 but reappear in List 26; the latter perhaps marks recoveries by Athens.

[38] Disciplinary measures against Poteidaia were taken possibly as early as 435/4; see above, pp. 64-65.

[39] That they were concessions is shown by the fact that the cities concurred in their assessments of 434/3; Miltoros, Chedrolos, and, we think, Gale accepted increases, Pharbelos was lowered (as was Othoros, whose behaviour is somewhat different; it passes into the ἰδιῶται rubric).

and Chedrolos, made no agreement with Athens and was indeed omitted entirely from the taktai's list. The town was promptly added by a citizen in the ekklesia.

One of the towns in the πόλεις αὐταί rubric is Thrakian Gale, which pays in Lists 21 and 22, only to default in List 23. Gale's first appearance is in List 19, V, 26 [40] and its record is so similar to the Thrakian ἄτακτοι, especially Miltoros, that we think it likely that it was unassessed but paid in Period V. We should then expect to find Γαλαῖοι ἄτακτοι in List 20 and we suggest not only that the entry stood in List 20 but that it is to be restored in V, 31: [Γαλαῖ]οι ἄτακτοι. [41] If this is right, then the quota [ΔΗΗΙΙ] may be restored against the name [Γαλ]αῖοι in 19, V, 26.

The five πόλεις ἄτακτοι are all Thrakian; there were no more in this district, for the panel of List 20 is full. Aioleion, Sarte, and Pleume, therefore, did not enter the Empire until 434/3; nor did the Thrakian cities whose first appearance is in the ἰδιῶται rubric of List 21. We know too that no Hellespontine city was ἄτακτος, for the full panel of List 20 shows no such designation. So the Hellespontine cities of the πόλεις αὐταί (Kallipolis) and ἰδιῶται (Bysbikos) rubrics were also new acquisitions in 434/3. The loss of the Ionic-Karic panels in Lists 19 and 20 makes certainty regarding ἄτακτοι πόλεις in this area impossible, while in the Islands we can draw no conclusions from the few names that survive in List 20. Our opinion, however, is that the ἄτακτοι πόλεις were confined to Thrace; this, in the middle 'thirties, was the area of possible disaffection and the evidence suggests that Athens watched it closely. Four of the five ἄτακτοι πόλεις, along with others from Thrace and cities from the Hellespont and Ionia-Karia, made special arrangements with Athens in 434/3 regarding assessment. The other πόλις ἄτακτος, Othoros, along with the πόλεις Κροσσίδος, other Thrakians, and one city from each of the remaining districts (Diakres, Syme, Bysbikos), was omitted from the list by the taktai of 434/3 and inserted by a member of the Athenian public. In the three classes (ἄτακτοι, πόλεις αὐταί, ἰδιῶται) we have twenty-five names; [42] all are new to the quota records except Pharbelos, Othoros, and Chedrolos, and these are cities that had returned to the roster as πόλεις ἄτακτοι in Period V.

[40] The restoration is not absolutely certain; see the note ad loc., A. T. L., I, p. 187.

[41] In A. T. L., I, note ad loc., p. 188, we abandoned [Γαλαῖ]οι, the reading of S. E. G., V, 20, "because the spacing is probably wrong and because the quota does not suit the name." It is impossible to measure the spacing accurately and we now feel that a lacuna of five letters is perhaps more likely than one of six (see A. T. L., I, Plate XX). The compelling reason for the restoration, however, emerges from the study of the rubrics and the behaviour of the names which belong to them. This study also eliminates the objection which we formerly admitted regarding the quota; the increase from ΔΗΗΙΙ (List 20) to Ⱶ (List 21) is paralleled by the known increases accepted by Miltoros and Chedrolos. There is one other possible restoration for 20, V, 31: [Σαρταῖ]οι ἄτακτοι. Sarte belongs to the same group of cities and might be expected in Lists 19 and 20; but the spacing now seems to us to favour [. .⁵. . .]οι rather than [. . .⁶. . .]οι. We suggest that normal spacing was maintained for the first four letters and that crowding began with the first iota; we note that the lettering is less crowded than the long entries (ἄτακτοι) in VI, 23, 24, 25, and 31. Sarte, therefore, did not pay in List 20 (the Thrakian panel is full) and probably not in List 19.

[42] Eleven πόλεις αὐταί (including the four πόλεις ἄτακτοι) and fourteen ἰδιῶται (including the missing name of 22, II, 99-100, which did not pay in List 21).

List	ἄτακτοι	πόλεις αὐταί	ἰδιῶται	βουλή
19 436/5	[ΔΓΗΙΙΙΙ] [Μιλτόρ]ιοι [ΔΓΗΙΙΙΙ] [Φαρβέ]λιοι [ΔΗΗΙΙ] [Γαλ]αῖοι [ΔΗΙΙΙΙ] ['Οθό]ριοι ΓΗΗΙΙ [Χεδρόλιοι]			
20 435/4	ΔΗΗΙΙ [Γαλαῖ]οι ⟶ ΔΓΗΙΙΙ[Ι] Φαρβέλιοι ⟶ ΔΗΙΙΙΙ 'Οθόριοι ⟶ ΓΗΗΙΙ Χεδρόλιοι ⟶ ΔΓΗΙΙΙΙ Μιλτόριοι ⟶			
21 434/3	Γ Κυστίριοι τάκται	ΓΗΗΙΙ Αἰολῖται ℟ Γαλαῖοι ℟ Μιλκό[ριοι] Η 'Αμ[όργιοι] ΔΓΗΙΙΙΙ Κ[άσιοι] ΔΓΗΙΙΙΙ Κα[λλιπολῖται] ΔΔΓ Σαρ[ταῖοι] ΔΓΗΙΙΙΙ 'Ετ[εοκαρπάθιοι] ΓΗΗΙΙ Φα[ρβέλιοι] ΔΓΗΙΙΙΙ [Χεδρόλιοι] ΔΓΗΙΙΙΙ Πλευ[μῆς]	Δ Πίλορος ΓΗΗΙΙ Κλεοναί ΔΔΓ Σίνος ΓΗΗΙΙ Διακρῆς ἀπὸ Χαλκιδέο[ν] ΓΗΗΙΙ Πίστασος ΔΔΔ Σύμε Τινδαῖοι ℟ Κίθας Σμίλλα Γίγονος ηαῖσα ℟ Βύσβικος ΓΗΗΙΙ 'Οθορος	
22 433/2		℟ Γαλαῖοι ΔΔΓ Σαρταῖοι Η 'Αμόργιοι ΔΓΗΙΙΙ 'Ετεοκαρπάθι[οι] ἐκ Καρπάθο ΔΓΗΙΙΙ Κάσιοι ΓΗΗΙΙ Αἰολῖται ℟ Μιλκόριοι ΓΗΗΙΙ Φαρβέλιοι [Δ]ΓΗΙΙΙΙ Καλλιπολῖτα[ι] [ΔΓΗΙ]ΙΙ Χεδρόλιοι	[Γ]ΗΗΙΙ Κλ[ε]οναί ΔΗΗΙΙ Δ[ια]κρῆς {ἀπὸ} Χαλκι[δέον] ΔΔΔ [Σύμε] ΓΗΗΙΙ – – – – – ΔΔΓ [Σίνος] ΔΔΔΗΗΙ[Ι] – – – – – (incomplete)	
23 432/1		ΔΔΓ [Σαρταῖοι] ΔΓΗΙΙΙΙ [Κάσιοι] Η ['Αμόργιοι] ΔΓΗΙΙΙ [Καλλιπολῖται] ΔΓΗΙΙΙ ['Ετεοκαρπάθιοι]	ΔΗΗ[ΙΙ] [Διακρῆς] [ἀπὸ Χαλκιδέον] ΔΔ[Δ] [Σύμε] (incomplete)	
24 431/0				
25 430/29	ΔΓΗΙΙ[ΙΙ] [Κ]αλλιπολῖται [Δ]ΔΓ Σαρταῖοι [Η] 'Αμόργιοι			ΓΗΗ[ΙΙ]℟ [Κλεοναί] [ΔΔΔ] [Συμαῖοι] [ΔΗΗΙΙ] [Διακρῆς ἀπὸ Χαλκιδέον] [℟] [Βυσβικενοί]
26 429/8	[ΔΓΗΙΙΙ] [Καλλιπολῖται] [ΔΔΓ] [Σαρταῖοι] [ΔΓΗΙΙΙΙ] [Κάσι]ο[ι] [ΔΓΗΙΙΙΙ] Π[λ]ε[υμ]ê[ς] [Η] 'Αμό[ργ]ι[οι] [ΓΗΗ]ΙΙ Α[ἰ]ο[λῖ]τ[α]ι			[ΔΔΔ] Συμαῖοι [ΔΗΗΙΙ] Διακρ[ês ἀ]πὸ Χαλκι[δέον] [℟] Β[υσβ]ι[κε]νο[ί] [ΓΗΗΙΙ] Κ[λε]ον[αί]

Fig. 3. The rubrics of Periods V-VII

To demonstrate clearly the interrelationship of the five rubrics here analysed we set them out graphically in Figure 3 (p. 87). We include [Μιλτόρ]ιοι and [Χεδρόλιοι] in List 19, even though we have not printed them in *A. T. L.*, II; the arrows indicate the passage of towns from one rubric to another. Kystiros, whose only appearance in the tribute records is as an ἄτακτος πόλις in List 21, does not affect the argument; the entry may be explained by apotaxis from Thasos.

As we have already remarked, all of these rubrics were swept away by A9 and even the tributaries which appealed their assessments were not placed in a special category in the record, as the list of the cities shows. In the quota lists after 425/4 the only rubrics which we should expect are those which indicate that sums of money were paid to commanders in the field and credited to the cities' tributes. We have no example from Period IX, but List 34, based upon the assessment of 421 (A10), proves that Hephaistia, Myrina, and Imbros paid their tributes (in whole or in part) to an Athenian force: [πόλ]ες αἵδε στρατιᾶι μισθὸν ἐτέλεσαν (I, 107-111, cut on the stone's reverse face). This practice was well-known, for in the past money had often been paid by cities of the Empire to field-commanders or to Athenian ἄρχοντες; see rubrics nos. I, VI, VIII, IX, and XI in *A. T. L.*, I, pp. 449-450, 453-454. In the early periods money levied in the field did not always have a special notation in the records at Athens; see above, Chapters I and III. As time went on, greater clerical accuracy was maintained, the development of which can be followed in the quota lists. These rubrics record the circumstances of collection and they could continue to exist, independent of the organization of the assessment list. Of particular interest is no. I, which perhaps reveals the formal procedure: αἵδε πόλεις καταδηλοῦσι τὸν φόρον (" these cities present a voucher for tribute "). Cities which paid money to generals in the field or to Athenian archontes in the Empire were given signed vouchers for presentation in Athens along with the due balance (if any) of the tribute. This rubric does not appear in the early periods; its absence testifies to the unsystematic nature of the bookkeeping.

Although with A9 the special rubrics were abolished, the list of the cities shows two new geographic panels: Ἀκταῖαι πόλεις and πόλεις ἐκ τοῦ Εὐξείνου. The Aktaian cities were taken from Mytilene after the suppression of the revolt in 427, as Thucydides (III, 50, 3 [T128]) tells us: παρέλαβον δὲ καὶ τὰ ἐν τῇ ἠπείρῳ πολίσματα οἱ Ἀθηναῖοι ὅσων Μυτιληναῖοι ἐκράτουν, καὶ ὑπήκουον ὕστερον Ἀθηναίων (cf. IV, 52, 3 [T131], and D22, quoted on p. 70 above). The assessment of the Aktaian cities, then, was realistic and the Athenians fully expected to collect tribute from them. In the early summer of 424 B. C. the Mytilenaian exiles on the mainland raided Rhoiteion and made their escape with 2000 Phokaian staters (Thucydides, IV, 52, 2 [T131]). Reckoned at 24 drachmai to the stater, this sum amounts to 8 talents, which is precisely the assessment of Rhoiteion in A9. It looks very much as if the Mytilenaians timed their raid perfectly, and made off with Rhoiteion's tribute just when it had been gathered together for transportation to Athens.

The Athenians also anticipated collection of tribute in the Euxine area, for in the summer of 424 Lamachos, in command of τῶν ἀργυρολόγων νεῶν, sailed with ten of the squadron into the Pontos and made his base at Herakleia, which had been assessed in A9 (Thucydides, IV, 75 [T133]).

When the Confederacy of Delos had originally been organized, the Athenians, no doubt, as part of their contribution to the allied undertaking, had promised to supply at their own expense ships and men. This Athenian squadron was the core of the Confederate fleet.[43] As members commuted their obligations from ships to money, Athens supplied the extra ships necessary and financed them from the tribute which came from the cities which had changed their status. But the Athenian core remained a charge upon Athenian funds, and was paid for by the demosion, the state treasury in the care of the kolakretai. This was the situation down to the Peace of Kallias: part of the Athenian fleet continued to be paid for by Athens herself, part by the tribute. Thus the annual reserve which accumulated first at Delos and later at Athens remained the same (about 200 talents a year), and by 450/49 had reached the sum of 5000 talents (cf. D13). The depositing of the 5000 talents with Athena in 450/49 and the proposal to transfer an annual 200 talents of tribute money to Athena for a period of fifteen years [44] show that Athens did not intend to jeopardize the programme of saving whose benefits she had experienced. The allies, however, did not apparently realize that Athens now could do as she liked with imperial funds. After the Peace of Kallias there was less campaigning and less expense; fewer ships needed to be kept on active service. Thus the Athenian naval core could be gradually decreased and more and more the fleet as a whole became genuinely imperial. The time came when the Athenians considered the entire fleet a charge upon imperial funds. The idea of a purely Athenian core (financially) disappeared and the Empire was expected to pay for the navy. We are not told when this happened, but we are sure that it did, probably some time before the Peloponnesian War. So in the war years the expenses of the fleet had to be borne by the tribute, which is one of the reasons why the tribute had become too small by 425 (cf. A9, lines 16-17: [τὸ δὲ φόρο, ἐπειδ]ὲ ὀλέζον ἐγ[ένε]το). Considerable emphasis is placed in A9 upon funds for the war and for military expeditions: if the prytaneis do not carry out instructions, each is subject to penalties [φό]ρο[ν hος] διακολύον ἐπιδ[όναι ἐς τὰ]ς στρα[τι]άς (line 38); the generals are to see to collection hίνα ἐι [τõι δέμοι ἀργύριον hικανὸν ἐς τὸμ] πόλ[εμον] (line 46); the generals each year are to compute [πόσ]α δεῖ ἒ ἐ[ς τὰς στρ]α[τιὰς ἒ ἐς ἄλλο τι ἀναλίσκεν] (line 48). The στρατιαί will be for the most part naval; the Athenian fleet by 425 is wholly imperial, so far as its financing is concerned.

---

[43] See further below, p. 229.
[44] D13, D1, D2; see below, pp. 281, 326-328.

The Tenth Assessment: 422/1

The circumstances and character of this assessment, and a consideration of its date, are given in detail on pp. 347-353.

The attribution here of A10 is quite certain, even though some of the arguments on which the attribution was first based are no longer valid.[45] For example, West believed that the Island panel belonged in the last column of A10 and that this geographic disposition was reflected in List 34, whereas we now hold that the disposition of geographical districts found in A9 was in all probability followed thereafter both in the quota lists and in the assessment decrees. There is nothing in the order of districts, therefore, to distinguish the tenth from the eleventh assessment period. Nor, as we shall observe below (pp. 348-352), will there be many changes in amounts of tribute in 418. Since these are the only two periods for which there can be any question about A10, it will be well to note specifically that the quota of Σομβία in 34, II, 86 at leasts permits the dating of A10 in 422/1 (cf. A10, IV, 3) and that the assessments of Mekyberna, Singos, and Gale in fact require it.

These three assessments of 10 drachmai each have been fully discussed by Meritt and West,[46] and West has further shown that they are closely tied to the clause in the Peace of Nikias (Thucydides, V, 18, 6 [T134]) which must be corrected to read: Μηκυβερναίους δὲ καὶ Γαλαίους καὶ Σιγγίους οἰκεῖν τὰς πόλεις τὰς ἑαυτῶν, καθάπερ Ὀλύνθιοι καὶ Ἀκάνθιοι.

These towns of Mekyberna, Gale, and Singos were in the possession of the Athenians when peace was made, but their citizens had been largely drawn away into the interior when Chalkidike revolted at the beginning of the war. They differed from the six towns named in the preceding paragraph of the treaty in that the Spartans had to return Argilos, Stageira, Akanthos, Stolos, Olynthos, and Spartolos, while the Athenians already held Mekyberna, Gale, and Singos. But the stipulations about all nine towns were the same. These three cities were to be repopulated, and—as the words καθάπερ Ὀλύνθιοι καὶ Ἀκάνθιοι prove—were to be autonomous and free from Athenian interference so long as they paid the tribute of Aristeides' day.[47] Akanthos and Olynthos have nothing more to do with Mekyberna, Gale, and Singos in the terms of the Peace of Nikias than to serve as convenient standards of reference. If the secretary of protocol had wished, he might have written in full: καθάπερ Ἀργίλιοι, Σταγιρῖται, Ἀκάνθιοι, Στώλιοι, Ὀλύνθιοι, Σπαρτώλιοι. And if there is perplexity because more than one city was named for reference (i. e., Ὀλύνθιοι καὶ Ἀκάνθιοι rather than

---

[45] Cf. West, Metr. Mus. Stud., III, 2 (1931), pp. 174-193.

[46] Meritt, A. J. A., XXIX (1925), pp. 26-28 (= Studies in the Athenian Tribute Lists, pp. 26-28); West, A. J. P., LVIII (1937), pp. 166-173.

[47] The great variety of speculation about this clause and its meaning is well summarized by West, op. cit., pp. 166-167.

simply Ὀλύνθιοι) we may suppose, as West did, quite tentatively, that the words καὶ Ἀκάνθιοι were an addition to the original text by some learned scribe who was himself already perplexed by the erroneous reading Σαναίους where he should have found Γαλαίους. But this is not necessary; the author of the treaty may have chosen two examples for no other reason than that it suited his fancy to give two examples instead of one, and that all six examples seemed to him unnecessary.

The Chalkidians did not accept the terms of the peace (Thucydides, V, 21, 2); Mekyberna, Gale, and Singos were not given the assessment of Aristeides in 422/1 (A10); and Athens kept her garrison in Mekyberna until the winter of 421/0, when the town was captured by the Olynthians (Thucydides, V, 39, 1). While the realistic assessment of a nominal 10 drachmai is intelligible if it applied to the few loyal Mekybernaians who stayed in their native city with the Athenian garrison, it is not intelligible if the city had been lost to the enemy, as was the case in 418; either there must then have been a full assessment or no assessment at all.[48] A10 must therefore be dated earlier than 421/0.

The Eleventh Assessment: 418/7

There was no demonstrable change in the scale of the assessment of A11 (cf. below, pp. 348-352), which we date to the Great Panathenaia of 418/7. The decree of A9 had ordered (lines 26-33) that future assessments be made at the time of the Great Panathenaia and heavy penalties had been prescribed in case of failure to comply with these orders. We therefore assume that, *ceteris paribus*, the orders were obeyed, and we thus posit assessments in 418/7, 414/3, and 410/09. In 422/1, circumstances were not normal, for talk of peace was in the air, and peace would affect the scale of the assessment. Even so, we think that the business of assessment was introduced at the Great Panathenaia of 422/1, although the allies paid at the Dionysia of that year (422/1) on the old scale and the actual reassessment was postponed until after peace was signed (Elaphebolion, 422/1).[49]

The Twelfth Assessment: 414/3

Instead of assessing tribute in 414 the Athenians imposed a five per cent tax on commerce (D24).[50]

The Thirteenth Assessment: 410/09

The reimposition of tribute for this assessment period is attested by Xenophon (*Hellenica*, I, 3, 9 [T160]) for the city of Kalchedon, and, in all probability, by the

---

[48] See West, *op. cit.*, p. 169.
[49] See below, pp. 347-348; Meritt, *A. F. D.*, pp. 15-16.
[50] Cf. Meritt, *A. F. D.*, pp. 15-17.

treasurers' record of 409/8 (*I. G.*, I², 301, lines 114-120) for Thasos.[51] Fragments of the assessment list have been preserved, some epigraphically, and some by Krateros of Makedon (A13). It is our belief that this was the last assessment of the Athenian Empire. Another assessment was due in 406, but there is no record of it and nothing has been preserved. Krateros, we believe, chose for illustration in his work the first and the last assessments. The fragments from the last assessment evidently come from book IX, which also contained the decree of 411/0, if we may judge from fragment 5 (Krech), on Andron's impeachment of Antiphon. The scope of Krateros' collection places the assessment fragments of the same book near in time to 411/0, and so we attribute them to the assessment of 410/09 B. C., which we assume to have been the last.[52]

[51] See List 46.
[52] See *A. T. L.*, I, p. 203.

PART II

THE OTHER EVIDENCE

CHAPTER I

THE SERPENT COLUMN AND THE COVENANT OF PLATAIA

The allies who " fought the war " against the Persian invaders in 480-479 B. C.[1] were inscribed by name on two monuments, the Delphic Serpent Column which is still extant in Istanbul (T68a) and the bronze Zeus at Olympia whose inscription Pausanias reports (V, 23, 1-2 [T90a]).[2] The few divergencies between the extant list from Delphi and the list which Pausanias reports from Olympia are perhaps due to inexact reporting of the Olympian copy, and in any case we may probably regard the Delphic list which survives as the master-copy.[3] The members of the alliance are here recorded as from the cities following: (1) Sparta, (2) Athens, (3) Korinth, (4) Tegea, (5) Sikyon, (6) Aigina, (7) Megara, (8) Epidauros, (9) Orchomenos (of Arkadia), (10) Phleious, (11) Troizen, (12) Hermione, (13) Tiryns, (14) Plataia, (15) Thespiai, (16) Mykenai, (17) Keos, (18) Melos, (19) Tenos (this name has been added in another hand, see note 3 below), (20) Naxos, (21) Eretria, (22) Chalkis, (23) Styra, (24) Elis, (25) Poteidaia, (26) Leukas, (27) Anaktorion, (28) Kythnos, (29) Siphnos, (30) Ambrakia, (31) Lepreon.

Herodotos says the monument was made from the booty of the battle of Plataia (IX, 81, 1; Thucydides' vaguer phrase in I, 132, 2 does not contradict this), but that the names included all who had helped defeat the barbarian (VIII, 82, 1; Thucydides, I, 132, 3, says the same; Pausanias, V, 23, 1, has no comparable authority). By " the barbarian " we must evidently understand the invasion whose defeat culminated at Plataia; the pursuit or counter-offensive which began with the campaign of Mykale brought in new allies whom the list did not include. It is likely then that the list was drawn up in 479, and this is confirmed to some extent by Thucydides' narrative in I, 132, 2-3. Thucydides there says that the original inscription was Pausanias' notorious couplet; that the Spartans deleted that " at once " and substituted the list of names; and that when Pausanias was in worse trouble (probably in 477) this earlier incident was remembered and compared. We may suppose that the offering was set up in the autumn of 479, and that the protests and change of inscription followed before the winter. The establishment of the list will belong, then, to the

[1] The heading in T68a is $[\tau]o[\emph{ίδε τὸν}]$ πόλεμον $[\emph{ἐ}]$πολ$[\emph{έ}]$μεον.

[2] A similar bronze Poseidon at the Isthmos was erected on the same occasion (Herodotos, IX, 81, 1 [T66c]) and may have had a similar inscription.

[3] This seems to be implied by Herodotos, VIII, 82, 1: " this deed won for the Tenians their inscription at Delphi amongst those who defeated the barbarian." On the Delphic Column the name Tenioi is clearly an addition; it breaks the symmetry and is in a different hand. The names not reported from Olympia are Thespiai, Eretria, Leukas, Siphnos. Plutarch, *Themistocles*, 20, 3, knows the list as of 31 names.

same series of deliberations as the question of refortifying Athens: to the autumn and winter of 479, before the Athenians who had fought at Mykale came home from Sestos.

It is probable that the names of the list fall into three groups, headed respectively by Sparta and her two chief allies, Athens and Korinth.[4] Roughly, the first group is Peloponnese, the second the Aegean, the third the Korinthian colonies; the main block of the first group is (4)–(13), of the second (17)–(23), of the third (25)–(27). The three categories are not kept systematically apart but they show through, in the same sort of way as the tribute districts show through in the quota lists of Periods II and III.[5] There are probably five names which are out of their categories: (24), (31), and perhaps (16) seem to be Peloponnesian cities whose questionable claims were allowed by afterthought; (28) and (29) are similar afterthoughts displaced from the Aegean group (see below, notes 20 and 21). If these five are placed in their proper categories the three lists resolve themselves thus:

Sparta	Athens	Korinth
Tegea	Plataia	Poteidaia
Sikyon	(Thespiai?)	Leukas
Aigina	Keos	Anaktorion
Megara	Melos	Ambrakia
Epidauros	Tenos	
Orchomenos	Naxos	
Phleious	Eretria	
Troizen	Chalkis	
Hermione	Styra	
Tiryns		
	Kythnos	
Mykenai	Siphnos	
Elis		
Lepreon		

Aigina and Megara fall into the Spartan list; it is interesting to notice that Melos falls into the Athenian. What then do these three categories represent?

Sparta's leadership of the whole alliance was never seriously contested until after the invader had been defeated.[6] The list is therefore a list of what is called, on

[4] This arrangement was observed by Domaszewski (his latest statement is in *Sitzungsber. Ak. Heidelberg*, XI [1920], 5, pp. 3-8); Franz Studniczka, *Zum platäischen Weihgeschenk in Delphi* (*Festgabe zur Winckelmannsfeier des archäologischen Seminars der Universität Leipzig*, December 12, 1928), suggests that the three serpents represent these three divisions of the alliance.

[5] See above, pp. 14, 30. In both cases it is probable that the categories once formed separate lists but additions were made after the consolidation.

[6] Herodotos, VIII, 3, 2 (T66a). See also below, pp. 184, 191-193.

especially formal occasions,[7] Λακεδαιμόνιοι καὶ οἱ (τούτων) σύμμαχοι, a designation which continues throughout the fifth century to be the formal designation of that alliance headed by Sparta which we commonly call the " Peloponnesian League," [8] and which had no doubt been the designation in the sixth century also.[9] This was the formal style, but in common parlance simpler designations were used. When the alliance was mainly [10] Peloponnesian (that is to say, before and after the Persian crisis) its usual name was Πελοποννήσιοι, " the Peloponnesians." [11] During the Persian crisis, when the alliance was much larger, its usual name was (οἱ) Ἕλληνες, " the Greeks." [12] Thus the formal title of Sparta's alliance is constant; " the Lakedaimonioi and their allies " fought against Persia in 480-479 and against Athens from 431 to 404. But the difference in the scope of Sparta's hegemony on those two occasions is recognized by the ordinary usage which calls the alliance of 480 " the

[7] Herodotos, VII, 157, 1; VIII, 142, 4.

[8] On formal occasions: Thucydides, III, 9, 1; 13, 1; 15, 1; 52, 4; 54, 2; 68, 1; cf. V, 26, 1 (T135). In formal documents: Thucydides, IV, 118, septies; 119, 1; V, 18, novies; VIII, 18, sexies; 37, septies; 58, undecies; cf. also V, 77, 2.

[9] No document or contemporary account is extant; Herodotos speaks of οἱ σύμμαχοι in V, 75, 3, and 91-93.

[10] Not of course exclusively; see Thucydides, II, 9, 2-3 (T116) and VIII, 3, 2.

[11] The " Peloponnesian War " has been so called, from the fourth century B. C. till today, because it was " the war against the Peloponnesioi." Thucydides' only adjective for it is Ἀττικός, the war " against the Athenians," from the Peloponnesian point of view; V, 28, 2; 31, 3 and 5. Both Herodotos (VII, 137, 1; IX, 73, 3) and Thucydides (I, 1, 1) describe it as " the war between Peloponnesians and Athenians," and Πελοποννήσιοι is Thucydides' regular term for the party which Athens was fighting, e. g., V, 9, 1; 26, 5; VIII, 44, 2 and 4; 46, 4-5; 48, 4. This usage is to be contrasted with the official style used in the passages quoted above in note 8, e. g., in the treaty of peace. The name Πελοποννήσιοι comes once in the Peace of Nikias, Thucydides, V, 18, 7, in a curious phrase: τοὺς ἐν Σκιώνῃ πολιορκουμένους Πελοποννησίων ἀφεῖναι καὶ τοὺς ἄλλους ὅσοι Λακεδαιμονίων ξύμμαχοι ἐν Σκιώνῃ εἰσὶ καὶ ὅσους Βρασίδας ἐσέπεμψε. The distinction here drawn was perhaps a delicate one: Brasidas had attempted to extend the alliance to this northern area, but by the treaty Sparta renounces that expansion, and Skione especially is left to Athens' discretion (V, 18, 8; 32, 1). It looks as if there had been some argument about delimiting exactly who, in Skione, should claim benefit as Sparta's ally; for the situation cf. Thucydides, III, 109, 2. Similar factual description of an enemy force as Πελοποννήσιοι occurs in I. G., I², 101, line 4 (possibly also in D18, line 7), Tod, Greek Hist. Inscr., I², no. 84, line 8, and Dittenberger, Syll.³, I, no. 73. A rather different documentary use of the name is in Thucydides, V, 77, 6: ὅπᾳ κα δικαιότατα δοκῇ τοῖς Πελοποννασίοις, corresponding more or less to ὅπᾳ κα δικαιότατα κρίναντας τοῖς ξυμμάχοις in 79, 3. These two documents (i. e., V, 77 and 79) broach ideas quite foreign to Sparta's normal hegemony; cf. Dittenberger, Syll.³, I, no. 181, lines 37-38.

[12] Herodotos, VII, 172-173; VIII, 56; IX, 106; and passim. In IX, 115-119 οἱ Ἕλληνες is used of Xanthippos' command, from which the " Peloponnesians " have withdrawn (IX, 114, 2). A year earlier, in VIII, 111-112, Herodotos seems to use both οἱ Ἕλληνες and Ἀθηναῖοι to designate the force which besieged Andros. These instances prepare us for the use of οἱ Ἕλληνες to designate what modern scholars call the Delian Confederacy (notably in the title hellenotamiai, but see also Thucydides, I, 139, 3; 140, 3; III, 62, 2, and especially III, 13, 1, with Larsen's observations in Harv. Stud. Cl. Phil., LI [1940], p. 202; cf. the probable fifth-century language in Plutarch, Pericles, 12, 1 [T96]: τὰ κοινὰ τῶν Ἑλλήνων χρήματα).

Greeks" and that of 431 (or 508) "the Peloponnesians." The Spartan alliance in fact was for most of the fifth century and the second half of the sixth an alliance whose centre of gravity was in Peloponnese, so that the modern name "Peloponnesian League" is not inapposite. But it is a modern name; the Greeks knew of one formal and constant style, "Lakedaimonioi and allies," and two informal and alternating designations, "Peloponnesioi" and "Hellenes."

A *de facto* distinction was clear, however, even in 480-479, between the "Peloponnesian" nucleus of this alliance and its "Hellenic" extension, and is responsible for the division of names on the Serpent Column. It may also be seen in such a phrase as Thucydides uses in I, 89, 2, where Leotychidas after Mykale "went home with the allies from Peloponnese," ἔχων τοὺς ἀπὸ Πελοποννήσου ξυμμάχους, or Herodotos of the same occasion (IX, 114, 2), τοῖσι μέν νυν ἀμφὶ Λευτυχίδην Πελοποννησίοισι, "the Peloponnesians with Leotychidas" decided to sail home. Constitutionally, the distinction was perhaps clear between the Peloponnesians whose alliance with Sparta was not for a particular war but in perpetuity,[13] and the other Greeks who had "sworn together against the Persian."[14] Historically, the distinction was in part a consequence of Sparta's realistic aversion to committing herself to alliances outside Peloponnese. This aversion led to the establishment of "subsidiary hegemonies." In the second half of the sixth century her impressive military strength made many parties seek her alliance, especially parties threatened by Persia, but Sparta seems not to have wanted to extend the area of those directly dependent on her: she preferred a system of buffer-states or "shock-absorbers." Thus Plataia asked for Spartan protection but was instructed to apply to Athens instead;[15] and Naxos, after Sparta had deposed the tyrant, exercised a hegemony of her own in the Aegean.[16]

In these cases Sparta seems to have erected friendly buffer-states, shock-absorbers, between the Persian advance and Peloponnese. Athens and Naxos had both been

[13] Thucydides, I, 71, 5-6; V, 30, 3. The Peloponnesian League was, in this, like the Delian Confederacy; see below, pp. 226-227, 232.

[14] Herodotos, VII, 148, 1, οἱ συνωμόται Ἑλλήνων ἐπὶ τῷ Πέρσῃ; cf. Thucydides, I, 102, 4; III, 63, 2. Herodotos' words in VII, 235, 4, πάντων Πελοποννησίων συνομοσάντων ἐπὶ σοί (*sc.* Xerxes), are constitutionally an understatement, apposite enough in their context. For the Spartan contention (Thucydides, II, 74, 2) that Plataia had broken her oath some time before the Spartan invasion of 427 see below, pp. 102-104.

[15] Herodotos, VI, 108. We do not go into the disputed chronology of this event. Nor do we argue the thesis, which we believe, that Sparta's main concern in Athens was that she should not medize; if her Hellenic loyalty could be assured, Athens was encouraged to form a small hegemony of her own.

[16] Plutarch, *Moralia*, 859d: Sparta deposes Lygdamis (again we do not go into the chronology). For the Naxian hegemony see Herodotos, V, 31, 2. That this hegemony was due to Sparta's action is perhaps indicated by the list of thalassocracies, which shows a Spartan thalassocracy in 516-515 and a Naxian in 515-505; Diodoros, VII, 11; cf. Myres, *J. H. S.*, XXVI (1906), p. 88; Helm, *Hermes*, LXI (1926), pp. 241-262. We follow Myres in supposing that the original author of the list put the fall of Eretria in 490 (not 485) and Xerxes' invasion in 480 (not 475).

" liberated " by Sparta and were perhaps bound to her by some sort of alliance, but they also had small hegemonies of their own whose members did not depend directly on Sparta. These arrangements were not very stable; by 480 Naxos was in the Persian sphere,[17] but Athens, after a good many vicissitudes, was at last firmly on the Greek side.

Thus the three categories of names on the Serpent Column no doubt indicate, first, the allies who depended on Sparta direct, and next, the two " subsidiary hegemonies " of Athens and Korinth. Korinth's small group is her northwestern colonies (which continue to be closely dependent on her in the Peloponnesian War),[18] and Poteidaia, which was first mobilized for Xerxes but, after Salamis, revolted from Persia, resisted a three-month siege late in 480, and provided 300 hoplites for the battle of Plataia (Herodotos, VII, 123, 1; VIII, 126-129; IX, 28, 3; these 300 hoplites were attached to the Korinthian contingent). Athens' group appears to be composed of (a) Plataia (and Thespiai?),[19] (b) the islands which never gave earth and water (Siphnos and Melos),[20] (c) Keos, Kythnos, and the three Euboic cities which had been won back to allegiance,[21] and (d) Naxos and Tenos, which were mobilized for Xerxes, but some of whose ships were taken by their trierarchs to the Greek side.[22]

[17] Naxos presumably gave earth and water in 491 (Herodotos, VI, 49, 1; cf. VIII, 46, 4); she was very roughly handled in 490 (Herodotos, VI, 96); in 480 her fleet was mobilized for Xerxes but four triremes deserted to the Greeks (Herodotos, VIII, 46, 3).

[18] Thucydides, I, 26, 1; 47, 3; 55, 1; II, 80, 3; III, 114, 4; IV, 42, 3; 49; VI, 104, 1; VII, 2, 1; 7, 1; 58, 3.

[19] Thespiai is often coupled with Plataia (Herodotos, VII, 132, 1; VIII, 50, 2; 66, 2) and may have looked to Athens in the same way as Plataia did. But the only Thespian action was at Thermopylai (Herodotos, VII, 202-227; VIII, 25, 1; Stephanos, s. v. Θέσπεια) and the Thespians were evacuated into Peloponnese (Herodotos, VIII, 50, 2; cf. IX, 30). Themistokles later had influence in Thespiai (Herodotos, VIII, 75, 1). Compare the case of Opous (note 22 below).

[20] Herodotos, VIII, 46, 4, adds Seriphos. Their contributions were very small, Melos two pentekonters, Siphnos and Seriphos one each (VIII, 48). This gained a firm place for Melos, a doubtful one (see the table on p. 96 above) for Siphnos, and none for Seriphos. Seriphos' grievance is possibly reflected in Plato's story, Rep., I, 329e-330a (contrast Herodotos, VIII, 125).

[21] I. e., Chalkis, Eretria, Styra. Neither Karystos nor Hestiaia was on the Greek side; the former was with Xerxes (VIII, 66, 2) and perhaps the latter too (VIII, 23). Eretria seems to have recovered from the disaster of 490; what exactly happened in 490 to the other Euboic cities (Chalkis, Styra) is not clear. Herodotos evidently thinks of the 20 Chalkidian ships " lent by Athens " as manned by the 4000 klerouchs (VIII, 1, 2; V, 77, 2; VI, 100, 1; 101, 1; for the computation cf., e. g., VII, 185, 1). Of the two islands, Keos provided two triremes and two pentekonters, Kythnos one of each (VIII, 1, 2 and 46, 4); this gained a firm place for Keos, a doubtful one (see the table on p. 96 above) for Kythnos. The " five island cities " referred to by Herodotos, VIII, 66, 2 (an inexact reference back to 46), are evidently Keos, Kythnos, Melos, Siphnos, Seriphos; he overlooks the Euboic cities.

[22] Tenos: Herodotos, VIII, 66, 2; 82, 1 (a single trireme ran the Persian blockade just before the battle. " This act won for Tenos her place in the list "). Naxos: VIII, 46, 3 (four triremes [probably not the whole contingent?] were destined by the government for Xerxes' fleet but the trierarch Demokritos brought them to the Greek fleet). Demokritos later distinguished himself at

These two subsidiary hegemonies bear witness to the reluctance which Sparta had felt about entangling herself directly in alliances outside Peloponnese; they also indicate lines of possible cleavage.[23] The two cases are by no means exactly parallel. Korinth was a Peloponnesian city, bound to Sparta by the same perpetually binding oaths as the Peloponnesian allies; she was no doubt one of Sparta's earliest allies.[24] Athens was outside Peloponnese and a much more recent ally. This meant that cleavage between Athens and Sparta was a good deal more likely than between Korinth and Sparta.[25]

We have called Athens " a much more recent ally." She had twice drawn close to Sparta, in 510-508 after the expulsion of Hippias, and in 493 when Miltiades came home and Themistokles was archon. But the first approach had led to the quarrel with Kleomenes in 508/7, and even after Marathon (in 490) Athens spent much time in an intensive war with Aigina who was certainly Sparta's ally.[26] Such collaboration as there was before and during the Marathon campaign is sufficiently explained by their common interest. The alliance in virtue of which Athens stands second on the Serpent Column is probably part of that great " sworn alliance against Persia " (Herodotos, VII, 148, 1) which put Sparta in command of the whole Greek force against Xerxes; this was made in the winter of 481/0. Those events form the first chapter of our narrative in Part III; we may anticipate to the extent of saying that the " Athenian group " on the Serpent Column is composed of those Greeks whom a strategy of defending Peloponnese would plainly abandon to Persia.

Salamis, destroying five enemy ships and rescuing one Greek ship; so Plutarch, *Moralia*, 869a-c, who quotes from a poem of Simonides. The exceptional nature of these two cases no doubt explains why Lemnos (VIII, 11, 3) was not included. The Peparethian feat of capturing two Karian ships (their dedication at Delphi is quoted in the note to *I. G.*, I², 523) was perhaps simply a minor instance of what Herodotos reports in VII, 190, and would not earn inclusion. The most surprising omission is the eastern Lokrians of Opous, whose record was good both at Thermopylai (VII, 203, 1 and 207; cf. Strabo, IX, 4, 2) and at sea (Herodotos, VIII, 1, 2), but not only are they not on the list of honour, they are not even excepted (as Thespiai and Plataia are) from the list of infamy in VII, 132. Is this perhaps because they belonged to no group, were not dependent on Korinth or Athens nor directly on Sparta, and so had no one to urge their claim? So too perhaps the Phokians, who are, however, absent from the list of infamy. The Ionic cities of Pallene which supported Poteidaia's revolt (Herodotos, VIII, 126, 3; 128, 2) are not included, no doubt because they sent no troops to Plataia.

[23] Korinth threatens to break off in 432 and 421 (Thucydides, I, 71; V, 30) and on the second occasion actually does; clearly her dependencies (cf. Thucydides, I, 68, 3, τοῖς ἡμετέροις ξυμμάχοις) are with her.

[24] A leading ally *ca.* 507 (Herodotos, V, 75); her collaboration in 525 probably means she is already an ally then (III, 49, 1). She is no doubt part of " the greater part of Peloponnese " which was already in Sparta's control *ca.* 545 (Herodotos, I, 68, 6).

[25] See especially Herodotos, VIII, 3, 2 (T66a).

[26] The narrative of these events is in Herodotos, V, 66-73, and VI, 103-120; for the war with Aigina see VI, 49-50, 61-93, and VII, 144-145. For Themistokles' archonship (Dion. Hal., *Ant. Rom.*, VI, 34, 1) see Wade-Gery, *B. S. A.*, XXXVII (1936-1937, published in 1940), p. 269.

The Covenant of Plataia is reported by Plutarch (*Aristides*, 21, 1-2 [T94b]) in the form of a decree proposed by Aristeides; we suspect that this covenant is not authentic. It contains the following four provisions:

1. Each year there shall assemble at Plataia probouloi and theoroi from Greece.
2. The games called Eleutheria shall be held every fourth year.
3. For the war against Persia the Greeks shall combine to contribute (εἶναι — — — σύνταξιν Ἑλληνικήν) 10,000 hoplites, 1000 cavalry, 100 ships.
4. The Plataians shall be left inviolable and sacred to Zeus (ἀσύλους καὶ ἱεροὺς ἀφίεσθαι τῷ θεῷ)[27] and shall offer sacrifice on behalf of Greece.

We take this clause by clause.

1. The yearly festival is firmly attested by Thucydides; it consisted of offerings to the fallen (III, 58, 4, κατὰ ἔτος ἕκαστον) and perhaps also of sacrifices to the gods and local heroes (58, 5, if this refers to the same occasion). Isokrates also mentions both the offerings to the fallen (XIV, 61) and the honours to the gods and heroes (XIV, 60). This would reasonably require the presence of theoroi from Greece. The probouloi suggest that Plataia was to act as military headquarters (cf. Herodotos, VI, 7; VII, 172, 1). If the decree is authentic, these probouloi will have lapsed when the Delian Confederacy was formed and Delos was made the place of the synods (Thucydides, I, 96, 2 [T109]); see further under clause 3.

2. Strabo (IX, 2, 31) says that the Eleutheria were an ἀγὼν γυμνικὸς στεφανίτης; the decree states that the games were to be quadrennial. This puts the Eleutheria on a level with the Olympia and Pythia and the absence of all trace of them in the fifth and fourth centuries is surprising. Neither Pindar nor Bakchylides mentions them,[28] and during the two Plataian catastrophes (427-386, 373-338; see note 39 below) we hear of no concern for their disappearance nor arrangement for their conduct. They were real enough in Hellenistic and Roman times. Besides Strabo and Pausanias,[29] and the passage of Plutarch now under consideration, an inscription of early Roman date (Dittenberger, *Syll.*³, III, no. 1064, line 10) records a victor, and the comic poet Poseidippos says that Plataia came alive only at the Eleutheria.[30]

[27] *Sc.* to Zeus Eleutherios. This dative may perhaps be construed with θύοντας rather than with ἱεροὺς ἀφίεσθαι, but this will not alter the sense materially.

[28] This can hardly be due to Pindar's Theban bias. Both poets write before the first Plataian catastrophe. The great event in the Eleutheria in Roman times was the hoplite race (Pausanias, IX, 2, 6); Telesikrates won that event at the Pythia of 474, and Pindar (*Pythia*, 9, 97-103) records his former victories but none at Plataia. Cf. also Dittenberger, *Syll.*³, I, no. 36.

[29] Strabo, IX, 2, 31; Pausanias, IX, 2, 6. The institution of the Eleutheria was associated with the "Hellenic Oath" (see below, pp. 104-105), and therefore dated before the battle of Plataia, in Diodoros, XI, 29, 1.

[30] Frag. 29 Kock:

ναοὶ δύ' εἰσὶ καὶ στοά, καὶ τοὔνομα,
καὶ τὸ βαλανεῖον, καὶ τὸ Σαράβου κλέος,
τὸ πολὺ μὲν ἀκτή, τοῖς δ' Ἐλευθερίοις πόλις.

Poseidippos writes after the second restoration. For Sarabos cf. Plato, *Gorgias*, 518b (whence

3. This provision of army and fleet envisages a continuation of the war, that is to say, a war of pursuit; and Pausanias and Aristeides, the two leading commanders present, did actually undertake a war of pursuit the next year. But the schematic figures given (10,000 hoplites, 1000 cavalry, 100 ships) do not suit such a campaign, and if the probouloi of clause 1 are part of the war plans, there is no sign that such a body met in 478.[31] The use of the word σύνταξις for contribution to a war effort seems to us perhaps suspicious.[32]

4. The Spartan contention in 427 is that Plataia had " deserted the covenant " at some time before this invasion.[33] The invasion therefore is justified in the first place; the siege and eventual punishment will be justified, because Plataia has refused many reasonable proposals. What covenant Plataia had deserted, when, and how, is made clear by certain words of the Theban speaker in 427 (Thucydides, III, 64. 2-3): " do not," he says to the Plataians, " appeal to the covenant of 479 (τὴν τότε γενομένην ξυνωμοσίαν) or claim that it should save you, for you have deserted it (ἀπελίπετε γὰρ αὐτήν) and in contravention of it you rather helped than hindered the subjection of Aigina and of others of the covenanters." And more generally, in III, 63, the Theban charges them with having joined in Athens' wars of subjection against the Greeks; the Plataians do not deny this but claim it was venial (III, 55, 3-4), and they plead that their alliance with Athens was dictated to them by Sparta (55, 1). They meet no other charges; their breach of covenant lay evidently in having joined in the reduction of such covenanters as Aigina in 457, Euboia in 446, and no doubt

Pollux, VII, 193 and Dion [of Prousa], IV, 98), and Achaios, in Athenaios, IV, 74 [173d] (who fixes his date); he was a famous restaurateur and perhaps kept the καταγώγιον established by the Spartans in 427 (Thucydides, III, 68, 3). The two temples will be (1) Athena's, built from the spoils of Marathon, no doubt after 479, with a statue by Pheidias and paintings by Polygnotos (Pausanias, IX, 4, 1-2), and (2) Hera's, built by the Spartans after 427 (Thucydides, III, 68, 3), for which Praxiteles made two statues (Pausanias, IX, 2, 7; presumably between 386 and 373). Both these were built long before Poseidippos and were there long after him. Zeus had an altar and image (Pausanias, IX, 2, 5 and 7) but Pausanias records no temple. The ἱερόν of Zeus mentioned by Strabo (IX, 2, 31) need not be a temple, nor that of Demeter in Pausanias, IX, 4, 3. The latter is distinct from the ναὸς ἀρχαῖος πάνυ (cf. Plutarch, Aristides, 11, 6), which was not at Plataia.

[31] Sparta appears to be military headquarters until they are shifted to Delos. Other questions which might have come before such probouloi are dealt with by the Amphiktyones (Plutarch, Themistocles, 20, 3; Cimon, 8, 4; cf. Herodotos, VII, 213, 2; 228, 4).

[32] It is used by Xenophon, in describing events of 382 B.C., of contributions to a similar total of 10,000 (Hellenica, V, 2, 37), and was soon after adopted by Kallistratos as a euphemism for φόρος in the Second Confederacy (T65a: Harpokration, s. v. σύνταξις, from Theopompos). It sounds to us like fourth-century language.

[33] Thucydides, II, 74, 2: οὔτε τὴν ἀρχὴν ἀδίκως, ἐκλιπόντων δὲ τῶνδε προτέρων τὸ ξυνώμοτον, ἐπὶ γῆν τήνδε ἤλθομεν --- οὔτε νῦν, ἤν τι ποιῶμεν, ἀδικήσομεν· προκαλεσάμενοι γὰρ πολλὰ καὶ εἰκότα οὐ τυγχάνομεν. We assume that ἤλθομεν refers to the invasion just perpetrated. Archidamos is answering the Plataian claim expressed in II, 71, 2-4.

Poteidaia in 430.[34] This agrees with the Spartan reasoning when the siege is over: they were entitled to ask the Plataians to name what service Sparta had received from them since 431, since before that (τόν τε ἄλλον χρόνον) Sparta had *expected* from Plataia the unaggressive behaviour implied in Pausanias' covenant.[35] Sparta claims in fact that by throwing in her lot actively with Athens, against Peloponnesians and revolted allies, Plataia has forfeited her privileges; and when Plataia actually rejected all the Spartan suggestions for preserving those privileges, Sparta felt herself released from the covenant (III, 68, 1: ἔκσπονδοι ἤδη).

Sparta in fact speaks as if the covenant had laid on Plataia certain obligations, not so much of neutrality, as of fostering (or at least not damaging) the other covenanters' freedom.[36] Plataia claims that her autonomy was guaranteed and that the covenanters were all bound to combine against any party which threatened it.[37] The parties had evidently pledged each other's freedom, and no doubt special guarantees were given to Plataia to defend her against Theban resentment. The clause in Plutarch seems to us to read quite differently from this, and to envisage the same sort of monkish sacrosanctity which was claimed for Elis in the fourth century.[38]

[34] Thucydides' phrase τὸ ξυνώμοτον refers probably not to the συνωμόται of 481 (Herodotos, VII, 148, 1), i. e., the ξυμμαχία ἐπὶ τῷ Μήδῳ (Thucydides, III, 63, 2), but to those ὅσοι μετασχόντες τῶν τότε κινδύνων — — — ξυνώμοσαν (II, 72, 1), i. e., the covenant of 479 (αἱ — — — μετὰ τὸν Μῆδον σπονδαί, Thucydides, III, 68, 1; cf. especially III, 64, 2, τὴν τότε γενομένην ξυνωμοσίαν, and III, 63, 3; 64, 3). This gives us agreement with III, 68, 1: ἠξίουν — — — αὐτοὺς κατὰ τὰς — — — σπονδὰς ἡσυχάζειν (see note 35 below); the Plataia covenant required some sort of " non-aggression." If we seek to make the Theban allusion in III, 63 concrete, it probably means that in 446, when ordered to follow Athens against Euboia, Plataia might have refused and appealed to Sparta and had her position secured in the Thirty Years' Peace; for Theban interest in Euboia see, *inter alia*, Thucydides, I, 113, 2; IV, 92, 4. Finally, we doubt if the alliance of 481 could have been claimed as perpetual, or binding on Plataia after Sparta had stopped fighting Persia; but the covenant of 479 clearly had perpetual elements in it.

[35] III, 68, 1: ἠξίουν δῆθεν αὐτοὺς κατὰ τὰς παλαιὰς Παυσανίου μετὰ τὸν Μῆδον σπονδὰς ἡσυχάζειν. Crawley here translates, " they had always invited them to be neutral [but see note 36 below], agreeably to the original covenant"; and Classen-Steup similarly, " zur Ruhe ermahnt hätten," observing further that the ironic δῆθεν expresses Thucydides' contempt for this contention. There is little doubt where Thucydides' sympathy was, but we think the δῆθεν is here dramatic: the Spartans " had *expected* indeed " that Plataia would stay still, and had been surprised to see the contrary.

[36] It can hardly be neutrality which was demanded, since Archidamos invites the Plataians to join him against Athens; his grounds are that the war is a war of liberation (πόλεμος — — — ἕνεκα — — — ἐλευθερώσεως), to liberate those covenanters who are now subjected by Athens (II, 72, 1: τοὺς ἄλλους ξυνελευθεροῦτε, ὅσοι μετασχόντες τῶν τότε κινδύνων ὑμῖν τε ξυνώμοσαν καὶ εἰσὶ νῦν ὑπ' Ἀθηναίοις; the allusion must be primarily to Euboia). Plataia will keep her oaths best by joining this war, next best by ἡσυχία. It is not easy to regard the Ithome war (III, 54, 5) as a " war of liberation," but no doubt Archidamos did so regard it; it was for Sparta's freedom. The actual obligation may perhaps be inferred from the words of the Theban speaker in III, 64, 3, μᾶλλον — — — ἢ διεκωλύετε (sc. δουλείαν).

[37] Thucydides, II, 71, 2: αὐτονόμους οἰκεῖν, στρατεῦσαί τε μηδένα ποτὲ ἀδίκως ἐπ' αὐτοὺς μηδ' ἐπὶ δουλείᾳ· εἰ δὲ μή, ἀμύνειν τοὺς παρόντας ξυμμάχους κατὰ δύναμιν. Douleia is here (as usually) the contrary of autonomy; see below, pp. 155-157.

[38] Ephoros, frag. 115 Jacoby (no. 70); cf. Wade-Gery, *Cl. Quart.*, XXXIX (1945), p. 23, note 2.

It is clause 4 which seems to us the hardest to believe authentic. Plataia was in fact twice destroyed, by Sparta in 427 and by Thebes in 373. The right and the wrong of the destruction of 427 is dealt with in detail by Thucydides, and the case against the destruction of 373 is argued at length in Isokrates, XIV (*Plataicus*).[39] In Thucydides the Spartans and Thebans use arguments which could hardly have been maintained in the face of the explicit formulation of clause 4; and the Plataians do not, either in Thucydides or Isokrates, appeal to it. In Thucydides they appeal to a clause which guaranteed their autonomy (see note 37 above), in Isokrates to the " oaths and agreements " of the King's Peace. Of the other clauses, clause 1 is unsuspicious except possibly for the probouloi, and against clause 2 we should be reluctant to press the *silentium* if it stood alone; but if clause 4 is (as we believe) a product of fourth-century propaganda, the other clauses are discredited.[40] The cavalry in clause 3 would be in place in a Persian war as contemplated in the fourth century. The proportion of 1 horseman to 10 infantrymen was standard until Makedonian times.

Our tentative conclusion, then, is that the decree of Aristeides is not authentic but a product of fourth-century controversy, composed later than Isokrates, XIV, but in pre-Makedonian times, that is, during the second catastrophe.

A quite different account of the Covenant of Plataia is implied in that " Hellenic Oath, which the Athenians say that the Greeks swore before the battle against the Persians at Plataia " (Theopompos, frag. 153 Jacoby). Theopompos, *loc. cit.*, asserts that this oath is not authentic. It is quoted by the orator Lykourgos (κατὰ Λεωκράτους, 80-81) and by Diodoros (XI, 29, 1-3) in virtually identical words. The fourth-century style (especially in the avoidance of hiatus) makes it likely that both writers are using the form given in Ephoros' *History*. Another version, which allows hiatus freely, has been recently discovered in a fourth-century Attic inscription from Acharnai.[41]

This oath or pledge is not the Thucydidean covenant. This is seen most clearly in the fact that Thucydides reports the covenant as made after the battle,[42] whereas

---

[39] The date of the second destruction is given by Pausanias, IX, 1, 8; the hypothesis to Isokrates, XIV, puts it after Leuktra, but the speech, which presupposes the destruction, was certainly written before Leuktra. The dates of the two restorations are also given by Pausanias (IX, 1, 4 and 8), as consequent on the King's Peace of 386 and the battle of Chaironeia of 338 respectively.

[40] Whether or not the quadrennial Eleutheria had yet existed, we imagine they were in suspense when this decree was formulated, and founded or refounded with special prestige when Philip restored Plataia.

[41] Robert, *Études épigraphiques et philologiques*, pp. 307-316; Klaffenbach, *Gnomon*, XV (1939), p. 505; Prakken, *A. J. P.*, LXI (1940), pp. 62-65; Daux, *Rev. Arch.*, 1941, I, pp. 176-183. Parke's paper, *Hermathena*, LXXII (1948), pp. 82-114, deals with the notions contained in this alleged oath.

[42] This is the sense of μετὰ τὸν Μῆδον in III, 68, 1; cf. also II, 72, 1: μετασχόντες τῶν τότε κινδύνων --- ξυνώμοσαν. And *a priori* there can be little doubt that the authentic covenant must have been made after the battle and not just before it.

all who speak of this " Hellenic Oath " put it either before the Greeks marched to
Plataia or just before they lined up for battle.[43] Its spuriousness is so generally allowed
that we need not argue it, nor discuss the various currents of propaganda which have
caused the variations in its form.[44] The original from which it has been developed is
the oath recorded by Herodotos in VII, 132. The loyal Greeks here swear to " tithe "
(δεκατεῦσαι τῷ ἐν Δελφοῖσι) those Greeks who wantonly submitted to the invader.
Herodotos' date is the date when these submissions were made, early in 480; the date
of the oath cannot have been the same, and Herodotos gives no clear indication of
when it was. Since the list of those who submitted is in fact a list of Amphiktyonic
peoples, the oath was no doubt sworn at an Amphiktyonic meeting. As Parke points
out, the words used by Herodotos imply that victory has not yet been secured,[45] while,
on the other hand, the list of names is clearly later than Thermopylai, so that the
meeting was no doubt the spring Pylaia of 479.

We note, finally, the remarkable likeness between the names in this list of traitors
and those in D12, Perikles' Congress Decree (see below, pp. 279-280 with note 21).
Boiotia, the Lokroi, the Oitaioi and the Malian Gulf, the Achaioi Phthiotai, and the
Thessalians correspond to five of Herodotos' nine names. Three Amphiktyonic names
are missing from Herodotos' list, since they are not traitors (Phokians, Ionians,
Dorians), and these three are all in Perikles' decree. There are four Amphiktyonic
names absent from D12, Dolopes, Enienes, Perrhaiboi, Magnetes, that is, the Thessalian fringe. Whether their omission is due to Plutarch or to Perikles himself, we can
in either case hardly doubt that the list of Greeks in Perikles' decree is drawn up in
Amphiktyonic terms. It was to be a quasi-Amphiktyonic meeting held in Athens.
From the day when Themistokles resisted the purging of medizers from the Amphiktyony,[46] Athens seems to have wished to preserve that organization of the Greek people
as something to counterbalance the pretensions which Sparta might base upon her
leadership in the war.

[43] Diodoros, XI, 29, 1-2: συναχθέντων δὲ τῶν Ἑλλήνων εἰς τὸν Ἰσθμόν, ἐδόκει τοῖς πᾶσιν ὅρκον ὀμόσαι.
Lykourgos, κατὰ Λεωκράτους, 80: ταύτην πίστιν ἔδοσαν αὐτοῖς ἐν Πλαταιαῖς πάντες οἱ Ἕλληνες, ὅτ' ἔμελλον
παραταξάμενοι μάχεσθαι πρὸς τὴν Ξέρξου δύναμιν. Theopompos, frag. 153 Jacoby: Ἑλληνικὸς ὅρκος κατα-
ψεύδεται, ὃν Ἀθηναῖοί φασιν ὀμόσαι τοὺς Ἕλληνας πρὸ τῆς μάχης τῆς ἐν Πλαταιαῖς πρὸς τοὺς βαρβάρους. The
inscriptional copy is headed ὅρκος ὃν ὤμοσαν Ἀθηναῖοι ὅτε ἤμελλον μάχεσθαι πρὸς τοὺς βαρβάρους. Daux
(op. cit., p. 182) has observed that this last does not imply that only Athenians swore, but, rather,
that this Acharnaian copy is concerned only with Athens' obligation.

[44] See Parke, Hermathena, LXXII (1948), pp. 92-114, especially 106-112.

[45] Καταστάντων σφι εὖ τῶν πρηγμάτων, " if they should be victorious " they would dedicate the
traitors to Apollo.

[46] Plutarch, Themistocles, 20, 3-4, probably in 478 when the question of implementing the
Herodotean oath came up; an example of Perikles' affinity to Themistokles.

CHAPTER II

THE LOSSES AT DRABESKOS

The two passages of Thucydides which describe the disaster of Drabeskos are as follows:

I, 100, 2-3: καὶ ναυσὶ μὲν ἐπὶ Θάσον πλεύσαντες οἱ Ἀθηναῖοι ναυμαχίᾳ ἐκράτησαν καὶ ἐς τὴν γῆν ἀπέβησαν, ἐπὶ δὲ Στρυμόνα πέμψαντες μυρίους οἰκήτορας αὐτῶν καὶ τῶν ξυμμάχων ὑπὸ τοὺς αὐτοὺς χρόνους ὡς οἰκιοῦντες τὰς τότε καλουμένας Ἐννέα ὁδούς, νῦν δὲ Ἀμφίπολιν, τῶν μὲν Ἐννέα ὁδῶν αὐτοὶ ἐκράτησαν, ἃς εἶχον Ἠδωνοί, προελθόντες δὲ τῆς Θρᾴκης ἐς μεσόγειαν διεφθάρησαν ἐν Δραβησκῷ τῇ Ἠδωνικῇ ὑπὸ τῶν Θρᾳκῶν ξυμπάντων, οἷς πολέμιον ἦν τὸ χωρίον [αἱ Ἐννέα ὁδοί] κτιζόμενον.

IV, 102, 2: τὸ δὲ χωρίον τοῦτο ἐφ' οὗ νῦν ἡ πόλις ἐστὶν ἐπείρασε μὲν πρότερον καὶ Ἀρισταγόρας ὁ Μιλήσιος φεύγων βασιλέα Δαρεῖον κατοικίσαι, ἀλλὰ ὑπὸ Ἠδώνων ἐξεκρούσθη, ἔπειτα δὲ καὶ οἱ Ἀθηναῖοι ἔτεσι δύο καὶ τριάκοντα ὕστερον, ἐποίκους μυρίους σφῶν τε αὐτῶν καὶ τῶν ἄλλων τὸν βουλόμενον πέμψαντες, οἳ διεφθάρησαν ἐν Δραβησκῷ ὑπὸ Θρᾳκῶν.[1]

Are these two passages materially inconsistent? We should not believe this except as a last resort. If they are, we should probably assume that one or the other is not as Thucydides wrote it. One minor problem is how to take the words (in IV, 102, 2) ἐποίκους μυρίους σφῶν τε αὐτῶν καὶ τῶν ἄλλων τὸν βουλόμενον. Crawley translates: " ten thousand settlers of their own citizens, and whoever else chose to go," but surely this is wrong; it would require a different order of the words (e. g., σφῶν τε αὐτῶν μυρίους καὶ ———), and in any case we should be reluctant to suppose that Thucydides here means to give figures materially inconsistent with what he gives in I, 100, 3, " 10,000 made up of themselves and their allies." We may question whether the words in IV, 102, 2 mean " 10,000, Athenians and volunteers from elsewhere," or " 10,000, volunteers from Athens and elsewhere "; that is to say, whether the partitive σφῶν τε αὐτῶν depends directly on ἐποίκους, or (like τῶν ἄλλων) on τὸν βουλόμενον, which is in apposition to ἐποίκους. The latter is more symmetrical, but we think the former is more likely; the asymmetry is of a kind which Thucydides does not much try to avoid. In either case, only a part of the 10,000 is Athenian. We are not told how large a part; in Amphipolis later the Athenians were probably a small minority (βραχὺ μὲν Ἀθηναίων ἐμπολίτευον, τὸ δὲ πλέον ξύμμεικτον, IV, 106, 1).[2]

---

[1] We change Powell's Δραβήσκῳ to Δραβησκῷ (cf. I, 100, 3).

[2] The Athenian component in the 10,000 must not be identified with the supporting military force.

The main question is, who were destroyed? Isokrates, VIII, 86, understood that all the 10,000 were and that they were all hoplites: ἐν Δάτῳ δὲ μυρίους ὁπλίτας αὐτῶν καὶ τῶν συμμάχων ἀπώλεσαν. Modern writers have compromised. Walker, in *C. A. H.*, V, p. 58, writes: " The settlers, only a part of whom were Athenians, were ten thousand in number; ――― the whole body of settlers advanced into the interior of the country, and found themselves compelled to give battle ―――. The Athenian force was annihilated, and in consequence of this defeat the colony had to be abandoned." Why, if the whole body gave battle, only the Athenians were annihilated, is not clear. Gomme, *Commentary*, I, p. 297, writes: " it would be absurd to suppose that the whole body of settlers marched farther into Thrace; the majority would stay at Ennea Hodoi and begin the settlement: only some of the armed forces went farther, presumably to forestall an attack. The whole colony was destroyed as a result of the defeat, that is, the settlers were withdrawn; but that is another matter." If only some of the armed forces went farther, what reason is there to say that " the whole colony was destroyed "? And is not this a strange term to use to describe the withdrawal of the settlers?

It is indeed hard to believe that Isokrates was right; but presumably that was how he understood Thucydides, who consequently can hardly be acquitted of ambiguous writing. Does he say that the 10,000 οἰκήτορες were destroyed? Whoever were destroyed, were destroyed ἐν Δραβησκῷ, so that if the 10,000 did not advance to Drabeskos, Thucydides does not say that the 10,000 were destroyed. If he says that the 10,000 were destroyed, then he says that the 10,000 advanced to Drabeskos.

The word αὐτοί in I, 100, 3, unless we emend it, shows that in this passage at least Thucydides *does* distinguish the force destroyed from the 10,000 settlers. In view of the words αὐτῶν καὶ τῶν ξυμμάχων immediately above, we agree with Gomme (*Commentary*, I, p. 296) that " the natural meaning of αὐτοί would be here the Athenians as opposed to their allies." The second passage (IV, 102, 2) is therefore crucial; must we understand the antecedent of οἵ (in οἳ διεφθάρησαν) as ἐποίκους μυρίους? If we must, then Thucydides says that the 10,000 settlers were destroyed in Drabeskos, and for this to happen they must have advanced to Drabeskos. No compromise, such as that the settlers were destroyed at Ennea Hodoi later, or that they were withdrawn later and that this is here described as " being destroyed," is true to the text; either of these things may have happened, but Thucydides does not here say so.[3] Isokrates evidently understood the antecedent of οἵ as ἐποίκους and drew the proper inference: the 10,000 were all soldiers, they all advanced to Drabeskos, and all were killed.

We believe that the solution lies in finding a different antecedent, in fact οἱ Ἀθηναῖοι. This will give to διεφθάρησαν in effect exactly the same subject as it has in I, 100, 3; there αὐτοί, and here οἵ, both signify οἱ Ἀθηναῖοι. In both places the

---

[3] Not unless we delete ἐν Δραβησκῷ, and we do not think that this will be seriously suggested.

phrase οἱ Ἀθηναῖοι changes its meaning by an implied partition. When the statement is made that the Athenians sailed to Thasos and won a naval battle, the implied partition is a figure of speech common enough to cause no difficulty. Not all the Athenians sailed and fought the battle: only those (relatively few) who sailed were engaged in the battle, and landed on Thasos. The Athenians also sent [4] colonists to Ennea Hodoi, some from their own number and some from their allies, but it was the partitive group (the relatively few who took part in the expedition) that occupied the place,[5] and, further on again, it was the partitive group (those who proceeded inland) who were destroyed. The passages may be freely paraphrased as follows:

I, 100, 2-3: " The Athenians sailed to Thasos, were victorious at sea and landed on the island; and at about the same time they sent 10,000 settlers (Athenians and allies) with the intention of colonizing Ennea Hodoi (as Amphipolis was then called). They captured Ennea Hodoi from the Edonians, but advancing into the interior were annihilated at Drabeskos, – – –."

IV, 102, 2: " This spot, where the city now stands, Aristagoras the Milesian had earlier tried to colonize, in his flight from King Dareios, but he was repulsed by the Edonians; then 32 years later the attempt was made by the Athenians, who sent 10,000 settlers (of their own people and any other who chose), and who were annihilated at Drabeskos by the Thrakians."

These sentences are not elegant and not unambiguous; quite clearly the writers of the fourth century understood them differently from this. We believe that an acceptable sense can be found in them if one looks for it hard, but there may be corruption. What we do not believe is that Isokrates' version is historically correct, or that Thucydides intended that meaning; nor do we think that the modern compromises are tenable.

It is commonly believed that the casualty list *I. G.*, I², 928 is to be associated with the defeat at Drabeskos.[6] The surviving fragments of the document, which is very incomplete, mention Athenian and allied casualties in the Chersonese (Kardia), near Sigeion, and in Thasos. We can be reasonably sure of [Μαδ]ύτιοι (line 34) and [Βυζά]ντιο[ι] (line 98). The squeeze of fragment *a* shows that [Μαδ]ύτιοι was cut as a heading, with larger letters than were the names of the fallen, and extended across the width of two columns, the first of which is now lost. We are convinced that [Βυζά]ντιο[ι] was similarly spaced across two columns in line 98 (frag. *c*), and our belief is strengthened by the wide spacing and large letters of the name as printed in *I. G.*, I, 432 (frag. *c*, line 20). The surviving letters of line 37, [– – –]ΝΙ, are

---

[4] Diodoros, XII, 68, 2, writes ἐξέπεμψαν, and so probably indicates that Ephoros understood the subject of πέμψαντες to be the Athenian State.

[5] This is not a necessary construction; one might hold that " the Athenians," *i. e.*, the Athenian State, won possession.

[6] See, *e. g.*, the notes in *I. G.*, I², pp. 242-243.

unusually large, like those of [Μαδ]ύτιοι in line 34, and the spacing, as computed on the squeeze, proves that the restoration [ἐμ Παιό]νι, given in *I. G.*, I², 928, must be discarded. What we have here is in fact not a place name, but an ethnic which extended across the width of two columns: [..⁵...]νι.

We note that the allies named in the inscription, Μαδύτιοι and Βυζάντιοι, are Hellespontine and that they died in the Hellespontine area (Kardia, Sigeion), none, so far as we can tell, in Thasos or Thrace. We therefore conclude that the Hellespontine allies were fighting with the Athenians in defense of their own territory against the Persians, rather than that their presence in the casualty list reflects the joint effort to found the colony at Ennea Hodoi, as Gomme suggests.[7] This means that for [..⁵...]νι we must seek a Hellespontine ethnic, and we accordingly suggest [Κεβρέ]νι(οι). Thus there were four Madytian casualties (two in each column) and two Kebrenian (one in each column).

The campaigns of *I. G.*, I², 928 all fall in a single season, 465 B. C.[8] Drabeskos is not named on the monument and we cannot be sure that it ever stood there; the battle may have been fought too late for the casualties to have been included in the list of 465. On the other hand, we cannot deny that the casualty list may originally have carried the sorry memorial of Drabeskos. We have stated our belief that the troops who fought at Drabeskos were the Athenian escort and not the colonists; we should not then expect the names of the Athenian colonists on the casualty list (non-Athenians would not as a rule merit such space) and the escort itself was probably not large. But there is plenty of room, on the basis of the surviving fragments, for those who died at Drabeskos and since for many of the extant names of the inscription no heading is preserved to indicate who they were or where they fell, we may have in them Athenian citizens who were slain by the Edonians at Drabeskos.

There is indeed some evidence for this view. That the casualties of Drabeskos were inscribed on a stele we know from Pausanias (I, 29, 4-5), who may have seen it.[9] His account begins as follows: πρῶτοι δὲ ἐτάφησαν οὓς --- Ἠδωνοὶ φονεύουσιν ---. It is natural to take πρῶτοι in a temporal sense (as Jacoby seems to, although cautiously), in which case Pausanias is telling us that this stele, bearing the names of those who died at Drabeskos, was the first public monument set up by the Athenians to honour their military casualties. " *The year 465/4 marked an epoch in the history of the Kerameikos; Pausanias has preserved from his learned source a historical date*

---

[7] *Commentary*, I, p. 297. The Hellespontine campaign (especially in the Chersonese) is no doubt part of the operations against Doriskos; see below, pp. 205-206 with note 55.

[8] For the chronology see below, pp. 170, 175-176 with notes 57, 58; cf. also Kolbe, *Hermes*, LXXII (1937), pp. 248-254, especially 250 and 254.

[9] Jacoby argues with cogency that Pausanias' description of the Kerameikos was not based on autopsy, but that he drew from a " learned source " (Diodoros, περὶ μνημάτων), whose information was full and accurate; *J. H. S.*, LXIV (1944), pp. 53-55 and note 12 on pp. 40-41.

of the first order." [10] We have elsewhere established that the revolt of Thasos belongs in 465 and we take *I. G.*, I², 928 as the record of the fighting of that year; [11] to the same year must be assigned the Hellespontine casualties of the inscription. The problem thus becomes more simple: Drabeskos followed the Thasian revolt (Thucydides), casualties on Thasos were commemorated on stone (*I. G.*, I², 928), the Drabeskos names were cut on the first such public monument (Pausanias), therefore the Drabeskos names stood (or stand) in the document catalogued as *I. G.*, I², 928.

This, in fact, is the interpretation which we adopt. It depends ultimately upon the credibility of Pausanias and our understanding of what he says; but if we read him correctly, the conclusion is inescapable. With this assumption, then, the battle at Drabeskos was fought early in the winter of 465/4, in time to be commemorated by the first λόγος ἐπιτάφιος, spoken for the Athenians who lost their lives in the busy season of 465 B. C.

[10] Jacoby, *J. H. S.*, LXIV (1944), p. 55.
[11] Thucydides, I, 101, 1: Θάσιοι δὲ νικηθέντες μάχῃ ---. But μάχαις is the reading of a good family of mss. and is considered preferable by Gomme, *Commentary*, I, p. 298. Jacoby's caution in his conclusions is dictated by his uncertainty regarding the chronology; he places the first λόγος ἐπιτάφιος (pronounced on the dead of Drabeskos) in 464 and states a little later (p. 55): " I at least would not dare to decide from § 4-5 [Pausanias, I, 29] the question whether the first casualty list preserved on stone contained, besides the dead of the Chersonnese and Thasos, those of Drabeskos too; or (to put it differently) whether in the ' first tomb ' of the *Mnema* only the dead of Drabeskos were buried, or also men from other theatres of war of the same year." We feel more confident of the chronology, and we regard the order of events (*i. e.*, Drabeskos followed the revolt of Thasos) as certain; see below, pp. 158-180, especially 175-176 with notes 57, 58.

CHAPTER III

KLEOPHANTOS IN LAMPSAKOS

Highby has rendered a valuable service by calling attention to the evidence of a real connection between Themistokles and Lampsakos. The most important piece of evidence is an inscription from Lampsakos of the late third century B. C. published by Lolling in *Ath. Mitt.*, VI (1881), pp. 103-105.[1] A person whose name is lost is given the usual honours of proxenos, and a second decree is added, containing two clauses. The second clause orders that the honours be inscribed on stone; the first is as follows:

$$[\kappa\acute{\nu}\rho\iota\alpha\ \hat{\epsilon}\iota]$$
$$\nu\alpha\iota\ \tau\grave{\alpha}\ \acute{\epsilon}\psi\eta\phi\iota\sigma\mu\acute{\epsilon}[\nu\alpha,\ \acute{\epsilon}\nu\ \delta\grave{\epsilon}\ \tau\hat{\eta}\iota\ \acute{\epsilon}o\rho\tau\hat{\eta}\iota]$$
$$\tau\hat{\eta}\iota\ \Theta\epsilon\mu\iota\sigma\tau o\kappa\lambda\epsilon\hat{\iota}\ [\grave{\alpha}\gamma o\mu\acute{\epsilon}\nu\eta\iota\ \delta\iota'\ \acute{\epsilon}\nu\iota\alpha\nu]$$
$$\tauο\hat{\upsilon}\ \epsilon\hat{\iota}\nu\alpha\iota\ \pi\acute{\alpha}\nu\tau\alpha\ \alpha[\acute{\upsilon}\tau\hat{\omega}\iota\ \tau\grave{\alpha}\gamma\alpha\theta\grave{\alpha}\ \grave{\alpha}\ \acute{\epsilon}\delta\acute{o}\theta\eta]$$
$$15\quad \sigma\alpha\nu\ K\lambda\epsilon o\phi\acute{\alpha}\nu\tau\omega\iota\ \kappa[\alpha\grave{\iota}\ \tauο\hat{\iota}\varsigma\ \grave{\alpha}\pi o\gamma\acute{o}\nu o\iota\varsigma].$$

" Let the previous vote be confirmed, and let him receive at the annual festival of Themistokles all the privileges which were accorded to Kleophantos and his descendants." This annual festival in honour of Themistokles, with special honours for Kleophantos and his descendants, was most probably instituted after Themistokles' death but in the lifetime of his son Kleophantos. So much indeed is virtually certain;[2] and it is evident that Themistokles and his family were regarded as benefactors. It is likely that Kleophantos was present at the first celebration at least, but Lolling's inference that Kleophantos and his family resided in Lampsakos is not self-evident and from Plato's reference (*Meno*, 93d) it can hardly be doubted that he resided in Athens.[3]

Highby's other witness is the author of the 20th of the *Letters* ascribed to Themistokles.[4] In this long narrative letter Themistokles records his escape from Argos and his further adventures till he reached Sousa, and was loaded with gifts by the king; he continues (p. 761):

καὶ μου ἤδη ᾿Αρτάβαζον ἧσσον ἐνόμιζε πιστὸν καὶ ἐπὶ θάλατταν με κατέπεμπεν ἐπὶ τὴν ἐκείνου στρατηγίαν, καὶ οὐκ ἐσθῆτας ἔτι ἡμῖν οὐδὲ χρυσόν, ἀλλὰ πόλεις τε ἤδη καὶ πολλὴν γῆν ἐχαρίζετο· ἀφελὼν γὰρ τῆς ἑαυτοῦ βασιλείας Μυοῦντα καὶ Λάμψακόν τε καὶ

---

[1] Highby, *Klio*, Beiheft XXXVI, p. 47. The stone is in Athens, E.M. 11544.

[2] Bauer, *Themistokles*, pp. 168-169, questions whether the festival goes back to Themistokles. To Themistokles surely not; but to Kleophantos it must. At no other date can the honours have been reserved for " Kleophantos and his descendants."

[3] Cf. Wilamowitz, *Aristoteles und Athen*, I, p. 147, note 44.

[4] Highby, p. 48; Hercher, *Epistolographi Graeci*, pp. 758-762.

111

τὴν ἐπὶ Μαιάνδρῳ Μαγνησίαν ἐμοὶ δίδωσι. καὶ Λάμψακον μὲν ἠλευθέρωσα καὶ πολλῷ φόρῳ βαρυνομένην ἅπαντος ἀφῆκα, Μυοῦντα δὲ τὴν ἐν Μαγνησίᾳ καὶ αὐτὴν Μαγνησίαν καρποῦμαι.

"The king now thought me more loyal than Artabazos and sent me to the coast to Artabazos' province and instead of clothes and money his gifts to me became cities and lands; detaching from his own kingdom Myous and Lampsakos and Magnesia he has given them to me. I have left Lampsakos free and remitted its heavy tribute, but the revenues of Myous and Magnesia I enjoy."

The author of this letter has gathered his data carefully, but he makes mistakes: Artabazos is taken from Thucydides (I, 129, 1 and 3; 132, 5) but is imagined as satrap of Sardis as well as of Daskyleion.[5] Has he some similar evidence for the remission of Lampsakos' tribute? Themistokles' adventures were probably first narrated by Charon of Lampsakos, and next by Thucydides,[6] and these two agree, against the later writers, that the king whom Themistokles encountered was Artaxerxes, Xerxes being dead. In this particular our author follows Charon and Thucydides,[7] and it is at least likely that he used Charon to supplement Thucydides. Charon was a Lampsakene and probably saw the founding of the Themistokles festival.

Themistokles was treated as a traitor for some years. Kimon's prosecution of Epikrates, who had sent Themistokles' family to join him in exile, was at some interval after the event (ὕστερον, Plutarch says, *Themistocles*, 24, 6, quoting Stesimbrotos) and perhaps in 450;[8] Epikrates was condemned to death. Until the Peace of Kallias, indeed, Themistokles' treason could hardly be overlooked. But the change of opinion is certain,[9] and his family was certainly recalled.[10] It is probable that the Lampsakos festival was instituted after this change of opinion and after the recall of Kleophantos to Athens.

[5] When Themistokles lands at Ephesos he finds Artabazos' men on guard there, though Artabazos himself is in Phrygia (p. 760). That there was any Persian garrison in Ephesos is no doubt false, but it should not in any case belong to the satrap of Daskyleion.

[6] See Jacoby's commentary on Charon, frag. 11 (no. 262), in *Frag. Gr. Hist.*, IIIa, p. 19: "der Lampsakener Ch(aron) sie als erster schriftlich fixierte."

[7] When landing at Ephesos Themistokles expects to find Xerxes alive (p. 760: Ξέρξῃ μὲν ἤδη ἀδεῶς εἶχον ὅστις εἴην λέγειν) but the king whom he actually encounters is Artaxerxes (not named, but cf. p. 761: αἴτιον ἐμοὶ γενέσθαι καὶ πατρὶ ἐμῷ μὴ ἄρχειν Ἑλλήνων). We cannot share Jacoby's apparent suspicion that the later writers had some better evidence. What they thought incredible was that Themistokles landed at Ephesos in 470 and did not reach Sousa till 465; they therefore made him either land in Asia later (at the time of the revolt of Thasos, Plutarch, *Themistocles*, 25, 2, where, however, νάξον is a variant reading), or reach Sousa earlier (*Themistocles*, 27, 1). We believe the long interval to be a fact which the letter-writer has not obliterated.

[8] See Wade-Gery, *Hesperia*, XIV (1945), p. 222, note 22.

[9] His treatment by Thucydides and the comedians is well known; the most striking passage is Thucydides, I, 74, 1, where the Athenians at Sparta in 432 cite him as one of Athens' main titles to glory.

[10] See Wilamowitz, *Aristoteles und Athen*, I, p. 147, note 44.

Had Themistokles any claims on revenue from Lampsakos? Had he exercised or waived such claims? Was the waiving of the claims the reason for the festival? Did Charon so report? Is Charon the source of our letter-writer? These questions will be hard to answer with certainty. They raise further questions about what happened to property and title when a city passed from one regime to another.[11] That Lampsakos was politically in the king's possession when he assigned certain Lampsakene revenues to Themistokles seems to us highly improbable; but there were surely some Persian titles to property in Greek cities which had to be adjusted when peace was made. We suggest that Kleophantos, when restored to Athens, retained property in Magnesia and possibly in Myous, but waived his doubtful title in Lampsakos.[12]

[11] For example, are the regulations for Selymbria in *I. G.*, I², 116 (Tod, *Greek Hist. Inscr.*, I², no. 88) exceptional?

[12] Or perhaps rather Kleophantos confirmed his father's alleged action.

CHAPTER IV

PERIKLES' PONTIC EXPEDITION

The expedition of Perikles into the Euxine is related by Plutarch, *Pericles*, 20, 1-2 (T97b), in a context which is perhaps timeless (though if any time be implied, it is earlier than the date now commonly assigned). Plutarch's words are:

εἰς δὲ τὸν Πόντον εἰσπλεύσας στόλῳ μεγάλῳ καὶ κεκοσμημένῳ λαμπρῶς, ταῖς μὲν Ἑλληνίσι πόλεσιν ὧν ἐδέοντο διεπράξατο καὶ προσηνέχθη φιλανθρώπως, τοῖς δὲ περιοικοῦσι βαρβάροις ἔθνεσι καὶ βασιλεῦσιν αὐτῶν καὶ δυνάσταις ἐπεδείξατο μὲν τῆς δυνάμεως τὸ μέγεθος καὶ τὴν ἄδειαν καὶ τὸ θάρσος, ᾗ βούλοιντο πλεόντων καὶ πᾶσαν ὑφ' αὑτοῖς πεποιημένων τὴν θάλασσαν, Σινωπεῦσι δὲ τρισκαίδεκα ναῦς ἀπέλιπε μετὰ Λαμάχου καὶ στρατιώτας ἐπὶ Τιμησίλεων τύραννον. ἐκπεσόντος δὲ τούτου καὶ τῶν ἑταίρων, ἐψηφίσατο πλεῖν εἰς Σινώπην Ἀθηναίων ἐθελοντὰς ἑξακοσίους καὶ συγκατοικεῖν Σινωπεῦσι, νειμαμένους οἰκίας καὶ χώραν ἣν πρότερον οἱ τύραννοι κατεῖχον.

Apart from the context (to which we shall return), the best and perhaps only indication of date is the mention of Lamachos. If, as can scarcely be doubted, this is the famous Lamachos, he died in Sicily in 414 B. C. Beloch advanced various reasons for thinking that he was not born before 470 B. C. and cannot therefore have held this command under Perikles before 440.[1] The Pontic expedition, consequently, is later than the Samian War. This is accepted by Busolt, Meyer, Rostovtzeff, Kirchner and Adcock.[2] Among the kings and dynasts whom Perikles wished to impress it is supposed that the most important was Spartokos, who founded the Spartokid dynasty in Pantikapaion in 438 or a little later, as " Archon " of the Greek city and " King " of the tribes around.

Lamachos is thus the kingpin of this chronology. This officer makes three main

---

[1] Beloch, *Attische Politik*, p. 325; *Gr. Gesch.*, II, 2², p. 216. The most important reason is that Lamachos is compared to νεανίαι by Dikaiopolis in Aristophanes, *Acharnians*, 601 (" youngsters like you "); he was therefore " offenbar noch nicht 50 Jahre alt " in 425. This may be so; the passage has a different sort of outrageousness from Demosthenes, XVIII, 136, where the 57-year old Aischines is called νεανίας (sarcastically; cf. 313); but it is outrageous, and rational inference is not quite simple. For Lamachos' age in Sicily and for the phrase ἡλικίᾳ προήκων in Plutarch, *Alcibiades*, 18, 2, see below, p. 115 with note 3.

[2] Busolt, *Gr. Gesch.*, III, 1, p. 585, note 2; Meyer, *Gesch. d. Alterthums*, IV, pp. 77-78; Rostovtzeff, *Iranians and Greeks*, p. 67 (" in the year 435 "); Kirchner, *P. A.*, no. 8981; Adcock, *C. A. H.*, V, p. 174 (" c. 437 B. C."). Duncker (*Sitzungsber. Ak. Berlin*, 1885, pp. 533-550, especially pp. 541-542) urged 444 B. C. (spring and summer) and is followed by Minns (*Scythians and Greeks*, pp. 447 and 561). Robinson, giving a false reference to Duncker and misquoting him (see above), places the expedition " probably soon after 444 " and " circ. 440 "; *Ancient Sinope*, p. 151 with note 3 (reprinted from *A. J. P.*, XXVII [1906], p. 151 with note 3).

appearances in history. The first is when he commands this detachment of Perikles' Euxine force. The second is in Aristophanes' *Acharnians*, which was played early in 425; Thucydides (IV, 75, 1-2 [T133]) mentions him as one of the strategoi of the following year, 425/4, when he took a tribute-gathering squadron into the Euxine (early summer of 424). His third important appearance is in 415, when he is appointed one of the three commanders for Sicily; he fell in battle there the following summer. Beloch's contention is based chiefly on the passage of Aristophanes discussed in note 1 above; he also suggests that he was probably not more than 55 years old on this last occasion.

Plutarch, *Alcibiades*, 18, 1-2, says that Nikias was chosen for the command in Sicily against his will because the Athenians thought it wiser to balance his prudence against Alkibiades' rashness; καὶ γὰρ ὁ τρίτος στρατηγὸς ὁ Λάμαχος ἡλικίᾳ προήκων ὅμως ἐδόκει μηδὲν ἧττον εἶναι τοῦ Ἀλκιβιάδου διάπυρος καὶ φιλοκίνδυνος ἐν τοῖς ἀγῶσι. "For Lamachos, the third commander, though eminent in years, yet seemed as fiery and as fond of danger in battle as Alkibiades himself." We must probably not attach too precise a meaning to Plutarch's phrase "eminent in years" (ἡλικίᾳ προήκων),[3] but men with the taste for danger here described (and this agrees well with Lamachos' character in Aristophanes) often carry their years very lightly. We note that Chabrias, who died in circumstances of particular gallantry about 356, was already a strategos in 390, well over 30 years before;[4] Miltiades was probably not less than 64 when he fought at Marathon, or 65 when he got his wound at Paros the next year.[5] Statistics could be easily collected to show that many Greek commanders remained in active service to much greater ages than 65. We believe then that Perikles' Euxine voyage cannot be tied by Lamachos' age to the 'thirties, but that so far as that goes a date in, *e. g.*, the early 'forties is not at all impossible.

The question next arises whether the landing of troops in Sinope was a violation of the Peace of Kallias; if it was, a date in the early 'forties becomes improbable. It may be that Artaxerxes made no claims in Sinope (or on the northern coast of Asia Minor in general) and was content for Athenian troops to interfere in its government. Unless we suppose this (and it is not a very likely supposition) we ought no doubt to place Perikles' voyage at some decent interval after the peace, or else before it. Can we put it as early as 450?

---

[3] "Dem 450 geborenen Alkibiades gegenüber ἡλικίᾳ προήκων" (Beloch, *Gr. Gesch.*, II, 2², p. 216; cf. Busolt, *Gr. Gesch.*, III, 1, p. 585, note 2). Προήκων has of course no explicitly comparative sense (it does not mean "ahead of" someone else), but means, absolutely, "advanced in age." It is used by Plutarch of Nikias in 418 (*Alcibiades*, 13, 1, ἤδη καθ' ἡλικίαν προήκοντα).

[4] For Chabrias' early commands see Kirchner, *P. A.*, no. 15086. The alleged command in 390/89 rests on the date of *I. G.*, II², 21, which is uncertain (*I. G.*, II², Addenda, p. 656), but those in the years immediately following are reasonably certain.

[5] The identity of the victor of Marathon with the archon of 524/3 (Dion. Hal., *Ant. Rom.*, VII, 3, 1; cf. *S. E. G.*, X, 352) is made probable by Herodotos' words (VI, 39, 1), ἐν Ἀθήνῃσι ἐποίευν εὖ.

It could hardly be put much earlier, but the date 450 should be seriously examined. Lamachos then, we must suppose, was born about 480, was 30 at the time of this command, 55 in Aristophanes' *Acharnians*, 65 when he was appointed to the command in Sicily, 66 when he died in action. We suggest that none of this is impossible. Quite apart from Lamachos' age, it is no doubt most unlikely that Perikles and a "large fleet" could be spared so far from home in the years just before 450, when Athens was still at war with Sparta and Peloponnese. But in 450, Athens was quit of the war in Greece (Thucydides, I, 112, 2); her major operation was in Kypros. As against Kimon's 200 ships meant for serious campaigning, Perikles' squadron, though "large and splendidly equipped" for its purpose, was no doubt of not more than about 50 ships. The native kings and dynasts who were to be impressed will have been not the Spartokidai but their predecessors the Archeanaktidai, and Timesileos, the tyrant in Sinope, will have been of the party of Nympharetos and those other Milesians named in Tod, *Greek Hist. Inscr.*, I², no. 35 (see below p. 256). It makes, we suggest, a good pendant to Kimon's campaign, and was sufficiently subordinate not to have infringed the Elpinike compact (Plutarch, *Pericles*, 10, 5).[6] The fact that peace was concluded with Persia in the following winter will explain why the expedition had so little result. If it belongs in 450, then no doubt we should understand the Kyaneai of the peace as the Kyaneai which mark the mouth of the Euxine;[7] the peace forbade such expeditions for the future. The colonists in Sinope no doubt remained, and in Amisos as well.[8]

If we date the voyage to *ca.* 435, the fact that no tribute was collected in Period VI or VII (434-428), but was in Period IX and probably X is rather surprising. This sequence is in any case not without difficulty. A9 assesses cities on the north coast of Asia Minor (Herakleia) and on the eastern coast of northern Thrace (Apollonia). These are the two certain names, and others are likely further north. This was very probably a breach of the treaty with Persia, and Lamachos' adventure at Herakleia in 424 (Thucydides, IV, 75, 2 [T133]) makes it certain that the attempt was made to collect money from the Asiatic coast. The embassy to Persia which turned back from Ephesos on the news of Artaxerxes' death (Thucydides, IV, 50) was perhaps

---

[6] Lamachos is, very probably indeed (see Kirchner, *P. A.*, no. 8981), of the same tribe (Oineis, VI) as Kimon. If Lamachos was strategos for 450/49, we must suppose that Kimon was elected ἐξ ἁπάντων; on this question see Ehrenberg, *A. J. P.*, LXVI (1945), pp. 113-134.

[7] The Kyaneai are described in detail in Dionysios, *Anaplus Bospori*, 86-90. Strabo, XII, 3, 11, mentions the seapower of Sinope: ἐπῆρχε τῆς ἐντὸς Κυανέων θαλάττης, καὶ ἔξω δὲ πολλῶν ἀγώνων μετεῖχε τοῖς Ἕλλησιν.

[8] Strabo, XII, 3, 14 = Theopompos, frag. 389 Jacoby (no. 115): Amisos was colonized for the third time by Athenokles and the Athenians and renamed Peiraieus. The parallel passages are named by Jacoby in his commentary; *Frag. Gr. Hist.*, IID, p. 400. For [Skymnos], 917-920, see Franz Miltner, in *Anatolian Studies presented to William Hepburn Buckler* (Manchester, 1939), p. 193. The fourth-century coins of Amisos still give the name as Peiraieus; Head, *Hist. Num.*², p. 496.

intended to settle this question; the embassy which went a year later and (as we believe, pp. 275-277 below) merely renewed the Kallias treaty should have put an end to such collection. The evidence for actual collection in Period X (34, III, 78) looks very tenuous, but we think that the Euxine rubric is the most probable supplement for this line; and Krateros' reference to Nymphaion (frag. 8 Krech; see the Register and Gazetteer, *s. v.* Νύμφαιον) makes it extremely likely that north Euxine cities were assessed as late as Period XIII.

We suggest as a possible solution that A9 in 425 was a frank breach of treaty (cf. the entry Κελένδερις) due to Athens' great confidence after the victory at Pylos, but that, after the renewal of the treaty in 423, Athens confined herself to the European coasts, and did not assess Euxine cities in Asia Minor. We think this likely, whether Perikles' voyage be put in 450 or *ca.* 435.[9]

---

[9] In the casualty list *I. G.*, I², 944 [ἐν Σιν]όπει has now more probably been restored as [ἐν 'Αλ]όπει; Raubitschek, *Hesperia*, XII (1943), pp. 25-27 (cf. *S. E. G.*, X, 415).

CHAPTER V

THUCYDIDES, II, 13, 2-9 (T117)

1. The Variant in II, 13, 3

While the enemy was on the march in 431 but had not yet entered Attica (about the middle of May, or early in Thargelion; Wade-Gery and Meritt, *A. J. P.*, LVII [1936], p. 379, note 10), Perikles gave an appreciation of the general outlook which Thucydides reports in this passage. It is not one of the usual Thucydidean speeches; it is not in *oratio recta*, but in *oratio obliqua* dependent on a series of narrative verbs (*e. g.*, παρῄνει, θαρσεῖν τε ἐκέλευε, ἔτι δὲ --- προσετίθει), and it is interrupted by three long parentheses in which Thucydides adds his own statements to corroborate Perikles' picture. In the following short précis these parentheses are especially inset; they are in fact in the nature of footnotes.

13, 2: He gave the same advice as before, to evacuate Attica, to fight no pitched battle, to nurse the fleet, to keep the allies in hand. Their strength, he said, depended upon receiving the allies' payments, and wars were won by policy and extra money.

13, 3: He spoke encouragingly of their 600 talents of annual revenue from the allies, and of their 6000 talents accumulated on the Akropolis,

> [That was in fact the sum even after the disbursements on buildings and for the siege of Poteidaia.] [1]

13, 4: and of their 500 talents in festival gear, trophies, dedications, etc.

13, 5: He added to this the contents of the other temples and as a last resort the actual gold of Athena's statue which was all detachable and weighed 40 talents of gold. All these they could use but must eventually repay.

13, 6: He gave this encouraging account of their money; in men, he said, there were 13,000 hoplites not counting the 16,000 garrison troops.

13, 7: [That was in fact the number of garrison troops during the invasions, made of oldest, youngest, and metoikoi. The length of wall to be garrisoned was 35 stades up from Phaleron, 43 of the city itself, 40 down to Peiraieus, 30 at Peiraieus.]

13, 8: He reckoned 1200 cavalry, 1600 archers, 300 ships fit for service.

[1] This may perhaps serve as a noncommittal précis of this crucial passage, not seriously misrepresenting any of the possible readings. We translate the introductory γάρ as "in fact," here as in 13, 7 and 13, 9.

13, 9: [These were in fact the figures, in each case,[2] at the moment of the first invasion.]

And he repeated his usual arguments for the likelihood of victory.

The passage which most concerns us (13, 3) is extant in two distinct versions: one in the " book texts," that is, in all the manuscripts of Thucydides (those which give Thucydides as a book, not in quotations), the other in an ancient quotation preserved in the scholia on Aristophanes, *Plutus*, 1193 (T38i). Book texts are usually superior to quotations, and scholiastic quotations are particularly liable to corruption. But it is always possible that an ancient quotation preserves a text older and better than that of the book texts.

The version of the book texts (T117 in *A. T. L.*, I) is as follows:

θαρσεῖν τε ἐκέλευε προσιόντων μὲν ἑξακοσίων ταλάντων ὡς ἐπὶ τὸ πολὺ φόρου κατ᾽ ἐνιαυτὸν ἀπὸ τῶν ξυμμάχων τῇ πόλει ἄνευ τῆς ἄλλης προσόδου, ὑπαρχόντων δὲ ἐν τῇ ἀκροπόλει ἔτι τότε ἀργυρίου ἐπισήμου ἑξακισχιλίων ταλάντων (τὰ γὰρ πλεῖστα τριακοσίων ἀποδέοντα μύρια ἐγένετο, ἀφ᾽ ὧν ἔς τε τὰ προπύλαια τῆς ἀκροπόλεως καὶ τἆλλα οἰκοδομήματα καὶ ἐς Ποτείδαιαν ἀπανηλώθη).

The quotation in the scholiast (T38i) begins at the word ὑπαρχόντων; it contains some errors and a few late spellings of the kind common in quotations (these we note in a brief apparatus).[3] It has three significant variants which change the sense radically:

ὑπαρχόντων δὲ ἐν τῇ ἀκροπόλει αἰεί ποτε ἀργυρίου ἐπισήμου ἑξακισχιλίων ταλάντων (τὰ γὰρ πλεῖστα τριακοσίων ἀποδέοντα περιεγένετο, ἀφ᾽ ὧν ἔς τε τὰ προπύλαια τῆς ἀκροπόλεως καὶ τἆλλα οἰκοδομήματα, καὶ ἐς Ποτείδαιαν ἐπανηλώθη).

> αἰεί ποτε V, ἄγει ποτὲ R.
> τριακοσίων R, τὰ V.
> εἴς τε τὰ V, εἰς τὰ R.
> εἰς VR.
> Ποτίδ (abbreviated) V, Ποτίδαιαν (corrected from Ποτιδαίαν?) R.

According to the book texts, Perikles said there were still (ἔτι τότε, *i.e.*, in May, 431) 6000 talents accumulated; according to the quotation, he said that there had

---

[2] Ἕκαστα τούτων: we understand this to refer to the three figures given in 13, 8, for cavalry, archers, and ships. It is perhaps possible to understand it as referring to the whole survey (13, 3-8), but we think this less likely.

[3] We report the Ravennas and the Venetus, using the published facsimiles (see the " Table of Abbreviations," *s. vv.*). We are indebted to Herbert Bloch and Werner Jaeger for help in reading these. We have omitted R's numerous interpuncts (see Rutherford's transcript in his *Scholia Aristophanica*, I, p. 117); V gives only the colon after περιεγένετο. We have added the marks of parenthesis.

been such an accumulation for several years (αἰεί ποτε). Thucydides' "footnote," according to the book texts, says that the accumulation at its highest had been of 9700 talents but certain special expenses had brought it down; according to the quotation, the "footnote" observes that in spite of these special expenses the accumulation still stood at something near its normal figure, namely, at 5700 talents.

The first contention of this study is that the quotation preserves the original text, and that the book texts give us a corrupted version. The most important fact alleged by the quotation is shown to be true by evidence of which no ancient reader of Thucydides is likely to have been aware: there *was,* from 449 to 431, an accumulation of money on the Akropolis which stood at a fairly level figure of 6000 talents. We believe it certain that there was never an accumulation of over 9000 talents (or anywhere near that amount). It is entirely probable (though here we have no exact corroboration) that the recent unusually high expenses had lowered the figure by May, 431, to 5700 talents.[4]

These considerations of fact could not, however, be decisive. Thucydides might have been misinformed, or it is conceivable that the version of the book texts could be understood as a "loose" statement; we do not indeed deny the possibility that we have misinterpreted the (mainly inscriptional) evidence which we understand as corroborating the quotation's text. More important is that the language of the quotation is more Thucydidean than that of the book texts. The meaning which the book texts require of τὰ πλεῖστα ("the amount at its greatest") would be unique in the more than fifty examples of πλεῖστος with the article in Thucydides; the meaning which the quotation requires ("most of this") is normal and in Thucydides is perhaps invariable. It is further worth noting that the phrase αἰεί ποτε given in the quotation is rare in most writers but relatively frequent in Thucydides.

These questions of usage are discussed below. Meanwhile, can any explanation be found of the book texts' variant? And, particularly, what is the origin of this figure of 10,000 (μύρια) which stands in the book texts? The figure of 10,000 talents as a sort of high point in fifth-century finance occurs elsewhere:

(a) in four passages of fourth-century orators: Isokrates, VIII, 69 (T79); XV, 234 (T82); Demosthenes, III, 24 (T47); [XIII, 26] (T49). All four are fairly close to 350 B. C.

(b) in three passages of Diodoros: XII, 40, 2 (T58); 54, 3 (T59); XIII, 21, 3 (T60).[5]

---

[4] For the inscriptional evidence in question see below, pp. 326-341, especially 337-341.

[5] The figure of 10,000 talents occurs also in Dion of Prousa, II, 36 (T60a) and Aelius Aristeides, XIII, 160 (Dindorf, I, p. 262 [T21a]). The passage of Dion is from a conversation between Philip and Alexander; the figure is the cost of the Propylaia plus the Olympieion. In Aristeides, the Akropolis is said to have been denuded of its "nearly 10,000 talents" before the reinforcement was sent to Sicily in 414. In both the figure seems to be purely conventional.

The third passage of Diodoros (XIII, 21, 3) is probably from Timaios; it is certainly not from Ephoros, since it is in the speech of the Syracusan Nikolaos in 413 and Ephoros' work did not contain such speeches. The second passage (XII, 54, 3), very similar to the third and also in a Sicilian context, is perhaps likewise from Timaios. The first (XII, 40, 2) is almost certainly from Ephoros[6] and represents his rewriting of our passage of Thucydides (II, 13).

Our suggestion is that it was Ephoros' rewriting of Thucydides, II, 13 which is responsible for the figure of 10,000. The orators write under his immediate influence,[7] Timaios draws from him later; the book-text reading in Thucydides is a corruption induced by the Ephoran version.[8]

2. THE VERSION OF EPHOROS

We have not Ephoros' own words, but Diodoros in XII, 38-40 gives what (he claims)[9] represents Ephoros' account of how the war started, and it includes a paraphrase of Thucydides, II, 13.[10] The paraphrase is fairly close but there are also some definite changes. One important change is that in Ephoros' account Perikles made his survey not in May, 431, but in the preceding autumn.[11] The change could be justified, since Thucydides points out (II, 13, 2; cf. II, 13, 9) that in May, 431, Perikles was largely repeating what he had said in the preceding autumn; and it enabled Ephoros to bring this survey into his story of the war's origins. More

---

[6] See XII, 41, 1: αἰτίαι μὲν οὖν --- τοιαῦταί τινες ὑπῆρξαν, ὡς Ἔφορος ἀνέγραψε.

[7] We have then to assume that Ephoros' history of the year 432 was published (not merely known to Isokrates) before the *de Pace*, which can hardly be after 354. Ephoros' publication is generally put a little later than this for two main reasons: frag. 119 (Jacoby [no. 70]) evidently presupposes Epameinondas' death in 362, and frag. 37 from book IV is most simply understood as presupposing Philip's renaming of Daton as Philippoi in 357 (see Jacoby, *Frag. Gr. Hist.*, IIC, p. 24; Barber, *Ephorus*, pp. 11-12). It is, however, uncertain whether this renaming is really quoted from Ephoros' fourth book, and the passage about Epameinondas may have come in a book considerably later than that (XV?) in which he dealt with the outbreak of the Peloponnesian War. The historical facts of the fifth century which appear as accepted in Isokrates, VIII and XV, seem to us to make the publication of Ephoros' history of the Periklean age virtually certain before Isokrates, XV (*Antidosis*; see note 14 below) and highly probable before VIII (*de Pace*). It is of course conceivable that the *de Pace* and Ephoros' Periklean history both draw from a common source; we do not think this likely.

[8] *I. e.*, μύρια is a *marginale* which has got into the text (being understood as a correction of περι-?). This would presumably not be deliberate, but the change of αἰεί ποτε to ἔτι τότε looks more deliberate—a consequential change.

[9] XII, 41, 1, ὡς Ἔφορος ἀνέγραψε. See note 12 below.

[10] XII, 40, 1-4 paraphrases Thucydides, II, 13, 3-8.

[11] Diodoros includes his whole story of the war's origins in his year 431 or 431/0 (Euthydemos archon), but says that he is going to dive into the past (38, 1); Ephoros will have named no archon. The survey is made a part of the speech in which Perikles refuses to revoke the Megarian decree. In Thucydides' account, the Athenians had, before the survey, voted not to discuss any proposals until the Spartans demobilized (II, 12, 2).

particularly it let him connect this survey with an anecdote about Alkibiades: Perikles had been worrying about how he should account for the moneys in his charge and Alkibiades advised him, instead of trying to give an account, to try to avoid giving one. These two very different motifs thus juxtaposed (the Thucydidean survey and the Alkibiades anecdote) produce a certain awkwardness, since Perikles makes war to avoid giving the account and then gives it after all.[12] Diodoros' words are as follows:

38, 2: Ἀθηναῖοι τῆς κατὰ θάλατταν ἡγεμονίας ἀντεχόμενοι τὰ ἐν Δήλῳ κοινῇ συνηγμένα χρήματα, τάλαντα σχεδὸν ὀκτακισχίλια, μετήνεγκαν εἰς τὰς Ἀθήνας καὶ παρέδωκαν φυλάττειν Περικλεῖ. οὗτος δ' ἦν εὐγενείᾳ καὶ δόξῃ καὶ λόγου δεινότητι πολὺ προέχων τῶν πολιτῶν [= Thucydides, I, 139, 4]. μετὰ δέ τινα χρόνον ἀνηλωκὼς ἀπ' αὐτῶν ἰδίᾳ πλῆθος ἱκανὸν χρημάτων καὶ λόγον ἀπαιτούμενος εἰς ἀρρωστίαν ἐνέπεσεν, οὐ δυνάμενος τῶν πεπιστευμένων ἀποδοῦναι τὸν ἀπολογισμόν.

38, 3: ἀδημονοῦντος δ' αὐτοῦ περὶ τούτων, Ἀλκιβιάδης ὁ ἀδελφιδοῦς --- ἀφορμὴν αὐτῷ παρέσχετο τῆς περὶ τῶν χρημάτων ἀπολογίας. θεωρῶν γὰρ τὸν θεῖον λυπούμενον ἐπηρώτησε τὴν αἰτίαν τῆς λύπης. τοῦ δὲ Περικλέους εἰπόντος, ὅτι τὴν περὶ τῶν χρημάτων ἀπολογίαν αἰτούμενος ζητῶ πῶς ἂν δυναίμην ἀποδοῦναι τὸν περὶ τούτων λόγον τοῖς πολίταις, ὁ Ἀλκιβιάδης ἔφησε δεῖν αὐτὸν ζητεῖν μὴ πῶς ἀποδῷ τὸν λόγον, ἀλλὰ πῶς μὴ ἀποδῷ.

38, 4: Perikles accepts this advice and determines on war; οὕτω γὰρ μάλιστα ὑπελάμβανε διὰ τὴν ταραχὴν --- ἐκφεύξεσθαι τὸν ἀκριβῆ λόγον τῶν χρημάτων. There are other embarrassments too.

39, 1-2: Pheidias and Anaxagoras are prosecuted by Perikles' enemies.

39, 3: Perikles sees that war will stop this trouble; ἔκρινε συμφέρειν αὐτῷ τὴν πόλιν ἐμβαλεῖν εἰς μέγαν πόλεμον, ὅπως --- μὴ προσδέχηται τὰς κατ' αὐτοῦ διαβολάς, μηδ' ἔχῃ σχολὴν καὶ χρόνον ἐξετάζειν ἀκριβῶς τὸν περὶ τῶν χρημάτων λόγον.

39, 4: The Megarian Decree; Sparta demands its repeal.

39, 5: συναχθείσης οὖν περὶ τούτων ἐκκλησίας, ὁ Περικλῆς, δεινότητι λόγου πολὺ διαφέρων ἁπάντων τῶν πολιτῶν [= Thucydides, I, 139, 4, as before], ἔπεισε τοὺς Ἀθηναίους μὴ ἀναιρεῖν τὸ ψήφισμα, λέγων ἀρχὴν δουλείας εἶναι --- [= Thucydides, I, 141, 1]. συνεβούλευεν οὖν τὰ ἀπὸ τῆς χώρας κατακομίζειν εἰς τὴν πόλιν καὶ θαλαττοκρατοῦντας διαπολεμεῖν τοῖς Σπαρτιάταις [= Thucydides, II, 13, 2].[13]

---

[12] The awkwardness is ironed out in 39, 3: war made the Demos too busy to scrutinize the statement *closely* (ἀκριβῶς, cf. ἀκριβῆ in 38, 4). Jacoby in his text of frag. 196 indicates both these passages as foreign to Ephoros; though Diodoros states (in XII, 41, 1) that he has taken his account of the origins of the war from Ephoros, Jacoby holds that the Alkibiades anecdote cannot have stood in the same narrative as the prosecutions of Pheidias and Anaxagoras. We feel, however, that the Alkibiades anecdote has been combined and integrated with Perikles' survey more thoroughly than Diodoros himself is likely to have done it; see below, p. 123.

[13] This is where Diodoros passes from the situation at the end of Thucydides' book I to that

40, 1: περὶ δὲ τοῦ πολέμου πεφροντισμένως ἀπολογισάμενος ἐξηριθμήσατο μὲν τὸ πλῆθος τῶν συμμάχων – – –, πρὸς δὲ τούτοις τὸ πλῆθος τῶν μετακεκομισμένων ἐκ Δήλου χρημάτων – – –.

At this point (XII, 40, 1) begins the paraphrase of Thucydides, II, 13, 3-8. The paraphrase is closer than appears from the opening words just quoted (Thucydides mentions no enumeration of allies nor says anything of the money having come from Delos); it is in fact very close indeed. But we have transcribed this long passage to make clear how different the context is. Ephoros takes an un-Thucydidean view of Perikles, and the intrusion of the cynical anecdote perhaps suited the temper of the day.[14] The changed point of view causes Ephoros to stress the facts that the accumulation was Greek money, not Athenian; that it had come from Delos; that Perikles had spent it on extravagant buildings. The anecdote and new context cause the one departure from the Thucydidean order (in Thucydides the *income* comes first, the accumulation second; Ephoros brings the *accumulation* to the front). It is perhaps symptomatic that we do not hear that there were 6000 talents left, but instead that there had once been 10,000 and that 4000 had been spent.

40, 1: ἐξηριθμήσατο μὲν τὸ πλῆθος τῶν συμμάχων – – –, πρὸς δὲ τούτοις τὸ πλῆθος τῶν μετακεκομισμένων ἐκ Δήλου χρημάτων εἰς τὰς Ἀθήνας, ἃ συνέβαινεν ἐκ τῶν φόρων ταῖς πόλεσι κοινῇ συνηθροῖσθαι.

40, 2: κοινῶν δ' ὄντων τῶν μυρίων ταλάντων ἀπανήλωτο πρὸς τὴν κατασκευὴν τῶν προπυλαίων καὶ τὴν Ποτιδαίας πολιορκίαν τετρακισχίλια τάλαντα.

Where did Ephoros get this figure of 4000? The answer depends on the answer to another question (the vital question): which version of Thucydides did he read? If he read the version of our book texts, then he got the 10,000 from that, and he computed the 4000 by *subtracting* Thucydides' 6000 from Thucydides' *ca.* 10,000. If he read the version quoted by the scholiast, then he will have computed the 4000 for himself and obtained his 10,000 by *adding* his 4000 to Thucydides' *ca.* 6000. This second alternative deserves, we suggest, serious consideration. He may (on this view) have obtained his 4000 by adding together (a) 2000 talents for Poteidaia, from

in II, 13; what follows in Diodoros (40, 1-4) is taken closely from II, 13, 3-8. But similar things to II, 13, 2 are found in, *e. g.*, Thucydides, I, 143; and in 40, 5 Diodoros comes back again to Thucydides, I, 141, 2–143, 2, thus finally telescoping the two occasions.

[14] Athenian morale was at its lowest between the death of Chabrias and the entry of Demosthenes into politics; it is not unfairly represented by Isokrates' *Areopagitica* (VII) and *de Pace* (VIII). No heroic view of Perikles was likely. The last sentence in XII, 40, 3 (τούς τε τῶν πολιτῶν βίους – – – εὐδαιμονίαν) has no Thucydidean original and is Ephoros' own addition; its likeness to the tone of the *de Pace* is noteworthy, *e. g.*, VIII, 124-125. Isokrates' *Areopagitica* and *de Pace* are the two speeches which show best the milieu in which Ephoros wrote; and the *de Pace* and *Antidosis* (XV) are the two which show most clearly the effect of his work. All our quotations from Isokrates are from VIII and XV.

Thucydides, II, 70, 2 (T120), and (b) *ca.* 2000 talents for the Propylaia, from the same documentary source as Heliodoros used, who gave the cost of the Propylaia as 2012 talents.[15]

This would not be a realistic computation. But it is important to recognize that Ephoros' computations are not realistic but (so to say) rhetorical or literary; he is interested in figures and finds them effective in making his picture vivid, but he is not so fastidious as a realistic computer must be concerning their exactness or their relevance. The 2000 for Poteidaia is of course not correct for the amount which has been expended when Perikles speaks; but Ephoros is indifferent to that *realistic* aspect, as is shown by his moving the occasion of the speech back from May, 431, to autumn, 432 (when the siege of Poteidaia had in fact only just begun). His *rhetorical* interest is in his point that Athens is spending money which is not hers; this is made effective by naming an actual sum: 4000 thus improperly spent, 6000 boasted of by Perikles as still left—that makes 10,000 talents of Greek money appropriated by Athens.

We do not suggest that we can be sure exactly how Ephoros computed his 4000.[16] The essential thing is that he *can* have computed in some other way than by subtracting 6000 from 10,000,—that is to say, that he *need* not have found both those figures in Thucydides, II, 13. On the other hand there can hardly be any doubt that the figure 10,000 has its origin in this Periklean survey: either Ephoros found it in Thucydides, II, 13, 3, or else (more likely, as we think) he put it into his own rewriting of that passage, as being the sum of Thucydides' 6000 and his own 4000. It is not a mere

[15] Harpokration and Suidas, *s. v.* Προπύλαια ταῦτα. Heliodoros' date is not known (see Jacoby, in P. W., *R. E., s. v.* Heliodoros[11]; Keil's very speculative article in *Hermes,* XXX [1895], pp. 199-240, must be taken with caution; cf. Drexel, *Ath. Mitt.,* XXXVII [1912], pp. 119-128). For his figure see Tod, *Greek Hist. Inscr.,* I², pp. 115-116. Most critics are agreed that it is too large for the Propylaia alone, and it is suggested that it includes the Parthenon (and Parthenos?). If so, we must suppose a statement not unlike *I. G.,* I², 324 (Tod, *Greek Hist. Inscr.,* I², no. 64), which is, as for its greater part, an account of loans between 433 and 422. So Heliodoros' presumed documentary source will have been primarily an account of the Propylaia expenses yet have concluded with a more comprehensive total. Was it in fact *I. G.,* I², 363-367? Or was it something more analogous to *I. G.,* I², 354 (as now restored by Dinsmoor in Ἀρχ. Ἐφ., 1937, II, pp. 507-511)?

[16] The computation we suggest (2000 Poteidaia + 2000 Propylaia; the former from Thucydides, II, 70, 2, the latter from a document, see note 15 above) may be borne out by the other changes which he has made in the figures of Thucydides, II, 13. He changes Thucydides' 600 talents of income to 460, evidently on the strength of Thucydides, I, 96, 2 (T109); and instead of Thucydides' 40 talents weight of gold in the statue he gives 50, which is perhaps a rounding-out of the documentary 44 talents (schol. Aristophanes, *Peace,* 605). This independence in figures is remarkable (he also changes the numbers of hoplites) and is perhaps due not to careless copying but to a genuine interest in figures, leading him to research. The research is not indeed always realistic, but we suggest that its results are apparent in Isokrates, XV, 111-113 (cf. T82a and 82b), where Isokrates evidently had a figure for Melos as well as for Samos and Poteidaia. Our reason for questioning the particular computation which we suggest is not that Heliodoros' figure may be wrong (we find little difficulty in supposing Ephoros made the same hasty reading) but that Isokrates (*loc. cit.*) gives 2400 for Poteidaia and one would think that this was Ephoros' figure.

" rounding-out " of the figure 8000 which Ephoros also used (Diodoros, XII, 38, 2, quoted above).

3. THE 10,000 AND THE 8000

It is not quite clear in Diodoros (it was no doubt clearer in Ephoros' own words) whether " the 10,000 talents " (XII, 40, 2 [T58]) was the same figure as the sum brought from Delos (XII, 38, 2 [T57]; 40, 1 [T58]). It was certainly the same money in principle, " accumulated out of the cities' tributes " and therefore common property of Greece; but did Ephoros conceive of it as growing, or static, between 454 when it was brought from Delos and 437 when the disbursement of the 4000 began? This is perhaps rather a realistic consideration, yet it seems to have occurred to Ephoros and his answer seems to have been that it grew. In Diodoros, XII, 38, 2 the amount " brought from Delos and entrusted to Perikles " is 8000, not 10,000; and XII, 54, 3 (T59) and XIII, 21, 3 (T60), where we hear of the Athenians " taking 10,000 talents from Delos," are, as we have seen, probably not Ephoros but Timaios. It looks as if Ephoros used both figures, and 8000 is the figure for what was " brought from Delos and entrusted to Perikles " in about 450, while 10,000 is the figure for the highest point which it reached while in his charge. Three considerations point to this:

(1) Diodoros gives both figures (XII, 38, 2; 40, 2) in that account of the war's origins which he expressly says is taken from Ephoros (XII, 41, 1).

(2) Isokrates gives both figures: in VIII, 126 (T80) Perikles placed 8000 talents on the Akropolis (" not counting the hiera "); in XV, 234 (T82) Perikles placed on the Akropolis not less than 10,000 talents.[17]

(3) The two figures not only refer to different occasions but are derived from different computations: the 10,000 from a computation based on Thucydides, II, 13, 3 (if it did not actually stand in that passage), the 8000 from the Papyrus Decree (D13).[18]

The Papyrus Decree is so called because the prime evidence for it is in the Strassburg Papyrus (*Anonymus Argentinensis*); see *A. T. L.*, I, T9 (D13 in *A. T. L.*, II). The writer (a commentator on Demosthenes) quotes the decree as moved by Perikles,

[17] This second passage requires serious attention. It is what lends most colour to the view that the 10,000 is a rhetorical rounding-out of the 8000. This view seems to us impossible (see note 18 below): the two figures rest on different computations and refer to different occasions. Those who find a marked increase of senility between the *de Pace* and the *Antidosis* (XV) will impute the latter figure to senile confusion; but what is he confusing with what? If Ephoros' story was what we suppose, Isokrates' use of both figures for what Perikles " placed on the Akropolis " becomes intelligible. For the " hiera " in VIII, 126 see note 20 below.

[18] This is fundamental and we think certain. The 10,000 *must* originate, one way or other, with Thucydides, II, 13, 3 and therefore is *not* a rhetorical rounding-out of the 8000. The 8000 cannot be derived from Thucydides, II, 13, 3 and must have some other origin.

as belonging to the year of " Euthydemos " (he means Euthynos, the archon of 450/49), and as being a preliminary to the great constructions on the Akropolis which started in 447. The decree authorizes the Athenians to " use for these constructions " (? the verb is missing) a fund consisting of 5000 talents of accumulated tribute. This was in 450/49; 16 years later, in 434/3, we read in one of the decrees of Kallias that a sum amounting to 3000 talents " has now been carried up to the Akropolis as was previously decreed " (D1, lines 3-4). This amount was not placed on the Akropolis in one sum but in instalments; we argue on pp. 327-328 below that there had been 15 annual instalments of 200 talents each in the years from 449/8 to 435/4 inclusive,[19] and that the payment of these annual instalments, up to the total of 3000, was ordered in the Papyrus Decree. In that decree, then, Perikles devoted to the Akropolis fund 5000 talents of tribute already accumulated and yearly instalments out of future tribute up to the total of a further 3000, or 8000 in all.

The sum of 8000 talents is mentioned explicitly not more than twice; Isokrates, VIII, 126 (T80) and Diodoros, XII, 38, 2 [T57] (it is also probably implied in Pausanias, I, 29, 16 [T90]). Isokrates' evidence is no doubt the most valuable, since we have his own words and they are reasonably precise; Diodoros follows Ephoros whose evidence would be even more important if we had his own words. Isokrates' words are (VIII, 126) : " Perikles placed on the Akropolis 8000 talents not counting the sacred moneys " (Περικλῆς --- εἰς --- τὴν ἀκρόπολιν ἀνήνεγκεν ὀκτακισχίλια τάλαντα χωρὶς τῶν ἱερῶν).[20] Diodoros' words are (XII, 38, 2) : " The Athenians maintaining their claim to sea-hegemony brought to Athens the money accumulated in Delos for the general use, some 8000 talents, and gave it into Perikles' charge." How well do these statements square with the Papyrus Decree?

They certainly do not represent the truth of it. The money brought from Delos was in fact a good deal less than 8000 talents, nor did Perikles at any one time place that sum on the Akropolis. Ephoros (or whoever read the decree for him) did not take in its provisions realistically; he was impressed with the total, but not impressed by the fact that nearly half was to come in instalments over 15 years. Perikles may have named his desired total first, and then defined the two components, 5000 in hand, 3000 to come. Perikles no doubt foresaw that the outgoings on his building projects would prevent the 8000 from actually accumulating; it is likely that he calculated his provision for feeding the fund so as to balance the expenditure which he contemplated, i. e., he meant the fund to keep at a fairly constant figure. But he is not likely to have

---

[19] Accordingly, Kallias confirms the assignment of a sum of 200 for the current year 434/3 (now that the 3000 is completed) to repayment of debts to the Other Gods (D1, lines 2-7, and D2, lines 21-23).

[20] The hiera are no doubt the moneys from Athena's own revenues, as distinguished from the secular moneys (i. e., tribute money) of which the 8000 was composed. We compute that these " sacred moneys " amounted in 449 to about 750 talents (see below, p. 337). A comparison with XV, 234 (T82) might suggest that the hiera were temples, but this seems to us unlikely.

gone into all that in the decree.[21] Ephoros was content to imagine the 8000 as a single sum; to be surprised at this is to mistake Ephoros' standards.

Diodoros' phrase sounds looser than Isokrates', yet it perhaps represents Ephoros fairly enough. Once he had entertained the false notion that the 8000 talents named in Perikles' decree of 450/49 was a single sum, it was natural to identify it with what came from Delos. We moderns believe ourselves to know (chiefly from the serial numbering of the quota lists) that the transfer from Delos was in 454, some five years before the Papyrus Decree. Ephoros was probably unconscious of this interval and will in any case hardly have thought it important. The unfolding of Perikles' plans (Papyrus Decree, Parthenon specification, etc.) put a new complexion on the transfer from Delos, and this fact disturbed his contemporaries;[22] but Ephoros will not have seen this process in its stages.

Ephoros, then, believed himself to know that (a) in about 450 the money lately come from Delos, some 8000 talents, was put on the Akropolis, on Perikles' motion, and Perikles was henceforward in charge (this on the evidence of the Papyrus Decree); (b) there was 6000 left in about 432 (this on the evidence of Thucydides, II, 13, 3); (c) a little before 432 it had stood at 10,000 (this on the evidence of Thucydides, II, 13, 3 combined with his own figures for the Propylaia and Poteidaia); (d) Perikles was continuously in charge and responsible; this is implied in the use of the Alkibiades anecdote. He will have made all this specific in the passage which Diodoros has condensed in XII, 40, 1-2 (quoted above, p. 123). Isokrates was entitled to name as the sum which " Perikles put on the Akropolis " either 8000 [on the strength of (a)], or 10,000 [on the strength of (c) and (d)]. He was entitled to name (in VIII, 69 [T79]) 10,000 as the sum which could not save the Periklean Empire; and Demosthenes was entitled, for his different purpose, to name (in III, 24 [T47] and [XIII, 26] [T49]) the same sum as the glory of that Empire. But Timaios' use of the figure 10,000 for the money brought from Delos is a piece of rhetorical looseness (Diodoros, XIII, 21, 3; XII, 54, 3); Dion of Prousa and Aelius Aristeides (see note 5 above) are looser still.

So much for those who drew on Ephoros. As to the actual facts, we summarize our hypothesis as follows. The 8000 is a real figure and was no doubt named by Perikles in the Papyrus Decree; Ephoros has only slightly misapplied it. The 10,000 is a chimaera, the product of Ephoros' own computations based on Thucydides, II, 13, 3; but 10,000 talents is a memorable figure and some reader of Thucydides put it in his margin.

---

[21] The specifications for Parthenon and Parthenos were still to come and their scale proved a surprise; Plutarch, *Pericles*, 12, 2 (T96).

[22] Plutarch, *Pericles*, 12, 1 (T96): ἣ δ᾽ --- εὐπρεπεστάτη τῶν προφάσεων --- ταύτην ἀνῄρηκε Περικλῆς. This must be from Ion or some contemporary.

4. Thucydidean Usages

The three places where the quotation differs significantly from the book texts are:

(1) περιεγένετο instead of μύρια ἐγένετο,

(2) αἰεί ποτε instead of ἔτι τότε,

(3) ἐπανηλώθη instead of ἀπανηλώθη.

(1) This is the fundamental variant; we conceive that it was the changing of περι- to μύρια which originated the book texts' corruption. The change (whichever way it was made) affects the meaning of the surrounding words. The version of the book texts, τὰ γὰρ πλεῖστα τριακοσίων ἀποδέοντα μύρια ἐγένετο, has to be translated, "the amount at its greatest had been 9700." The numeral is sufficiently supported by IV, 38, 5, ὀκτὼ ἀποδέοντες τριακόσιοι, though (as the commentators observe) Thucydides elsewhere always uses δέοντα, not this slightly more emphatic ἀποδέοντα. The difficulty is τὰ πλεῖστα. " Antea τὰ πλεῖστα iam Portus maxima pecuniae summa, quae fuerat in aerario, recte interpretatus erat, ut mirum sit Reiskium hic haerere potuisse," wrote Poppo in 1834; [23] since Reiske no one apparently has felt the difficulty and all have accepted Portus' rendering. The nearest parallels we can find are (a) Isokrates, IX, 28: παρακαλέσας ἀνθρώπους, ὡς οἱ τοὺς πλείστους λέγοντες, περὶ πεντήκοντα (Euagoras gathered a band " of 50 men according to those who put the figure highest "), and (b) Herodotos, VI, 46, 3: προσήιε – – – ἔτεος ἑκάστου διηκόσια τάλαντα, ὅτε δὲ τὸ πλεῖστον προσῆλθε, τριηκόσια (" 200 talents or at its highest 300 "). Against these rare examples in other writers we have to put the constant usage of Thucydides, who employs some form of ὁ πλεῖστος, οἱ πλεῖστοι, close upon fifty times, and without any exception it denotes " the greater part " of something.[24]

---

[23] *Commentarii*, II, p. 56. The difficulty becomes flagrant as soon as one observes (as Reiske no doubt did) the parallelism of τὰ γὰρ πλεῖστα, τοσοῦτοι γάρ, and ταῦτα γάρ – – – καὶ οὐκ ἐλάσσω – – – τούτων in II, 13, 3, 7, and 9.

[24] The examples are here arranged in categories. (1) Singular, with the partitive genitive expressed, type ἡ πλείστη τῆς στρατιᾶς: I, 5, 1; 30, 3; II, 98, 4; IV, 34, 1; VII, 3, 4. (2) The same, type τὸ πλεῖστον τῆς στρατιᾶς: I, 12, 4; III, 31, 2; IV, 35, 4; VIII, 17, 3. (3) Plural, with genitive expressed, type τὰς πλείστας τῶν νήσων: I, 8, 1; IV, 31, 2; 44, 2; 54, 4; VI, 15, 1; 30, 1; VII, 30, 2. (4) Singular, with noun in direct agreement, type τὸν πλεῖστον φθόρον: II, 51, 4; III, 1, 2; VII, 78, 2. (5) Plural, with noun in direct agreement, type οἱ πλεῖστοι στρατιῶται: I, 60, 2; II, 84, 4; IV, 90, 4; VII, 4, 5; VIII, 40, 2; 92, 10. (6) Singular, with no genitive and no noun in agreement, type τὸ πλεῖστον: II, 4, 5; IV, 109, 4; VII, 57, 4. (7) Plural, with no genitive and no noun in agreement, unspecific neuter plurals, type τὰ πλεῖστα: I, 115, 5; III, 104, 6; IV, 90, 4; VIII, 65, 2. (8) Plural, with no genitive and no noun in direct agreement, type τὰ πλεῖστα (*sc.* τάλαντα or τῶν ταλάντων): I, 18, 1; 50, 3; 110, 1; II, 49, 6; 96, 2; IV, 25, 9; 26, 2; 38, 1; 131, 3; VI, 5, 1; 27, 1; VII, 71, 6: 75, 5; VIII, 28, 4. Our instance, in II, 13, 3, will belong to category (8). I, 60, 2 may belong to (8) rather than (5), if it means " most of the 2000 were Korinthians," not " most of the Korinthians were volunteers." Category (4) is the least typical: II, 51, 4, " most of the mortality," but III, 1, 2, τὸν πλεῖστον ὅμιλον (τῶν ψιλῶν) = τὸ πλεῖστον, and so too τὸν πλεῖστον ὄχλον in VII, 78, 2; cf. Plato, *Rep.*, III, 397d.

This sense is much the commonest in other writers too;[25] when, as in the two examples just cited, the words are to denote a "maximum," the phrase is formed so as to exclude ambiguity. When Thucydides wishes to speak of a "maximum" or of "the greatest" or "the most numerous" among a number of examples, he omits the article;[26] Thucydidean Greek for the sense required by the book texts is perhaps ὅτε γὰρ πλεῖστα ἦν.

The version in the quotation is, τὰ γὰρ πλεῖστα τριακοσίων ἀποδέοντα περιεγένετο. This allows τὰ πλεῖστα to have its normal sense, the sense it invariably bears in Thucydides. The tense of περιεγένετο may seem surprising; we might expect περιεγίγνετο, "were surviving," or "were still there." But the aorist is correct in a statement of accounts; in *I. G.*, I², 338 we hear each year of λέμμα περιγενόμενον and that so much περιεγένετο τὸ λέμματος.[27] As a Thucydidean parallel compare III, 98, 3, οἱ περιγενόμενοι, "those who had survived the disaster." The notion is, the quantity which *has survived* at the moment while the line is drawn.[28]

(2) The phrase αἰεί ποτε, "as a regular thing for some time past," is almost a mannerism in Thucydides. It is not common elsewhere; Ast (*s. v. πότε*) quotes one example in Plato,[29] there is none (we believe) in Isokrates or Demosthenes, Sturz (*s. v. ποτὲ*) quotes 6 examples from Xenophon.[30] Bétant (*Lexicon*, I, pp. 16-17, *s. v. ἀεί*) gives 12 in Thucydides (13 if we include II, 13, 3; we believe this is exhaustive); this is about 10 per cent of his total uses of αἰεί. It occurs mostly with the imperfect or present indicative, or present participle, of εἰμί (7 times: ἦν, I, 60, 2, VIII, 85, 3; ἐσμέν, VI, 89, 4; εἰσίν, I, 47, 3, VI, 82, 2; ὄντας, II, 102, 2; ὄντες, IV, 103, 4) or ὑπάρχω (IV, 78, 2, ὑπῆρχεν). Twice where it is used adjectivally (III,

[25] Certainly in Attic prose. Herodotos uses the article sometimes where Thucydides would not; I, 136, 1, τῷ δὲ τοὺς πλείστους ἀποδεικνύντι, "the man who produces most sons" gets the prize; VII, 25, 2, τὸν δὴ ὧν πλεῖστον ⟨σῖτον⟩ (*nisi legendum* ⟨σῖ⟩τον δὴ ὧν πλεῖστον) means "the largest dump," not "most of the corn"; in I, 32, 8, ἣ δὲ ἂν τὰ πλεῖστα ἔχῃ, the words τὰ πλεῖστα are exactly equivalent to the anarthrous πλεῖστα just below (I, 32, 9). We believe that these three and VI, 46, 3 quoted above are the only cases; in VIII, 89, 2 and IX, 65, 2 we should probably understand "most (of the ships destroyed) were destroyed here," "most (of those who fell) fell here."

[26] Notably in III, 17, 1 and 4; cf., *e. g.*, I, 9, 4; IV, 26, 4; VII, 70, 4. We think he would have omitted the article in the two phrases quoted (*i. e.*, Isokrates, IX, 28 and Herodotos, VI, 46, 3). For Herodotos' use of the article in such cases see note 25 above.

[27] See Meritt's complete text in *Hesperia*, V (1936), pp. 366-368: col. II, lines 22, 28, 51, 57, 75, and col. III, 28, 35, 59, 65. The word is never complete, but its frequent occurrence makes the restoration certain. The new fragment published by Schweigert in *Hesperia*, VII (1938), pp. 264-268, and the fresh readings by Raubitschek in *Hesperia*, XII (1943), pp. 12-17, do not affect this question.

[28] A similar pluperfect sense is found in VII, 28, 4, ἀδύνατοι ἐγένοντο, "they had become pinched" for money.

[29] *Amatores*, 133a; this is like the Thucydidean usage.

[30] *Hellenica*, (1) II, 3, 45; (2) III, 5, 11; (3) IV, 5, 11; (4) VI, 3, 15; (5) *Convivium*, VIII, 41; (6) *de Vectigalibus*, I, 1. These examples are all fairly close to the Thucydidean use, though Xenophon employs it with other verbs than εἰμί (5) and ὑπάρχω (2).

95, 1, κατὰ τὴν Ἀθηναίων αἰεί ποτε φιλίαν; IV, 57, 4, διὰ τὴν προτέραν αἰεί ποτε ἔχθραν) we have to supply οὖσαν or ὑπάρχουσαν; in the two places where it is used with other verbs (I, 13, 5, αἰεὶ δή ποτε ἐμπόριον εἶχον; VIII, 73, 5, αἰεὶ δήποτε ὀλιγαρχίᾳ — — — ἐπικειμένους) it so happens that Thucydides inserts the particle δή, which is perhaps accidental.

As against this, the phrase ἔτι τότε occurs in Thucydides twice: V, 43, 2, ἡλικίᾳ μὲν ἔτι τότε ὢν νέος; VIII, 50, 2, ναύαρχον ἔτι ὄντα τότε.[31]

From this we may infer that while Thucydides may well have written in our passage either ἔτι τότε or αἰεί ποτε (according to which he meant), yet it is improbable that anyone misquoting him should have hit on what is in fact almost a Thucydidean mannerism.

(3) The verb ἐπαναλίσκω does not occur in Thucydides (outside II, 13, 3), while ἀπαναλίσκω occurs 3 times: VII, 11, 3; 14, 2; 30, 3. This might be held to outweigh the greater frequency of αἰεί ποτε; but we think we shall be conceded the fact that there is no true analogy between the frequency of these comparatively rare verbs, and that of such particles as ἔτι τότε, nor any question here of a " mannerism." Indeed, in view of the rareness of the verb, ἐπανηλώθη may count as a *lectio difficilior*. The only occurrence of it which we know in classical Greek is in [Demosthenes], L, 42, τὸ ἐπιτριηράρχημα ἀπέδωκεν τῷ Ἁγνίᾳ τοῦ χρόνου οὗ ἐπανήλωσεν ὑπὲρ αὐτῶν, repeated almost verbatim in 54, ἐκέλευον αὐτὸν — — — τὸ ἐπιτριηράρχημα ἀποδιδόναι τοῦ χρόνου οὗ ἐπανήλωσα ὑπὲρ τούτου ἐπιτριηραρχῶν (" I told him to pay the epitrierarchema for the time for which I, as epitrierarch, had made extra disbursement on his behalf "). When the new trierarchs turn up late, the old ones continue as epitrierarchs, and are entitled to a cash sum (the epitrierarchema) when they are relieved, the sum varying with the length of their extra service. The verb ἐπαναλίσκω is used with no direct object, but with a genitive of the time involved: " I had made extra disbursement for so many months." Though it no doubt could if necessary have a direct object, this absolute usage accords exactly with the impersonal passive which Thucydides uses: ἐπανηλώθη, " extra disbursements had been made."

For these reasons we feel confident that the quotation preserves the true reading and the book texts have a corrupted reading. This is not scholiast's Greek, and it is unusually free of those casual changes in the order of words, and omissions, not affecting the sense, which commonly mark quotations. Here we have three significant changes which cannot be casual since they cohere and radically change the text. It is evidently the version intended by the original annotator, who saw, in Thucydides' αἰεί ποτε, an illustration of the poet's ἀεὶ φυλάττων.

---

[31] That a phrase expressing so simple a notion should be so rare means that it is not the writer's only way of expressing that notion. Thucydides in fact uses the simple ἔτι in, *e. g.*, II, 59, 3, ἔτι δ' ἐστρατήγει.

The quotation's version may be translated as follows:

" And there was, he said, a regular standing amount of 6000 talents on the Akropolis. [The greater part of this, actually 5700 talents, was in fact still there. There had been extra disbursements from it for the Propylaia and other buildings and for Poteidaia.] "

What is the antecedent of ἀφ' ὧν? Perhaps αὐτῶν, to be understood with τὰ πλεῖστα. The qualification which follows τὰ πλεῖστα is slightly illogical, " most of them [that is to say, all] minus 300 "; we may compare VII, 57, 4, καὶ τὸ πλεῖστον Ἴωνες – – – πάντες – – – πλὴν Καρυστίων, and I, 18, 1, οἱ πλεῖστοι καὶ τελευταῖοι πλὴν τῶν ἐν Σικελίᾳ.

There is one other question of Thucydidean usage in II, 13, 3: the phrase ὡς ἐπὶ τὸ πολύ. It occurs in three other places in Thucydides; it is fairly common in Xenophon, Isokrates, Plato.[32] There is no room for doubt concerning its meaning: " usually," " on an average," " more often than not." Isokrates, IV, 154, distinguishes it from καθ' ἓν ἕκαστον, " not each case but the average "; Plato, Politicus, 295a, enunciating the principle that hard cases make bad law, says that legislation will be appropriate only in the bulk, a sort of average justice (καὶ ὡς ἐπὶ τὸ πολύ) which may be a bit rough and ready in particular cases. The Thucydidean examples are:

I, 12, 2: καὶ στάσεις ἐν ταῖς πόλεσιν ὡς ἐπὶ τὸ πολὺ[33] ἐγίγνοντο, " there were usually factions in the cities."

V, 107: ὃ Λακεδαιμόνιοι ἥκιστα ὡς ἐπὶ τὸ πολὺ τολμῶσιν, justice may involve danger " and that is a risk which Spartans are usually the last to take."

VI, 46, 4: καὶ πάντων ὡς ἐπὶ τὸ πολὺ τοῖς αὐτοῖς χρωμένων, " and since all of them more or less used the same " gold and silver plate, the impression made was considerable.

II, 13, 3: προσιόντων μὲν ἑξακοσίων ταλάντων ὡς ἐπὶ τὸ πολὺ φόρου κατ' ἐνιαυτὸν ἀπὸ τῶν ξυμμάχων τῇ πόλει ἄνευ τῆς ἄλλης προσόδου.

There had no doubt been some city without faction; Sparta had sometimes taken a risk for justice; there were some variations in the display of plate. What particular exception is safeguarded in the fourth passage? It has generally been understood that there was no doubt some year when the income was not exactly 600 talents. Nesselhauf[34] published Kolbe's suggestion that the phrase especially qualifies φόρου: there was some of the 600 talents which was not tribute. This is almost certainly true factually; and the position and construction of φόρου is certainly such (whether we

---

[32] Xenophon, Anabasis, III, 1, 42; 4, 35; Cyropaedia, I, 6, 37; V, 5, 39; VIII, 8, 5; Oeconomicus, 3, 11; 3, 15; 9, 5; 11, 20. Isokrates, II, 34; IV, 154; VII, 5; VIII, 35; XII, 30; 165; XV, 184; 271. Plato, Rep., II, 377b; Politicus, 294e; 295a; Laws, VII, 792b; IX, 875d.

[33] Some mss. omit τό but P. Oxy., XIII (1919), 1620 has it.

[34] Klio, Beiheft XXX, p. 117.

call it emphatic or awkward) that practically every editor has felt bound to offer some explanation of it. No doubt the words can be taken as Kolbe suggests. But Nesselhauf overstates the case when he says the words *must* bear this meaning, and (citing VI, 46, 4) writes, " ein Begriff wird durch *vorangestelltes* [35] ὡς ἐπὶ τὸ πολύ eingeschränkt." This is only questionably true of VI, 46, 4,[36] and is untrue of the other examples.

Thucydides may have been misinformed, or he may perhaps have used the word φόρου here in a looser sense than, strictly, " tribute " (as he has been thought to do in VII, 57, 4, where the Samians are said to be φόρου ὑποτελεῖς). There is also the possibility that Thucydides did not write φόρου (*i. e.*, that it is either an editor's addition or, more likely, a gloss). Its deletion would let us give to ὡς ἐπὶ τὸ πολύ what we think is its normal usage without bringing Thucydides into conflict with the tribute lists.

With φόρου deleted, the phrase aptly particularizes what is said in II, 13, 2: τὴν ἰσχὺν αὐτοῖς ἀπὸ τούτων (*sc.* ξυμμάχων) εἶναι τῶν χρημάτων τῆς προσόδου. Moreover ὡς ἐπὶ τὸ πολύ gives now the same sort of qualification to its clause as αἰεί ποτε gives to the clause following. We suggest therefore that φόρου may be a *marginale* which, like μύρια, at some time intruded into the text.[37] We do not, however, regard the case as certain and so we have retained φόρου in our version of the passage (see T117 in *A. T. L.*, II).

The following is the resulting text of Thucydides, II, 13, 3: θαρσεῖν τε ἐκέλευε προσιόντων μὲν ἑξακοσίων ταλάντων ὡς ἐπὶ τὸ πολὺ φόρου κατ᾽ ἐνιαυτὸν ἀπὸ τῶν ξυμμάχων τῇ πόλει ἄνευ τῆς ἄλλης προσόδου, ὑπαρχόντων δὲ ἐν τῇ ἀκροπόλει αἰεί ποτε ἀργυρίου ἐπισήμου ἑξακισχιλίων ταλάντων (τὰ γὰρ πλεῖστα τριακοσίων ἀποδέοντα περιεγένετο, ἀφ᾽ ὧν ἔς τε τὰ προπύλαια τῆς ἀκροπόλεως καὶ τᾶλλα οἰκοδομήματα καὶ ἐς Ποτείδαιαν ἐπανηλώθη), χωρὶς δὲ χρυσίου — — —.

---

[35] Our italics.

[36] The phrase could perhaps be taken here as qualifying especially τοῖς αὐτοῖς (so Nesselhauf wishes), but it might equally qualify πάντων; and in fact it surely, like the other examples, qualifies the whole notion.

[37] Φόρου was probably (not quite certainly) written in the papyrus; Nicole, *Textes grecs inédits de Genève*, 2 (p. 17); *P. Rylands*, III (1938), 548 is part of the same sheet.

CHAPTER VI

THE METHONE DECREES (D3–D6)

The Methone inscription (D3-D6) contains two decrees virtually complete (D3, D4) and the opening of a third (D5); we must presume a fourth also (D6), since the secretary named at the top of the whole is different from the secretaries of the three whose prescripts are extant, and must therefore be the secretary of a concluding decree. This concluding decree will (among other things, no doubt) have ordered the inscribing of its three predecessors and itself.

We thus have the names of all four secretaries,[1] and two of them can be probably identified. D4 was passed in the first prytany of its year (lines 51-54; orders are there given to the second prytany, whose name is as yet undetermined), and its secretary was Megakleides. The year 426/5 is described in two places (*I. G.*, I², 324, lines 4-5; 368, lines 2-5) as the year of the Boule whose first secretary was Megakleides. The identity is confirmed by the fact that the second prytany of this year was Kekropis (*I. G.*, I², 324, line 6) and the order given to the second prytany is executed by Kekropis in D8.[2] We can therefore be confident that D4 is of the first and D8 of the second prytany of 426/5 (July-August and August-September, 426).

The secretary of D6 was Phainippos. His identity with the Phainippos who was secretary of Akamantis in 424/3, in the month Elaphebolion (Thucydides, IV, 118, 11-12; Akamantis will have been the eighth prytany,[3] March-April, 423), is not perhaps as dead certain as is the identity of Megakleides, but it is hardly open to doubt.

D5, then, comes between Prytany I of 426/5 and Prytany VIII of 424/3. It cannot, further, belong to the year 426/5, since the secretary of Kekropis in that year was Polemarchos (D8), while our secretary's name was of 9 letters, ending in -es. Nor can it come in the first four prytanies of 425/4, none of which was Kekropis.[4]

[1] Of the secretary of D5 we know only that the name was of 9 letters and ended in -es (this is enough to show that he is not the Polemarchos of D8).

[2] The three facts following may be called certain: (a) D4, being of 426/5, contains orders for the second prytany, (b) the second prytany of 426/5 was Kekropis, and (c) the prytany of D5 is Kekropis. These three facts misled Kirchhoff into supposing that Kekropis in D5 was the second prytany of 426/5 and was fulfilling the orders given in D4. But in fact Kekropis in D5 belongs to the following year; the fulfillment of the orders in D4 is extant as D8. D4 and D8 are both moved by Kleonymos.

[3] Cf. *I. G.*, I², 324, line 33.

[4] The first secretary of the year was Pleistias; A9, lines 58-59; *I. G.*, I², 324, lines 17-18 (in Meritt's text, *A. F. D.*, p. 138). Prytany II was Oineis (A9, line 34; Wade-Gery and Meritt, *A. J. P.*, LVII [1936], pp. 384-391), Prytany III Leontis (A9, line 3; Meritt, *Hesperia*, XIV [1945], pp. 118-119), Prytany IV Aigeis (*I. G.*, I², 324, lines 18-19; Meritt and West, *Ath. Ass.*, pp. 55-56).

We believe that D5 is the special decree, the *privilegium* naming Methone, which was required (D4, lines 44-46) before Methone's name could be included in A9. We therefore ascribe it to 425/4, and its orator may well have been Thoudippos, the orator of A9. The list of names in A9 (including, we believe, Methone's) was published before the end of the sixth prytany; Kekropis was therefore Prytany V or perhaps VI, about December, 425, or January, 424.

The date of D3 is a more complicated question. We believe, indeed, that " the previous Panathenaia " which are mentioned twice (lines 8-9 and 31, τοῖς προτέροις Παναθεναίοις) should be understood as contrasted with " the present Panathenaia," and that these two occasions are the Great Panathenaia of 434 and 430. This reasoning is cogent, if we are right in supposing that two celebrations are in question and both of them are Great Panathenaia; the Great Panathenaia of 426 came late in the same prytany as D4, and thus, in the different prytany of D3, cannot have been " the present Panathenaia." The crucial question, then, is whether two celebrations of the Great Panathenaia (*sc.* the " previous " and the " present " occasions) are really required by the wording of D3, and to determine this we must look at the contents of this decree, and particularly at the first clause which contains the reference to " the previous Panathenaia."

A. The ekklesia is asked to vote straightway between two alternatives in regard to Methone's tribute (lines 5-9), and a note is appended that the ekklesia did so vote and chose the second alternative (lines 29-32). The two alternatives are these:

(a) shall a new assessment for Methone be made at once? Or
(b) shall Methone pay no more than Athena's quota on the amount assessed " at the previous Panathenaia "?

The phrase " the Panathenaia " clearly denotes the occasion when tribute is assessed. The Greek adjective πρότερος is a comparative, and implies priority to something *in pari materia*; ὁ πρότερος ἐνιαυτός is the year before the present year, τὰ πρότερα Παναθήναια are the Panathenaia before the present Panathenaia.[5] Kirchhoff's conclusion, that D3 belongs to the time of the Panathenaia (that is, most likely, to the first prytany of the year), seems to us cogent.[6] He believed it was the celebration of

---

[5] This has been well argued by Kirchhoff, *Abh. Ak. Berlin*, 1861, p. 589. We are not prepared to assert that πρότερος has invariably this strict comparative sense, but it is because it is to be expected that we have questioned the reading [πρότε]ρον in D14, VI, lines 9-10 (*A. T. L.*, II, p. 67). West's formulation, therefore, " the decree states that there had been an assessment *at the last Panathenaic festival* " (our italics), is in our opinion wrong; *A. J. A.*, XXIX (1925), p. 440.

[6] West rejected this, because the decree provides that ambassadors shall go to Perdikkas and attempt to settle the points at issue between him and Methone, and if they fail then Perdikkas and Methone are both to send ambassadors to Athens for the Dionysia (March). " It is inconceivable that the decree contemplated deferring the settlement of the question nine months or more " (*A. J. A.*, XXIX [1925], p. 441). He thought that the decree could not have been voted more

429, the " previous Panathenaia " being that of 430, which was an assessment year.[7] It is not impossible *per se* that tribute questions (particularly, as here, an exceptional question regarding one special city) could arise in off years, at the lesser Panathenaia. But such questions would not, we think, make of those lesser Panathenaia a *comparandum* which would justify προτέροις; to put this more simply, we think that in such a case the normal Greek would be τοῖς πέρυσι Παναθηναίοις or τοῖς Παναθηναίοις τοῖς μεγάλοις. The reference to " the previous Panathenaia " implies, we believe, that the present occasion is a celebration of the Great Panathenaia.[8]

Methone, then, had been assessed in 434 but had found payment difficult and was in debt (lines 9-16). In 430 the question rises, how to lighten the burden? Shall Methone's tribute be lightened?[8] Or shall the old figure be kept with remission of all except Athena's quota? The ekklesia votes for the second course.[10]

We pass to the other clauses of D3:

B. The debts recorded against Methone in the sanides (see above, pp. 15-16) shall be treated with benevolence if Methone stays loyal, and no steps for recovery of such debts shall apply to Methone without a separate decree (another *privilegium*) in which Methone shall be named (lines 9-16).

C. Perdikkas shall be requested to allow free movement to the Methonaioi by sea and land and not to march troops through Methone's territory without leave; if no agreement is reached, Methone and Perdikkas shall both send envoys to Athens next spring (Dionysia).

than two or three months before the Dionysia. The question in fact dragged for several years. We do not think that the seven and a half months, between Panathenaia and Dionysia, were an excessive time to allow for the start of the first negotiations, their breakdown, and the preparations for the second; for the appointment of fresh delegates, their briefing, and their journey to Athens. What in fact is allowed is the remainder of summer (September-October) for the first negotiations, and if they break down the new ones shall start first thing in the spring. The ambassadors (elderly men, line 17) are probably not expected to travel in winter.

[7] *Op. cit.*, pp. 591-592.

[8] Compare the phrase ἐκ Παναθηναίων ἐς Παναθήναια in connection with the financial quadrennium, *e. g.*, D2, lines 27-28. Down to 430, there had been an assessment regularly at the Great Panathenaia since 454 with the single exception of A4 in 443, for which see p. 306 below.

[9] The phrase used is εἴτε φόρον δοκεῖ τάττεν (line 6). This makes it likely that in this and earlier assessments the taktai did not make an assessment for every city but only when there was a change in amount. *Ceteris paribus*, in fact, the traditional or Aristeidean figure was retained without comment. The procedure in A9 was notoriously different, and so perhaps was it in A8 (428 B. C.) also.

[10] Similar *privilegia* were no doubt passed for Dikaia and Haison as well; these will not have been published on stone, as Methone's was not until 423 when the long series of Methone decrees was published as a whole. The consequence of D3 (and the *privilegia* for Dikaia and Haison) is seen in the ἀπαρχήν rubric of Lists 25 and 26. This gives a satisfactory clinch to our chronology, but we did not choose to argue from it, since in List 25 the rubric is restored, and the date of List 26 (though we believe it correct) is hardly certain enough to build on.

D. Perdikkas shall be informed that his credit in Athens depends on good reports from the troops at Poteidaia.

The Greek phrase in this last clause is ℎοι στρατι[ôται ℎοι] ἐμ Ποτειδ[ά]αι, and we take this to mean the army besieging Poteidaia (which did not surrender till some months later, in the winter of 430/29; Thucydides, II, 70). The phrase would be hard to understand if the Athenian colony were in existence.[11] Finally, Methone's debts (ὀφελεμάτον, plural) make it likely that Methone has been a tributary for more than one year;[12] if our interpretation of the Panathenaia is right, she was first assessed in 434. She was assessed then for 3 talents, as we know from the fact that after D3 she continues to pay a quota of 300 drachmai (List 26, II, 53), and we have restored her name against that figure in 23, II, 67.

Methone's presence in the Athenian Confederacy was evidently resented by Perdikkas (lines 18-23) and we may presume that her inclusion had been a hostile act. The first alliance between Athens and Perdikkas was probably in 436,[13] and the first breach was before 433. It was probably in 434 that Athens made her alliance with the rebel princes Derdas and Philip, and the alliance with Methone (and her assessment for tribute) in 434 was no doubt part of the same policy. There was a brief second alliance with Perdikkas in 432, and a third in 431, which lasted without open breach till 424, but was extremely hollow.[14] The two decrees of which we have substantial remains, D3 and D4, belong to this period; the covert hostility of Perdikkas is evident, and causes constant trouble to Methone. The envoys sent to compose the trouble in 430 (D3) evidently achieved little (see below, pp. 323-325) and there are two more Athenian embassies in Makedonia in 426 (D4); one of these is led by Leogoras (line 51), which is interesting in view of the relations of his son Andokides with Archelaos.[15]

The victory of Pylos momentarily restored Athens' prestige, and her confidence even more. The chief monument of this confidence is A9, and D5 is (we believe) a pendant to A9, and presumably ordered that Methone should pay tribute like other cities; since it is included in this series of documents which for the most part favour Methone (and which were no doubt inscribed at Methone's expense), the assessment

[11] West argued (*op. cit.*, p. 442) that " before the capture of the city, there were no soldiers in Potidaea "; but ἐμ Ποτειδάαι does not mean " inside the city," as *I. G.*, I², 945, line 1, shows. This was set out by Nesselhauf, *Klio*, Beiheft XXX, p. 83, note 1.

[12] So West, *op. cit.*, pp. 442-444, who, however, was reluctant to draw the full inference. We have frequently cited West's paper (written when the evidence which he did so much to put in order was still in great confusion), mostly to signify disagreement. His paper was concerned to disprove any date later than 429; we have been concerned to indicate the misapprehensions which prevented him from going back to 430. Meritt, *A. F. D.*, p. 23, followed West's chronology.

[13] For the history of Athens' relations with Perdikkas see below, pp. 313-325.

[14] In 429 Perdikkas sent 1000 troops to join the Spartan Knemos; Thucydides, II, 80, 7.

[15] Andokides, II, 11; see below, p. 325 with note 106.

may have been more moderate than most in A9. In 423, finally, Perdikkas had quarrelled with Sparta and was therefore becoming more amenable for Athens. D6 perhaps recorded some concessions gained from Perdikkas for Methone's relief, sufficiently satisfactory to justify the publication on marble of the whole series of decrees. Methone remained loyal; she provided troops against Mende in 423 (Thucydides, IV, 129, 4) and was the base for the successful invasion of Makedonia at the time of Perdikkas' last defection (VI, 7, 3).

The traditional text of D3, lines 12-13, has been ἐπι[τρέπεν τε τ]άχσιν περὶ τês πράχσεος Ἀθεναίος, meaning that, under favourable conditions, the Athenians would allow an accommodation about the collection of Methone's debts. We wish to suggest ἐπι[χορêν ἀπότ]αχσιν as a possible alternative, in which case the entire sentence would read: " As to the debts outstanding which the Methonaioi have been written down as owing to the public treasury, if they are coöperative with the Athenians as they now are and become even more so, the Athenians shall grant separate consideration about the collection of them, and if any general decree is passed about the debts on the panels it shall have nothing to do with the Methonaioi, unless there is a separate decree about the Methonaioi." We know of ἀπόταξις as the separate assessment of tribute (T19, T101a), singling out for individual treatment a city that had once been one of a group; it is a very slight extension of meaning to let the same word refer to singling out from a group one city that is to have separate treatment respecting the payment of its arrears.

CHAPTER VII

THE DELIAN SYNODS

Thucydides records that, when the Athenians assumed the hegemony, "Delos was their treasury, and the councils (synods) used to meet at the temple. At first the allies whom they led (whose hegemon they were) were autonomous and debated policy in common council (by means of synods in which all shared)" (I, 96, 2 and 97, 1 [T109]). There is no vestige of these Delian synods in the time (from 433 onwards) when Thucydides gives us a full narrative of events; the policy-making organ for the Confederacy at this time appears to be the Athenian Boule and ekklesia.[1] The disappearance of the synods is evidently a cardinal stage in Athens' usurpation of sovereignty, but Thucydides tells us no more. From the first of the two sentences quoted above it may perhaps be inferred that the Delian synods did not survive the transfer of the treasure from Delos to Athens in 454. Plutarch, *Aristides*, 25, 3 (T94), reports (probably on Theophrastos' authority) that at some time "there was a question of moving the treasure from Delos to Athens, contrary to the agreements, and the Samians made a motion to that effect; Aristeides observed that this would not be right, but it would be expedient." The scene is evidently a meeting of the synod.[2] The evidence cannot be called good, but such as it is it suggests that there was a meeting of the synod in 454, just before the treasure was moved. On this supposition, it is likely that the Delian synod was immediately replaced by the assembly of allies at the quadrennial Great Panathenaia at Athens, which we know as the occasion for the revision of tribute assessments. If so, should we suppose that in these meetings also there was (at least at first) discussion of policy, and voting?

The evidence about the voting comes from Thucydides, III, 10-11, the speech of the Mytilenaian at Olympia in 428. He makes two references to the voting, as follows:

(1) III, 10, 4-5 (T122): καὶ μέχρι μὲν ἀπὸ τοῦ ἴσου ἡγοῦντο, προθύμως εἱπόμεθα· ἐπειδὴ δὲ ἐωρῶμεν αὐτοὺς τὴν μὲν τοῦ Μήδου ἔχθραν ἀνιέντας, τὴν δὲ τῶν ξυμμάχων δούλωσιν ἐπαγομένους, οὐκ ἀδεεῖς ἔτι ἦμεν. ἀδύνατοι δὲ ὄντες καθ' ἓν γενόμενοι διὰ πολυψηφίαν ἀμύνασθαι οἱ ξύμμαχοι ἐδουλώθησαν πλὴν ἡμῶν καὶ Χίων· ἡμεῖς δὲ αὐτόνομοι δὴ ὄντες καὶ ἐλεύθεροι τῷ ὀνόματι ξυνεστρατεύσαμεν.

"So long as Athens led us like equals, we were eager to follow; but when we saw her becoming less interested in the war against Persia than in the subjection of her allies, we began to feel nervous. Since the *system of many votes* had made them

---

[1] For the original constitution of the Confederacy see below, pp. 225-233.

[2] This anecdote is further discussed below, p. 262 with notes 90-92.

138

incapable of combining to protect themselves, all of the allies except us and Chios were subjected; we two continued to serve in her campaigns, the so-called ' free and autonomous allies '."

(2) III, 11, 3-4 (T123) : αὐτόνομοί τε ἐλείφθημεν οὐ δι' ἄλλο τι ἢ ὅσον αὐτοῖς ἐς τὴν ἀρχὴν εὐπρεπείᾳ τε λόγου καὶ γνώμης μᾶλλον ἐφόδῳ ἢ ἰσχύος τὰ πράγματα ἐφαίνετο καταληπτά. ἅμα μὲν γὰρ μαρτυρίῳ ἐχρῶντο μὴ ἂν τούς γε ἰσοψήφους ἄκοντας, εἰ μή τι ἠδίκουν οἷς ἐπῆσαν, ξυστρατεύειν · ἐν τῷ αὐτῷ δὲ καὶ τὰ κράτιστα ἐπί τε τοὺς ὑποδεεστέρους πρώτους ξυνεπῆγον καὶ τὰ τελευταῖα λιπόντες τοῦ ἄλλου περιῃρημένου ἀσθενέστερα ἔμελλον ἕξειν.

" Our autonomy was spared for reasons of propaganda; Athens realized that opinion counts in power politics far more than force. We were standing witnesses to her character (surely allies who have an equal vote could not be forced [3] to take part in campaigns unless the parties attacked were in the wrong) ; and at the same time,[4] while she was using us (the strong to crush the weak) she was also reserving us to the last, knowing that the strong when isolated would no longer be so strong."

For the system of voting, we may infer from these passages that every city, small and great, had one vote, and probably that Athens had the same. The " system of many votes " caused the powerful cities (Mytilene, Chios, etc.) to be outvoted by the many insignificant cities which were under Athens' thumb; Mytilene's " equal vote " is no doubt (in the context of the second passage) equal in particular to Athens' vote (cf. III, 79, 3), but that it was also equal to the vote of any other city is perhaps a fair inference from the use of the same word in I, 141, 6.[5] Such a general equality is also implied, of course, in " the system of many votes."

Perikles (in I, 141, 6) names this system of voting as one of the disadvantages of the Peloponnesians in comparison with Athens. We may conclude with certainty that neither the Delian synod nor its Panathenaic successor (if such there was) still voted in this way in 432, nor consequently in 428, when the Mytilenaian makes his speech. The Mytilenaian, then, insists on the hollow speciousness of a system which the audience he was addressing did in fact use, and does not make the much simpler point that Athens had abolished even that show of liberty.

Nothing much can be inferred concerning date. It is surprising that the speaker dwells so much on the past and especially on a system of voting which was certainly obsolete when he spoke. One possible reason for the obliqueness of his whole argument

---

[3] The exact sense of this difficult ἄκοντας is not material for our purpose.

[4] The words ἅμα μέν — — — ἐν τῷ αὐτῷ δέ (cf. IV, 73, 2) combine to make these two processes (the standing witness to character, and the strong helping to crush the weak) parallel, if not strictly contemporaneous.

[5] From this passage (I, 141, 6) we learn that the cities of the Peloponnesian League were also all ἰσόψηφοι, " equal-voting "; and this is confirmed in I, 125, 1, ψῆφον ἐπήγαγον τοῖς ξυμμάχοις ἅπασιν ὅσοι παρῆσαν ἑξῆς, καὶ μείζονι καὶ ἐλάσσονι πόλει.

may be suggested, namely, that he is meeting the criticism, " Why did Lesbos do what she did in the Samian War? " Lesbos and Chios had joined with Athens in that war, providing 25 ships.[6] His answer is, " We had no choice, it is a mere pretense that we had ever had freedom of choice." Both the passages quoted above describe a process which culminated in the Samian War. In the first, the subjection of all the allies except Lesbos and Chios must include the Samian War; the helplessness which let Athens subject them one by one was a consequence of the system of voting. In the second, the time for protesting against Athens' encroachments had been while she was still dealing with weaker powers, before the Samian War; but again the system of voting had made that impracticable. It is not unlikely that the participation of Chios and Lesbos had weighed in the discussion in the Peloponnesian synod in 440, as an indication that Samos had a bad case; why had not Lesbos protested? The speaker makes the rather poor point that in the past such protests had always been outvoted.

It is most improbable that there was any sort of synod, whether at Delos or Athens, which voted upon the Samian War.[7] On the other hand, the speaker does not specify that the voting he mentions was at Delos; and the later we can bring the actual practice of voting the less irrelevant the references to it become. We suggest tentatively that the system of voting was not dropped abruptly in 454, when the treasure was moved and the Delian routine was exchanged for a new Athenian routine. Votes may have been taken at the Great Panathenaia in 454 and 450, and perhaps at Lesser Panathenaia or Dionysia. We see no way of judging when the last vote was taken; but between 449 and 445 the signs accumulate that Athens is purposing to usurp sovereignty, to exchange her " hegemony " for " tyranny," and by 432 the system was certainly obsolete.

Is it possible that the Spartan demand in 432 that Athens restore autonomy to the Greeks (I, 139, 3; 140, 3) concealed a demand for the restoration of the synod?[8] If so, Perikles' answer (I, 144, 2) is partly that the synods had lapsed before the Thirty Years' Peace, partly that the Peloponnesian synods were manipulated for Sparta's interests.

Of the exact limits of the synod's competence we are very ill-informed. *A priori* it is likely that its competence resembled that of the Peloponnesian synod; if it did

---

[6] Thucydides, I, 116, 2. The demand was sent during the battle of Tragia (116, 1); it was perhaps Sophokles who fetched the Lesbian contingent (see Ion, in Athenaios, XIII, 81 [603e-f]). The first Lesbian proposals to Sparta (before 431, Thucydides, III, 2, 1 and 13, 1) were no doubt later than this.

[7] There was no doubt a vote in the ekklesia. Plutarch's words (*Pericles*, 25, 1), τὸν δὲ πρὸς Σαμίους πόλεμον --- τὸν Περικλέα ψηφίσασθαι, may mean that this was one of Perikles' psephismata (*Pericles*, 8, 7). A vote in the ekklesia would not of course exclude a synod vote.

[8] See the association of autonomy and synods in Thucydides, I, 97, 1; and perhaps of αὐτόνομοι and ἰσοψήφους in III, 11, 3-4. It would give added point to Perikles' jibes at the Peloponnesian synods in I, 141, 6-7.

not, then Thucydides' very general phrase, ἀπὸ κοινῶν ξυνόδων βουλευόντων, will not help us to determine the exact difference.[9] The hegemonic power was surely protected somehow against being outvoted and compelled to execute a policy which it disapproved (against finding itself, in fact, in the position of Archidamos in 432/1, or Nikias in 415). Possibly the members trusted in what the Romans called *auctoritas*. Larsen (note 2 on p. 194) observes that, *e. g.*, in 432 the vote of the Peloponnesian synod was preceded by a vote of the Spartan ekklesia (Thucydides, I, 87; 118, 3; 119; 125, 1); but certain things (*e. g.*, the word βούλεσθαι in I, 87, 4) suggest that this was not an automatic routine. The Spartan members presided in the Peloponnesian synod (I, 125, 1: οἱ δὲ Λακεδαιμόνιοι - - - ψῆφον ἐπήγαγον; cf. 87, 4) and we do not doubt that the Athenian members did in the Delian; perhaps the simplest is to suppose that neither of them would put a motion of which they disapproved. The hegemon, then, had what in Athens would be called " probouleutic " power.

[9] Larsen, *Harv. Stud. Cl. Phil.*, LI (1940), p. 196, note 1, says that this word βουλευόντων, " unless the reader is misled by the usage in other symmachies, can mean only that the policy of the League was determined by the assembly " (*i. e.*, by what we call the synod). We think indeed that it was; but we cannot see how the word compels this, nor how so general a word as βουλευόντων can be given precise content in any other way than by the analogy of comparable (but better known) institutions.

CHAPTER VIII

EXTERNAL CONTROL AND TRIBUTE COLLECTION [1]

The relations between Athens and the cities of the Confederacy were essentially individualistic. Even in the beginning, when the synod first met on Delos to discuss common policy, the Athenians were given the mandate of deciding which cities should furnish ships and which should pay money in support of the war against Persia.

The position of direct administrative responsibility thus created was strengthened with the changing development of the Confederacy, which served only to weaken the bonds of common administrative effort and to emphasize the separate status of each member. Rebellion was individually suppressed, and commutation of ships to money in fulfillment of confederate pledges was individually negotiated.

When the synod no longer met on Delos, there were, it is true, Athenian decrees and regulations which applied generally to all cities,[2] or to groups of cities,[3] but each city was held individually responsible for obedience even to a general rule. The paramount agent for the enforcement of law and order was, of course, the Athenian navy, which also played a considerable rôle, especially during the Archidamian War, in the collection of the tribute.[4] Aristotle speaks of twenty patrol ships after the commencement of the war,[5] but the duties of the navy went far beyond what these could do, and are sufficiently obvious and so well attested that they need no further documentation here.

The first evidence of the more intimate details of the Athenian pattern of control is found in the Regulations for Erythrai (D10),[6] which mention the presence of

---

[1] See Gomme, *Commentary*, I, pp. 380-385.

[2] *E. g.*, D7, D8, D14, *I. G.*, I², 76. Reference to these κοινὰ ψηφίσματα περὶ τῶν ξυμμάχων appears in D4, lines 41-44 (cf. also D3, lines 13-15). Every assessment decree was generally applicable, though the amounts of tribute were individually assessed.

[3] Like the cities in Thrace; *I. G.*, I², 45, lines 16-17 (T78c).

[4] See Thucydides, II, 69, 1; III, 19; IV, 50, 1; IV, 75, 1-2 (T119, T125, T130, T133); Aristophanes, *Knights*, 1070-1072, with scholia (T35-37); Xenophon, *Hell.*, I, 1, 8 (T158); cf. also Aristotle, Ἀθ. Πολ., 24, 3, ἄλλαι δὲ νῆες αἱ τοὺς φόρους ἄγουσαι τοὺς ἀπὸ τοῦ κυάμου δισχιλίους ἄνδρας, where φόρους has sometimes been emended to φρουρούς. But see above, p. xi.

[5] Ἀθ. Πολ., 24, 3: νῆες δὲ φρουρίδες εἴκοσι.

[6] One can make only the most general inference from the mention of a φυλακή in the early decree which deals with Aigina (*I. G.*, I², 18). Hiller's note (*ad loc.*) suggests that this φυλακή was a garrison of Peloponnesians which the terms of capitulation expelled from the island, and Cloché, *Rev. Belge*, XXV (1946-1947), p. 54, note 2, assumes much the same thing: "Cette inscription, très mutilée, fait allusion, semble-t-il, à la garnison que les Péloponésiens avaient installée dans Egine (l. 3 et l. 9-10), aux stipulations de la capitulation (l. 4) et à la défense de porter préjudice aux intérêts d'Athènes (l. 6)." It seems to us more probable that it refers to Athenian

inspectors and a garrison-commander. They were to choose by lot and then establish the new Erythraian Council.[7] The existence of the garrison-commander implies also a garrison of military personnel (φρουροί), and these are, in fact, named in the same inscription.[8] The inspectors and the commander had other duties as well, the nature of the former's being now lost to us because of the fracture of the stone (line 50) but those of the latter having to do with the security of Erythrai (lines 38-39), the receiving of the oath, and the setting up of the stele,[9] and, in time to come, with assistance to each retiring Council in the choice by lot of its successor.[10] We know also of Athenian φρουροί in Miletos in 450,[11] and of φρουροί in Samos in 440 who were taken by the rebellious Samians and handed over to Persia.[12] The establishment of garrisons must have been a common practice in enforcing discipline as well as in securing military control,[13] and they were among the instruments of Athenian supremacy which earned the odium of later generations.[14] These garrisons were an infringement of the sovereignty of the cities on whom they were quartered, and it was primarily against them that provisions for " autonomy " of the cities of Asia Minor were written into the terms of the Peace of Kallias, as stipulated by the Great King, and into the Peace of Nikias, as stipulated by the Spartans for certain cities which had sided with her in Thrace against the Athenians. In point of fact φρουροί and φρούραρχοι are not known in Asia Minor while the Peace of Kallias was valid.[15] The garrison-commander whose duties at Erythrai were laid down " for the future " in 452 could not have survived 449. But the Athenians were able to circumvent this

defense after the subjugation, like the φυλακή in D17, lines 76-77, after the suppression of Euboia. Cf. Gomme, *Commentary*, I, p. 319.

[7] D10, lines 12-14: [ἀπο]κναμεῦσαι [δ]ὲ καὶ καταστῆσαι τὲν μὲν νῦν βολὲν τός τ' [ἐπισκ]όπος καὶ [τὸν] φρ[ό]ραρχον.

[8] D10, line 55: φρορο͂ις.

[9] If the restorations in D10, lines 69 and 75, are correct.

[10] D10, lines 14-15: τὸ δὲ λοιπὸν τὲν βολὲν καὶ τὸν [φρόρ]αρχον.

[11] D11, line 77: φρουρόν. See also φρορίδε in line 87 and [φ]ύλακες in line 85; this latter might be read as [φ]υλακὲς (cf. D10, line 39; *I. G.*, I², 105, line 19; and note 6 above).

[12] Thucydides, I, 115, 5: καὶ τοὺς φρουροὺς τοὺς Ἀθηναίων καὶ τοὺς ἄρχοντας οἳ ἦσαν παρὰ σφίσιν ἐξέδοσαν Πισσούθνῃ (T112).

[13] Lykon of Achaia was granted a dispensation by the Athenians (*I. G.*, I², 93, lines 11-17): τὴν δὲ ναῦν ἣν δῆται ἐκκομίσασθαι ἐξ Ἀχαΐας ἐκκομισάσθω καὶ ἐξεῖναι αὐτῶι πλὲν καὶ χρήματα ἐσάγεν ὅσης Ἀθηναῖοι κρατο͂σι, καὶ ἐς τὰ Ἀθην[α]ίων φρόρια.

[14] Plutarch, *Solon*, 15, 2 (T97e): ἃ δ' οὖν οἱ νεώτεροι τοὺς Ἀθηναίους λέγουσι τὰς τῶν πραγμάτων δυσχερείας ὀνόμασι χρηστοῖς καὶ φιλανθρώποις ἐπικαλύπτοντας ἀστείως ὑποκορίζεσθαι, τὰς μὲν πόρνας ἑταίρας, τοὺς δὲ φόρους συντάξεις, φυλακὰς δὲ τὰς φρουρὰς τῶν πόλεων, οἴκημα δὲ τὸ δεσμωτήριον καλοῦντας. Cf. Gomme, *Commentary*, I, p. 385.

[15] The garrison at Samos in 440 (Thucydides, I, 115, 5 [T112]) was not, by definition, in the King's domain; the terms of the peace applied to garrisons on the mainland only. In the fourth century Timotheos, though acting under explicit orders to respect the terms of the Peace of Antalkidas, yet besieged and conquered Samos (cf. Klee, in P. W., *R. E.*, *s. v.* Timotheos [3], p. 1327).

embarrassment by the expedient of colonization. The colony which went out to Erythrai a year or two later took, in effect, the place of the garrison.[16]

The inspectors, likewise, infringed on sovereignty, potentially, at least, wherever they were sent. Theophrastos, at any rate, linked them with the φρουραί,[17] as did also D10 (453/2) in a context which leaves no doubt about their interference in matters of local government. In D7 they were given joint responsibility with the ἄρχοντες ἐν τῇσι πόλεσι and the Council in making sure each year that the tribute was paid to Athens. Aristophanes ridiculed them in the *Birds* as pompous officials, and the treatment of the inspector who arrived at Cloud-Cuckoo-land proves how little welcome they found in the cities of the Empire.[18] But Aristophanes also shows that they counted on the support of local Athenian proxenoi, that they were interested in legal and political affairs, and that they expected to be treated with deference. We do not know whether there were inspectors in the cities of Asia Minor after the treaty with Persia. They were not soldiers, or even police, and the terms of the treaty seem to have been directed against Athenian military occupation. If a colony could remain, or be established, on the mainland of Asia after 449, as we now know to have been true at least in Erythrai and Kolophon, it is likely that an inspector could remain. His influence probably depended on moral suasion and influence through friends (proxenoi), supported by the threat of force if Athenian laws about the Empire were not obeyed or if the tribute was not duly paid. The Decree of Kleinias (D7) emphasized the duty of the inspectors in guaranteeing the collection of tribute;[19] doubtless the question of " autonomy " did not arise so long as the tribute was regularly sent to Athens.[20] One thinks inevitably of the well-known phrase of the later Peace of Nikias (T134): τὰς δὲ πόλεις φερούσας τὸν φόρον τὸν ἐπ' Ἀριστείδου αὐτονόμους εἶναι. We believe that a city subject to a garrison was not autonomous, but

[16] See below, pp. 283-284 with note 39.

[17] Harpokration cites Antiphon for his use of the word ἐπίσκοπος and quotes from Theophrastos (T65): Θεόφραστος γοῦν ἐν α′ τῶν πολιτικῶν τῶν πρὸς καιρούς φησιν οὕτω· πολλῷ γὰρ κάλλιον κατά γε τὴν τοῦ ὀνόματος θέσιν, ὡς οἱ Λάκωνες ἁρμοστὰς φάσκοντες εἰς τὰς πόλεις πέμπειν, οὐκ ἐπισκόπους οὐδὲ φύλακας, ὡς Ἀθηναῖοι. Theophrastos used the fourth-century word (see note 14 above), whether φύλακας or φυλακάς, instead of φρουρούς or φρουράς. Suidas (T102) has a definition almost the same as that of Harpokration, and obviously derived also from Theophrastos: ἐπίσκοπος· οἱ παρ' Ἀθηναίων εἰς τὰς ἐπηκόους πόλεις ἐπισκέψασθαι τὰ παρ' ἑκάστοις πεμπόμενοι ἐπίσκοποι καὶ φύλακες ἐκαλοῦντο· οὓς οἱ Λάκωνες ἁρμοστὰς ἔλεγον. But Suidas has contaminated the definition by giving to φύλακες and ἐπίσκοποι the explanation which belongs to ἐπίσκοποι alone. The φρουροί, who were called φύλακες by later writers, were under a military commander (φρούραρχος); the ἐπίσκοποι, by definition and function, seem rather to have been civilian personnel.

[18] Aristophanes, *Birds*, 1021-1034 (cf. T29).

[19] D7 also implies that they were general imperial officers, and gives no hint that they were excluded from Asia.

[20] There were plural ἐπίσκοποι in Erythrai (D10, lines 13-14); Aristophanes, *Birds*, 1033-1034, implies that this was the general rule: οὐ δεινά; καὶ πέμπουσιν ἤδη ἐπισκόπους εἰς τὴν πόλιν, πρὶν καὶ τεθύσθαι τοῖς θεοῖς;

that a city with inspectors might be, so long as good behaviour permitted them, as it were, to remain aloof.

Closely associated with the inspectors were the " archons in the cities." They had general supervision of Athenian interests, numbering among their obligations not only the enforcement of Athenian decrees which affected the Empire [21] and assistance in sending the tribute to Athens,[22] but also the protection of individuals to whom the Athenian state extended its special care.[23] The archons, as a magistracy of Athenians, are specifically attested for Miletos,[24] Samos,[25] Lesbos,[26] Skiathos,[27] Kos,[28] Methone,[29] and indirectly for Limnai and Agora.[30] It is evident from the Decree of Klearchos (D14) that not every city had an Athenian board, for provision is there made for enforcement by local archons in those cities where no Athenian archons were in residence (§ 4), and it is also clear, we believe, from the terms of D21 [31] that there was no Athenian board in, for example, Therambos. Therambos was a small town, and could hardly have been expected to contribute to the support of the Athenian board in Aphytis if it maintained at the same time an Athenian board of its own. The

[21] Like the Decree of Klearchos (cf. D14, §§ 1 and 4). We have assumed also that they assisted the heralds in the proclamation of the tribute assessment of 425 B. C. (A9, line 42); cf. above, p. 76.

[22] D7, lines 5-11: [τὲ]μ βολὲν καὶ τὸς ἄρχ[οντας ἐν] τῆσι πόλεσι καὶ τὸς [ἐπισκό]πος ἐπιμέλεσθαι hόπ[ος ἂν χσ]υλλέγεται ho φόρος κ[ατὰ τὸ ἔ]τος hέκαστον καὶ ὑπά[γεται] Ἀθέναζε. Probably this function of the ἄρχοντες lies behind the statement in Bekker's *Anecdota* (T44): ἐκλογεῖς· οἱ ἐκλέγοντες τοὺς φόρους, ἵνα οἱ ἄρχοντες λάβωσιν.

[23] See *I. G.*, I², 56, lines 2-9 (cf. T78b), a decree in honour of Leonidas of Halikarnassos: ἐ[π]ιμέλεσθαι δὲ αὐτῦ Ἀθένεσι μ[ὲ]ν τὸς πρυτάνες καὶ τὲμ βολέν, ἐν δὲ τῆσι ἄλλεσι πόλεσι hοίτινες Ἀθεναίον ἄρχοσι ἐν τῆι hυπεροψίαι hό, τι ἂν hέκαστοι δυνατοὶ ὄσιν, hος ἂμ μὲ ἀδικῶνται; *I. G.*, I², 108, lines 45-46 (T77), a decree honouring the city of Neapolis in Thrace: καὶ τὸς ἄρχ[οντ]ας τοὺς Ἀθεναίον hοὶ ἂν hεκ[άστοτε ἄρχοσι τὸν συμμάχ]ον (sc. ἐπιμέλεσθαι αὐτόν); *I. G.*, I², 118, lines 15-20 (T78), a decree honouring Oiniades of Palaiskiathos: καὶ ὅπως ἂν μὴ ἀδικῆται ἐπιμέλεσθαι τήν τε βολὴν τὴν ἀεὶ βουλεύοσαν καὶ τοὺς στρατηγὸς καὶ τὸν ἄρχοντα τὸν ἐν Σκιάθωι ὃς ἂν ἦι ἑκάστοτε. Cf. also *I. G.*, I², 68/69, lines 12-14, for protection to the Boiotians, as restored by Meritt in *S. E. G.*, X, 81.

[24] D11, line 41: [π]ρὸς τὸς ἄρχοντας τὸς Ἀθ[εναίον], and line 47: [h]οι ἄρχοντες hοι Ἀθενα[ίον].

[25] Thucydides, I, 115, 5 (T112): καὶ τοὺς φρουροὺς τοὺς Ἀθηναίων καὶ τοὺς ἄρχοντας οἳ ἦσαν παρὰ σφίσιν ἐξέδοσαν Πισσούθνῃ. Aristotle's notice (Ἀθ. Πολ., 24, 2 [T40]) that the Athenians did not interfere in the government of Samos must apply to a time earlier than 440 B. C.: πεισθέντες δὲ ταῦτα καὶ λαβόντες τὴν ἀρχὴν τοῖς [τε] συμμάχοις δεσποτικωτέρως ἐχρῶντο, πλὴν Χίων καὶ Λεσβίων καὶ Σαμίων· τούτους δὲ φύλακας εἶχον τῆς ἀρχῆς ἐῶντες τάς τε πολιτείας παρ' αὐτοῖς, καὶ ἄρχειν ὧν ἔτυχον ἄρχοντες.

[26] Antiphon, περὶ τοῦ Ἡρῴδου φόνου, 47 (T10): τοῖς ἄρχουσι τοῖς ὑμετέροις παραδοῦναι. Aristotle's reference to Lesbos, quoted in the preceding note, refers to a time earlier than 428 B. C.

[27] *I. G.*, I², 118 (T78); see above, note 23.

[28] Thucydides, VIII, 108, 2 (T153): ταῦτα δὲ πράξας (Alkibiades) καὶ ἄρχοντα ἐν τῇ Κῷ καταστήσας.

[29] D21, lines 6-8: τὸς δὲ ἄρχοντας σι[τοδοτό]ντων τὸς ἐν Ἄ[φυτι παρ' ἑαυτῶ]ν Θραμβαῖοι κατὰ [τ]ὸ πλῆθος· σ[υντελ]όντων δὲ καὶ α[ἱ ἄλλαι πόλε]ις καθάπερ Μεθωναίοις κατὰ τὸ [αὐτὸ]ν ψήφισμα. For the interpretation of the text see Meritt, *Hesperia*, XIII (1944), pp. 218-219.

[30] Cf. rubric XI (*A. T. L.*, I, p. 454: πόλεις αἵδε ἀρχαῖς ἔδοσαν τὸν φόρον). See also the commentary on rubric I, *A. T. L.*, I, p. 449.

[31] See note 29 above.

archons in Therambos thus furnish one certain example of the contingency envisaged in the clause of D14: [καὶ εἰ μ]ή εἰσι[ν] ἄρχοντες Ἀθηναίων (§ 4). The decision about which cities should have an Athenian (or Athenians) quartered upon them was in the competence of the Athenian assembly, and measures to ensure their support were stipulated in Athenian decrees.[32] Altogether, the " archons of the Athenians " and the inspectors must have counted for some hundreds of Athenian citizens serving in an official capacity as magistrates overseas. Aristotle says categorically that the ὑπερόριοι ἀρχαί occupied 700 Athenians, and though the figure has been questioned because it repeats his earlier estimate of the number of Athenian magistrates at home we see no reason to doubt that it may have been substantially correct.[33]

The decrees by which Athens controlled her Empire were sometimes proposed by individual orators, and, if so, they came to be known in the usual terminology by the authors' names, each decree being called τὸ ψήφισμα ὃ ὁ δεῖνα εἶπε. The Decree of Klearchos (D14) is a good example of this type of reference (§ 12). But frequently the regulations of the Empire were drafted by commissioners (ξυγγραφεῖς). Under these circumstances the resultant decree could not be named for any one man; it had to be named in the next best way, possibly by the name of the archon, or by the name of the secretary, in whose term of office it was passed. The covenant between Athens and the cities of Bottike (I. G., I², 90), for example, was to be inscribed on stelai which carried the name of the archon (lines 21-30):[34] τὰς δὲ χσυνθέκας τά[σδε καὶ] τὸν [hόρκον κατα]θέναι Ἀθεναῖος μὲν ἐμ πόλε[ι ἀναγρά]φσ[αντας ἐστέλει] λιθίνει καὶ τὰ ὀν[ό]ματα τὸν [πόλεον] τὸ[ν Βοττιαίον τ]ὸν χσυντιθεμένον τὲν φιλία[ν καὶ τὲν χσυμμαχίαν· κα]ὶ ἐπιγράφσαι ἐν τ[ε͂]ι στέλει τὸ ἄ[ρχοντος τὸ ὄνομα, ἐφ' ὅ] ἐγένοντο αἱ χσ[υ]ν[θ]ε͂και· Βοττια[ῖοι δ' ἐν στέλαις λιθί]ναις ἀναγράφ[σαντ]ες καταθέντ[ον ἐν τοῖς hιεροῖς κ]ατὰ πόλες, ἐπι[γράφσ]αντες ἐν ταῖ[ς στέλαις τὸν ἀρχόν]τον τὰ ὀνόμα[τα τὸν Β]οττιαίον. Such a covenant could be referred to later in Athens as αἱ ξυνθῆκαι αἳ ἐγένοντο ἐπὶ τοῦ δεῖνος ἄρχοντος. Or, to distinguish it from other covenants of the same year, the reference might have been more full, including a brief description: αἱ ξυνθῆκαι αἳ ἐπὶ τοῦ δεῖνος ἄρχοντος ἐγένοντο περὶ τῶν πόλεων τῶν Βοττιαίων. Sometimes the secretary, rather than the archon, gave his name to the decree. No archon is named, for example, in I. G., I², 76, which deals with the first-fruits to be consecrated at Eleusis. Nor is there an orator; the decree was introduced on motion of the commissioners. When Lampon moved an amendment in the ekklesia he quite correctly and precisely called the original motion ξυγγραφαί and his own amendment a ψήφισμα. He had no need to bother about a date, for everyone knew the motion to which he

---

[32] Cf. D21, lines 12-14, with the reference to an Athenian ψήφισμα. Aristophanes alludes to the establishment of these Athenian boards when he represents the ψηφισματοπώλης (Birds, 1049-1050 [T31]) as quoting from a decree: " ἐὰν δέ τις ἐξελαύνῃ τοὺς ἄρχοντας καὶ μὴ δέχηται κατὰ τὴν στήλην - - -."

[33] Ἀθ. Πολ., 24, 3: ἀρχαὶ δ' ἔνδημοι μὲν εἰς ἐπτακοσίους ἄνδρας, ὑπερόριοι δ' εἰς ἐπτακοσίους.

[34] For the text see also Meritt, Hesperia, VII (1938), p. 81.

was speaking; but he did specify that the regulations were those which dealt with the grain (lines 47-48: αἱ χσυγγραφαὶ τὲς ἀπαρχὲς τὸ καρπὸ τοῖν θεοῖν) because he himself intended to introduce new ξυγγραφαί about olive oil at a subsequent session. For the Athenians in antiquity the full reference to *I. G.*, I², 76 was αἱ ξυγγραφαὶ αἳ ἐπὶ Τιμοτέλους γραμματεύοντος ἐγένοντο περὶ τῆς ἀπαρχῆς τοῦ καρποῦ τοῖν θεοῖν.

So it is with the ξυγγραφαί mentioned in *I. G.*, I², 45, lines 13-17 (T78c). Like the ξυγγραφαί of *I. G.*, I², 76, these ξυγγραφαί must have been dated by the name of the secretary in whose prytany the decree was passed, and whose name (as in *I. G.*, I², 76) presumably stood in large letters at the top of the stele. There are several possibilities of restoration of the name; so we read simply: ἐὰν δέ τις ἐπιστρα[τεύει ἐπὶ τὲν γὲ]ν τὲν τὸν ἀποίκον, βοεθὲν τὰ[ς πόλες hος ὀχσύ]τατα κατὰ τὰς χσυγγραφὰς ha[ὶ ἐπὶ ....⁸....]το γραμματεύοντος ἐγένον[το περὶ τὸν πόλε]ον τὸν ἐπὶ Θράικες.³⁵

The naming of "cities Thraceward" does not imply that there was a Thrakian administrative district,³⁶ but the fact of the ξυγγραφαί shows that some cities in Thrace had been grouped together with an obligation to defend Athenian outposts in case of attack. We learn from D21 that cities in geographical proximity to Methone were grouped in one decree, and D21 itself uses the Methone decree for reference and defines the same group, adding Therambos. These references were all picked up later in D4 (426/5), in which Methone was excused from blanket imperial regulations (lines 41-47): hό, τι δ' ἂν κοινὸν φσήφ[ισμα π]ερὶ τὸν χσυμμάχο[ν] φσεφίζονται Ἀθεναῖοι πε[ρὶ βοε]θείας ἒ ἄ[λ]λο τι προ[σ]τάττο[ν]τες τὲσι πόλεσι ἒ [περὶ σ]φὸν [ἒ] περὶ τὸν πόλεον, hό, τι ἂν ὀνομαστὶ περὶ τ[ὲς πόλε]ος τὲ[ς] Μεθοναίον φσεφίζονται τοῦτο προσέ[κεν αὐτοῖ]ς, τ[ὰ] δὲ ἄλλα μέ, ἀλλὰ φυλάττοντες τὲν σφετ[έραν αὐτὸν ἐ]ν τὸι τεταγμένοι ὄντον. Here, as in *I. G.*, I², 45, the requirement of military aid was paramount.

At the outbreak of the Archidamian War, the Athenians established a number of permanent garrisons.³⁷ One of these, we happen to know, was on the small island of Atalante off the coast of Opountian Lokris.³⁸ We know also of the garrisons which later blockaded the Peloponnesos, but they belong to the story of the war rather than to the management of the Empire, and are not here discussed. It is possible that the Ἑλλησποντοφύλακες, the garrison of the Hellespont, were established at this time. They appear in D4, lines 36-37 (426/5), and had control of shipments of grain through the straits.

Well into the Archidamian War the Athenians had depended on their inspectors,

³⁵ See now *S. E. G.*, X, 34.

³⁶ Schaefer, *Hermes*, LXXIV (1939), pp. 246-247, lays correct emphasis on the exclusively geographical significance of the reference.

³⁷ Thucydides, II, 24, 1 (D20): ἀναχωρησάντων δὲ αὐτῶν οἱ Ἀθηναῖοι φυλακὰς κατεστήσαντο κατὰ γῆν καὶ κατὰ θάλασσαν, ὥσπερ δὴ ἔμελλον διὰ παντὸς τοῦ πολέμου φυλάξειν.

³⁸ Thucydides, II, 32: ἐτειχίσθη δὲ καὶ Ἀταλάντη ὑπὸ Ἀθηναίων φρούριον τοῦ θέρους τούτου τελευτῶντος, ἡ ἐπὶ Λοκροῖς τοῖς Ὀπουντίοις νῆσος ἐρήμη πρότερον οὖσα, τοῦ μὴ λῃστὰς ἐκπλέοντας ἐξ Ὀποῦντος καὶ τῆς ἄλλης Λοκρίδος κακουργεῖν τὴν Εὔβοιαν.

the archons in the cities, and (when needed) on the fleet, to insure the payment of tribute. But early in 426/5 a decree was proposed by Kleonymos (D8) establishing in the cities of the Empire local boards of " collectors " (φόρου ἐκλογεῖς) who would underwrite the contributions of their respective cities and see that the collections were made.[39] These have been cited by the lexicographers,[40] and we believe that in D23 there is an epigraphical reference (though the text is restored) to the local board at Knidos. It is surprising that the dictionaries refer only to collectors of the tribute, for there were also similar boards of collectors of the grain. In I. G., I², 76 the allied cities were ordered to select such boards (lines 14-16): τὰς δὲ πόλες [ἐγ]λ[ο]γέας hελέσθαι τὸ καρπὸ, καθότι ἂν δοκεῖ αὐτέσι ἄριστα ὁ καρπὸ[ς] ἐγλεγέσεσθαι. The rendering of first-fruits at Eleusis was made compulsory for the allies, but an invitation was extended to the whole Greek world (line 30-31: καὶ τέσι ἄλλεσι πόλεσιν [τ]ê[σι] hε[λ]λενικêσιν ἁπάσεσι). These two aspects of the decree, compulsion for the Empire and a hospitable welcome for all others, bring to mind the earlier Decree of Klearchos about uniform coinage, weights, and measures. The allies were ordered to conform; an invitation to do so was extended to the rest. It is quite probable also that Lampon's proposed decree about the first-fruits of olive oil became law, that the same opportunity for participation was given to the Greeks at large, and that there were within the Empire ἐκλογεῖς τοῦ ἐλαίου as well as τοῦ φόρου and τοῦ καρποῦ. These offerings at Eleusis were an additional religious bond between Athens and her allies, supplementing the already long-standing obligation, which they shared with colonists,[41] of sending a cow and a panoply of arms to the Great Panathenaia.[42]

After 414 B. C. the adoption of the 5 per cent tax made necessary the appointment of new collectors. Aristophanes (*Frogs*, 363 [T34]) speaks of an εἰκοστολόγος on Aigina in 406/5. Evidently the tax was being collected even where tribute had not been assessed, for Aigina had paid no tribute since its colonization in 431. But we do not know whether the tax was collected after 410 from cities that also paid tribute according to the reassessment of that year.[43]

---

[39] See Meritt, *D. A. T.*, pp. 3-42.

[40] Bekker's *Anecdota*, *s. v.* ἐκλογεῖς (T44), has: οἱ ἐκλέγοντες τοὺς φόρους, ἵνα οἱ ἄρχοντες λάβωσιν. ὠνομάσθησαν ἀπὸ τοῦ ἐκλέγειν, ὅ πέρ ἐστι πράττεσθαι καὶ ἀπαιτεῖν; the *Etymologicum Magnum* (T62) reads: ἐκλογεῖς· οἱ ἐκλέγοντες τοὺς φόρους· ἀπὸ τοῦ ἐκλέγειν τὸ πράττεσθαι καὶ ἀπαιτεῖν; Harpokration (T66): νῦν δὲ πρὸς τοὺς ἐκλογέας τοῦ φόρου ἅπαντα ἀπογραφόμεθα; and Suidas (T100): ἐκλογεῖς· οἱ ἐκλέγοντες καὶ εἰσπράττοντες τὰ ὀφειλόμενα τῷ δημοσίῳ. ὁπότε δέοι χρήματα τοὺς πολίτας εἰσφέρειν, τούτους κατὰ δύναμιν οἱ καλούμενοι ἐκλογεῖς διέγραφον. ἀλλὰ καὶ οἱ τοὺς φόρους ἀπὸ τῶν ὑπηκόων ἀθροίζοντες πόλεων οὕτως ἐλέγοντο.

[41] I. G., I², 45, lines 11-13 (of the colony sent to Brea in 447/6): βοῦν δὲ καὶ π[ανhοπλίαν ἀπά]γεν ἐς Παναθέναια τὰ μεγάλ[α καὶ ἐς Διονύσι]α φαλλόν. Cf. also A9, lines 57-58 (of the duties of the allies): πεμπόντον δ[ὲ ἐν] τêι πομπêι [καθάπερ ἄποι]κ[οι]. We do not follow Wilhelm's suggestion (*Abh. Ak. Berlin*, 1939-1940, no. 22, p. 5) that [μετὰ τὸς ἀποί]κ[ος] should be restored, signifying the order of precedence in the festival procession.

[42] D7, lines 41-42; A9, line 57.

[43] Cf. Meritt, *Hesperia*, V (1936), p. 389.

CHAPTER IX

DEMOCRACY IN THE ALLIED CITIES

The charge that Athens insisted upon democratic constitutions in the cities of the Empire has often been made,[1] and, despite occasional refutation,[2] has become standard in the textbooks and among lay students of Greek history. Since the evidence scarcely justifies so dogmatic a belief, we think it profitable at least to review that evidence. We set out the pertinent literary passages which are usually cited:

1. [Xenophon], I, 14: The writer says that, if the oligarchs gain power in the cities, the Empire of the Athenian Demos will not last long.[3]
2. [Xenophon], III, 10-11: The writer says that the Athenians deliberately side with the worse element in the cities in which stasis arises; like favours like. Whenever they did choose the best element (the oligarchs), it brought them no advantage. Within a short time the demos in Boiotia was subjected, and the same happened when they favoured the Milesian oligarchs; within a short time the latter revolted and massacred the demos.[4]
3. Thucydides, I, 19 (T104): The Lakedaimonians did not impose tribute on their allies, but established oligarchies to ensure loyalty; the Athenians gradually took away their allies' ships (except the Chians' and Lesbians') and imposed tribute on them all.
4. Thucydides, I, 115, 3: In 440 B.C., at the time of the revolt, the Athenians established a democracy in Samos.[5]
5. Thucydides, I, 56, 2 (T105): The Athenians ordered Poteidaia to expel its magistrates who had come from the mother-city (Korinth) and no longer to receive these annual officials. (This passage is not specifically cited by Walker.)
6. Thucydides, VIII, 21: The democrats in Samos (412 B.C.), aided by the Athenians who were there (in three ships), rose against the oligarchs.[6]

---

[1] E. g., Walker, C. A. H., V, pp. 471-472.

[2] E. g., Robertson, Cl. Phil., XXVIII (1933), pp. 50-53.

[3] Εἰ δὲ ἰσχύσουσιν οἱ πλούσιοι καὶ οἱ χρηστοὶ ἐν ταῖς πόλεσιν, ὀλίγιστον χρόνον ἡ ἀρχὴ ἔσται τοῦ δήμου τοῦ Ἀθήνησι.

[4] Τοὺς χείρους αἱροῦνται ἐν ταῖς πόλεσι ταῖς στασιαζούσαις. --- οἱ γὰρ ὅμοιοι τοῖς ὁμοίοις εὖνοί εἰσι. --- ὁπασάκις δ' ἐπεχείρησαν αἱρεῖσθαι τοὺς βελτίστους, οὐ συνήνεγκεν αὐτοῖς, ἀλλ' ἐντὸς ὀλίγου χρόνου ὁ δῆμος ἐδούλευσεν ὁ ἐν Βοιωτοῖς· τοῦτο δὲ ὅτε Μιλησίων εἵλοντο τοὺς βελτίστους, ἐντὸς ὀλίγου χρόνου ἀποστάντες τὸν δῆμον κατέκοψαν. This passage is not specifically cited by Walker.

[5] Πλεύσαντες οὖν Ἀθηναῖοι ἐς Σάμον --- δημοκρατίαν κατέστησαν.

[6] Ἐγένετο δὲ κατὰ τὸν χρόνον τοῦτον καὶ ἡ ἐν Σάμῳ ἐπανάστασις ὑπὸ τοῦ δήμου τοῖς δυνατοῖς μετὰ Ἀθηναίων, οἳ ἔτυχον ἐν τρισὶ ναυσὶ παρόντες.

7. Thucydides, VIII, 64, 1 and 65, 1: Peisandros and his fellows (411 B. C.) are ordered to establish oligarchies wherever they put in at allied cities during their voyage. This they do.[7]

8. Xenophon, *Hell.*, III, 4, 7: Agesilaos finds the Greek cities of Ionia in political confusion, with neither democracy, as under the Athenians, nor dekarchies, as under Lysandros.[8]

9. Aristophanes, *Acharnians*, 642 (T27a): The poet has shown how the allied cities are governed by the democracy (*i. e.*, the Athenian). (This passage is not cited by Walker.)

10. Isokrates, IV, 104-107 (T80c): As a favour to them Athens established in all the cities the same laws and her own type of constitution. Cf. VIII, 79 (T79b); XII, 54 (T81a) and 68 (T81d).

11. Aristotle, *Pol.*, 1307b (T41e): The Athenians destroyed oligarchies everywhere.

To the literary evidence we add the testimony of the inscriptions:

12. Regulations for Erythrai (D10): After the revolt a democratic constitution is established by Athens (453/2 B. C.); see D10, line 7.

13. Regulations for Miletos (D11): After the revolt an oligarchic constitution is tolerated by Athens (450/49 B. C.); see D11, lines 6-7.

14. The Treaty with Kolophon (D15): Democracy is established (or continued) in Kolophon (447/6 B. C.); see D15, line 48.

15. The Treaty with Chalkis (D17): After the revolt a democratic constitution is established (or continued) by Athens (446/5 B. C.); see D17, lines 62, 66-67, 71-72.

16. The Treaty with Samos (D18, cf. no. 4 above): After the revolt a democratic constitution is established by Athens (439/8 B. C.); see D18, lines 21-22.

17. Athens and Lesbos (D22): After the revolt a democratic constitution is established by Athens in Mytilene (427/6 B. C.); see D22, lines 6-7.

18. Treaty with Selymbria (*I. G.*, I², 116): The Selymbrians (409/8 B. C.) are to choose the form of constitution they wish (lines 6-8).[9]

" The evidence," says Walker, " warrants two conclusions; firstly, that democracy was universal in the subject states, and secondly, that no other form of constitution was tolerated by Athens." Clearly, the evidence is not consistent and the passages listed above merit further examination.

It is true that [Xenophon], in his generalizations, suggests that Athens always

---

[7] Τὸν μὲν Πείσανδρον εὐθὺς τότε — — — ἀπέστελλον ἐπ' οἴκου — — — καὶ εἴρητο αὐτοῖς τῶν ὑπηκόων πόλεων αἷς ἂν προσχῶσιν ὀλιγαρχίαν καθιστάναι. — — — οἱ δὲ — — — τοὺς δήμους ἐν ταῖς πόλεσι κατέλυον.

[8] Οὔτε δημοκρατίας ἔτι οὔσης, ὥσπερ ἐπ' Ἀθηναίων, οὔτε δεκαρχίας, ὥσπερ ἐπὶ Λυσάνδρου.

[9] [Καταστέσασθαι δὲ Σελυμβ]ριανὸς τὲμ πολι[τείαν αὐτονόμος τρόποι h]ότοι ἂν ἐπίστοντ[αι].

supported the democrats; no. 1 above is illustrative of his point of view. This theory is in fact part of the thesis of the essay. Yet when he mentions specific examples, he cites occasions when Athens took sides with the oligarchical element. Of particular interest to us is Miletos, which was a tributary member of the Empire; here Athens supported the oligarchic faction (see no. 2). As it happens, we know epigraphically (see no. 13) that Miletos was left by Athens with an oligarchic constitution in 450/49; this may be, and probably was, the occasion to which [Xenophon] makes reference.[10] Of the later stasis mentioned by him we know nothing. Before leaving [Xenophon], we note that, according to him (no. 2), the Athenians chose the worse element *when civil strife arose*. This *may* imply no previous interference; it surely reflects no strong earlier support of the democrats. [Xenophon] does not prove that the Athenians imposed democracy on all the cities.

Nor, indeed, does Thucydides. Walker writes of no. 3: " The obvious implication is that Athens not only insisted on a democratic government in the cities in her alliance, but that she still further interfered with their autonomy." We are unable to infer this from Thucydides. The contrast between Lakedaimonian and Athenian treatment of their respective allies is not a political contrast at all, it is financial: " the Lakedaimonians did not compel their allies to pay money, the Athenians on the other hand did; the Lakedaimonians maintained security and loyalty through subservient oligarchies, the Athenians held their position by gradually stripping their allies of ships and assessing them money." If anything, the passage shows that Lakedaimonian interference was political, whereas Athenian was naval (and, therefore, financial).

We learn from no. 4 that Athens established democracy in Samos (cf. also no. 16); the significant point is that down to this time (440 B. C.) Samos had lived under an oligarchy. It may justly be said that Samos, one of the three remaining naval allies, was autonomous and, like Chios and Lesbos, was allowed to choose its own constitution. More significant, however, is no. 6, in which we find Samos, in 412 B. C., oligarchic once again. So between 439/8 and 412 an oligarchic revolution in Samos had been countenanced by Athens; this was after Samos had lost her privileged position.[11]

Until the revolt of Poteidaia, the city had received annual magistrates from Korinth (no. 5); this means that Athens had not interfered with the constitution of Poteidaia, which was in all probability oligarchic.

---

[10] If the known revolt of Miletos, *ca.* 457/6 (see below, pp. 253-254), was caused by oligarchic defection from Athens and massacre of the democrats, Athens would scarcely have left an oligarchy in Miletos in 450/49. In addition, the government which immediately preceded the crushing of the revolt was probably a tyranny. So [Xenophon]'s reference is to an event after 450/49, about which we have no further knowledge. Meiggs, on the evidence of the quota lists, which we interpret differently, dates this second defection in 448/7; *J. H. S.*, LXIII (1943), p. 27.

[11] Meyer, *Gesch. d. Alterthums*, IV, pp. 564-565, does not think that Thucydides' words

We are left with a single passage (no. 7) from Thucydides in which there is supposed to be evidence for universal democracy. But Peisandros, on his voyage from Samos to Athens, would not call at every subject city or touch every area of the Empire; no doubt the very great majority of the cities along the route were democratic, and this justified the categorical orders given to Peisandros. We note that in VIII, 64, 2-5 Dieitrephes establishes oligarchy in Thasos and the oligarchs then plan complete freedom from Athens, a step which the Athenian oligarchs have not foreseen; " and I believe," adds Thucydides, " that this happened in many other subject cities." [12]

Xenophon's testimony (no. 8) applies only to Ionia and is obviously a generalization. We should need more specific evidence than this to argue that every Ionian city, let alone every city of the Empire, was democratic under Athens and received a dekarchy under Lysandros. Nor does the passage of Aristophanes (no. 9) reveal that democracy was the prevalent form of polity in the states; rather, the poet says, " I showed what (our) democracy means to them (the allies)." Rogers translates, " The way that our wise democratic allies are ruled by our State democratic " (B. B. Rogers, *The Acharnians of Aristophanes* [London, 1910]). The line is therefore irrelevant to this enquiry.

Isokrates is quite specific (no. 10): Athens instituted democracies in the allied cities. The problem here is not what he says, but whether we can believe what he says. It must be admitted that his comments on the history of the fifth century and on the Athenian Empire do not inspire an implicit confidence. In XII, 67-68 (T81d), for example, he is discussing the tributes paid by the allies to Athens, " which, in the first place, they paid of their own free will when they conferred naval hegemony upon Athens "; this is true enough. " Then," he continues, " they paid not to preserve Athens, but to preserve their democracies and their freedom and to avoid the great evils of oligarchy "; this ridiculous statement, which equates democracy with a sort of Utopia, has little relation to the historical situation of the Empire, plausible as it may have sounded to the readers of the *Panathenaicus*. For our immediate problem, and for many others concerning the history of the fifth century, Isokrates is not a reputable witness, as a glance through the Testimonia (T79-T82c) will prove. [13]

Aristotle (no. 11) is the only author to report categorically that the Athenians put down oligarchies *everywhere* (πανταχοῦ), and so, we may justly infer, established democracies *everywhere*. Yet the statement is proved false by exceptions which no one can doubt, and we can only believe that Aristotle, writing a century after the events, has made a careless and dogmatic generalization.

necessarily imply an oligarchy ruling in Samos before the rising of 412. We see no reason to take the passage in other than its natural sense.

[12] Δοκεῖν δέ μοι καὶ ἐν ἄλλοις πολλοῖς τῶν ὑπηκόων (*i. e.*, not in all of them).

[13] For another example of his gross exaggeration see below, note 29 on p. 251 (on T79b and the mercenary crews of Athenian ships).

To the evidence so far adduced something may be added. The Mytilenaians and Chians are called autonomous by the envoys of the former who seek aid at Sparta in 428 B. C. (Thucydides, III, 10, 5 [T122]); this means that Athens had not interfered politically, for such interference would have been a flagrant breach of autonomy. The autonomy of Aigina had been guaranteed by the Thirty Years' Peace (446/5), and later, just before the Peloponnesian War, the Aiginetans claimed that their autonomy had been encroached upon (Thucydides, I, 67, 2); the complaint could at least be debated and, to judge by the care which the Athenians elsewhere took (I, 44, 1) not to breach the treaty, it is unlikely that they had imposed a constitution on Aigina. In the Peace of Nikias (421 B. C.) Athens guaranteed autonomy to nine Thrakian cities (Thucydides, V, 18, 5-6 [T134]): Argilos, Stageira, Akanthos, Stolos, Olynthos, Spartolos, Mekyberna, Gale, Singos.[14] The guarantee was to protect rebels from punishment; it does not prove anything about the pre-war status of the cities.

Within the Empire, and paying tribute to Athens, at least in the early years, were dynasts, all of whom were in the Karian district: Paktyes (named in Lists 2 and 4; his seat, Idyma, pays as late as 13 and is assessed in A9), Pikres (1, 5, 23, 28; his seat, Syangela, appears regularly), Sa --- (assessed in A9; his seat, Killara, appears in 4), Sambaktys (1 and 3), Tymnes (10, 13, 14, 15, assessed in A9), an unknown (assessed in A9; his seat, Kindye, appears in 2, 5, 8, 12, 13, 15). A dynast is incompatible with democracy. The record as a whole is sporadic, but Syangela and Kindye are fairly regular.

We may now summarize the specific evidence, both literary and epigraphic:

Erythrai: democracy established in 453/2, after revolt (no. 12 above); previously under a tyrant.[15]

Miletos: oligarchy allowed in 450/49, after revolt (nos. 2 and 13); previously under a tyrant.[16]

Kolophon: democracy established in 447/6, after revolt (no. 14).

Chalkis: democracy established in 446/5, after revolt (no. 15).[17]

Samos: democracy established in 440 and reëstablished in 439/8, after revolt (nos. 4, 16); but by 412 the city had become oligarchic once again, without interference by Athens (no. 6).

Poteidaia: autonomous (and oligarchic) until her disaffection, ca. 433 (no. 5).

---

[14] For the last three see above, pp. 90-91.

[15] See below, pp. 254-255.

[16] See below, pp. 255-256.

[17] The oligarchic Hippobotai were expelled from Chalkis (Plutarch, Pericles, 23, 4), which may indicate that the constitution had been oligarchic; they undoubtedly played an important part in the revolt. Democracy was probably established in Eretria at the same time (see D16, whose oath was the model for the oath of D17).

Aigina: autonomy guaranteed by the terms of the Thirty Years' Peace in 446/5; constitutional interference before 431 unlikely (Thucydides, I, 67, 2).

Mytilene: autonomous (and oligarchic) to 427 (Thucydides, III, 10, 5); democracy then established, after revolt (no. 17).

Thrace: autonomy of nine cities guaranteed by the Peace of Nikias in 421 (T134), after revolt.

Selymbria: political autonomy guaranteed in 409/8 (no. 18).

Chios: autonomous (Thucydides, III, 10, 5).

Dynasts: at least six dynasts appear in the records of assessment and collection, extending from List 1 to A9.

On the basis of this evidence we may fairly claim that at all periods there were non-democratic states in the Empire. More than that, on at least one occasion Athens supported an oligarchy (Miletos), and on another she allowed the unseating of a democracy by an oligarchy (Samos). Significantly, it is never charged by her enemies that Athens imposed democracies upon her allies; she is said to have robbed them of their autonomy, it is true, but this could take many forms, such as the installation of a garrison or Athenian officials without respect to the form of constitution [18] (democratic Erythrai and oligarchic Miletos received garrisons). Walker's two conclusions ("democracy was universal in the subject states" and "no other form of constitution was tolerated by Athens"), with which we began our enquiry, are not warranted by the evidence.

That Athens interfered with the polities of the subject cities, however, is demonstrably true. Such interference could be provoked by revolt from Athens, civil strife within the city, or by wars among members of the Empire; sometimes stasis and internal wars led to revolt. Probably Athens was not slow to move, although, apparently, she sometimes did not move at all (Samos). When she did restore peace or loyalty in a state, she would naturally choose the side of the democrats or institute a democratic constitution; the demos, as [Xenophon] repeatedly says, would be more loyal to her than would the oligarchs. Yet even here there were exceptions (Miletos), although in all probability very few.

We believe that the cities of the Empire were, for the most part, under democratic constitutions; some had had these constitutions imposed by Athens, others (probably a great many) had adopted that form of polity without pressure from Athens. There was no rule, and, just as some of the cities lived without Athenian archontes in their midst,[19] so some existed in peace under non-democratic constitutions. But during the Empire democracy was not only the fashion, it was no doubt expedient.

[18] See further below, pp. 228-229.
[19] See D14, § 4, and above, pp. 145-146.

CHAPTER X

THE MEANING OF DOULEIA

In I, 98, 4 Thucydides describes the fate of Naxos: πρώτη τε αὕτη πόλις ξυμμαχὶς παρὰ τὸ καθεστηκὸς ἐδουλώθη. What is this douleia? It is certainly distinct from the ἀνδραποδισμός suffered by Eion (I, 98, 1) and Skyros (I, 98, 2).

Δουλεία (δουλεῦσαι, δουλωθῆναι, etc.) is used of Persian intentions towards the Greek cities and so of the status of Persian subjects in the following passages: I, 16; 18, 2 (ὁ βάρβαρος — — ἐπὶ τὴν Ἑλλάδα δουλωσόμενος ἦλθεν); 74, 2; 138, 2; III, 56, 4; VI, 82, 4; VIII, 43, 3; 84, 5.

At the time when Thucydides wrote, douleia had become the normal status of Athenian allies. In V, 9, 9, before the battle of Amphipolis, Brasidas tells his new allies that, in case of defeat, the best they can hope for, if they escape ἀνδραποδισμός or θανάτωσις, is to be δοῦλοι of the Athenians, and with a heavier (χαλεπωτέραν) douleia than they had before. And so we find it constantly of the situation of Athenian allies: I, 68, 3; 69, 1; 121, 5; 124, 3; III, 10, 3-5; 13, 6; 63, 3; IV, 86, 1; 87, 3; 92, 4; V, 86; 92; 100; VI, 76, 2; 76, 4 and 77, 1 (Hermokrates says that the Ionians exchanged Persian for Athenian δουλεία); 82, 3; VIII, 48, 5.

The word is used of Athenian intentions in Sicily or Peloponnese: I, 122, 2; VI, 80, 5; 88, 1; VII, 66, 2; 68, 2; 75, 7. Douleia to Athens is alleged in III, 70, 3 and 71, 1. Euphemos denies the intention in Sicily (VI, 83, 4) but appears to admit the status in Ionia (VI, 84, 3). The Peloponnesians fear, after the Peace of Nikias, that Athens and Sparta intend such a status for Peloponnese: V, 27, 2 and 29, 3 (cf. IV, 20, 4 and Aristophanes, *Peace*, 1082). The Kerkyraian, in I, 34, 1, says that it is not a proper status for a colony.

Douleia is of course the natural opposite of eleutheria. For individuals it means personal slavery: I, 55, 1; 103, 1; II, 78, 4; III, 73; IV, 118, 7; VI, 27, 2; VII, 85, 4; VIII, 15, 2; 28, 4. In V, 23, 3, in the text of the Athenian treaty with Sparta, ἡ δουλεία means the helots. In I, 101, 2 Thucydides says that most of the helots are οἱ τῶν παλαιῶν Μεσσηνίων τότε δουλωθέντων ἀπόγονοι, and this is the only passage in which the personal sense (slavery) and the political (subject status) cause any ambiguity at all; perhaps we should apply the political meaning here and translate δουλωθέντων as "conquered," but the ambiguity cannot be denied and is possibly not unintentional. In a few passages douleia is metaphorical: I, 81, 6; III, 38, 5; IV, 34, 1; VII, 71, 3. Twice (as in [Xenophon], III, 11) it is used of the subjection of one party within a city to another: IV, 86, 4 and VI, 40, 2 (in the latter it practically means τυραννίς, and we may compare the converse figure in II, 63, 2 and III, 37, 2).

In all other passages δουλεία is the political subjection of one state to another. As such, it is the opposite of political ἐλευθερία: I, 124, 3; II, 63, 1; III, 10, 3; 58, 5; 63, 3; IV, 92, 4 and 7; 114, 3; V, 9, 9; 100; VI, 20, 2; 84, 3; VIII, 43, 3; 48, 5. It is the passive state answering to the active state of ἀρχή (i. e., δουλεύειν = ἄρχεσθαι), and this contrast is expressed or indicated in II, 63, 3; V, 69, 1; 92; 100; VI, 20, 2; VII, 66, 2; cf. VI, 87, 2; VIII, 43, 3. The intention of imposing douleia is disclaimed by Euphemos in Sicily (VI, 83, 4, see above), by Brasidas at Torone (IV, 114, 3), by the Boiotian Pagondas before the battle of Delion (IV, 92, 7; cf. Plataian fears in II, 71, 3 and III, 58, 5). Nikias says there is no douleia in Sicily (VI, 20, 2), but Euphemos works on the fear of it (VI, 83, 4). It is of course the opposite of the famous autonomia of the Peloponnesian League, yet Mantineia is conscious of having escaped it by withdrawal (V, 69, 1).

These ambiguities arise from its popularity as a propaganda word and also from its very wide range of meaning: from the severest type of subjection, ἐν ᾧ, εἰ κατώρθωσαν, ἀνδράσι μὲν ἂν τἄλγιστα προσέθεσαν, παισὶ δὲ καὶ γυναιξὶ τὰ ἀπρεπέστατα, πόλει δὲ τῇ πάσῃ τὴν αἰσχίστην ἐπίκλησιν (VII, 68, 2, Gylippos on Athens' plans for Syracuse), to a simple loss of sovereignty, which may seem a rather comfortable state to the unambitious; II, 63, 3 (ἀσφαλῶς δουλεύειν), VI, 80, 5 (τὴν αὐτίκα ἀκινδύνως δουλείαν), cf. VI, 88, 1, where the suspicion of Athenian intentions hardly affects Kamarina's εὔνοια.

Speaking of the days of Minos, Thucydides (I, 8, 3) uses δουλεία as the noun of ὑπήκοος: δουλεύειν is merely a rather forceful synonym for ὑπακούειν. Dictation from one sovereign state to another, on any matter, large or small, constitutes δούλωσις (I, 141, 1, tinged by rhetoric). Phrynichos (VIII, 48, 5) says that an imposed oligarchy will give as much sense of δουλεύειν as an imposed democracy. The recommended establishment of a full defensive and offensive alliance with Athens (III, 70, 6, cf. I, 44, 1) seemed fraught with δουλεία (III, 71, 1, cf. 70, 3). Allies who revolt will receive δουλείαν χαλεπωτέραν ἢ πρίν (V, 9, 9), but even this is clearly distinguished from ἀνδραποδισμός (loc. cit.). Pausanias guarantees to Plataia not that she shall never be attacked (an enemy with a fair grievance might go to war with her), but that, if attacked and beaten, she shall not be " subjected ": στρατεῦσαί τε μηδένα ποτὲ ἀδίκως ἐπ' αὐτοὺς μηδ' ἐπὶ δουλείᾳ (II, 71, 2); the sentimental basis of the guarantee is explained in III, 58, 5: γῆν ἐν ᾗ ἠλευθερώθησαν οἱ Ἕλληνες δουλώσετε. It was violated grossly; the Plataians in their most moving speech minimize their own execution (which goes beyond δουλεία, cf. V, 9, 9) in comparison with the extreme breach of the guarantee: τὴν Πλαταιίδα Θηβαΐδα ποιήσετε (III, 58, 5).

What then does Thucydides say of Naxos? " She was the first allied city to be treated as a subject, in breach of the constitution " (πρώτη τε αὕτη πόλις ξυμμαχὶς παρὰ τὸ καθεστηκὸς ἐδουλώθη). The constitution guaranteed autonomy (cf. I, 97, 1, and below, pp. 228-229), and this douleia in some way infringed upon that autonomy. Thucydides does not say exactly how. Perhaps Naxos was compelled (rather than agreed) to provide χρήματα instead of ναῦς; perhaps she received a garrison (the most typical breach of autonomy, cf. D10, D11, and below, pp. 252-258), perhaps even a klerouchy. The particular form was of no importance for Thucydides' point: that this was a precedent for treating the allies as subjects. Athens' (or, better, the Confederacy's) case against Naxos was a good one: she had broken her oaths by seceding (see below, p. 228) and a new Persian attack was imminent. What was unfortunate, for the working of the Confederacy, was that such incidents gave too much power and opportunity to the executive, i. e., to Athens, the hegemon. In suppressing revolt, by which the oath was automatically broken, Athens herself went too far. This revealed the inequality of the alliance; but the disparity of energy between Athens and her allies was the fundamental fact, and it was bound to tell. Such is Thucydides' verdict in I, 99 (see below, pp. 244-252).

CHAPTER XI

THE CHRONOLOGICAL BACKGROUND OF THE FIFTY YEARS

In the course of the narrative of Part III we shall argue that the allies made every effort to complete the arrangements begun on Delos, including the first assessment, by the spring of 477 B. C.; they would then be ready to turn their attention to the offensive war against Persia during the campaigning season of 477. We are thus led to anticipate almost immediate operations.

Thucydides, after describing the Confederate machinery in I, 96 and after presenting his chronological principles in I, 97, commences his account of the Fifty Years by naming as the first event [1] of the period the capture of Eion: πρῶτον μὲν Ἠιόνα τὴν ἐπὶ Στρυμόνι Μήδων ἐχόντων πολιορκίᾳ εἷλον καὶ ἠνδραπόδισαν, Κίμωνος τοῦ Μιλτιάδου στρατηγοῦντος. The capture of Eion is placed in the archonship of Phaidon by the scholiast to Aischines, II, 34.[2] The siege was grim and Eion was eventually reduced by starvation; the detail of the ancient accounts [3] implies strongly that the siege lasted through a winter and the final surrender has therefore been placed in the spring of 475.[4]

We may well ask what the Confederates were doing in 477, when their enthusiasm was high and the navy was ready and eager to press the advantage against the demoralized Persians. This was not the time for a suspension of offensive operations. Walker finds [5] the answer to the question in the eviction of Pausanias from Byzantion, a necessary task which was completed by the end of 477. With much of his argument we agree: " To gain possession of Byzantium, and with it the control of the Bosporus, was a matter of first importance to the Athenians and their allies, and although Pausanias must have had at his disposal a garrison of some sort or other, he had not the moral authority of Sparta behind him. He had been superseded in his command,

---

[1] We believe that in I, 98, Thucydides sets out first examples of types of allied operations: Eion is the first Persian fortress to be captured (there were others); Skyros is the first example of the subjugation and colonization of territory not held by Persia; Karystos is the first Hellenic city to be forced into the Confederacy; Naxos is the first example of the revolt and suppression of a member of the Confederacy (ἔπειτα δὲ καὶ τῶν ἄλλων ὡς ἑκάστῃ ξυνέβη). I, 99 is a brief explanatory digression on revolt and its causes, and the narrative is resumed in I, 100 with the Eurymedon campaign, which we date in 469. Thus, from the beginning of Confederate activity to 469, Thucydides mentions specifically only four events, each, we hold, by way of example, for these years must have been busy indeed for the naval squadrons. Thucydides, I, 96-99 is printed in *A. T. L.*, II as T109.

[2] Τὸ πρῶτον μὲν Λυσιστράτου καὶ Λυκούργου καὶ Κρατίνου στρατευόντων ἐπ' Ἠϊόνα τὴν ἐπὶ Στρυμόνι διεφθάρησαν ὑπὸ Θρακῶν, εἰληφότες Ἠϊόνα, ἐπὶ ἄρχοντος Ἀθήνῃσι Φαίδωνος.

[3] Herodotos, VII, 107; Plutarch, *Cimon*, 7.

[4] Walker, *C. A. H.*, V, p. 50 with note 1.

[5] *C. A. H.*, V, pp. 466-467.

and in those distant waters he was a mere adventurer playing for his own hand." We are compelled, however, to place the expulsion of Pausanias and the investment of Eion (but not its capture) in the same campaigning season because of a papyrus fragment of Ephoros: [6] Ἀθηναῖοι δὲ Κίμωνος τοῦ Μιλτιάδου στρατηγοῦντος ἐκπλεύσαντες ἐκ Βυζαντίου μετὰ τῶν συμμάχων Ἠιόνα τὴν ἐπὶ Στρυμόνι Περσῶν ἐχόντων εἷλον καὶ Σκῦρον. Both events must be set in 477 or in 476, along with the second capture of Sestos, by Kimon, if this is historical.[7]

The assault on Eion was the first major offensive against the Persians after the formation of the Confederacy and it must have been given a very high priority. There is therefore a good argument for placing the beginning of the siege in 477. Nor does this date demand an unreasonable reconstruction of the adventures of Pausanias. After his first acquittal at Sparta (478/7, winter), he sailed off to the Hellespont in a single trireme and established himself in Byzantion.[8] He may have made his way to Byzantion even as the allies were engaged in their deliberations on Delos; at all events they had already left Byzantion. But Pausanias' stand in Byzantion was only temporary and the siege which resulted in his expulsion was not a major operation.[9] We know (from Ephoros) that the affair at Byzantion preceded the siege of Eion; yet Eion is named by Thucydides as the first Confederate undertaking.[10] Byzantion, however, should perhaps be regarded as belonging to domestic affairs, and the second capture of Sestos, if we accept it, was scarcely a major campaign. We might call Byzantion the first Confederate undertaking, but Thucydides takes as his starting point the onslaught upon Eion, the beginning of the full-scale offensive against the Persians.

The Athenian commander against Byzantion, Sestos, and Eion was Kimon, whose age now becomes a matter of concern. We cannot assume that he became

[6] Frag. 191 Jacoby (no. 70), 37-46.

[7] Plutarch, *Cimon*, 9, 3 [T95c] (in the same campaign as the capture of Byzantion from Pausanias). Walker, *C. A. H.*, V, p. 467, rejects it; but see below, note 55 on p. 206.

[8] Thucydides, I, 128, 3: δημοσίᾳ μὲν οὐκέτι ἐξεπέμφθη, ἰδίᾳ δὲ αὐτὸς τριήρη λαβὼν Ἑρμιονίδα ἄνευ Λακεδαιμονίων ἀφικνεῖται ἐς Ἑλλήσποντον – – –. Cf. I, 131, 1: καὶ ἐπειδὴ τῇ Ἑρμιονίδι νηὶ τὸ δεύτερον ἐκπλεύσας οὐ κελευσάντων αὐτῶν τοιαῦτα ἐφαίνετο ποιῶν, καὶ ἐκ τοῦ Βυζαντίου βίᾳ ὑπ' Ἀθηναίων ἐκπολιορκηθεὶς ἐς μὲν τὴν Σπάρτην οὐκ ἐπανεχώρει – – –.

[9] Gomme (*Commentary*, I, p. 433) quotes Forbes' note: " the words imply a forcible expulsion, of which we should like to know more, but we have no right to assume, on very doubtful and indirect evidence, that he installed himself in full possession of Byzantium and was regularly besieged by the Athenian forces. Thucydides uses the same strong word (ἐξεπολιόρκησαν λιμῷ, 134. 2) of his starvation in the temple of Athene."

[10] See also the epigram cited by Plutarch, *Cimon*, 7, 4:

ἦν ἄρα κἀκεῖνοι ταλακάρδιοι, οἵ ποτε Μήδων
παισὶν ἐπ' Ἠιόνι, Στρυμόνος ἀμφὶ ῥοάς,
λιμόν τ' αἴθωνα κρυερόν τ' ἐπάγοντες Ἄρηα
πρῶτοι δυσμενέων εὗρον ἀμηχανίην.

strategos before reaching the age of 30, and if we take 477/6 as his first year of command we must set his birth no later than 507 (spring). Now when his father Miltiades died, Kimon, according to Plutarch,[11] was not yet a man. In this year, 489, he was, according to our scheme, 18 or 19 years of age. This suits the usage and phraseology in the texts of Plutarch well enough. So we date the expulsion of Pausanias and the fighting at Sestos after midsummer of 477. We posit that the fleet proceeded to Eion late in the season and there invested the city, thus beginning the major tasks of the Confederacy. The siege lasted through the winter of 477/6 and well into the summer of 476; at last Eion capitulated, in the late summer of 476, in the archonship of Phaidon (476/5). This reconstruction makes a logical pattern of the ancient testimony and has the very great advantage of explaining what the Confederates did in the season of 477 as well as that of 476. That is a real problem; but with the siege of Eion Thucydides begins his deliberate policy of omission, naming only first examples, and consequently the meagreness of our information about Confederate campaigns from Eion to the Eurymedon is not a comparable problem, tantalizing as our ignorance may be.

The colonization of Skyros followed the capture of Eion and we are probably safe in assigning both to the same archon-year on the basis of the fragment of Ephoros cited above and Plutarch's report that the oracle instructing the Athenians to recover the bones of Theseus came in the archonship of Phaidon.[12] So we may place the Skyros incident in the autumn of 476 or the spring of 475. Of the war against Karystos we can say only that it fell sometime between 475 and 470, and that it took time (χρόνῳ ξυνέβησαν καθ' ὁμολογίαν). The revolt of Naxos followed (μετὰ ταῦτα) and we tentatively assign it to 470. It could scarcely have occurred later, because the next event listed by Thucydides was the battle of the Eurymedon (ἐγένετο δὲ μετὰ ταῦτα), for which the evidence points to 469. Plutarch, after describing how Kimon brought Theseus' bones back from Skyros and his resultant popularity, goes on to another famous incident which was cherished by the people: when Sophokles competed with Aischylos for the first time, in the archonship of Apsephion (469/8), the entry of Kimon and his nine colleagues into the theatre occasioned a departure from custom and the whole board of generals was prevailed upon to sit as judges.[13] It was a special occasion (ὁ μὲν οὖν ἀγὼν καὶ διὰ τὸ τῶν κριτῶν ἀξίωμα τὴν φιλοτιμίαν ὑπερέβαλε) and we find the cause of the demonstration most satisfactorily in the prestige won by Kimon and his colleagues in the offensive which culminated in the overwhelming victory of the Eurymedon. So we place the battle in 469 B. C.

Thucydides promises, in effect (I, 97, 2), that he will set forth the record of the

---

[11] *Cimon*, 4, 4: μειράκιον παντάπασιν. In the *Brutus*, 27, 2, Plutarch says that Octavius Caesar was made consul οὔπω πάνυ μειράκιον ὤν, ἀλλ' εἰκοστὸν ἄγων ἔτος.

[12] Plutarch, *Theseus*, 36, 1-2.

[13] Plutarch, *Cimon*, 8, 7-9.

Fifty Years in chronological order. Inasmuch as those who assume irregularities in his chronological order of events claim either that the promise was not implied, or (if implied) was not kept, it is necessary in any resumé of the argument to begin by observing closely what Thucydides did in fact say. He states categorically his reasons for writing the excursus on the Fifty Years:

(1) Earlier writers without exception (ἅπασιν) had failed to touch on the period.

(2) Hellanikos, who did touch on it, did so briefly and not with chronological accuracy (βραχέως τε καὶ τοῖς χρόνοις οὐκ ἀκριβῶς).

These are the first two reasons which Thucydides gives for undertaking the excursus, but he adds a third, in the light of his whole history certainly one of equal importance, that the excursus will show at the same time how the Athenian Empire was established. The modern historian wishes that Thucydides had written more,[14] but our disappointment does not entitle us to doubt that, in the opinion of its author, the excursus accomplished its purpose. Thucydides says that Hellanikos' account was brief and was inexact in chronology, and that therefore there was still room for his own; we are consequently bound to believe that he meant his own account to be fuller than that of Hellanikos and to possess some chronological virtue which Hellanikos lacked. That it is fuller than Hellanikos (even if not so full as we should have liked) there is no serious warrant for doubting. It is important that unwarranted doubt about this should not lead to a general doubt about the whole implied claim, especially the claim to chronological precision.

Hellanikos used archon dates. Thucydides gives no single archon date in the whole excursus, and he tells us elsewhere[15] that archonships are of no use to his purpose, apparently because they split the campaigning year into two, or (rather) because an archonship contains parts of two campaigning years. For his continuous history, therefore, he employs summers and winters, that is to say, campaigning seasons and the intervals between campaigning seasons. In the excursus he does not do even that, and the complaint that he failed of his promised precision is often heard.[16] We happen to possess (in Diodoros, XI-XII) a list of fifth-century archons, and it would have been useful if Thucydides had named some of them. No doubt he thought Hellanikos had done enough of that (he of course did not know that Hellanikos' book was going to perish); he seems to have judged that relative chronology is what matters for the real understanding of a narrative and he left absolute chronology to look after itself.

[14] Gomme has made a convenient list of the more important events omitted, which, in his opinion, show the gaps in Thucydides' narrative (Commentary, I, pp. 365-369).

[15] V, 20, 2-3.

[16] Gomme, Commentary, I, p. 363, comments on the absence of dates by archons in the Fifty Years and says that " his narrative is not only, in this sense, τοῖς χρόνοις οὐκ ἀκριβές, but βραχύ." What Gomme says may be true, but the judgment it implies is mistaken.

How has he sought precision, or what kind of precision has he sought, in relative chronology? His improvement is to set events in proper order.[17] It is our belief that in his excursus Thucydides has done this without any deviation whatever.[18]

It is this " order of events " which is the touchstone of historical reality. When the Fifty Years were over and Thucydides began the story of the war itself he again laid emphasis on his adherence to the principle of chronological order (II, 1): γέγραπ-ται δὲ ἑξῆς ὡς ἕκαστα ἐγίγνετο κατὰ θέρος καὶ χειμῶνα. The language of the excursus itself bears out the promise for the Fifty Years as well: πρῶτον μὲν Ἠϊόνα (I, 98, 1); ἔπειτα Σκῦρον (I, 98, 2); πρὸς δὲ Καρυστίους (I, 98, 3); Ναξίοις δὲ ἀποστᾶσι μετὰ ταῦτα (I, 98, 4); and so on. If at any point Thucydides failed to make his account chronologically accurate, that is something that must be proved against him. The first real crux in the excursus comes with the fall of Ithome and the settlement of Nau-paktos, in the tenth year after the revolt of the Messenians from Sparta. Here the text of Thucydides (I, 103, 1-3) is quoted as evidence against him. The issue is clearly drawn. Thucydides narrates these events between the alliances that Athens made with Argos and Thessaly (I, 102, 4) and the alliance that she made with Megara (I, 103, 4). Either Thucydides has violated his order, or " tenth " must be wrong. It has been pointed out many times, since Krüger's emendation of δεκάτῳ to τετάρτῳ, that the correction of the numeral is easily made and readily explainable. If we accept Krüger's correction, we can impute the error not to Thucydides himself but to an early copyist (perhaps his editor).[19] The alternative is to assume that Thucydides has violated the order, that he has misplaced an event of great importance by as much as six years just after he has been chiding Hellanikos for inaccuracy, and after he has started the excursus on the pattern of true chronological sequence. We therefore accept the correction of the text.

This is a change made necessary by the order of the narrative, and it is further supported by the text of I, 103, 4. When the settlement at Naupaktos has been noted, Thucydides proceeds to the story of the Megarian alliance with these words:

---

[17] Correct sequence of events is meticulously observed both in the *Iliad* and the *Odyssey*; the poet in his narrative almost never either goes back in time or anticipates (*Iliad*, XII, 13-33, is quite exceptional). Historians had found this impracticable (as any reader of Herodotos knows); the annalistic system of dealing with all the events of one archonship before going on to the next was a rather mechanical means of keeping some sort of sequence. Thucydides evidently found it too mechanical; the events of two campaigning years might be jumbled within one archonship.

[18] Gomme (*Commentary,* I, p. 361) quite rightly points out that the insistence which Thucydides lays upon order shows lack of order to be the fault he criticized in Hellanikos; for the preservation of a correct order in Thucydides see Gomme, pp. 361-362, 392.

[19] The error is as old as Ephoros, for Diodoros says (XI, 63-64) that the Messenian war lasted ten years. If the original ms. had Δ, this can have been expanded correctly only to τετάρτῳ. There is no evidence, we believe, for the expansion of the acrophonic numerals as ordinals. But the mistake may have arisen because Δ can mean δέκα as well as τέταρτος.

προσεχώρησαν δὲ καὶ Μεγαρῆς Ἀθηναίοις ἐς ξυμμαχίαν Λακεδαιμονίων ἀποστάντες. The particles δὲ καί are used, as is correct, for the next item in a cumulative series in his continuous narrative. They mean " and also." They do *not* mean that the Megarian alliance came next after the alliances with Argos and Thessaly, with disregard for the alliance with the Messenians, which must be thought away as something to which the words " and also " do not apply; they mean that the Megarian alliance came next after the acceptance of the Messenians and the founding of Naupaktos. It is with these events fresh in mind that the words " and also " are used. To read the text in any other way is to misconstrue. Thucydides knew how to come back to the main theme of an interrupted narrative, if in fact there was an interruption; witness the resumed account of affairs at Thasos after the interlude of the Messenian revolt (I, 101, 3 [T110]): πρὸς μὲν οὖν τοὺς ἐν Ἰθώμῃ πόλεμος καθειστήκει Λακεδαιμονίοις, Θάσιοι δὲ τρίτῳ ἔτει πολιορκούμενοι ὡμολόγησαν – – –. If he has resumed an old narrative in I, 103, 4 after a digression six years into the future, some warning like ταῦτα μὲν οὖν πρὸς Μεσσηνίους ὕστερον ἐγένετο would be essential to the intelligibility of the text before he goes on to the alliance with Megara. The burden of proof lies with those who still hold to δεκάτῳ and who read from the present text something different from its obvious and *prima facie* meaning to explain why the Megarian alliance, syntactically, follows immediately upon the founding of Naupaktos as a Messenian refuge.

Cloché, following the long tradition of those who hold to δεκάτῳ,[20] thinks (as others have thought before him) that Thucydides merely wanted to finish his tale about Ithome, though he knew it was quite out of order: " Certes, il est regrettable que l'historien n'en ait point averti ses lecteurs; mais il n'a pas davantage expressément déclaré que la capitulation d'Ithome avait eu lieu exactement au temps où il paraît la situer, c'est-à-dire à la veille de l'accord athéno-mégarien." Why should he? One cannot expect of Thucydides that he will pause with each incident of his history to inform the reader " expressément " that he is putting it in its proper place. He set out in the beginning to do this for all events; his failure to make reference to an exception here is not regrettable, it merely means there is no exception.[21]

The view that Thucydides may have wanted to finish the story of Ithome all at once, even though in so doing he placed it out of order, is quite contrary to his method.

---

[20] *L'Antiquité Classique*, XI (1942), p. 32.

[21] West, *Cl. Phil.*, XX (1925), p. 229, summed up the value of the order as evidence when he wrote: " Though the chronological indications given by Thucydides are few and difficult to use, yet the accuracy of his account, especially as to the order of events, is unquestionable, since his purpose, in part at least, was to correct the chronology of Hellanicos. Consequently, in our attempts to date events between 466 and 450 precisely, we must follow the order of events found in Thucydides, interpreting his chronological indications as best we may." Having formulated the principle, it required no more than a footnote for West to reject δεκάτῳ in favour of τετάρτῳ (*op. cit.*, p. 234). Gomme, *Commentary*, I, p. 402 (cf. p. 303), after a longer account, decides also to abandon δεκάτῳ.

In the main body of the work there are frequent examples of the interruption of a narrative for the purpose of inserting some extraneous event in chronological order. The story of Pylos, for example, is interrupted to make way for events in Sicily (IV, 24-25). But if we confine our attention to the Fifty Years we discover that the Egyptian campaign is divided between I, 104 and I, 109-110; the building of the Long Walls is divided between I, 107, 1 and I, 108, 3 (with an intermediary reference in I, 107, 4); the war with Aigina, and its siege and capture, is divided between I, 105, 2 and I, 108, 4; the revolt of Thasos, which lasted less than three years, not ten, is so conspicuously divided by the revolt of Messene as to carry great weight against the hypothesis that Thucydides finished the story of Ithome *out of order* merely for the sake of being done with it before going on to something else. Even in the case of Ithome, the story has already been broken down accurately into its component parts: the revolt and retreat to Ithome are separated from the siege and the insult to the Athenians by the fall of Thasos; and the insult to the Athenians is separated from the fall of Ithome by the alliance between Argos and Athens and the alliances of Argos and Athens *vis-à-vis* Thessaly. Those who hold to the reading δεκάτῳ impute to Thucydides a method which he nowhere (except hypothetically here) practises, and even so they do not attain to that unity of subject which they claim as the excuse for the irregularity.

Busolt has reviewed much of the other evidence for abandoning the reading δεκάτῳ. He emphasized the significance of ἤδη, rightly, we think, in the phrase κατ' ἔχθος ἤδη τὸ Λακεδαιμονίων (I, 103, 3). The Athenians took the Messenians and put them in Naupaktos " in keeping with the hatred they now bore the Lakedaimonians." [22] The emphasis is on the fact that enmity had now replaced friendship, and it seemed appropriate to Thucydides to call attention to the change. The use of ἤδη would have been out of place if the settlement of Naupaktos had come at the end of the bitter (and bloody) struggles of the First Peloponnesian War; it is quite in place if the settlement is dated where Thucydides puts it, between the alliances with Thessaly and with Megara.

Thucydides leads up to the First Peloponnesian War not only by giving the facts of national hatred (Athenians vs. Spartans, I, 103, 3; Korinthians vs. Athenians, I, 103, 4) but also by naming the effective allies. This is in the best epic and historic tradition, the review of the allies before the battle is joined. The allies of Athens are named in order from I, 102, 4 through I, 103: Argos, Thessaly, Messenians in Naupaktos,[23] Megara. Thucydides has misled his readers if he has enumerated here allies

---

[22] Busolt, *Gr. Gesch.*, III, 1, note 2 on pp. 298-300. Gomme, *Commentary*, I, p. 304, translates, " in accord with their new hostility to Sparta "; this seems to us correct, and we agree with the conclusions that he draws.

[23] The Messenians οἱ ἐν Ναυπάκτῳ are listed as formal allies in II, 9, 4, before the Second Peloponnesian War.

who came in long after the war had begun. Moreover, the words αὐτοὺς (i. e., the Messenians) οἱ Ἀθηναῖοι δεξάμενοι prepare the way for the next sentence: προσεχώρη-σαν δὲ καὶ Μεγαρῆς Ἀθηναίοις ἐς ξυμμαχίαν Λακεδαιμονίων ἀποστάντες. The earlier allies, the Argives and Thessalians, had not come over in defection from Sparta; the Messenians had, and so also (next in order) had the Megarians.

Other arguments, implicit in the narrative of Thucydides, show that Naupaktos must have been in Athenian hands before the outbreak of the war. A consideration of Athenian tactics indicates that it was used by the Athenians as a base. When the Lakedaimonians crossed the Gulf of Korinth and with their allies rescued Doris from the Phokians (I, 107, 2) they were cut off from their return home by the Athenians. With control of Megara and Pegai the Athenians were able to guard the land route through the Geranian mountains, and by sending a fleet around the Peloponnesos they planned also to prevent a Lakedaimonian retreat by sea from the Krisaian Gulf (I, 107, 3). The effective base for this naval blockage was Naupaktos, not Pegai. Phormion used Naupaktos to blockade the Krisaian Gulf in 430 (II, 69, 1), and it may indeed be argued that he did it of necessity, for he did not hold Pegai. But, on the other hand, if the Athenians in 458 had held only Pegai (and not Naupaktos as well) it would have been useless in preventing the Spartans from crossing the Gulf for home. They could have sailed unmolested on any calm night from the alluvial plain at the mouth of the Mornos river, on one of the direct routes from Doris to the sea, within sight of Naupaktos, and quite safe from Pegai. If their boats were in the Krisaian Gulf, as the text implies, they could still have taken them to the mouth of the Mornos, if the crossing direct from Krisa seemed dangerous and they wished a shorter passage across open sea, and no Athenian patrol from Pegai could have prevented the successful issue of any part of the operation. But an Athenian fleet at Naupaktos would have blocked the short alternative route, for it would have controlled the delta of the Mornos river, and it would have made possible an attack at any time on the only other route left open to the Spartans, the long passage direct from Krisa. This is what the Spartans feared, and there was no reason for fear unless the Athenians held Naupaktos. The text of Thucydides shows not only that the Spartans anticipated interception on the long route but also that they did not even contemplate the possibility of a crossing further west than Krisa.

So the internal evidence of Thucydides, which carries adversely only the corruption of text in I, 103, 1 from δ′ (probably) to δεκάτῳ, is overwhelmingly in favour of adherence to the order of events: the settlement of Naupaktos came before the Megarian alliance.[24] The external evidence for placing the settlement of Naupaktos

---

[24] Fritz Taeger, *Ein Beitrag zur Geschichte der Pentekontaetie* (Stuttgart, 1932), p. 6, says that the change in reading, once proposed, from δεκάτῳ to τετάρτῳ " musste aus inneren Gründen wieder aufgegeben werden." We do not know what Taeger means; he offers no further explanation.

after the battle of Tanagra amounts to Diodoros and Pompeius Trogus, whereas Herodotos and [Xenophon] put it before Tanagra. In spite of Taeger's claim that one must hold fast to the order as set forth by Trogus,[25] we treat here as serious only the statement of Diodoros (XI, 84, as confirmed by schol. Aischines, II, 78), who puts the periplous of Tolmides in the archonship of Kallias (456/5) and ascribes to him in this order a series of exploits: (1) the capture of Methone in Lakonia, (2) the plundering of Gytheion and the burning of the dockyards, (3) the subjugation of Zakynthos and winning over of all the cities of Kephallenia, (4) the storming of Naupaktos, and (5) the settling of the Messenians there. Inasmuch as Thucydides describes the same periplous (I, 108, 5) there is some control over the credibility of Diodoros. What Thucydides (I, 108, 5) says is: καὶ Πελοπόννησον περιέπλευσαν Ἀθηναῖοι Τολμίδου τοῦ Τολμαίου στρατηγοῦντος, καὶ τὸ νεώριον τῶν Λακεδαιμονίων ἐνέπρησαν καὶ Χαλκίδα Κορινθίων πόλιν εἷλον καὶ Σικυωνίους ἐν ἀποβάσει τῆς γῆς μάχῃ ἐκράτησαν. The scholiast on Aischines (II, 78) adds other details: οὗτος (Tolmides) περιπλεύσας Πελοπόννησον μετ' Ἀθηναίων ηὐδοκίμησε λαμπρῶς καὶ Βοιὰς καὶ Κύθηρα εἷλεν ἄρχοντος Ἀθήνησι Καλλίου. ἐνέπρησε δὲ ὁ Τολμίδης καὶ τὰ νεώρια Λακεδαιμονίων. Pausanias also (I, 27, 5) recounts the exploits of Tolmides: he ravaged the coast of the Peloponnesos, burned the docks at Gytheion, captured Boiai and Kythera, and landed in Sikyonia and ravaged the countryside. The one event that these accounts all have in common is the destruction of the dockyards. The most striking event, the capture and settlement of Naupaktos, is mentioned by Diodoros alone. Gomme takes the silence of Thucydides on Tolmides' capture of Naupaktos to prove that Diodoros was mistaken.[26] It is indeed almost incredible that Thucydides should have passed over the capture of Naupaktos and the settlement of the Messenians there if these were events that belonged to Tolmides' campaign after the conquest of Aigina, especially as he does mention the capture of Chalkis (some four miles from Naupaktos). Our incredulity is not allayed by the silence of the other sources. It does little good to try to salvage the account in Diodoros by saying that he got it from Ephoros. Undoubtedly he did, though his date for the expedition was probably his own affair, drawn from a chronological table which named one of the exploits of Tolmides in the archonship of Kallias.[27] What Ephoros had done in the matter of dating can only be conjectured, but it is probable, to judge from what we know of his work, that he wrote out the deeds of Tolmides with no regard for absolute dates and that it was Diodoros who equated this segment of Ephoros with 456/5. It is clear that even within the exploits themselves Diodoros (or Ephoros) failed to achieve a proper order. The capture of Methone cannot have come before the burning of

---

[25] Taeger, *op. cit.*, p. 14.

[26] Gomme, *Commentary*, I, p. 304.

[27] For Diodoros' dates see Gomme, *Commentary*, I, p. 52, and, in general, Kolbe, *Hermes*, LXXII (1937), pp. 241-269.

Gytheion, for example, unless it was part of a different, and earlier, campaign. If indeed Tolmides had at some time captured Naupaktos, there is no guarantee, from what we know of Ephoros, that this did not also precede the later periplous. The dislocation of order need not have been one of months; it may have been one of years. And a possible explanation of the ascription to Tolmides is that in very truth Tolmides did capture Naupaktos, perhaps in 461, and that Ephoros, or Diodoros, muddled the career of Tolmides so completely that this event came into the final story as the culmination of the later campaign.[28] We need only to read Diodoros on the exploits of Kimon in Kypros to realize that such confusion is entirely possible.[29]

The external evidence from Herodotos which favours putting the settlement of Naupaktos before the battle of Tanagra is in IX, 35. It amounts to very little. In the list of the ἀγῶνες of Sparta, that against the Messenians at Ithome precedes that against the Athenians and Argives at Tanagra. The ms. reading is not Ἰθώμῃ, but ἰσθμῷ; however, the emendation seems sound. But all that Herodotos shows is that Ithome revolted before the battle of Tanagra. We knew this anyway.

The evidence from [Xenophon] is better. Here the author gives examples of how the Athenians had come to grief in trying to support the βέλτιστοι in other states (Ἀθ. Πολ., III, 11): ὁποσάκις δ' ἐπεχείρησαν αἱρεῖσθαι τοὺς βελτίστους, οὐ συνήνεγκεν αὐτοῖς, ἀλλ' ἐντὸς ὀλίγου χρόνου ὁ δῆμος ἐδούλευσεν ὁ ἐν Βοιωτοῖς· τοῦτο δὲ ὅτε Μιλησίων εἵλοντο τοὺς βελτίστους, ἐντὸς ὀλίγου χρόνου ἀποστάντες τὸν δῆμον κατέκοψαν· τοῦτο δὲ ὅτε εἵλοντο Λακεδαιμονίους ἀντὶ Μεσσηνίων, ἐντὸς ὀλίγου χρόνου Λακεδαιμόνιοι καταστρεψάμενοι Μεσσηνίους ἐπολέμουν Ἀθηναίοις. Gomme (*Commentary*, I, note 3 on pp. 402-403) speaks of [Xenophon] " for what he is worth " as favouring a date for the fall of Ithome before the battle of Tanagra. His evidence is worth a very great deal, for it is an unequivocal statement that the Lakedaimonians subjugated the Messenians before they went to war with Athens. Moreover, it comes from a writer of the fifth century earlier than Thucydides and well in a position to know the facts. It is testimony incomparably superior to anything in Trogus (or Justin) or Diodoros, and it supports the order of the Thucydidean narrative rather than the numeral δεκάτῳ.

An attempt to brush aside this evidence, which has not had the recognition it deserves, has been made by Stier,[30] who writes as follows: " wer etwa die bekannten Worte in der pseudoxenophontischen Ἀθηναίων Πολιτεία III 11: ἐντὸς ὀλίγου χρόνου Λακεδαιμόνιοι καταστρεψάμενοι Μεσσηνίους ἐπολέμουν Ἀθηναίοις als Stütze für τετάρτῳ anführen wollte, reisst sie aus ihrem Zusammenhange heraus und verbindet ἐντὸς

---

[28] Cf. Gomme, *Commentary*, I, p. 405. He states elsewhere (p. 304) what we believe to be the fact, that Diodoros deserves no credence for putting the capture of Naupaktos among the exploits of Tolmides on this campaign. Why he did so is a question that should be answered by literary, rather than historical, criticism.

[29] Cf. Gomme, *Commentary*, I, p. 286.

[30] Hans Erich Stier, *Eine Grosstat der attischen Geschichte* (Stuttgart, 1934), pp. 12-13.

ὀλίγου χρόνου mit καταστρεψάμενοι, während es zu ἐπολέμουν Ἀθηναίοις gehört." This
is not true. The crux of the passage is that καταστρεψάμενοι is an aorist participle,
which shows the subjugation of the Messenians to have come before the fighting with
the Athenians. There may be a difference of opinion about how long a time is implied
by ὀλίγου χρόνου and about what absolute dates, if any, the author may have had in
mind, but there can be no justifiable difference of opinion about the order of events.
The important fact is the existence of independent evidence from the fifth century to
prove that the fall of Ithome preceded the battle of Tanagra.

The only escape from this conclusion lies in mistranslating the Greek or in dis-
crediting the author. One cannot argue that καταστρεψάμενοι does not mean " having
subjugated "; it means nothing less than final and complete reduction to the will of
the conqueror. One cannot argue that the skirmish at Tanagra does not prove the
existence of a war or justify ἐπολέμουν; Tanagra was a hard and bloody fight, and
Theopompos at least (frag. 88 Jacoby) called it a war: οὐδέπω δὲ πέντε ἐτῶν παρεληλυθότων πολέμου συμβάντος πρὸς Λακεδαιμονίους ὁ δῆμος μετεπέμψατο τὸν Κίμωνα ---.
So did Plutarch (Cimon, 18, 1 [T95h]), probably following Theopompos: εὐθὺς μὲν
οὖν ὁ Κίμων κατελθὼν ἔλυσε τὸν πόλεμον ---. And whatever we think of [Xenophon]'s
Tendenz, there is nothing he gains in his Tendenzschrift by distorting the truth about
Ithome and Tanagra. The fact remains that he is the earliest author whose reference
to them is extant.

Another chronological crux comes in I, 109, where Thucydides is supposed to
have misplaced certain events leading up to the Egyptian disaster. It is not that they
are out of order within the story of Egypt itself, but the assumption has been that
Thucydides, after relating the expedition of Tolmides in 456/5,[31] picks up the narrative of Egyptian affairs with the journey of Megabazos to Sparta, and that this
diplomatic mission must have preceded the periplous of Tolmides. In other words,
here again the narrative as a whole was τοῖς χρόνοις οὐκ ἀκριβές.[32]

It is true that the events which Thucydides narrates between the periplous of

---

[31] This date, which we do not accept, depends on Diodoros and on the scholiast to Aischines,
II, 78; see above, pp. 166-167, and below, pp. 169-171.

[32] It is an arbitrary refuge to say that in I, 109, 1-3 Thucydides is merely making a brief
reference to the period which has intervened since his last account of Egypt in I, 104, 2, that the
intrigues of Megabazos are not properly part of the res gestae and so lie outside the channel of
chronological sequence. It is quite clear that in I, 109, 2 the references to the past are concluded
with the words τὸ μὲν γὰρ πρῶτον ἐκράτουν τῆς Αἰγύπτου οἱ Ἀθηναῖοι and that a new fact is introduced
with καὶ βασιλεὺς πέμπει ἐς Λακεδαίμονα Μεγάβαζον. His coming, the failure of his mission, and his
return are all told with the necessary detail to justify the belief, not that Thucydides is alluding
briefly to the interim, but that he is giving a full account which belongs properly in the resumed
narrative. Meyer, Gesch. d. Alterthums, III, pp. 603-605, even puts the visit of Megabazos earlier
than the battle of Tanagra, and he suggests that the Lakedaimonians may have financed their campaign with his bribes. This is a striking example of erroneous reconstruction dependent upon false
chronology.

Tolmides and the catastrophe in Egypt cannot be compressed between 456/5 and 454. Partly on this account Meritt has been disposed (with others) to date the disaster one year later, in 453.[33] But the difficulties in the way of this solution are so considerable that the late date must be abandoned. Rather than abandon also the chronological order of the Thucydidean narrative, we may question whether the periplous of Tolmides, alternatively, may not have been earlier than 456/5.

It has been the tradition to place considerable reliance on the date given by the scholiast on Aischines, II, 78 for this expedition. Most recently, Gomme, for example, refers to the scholiast as " generally a good authority," [34] and again to the scholion here in question as " a learned note, from the *Atthis*." [35] Respect for this alleged *Atthis* is great, and the scholiast's date has been generally accepted. Cloché writes, in a recent study of the Pentekontaetia,[36] " Personne ne songe à rejeter l'assertion du scholiaste d'Eschine—empruntée selon toute vraisemblance, à une Atthide—sur l'année de l'expédition du stratège Tolmidès autour du Péloponèse (456-455)." Inasmuch as this date is one of the cornerstones for every reconstruction of fifth-century chronology, it is essential to know as nearly as possible how much credence it deserves.

The scholia, as now extant, seem to have been compiled about the end of the fifth century of our era,[37] but the dates by Athenian archons are supposed to go back to a chronological table that had become the accepted standard as a result of the researches of Alexandrian scholarship, based perhaps on Philochoros' latest and most comprehensive *Atthis* (or possibly but less probably on Istros' Ἀτθίδων Συναγωγή). So, admittedly, the sanction of a date from the scholia is very great. This source must also have been the kind of aid that Diodoros used for Athenian archons.[38] To transfer segments of the narrative of Ephoros into the annalistic framework of archon-years led, as is well-known, to innumerable errors in Diodoros' dating of individual events, and it is not unjust to say of him that his dates in the fifth century have very little independent value.[39] It is of no great importance, chronologically, that Diodoros put the expedition of Tolmides, for example, in 456/5. He has been taken to be right partly because this is the date given also by the scholiast on Aischines. But if both Diodoros and the scholiast get their dates from the same source, they do not do more than merely show that the source has not been misquoted.

[33] Cf. Gomme, *Commentary*, I, note 2 on pp. 412-413, with the bibliography there cited.

[34] *Commentary*, I, p. 320.

[35] *Commentary*, I, p. 405, note 1.

[36] *L'Antiquité Classique*, XI (1942), p. 26.

[37] W. Dindorf, *Scholia Graeca in Aeschinem et Isocratem* (Oxford, 1852), pp. iv-v.

[38] Cf. Gomme, *Commentary*, I, p. 52: " He took the chronological tables, in which the Athenian archons had long been equated with the Olympiads and, more recently, with the Roman consuls, and cut up his narrative accordingly—every event is dated."

[39] Gomme, *Commentary*, I, pp. 51-54.

The dates given in the scholia on Aischines by Athenian archons are as follows:

I, 39: τῶν τριάκοντα]. The scholiast comments on the restoration of the laws after the return of democracy: καὶ ἐψηφίσαντο καινοὺς νόμους εἰσφέρειν ἀντὶ τῶν ἀπολωλότων ἐπ᾽ ἄρχοντος Εὐκλείδου (403/2), ὃς πρῶτος ἦρξε μετὰ τοὺς τριάκοντα.

I, 53: Σάμῳ] εἰς Σάμον κληρούχους ἔπεμψαν Ἀθηναῖοι ἐπ᾽ ἄρχοντος Ἀθήνησι Νικοφήμου (361/0).

I, 109: Νικοφήμου (361/0)] οὗτος ἦρξε πρὸ Θεμιστοκλέους (347/6), ἐφ᾽ οὗ βουλεῦσαι τὸν Τίμαρχον. ἦν δὲ ἐπὶ τοῦ αὐτοῦ ἄρχοντος (361/0) καὶ Ἡγήσανδρος τῆς θεοῦ ταμίας.

II, 34: Ἐννέα ὁδῶν]. The scholiast names the nine failures of the Athenians, and in five of them he gives the dates by the Athenian archons:

1. ἐπὶ ἄρχοντος Ἀθήνησι Φαίδωνος (476/5).
2. οἱ μετὰ Λεάγρου [λεογόρου, λεωγόρου codd.] κληροῦχοι ἐπὶ Λυσικράτους (453/2).
4. οἱ μετὰ Κλέωνος, ἐπὶ ἄρχοντος Ἀλκαίου (422/1).
8. Ἀλκίμαχος ἀπέτυχεν, – – – ἐπὶ Τιμοκράτους Ἀθήνησιν ἄρχοντος (364/3).
9. Τιμόθεος ἐπιστρατεύσας ἡττήθη ἐπὶ Καλλιμήδους ἄρχοντος (360/59).

The scholiast also mentions the successful settlement of Amphipolis in 437/6: ἐπὶ ἄρχοντος Ἀθήνησιν Εὐθυμένους.

II, 78: Τολμίδου] οὗτος περιπλεύσας Πελοπόννησον μετ᾽ Ἀθηναίων ηὐδοκίμησε λαμπρῶς καὶ Βοιὰς καὶ Κύθηρα εἷλεν ἄρχοντος Ἀθήνησι Καλλίου (456/5). ἐνέπρησε δὲ ὁ Τολμίδης καὶ τὰ νεώρια Λακεδαιμονίων.

II, 186 (T3a): καὶ πάλιν] μετῆκται τὰ πλεῖστα ἐκ τῶν Ἀνδοκίδου, ἐστὶ δὲ ψευδῆ. ἡ μὲν γὰρ Νικίου εἰρήνη ἐπὶ ἄρχοντος Ἀρίστωνος (421/0) ἐγένετο τῷ τετάρτῳ[40] ἔτει τῆς ὀγδοηκοστῆς ἐνάτης ὀλυμπιάδος· ἐν δὲ ταύτῃ οὐχ ὅτι ἐννακισχίλια τάλαντα εἰς ἀκρόπολιν ἀνήγαγον, ἀλλὰ καὶ τὰ προανενηνεγμένα ἐκ Δήλου μύρια πεντακισχίλια προσανάλωσαν. περὶ τῶν ἀποικιῶν δὲ ψεύδεται· οὐ γὰρ ἐπὶ τῆς Νικίου εἰρήνης ἐγένετο, ἀλλὰ πολλοῖς χρόνοις πρότερον.

It has been known for a long time that this catalogue contains an obvious inaccuracy in the date of Leagros' failure at Ennea Hodoi. He died in the disaster of Drabeskos (Datos) in 465,[41] and the most plausible explanation of the scholiast's error is that he confused the archon of 453/2 with the archon of 465/4, or perhaps of 466/5, because of the similar beginnings of the names Lysanias (466/5), Lysitheos (465/4), and Lysikrates (453/2). So the scholiast was not infallible. But the nature of the error here is such that the blame may fall on him rather than on his source.

On the other hand, the date for the Peace of Nikias compromises not only the

---

[40] Τετάρτῳ is Sauppe's reading for τεσσαρεσκαιδεκάτῳ.
[41] Herodotos, IX, 75; Thucydides, I, 100, 3 and IV, 102, 2.

scholiast but his source as well. It is not a sufficient explanation to say simply that the scholiast may have written the archon's name as Ariston when he meant Alkaios, for in dealing with the events of this year Diodoros has made a similar error, even to the misspelling Ariston where he should have written Aristion. It seems probable that the scholiast and Diodoros were here dependent on the same chronological tables, and if this was generally true no date in Diodoros receives more confirmation from a scholiast than the presumption that it comes from his chronological source.

Diodoros, however, got the Peace of Nikias in the proper archonship (XII, 73-74) and was mistaken (XII, 75) only about the separate peace between Athens and Sparta. There can be no doubt about either, for Thucydides gives the dates of both by the Spartan ephor Pleistolas and the Athenian archon Alkaios (V, 19 and 25). If the common source of the scholiast and of Diodoros was wrong, one has the paradoxical phenomenon of Diodoros improving on the tradition of the *Atthis*. If the scholiast drew from a source different from that of Diodoros it was in this case a worse source, and may well also have been bad for the date of Tolmides' expedition. If his source was good and he merely made another blunder there is not much to be said for his own credibility. The traditional year 456/5, therefore, is not well founded, and the expedition may be dated with more confidence where it comes in the chronological sequence of Thucydides, immediately after the surrender of Aigina (spring of 457) and before the journey of Megabazos to Sparta (not later than winter of 457/6).[42]

This close juxtaposition of the periplous of Tolmides with the surrender of Aigina is corroborated by the use of the connective καί in the text of Thucydides. Presumably Tolmides, in going about the Peloponnesos, used ships that no longer had to be held at home for the siege and blockade of Aigina. The battles of Tanagra and Oinophyta must now be put in the previous year (458), and there is in fact no

---

[42] The decree banishing Arthmios of Zeleia for his implication in bringing Persian gold into the Peloponnese (Demosthenes, IX, 42) has been dated in 457/6 by those who would connect it with the affair of Megabazos. A scholion to Aristeides, first published by Wilamowitz (*Coniectanea* [1884], p. 10), tells us on the authority of Krateros that Kimon was the author of the decree: Κρατερός τις ἐγένετο, ὃς συνῆξε πάντα τὰ ψηφίσματα τὰ γραφέντα ἐν τῇ Ἑλλάδι. καὶ τοῦτο τὸ γραφὲν εἰς τὴν στήλην Κίμωνός ἐστιν. ὁ δὲ Ἀριστείδης Θεμιστοκλέους τοῦτο λέγει. See Gomme, *Commentary*, I, note 1 on p. 327, with the bibliography there cited; cf. note 1 on p. 292. A useful survey of the evidence and of the various dates proposed is given by Cary, *Cl. Quart.*, XXIX (1935), pp. 177-180, who follows Grote in associating the decree with Pausanias' sojourn in Byzantion in 477. We see no objection to placing the decree in 451, after Kimon's return from ostracism; malefactors were not always punished promptly, and Kimon's negotiation of the Five Year Truce might have had as a by-product the banishment of the men who had tried earlier to bribe the Lakedaimonians into a renewal of open warfare. Kimon's prosecution of Epikrates, Themistokles' friend, followed some time after Epikrates' offense (ὕστερον, Plutarch, *Themistocles*, 24, 6) and may belong in the same context as the prosecution of Arthmios; see above, p. 112. We do not believe that Kimon was in Athens in 457/6; see Wade-Gery, *Hesperia*, XIV (1945), note 21 on p. 221 (for Kimon's recall) and note 22 on p. 222 (for Arthmios).

reason why they should not be dated there except that Diodoros has them in 458/7 and 457/6 respectively. This is not of sufficient moment to carry conviction if there are considerations that demand an earlier date. More important is the evidence of Theopompos, who has been held to confirm this date of 457 for Tanagra. His words are (frag. 88 Jacoby [no. 115]): οὐδέπω δὲ πέντε ἐτῶν παρεληλυθότων πολέμου συμβάντος πρὸς Λακεδαιμονίους ὁ δῆμος μετεπέμψατο τὸν Κίμωνα, νομίζων διὰ τὴν προξενίαν ταχίστην ἂν αὐτὸν εἰρήνην ποιήσασθαι. ὁ δὲ παραγενόμενος τῇ πόλει τὸν πόλεμον κατέλυσε. We hold, along with others, that he is wrong about Kimon's recall, but we allow that this need not invalidate his chronological framework. It is often said that in this framework the battle of Tanagra stood in 457. Gomme,[43] for example, taking the probable date of Kimon's ostracism as spring of 461, calculates that the war between Athens and Sparta (that is, Tanagra in the summer of 457) came more than four years and less than five years later, and that this accords with Theopompos' phrase οὐδέπω πέντε ἐτῶν παρεληλυθότων. But it is not the war that Theompompos dates; it is the recall of Kimon. The temporal phrase οὐδέπω πέντε ἐτῶν παρεληλυθότων need not modify the other temporal (or causal) phrase πολέμου συμβάντος; it modifies the main verb μετεπέμψατο.[44] Kimon, on Theopompos' view, came home in 457 and put an end to the war (παραγενόμενος – – – τὸν πόλεμον κατέλυσε), and Plutarch (*Cimon*, 18, 1) says explicitly that he did this at once: εὐθὺς – – – κατελθὼν ἔλυσε τὸν πόλεμον. If this view is to be fitted to a real chronology, then we shall have to put Tolmides' expedition (and the burning of the Spartan dockyards) in 457; it cannot be placed a whole campaigning season later than Kimon's alleged return. The story is nonsense if Tolmides burned the Spartan dockyards and ravaged Lakonian territory *after* the war was officially ended in Kimon's Peace. Whether Plutarch's mention of Tanagra in this connection (*Cimon*, 17, 8) is derived from Theopompos[45] is uncertain; that Kimon was recalled on Perikles' motion (Plutarch, *loc. cit.*: τὸ ψήφισμα γράψαντος αὐτοῦ Περικλέους) was probably not in Theopompos.[46]

The dating of Tanagra in 458 is supported also by Pindar's seventh Isthmian ode, written in honour of Strepsiades of Thebes, whose uncle of the same name had died in battle, in the Peloponnesian War, according to the scholiast. The ode is a late one (see line 41) and the battle has been reasonably identified as Tanagra and the poem dated to 456.[47] The identification is made more attractive by the similarity of

[43] *Commentary*, I, p. 326.

[44] This observation was made by Meyer, *Gesch. d. Alterthums*, III, p. 570.

[45] See Gomme, *Commentary*, I, p. 326.

[46] Wade-Gery, *Hesperia*, XIV (1945), note 21 on p. 221; on Plutarch's general dependence on Theopompos for his main narrative see Wade-Gery, *A. J. P.*, LIX (1938), pp. 131-134.

[47] See, *e. g.*, J. B. Bury, *The Isthmian Odes of Pindar* (London and New York, 1892), p. 120; Sir John Sandys, *The Odes of Pindar* (*The Loeb Classical Library*, Cambridge, Mass., and London, 1937), pp. 488-489; Gomme, *Commentary*, I, pp. 318-319 with notes 3 and 1.

language which may possibly exist between Pindar's poem and the epigram which was carved on the monument of the Argives who fell at Tanagra and whose names were inscribed in the public cemetery at Athens.[48] The ode also expresses the wish that Strepsiades may be victorious at the Pythian games. Since the Pythia were penteteric, it has followed that the Pythia in question were those of 454, still two years in the future at the time the poem was composed.[49] With Tanagra now set in 458, however, a more convincing interpretation is possible. Strepsiades won his victory at the Isthmia in the spring of 458 and the poem was written shortly after the battle of Tanagra (June?) but before Oinophyta (August?); the poet's hope that Strepsiades will triumph at the Pythia (August) of the same year is opportune and graceful.[50]

Comment has already been made on the relatively close sequence in time between the surrender of Aigina and the expedition of Tolmides as indicated by the connecting particle καί which occurs in I, 108, 5. Throughout the excursus on the Fifty Years the various connecting links give some clue, though of course they are not necessarily precise, to the relative disposition of events. The use of τε, for example, in I, 108, 3, indicates a close sequence between the taking of hostages from Opous and the completion of the Long Walls of Athens. Gomme gives a useful summary of the devices used to indicate lapse of time.[51] The relatively colourless καί and δέ show " immediately following or logically connected or contemporaneous events," and there are more circumstantial locutions like πρῶτον μέν, ἔπειτα, μετὰ ταῦτα, χρόνῳ δὲ ὕστερον, δὲ — — — ὑπὸ τοὺς αὐτοὺς χρόνους, εὐθὺς ἐπειδή, ἅμα, καὶ ὕστερον, δὲ — — — κατὰ τοὺς χρόνους τούτους, καὶ τέλος, μετὰ δὲ ταῦτα οὐ πολλῷ ὕστερον, ὕστερον δέ, καὶ αὖθις ὕστερον, χρόνου ἐγγενομένου μετὰ ταῦτα, καὶ μετὰ τοῦτο, οὐ πολλῷ ὕστερον, and μετὰ ταῦτα οὐ πολλοῖς ἔτεσιν ὕστερον. Of these, οὐ πολλῷ ὕστερον links events which were no great distance apart, probably within the same campaigning season. This is true of the interval between the Athenian campaign to Thessaly (I, 111, 1) and Perikles' voyage through the Gulf of Korinth (I, 111, 2-3), which came in the summer and autumn of 454 after the Egyptian disaster. It is also true of the interval between the Athenian reduction of Euboia in the autumn of 446 (I, 114, 3) and the ratification of the Thirty Years' Peace in the winter of 446/5 (I, 115, 1). Since the same phrase separates the

---

[48] Meritt, *Hesperia*, XIV (1945), pp. 134-147, especially p. 146 with note 21.

[49] Gomme, *loc. cit.*, perceives the difficulty and suggests that the ode was composed for a victory at the Isthmia of 454, the memory of Tanagra and Oinophyta remaining fresh in the minds of Boiotians during the intervening three years.

[50] Pindar's fifth Pythian ode celebrates the victory of Arkesilaos of Kyrene in the chariot race of 462 and concludes with the wish that he may be victorious also at the Olympic festival, which fell next in 460. So an interval of two years between Strepsiades' contests can be documented. But that Arkesilaos, who maintained elaborate stables, would enter again was a foregone conclusion. Not so sure were the plans of a private individual who competed in the pankration.

[51] *Commentary*, I, p. 361.

battle of Koroneia (I, 113, 2-4) from the revolt of Euboia (I, 114, 1) in the early summer of 446, we may conclude that the battles of Chaironeia (I, 113, 1) and Koroneia belong properly only a few months earlier, in the spring of 446 rather than in 447 as has been generally supposed. This view has much to recommend it historically, in that it allows the revolt of Euboia to come soon after the defeat of Tolmides in Boiotia and makes unnecessary any attempt to explain a long-delayed Euboian reaction to events on the mainland.[52]

It is not claimed that Thucydides deliberately gauged these connecting phrases in terms of days or months, but he does seem to have felt a general applicability of certain usages which betrays his mode of thought. From I, 104, 2 to I, 105, 3 the particle δέ joins Egypt to Kypros, and Halieis to Egypt, but καὶ ὕστερον unites Halieis with Kekryphaleia and δὲ – – – μετὰ ταῦτα marks the transition to the Aiginetan war and the first decisive battle. Between the commencement of the siege of Aigina and the invasion of Megara Thucydides uses ἔπειτα. The longer breaks in time in this sequence are those between Halieis and Kekryphaleia, between Kekryphaleia and the battle of Aigina, and between the battle of Aigina and the invasion of Megara. The invasion of Egypt, according to the indications of these connectives, came closer before the descent on Halieis than Kekryphaleia did after it: consequently, it came in the same campaigning season, and did not belong to an earlier year. Since Halieis is thus dated in the same year with the invasion of Egypt and the expedition to Kypros, the other events known to have been in the same year with Halieis are dated there too, and the whole passage here under discussion (I, 104-106) belongs in one year. This year is that which began six years before the Egyptian debacle (I, 110, 1) and to it (460) must be assigned the record of battles in *I.G.*, I², 929, which names the dead from the phyle Erechtheis ἐν Κύπροι ⫶ ἐν Αἰγ[ύ]πτοι ⫶ ἐν Φοινίκει [⫶] ἐν ʽΑλιεῦσιν[⫶] ἐν Αἰγίνει ⫶ Μεγαροῖ· τὸ αὐτὸ ἐνιαυτὸ. There need no longer be any doubt that this inscription belongs to the first year of the war.[53] The casualties in Phoinike were possibly suffered during the establishment of a foothold in Doros, the Athenian way-

---

[52] See Nesselhauf, *Klio*, Beiheft XXX, pp. 23-24, and below, note 65 on pp. 178-179.

[53] Meiggs, *J. H. S.*, LXIII (1943), p. 22, note 10, with hesitation has accepted 459. Hondius, *N. I. A.*, p. 5, dates the inscription *ca.* 460, which Klaffenbach, *Gnomon*, II (1926), p. 708, wishes to correct to 458, with a reference to Beloch, *Gr. Gesch.*, II, 2², pp. 199-200. See also De Sanctis, *Atthis²*, p. 485, and *Riv. di. Fil.*, LXIII (1935), pp. 71-72; Wallace, *T. A. P. A.*, LXVII (1936), pp. 252-260; Meritt, *D. A. T.*, p. 92, note 59. Gomme, *Commentary*, I, p. 311, records the fact that ἐνιαυτός in the inscription must mean a campaigning year (cf. Kolbe, *Hermes*, LXXII [1937], p. 247), but he did not use the evidence of the particles when he wrote, " It does not follow from this that the Athenian campaign in Egypt was *begun* in the same year as the fighting at Halieis, Aigina, and Megara (as, e. g., Busolt, iii. 305 n., 308 n., Kolbe, *Herm.* lxxii, 1937, 266-7, and Wallace assume: see below, p. 412, n. 2); there may well have been casualties in Cyprus, Egypt, and Phoenicia in the second or third as in the first year of the Egyptian War." The evidence of the particles favours the *first* year of the war; it is unfortunate that the artificial device of a new chapter and a new paragraph in modern publications misleads the reader at I, 105.

station between Egypt and Kypros; and the absence of Kekryphaleia from the Erechtheid inscription merely means that no members of this phyle lost their lives there.

We give here our table of events for the Fifty Years; events not mentioned by Thucydides are placed in brackets and the references in the right margin are to Thucydides, I: [54]

CHRONOLOGICAL TABLE

479 summer	[Battle of Plataia]	
	[Covenant of Plataia]	
479 summer	Battle of Mykale	89, 2
	[Congress of Samos]	
479 autumn	Departure of Peloponnesians	89, 2
	Siege of Sestos begins	
479/8 winter	Capture of Sestos	89, 2
479/8	Rebuilding of Athenian walls begins	89, 3; cf. 93, 2
478	Rebuilding of walls in Peiraieus begins	93, 3-8
478 spring and summer	Campaigns to Kypros and Byzantion	94
478 summer	Recall of Pausanias	95, 3
478 late summer	Dorkis replaces Pausanias, but soon, with	95, 6
	Peloponnesian forces, goes home	95, 7
478 late summer	Allies negotiating with Athenians	95, 1-4, 7
478/7 winter	Organization of the Confederacy of Delos	96
478/7	The first assessment [55]	96
477 summer	Expulsion of Pausanias from Byzantion	131, 1
	[Second capture of Sestos]	
477 autumn	Siege of Eion begins	
476/5	Capture of Eion	98, 1
476/5	Capture of Skyros	98, 2
475-471	War with Karystos	98, 3
	Its capitulation	
470	Revolt of Naxos	98, 4
469	Eurymedon campaign [56]	100, 1
465 midsummer	Revolt of Thasos	100, 2
465 late summer	Athenian naval victory and landing on Thasos	100, 2
465 autumn	Colony to Ennea Hodoi	100, 3

[54] Gomme gives a similar table, *Commentary*, I, pp. 394-396.

[55] For the chronology of Pausanias and Dorkis see below, pp. 191-193; for the first assessment, pp. 234-243.

[56] Kolbe, *Hermes*, LXXII (1937), p. 253, favours 467.

465/4 early winter	Defeat at Drabeskos [57]	100, 3
465/4 winter	Thasian appeal to Sparta	101, 1
464	Earthquake at Sparta	101, 2
464/3	Revolt of Messene [58]	101, 2
463/2	Subjugation of Thasos	101, 3
(τρίτῳ ἔτει)		
462	Spartan appeal to Athens	102, 1
462	Athenian response	102, 1
462	Spartan dismissal of Kimon	102, 3
462/1	Athenian alliance with Argos	102, 4
462/1	Athenian alliance with Thessaly	102, 4
461/0	Fall of Ithome [59]	103, 1-2
(τετάρτῳ ἔτει)		
461/0	Settlement at Naupaktos	103, 3
461/0 winter	Athenian alliance with Megara	103, 4

[57] The scholiast to Aischines, II, 34 gives ἐπὶ Λυσικράτους, 453/2 (see above, p. 170). We suggest that Λυσικράτους was read by error for Λυσιθέου; cf. I. G., I², p. 278. The corruption from Λυσιστράτου (467/6) would be easier, but the intervals given by Thucydides in IV, 102, 2-3 would then necessitate dating the failure of Aristagoras in 499 and the founding of Amphipolis in 439. Both are impossible: Aristagoras cannot have left Miletos for Thrace so early as 499 and the scholiast's date for the founding of Amphipolis (437/6) now has the support of the quota lists. As late as 438/7 Argilos still pays 1 talent (List 17, VI, 15); its next appearance shows an assessment of 1000 drachmai (List 22, II, 54), a decrease occasioned by the founding of Amphipolis. Any date between autumn, 437, and autumn, 436, would fall in the 29th year after Drabeskos. Kolbe, *Hermes*, LXXII (1937), pp. 249-250, urges that to Thucydides the sending of the colony rather than the defeat at Drabeskos was the event of primary chronological importance. This may be true, but the narrative sequence in I, 100, 3 shows that Drabeskos belongs earlier than the Thasian appeal to Sparta. The disaster may have occurred too late in the winter of 465/4 for the casualties to be listed in I. G., I², 928 and yet still be in the 29th year before the founding of Amphipolis; see further above, pp. 108-110, where we prefer to believe that I. G., I², 928 is the record of 465 and originally bore the casualties of Drabeskos. Kolbe concludes that Thasos revolted in the second half of 465 and that I. G., I², 928 belongs to this year. For fighting in the Chersonese in the same year see below, pp. 205-206 with note 55.

[58] Placed by Pausanias, IV, 24, 5, in the 79th Olympiad, in the archonship of Archimedes (*i. e.*, Archedemides, 464/3). We prefer this to Plutarch's τέταρτον ἔτος (*Cimon*, 16, 4) of Archidamos, the date of whose accession depends on Diodoros and is not absolutely certain; it is generally taken to be 469/8. Plutarch's τέταρτον ἔτος (for the earthquake) would be 466/5 and would necessitate placing the revolt of Thasos in 466, which might be interpreted as 467/6 and would allow the simplest correction of the scholiast to Aischines (*i. e.*, Λυσιστράτου, 467/6; see note 57 above). Pausanias' date, on the other hand, accords well with the narrative of Thucydides and agrees with his chronological indications (see note 57 above). Gomme, *Commentary*, I, pp. 405-407, especially note 1 on p. 406, emphasizes the unreliability of Diodoros and urges that τέταρτον ἔτος could mean 464/3. He dates the revolt of Thasos in the summer of 465 (p. 395).

[59] Palaeographically, the correction from δεκάτῳ to ἕκτῳ has much to recommend it; historically, however, it is open to the objections discussed in note 57 above.

	Occupation of Megara and Pegai	
	Building of long walls to Nisaia	
461/0 winter	Revolt of Egypt (Inaros)	104, 1
460 spring	Expedition to Kypros	104, 2
460 spring	Campaign to Egypt [60]	104, 2
460 spring	[Fighting in Phoinike]	[*I. G.*, I², 929]
	(Doros an Athenian base)	
460 spring	Attack on Halieis	105, 1
460 summer	Battle of Kekryphaleia	105, 1
460 summer	War with Aigina	105, 2
460 late summer	Great battle and siege of Aigina	105, 2
460 autumn	Spartan and Korinthian invasion of the	105, 3-106
	Megarid, Korinthian defeat by Myronides	
460/59 winter	Beginning of the Long Walls at Athens	107, 1
459 summer	Phokian attack on Doris	107, 2
459/8	Spartan invasion of north Greece	107, 2
459/8	Spartan delay in Boiotia [61]	107, 3-4
458 (June?)	Battle of Tanagra	108, 1
458 (August? δευτέρᾳ	Battle of Oinophyta	108, 2-3
καὶ ἑξηκοστῇ ἡμέρᾳ)		
458/7	Subjugation of Boiotia and Phokis	108, 3
458/7	Dismantling of the walls of Tanagra	108, 3
458/7	Hostages taken from Opous	108, 3

[60] The date is fixed with reference to the disaster in Egypt, for fully six years intervened between the two events (Thucydides, I, 110, 1). With the collapse of Egypt dated in 454 there is no legitimate method of counting ἓξ ἔτη that gives a date other than 460. An erroneous count has often been made, as, for example, by Kolbe, *Hermes*, LXXII (1937), p. 267, who still advocates 459.

[61] In 460 the Korinthians invaded the Megarid, νομίζοντες ἀδυνάτους ἔσεσθαι Ἀθηναίους βοηθεῖν τοῖς Μεγαρεῦσιν ἔν τε Αἰγίνῃ ἀπούσης στρατιᾶς πολλῆς καὶ ἐν Αἰγύπτῳ· ἢν δὲ καὶ βοηθῶσιν, ἀπ᾽ Αἰγίνης ἀναστήσεσθαι αὐτούς. The Athenians, however, refused to lift the siege of Aigina and Myronides fought in the Megarid commanding the oldest and the youngest. The Spartan invasion of northern Greece, across the Gulf of Korinth, was apparently unopposed. Yet the Spartans feared Athenian interception by sea or by land upon their return to the Peloponnese. Further, the Athenians, who had been demonstrably short of manpower, marched into Boiotia πανδημεί to fight Tanagra and can, even after that defeat, resume battle at Oinophyta. The siege of Aigina was in the meantime continuing. It seems clear that reinforcements had arrived in Athens between the Spartan march north and their projected return. These would reinforce the garrison in the Megarid and would furnish naval strength, based on Naupaktos, in the Korinthian Gulf; the Spartans had provided a convoy strong enough to contain Naupaktos but not strong enough to face the reinforced Athenian fleet. The reinforcements came from Egypt, as Wallace has urged, accepting the figure of 40 ships from Ktesias (*Persica*, 32 Baehr) as the size of the squadron which remained in Egypt; *T. A. P. A.*, LXVII (1936), pp. 252-260. The weight of our argument. it should be noted, comes from Thucydides, not from Ktesias.

458/7 winter	Completion of the Long Walls	108, 3
457 spring	Surrender of Aigina	108, 4
457 summer	Periplous of Tolmides	108, 5
457/6 late autumn	Journey of Megabazos to Sparta	109, 2
456 spring	Campaign of Megabyxos to Egypt	109, 3
456 autumn (τέλος)	Siege of Prosopitis begins	109, 4
454 summer (ἐνιαυτὸν καὶ ἐξ μῆνας)	Siege of Prosopitis ends	109, 4
454 summer (ἐξ ἔτη πολεμήσαντα)	Hellenic collapse in Egypt	110, 1
454 summer	Crucifixion of Inaros [62]	110, 3
454 summer	Fate of the last squadron	110, 4
454 summer	Expedition to Thessaly	111, 1
454 autumn	Perikles' campaign in Sikyonia, Achaia, Akarnania	111, 2-3
451/0 (ὕστερον δὲ δια- λιπόντων ἐτῶν τριῶν)	Five Years' Truce	112, 1
450 spring	Kimon's campaign to Kypros	112, 2
450 spring	Despatch of 60 ships to Egypt	112, 3
450 summer	Death of Kimon	112, 4
450 summer	Athenian naval and land victories in Kypros	112, 4
450 autumn	Return of the fleet from Kypros and Egypt	112, 4
450/49	[Peace of Kallias] [63]	
449 summer	Sacred War: Spartan attack [64]	112, 5
447/6	Sacred War: Athenian reprisal [65]	112, 5

[62] See further below, p. 180.

[63] For the Peace of Kallias see below, pp. 275-278, 281, and for the chronology of Athenian imperial reconstruction between 450 and 446, pp. 298-300.

[64] The date must be later than the Athenian invitations to a Panhellenic Congress, for Athens could scarcely have sent an invitation to a state which had just ousted the Phokians, allies of Athens, from Delphi. For the congress see further below, pp. 279-281, and for the chronology, p. 299.

[65] Gomme, *Commentary*, I, pp. 337 and 409 with note 2, discusses the chronology of the Sacred War. The dates here proposed have the advantage of allowing the retention of the time interval given by Philochoros (frag. 88 Müller), who places the Athenian attack τρίτῳ ἔτει after the Spartan campaign. The emendation to τρίτῳ μηνί brings the two expeditions so close together as to clash, perhaps, with Thucydides' καὶ αὖθις ὕστερον; the same is true of Plutarch's account (*Pericles*, 21, 2), which says that Perikles answered the Spartan attack at once (εὐθὺς --- ὁ Περικλῆς ἐπιστρατεύσας). But there is no need to jettison the reading of the manuscript. A whole year elapsed between the death of Kimon and the Spartan incursion (Thucydides writes δὲ --- μετὰ ταῦτα) and an autumn and winter passed between the Athenian retort and the fighting in Boiotia (Thucydides says χρόνου ἐγγενομένου μετὰ ταῦτα). Rather, Philochoros argues for dating Chaironeia in the spring of 446. Cloché, *Les Études Classiques*, XIV (1946), pp. 23-24, writes copiously but not persuasively in favour of dating both Athenian and Spartan campaigns in 448, on the assumption that Philochoros

446 spring	Battle of Chaironeia	113, 1
446 spring	Battle of Koroneia	113, 2
446 early summer	Revolt of Euboia	114, 1
446 summer	Revolt of Megara	114, 1
446/5 (after expiration of the truce)	Spartan invasion of Attica	114, 2
446/5	Reduction of Euboia	114, 3
446/5 winter	Thirty Years' Peace	115, 1
441/0 (ἕκτῳ ἔτει)	Samian War begins	115, 2
441/0	Revolt of Byzantion	115, 5
440/39	Siege of Samos begins	116, 2
439 spring or early summer (ἐνάτῳ μηνί)	Subjugation of Samos	117, 3
439 spring or early summer	Capitulation of Byzantion	117, 3
μετὰ ταῦτα ––– οὐ πολλοῖς ἔτεσιν ὕστερον	Affairs of Kerkyra and Poteidaia	118, 1

The guiding principle of this table has been to place events in chronological order and to demonstrate visually how Thucydides accomplished the purpose implied in I, 97, 2. Two minor points require further comment.

The revolt of Thasos was followed by an Athenian military attack. The Athenians were victorious in the initial battle on sea and landed a force on the island. Here Thucydides breaks off the story of events on Thasos, for chronological accuracy compelled him to turn to the fortunes of the colony at Nine Ways. These colonists reached Thrace later than the squadron which attacked Thasos, but the phrase ὑπὸ τοὺς αὐτοὺς χρόνους indicates that the activities of colonization were undertaken at a time when the fighting on Thasos was going on. The disaster at Drabeskos followed soon after the arrival of the colony. Thucydides mentions next the summoning of aid from Sparta by the defeated and besieged Thasians. He does not attempt to date the battle (or battles) [66] on land or the beginning of the siege. This might have involved

was ill-informed. L. Pearson, *The Local Historians of Attica* (*Philological Monographs published by the American Philological Association*, XI, Philadelphia, 1942), pp. 122-123, retains the ms. reading without question and speaks of " the more accurate indication of date given by Philochorus." See above, pp. 173-174.

[66] One group of manuscripts (ABEFM) reads μάχαις, where the traditional texts have μάχῃ, in I, 101, 1. Gomme, *Commentary*, I, p. 298, prefers μάχαις.

a chronological anomaly, but Thucydides avoids it by making the next main finite verb refer to something that took place well after Drabeskos. The land battles, which would have been an awkward problem if mentioned as events in their own right, are not part of the current of the narrative. Similarly, in I, 103, 3, the capture of Naupaktos, told by Thucydides in an explanatory dependent clause, does not interrupt the continuous chronological order of the narrative, and it is not to be counted a part of it.

The second point has to do with the crucifixion (or impaling) of Inaros. Ktesias (33-36) says that he was not killed until five years after the Egyptian disaster. Clearly this conflicts with anything like a continuous chronological order in Thucydides. The account of Ktesias is very circumstantial,[67] and it would have more weight than it has if his historical credit were better and especially if he were not patently wrong in much of the story about the Egyptian disaster. Ktesias says that the last stand of the Greeks was made in Byblos; Thucydides has the final siege in Prosopitis. Ktesias says that the stronghold could not be captured (ἐπειδὴ δὲ ἐκείνη ἀνάλωτος ἐδόκει) and that Mega-byxos made a truce with the garrison; Thucydides says that the Persians diverted the water from the canal which protected the island, left the Athenian ships beached on dry land, and captured the island in an infantry attack. There has never been any disposition on the part of historians to prefer Ktesias' account of the final disaster to that of Thucydides on these two items of difference, and our preference is to believe that Thucydides was right also about the death of Inaros. The alternative is to believe that Thucydides had been misinformed (if Inaros did in fact live on for five years), not that he abandoned the chronological sequence of the narrative.

[67] See Gomme, *Commentary*, I, pp. 322-323 and (on his estimate of the reliability of Ktesias) 30.

PART III

THE ATHENIAN NAVAL CONFEDERACY

CHAPTER I

THE ALLIANCE AGAINST PERSIA

The Spartans assembled representatives of their allies at the Ko:
in the winter of 481/0, when it was known that the Persians were ␣ ␣␣␣␣␣␣␣ ␣␣ ␣␣␣
other side of the Aegean.[1] As in 490, the city immediately threatened was Athens;
but in 490 Sparta had been willing (if not very prompt) to give Athens support, and
the same considerations were still valid. The more formidable scale of the Persian
preparations increased the danger; it made it more dangerous to give support but also
more dangerous to withhold it. Sparta's own most immediate concern was probably
to defend Peloponnese.

From Herodotos' story it looks as if Athens took the initiative in proposing a
grand alliance, acting in this as the spokesman of the non-Peloponnesians who lay
in the path of the invader (the " Athenian group " in the list of cities on the Serpent
Column). The passage in Herodotos is plainly controversial and should be compared
with the similarly controversial speech of the Athenian at Sparta in 432 in Thucydides,
I, 73-74.[2] Herodotos says that Athens was the enemy's avowed objective, but all
Greece was in fact threatened (VII, 138, 1), and that if Athens had submitted
Peloponnese could not have been defended, so that " the Athenians may truly be called
the saviours of Greece "; their decision turned the balance, it was they who " roused
all the rest of Greece which did not medize " and next to the gods were responsible
for Xerxes' defeat (VII, 139). The Athenian decision was " to oppose the invader
with their whole force, by sea, together with such other Greeks as were willing "
(VII, 144, 3).

This Athenian decision no doubt went further than what Sparta had intended.
The Korinthian in Thucydides, I, 69, 5 complains in general terms of the Spartans'
lack of enterprise on this occasion; Herodotos implies that they meant simply to
fortify the Isthmos and evacuate all territory outside.[3] This can hardly have seemed

---

[1] At first these allies were in the main, probably, Peloponnesians: the " Spartan group " of the
Serpent Column plus Korinth. For the grouping of the allies on the Serpent Column (T68a) see
above, Part II, Chapter I. Korinth's northwestern allies were also perhaps there from the start,
certainly before the envoy was sent to Kerkyra (Herodotos, VII, 145, 2). Herodotos speaks of this
assembly in VII, 145, 1 and 172, 1 (the representatives are there called probouloi). He nowhere
says explicitly that the Peloponnesians assembled first, but we think it is implied by his general
narrative.

[2] According to Powell, *Herodotus*, p. 83 and *passim*, Herodotos wrote books VII-IX soon after
the delivery of this speech, and in the same controversial atmosphere. Note that with his usual
candour Herodotos also gives the Spartan view (in a speech, VIII, 142, 2): that Athens had provoked the war without Sparta's approval (this presumably refers to the burning of Sardis).

[3] VII, 139, 4: "no one can tell me what use it was to fortify the Isthmos while the enemy

satisfactory to Aigina, but Athens and Aigina were engaged in a truceless war and the alternative of joining Athens must have seemed impracticable. The initiative would come most appropriately from Athens, who had just built an overwhelmingly strong fleet which gave her good prospects in that war [4] and also made her the natural rallying point of those non-Peloponnesians (mainly islanders) who wanted a more forward strategy. If it was really proposed that Athens should have the naval command against Persia,[5] these islanders will have been the proposers. But Themistokles, who at this time led Athenian policy, saw with unique clearness the need for collaboration and was prepared to subordinate everything to it. There could be no question of Aigina's fleet serving under an Athenian admiral; so Sparta must command by sea as well as by land.

At the Isthmos, then, still in the winter of 481/0, the Peloponnesians were joined by representatives (probouloi, see note 1 above) of the other Greeks, and the parties now assembled pledged their faith to each other and discussd the alternative courses of action,[6] whether to hold the line of the Isthmos or to advance and meet the enemy by sea (and this meant also advancing the line on land). As is familiar, the Spartans agreed to the Athenian plan, to the extent of first reconnoitring the northern approaches to Thessaly and then attempting to hold the pass of Thermopylai, the entrance to Central Greece. The first was judged too difficult, the second proved too difficult in fact; Thessaly and all Central Greece had to be abandoned. After these failures, the controversy became acute, whether the fleet should still be kept so far north as Salamis or should be brought back for the immediate defense of Peloponnese. Themistokles threatened to withdraw the whole Athenian fleet from the alliance unless the former plan were adopted, and no doubt much of the " Athenian group " would have followed him. The Spartan command again consented, and at Salamis in the late summer of 480 the invaders' fleet was put out of action.

The victory of Salamis justified Athens' strategy and enhanced her prestige, but it was not yet decisive. The Persian fleet withdrew immediately to Phaleron in Attica and soon afterwards recrossed the Aegean and covered Xerxes' crossing into Asia;

controlled the sea "; cf. this whole chapter and Thucydides, I, 73, 4. Herodotos' thesis, that only Salamis prevented the Persian fleet from reducing Peloponnese city by city, was perhaps maintained by those who believed (in 432) that Athenian sea-power would be able to do the same. The latter belief proved to be untrue; cf. Thucydides, III, 56, 4. We do not, however, think that Herodotos' controversial tone affects the credit of his basic facts, namely, that Athens pressed for a forward strategy which the Peloponnesians did not much want. The association of allies on the Serpent Column illustrates this grouping of interests.

[4] Herodotos, VII, 144; Aristotle, Ἀθ. Πολ., 22, 7.

[5] Herodotos, VIII, 3, 1-2 (T66a); cf. VIII, 92, 2. He implies some continuity between this original proposal and the final secession in 479.

[6] Herodotos, VII, 145, 1: διδόντων σφίσι λόγον καὶ πίστιν. This is almost the same phrase as he uses to introduce the famous Persian conspirators' debate in III, 71, 1: ἐδίδοσαν σφίσι λόγους καὶ πίστις.

after that it wintered, part at Kyme and part at Samos. The west and the south of the Aegean were left at the disposal of the allies.[7] But until the strong Persian army which had been left in Greece under Mardonios had been defeated the final decision was still uncertain.[8] One immediate consequence was the revolt, led by Poteidaia, of the peninsula of Pallene in Chalkidike. The Persians spent three months trying to recover it but failed; Poteidaia (a Korinthian colony) was received into the " Korinthian group " on the Serpent Column, and sent 300 hoplites who fought beside the Korinthians at Plataia.[9] The Persian fleet was not pursued, but the medizing islands were visited and made to contribute to war expenses. Themistokles was the moving spirit in this and had to bear some odium for it. Herodotos records that no money could be obtained from Andros, that Karystos paid but did not thereby escape maltreatment, and that Paros sent a contribution and was therefore not visited; he believes that other islands contributed likewise, but knows no exact amounts and no further names (VIII, 110-112; 121). The contemporary Timokreon says that Themistokles came on this occasion [10] as far as Rhodes, and that he collected 3 talents from Ialysos [11] and sailed to many other places " bursting with money " and punishing traitors.

Such was the rather unfortunate precedent for the later collection of tribute. It was arbitrary, disciplinary, unpopular. It is no doubt of this (and possibly of other similar collections) that Plutarch speaks in *Aristides*, 24, 1 (T94), saying that the Greeks made some contribution to the war whilst the Spartans retained hegemony, but wished for a regular assessment and entrusted Aristeides with that task. The need for some such contributions, on one basis or the other, could not be denied, for the booty of Salamis could not meet all the expenses of the naval war.

The land strategy of the next year, 479, need not detain us. The summer was far advanced before the decisive land battle was fought at Plataia (August or September). Plutarch reports, in *Aristides*, 21, 1-2 (T94b), that after the battle an assembly (ἐκκλησία κοινή) of the Greeks was held and that Aristeides moved a decree

[7] Themistokles went as far as Rhodes in the autumn of 480; see below, note 26 on p. 191.

[8] Pindar, *Isthmia*, 5, written just after Salamis, refers to the battle (lines 46-50) and then adds (51-53) : ἀλλ' ὅμως καύχαμα κατάβρεχε σιγᾷ· Ζεὺς τά τε καὶ τὰ νέμει, Ζεὺς ὁ πάντων κύριος.

[9] Herodotos, VIII, 126-129; IX, 28, 3.

[10] See T97d and below, notes 15 and 26 on pp. 189 and 191. Timokreon's story is that after leaving Rhodes Themistokles went around dealing punishment and gathering money, and returned to the Isthmos where his unpopularity was seen. This last is evidently the same occasion as Herodotos describes in VIII, 123. From Herodotos one would infer that the fleet went no further east than Andros. It may be that on his further voyages Themistokles took only a small detachment. Unless the Persians were very badly demoralized this sounds rather risky; it is in any case in striking contrast with Leotychidas' timidity in the following year.

[11] The tribute of Ialysos was 10 talents in Periods [I], II, and VIII, 6 talents in IV and VI. and 5 talents in X.

(ψήφισμα) providing among other things for the contributions which the Greeks should make for continuing the war against Persia (σύνταξιν Ἑλληνικὴν – – – ἐπὶ τὸν πρὸς τοὺς βαρβάρους πόλεμον). If the decree is authentic this change will have done something towards regularizing the demands which the war was to make, but will not otherwise have much altered the nature of the alliance; it will not, for instance, have converted a war alliance into a permanent confederacy.[12] But we believe that it is probably not authentic, and from Thucydides we get the impression that, although a covenant was indeed made on the battlefield of Plataia, it was of a different kind.[13] Some sort of permanent obligations were assumed among themselves by the parties who conceived that they " had fought the war " and that it was over: they would for the indefinite future defend one another's freedom.[14] But though Sparta and Plataia could later charge each other with breaches of these obligations, the Covenant of Plataia did not create a viable union. The old union, on the other hand, was at that very moment on the threshold of its new life, when the fleet started to cross the Aegean and the liberation of the Asiatic Greeks began.

[12] Larsen, Cl. Phil., XXVIII (1933), pp. 262-265, and Harv. Stud. Cl. Phil., LI (1940), p. 176, believes the decree authentic and sees in it the creation of the " Hellenic League." In our belief, the " Hellenic League " (i. e., οἱ συνωμόται ἐπὶ τῷ Πέρσῃ, more usually called οἱ Ἕλληνες; see above, pp. 97-98 with note 12) came into existence in 481.

[13] See above, pp. 101-105.

[14] This is the implication, we believe, of Thucydides, II, 72, 1; 74, 2; 71, 2. See above, pp. 102-104.

CHAPTER II

TRANSITION

The spring of 479 B. C. found a Greek fleet of 110 ships under the command of the Spartan Leotychidas mustered at Aigina. While they lay there, Chian envoys reached them with the plea that they free Ionia. These Chians had failed in their attempt to produce revolution at Chios and had fled first to Sparta. The Hellenes reluctantly escorted the Chians eastward to Delos but beyond this they dared not sail, despite the Chian entreaties. Since the Persian fleet, based at Samos, felt a similar timidity, a stalemate existed at sea.[1]

As the Greeks lingered at Delos, they were visited by representatives from Samos who urged Leotychidas and the other generals to seek out the Persians on the coast of Asia Minor and thus to liberate that territory from foreign rule. The Samians were apparently more persuasive than the Chians, for Leotychidas accepted them and their pledge of Samian alliance with the Greeks.[2] The Samians kept their mission and presumably their alliance secret;[3] if the Greek effort should fail, the Samian situation would be desperate and the islanders were anxious not to commit themselves openly. In view of the earlier unwillingness of the Greek squadron to risk manoeuvres in eastern waters at all, one may well be surprised that the Samians were so successful, especially after the Chian failure. It is possible, however, that events on the mainland of Greece influenced the decision. Plataia might by this time have been fought and the news, reaching Delos, could have inspired the naval forces with a new courage. At any rate, they sought out the Persians and inflicted upon them a decisive defeat at Mykale.[4]

---

[1] Herodotos, VIII, 131-132.

[2] Herodotos, IX, 90-92. The Samian pledge was made πρὸς τοὺς Ἕλληνας.

[3] Herodotos, IX, 90, 1: ἄγγελοι ἀπὸ Σάμου – – –, πεμφθέντες ὑπὸ Σαμίων λάθρῃ τῶν τε Περσέων καὶ τοῦ τυράννου – – –, τὸν κατέστησαν Σάμου τύραννον οἱ Πέρσαι. The Persians nevertheless suspected the Samians; IX, 99, 1.

[4] Herodotos places the battles of Plataia and Mykale on the same day, in the morning and afternoon respectively; IX, 90, 1 and 100-101. The report of the victory at Plataia reached Mykale in time to spur the allies to greater efforts. The synchronism is no doubt romantic and may have come from the *Phoinissai* of Phrynichos, in which, as Marx has shown, a description of the battle of Mykale was an incident; *Rh. Mus.*, LXXVII (1928), pp. 337-360, especially pp. 359-360. That the battles were fought on the same day and that news of Plataia reached Mykale in time to stimulate the allied combatants Herodotos regards as a miracle; it would be a very effective dramatic device. Larsen, *Cl. Phil.*, XXVIII (1933), p. 264 with note 23, discards the synchronism and even proposes that the Samians at Delos were admitted into the Hellenic League as reorganized at Plataia. This we doubt; it makes more difficult the later acceptance of the Samians and it is not necessary to account for the Greek advance. Larsen has more recently modified his views; *Harv. Stud. Cl. Phil.*, LI (1940), p. 180 with note 2, and see below, p. 188.

After the battle of Mykale, the Greeks destroyed the Persian camp, burned the Persian ships, gathered available booty, and sailed away to Samos.[5] This victory precipitated the second Ionian revolt.[6] At Samos a conference was held to debate the possibility of transplanting the Ionians from Ionia to Greece. This would abandon Ionia to the Persians, but the allies could not guard the territory forever and the Ionians could do little in their own defense. The Spartan policy of non-intervention is clear, although Herodotos tells us that the Peloponnesian (not merely Spartan) leaders [7] were in favour of dispossessing Greek states at home which had medized and giving their land to the Ionians. The Athenians, on the other hand, opposed the suggestion and indeed resented the Peloponnesian willingness to make plans about people who were after all colonists of Athens. They maintained this point of view with vigour, until their opponents yielded. So Ionia was not abandoned and under pledge and oath the Hellenes accepted into the alliance the Samians, Chians, Lesbians, and other islanders, who, as it happened, were with them in the campaign. Their business finished, they set out towards the Hellespont to destroy the bridges.[8]

The Samians had now been accepted twice by the allies, once at Delos before Mykale and again at Samos after the battle. According to Larsen, " the natural explanation is that the first time the Samians were accepted as allies by the organization conducting the war; the second time they were admitted into the Hellenic League as reorganized at Plataea." [9] Rather, we believe that whatever reorganization was carried out at Plataia automatically embraced all of those who had been officially accepted by the fighting forces (by land and by sea) and that, if oaths were sworn, they were sworn at Plataia before the generals by current members, not before the naval arm, which was already part of the organization. The new allies at Samos were recent acquisitions. A better explanation of the Samian incident lies in the secrecy of the negotiations at Delos. Leotychidas and the generals, on behalf of the Hellenes, accepted the Samians through envoys whose mission could not be made public. These commitments, on both sides perhaps,[10] had to be ratified; hence the ceremony at Samos, when the danger of Persian reprisals had disappeared.

Who " the other islanders " were we are not told; along with the Samians, Chians, and Lesbians, they were too late to win a place on the Serpent Column at Delphi.[11]

[5] Herodotos, IX, 106, 1.

[6] Herodotos, IX, 104: οὖτω δὴ τὸ δεύτερον Ἰωνίη ἀπὸ Περσέων ἀπέστη.

[7] Herodotos, IX, 106, 3: Πελοποννησίων μὲν τοῖσι ἐν τέλεϊ ἐοῦσι ἐδόκεε — — —.

[8] For the conference see Herodotos, IX, 106. We accept the proposal to transplant the Ionians as historical (cf. Larsen, Harv. Stud. Cl. Phil., LI [1940], p. 181); it is named as the first order of business. For the acceptance of new allies see 106, 4: καὶ οὖτω δὴ Σαμίους τε καὶ Χίους καὶ Λεσβίους καὶ τοὺς ἄλλους νησιώτας, οἳ ἔτυχον συστρατευόμενοι τοῖσι Ἕλλησι, ἐς τὸ συμμαχικὸν ἐποιήσαντο, πίστι τε καταλαβόντες καὶ ὁρκίοισι ἐμμενέειν τε καὶ μὴ ἀποστήσεσθαι. We understand ἐμμενέειν to indicate permanency.

[9] Harv. Stud. Cl. Phil., LI (1940), p. 180; cf. note 4 above.

[10] In Herodotos Leotychidas personally accepts the Samians; IX, 91-92.

[11] T68a; cf. Herodotos, VIII, 43-48 and IX, 28-30.

They were of course territories early lost to Persia, although loss to Persia did not of itself mean gain to the Hellenic League. Andros is a case in point, for she successfully resisted a Greek naval squadron shortly after the battle of Salamis. No longer Persian, she was nevertheless not collaborating with the Greek fleet which broke off pursuit of the Persians at the island. Andros, unlike Paros and Karystos, refused to make payments to Themistokles, and the Greeks, after failing to take the town by siege, turned aside to Karystos, which they ravaged, before sailing back to Salamis.[12] The Andrians, no doubt, were not yet convinced, despite the victory at Salamis, that the allied cause would prevail and preferred a safe neutrality.[13] Here again they differed from the Parians, who, after waiting at Kythnos to see how the battle at Salamis would turn out,[14] now surrendered (not unwillingly, we may assume) to the demands of Themistokles. In the following year (479) the Samians too, whose danger to be sure was more urgent, did not commit themselves publicly before Mykale, as we have seen. In addition, the Andrians objected to the behaviour of Themistokles, which seemed to them high-handed.

It is entirely probable that the Andrians were no differently disposed in 479 when the Greek fleet gathered at Aigina or while it lay at Delos. The factors which must have governed many minds were the twin victories of Plataia and Mykale, and of these Mykale was to the islanders the more important. The islands, says Herodotos, were in part the prizes (ἄεθλα) of victory.[15]

The route from Aigina to Samos passes some islands that were represented at the Isthmos in 481/0, that were original members of the Hellenic League, and whose records entitled them to a place on the Serpent Column.[16] But it passes also other islands, which, like Samos, Chios, and Lesbos, may have been new recruits. Mykonos was immediately adjacent to the Greek base at Delos, Syros and Rhenaia were on the

[12] Herodotos, VIII, 111-112 and 121, 1. For the conference on the island, VIII, 108, 1: οἱ Ἕλληνες — — — διώξαντες μέχρι Ἄνδρου, ἐς δὲ τὴν Ἄνδρον ἀπικόμενοι ἐβουλεύοντο.

[13] The allies themselves, in the spring of 479, were not aggressive in attitude; see above, p. 187.

[14] Herodotos, VIII, 67, 1.

[15] IX, 101, 3 (the passage is quoted in full in note 23 below). Mykale was decisive to many of the islanders, but the Andrian objection to the forced levies of money remained. Of the activities leading to the formation of the Delian Confederacy in 478 B. C. Plutarch writes, *Aristides*, 24, 1 (T94): οἱ δ' Ἕλληνες ἐτέλουν μέν τινα καὶ Λακεδαιμονίων ἡγουμένων ἀποφορὰν εἰς τὸν πόλεμον, ταχθῆναι δὲ βουλόμενοι καὶ κατὰ πόλιν ἑκάστοις τὸ μέτριον ᾐτήσαντο παρὰ τῶν Ἀθηναίων Ἀριστείδην (this cannot refer to any time before Salamis). The allies wanted their contributions assessed on a regular and equitable basis to replace the spasmodic and arbitrary exactions made during Lakedaimonian hegemony. We consider that the complaint is directed against such conduct as that of Themistokles in 480. The new arrangements would have disposed of Andrian objections and there is no reason to believe that the island did not enter the Confederacy of Delos at its inception in 478/7 B. C. Karystos was a different case; she was suspected of medism and even her surrender to Themistokles did not save her from chastisement.

[16] T68a: Keos, Kythnos, Melos, Naxos, Seriphos, Siphnos, and Tenos were all reasonably close; cf. Herodotos, VIII, 46 and 48.

direct route, and Paros had presumably thrown in its lot with the Hellenes the previous year; these four might perhaps be considered among " the other islanders." But there were also states to whom the result of Mykale was particularly decisive in terms of their own immediate future.[17] West of Samos lies Ikaros, the home of the Oinaioi (ἐξ Ἰκάρου) and the Thermaioi (ἐξ Ἰκάρου) of the quota lists. These have a primary claim to be considered among " the other islanders," and they might have joined the Hellenes either before or after the battle; perhaps their conduct was similar to that of the Samians and their acceptance at the congress a form of ratification.

There may have been others,[18] but an attempt to define them precisely would be hazardous; we should expect them to lie fairly near to the scene of action or on the direct route taken by the fleet. Leotychidas had employed a strategem before the battle to win over the Ionians in the Persian camp[19] and Herodotos, in his description of the engagement, tells us of Milesians and Samians who deserted the Persians, and mentions " the other Ionians " who followed the lead of the Samians in revolt.[20] The Ikarians were Ionian and there must have been " other Ionians " from the mainland who abandoned Persia: " in this way Ionia revolted for the second time from the Persians " (οὕτω δὴ τὸ δεύτερον Ἰωνίη ἀπὸ Περσέων ἀπέστη). It does not follow that all the rebels joined the Hellenic League, but some may have done so.[21]

The fleet moved from Samos to Abydos, where the Greeks found that the bridges were already down. At this Leotychidas and the Peloponnesians sailed home but the Athenians, under Xanthippos, decided to remain and to attack the Chersonese. They thereupon crossed the strait and besieged Sestos.[22] Thucydides describes this force as " the Athenians and the allies from Ionia and the Hellespont who had already revolted from the King " (οἱ δὲ Ἀθηναῖοι καὶ οἱ ἀπὸ Ἰωνίας καὶ Ἑλλησπόντου ξύμμαχοι ἤδη ἀφεστηκότες ἀπὸ βασιλέως). At first sight there is a discrepancy between this and " the other islanders " of Herodotos. The Hellespontine allies, it is easy to understand, joined the fleet when it arrived, and, if " the other islanders " of Herodotos were the Thermaioi and Oinaioi, who could well have been listed as " from Ionia "

---

[17] The word συστρατευόμενοι in Herodotos, IX, 106, 4 (see note 8 above, where the passage is quoted in full) need not mean (and does not deny) that the new recruits had fought at Mykale on the Greek side; they must have joined the fleet in time to participate in the conference at Samos after the battle.

[18] Gomme, *Commentary*, I, p. 257, would include the Dorian islands.

[19] Herodotos, IX, 98.

[20] Herodotos, IX, 103-104.

[21] From the mainland Herodotos names only the Milesians as having actively assisted the Greeks; he does not include them at Samos. The Spartans may have hesitated to accept into the League continental states whom they were unwilling to defend (Gomme, *Commentary*, I, p. 257) ; yet it is difficult to see how such states at this time could join the Athenians without joining the League. It may be that Leotychidas, soon after Mykale, went to Miletos and expelled Aristogenes, probably the pro-Persian tyrant there; Plutarch, *Moralia*, 859d.

[22] Herodotos, IX, 106, 4; 114; Thucydides, I, 89, 2.

(ἀπὸ Ἰωνίας) by Thucydides, there is of course no discrepancy. It is even more likely, however, that Ionians from the mainland had entered the Hellenic League after the conference at Samos and were contributing to naval operations. Events at Samos followed so closely upon Mykale that all the new recruits (islanders and mainlanders) did not have time to be sworn into the League on that occasion. Before Mykale, both Greeks and Persians had realized that the islands and the Hellespont were the prizes of victory.[23]

The siege of Sestos, which lasted into the winter of 479/8, ended in its capture, after which the Athenians and the allies sailed away to their several homes.[24]

The spring of 478 B. C. saw a resumption of naval operations in eastern waters under the leadership of the Spartan Pausanias. The Peloponnesians contributed 20 ships, the Athenians 30; a sizable force of the other allies rounded out the naval squadron which now represented the Hellenic League. During this year the campaigns of Pausanias struck as far east as Kypros and led up to, and included, the siege and capture of Byzantion.[25]

Undoubtedly there were along the route from Greece to Kypros and then back to Byzantion many cities that threw off the yoke of Persia. Those of Rhodes were among them,[26] and Thucydides tells us that the greater part of Kypros was subjugated by the Greeks. Other names are not known and we are not told whether any become members of the Hellenic League. Some probably did (e. g., the cities of Rhodes), but some probably refrained.[27]

At Byzantion the conduct of Pausanias became such that the allies appealed to Athens, " trading on their kinship " (κατὰ τὸ ξυγγενές), to assume the hegemony.[28] The result of the trouble was that Pausanias was recalled to face charges at Sparta

---

[23] Herodotos, IX, 101, 3: οἱ μὲν δὴ Ἕλληνες καὶ οἱ βάρβαροι ἔσπευδον ἐς τὴν μάχην, ὥς σφι καὶ αἱ νῆσοι καὶ ὁ Ἑλλήσποντος ἄεθλα προέκειτο. One could argue that the western islanders like the My-konians and Parians, νησιῶται to Herodotos but not ἀπὸ Ἰωνίας to Thucydides, had withdrawn from the campaign by the time operations began in the Hellespont; but this we do not regard as likely, especially in view of the tremendous stimulus given to Greek morale by the victories at Plataia and Mykale. Cf. Thucydides, VII, 57, 4 (T143): ἐκ δ' Ἰωνίας Μιλήσιοι καὶ Σάμιοι καὶ Χῖοι.

[24] Thucydides, I, 89, 2: οἱ δὲ Ἀθηναῖοι καὶ οἱ ἀπὸ Ἰωνίας καὶ Ἑλλησπόντου ξύμμαχοι ἤδη ἀφεστηκότες ἀπὸ βασιλέως ὑπομείναντες Σηστὸν ἐπολιόρκουν Μήδων ἐχόντων, καὶ ἐπιχειμάσαντες εἷλον αὐτὴν ἐκλιπόντων τῶν βαρβάρων, καὶ μετὰ τοῦτο ἀπέπλευσαν ἐξ Ἑλλησπόντου ὡς ἕκαστοι κατὰ πόλεις. This passage proves that Ionian allies had ships at their disposal at least a year before the Confederacy of Delos was organized (cf. Gomme, Commentary, I, p. 272).

[25] Thucydides, I, 94, especially 2: ἐν τῇδε τῇ ἡγεμονίᾳ.

[26] See Timokreon's poem in Plutarch, Themistocles, 21, 4 (T97d); Aristeides accompanied Pausanias. The lines also show that Themistokles was in Rhodes, where (in Ialysos) he took 3 talents. This belongs in 480 and gives us an indication of the extent of Themistokles' fund-raising expedition of that year (see note 15 above); the indignation of the allies, Λακεδαιμονίων ἡγουμένων, is understandable.

[27] For Kypros, which did not join the League, see below, pp. 207-209.

[28] Thucydides, I, 95.

while the allied pleas to the Athenians, in which the Peloponnesian forces took no part,[29] fell upon willing ears. Pausanias was acquitted on the major charges but he was not sent out again to command; instead Dorkis with colleagues and a small force was despatched to the allied fleet. The damage, however, had been done and when the allies refused to acknowledge Spartan leadership, through Dorkis, the latter departed. No further attempt was made by the Spartans to maintain command of the naval arm. They feared the effects of such experience upon their generals and, typically enough, they wished to be free of the war against the Mede. In any case the Athenians, they felt, were competent to command and satisfactory to Sparta.[30]

It is our belief that Dorkis, whose mission is generally placed in the spring of 477, was sent as a replacement for Pausanias in the summer of 478. When Pausanias was recalled the campaigning season had not yet come to a close and the Spartans, unaware of the extent of allied defection, believed that the responsibility of leadership was still theirs. It was their duty to provide a commander to take up the work begun by Pausanias.

The negotiations and arrangements that were to transform the naval arm of the Hellenic League into the Confederacy of Delos began in the summer of 478 and continued throughout the winter of 478/7. By the spring, we may be sure, all was ready for the season's campaign under the leadership of Athens. Sparta was anxious to withdraw and she must have realized what the allies and the Athenians were doing. Thus Sparta's conduct would be unaccountable if in the spring of 477, in the face of her own desire to withdraw and the Athenian willingness to lead willing allies in a newly organized body, she persisted in sending out new commanders for the fleet.[31] The Spartan retreat belongs in the autumn of 478 and this retreat was one of the factors which allowed the Athenians to proceed apace with their reorganization in the winter of 478/7 B. C.

The retirement of Dorkis meant not only that Spartan participation in the war was at an end but also that some other members of the Hellenic League returned to their homes and played no part in the formation of the new Confederacy. These naturally included the Peloponnesians, who were followed, we may be sure, by other

---

[29] Thucydides, I, 95, 4: ξυνέβη --- τοὺς ξυμμάχους --- παρ' Ἀθηναίους μετατάξασθαι πλὴν τῶν ἀπὸ Πελοποννήσου στρατιωτῶν. Presumably the Peloponnesian forces did not return with Pausanias; they awaited his replacement.

[30] Thucydides, I, 95, 7: --- ἀπαλλαξείοντες δὲ καὶ τοῦ Μηδικοῦ πολέμου καὶ τοὺς Ἀθηναίους νομίζοντες ἱκανοὺς ἐξηγεῖσθαι καὶ σφίσιν ἐν τῷ τότε παρόντι ἐπιτηδείους. The Athenians assumed their hegemony ἑκόντων τῶν ξυμμάχων; Thucydides, I, 96, 1 (T109). Gomme, Commentary, I, p. 272, proposes that ἀκόντων τῶν Λακεδαιμονίων, in Aristotle, Ἀθ. Πολ., 23, 2, means " Sparta being unwilling to keep the leadership "; this, we believe, is right.

[31] Thucydides, I, 95, 4 makes it clear that the negotiations of the allies with the Athenians were in progress even as Pausanias was obeying the summons to return to Sparta; this was in the summer of 478; the interval to the spring of 477 is too long to suppose Spartan ignorance of the allied temper.

Dorians (*e. g.*, the Melians and the Aiginetans). Membership in the Hellenic League does not guarantee membership in the Confederacy of Delos.[32]

By the end of the season in 478 the formal organization of the Confederacy had been begun; during the winter the proposals were ratified at Delos and the Confederacy entered upon its formal existence; by the spring of 477 the first tributes had been assessed, if not paid, and the confederates, under the aggressive leadership of Athens, were ready to continue the liberation of Greek territories from Persia.[33]

---

[32] Those who retired may have included some who joined the Hellenic League during the campaigns of Pausanias in 478.

[33] Of Aristeides Aristotle says, Ἀθ. Πολ., 23, 5 (T39): " And so it was Aristeides who laid the first assessments of phoroi on the cities, in the third year after the battle of Salamis, in the archonship of Timosthenes " (διὸ καὶ τοὺς φόρους οὗτος ἦν ὁ τάξας ταῖς πόλεσι τοὺς πρώτους, ἔτει τρίτῳ μετὰ τὴν ἐν Σαλαμῖνι ναυμαχίαν, ἐπὶ Τιμοσθένους ἄρχοντος). This date is a cornerstone of the early history of the Confederacy.

CHAPTER III

THE ORIGINAL MEMBERSHIP OF THE CONFEDERACY

We are nowhere given a list of the original members of the Confederacy of Delos, any more than we are told which states supplied ships and which money. We are therefore obliged to combine the evidence of the Serpent Column (T68a), of the quota lists, and of the literary authorities if we wish to determine approximately the membership of 478/7 B. C.[1] A complete roster of all the identifiable names which appear in the assessment and quota lists is set out by districts in *A. T. L.*, I, pp. 457-460. Our references will be to this and to the map which accompanies *A. T. L.*, I.

Many of the states, we know, were not associated with the Confederacy at the beginning; the task is to identify and to eliminate these. Much of the evidence is negative, for, though we can often be certain that given towns were not original members, we are seldom positively informed about those that were. Again, we are sometimes told, or we can safely deduce, that states had thrown off Persian control; but it does not follow that they immediately attached themselves to the Confederacy. In most cases they surely did, for it is difficult to see what other course was open to them if they hoped to retain their freedom. Still, the nature of the problem creates a possible margin of error with which we must always reckon.

In estimating the extent of the first membership (the cities included in Aristeides' assessment)[2] we are conscious that we apply some criteria which are not decisive. We therefore state these criteria at the outset in order that the reader may form his own judgment of them.

We consider that names found in the quota and assessment lists are not likely to have appeared in the first assessment if

    (A) they lie far inland,
    (B) they lie beyond the other geographic limits which we believe credible for the first assessment,
    (C) their record in the tribute lists is sporadic or begins late.

Under (A) we exclude more particularly cities of the Marsyas valley in Karia, of the upper Skamandros valley in the Troad, of the upper Strymon (especially Berge) in Thrace. Such areas were not easily accessible to the Confederacy, which at its inception was essentially maritime.

---

[1] For the assessment of 478/7 see below, Chapter V.

[2] Contributions were made in ships or in money. For our purposes, whether a city's status was tributary (cash) or non-tributary (ships) is irrelevant.

Under (B) we judge that the Confederacy did not at first extend into the Levant or the Black Sea, nor to those Dorian islands of the south Aegean which do not group themselves naturally with the Ionian Islands or with the Asiatic Greeks; we do not carry the Confederacy's jurisdiction north or west of Cape Aineia at the entrance to the Gulf of Salonika, and, though the route through the Dardanelles and Hellespont was secured, we posit that much of the Propontis coast remained at first under the influence of the Thrakians (between Tyrodiza and Didymoteichitai) or the satrap of Daskyleion (east of Kyzikos).

Criterion (C) is rather more complex and might very easily be subdivided. First, there are the cities whose payments in the quota lists are so sporadic as to suggest that they were never regular members of the Confederacy at all; they paid occasionally, perhaps when Athens applied compulsion, but as a rule they disappear from the records early. Most of them are in the Karic district, and most of them were deliberately allowed to drop from the roll about 440; lying inland, as the majority do, they would fall also under criterion (A). Similarly we dismiss from original membership cities which were acquired late; this is sometimes reflected in the quota lists, sometimes attested by the literary sources (e. g., Phaselis).

In List 21 there commence the special rubrics which mark the adoption of a new policy by Athens. The πόλεις αὐταί and the ἰδιῶται rubrics [3] contain peripheral cities and cities which have been assessed separately by apotaxis.[4] These we eliminate from the original roster on the ground that peripheral cities were not members, and states to whom apotaxis was applied later have no right to independent membership in the early years. At the time of the first assessment, and for many years afterwards, Athens was not concerned with the dependencies of her allies. If a large state in a given area chose to farm out part of its financial obligation, this was not the business of Athens. In 478/7, indeed, many of the dependencies could not yet have developed. In Thrace, for example, the Persian march and flight must have produced chaotic conditions, to which stability was brought only with time. Apotaxis, which was not employed on a large scale until after 440, was a means of increasing Athenian revenues; the assessment of the large city might decrease, but the sum total realized by Athens, when she took over direct assessment of the small dependencies, increased.

The separate assessment of an island's peraia was a form of apotaxis;[5] witness Samothrake, whose mainland towns (Drys, Zone, Sale) do not appear in the records until A10. It is extremely doubtful whether Thasos and Samothrake exercised control on the mainland until eastern Thrace had been cleared of the Persians. Thasos, however, lost her peraia early, for Athens stripped it from her after the revolt (463/2).[6]

[3] *A. T. L.*, I, pp. 455-456; see also above, pp. 80-88.

[4] Cf. Antiphon, frag. 55 Thalheim (T19): ἀπόταξις· τὸ χωρὶς τετάχθαι τοὺς πρότερον ἀλλήλοις συντεταγμένους εἰς τὸ ὑποτελεῖν τὸν ὡρισμένον φόρον.

[5] The definition quoted in note 4 is from Antiphon's speech περὶ τοῦ Σαμοθρᾴκων φόρου.

[6] Thucydides, I, 101, 3 (T110); for the date see above, pp. 175-176 with notes 57, 58.

In Asia Minor Lesbos, Chios, and Samos had possessions on the mainland.[7] Lesbos lost hers after the revolt of 428/7 (Thucydides, III, 50, 2-3 [T128]) and the assessment of 425/4 reveals the names of no fewer than thirteen of these towns (A9, III, 125-137); we know that there were more. The peraia of Chios, which extended north of Atarneus, adjoined or perhaps overlapped that of Lesbos.[8] The Samian peraia lay due east of the island and centred about Anaia (Thucydides, III, 32, 2; IV, 75, 1). Samos and Chios never paid tribute and the unmarked areas on our map east of Samos and Lesbos (the Chian peraia) are explained by this fact. If all the names which occur late by reason of apotaxis were removed from the map, it would reveal many sparsely marked areas. Conversely, we are sure that other dependencies existed, at present unknown to us, which contributed indirectly to the Athenian treasury. Independent membership in the Confederacy, however, we hold to have been based upon individual assessment; we shall therefore list as original members only those cities which we suppose to have been assessed, not their dependencies.

In A9 or in A10, or in both, we meet many names without tribute records before the Archidamian war. Some of these too are to be explained by apotaxis; others by the fact that A9 was an unrealistic assessment which contained cities from whom Athens could scarcely expect payments. They cannot be included in the original membership of the Confederacy.

In tabulating names which are to be removed from the roster of 478/7 under criterion (C), we shall add in each case the lists and assessments in which sporadic tributaries are entered; for those who do not occur until later in the records we shall refer to the list or assessment in which the first appearance is made. The reader will already have observed that a city may well fall under more than one category; for example, many sporadic records come from inland territory, and the location will often explain the record. So too under criterion (C) there will be much overlapping. We shall attempt to give some indication of these facts.

Some scholars may hold that the true explanation of Thucydides' figure of 460 talents for the first assessment is that the membership was vastly larger than we are supposing. They may point to the fact that the Persian forces after Mykale retreated to Sardes;[9] to Pausanias' reduction of Kypros in 478;[10] to Aristeides' mission into the Black Sea;[11] to the possible appearance of Kretan names in A9[12] and of Melos in the "Athenian group" on the Serpent Column.[13] They may contend that sporadic

---

[7] Rhodes had apparently not yet acquired a peraia. The towns of the peninsula which was later Rhodian seem to have formed a syntely of their own in the Karic Chersonese; see below, note 73.

[8] See the Gazetteer, s. v. Καρηναῖοι, in A. T. L., I, pp. 495-496.

[9] Herodotos, IX, 107, 1.

[10] Thucydides, I, 94, 2.

[11] Plutarch, Aristides, 26, 1.

[12] See the note on A9, II, 158-160, in A. T. L., I, pp. 206-207.

[13] See above, pp. 96, 99.

appearance in and after the middle of the century, when Athens' popularity was on the wane, does not preclude enthusiastic participation in the formation of the Confederacy when morale was high.[14] We cannot disprove such a position and we concede in principle that it may be right; but we have weighed it carefully and do not find it convincing.

ISLANDS

For the islands who were charter members of the Confederacy we have an important piece of positive evidence in the Serpent Column,[15] on which the " Athenian group " contains eight island cities which later pay tribute; to these we should add as a ninth Seriphos, which fought on the right side at Salamis.[16] Aigina, in the " Spartan group," paid later, but with Melos, in the " Athenian group," no doubt withdrew from naval operations along with the Peloponnesians at the end of 478.[17] Poteidaia, in the " Korinthian group," belongs to the Thrakian district. The revised Insular list, with the date of the first recorded payment of tribute added to each name, is as follows: Chalkis (448/7), Eretria (448/7), Keos (451/0), Kythnos (450/49), Naxos (450/49), Seriphos (451/0), Siphnos (450/49), Styra (450/49), Tenos (450/49). That no payment for this group is recorded before 451/0 cannot, in West's view, be ascribed to the accident of survival and he would consider them charter members of the Confederacy who contributed ships in the early years and commuted their obligations to cash about 450 B. C.[18] These names give us a good start towards identifying the original Insular membership.

We follow West in adding to the list of original members Andros (first preserved payment, 451/0) and Hestiaia (450/49).[19] We have already seen that the refusal of Andros to join the Hellenic League in 480 (and 479) does not preclude her membership in the Confederacy of Delos in 478/7, after a regular method of assessment had

---

[14] We argue in detail against some of these suggestions below.

[15] T68a; cf. Herodotos, VIII, 46 and 48. For the grouping see above, pp. 96-100.

[16] Herodotos, VIII, 46, 4 and 48.

[17] See above, pp. 192-193. Aigina became tributary in 457; Thucydides, I, 108, 4 (T111), and for the date see above pp. 171-173, 178.

[18] West, *Am. Hist. Rev.*, XXXV (1929-1930), pp. 267-275. Plutarch, *Cimon*, 11 (T95), tells us of Kimon's conciliatory policy towards the allies: he accepted money and empty ships instead of the burdensome service and so the allies became tributary (ἔλαθον ἀντὶ συμμάχων ὑποτελεῖς καὶ δοῦλοι γεγονότες). West proposes that the story may belong to 451 and 450, after Kimon's return from ostracism, where it fits well with the evidence of the quota lists; *op. cit.*, especially pp. 269-272 and 275. We believe, however, that Plutarch, *Cimon*, 11 is based very largely on Thucydides, I, 99, and that Plutarch exaggerates the rôle of Kimon; nor is the dating of the story vital to West's thesis, which we accept in general. See further below, pp. 244-250. For Naxos, a charter member which became tributary after her revolt *ca.* 470, see above, pp. 65-66. Chalkis and Eretria probably paid tribute in 450/49; see above, note 7 on p. 31.

[19] *Op. cit.*, pp. 274-275 with note 26.

been instituted.[20] As for the towns of Euboia, Karystos alone is eliminated by the literary sources. Despite her submission to Themistokles in 480 she was ravaged by the allies in the same year (she was suspected of medism), and some time after 478/7 she was attacked by the Confederate forces. Eventually she surrendered and, we may be sure, was enrolled as tributary.[21] She had probably refused to join the Confederacy earlier; she was perhaps embittered by her fruitless appeasement of the Greeks in 480.[22]

We have previously nominated Mykonos, Syros, and Rhenaia for membership in the Hellenic League in 479, and Paros a year earlier;[23] there is no reason to doubt that these Ionians participated in the negotiations on Delos.

According to criterion (B) we may now eliminate the Dorian islands: Melos (only in A9), Kimolos (first in A9), Thera (first in List 25), Pholegandros (first in A9), Anaphe (first in List 27), Kythera (first in List 31).[24] These Dorians, along with Aigina, if they participated in the naval war, probably followed the Peloponnesians in the withdrawals of 479 and 478.[25]

Criterion (C) may now be applied to strike from our roll: Posideion (Euboic, only in A9), the Euboic Diakres (first in the ἰδιῶται rubric of List 21, perhaps by apotaxis from Chalkis) and Diakrioi (first in List 26, perhaps by apotaxis from Chalkis), Belbina (only in A9), Keria (only in A9, perhaps by apotaxis from Naxos, although it is assessed with Anaphe), Sikinos (first in A9), Koresia (only in List 4, elsewhere included in the payment of Keos).

We are left with the following Insular candidates for the roll of 478/7 B. C.:

Andros	Ios	Rhenaia
Athenai Diades	Keos	Seriphos

[20] See above, p. 189 with note 15.

[21] Herodotos, VIII, 112, 2-3 and 121, 1; Thucydides, I, 98, 3 (T109): πρὸς δὲ Καρυστίους αὐτοῖς ἄνευ τῶν ἄλλων Εὐβοέων πόλεμος ἐγένετο, καὶ χρόνῳ ξυνέβησαν καθ᾽ ὁμολογίαν. The other Euboian towns did not participate (they were not recalcitrant, they belonged to the Confederacy).

[22] Gomme, Commentary, I, p. 291, says that the reduction of Karystos fell so soon after the formation of the Confederacy that her exclusion at the beginning is of no importance in the computation of the initial tribute. This, however, is an understatement of the significance of Thucydides' text (I, 98). Thucydides names in order the events of importance after the founding of the Confederacy. First is the conquest of Eion, after a siege, then the taking of Skyros at a later date (ἔπειτα) and its colonization, and only then the conquest of Karystos, which itself took time (χρόνῳ); he goes on to describe the subjugation of Naxos, which may, we think, have been as early as 470. The capture of Eion is dated to 476/5 by the scholiast to Aischines, II, 34. For the chronology and the text of the scholiast see above, pp. 158-160 with the notes; cf. p. 175.

[23] See above, pp. 189-190.

[24] Melos, with whom Kimolos should be associated, was never tributary and was destroyed in 416/5; Thucydides, V, 116, 2-4. Thera was independent in the spring of 431 B. C. (Thucydides, II, 9, 4 [T116]) and was soon afterwards taken by Athens; Meritt, D. A. T., pp. 35-37. Pholegandros and Anaphe were her neighbours. Kythera became Athenian in 424; Thucydides, IV, 57, 4 (T132). It will be noted that all these fall under criterion (C).

[25] See above, pp. 190, 192-193.

Chalkis	Kythnos	Siphnos
Dion (Euboia)	Lemnos (Hephaistia, Myrina)	Styra
Eretria	Mykonos	Syros
Grynche	Naxos	Tenos [26]
Hestiaia	Paros	

IONIA

To eliminate names from the complete Ionic panel of *A. T. L.*, I, p. 457 is more difficult. Larisa (only in A9, perhaps by apotaxis from Kyme or Phokaia) falls under criterion (C). Karene is mentioned by Krateros and we have assigned it to the assessment of 454/3 (A1). Its precise location is not known and we have placed it on the mainland and somewhat inland, on the borders of the continental territories of Lesbos and Chios, one of which may have later acquired it.[27] It may therefore have joined the Confederacy in 478/7.

The conduct of the Milesians at Mykale would certainly suggest that the city joined the Greeks as soon as possible.[28] A great many others must have done the same, for otherwise Herodotos' statement that the second Ionian revolt occurred now would lose much of its point; [29] and Thucydides' mention of Ionian allies who coöperated at the siege of Sestos in 479 supports this view.[30]

Yet there is a grave difference of opinion among historians concerning the status of the Ionian cities. Walker is typical of those who would deny original membership to important cities in Ionia (and, to be sure, in the Hellespont as well); " It is more than probable that from ––– Ionia and the Hellespont, serious deductions have to be made. It is not disputed that Ephesus and Myus in the former, and Byzantium, Lampsacus, and the greater part of the Thracian Chersonese, in the latter, were not yet in the possession of the League. ––– It is by the merest accident that we happen to know that the places mentioned were still in Persian hands ––– what warrant can there be for the assertion that from every other place in these two districts the Persian garrisons had been expelled? We may conclude then that the Confederacy ––– comprised ––– most, although by no means all, of the cities on the mainland of Ionia, and a majority of the cities in the Hellespontine district." [31] To the list of Ionic absentees Highby

---

[26] Imbros, in the early quota lists, was a member of the Thrakian Chersonese syntely and so must be considered Hellespontine until the breakdown of the syntely. In Period I a single payment seems to cover the island of Lemnos, in the name of Hephaistia in List 2, Λήμνιοι in List 3. Myrina does not appear until List 5 and is perhaps not entitled to independent membership in 478/7.

[27] *A. T. L.*, I, pp. 495-496.

[28] Herodotos, IX, 104; cf. above, p. 190 with note 21.

[29] Herodotos, IX, 104.

[30] I, 89, 2; see also above, pp. 190-191. A significant rôle was played in the appeal to Athens in 478 by οἱ Ἴωνες καὶ ὅσοι ἀπὸ βασιλέως νεωστὶ ἠλευθέρωντο; Thucydides, I, 95, 1.

[31] Walker, *C. A. H.*, V, pp. 43-44.

would add Erythrai, Kyme, Myrina, Pitane, Gryneion, Elaia; the last five of these are Aiolic, but they are classified as Ionic for purposes of tribute payment.[32]

The case against including Ephesos, Myous, and Lampsakos among the original members is based upon the experiences of Themistokles after his flight from the mainland of Greece (ca. 470 B. C.). Carried by a storm to Naxos, which was then under blockade, he persuaded the captain of the vessel to make a quick escape and was landed at Ephesos. Later the Persian King made him governor of Magnesia, which was to supply him with bread, and gave him authority to draw wine from Lampsakos and other food from Myous.[33] All of these towns, it is claimed, must have been in Persian hands and could not have belonged to the Confederacy at the time. Had Ephesos belonged, she must have surrendered an Athenian fugitive with a price on his head. Highby's case for Erythrai rests upon his interpretation and dating of the Erythrai decree,[34] which he places about 465 or perhaps earlier; Erythrai, he believes, could not have joined the Confederacy until shortly before the enactment of the decree, which in his opinion should not be connected with a revolt. In dismissing the Aiolic cities from the earliest roster of members Highby employs also the fact that neither Herodotos nor Thucydides expressly names the Aiolians as adherents of the Greek cause in the operations that followed the battle of Mykale. Herodotean usage, he urges, is to distinguish between Ionians and Aiolians; thus Aiolis is excluded when Herodotos writes, " for the second time Ionia revolted from the Persians."[35] The conduct of the Aiolians in earlier revolts also suggests that they refrained in 479 B. C. Concerning Myrina and Gryneion, Xenophon[36] reports that these cities, along with Gambreion and Palaigambreion, were given by the Persian king to the Eretrian Gongylos who had abetted the Spartan Pausanias in his treasonable relations with Persia in 479. If the states were within the gift of the king after 476 (Highby would not place Pausanias' eviction from Byzantion earlier), they could not have been constituent members of the Confederacy. Finally, since Plutarch says (*Themistocles*, 26) that Themistokles came to Kyme as a refugee, Kyme must be classed with Ephesos; and if Kyme, Myrina, and Gryneion did not free themselves from Persia and join the allies after Mykale, then Pitane and Elaia, which are further away from Mykale, did not do so.

The contrary opinion is well represented by Gomme,[37] many of whose views

[32] Highby, *Klio*, Beiheft XXXVI, especially pp. 34-35 and 43-57.

[33] Thucydides, I, 137, 2 and 138, 5 (T115); to Magnesia, Lampsakos, and Myous Plutarch (*Themistocles*, 29, 11), on the authority of Neanthes of Kyzikos and Phanias, adds Perkote and Palaiskepsis.

[34] *I. G.*, I², 10 + 11 + 12/13a; numbered by us D10 (Regulations for Erythrai) in *A. T. L.*, II, where we offer a revised text.

[35] IX, 104: τὸ δεύτερον Ἰωνίη ἀπὸ Περσέων ἀπέστη.

[36] Xenophon, *Hell.*, III, 1, 6; for Gongylos, Thucydides, I, 128, 6.

[37] *Commentary*, I, pp. 290-295.

we adopt in what follows. As for Themistokles, the fact that he landed at Ephesos and was not arrested says nothing of the status of Ephesos. He was wanted by both the Greeks and the Persians [38] and his escape proves only that he succeeded in staying hidden. Thucydides states that he was not recognized on the ship and Plutarch adds that he kept his incognito in Aiolis.[39] To suppose that Ephesos was at this time Persian does not explain Themistokles' escape and robs Herodotos' statement (τὸ δεύτερον Ἰωνίη --- ἀπέστη) of any significant meaning.

There is equally little reason for refusing to admit Kyme to the Confederacy, if (as we think) Themistokles really called there. Thucydides gives no details of how he journeyed to Sousa (πορευθεὶς ἄνω) except that he waited for money from home in Ephesos and then went to Sousa with a Persian escort.[40] Plutarch (*Themistocles*, 25,2 - 27) cites from Thucydides the story of the escape from Naxos and then brings the fugitive to Asia (παραπλεῦσαι καὶ λαβέσθαι τῆς Ἀσίας), where he received his funds from home. When he landed at Kyme and learned that there were many persons on the coast watching for him, he fled to Aiolic Aigai, where he remained in hiding before continuing his journey inland. The stories do not conflict [41] and in both it is clear that Themistokles' purpose was to make himself known only to persons whom he could trust, and that he succeeded. In both accounts the impression is of a hasty flight through territory that is essentially unfriendly.

We come now to Myous and Lampsakos (and perhaps Perkote and Palaiskepsis), whose produce Themistokles was to enjoy, thanks to the Persian king, along with the revenues of Magnesia. That the king had made such gifts proves nothing. The Persian maintained his *claims* for over half a century to territories he had formerly held; in the 460's, before any treaty had been signed, he still felt that they were within his gift. But the fact is that Themistokles lived at Magnesia (which was beyond question outside the Confederacy), " drew his revenue from there, issued coins there, and was there buried; we need not suppose he ever visited either of the other places after his exile." [42]

The four cities given by the Persian king to Gongylos as a reward for his treason may be treated in a similar fashion. The descendants of Gongylos are found in 399

---

[38] Plutarch, *Themistocles*, 26, 1 : --- πολλοὺς ᾔσθετο τῶν ἐπὶ θαλάττῃ παραφυλάττοντας αὐτὸν λαβεῖν, --- ἦν γὰρ ἡ θήρα λυσιτελὴς τοῖς γε τὸ κερδαίνειν ἀπὸ παντὸς ἀγαπῶσι, διακοσίων ἐπικεκηρυγμένων αὐτῷ ταλάντων ὑπὸ τοῦ βασιλέως.

[39] Thucydides, I, 137, 2 (ἦν γὰρ ἀγνὼς τοῖς ἐν τῇ νηί) ; Plutarch, *Themistocles*, 26. He had most to fear from individual professional informers.

[40] Μετὰ τῶν κάτω Περσῶν τινός (the Persian was from Sardes? Or from the coast?).

[41] Thucydides' ἄνω can only mean " up to Sousa "; he is not interested in the route. Certainly Themistokles found sanctuary at Aigai and the best way to Aigai from Ephesos was via Kyme by sea. It may have taken him some time to reach Sousa; see above, note 7 on p. 112.

[42] Gomme, *Commentary*, I, p. 292. For the benefaction of Kleophantos to Lampsakos and for the possibility of his having held property there see above, pp. 111-113.

B. C. holding as a hereditary gift four cities, of which two, Myrina and Gryneion, paid regular tribute to Athens. It is therefore impossible that the gift had been continuously operative. It is probable that Gongylos lived in Gambreion (or Palaigambreion), which is inland, and enjoyed its revenues, while Myrina and Gryneion, members of the Delian Confederacy at the beginning, belonged to him only nominally. *i. e.*, according to the word of the Persian king. The evidence is not strong enough to exclude Myrina and Gryneion (or, consequently, Pitane and Elaia) from the Confederacy in the year of its formation.

With regard to Erythrai, we date and interpret the decree quite differently from Highby. We date it to the year 453/2 B. C. and we do not believe that it has anything to do with the city's original adherence to the Confederacy; rather, it marks the recovery of Erythrai by Athens after the revolt, which we place a year or two after 460 (the Egyptian campaign).[43] If these dates and interpretations are accepted, Highby's reasons for excluding Erythrai from early membership in the Confederacy have disappeared.

To return to Aiolis, we consider it without significance that Thucydides names allies from Ionia and the Hellespont but not from Aiolis in his description of the campaign at Sestos in 479. Writing in the last quarter of the century, he would naturally speak of the Empire in terms of the official tribute districts. The Aiolic towns of the mainland were classified in the Ionic panel and " the allies from Ionia " (οἱ ἀπὸ Ἰωνίας) need never be thought to exclude Aiolians. Besides, the crucial year is 478/7, not 479.

Highby's conclusions from Herodotos are no more convincing. Herodotos distinguishes between Ionians and Aiolians, but that does not mean that when he says Ionians he necessarily excludes Aiolians.[44] In any case, when he tells us of the second revolt of Ionia (τὸ δεύτερον Ἰωνίη --- ἀπέστη) he is describing the battle of Mykale

---

[43] For the text see D10 in *A. T. L.*, II, pp. 54-57; for the revolt and the dates see below, pp. 252-255.

[44] Against Kyros the Aiolians are incidentally mentioned as accepting Ionian hegemony; Herodotos, I, 151, 3. In the great Ionic revolt Highby (*op. cit.*, pp. 53-54 with note 2 on p. 53) must explain away (1) the eviction of their tyrant by the people of Kyme (Herodotos, V, 38, 1, where, incidentally, the Aiolic Mytilenaians stone their tyrant), (2) the recapture of Kyme by the Persians (V, 123, where, we may add, Persian generals campaign ἐπὶ τὴν Ἰωνίην καὶ τὴν προσεχέα Αἰολίδα), (3) the defection of the Aiolic cities of the Troad (covered, perhaps, by Herodotos, V, 103, 2), (4) their recapture by Hymaies (V, 122, 2: εἷλε μὲν Αἰολέας πάντας ὅσοι τὴν Ἰλιάδα νέμονται), (5) the presence of Lesbians along with the Ionians at Lade (VI, 8, 1). Yet, in the face of these notices, Highby can write, " --- the cities of Aeolis proper on the coast north of Ionia did not, excepting only Cyme, revolt." " --- the remaining Aeolians played no part. --- it is certain that the Aeolians of the Aeolid played an altogether passive role ---." If all of this is evidence at all for the behaviour of the Aiolians in 478/7, it suggests rather that the Aiolians welcomed a Confederacy which would safeguard their freedom from Persia. Highby assigns too little importance to Kyme; to except Kyme from continental Aiolis is like excepting Athens from Attica.

(summer, 479). We have before this [45] shown that the Hellenic League may have increased its membership in the interval between the conference at Samos which followed Mykale and the campaigns in the Hellespont later in the season. Another full year elapsed before the Confederacy began to take shape and during the year the Greeks had campaigned actively from Kypros to Byzantion; by the end of 478 the threat of Persian reprisal was receding and the allies were proposing aggressive warfare against the barbarian. The League must have been gaining new recruits constantly. The question is not whether the Aiolians revolted after Mykale, but whether they stayed outside the Confederacy over a year later. Herodotos does not answer this specific question; in our judgment it is probable that the cities of Aiolis that are found in the early quota lists followed their Ionian neighbours in attaching themselves to the Confederacy at its inception; some may have already belonged to the old Hellenic League, whose naval arm it replaced.

More general considerations support the view that most of the Ionian tributaries of the quota lists were early adherents of the Greek alliance (whether Hellenic or Delian). The victory at Mykale, following so closely the victory at Plataia, which was already known, was a great moment for the Greeks and the enthusiasm must have been reflected in a marked increase in the number of allies.

The Persian survivors fled to Sardes [46] (this may mean at least a partial withdrawal from the coast) and the Greeks at Samos debated the future of Ionia. The very fact that the transplanting of the Ionians could be proposed is in logical sequence to Herodotos' report of the second revolt of Ionia and suggests that the Ionians had freedom of action. We cannot say how many of the cities joined the allies at this time but the debate itself gives us an important clue to the basic difference between Spartan and Athenian policy: Sparta was unwilling to maintain a defense of Ionia, Athens was willing. The change in leadership, then, in the following year, meant to the Greeks of Asia Minor that their freedom was to be protected and must have swept away the doubts of many who had wavered. Ionia was the very area which most needed guarantees; few could have remained aloof in 478/7.

Even if, in 479, there were many Ionians who had not made up their minds, we can question whether they were still under Persian rule. And as allied operations proceed during the next few years it becomes increasingly difficult to believe that important cities on the coast of Ionia are still garrisoned by Persians.

Our conclusion is that in the year of the formation of the Confederacy very nearly all of the cities that comprise the Ionic panel in the quota lists had entered the organization. There may have been a few recalcitrants but we are not told who they were and we are not justified, on the basis of the evidence, in striking names from the lists. The following roster is a maximum, we admit, but is not far beyond the truth: [47]

---

[45] See above, pp. 190-191.   [46] Herodotos, IX, 107, 1.

[47] If we were to mark any of the names as doubtful we should choose Maiandros and Kolophon,

Assos	Ikaros (Therme, Oine)	Myrina
Astyra	Isinda	Nisyros
Boutheia	Karene (?)	Notion
Chios (never tributary)	Klazomenai	Phokaia
Dioseritai	Kolophon	Pitane
Elaia	Kyme	Polichna
Elaiousa	Lebedos	Priene
Ephesos	Lesbos (never tributary)	Pteleon
Erythrai	Maiandros	Pygela
Gargara	Marathesion	Samos (never tributary)
Gryneion	Miletos	Sidousa
Hairai	Myous	Teos [48]

HELLESPONT

From the complete Hellespontine roster of *A. T. L.*, I, pp. 458-459, we may, in seeking the original members of the Confederacy, eliminate the following names in accordance with criterion (C): Artaioteichitai (first in List 27), Astyra Troika (only in A9), Bisanthe (only in A9, A10, A13), Brylleion (first in List 22), Bysbikos (first in the ἰδιῶται rubric of List 21), Dareion (only in A9), Halone (only in A9, by apotaxis from Prokonnesos), Kallipolis (first in the πόλεις αὐταί rubric of List 21), Kolonai (only in A9), Markaioi (only in A13), Metropolis (only in A9 and A10), Miletoteichos (only in A13), Mysoi (only in List 1 and A9),[49] Otlenoi (first in A9), Polichne (only in A9), Pythopolis (only in A9 and A10), Serioteichitai (first in List 27), Sombia (first in List 27), Tereia (only in A9 and A10), Zeleia (only in List 14 and A9). Some of these (e. g., Dareion, Pythopolis, Polichne) fall also under criterion (A), which may be employed to remove the following: Berytis, Skepsis, Kebrene, Gentinos.[50]

because of their inland positions. Note that Myous, which has been questioned, is very near to Miletos and the Milesians were perhaps the ringleaders in 479, as they were in the great Ionian revolt. Later, Myous may have followed Miletos in revolt; see below, pp. 255-256 with note 49. The notable absentee is Magnesia, which was inland and held by the Persians.

[48] Boutheia, Elaiousa, Polichna, Pteleon, Sidousa were later members of the Erythraian syntely; perhaps Elaiousa was last to join, for the name is absent from the syntelic payment of 450/49 and does not occur until 448/7. Isinda, Marathesion, Pygela do not appear in the first two assessment periods but are included here because, although they were assessed in Periods I and II with Ephesos, their status in relation to Ephesos in 478/7 cannot be determined. Teichioussa and the island of Leros were Milesian and do not merit independent membership; see *A. T. L.*, I, p. 448, s. v. Μιλήσιοι.

[49] We have equated Μυσ[οὶ hοι] ἐ[ν τ]ι̑ X[ερρονέσοι] (A9, III, 69-70) with the Μυσοί of List 1 and have placed them on the peninsula of Mt. Arganthonios, which separates the Olbian Gulf from the Kian in the eastern Propontis; *A. T. L.*, I, pp. 523-524. In this area Kios is the only consistent tributary.

[50] The exact site of Gentinos is not known, but it lay in the Troad, probably inland. The four

On the northwestern coast of the Propontis lay Tyrodiza and Neapolis. The last recorded payment of Tyrodiza is in List 10; but in List 13 Neapolis occurs for the first time and has apparently replaced Tyrodiza. The listing of both in A9 is a form of apotaxis. Neapolis, we believe, was " a small colony associated with the larger klerouchy in the Chersonese. --- a portion of the territory of Tyrodiza was requisitioned for the colony ---, probably about 450 B. C." [51] Neapolis, therefore, could not have been included in the original membership; we retain Tyrodiza and look upon it as the limit to the northeast of the Athenian power based upon the neck of the Chersonese, just as we look upon the Didymoteichitai as the limit of influence extending west on the same coast from Byzantion. The interval we leave to the Odrysian power.

When the allies sailed to the Hellespont in 479 they found the bridges at Abydos already broken; after the departure of Leotychidas the Athenians decided to assail the Chersonese (πειρᾶσθαι τῆς Χερσονήσου). They thereupon besieged Sestos where the Persians from the other towns of the neighbourhood (τῶν ἀλλέων τῶν περιοικίδων) had gathered. When the Persians evacuated Sestos, the Athenians took the town and pursued the fugitives. Oiobazos escaped towards Thrace but Artaÿktes was caught near Aigospotamoi and, at the request of the Greeks of Elaious, was executed near the town of Madytos.[52]

The narrative of Herodotos seems plainly to imply that the Persians fled the Chersonese, which fell into the hands of the Athenians. The straits were of the utmost importance and we cannot believe that the Athenians, after the formation of the Confederacy, allowed Persians to hold out in any organized form on the Chersonese. So Plutarch must not be misunderstood when he reports (Cimon, 14, 1 [T95f]), after the campaign of the Eurymedon, that Kimon expelled Persians and turned over the whole of the Chersonese for colonization to Athens.

Gomme calls these Persians stragglers (τῶν Περσῶν τινες), who had to be " mopped up "; [53] but the Chersonese had been in the Confederacy for some time and ten years is a long interval for stragglers to maintain resistance.[54] If the Persians did manage to retain points in the Chersonese, we should have to place them on the

cities have similar records: all are absent from the full panels of Lists 12, 13, 20, 22. The last recorded payment is by Skepsis in List 14 (441/0 B. C.). All are assessed in A9, Skepsis in A1 and A13.

[51] A. T. L., I, p. 525. These Athenian colonists, of course, did not themselves pay tribute.

[52] Herodotos, IX, 114-115 and 118-120. In 118, 2 the Χερσονησῖται give the signal to the Athenians that the town has been evacuated; in 120, 1 Χερσονησῖται are guarding Artaÿktes. Oiobazos was probably making for Doriskos when the Apsinthioi caught him. He was killed at Hieron Oros; A. T. L., I, p. 545, note 2.

[53] Commentary, I, p. 293.

[54] In Plutarch, Cimon, 14, 1, Kimon's work in the Chersonese follows the campaign of the Eurymedon.

west coast, at Limnai and Alopekonnesos, or perhaps at Alopekonnesos alone, the only town to remain outside the Chersonese syntely. But we consider it much more probable that the Chersonese was cleared of Persians in 479 and that the few Persians found there later by Kimon were members of raiding parties, despatched from Doriskos to conduct guerrilla warfare against the Greeks of the peninsula.[55] We include all the settlements of the Chersonese in the original membership of the Confederacy.[56]

The capture of Byzantion in 479 by Pausanias and the allies of the Hellenic League carried with it the Hellespont and much of the Propontis. Byzantion's membership in the Confederacy of Delos was perhaps affected between Pausanias' return in 477 and his eviction in the same year, but there is no reason to doubt that she was included in the first assessment in 478/7.[57]

The resulting list of those whom we deem original members in the Hellespontine district is as follows:

Abydos	Daunioteichitai	Parion
Agora (Cherronesitai)	Didymoteichitai	Perinthos
Alopekonnesos	Kalchedon	Perkote
Arisbe	Kios	Priapos
Artake	Kyzikos	Priapos
Astakos	Lamponeia	Selymbria

[55] For Doriskos see below, pp. 214-216. Plutarch says that these Persians were unwilling to leave (ἐκλιπεῖν) the Chersonese and invited assistance from Thrakians in the north. Operations were probably directed from Doriskos. With Kimon's campaign we connect the casualty list, *I. G.*, I², 928, which mentions fighting in Thasos, in the Chersonese and in the vicinity of Sigeion. Kolbe dates the casualties to 466/5; *Hermes*, LXXII (1937), pp. 248-254. We have placed the losses recorded in *I. G.*, I², 928 in 465 B. C.; for further discussion of the monument see above, pp. 108-110. It is entirely likely that the second capture of Sestos, by Kimon, in the same year as the second capture of Byzantion (Plutarch, *Cimon*, 9, 2-3), should be interpreted as an operation directed against Persians based at Doriskos; the captives were Persians. It is less likely that Sestos, as well as Byzantion, was taken from Pausanias and Gongylos. Fighting near Sigeion brings to mind *I. G.*, I², 32 (new fragment and complete text published by Meritt, *Hesperia*, V [1936], pp. 360-362), of 451/0 B. C., praise of the Sigeians which names an enemy ἐν τῆι ἐπείροι (lines 15-16). The enemy must have been the Persian satrap of Daskyleion. Earlier, the Persian bands in the Chersonese were perhaps trying, from Doriskos, to reach the satrap. We believe, however, that Sigeion was Greek in 478/7 and in 466/5.

[56] In the early quota lists the Χερρονῄσῖται make a syntelic payment which covers the obligations of Sestos, Madytos, Elaious, Limnai, and the island of Imbros. Alopekonnesos makes separate payments in Lists 3 (partially restored) and 5 and this suggests that the town was not a member of the syntely. When the members are separately treated, however, Alopekonnesos appears often with the erstwhile members of the syntely; see Lists 10 (restored), 11, 12 (restored), 13, 14, 15 (restored), 20, 22 (restored), 23 (restored), 26 (restored), 34. This may be a geographic matter only. After the breakdown of the syntely Imbros was classified as Insular. In our original panel above we list only Agora (Cherronesitai), on the assumption that the syntely existed from the beginning and the Chersonese (except Alopekonnesos) was assessed as a whole. This is not certain.

[57] Pausanias' stand in Byzantion was temporary; he was forcibly expelled (βίᾳ ὑπ᾽ Ἀθηναίων ἐκπολιορκηθείς, Thucydides, I, 131, 1). For the date see above, pp. 158-160.

Azeia	Lampsakos	Sigeion
Byzantion	Neandreia	Tenedos
Dardanos	Paisos	Tyrodiza [58]
Daskyleion	Palaiperkote	

KARIA

The chief problems of the Karian district lie to the east of Rhodes and the Karic Chersonese as far as Kypros and Doros (in Phoinike). It may be said at once that there is no direct evidence that Kypros was ever claimed as part of the Delian Confederacy. Those who would include it must go to Aischylos, whose *Persians*, produced in 472 B. C., contains a chorus (852-906 [T5a]) which recalls the blessings of the reign of Dareios. That monarch's acquisitions in the prosperous days include: the Acheloian cities of the Strymonian sea (*i. e.*, the islands of Imbros, Thasos, Samothrake?); the cities of the mainland (*i. e.*, of Thrace, moving east); the cities on both sides of the Hellespont; the Propontis; the entrance to Pontos; islands such as Lesbos, Samos, Chios, Paros, Naxos, Mykonos, Andros the neighbour of Tenos; Lemnos, Ikaros, Rhodes, Knidos, the cities of Kypros (Paphos, Soloi, Salamis); the Hellenic cities of Ionia.

From this passage one might argue not only that all these territories had been lost by Persia during the great campaigns of 480 to 478, but also that they had not been recovered by 472, the date of the play; it is a short step to assume that they lay in Athenian hands. For it cannot be denied that all the places named (excepting Kypros for the moment) had been lost to Persia and, we believe, acquired by the Delian Confederacy before 472; in fact, most of them were original members of the Confederacy in 478/7 (there is doubt about the area in Thrace between the Strymon and the Chersonese). Kypros, one could urge, must not be allowed to serve as an exception and must therefore have been brought into the Confederacy before 472 (presumably as the result of the campaign of Pausanias in 478).

Such an interpretation of Aischylos makes a powerful scene indeed, and if all of these Persian losses were valid not only during the campaigns of 480 and the next two or three years but also in 472, then the play of dramatic irony is admirable. But this we do not believe; we posit, rather, that they represent the maximum Persian loss, that is, the maximum extent of allied (Athenian) penetration. The scene, if this is the author's intention, is still powerful before an Athenian audience of 472. The cities of Kypros enter the list because they show the audience how far the Greek offense had reached in one direction.

[58] Harpagion does not enter the records until List 7, but, since it was a coastal city, we omit it with hesitation. Its membership may have been included in that of a neighbour (Kyzikos?). Palaiperkote is a little inland for 478/7 and may be regarded with suspicion.

We are not wholly ignorant, however, of the status of Kypros in 472, and what evidence there is denies that it was a member of the Confederacy or controlled by Athens. On the positive side, we know that in 478 it was in a large part reduced by the combined Lakedaimonian and Athenian fleets, with their allies,[59] and that it was being used once more by the Persian fleet as a naval base [60] at the time of the battle of the Eurymedon in 469 B. C.[61] Indeed, the attack in 478 may be interpreted as part of a strategic plan to cripple Persian sea-power, which had as its purpose rather the destruction of a Persian naval base than the liberation of Greek cities.[62] The allies left Kypros after the attack had achieved success, and proceeded to the Hellespont. In the absence of specific evidence, we doubt whether any Greek fleet was again in these waters before the battle of the Eurymedon.

Pausanias may have left garrisons in Kypros; we are not told and we are doubtful. At the congress of Samos (479), there had been debates concerning the possibility of holding Ionia without constant patrol. Kypros was far more remote; and when the Confederacy of Delos was formed in the following year the people of Kypros could not join with the Ionians in a plea to the Athenians " on the basis of kinship " (κατὰ τὸ ξυγγενές). When Kimon won his glorious victory at the Eurymedon he made no effort to add Kypros to the roster of the Confederacy.

This campaign of Kimon sheds more light on the status of Kypros. No one would deny that the island was a Persian base in the year of the Eurymedon (469 B. C.). Thus, whoever assumes that Kypros was a member of the Confederacy in 472 (the year of the *Persians*) must also assume that Persia had recovered it between 472 and 469; in other words, that Kypros had experienced very nearly a decade of membership in the Confederacy under Athenian leadership. This makes us sceptical of believing that Kimon, having defeated the Persians at the Eurymedon by land and sea, returned home with the spoils without first liberating once more and regaining the Greek cities of Kypros, his allies *ex hypothesi* only a year or so earlier. The shame and ignominy of such a retreat must have become proverbial. If Kypros with all her wealth had just been lost to the Confederacy, for what other reason than to recover it did Kimon go out to fight? And after the battle, the island was defenseless, so far as the Persians were concerned. Yet Kimon returned in triumph,[63] content, it would seem, with the Anatolian coast as far as Phaselis. There is only one conclusion: that

[59] Thucydides, I, 94, 2: καὶ ἐστράτευσαν ἐς Κύπρον καὶ αὐτῆς τὰ πολλὰ κατεστρέψαντο.

[60] Diodoros, XI, 60, 5: οἱ δὲ Πέρσαι τὸ μὲν πεζὸν στράτευμα δι᾽ ἑαυτῶν κατεσκεύασαν, τὸ δὲ ναυτικὸν ἤθροισαν ἔκ τε Φοινίκης καὶ Κύπρου καὶ Κιλικίας. Cf. Plutarch (*i. e.*, Kallisthenes), *Cimon*, 12, 5: – – – ὀγδοήκοντα ναῦς Φοινίσσας ἀπὸ Κύπρου προσπλεούσας.

[61] For the date of the battle see above, p. 160.

[62] Cf. Gomme, *Commentary*, I, p. 271: " the reason why the Greeks went so far afield before attacking those places nearer home which were still held by Persia was presumably that it was an important basis for the Persian fleet. They did not hold Cyprus permanently."

[63] For the spoils, Plutarch, *Cimon*, 13, 5-7.

Kypros was not, and never had been, a member of the Confederacy (or of the Hellenic League). Her subjugation to Athens came later, as Athenian power was pushed steadily eastward, probably in the campaigns that began in 460 B. C. Kimon, however, had no intention of bringing Kypros into the Athenian orbit.[64] The argument is not entirely from silence. Kallisthenes (Plutarch, *Cimon*, 13, 4 [T95e]) reports that the effect of the Persian defeat at the Eurymedon was so great that Perikles with 50 and Ephialtes with only 30 ships could sail beyond the Chelidonian islands without meeting a single barbarian vessel. We take it that he is giving a methodical account of voyages in these waters after the Eurymedon. If this is so, east of the Chelidonian islands was looked upon as a Persian sphere.

In enumerating the cities which he thought were not in the Confederacy from the first Walker claimed the whole of Karia except Rhodes and some of the adjacent islands. This district, " it is generally admitted," was retained by the Persians until after the campaign of the Eurymedon.[65] Precise evidence for most of the Karian towns is not available and Gomme has argued that the Greek cities of the Karian mainland, such as Halikarnassos and Knidos, are as likely as Miletos and Rhodes to have joined the Greeks.[66] But that the Karians, because they joined the earlier revolt, all associated themselves immediately with the allies in 479 and later with Athens in 478/7, we are not justified in claiming.[67] Gomme believes that " the Hellenized and semi-hellenized cities are as likely to have revolted again in 478 as in 465 " (*i. e.*, after the battle of the Eurymedon) ; no doubt many of them did, although we must repeat the warning that attachment to the allies or Athens was not the necessary consequence, even if it was the most likely.

The vital evidence for the cities of the Karic tributary district is to be found in the accounts of the Eurymedon campaign.[68] Diodoros writes as follows: " Kimon, sailing with his whole fleet towards Karia, at once persuaded those coastal cities which had been colonized from Hellas (ὅσαι μὲν — — — ἀπῳκισμέναι) to revolt from the Persians, and laid violent siege to those which were bilingual and held Persian garrisons (ὅσαι δ᾽ ὑπῆρχον δίγλωττοι καὶ φρουρὰς ἔχουσαι Περσικάς). Having taken over the cities on the coast of Karia, he applied similar persuasion to the Lykian cities too

---

[64] Kypros may have been free for a time as the result of Pausanias' campaign of 478. This freedom, however, was temporary, and we judge that the Persians lost no time in reëstablishing their authority, long before 472.

[65] *C. A. H.*, V, pp. 42-43.

[66] *Commentary*, I, p. 291.

[67] Even earlier, if the argument from analogy is to be pressed, the revolt of Karia was not immediate, nor for that matter complete; see Herodotos, V, 103, 2: ['Ίωνες] ἐκπλώσαντές τε ἔξω τὸν Ἑλλήσποντον Καρίης τὴν πολλὴν προσεκτήσαντο σφίσι σύμμαχον εἶναι· καὶ γὰρ τὴν Καῦνον πρότερον οὐ βουλομένην συμμαχέειν, ὡς ἐνέπρησαν τὰς Σάρδις, τότε σφι καὶ αὕτη προσεγένετο.

[68] Diodoros, XI, 60, 4; Ephoros, *P. Oxy.*, XIII (1919), no. 1610 (= frag. 191 Jacoby [no. 70]) ; Plutarch, *Cimon*, 12.

and won them." The account is essentially credible on historical grounds and, in the absence of evidence to the contrary, should be believed. True, it implies that Kimon at this time brought over to Athens *all* the Karian cities, which was certainly not the fact. It is quite specific that Kimon gained some adherents to the Confederacy, not only in Karia but also in Lykia, and that in so doing he expelled Persian garrisons from some of them. These Lykian accessions (except Phaselis) were, we imagine, tenuously held, as the record of Lykioi and Telmessos in the quota lists would suggest.[69] They could not have been members of the Confederacy at the beginning and it would be a mistake to assume it merely because an allied fleet passed along the coast of Lykia in 478 and " showed the flag," as it were, after the reduction of Kypros.

It is difficult to bring precision into the account of Karian accessions, for some Karian towns were members of the Confederacy at the start. The text of Diodoros shows that some were not, and tentatively at least we posit that the additions at the time of the Eurymedon all lay east of the Karic Chersonese and included perhaps Kaunos, Pasanda, Kalynda, Krya, Karbasyanda, Telandria, and Phaselis.[70]

The evidence thus far adduced, of which the most substantial is that of Diodoros, persuades us that nothing beyond Rhodes and the Karic Chersonese belonged to the Confederacy before Kimon's successful campaign [criterion (B)]. We are therefore ready to eliminate the following names from the Karic panel: Doros, Kelenderis, Aspendos, Sillyon, Perge, Ityra, Milyai, Phaselis, Lykioi, Iera, Telmessos, Telandria, Krya, Tymnessos, Kalynda, Pasanda, Karbasyanda, Kaunos. Most of these fall also under criterion (C).[71]

A further application of criterion (B) will render ineligible for original membership the Dorian islanders: Saros (first in List 27), Kasos (first in the πόλεις αὐταί rubric of List 21), Brykous (Lists 7, 8, 26, A9), Arkesseia (first in List 5), Karpathos (first in List 10) and Eteokarpathioi (first in the πόλεις αὐταί rubric of List 21), Astypalaia. The parenthesized notations indicate that some of these could be classed under criterion (C).

Without more ado we may employ criterion (C), which, it will be recalled, deals with sporadic appearances and apotaxis, to dismiss the following: Amorgos (first in the πόλεις αὐταί rubric of List 21), Syme (first in the ἰδιῶται rubric of List 21), Edries (inland, only in A9), Krousa (only in A9, by apotaxis from Bargylia), Taramptos

[69] See the record in the Register of *A. T. L.*, I; the restorations of Τελεμήσσιοι and Λύκιοι in 3, I, 29-30 and 4, V, 32-33 (see *A. T. L.*, II) give us a total of only three appearances. The Τελεμήσσιοι are assessed in A9.

[70] The evidence for Phaselis is specific; the city submitted to Kimon and paid 10 talents shortly before the battle; Plutarch, *Cimon*, 12, 3-4 (T95d). Kimon, says Plutarch (*Cimon*, 12, 1 [T95d]), cleared Asia of Persian garrisons from Ionia to Pamphylia.

[71] Only in A1: Doros. Only in A9: Kelenderis, Aspendos, Sillyon, Perge, Ityra, Milyai, Iera, Tymnessos. Lists 11-15 and A9: Kalynda.

(only in A9, by apotaxis from Bargylia), Arlissos (probably inland, only in List 10),[72] Kares ruled by Tymnes (inland, first in List 10), Telos (first in List 28), Euromos (inland, first in List 5), Amos and Ler[....]i (only in List 27),[73] Erines (Lists 2, 5, 9, 11, A9; see note 73), Oiai (only in Lists 1 and 3, elsewhere included under Lindos), Pedies (first in List 7, dependency of Lindos), Diakrioi (Rhodian, first in List 25, by apotaxis), Brikindarioi (Rhodian, first in List 26, by apotaxis), Pargasa (inland, Lists 5, 9, 10, 11), Polichne (site unknown, only in List 4), Sambaktys (site unknown, only in Lists 1 and 3), Hylima (site unknown, Lists 5, 7, 8), " Milesian " Pedasa (inland, Lists 2, 4, 7, 8), " Halikarnassian " Pedasa (only in A9),[74] Tarbanes (site unknown, Lists 2, 13, 14, 15, A9), Chios (Χῖοι Κᾶρες, in Knidian territory, Lists 1, 7, 8, A9),[75] Karya (only in A9).

We come now to certain groups of cities which could be treated under criteria (A) and (C), but which merit comment. In the fifth column of List 4 (lines 21-33) we find an instructive bloc of names from the Karic district:[76] Alinda (inland, here only), [.]ssyri − − − (here only), Chalketor (inland, no record between List 15 and A9), Kydai (inland, no record between List 8 and A9), Hyblissos (site unknown, elsewhere only in A9), Ouranion (elsewhere in List 2 and A9),[77] Killara (inland, elsewhere only in A9), Thydonos (inland, here only), Siloi (site unknown, here only), Telandria (Lykian), Telmessos and Lykioi (Lykian, elsewhere in Lists 3, 9, Tel-

[72] The site of Arlissos is unknown; it may be the name of a dynast (A. T. L., I, p. 470).

[73] These two and a missing name are entered in 27, III, 31-35 under the heading ἥαιδε τὸν πόλεον Χερρονεσίοις συντελὲς ὅσαι ἀπέδοσαν. The separate listing of the regular syntelic members was due to defection among the Χερρονήσιοι; Athens collected what she could (see the note on the passage in A. T. L., I, p. 198). These Χερρονήσιοι are a regular entry in the quota lists and occupied the peninsula which lies just north of Rhodes and which has Loryma at its tip; there were probably other members of the syntely. In the Gazetteer, s. v. Χερρονήσιοι, we have suggested that Τύμνιοι, Λωρυμῆς, Ἐρινῆς, and the island of Σύμη belonged to the syntely. [Λ]ορυμεῖς may be the correct restoration in 9, V, 9 (see the note ad loc., A. T. L., I, p. 179); Τύμν[ιοι] we have rejected in A9, I, 141 (see the note ad loc., A. T. L., I, p. 206). The payments of Ἐρινῆς are irregular and cease after List 11, although they are assessed in A9. The amount in 2, I, 13 is in reality for the previous year and a small fine has been added; see above, pp. 7-9. In 5, V, 11 they make a payment which is obviously complementary. This record suggests a reluctance to pay.

[74] The Pedasa of the quota lists we believe to be " Milesian " and different from the " Halikarnassian " Pedasa of A9. The Persians settled the " Milesian " site from the " Halikarnassian " and the settlers were probably Persian in sympathy. For the sites and for the transfer see the Gazetteer, s. v. Πηδασῆς, in A. T. L., I, pp. 535-538.

[75] Chios was coastal and on a peninsula; it should have been easily accessible and we eliminate it from original membership with some hesitation. It may have been dominated by Knidos.

[76] Keos in line 22 is intrusive and for the purposes of this argument may be ignored. The broken name in line 20 was probably Karic and belongs with the rest in this discussion; A. T. L., I, p. 173. It may well be that these tributaries should be restored in List 2, I; see above, pp. 7-9.

[77] Ouranion we have placed tentatively on the Iasian Gulf, slightly inland; see the Gazetteer, s. v. Οὐρανιῆται, and the additional note in Vol. II. For a map of part of this area, showing the Karian syntely, see A. T. L., I, p. 554.

messos in A9). Of these cities Ouranion is found in the first column of List 2, paying its assessed tribute plus an increment; we have suggested [78] that the others should perhaps be restored in the same column. Our interpretation is that they were reluctant to pay and that their appearance in List 4 is to be associated with Kimon's operations in 451/0.

These cities (apart from the Lykians) seem to centre about the Marsyas valley and we therefore proceed to eliminate, under criterion (A), the other tributaries of the area: Bolbai, Kindye, Mydones, Mylasa, Narisbara, Naxia, Parpariotai, Thasthara, Ydissos, Ymissos. Moving south, and employing the same criterion, we add: Idyma, Kasolaba, Kyllandos, Kyrbissos, Oula, Pladasa.

About 440 B. C. Athens deliberately removed from the rolls some forty Karian communities.[79] This should be connected with the general consolidating of the empire which is reflected by the merging of the Ionic and Karic panels in the next period, beginning in 438/7. Those whose membership was allowed to lapse are, for the most part, towns which were considered difficult of access and to which it was not worth while to apply compulsion. The retirement of Athens and the sporadic records of many of these Karian tributaries may also be indicative of the waning loyalties of inland Karia, which was bound to feel the influence of the Persian satraps. It is remarkable that, of the forty names, we have already eliminated, on one ground or another, all but three: Bargylia, Kodapes, Lepsimandos. Of these, the record of Kodapes (2, 4, 7, 8, 10, A9) is like that of " Milesian " Pedasa; the site is unknown but we are inclined to believe that the state was merely a temporary member of the Confederacy. We are left with Bargylia and Lepsimandos, whose records guarantee steady membership from 454 to about 440 B. C.

One might argue, from the disappearance of the names after Period IV, that these forty communities were perhaps brought into the Confederacy after its formation, that they were not easy to reach, that some (under Persian influence?) were reluctant to pay and did so irregularly, and that eventually the Athenians abandoned the effort to compel them. The argument may well be a good one, but we shall have to except from it Bargylia and Lepsimandos. Bargylia was a coastal city on the Iasian Gulf, perhaps important enough to be given the responsibility of collecting moneys

---

[78] Above, pp. 7-9.

[79] We count forty: Alinda, Arlissos, Bargylia, Bolbai, Chalketor, Chios (Χῖοι Κᾶρες), Erines, Euromos, Hyblissos, Hylima, Idyma, Kalynda (Κλαυνδῆς), Kares (Tymnes), Kasolaba, Killara, Kindye, Kodapes, Kydai, Kyllandos, Kyrbissos, Lepsimandos, Lykioi, Mydones, Mylasa, Narisbara, Oula, Ouranion, Pargasa, Parpariotai, " Milesian " Pedasa, Pladasa, Polichne, Sambaktys, Siloi, Tarbanes, Telmessos, Thasthara, Thydonos, Ydissos, Ymissos. Significant is the fact that, apart from unknown sites, all are well inland except Bargylia, Erines, Lepsimandos, Chios, Lykioi, Telmessos; the last two (Lykians) are not in question here. Ouranion and Pargasa are not far from the coast. Erines, as we have noted, were perhaps included in the Χερρονήσιοι at the time of the formation of the Confederacy, and, although we eliminated Chios from the early roll, we did so with hesitation.

from some of the inland states in Period II; the island of Lepsimandos faced the Halikarnassian peninsula. Their locations and their records lead us to retain Bargylia and Lepsimandos as original members of the Confederacy of Delos.[80]

In Ionia our fear was that we had included too many names in the original membership and our list should be regarded as a maximum. In Karia the opposite is true; we may have been too rigorous in our exclusions and the list of survivors is rather to be read as a minimum. The Karians, after all, had joined in the Ionian revolt at the beginning of the century and undoubtedly many did the same in 479. In 478/7 the inland communities in particular may have felt that their choice lay between accession to the Confederacy and a return to Persian rule; perhaps some chose the former. Herakleides of Mylasa certainly annihilated a Persian army ca. 497 (Herodotos, V, 121) and we formerly believed that he fought for the Greeks at Artemision in 480. On this understanding Mylasa might have maintained a continuous active alliance with the Greeks and might have exerted influence upon her neighbours in the Marsyas valley. But we now are disposed to accept Munro's conjecture that the Artemision mentioned by Sosylos can scarcely be the battle of 480; rather, Herakleides escaped after the Ionian revolt, with Dionysios the Phokaian (Herodotos, VI, 17), and assisted the Massiliotes against the Carthaginians off Iberian Artemision.[81] Thus the alliance with Athens was not made by Herakleides, who was " King " only at a distance, and the evidence for a pro-Greek element in Mylasa has gone. Furthermore, the synod at Delos in 478/7 was a conference of Hellenes whose primary purpose was the permanent protection of Hellenes; and there is no denying that Mylasa is a good distance from the coast. The weight of the evidence, we believe, supports our omission of Mylasa and her neighbours from our list of original Karian members of the Confederacy, but is not absolutely conclusive.

The survivors, whom we accept as the first Karic panel, are as follows:

Amynanda	Kalydnioi	Lepsimandos
Auliatai	Kameiros	Lindos
Bargylia	Karyanda	Madnasa
Chalke	Kedreai	Myndos
Cherronesioi	Keramos	Pelea (in Kos)
Halikarnassos	Knidos	Pyrnos (?)
Ialysos	Kos	Syangela (?)
Iasos	Latmos	Termera[82]

[80] The geographical argument holds good for Χῖοι Κᾶρες, but that of the record does not. For Bargylia in Period II see above, notes 14 and 54 on pp. 33 and 59.

[81] The evidence is assembled in A. T. L., I, p. 498, note 4; cf. p. 522, s. v. Μυλασῆς: " The alliance with Athens no doubt began with his reign " (i. e., Herakleides', after 480/79). For the more likely interpretation see Munro, C. A. H., IV, p. 289; cf. Bosch-Gimpera, Cl. Quart., XXXVIII (1944), p. 56.

[82] Syangela lies well inland but we conjecture that it may have entered the Confederacy through

THRACE

In the district of Thrace there is again a clash of opinion between Walker and Gomme. As Walker states the case,[83] " It may ––– be inferred with certainty from a comparison of a passage in Herodotos (VII, 105-7) with a statement in Thucydides (I, 98) that the whole coastline from the Hebrus to the Strymon, or more probably to the peninsula of Acte, was still in Persian hands," when the Confederacy was formed. Gomme [84] replies that the Thrakian coast was reconquered so soon after the organizing of the Confederacy that its " exclusion at the beginning is of no importance. ––– even if there were any reason—which there is not—to suppose that, because two brave Persians held on to two fortified positions for a year or two after Xerxes' retreat, the Greek cities in the neighbourhood did not join the League; they would be all the more likely to, for the sake of protection." Elsewhere [85] Gomme notes that " Eion and Doriskos were the two strongholds in Thrace held by the Persians after their retreat from Europe; according to Herodotos (vii. 106. 2) the latter, defended by Maskames, was never captured by the Greeks in spite of many efforts. But we are not to conclude from this that it remained long in Persian hands after the fall of Eion; nor that the coast of Thrace in general, with its many Greek cities, did not form part of the Delian League at its commencement." Gomme, of course, looks upon the first assessment as a process that lasted over several years, whereas we, on the other hand, place the fall of Eion itself after the first assessment.

Herodotos tells us that Xerxes, on his march through Thrace in 480, appointed Maskames governor of Doriskos. He was one of many hyparchs in the satrapy, " for even before this campaign hyparchs had been established throughout Thrace and the Hellespont. All these, both in Thrace and the Hellespont, with the exception of the hyparch in Doriskos, were eliminated by the Greeks after this expedition." [86] One of these was Boges, the hyparch of Eion, which was not recovered by the Greeks until 476/5,[87] that is, dispossession of the Persians did not follow immediately upon the retreat of Xerxes or even the Persian retreat after Plataia. Eion itself was taken after a long siege, which lasted through at least one winter.[88]

The assault upon Eion was Kimon's first move to bring the coast of Thrace into

Amynanda. Later the two pay together or Syangela includes Amynanda; see the Register, s. vv. Συαγγελῆς, Ἀμυνανδῆς. We question Pyrnos because it is to be located on what we believe to be the very borders of the Confederacy's territory, rather east of the Karic Chersonese. In Rhodes the larger cities probably stood for Diakrioi (Lindos or Kameiros?) and Brikindarioi (Ialysos?).

[83] C. A. H., V, p. 43.
[84] Commentary, I, p. 291.
[85] Commentary, I, p. 281.
[86] Herodotos, VII, 106.
[87] Schol. Aischines, II, 34 (ἐπὶ ἄρχοντος Ἀθήνησι Φαίδωνος).
[88] Walker, C. A. H., V, p. 50 with note 1, suggests the winter of 476/5. For the chronology see above, pp. 158-160, where we propose the winter of 477/6.

the control of Athens. Thucydides' words (I, 98, 1) are: " First of all, under the command of Kimon son of Miltiades, they took by siege Eion on the Strymon, which was held by the Medes, and enslaved its inhabitants." [89] It is our belief that in this chapter Thucydides is describing first examples of types of Athenian activity, in correct chronological sequence.[90] Later, in his brief excursus, he admits to his narrative only the more important events. If this interpretation is sound, then the attempt to drive Maskames from Doriskos, and indeed the other Persian commanders from Thrakian forts, must have followed the siege of Eion.[91] And since Doriskos resisted the Athenians for many years, it is legitimate to assume that other garrisons along the Thrakian coast may have held out for some time.[92] Herodotos and Thucydides make no report, although their silence is not conclusive to the argument.

The weight of the evidence is against including Thrace east of the Strymon in the Confederacy before the conquest of Eion, which came nearly two years after the first synod at Delos. The savage treatment of Eion by the Athenians (ἠνδραπόδισαν) may indicate that they intended to make of the town an example of what others might expect from continued resistance; this display of power was scarcely worth while if Doriskos was the only city to be impressed. The Athenians were aiming at other garrisons along the coast, and how effective their ruthlessness was is implied by the low opinion entertained by Xerxes of Persian commanders in towns other than Eion.[93]

It cannot be denied that some of the Thrakian cities might have freed themselves from Persia, either through their own efforts or because the Persians abandoned them, without Athenian help. That such cities immediately joined the Confederacy we cannot assume; the evidence, especially the lapse of time before the attack on Eion, suggests that some years passed before the whole district east of the Strymon was gathered into the fold.

At the mouth of the Hebros river was Ainos, a mere eleven miles away from

---

[89] I, 98, 1 (T109): πρῶτον μὲν Ἠιόνα τὴν ἐπὶ Στρυμόνι Μήδων ἐχόντων πολιορκίᾳ εἷλον καὶ ἠνδρα-πόδισαν, Κίμωνος τοῦ Μιλτιάδου στρατηγοῦντος. Πρῶτον does not indicate priority among Kimon's Thrakian campaigns; it means, of course, first of the varied activities in the long period Thucydides is about to describe.

[90] Eion was the first city taken from the Persians after the formation of the Confederacy, Skyros was the first conquest and colonization of territory not held by the Mede, Karystos was the first conquest of new territory for the Confederacy, Naxos was the first suppression of a revolt; see also above, note 22, and p. 158 with note 1.

[91] The capture of Sestos, of course, preceded the formation of the Confederacy; that of Eion was the first to succeed it.

[92] Herodotos does not actually say that Doriskos was never captured by the Greeks, only that the Greeks were never able to expel Maskames. No doubt the Maskameioi (Herodotos, VII, 106) were withdrawn by the terms of the Peace of Kallias (450/49). Doriskos was never a member of the Confederacy, however.

[93] Herodotos, VII, 107, 1: τῶν δὲ ἐξαιρεθέντων ὑπὸ Ἑλλήνων οὐδένα βασιλεὺς Ξέρξης ἐνόμισε εἶναι ἄνδρα ἀγαθὸν εἰ μὴ Βόγην μοῦνον τὸν ἐξ Ἠιόνος.

Persian Doriskos, for some time a centre of Persian resistance and, we may be reasonably confident, influence in the neighbourhood. It would be surprising to find Ainos among the allies when the Confederacy was organized. Yet the appearance of the city in the quota lists with a tribute of 12 talents as early as 454/3 guarantees its importance. This, however, only reflects the insignificance of Doriskos; when Doriskos was strong Ainos was weak. In the time of Xerxes it was Doriskos (not Ainos) which controlled the mouth of the Hebros and the adjacent fertile plain and here the Persians stopped, army and fleet,[94] having passed Aiolian Ainos on the way.[95] Herodotos mentions Ainos only once elsewhere, again casually, as the point at which the Hebros flows into the sea.[96] Thucydides, on the other hand, though he notes Ainian peltasts at the siege of Sphakteria and Ainians (Αἴνιοι ὑποτελεῖς) as unwilling allies in Sicily,[97] does not name Doriskos. The measure of the greatness of Ainos is its early tribute of 12 talents, and the reduction of Doriskos is attested not only by the silence of Thucydides but by the later scornful reference to it by Aischines, who could say that Demosthenes had ferreted out the town, though it was so obscure that nobody before had known even its name.[98]

Apparently the Athenians, who failed to take Doriskos while Maskames, its Persian commander, lived, used Ainos as their base. From it they absorbed the river valley and the coastal plain. Doriskos was starved to death but the change in relative wealth between the two cities came about only after some delay and considerable attrition. In 478/7 Ainos was insignificant.

When Artabazos and his remnants escaped after the battle of Plataia through Thessaly and across Makedonia and Thrace, their speed was great and we are not told where they halted in Thrace for refreshment.[99] The retreat of Xerxes in the previous year had also been hasty,[100] but he stopped at Eion and also at Abdera.[101] Here certainly is one of Xerxes' cities. It is altogether likely, a priori, that Abdera was the seat of a Persian hyparch; Herodotos does not say this categorically, but Xerxes' entertainment there and the later boast of the people that in Abdera Xerxes

[94] Herodotos, VII, 59.

[95] Herodotos, VII, 58, 3.

[96] IV, 90, where his interest is in the river.

[97] Thucydides, IV, 28, 4; VII, 57, 5 (T143). For the effect of Odrysian power upon Ainos note the reductions of tribute; for this and for the coinage (ca. 450) see the Gazetteer, s. v. Αἴνιοι, in A. T. L., I, p. 465, with the references there cited.

[98] Aischines, III, 82: οὗτός ἐστιν ὦ ἄνδρες Ἀθηναῖοι ὁ πρῶτος ἐξευρὼν Σέρριον τεῖχος καὶ Δορίσκον καὶ Ἐργίσκην καὶ Μυργίσκην καὶ Γάνος καὶ Γανιάδα, χωρία, ὧν οὐδὲ τὰ ὀνόματα ᾔδεμεν πρότερον. Cf. the Gazetteer, s. v. Σεριοτειχῖται, in A. T. L., I, p. 545.

[99] Herodotos, IX, 89 (ἀπήλαυνε σπουδῇ --- ὡς ἀληθέως ἐπειγόμενος).

[100] Herodotos, VIII, 115, 1: κατὰ τάχος.

[101] Herodotos, VIII, 118, 1 and 120.

was first able to " loosen his girdle " in safety [102] mark it as a garrison town. We may be sure that Abdera did not enter the Confederacy until after the conquest of Eion.

We are now ready to list the cities east of the Strymon which, although they appear in the tribute records, are excluded from the Confederacy at the beginning by criterion (B): Deire (only in A1 or A13),[103] Ainos, Sale (only in A10, by apotaxis), Zone (only in A10, by apotaxis), Drys (only in A10, by apotaxis),[104] Kystiros (only in List 21, ἄτακτος), Neapolis (παρ' Ἀντισάραν), Pergamon Teichos (only in A9, by apotaxis), Pieres (only in A9, by apotaxis), Galepsos,[105] Abdera, Dikaia (παρ' Ἄβδηρα), Maroneia.[106]

Criterion (C) will apply to so many Thrakian cities that it will be less confusing to take them up by groups. We start with the cities of Krousis (πόλεις Κροσσίδος) and the cities of Bottike, which were dependent on Spartolos. This is shown for Bottike by the entry Bottiaioi and syntely (Βοττια[ῖοι καὶ σ]) in 9, II, 19, which we have catalogued under Spartolos (Σπαρτώλιοι). The cities of Krousis are the first to appear in the lists, in 434/3, just when trouble is developing in Spartolos, as is suggested perhaps by her increased assessment. The Bottic communities and, no doubt, the cities of Krousis joined Spartolos in the revolt of 432/1. The first five of the following are the cities of Krousis (so entered in A10), which occur by name as a group in the ἰδιῶται rubric of List 21 and in A9; the others are Bottic: Tindaioi, Kithas, Smilla, Gigonos, Haisa, Kalindoia (only in T74, the treaty between Athens and Bottike), Tripoai (only in List 34 and T74), Kamakai (only in List 34 and T74), Prassilos (only in List 34), Pleume (first in the πόλεις αὐταί rubric of List 21), Aioleion (first in the πόλεις αὐταί rubric of List 21), Sinos (first in the ἰδιῶται rubric of List 21).[107]

[102] VIII, 120: πρῶτον ἐλύσατο τὴν ζώνην φεύγων ἐξ Ἀθηνέων ὀπίσω, ὡς ἐν ἀδείῃ ἐών. It is significant that Herodotos reports the claim, even though he does not believe it. He probably thought that Xerxes could feel safe with Boges at Eion.

[103] Deire was like Ainos in that it lay in a strong Persian sector near Doriskos; whether the citation from Krateros belongs in A1 or A13, there is no evidence that it ever paid tribute.

[104] Sale, Zone, and Drys were in the Samothrakian peraia; see the Gazetteer, s. v. Μαρωνῖται, in A. T. L., I, pp. 517-519.

[105] Kystiros, Neapolis, Pergamon Teichos, Pieres, and Galepsos were in the Thasian peraia. Thasos lost her peraia after her revolt (Thucydides, I, 101, 3 [T110]: Θάσιοι — — — τήν τε ἤπειρον καὶ τὸ μέταλλον ἀφέντες), although the late apotaxis of Pergamon Teichos, Pieres, and Kystiros suggests that she was not entirely stripped of holdings on the mainland; since they do not appear in the first two periods we cannot argue that they were restored by the terms of the Thirty Years' Peace.

[106] We have taken the capture of Eion as a terminus post quem for Athenian accessions along this coast. If any isolated communities could have joined the Greeks before this, Maroneia is perhaps the best candidate; a town or two on the mainland might have been held by Thasos and Samothrake.

[107] For Αἰολῖται and Πλευμῆς see the Gazetteer, s. vv., in A. T. L., I, pp. 465 and 538-539. Sinos we equated with the Σίνδος of Herodotos, VII, 123, 3, placed it rather north of Therme (Gazetteer, s. v. Σίνος, pp. 548-549), and suggested separation from Serme by apotaxis. Edson, however, would

We further eliminate, according to criterion (C): Piloros (only in the ἰδιῶται rubric of List 21, by apotaxis from Assera or Singos), Kleonai (first in the ἰδιῶται rubric of List 21, by apotaxis from Thyssos),[108] Pistasos (first in the ἰδιῶται rubric of List 21, site unknown), Gale (first in List 19, by apotaxis from Torone),[109] Sarte (first in the πόλεις αὐταί rubric of List 21, by apotaxis from Torone), Miltoros (first in List 20, ἄτακτος),[110] Akrothoon (only in A10, by apotaxis from Thyssos), Bormiskos (only in A9 and A10, by apotaxis from Argilos), Trailos (only in A9 and A10, by apotaxis from Argilos), Zereia (only in A10), Thestoros (only in A10), Kossaia (only in A9),[111] Posideion (only in A10, by apotaxis, perhaps from Akanthos), Herakleion (only in A9 and A10).[112]

On the map which accompanies Volume I, we sited four cities on the west coast

consider it a Bottic town (*Cl. Phil.*, XLII [1947], pp. 104-105) and locate it rather to the south of Therme. We are now disposed to agree with this judgment; see *A. T. L.*, II, p. 87, *s. v.* Σίνος.

[108] For the apotaxis of Piloros and Kleonai respectively see the Gazetteer of *A. T. L.*, I, *s. vv.* Ἀσσηρῖται and Ἄθως, pp. 471, 464.

[109] We read [Γαλ]αῖοι in 19, V, 26, where the alternative is [Σίγ]γιοι; see the note *ad loc.*, *A. T. L.*, I, p. 187. In Period V we have [Φαρβέ]λιοι in 19, V, 21 and Φαρβέλιοι ἀτακ[τοι] in 20, VI, 23; the record of their neighbour Othoros is similar, [Ὀθό]ριοι in 19, V, 28 and Ὀθόριοι ἄ[τακτοι] in 20, VI, 24. Another neighbour, Chedrolos, is grouped with Pharbelos and Othoros as Χεδρόλιοι [ἄτακτοι] in 20, VI, 25. We believe that these cities were not assessed in the fifth period, for though the indication (ἄτακτοι) was not entered in List 19, it seems clear that they were ἄτακτοι in fact. These three, along with Gale, are the only names from the πόλεις αὐταί and ἰδιῶται rubrics of List 21 which have any previous record. We believe that Gale too was not assessed in Period V (or earlier) and that [Γαλ]αῖοι in 19, V, 26 (if the restoration is right) should be understood as representing Γαλαῖοι ἄτακτοι; in 436/5 (List 19) the designation ἄτακτοι was not entered in the public record of the quotas. Partly on these grounds we have restored [Γαλαῖ]οι ἄτακτοι in 20, V, 31; see further above, p. 86 with note 41. Not one of the cities of these rubrics in List 21 had been assessed in the previous period; most are new to the records of tribute payment.

[110] Miltoros should probably be sought in the interior of Chalkidike, somewhere near Pharbelos and Chedrolos. Othoros was tentatively sited on the map and in the Gazetteer (*s. vv.* Ὀθώριοι and Ἡράκλειον, pp. 528 and 489) of *A. T. L.*, I, near Methone on the west coast of the Thermaic Gulf. This location has been criticized by Edson (*Cl. Phil.*, XLII [1947], p. 99). We now place the town in the interior of Chalkidike, or perhaps even further north, towards Argilos, and associate it, on the basis of its position and payment in the quota lists, with Pharbelos and Chedrolos. To this group, on the same basis, we add Miltoros. The Ἐρόδιοι of 5, IV, 18 we have equated with Χεδρώλιοι (Ἑδρώλιοι) and the two records, catalogued separately in the Register of *A. T. L.*, I, have been merged and Ἐρόδιοι stricken from the Thrakian panel of *A. T. L.*, I, p. 459. It looks as if all four (Pharbelos, Chedrolos, Miltoros, Othoros) participated in the revolt of 432/1 B. C. See also above, pp. 61-63.

[111] The locations of Zereia (in the Chalkidic state?), Thestoros (in Olynthian territory?), and Kossaia are unknown; see the Gazetteer, *s. vv.* Ζερεία, Θέστωρος, Κοσσαῖοι, *A. T. L.*, I, pp. 488-489, 490, and 506.

[112] Edson argues convincingly that Herakleion (on the west coast of the Thermaic Gulf) was a Makedonian town acquired by Athens after 430/29 in the course of her hostilities with Makedonia; *Cl. Phil.*, XLII (1947), pp. 96-98. He suggests the same of Bormiskos, which controlled the chief land route (later the Via Egnatia) from Makedonia to the lower Strymon and the west coast of the Gulf; *op. cit.*, p. 98.

of the Thermaic Gulf: Herakleion, Haison, Methone, and Othoros (tentatively). We now believe that Othoros should be placed elsewhere,[113] and we have just discussed Herakleion. There is no doubt that Methone was not assessed as a member of the Confederacy before 434/3.[114] We are left with Haison. Now this whole territory of Pieria was Makedonian and Edson has even denied " Athenian control of any place on the north coast of the Thermaic Gulf north of Cape Aineia during the fifth century or on the west coast of the gulf before the outbreak of the Peloponnesian War." [115] This sweeping statement we are not disposed to accept, for we still believe that Haison, with its steady tributary record from 451/0, must be associated with Plutarch's river Aison (Αἴσων) and placed on the west coast of the Thermaic Gulf.[116] Haison cannot possibly be equated with Haisa, one of the cities of Krousis, on the eastern coast of the Gulf.[117]

Edson's thesis is based upon the undeniable fact that Pieria was Makedonian. But so was Bisaltia, and here, more than twenty miles inland on the west bank of the Strymon, was Berge. The site is not disputed; nor is Berge's payment of tribute as early as 452/1, " an extension of Athens' power deep into territory recently added to the Argead kingdom by Alexander I." But Edson is not happy about it: " Were it not for the incontrovertible evidence of the tribute lists, one would hardly have thought any such Athenian intervention possible." Haison is no more difficult to explain than Berge. If " diplomatic pressure, backed by the threat of naval action, such as the blockade and raids on the coasts of the Macedonian homeland around the Thermaic Gulf," [118] won the concession of Berge for Athens, the same can be said of Haison.

The ἀπαρχήν rubric of Lists 25 and 26 (430/29 and 429/8), which shows that

---

[113] See note 110 above.

[114] See the Register, s. v. Μεθωναῖοι. Cf. also D3-6; Edson, op. cit., p. 92 with note 41 on pp. 92-93, and above, pp. 133-137.

[115] Op. cit., p. 88.

[116] But we acknowledge Edson's well-taken objections (op. cit., p. 92 with note 34) to our placement of the battle of Pydna.

[117] The evidence of the quota lists, which Edson (op. cit., p. 93 with note 46 on pp. 93-94) adduces for the equation, is conclusively against it. In Period VI the five cities of Krousis pay a joint quota of 50 drachmai in 21, VI, 29-33 and Haison 16⅔ in 22, II, 66 and 23, II, 62. Apart from the differences in the quota within the same period (Edson's explanation is not convincing), Edson has here failed to note that in List 21 the five πόλεις Κροσσίδος are catalogued in the ἰδιῶται rubric, whereas Haison in 22 and 23 is in the main body of the Thrakian panel. The Thrakian panel of List 21 is fragmentary and Haison may well have discharged its obligations in this year (434/3). Similarly, the ἰδιῶται rubric of 22 and 23 has not survived in its entirety and we cannot say that the five πόλεις Κροσσίδος were absent, especially in 433/2 (List 22), where they could have stood towards the end of the column; in 432/1 the outbreak of the war affected this region. In any case, cities catalogued within rubrics in 434/3 remained in those rubrics for the balance of the period; for further discussion of the rubrics see above, pp. 80-88.

[118] Edson, op. cit., pp. 95-96.

Methone,[119] Dikaia (Eretrion), and Haison paid in these war years only the quota of their assessed tribute, reflects Makedonian pressure upon these peripheral cities. It also shows that Athens could hold places in or on the borders of Makedonian territory;[120] Dikaia and Haison have tribute records which go back to the first period.

The discussion has so far concerned the years after 454/3, the year of Athens' greatest power. If it has demonstrated that Athens could encroach then upon Makedonia, it should also have cast doubt upon her ability to have done so when the Confederacy was in the process of formation. Our objection to Edson's initial thesis is that it is too sweeping; but, we believe, if it is applied to the earliest years of the Confederacy, it defines the situation on the coast of the Thermaic Gulf precisely. We do not hesitate to eliminate from the original panel the cities of Pieria (Haison, Methone, Herakleion), Berge[121] in Bisaltia, Strepsa,[122] Dikaia, and Serme.[123] The

[119] Cf. D3-6, which grant special privileges to Methone. We believe that Methone was assessed as early as 434/3; see above, pp. 133-137.

[120] [Demosthenes], VII, 12 (T48), says that the Makedonians paid tribute to Athens: ὑφ' ἡμῖν γὰρ ἦν ἡ Μακεδονία καὶ φόρους ἡμῖν ἔφερον. This is of course an exaggeration, although not so great perhaps as Gomme proposes and not based solely upon the tributary status of Methone; *Commentary*, I, p. 238, note 3.

[121] Berge was completely isolated, at least in 478/7, before the capture of Eion.

[122] In the Gazetteer, *s. v.* Στρεψαῖοι, in *A. T. L.*, I, pp. 550-551, we tentatively placed Strepsa northwest of Therme (as located on our map). Gomme (*Commentary*, I, pp. 215-218) would site it south of Therme, in Chalkidike or Bottike or near by: (1) " it revolted (at least did not pay its tribute) along with Poteidaia and the rest," (2) " there is very little evidence for supposing any town beyond C. Aineia – – – to have belonged to the Delian League " (pp. 216-217, cf. pp. 214-215). We have already examined (2); as for (1), the revolt need not be confined strictly to Chalkidike and Bottike (if our identification of Serme and Therme is right, then the capture of Therme in Thucydides, I, 61, 2 is the recovery of a rebel town well outside Chalkidike and Bottike). We see no reason to change our tentative assignment of Strepsa. See also below, pp. 314-316 with notes 62 and 64.

[123] In the Gazetteer, *s. v.* Σερμαῖοι, in *A. T. L.*, I, p. 546 with note 3, we equated Serme with Therme, which we placed at Sedes, six miles southeast of Thessalonike. Edson, *Cl. Phil.*, XLII (1947), pp. 100-104, objects to the equation (cf. Gomme, *Commentary*, I, p. 214) and to the placement. We believe that in putting Therme " at, or very near, Salonica " Edson is right; we are not so ready to abandon the equation. The identification means that Athens " maintained an enclave in Macedonian territory "; this runs contrary to Edson's *a priori* argument, which, in our opinion, is untenable. Edson says (*op. cit.*, note 85 on p. 100) that the use of ἀποδοῦναι in Thucydides, II, 29, 6 (the Athenians hand over Therme to Perdikkas) " definitely implies that Therme had previously been a Macedonian possession "; it may have been merely garrisoned by Makedonians when Perdikkas was encouraging revolt (Thucydides, I, 57, 4-5 and 58, 2). But this is not relevant, for Athenian holdings in Makedonian territory are not only possible (Haison) but proved (Berge). The philological argument is not decisive (Σέρμη in the tribute lists, Θέρμη or Θέρμα in the authors and *I. G.*, I², 302, line 68); the theta perhaps goes back to Ionian geographers, the sigma represents contemporary notation. We observe too that fifth-century Syangela became Hellenistic Theangela; *A. T. L.*, I, pp. 551-552, *s. v.* Συαγγελῆς. The smallness of the tribute is perhaps the strongest objection to equating Therme and Serme (Gomme). But in a peripheral town Athens may have been lenient; cf. the privileges enjoyed by Haison, Methone, and Dikaia in Lists 25 and 26 (they paid ἀπαρχή only). The town may not, in the fifth century, have been wealthy or important. It is

northwestern limit of the Confederacy in 478/7 we conceive to have been Aineia.[124]

The terms of the Peace of Nikias named certain Thrakian towns which were to be autonomous and pay " the tribute of Aristeides " (as it is usually translated).[125] The expression " the tribute of Aristeides " (τὸν φόρον τὸν ἐπ' Ἀριστείδου) ought to mean, literally, " the tribute of Aristeides' time " and if this is interpreted strictly then cities which paid Aristeides' tribute were original members of the Confederacy; the phrase should not apply beyond the lifetime of Aristeides, and surely the " assessment of Aristeides " in later years connoted the famous assessment of 478/7, " the first tribute assessed " (ὁ πρῶτος φόρος ταχθείς) of Thucydides, I, 96, 2 (T109). The Papyrus Decree (D13, formerly T9) mentions the money gathered " according to the assessment of Aristeides " (κατὰ τὴν Ἀριστεί[δου τάξιν]), which shows that, whatever additions or adjustments had been made, the assessment of Aristeides was still valid down to that time (450/49); [126] all exactions had been " on the scale of Aristeides' assessment." Cities which were assessed later than 477, like Doros in Phoinike, might be said to have paid " on the scale of Aristeides' assessment " (κατὰ τὴν Ἀριστείδου τάξιν), but hardly " the tribute of Aristeides' time " (τὸν ἐπ' Ἀριστείδου φόρον). Those who paid the latter were charter members of the Confederacy.

This interpretation does not preclude the possibility that " the tribute of Aristeides' time " (τὸν φόρον τὸν ἐπ' Ἀριστείδου) was used loosely in the Peace of Nikias to denote the pre-war figures. The record of Argilos may be considered to support this view. The town paid 1½ talents in the first period, 1 talent from 446/5 to 438/7, and, after and as a result of the founding of Amphipolis, 1,000 drachmai.[127] It may not have been the intention of the clause in the peace to return to the 1½ talents, which

true that the Gulf was named after the town. Yet even this does not have to mean wealth or importance; it depends rather upon physical characteristics, as Edson himself reveals (" It is also possible that prominent physical features associated with its site may have caused ancient sailors to name the gulf from the city. Cape Mikro Karaburnu, the only important promontory along the northern coast of the gulf, can have been the cause of the name. --- the citadel of Salonica --- is the last high point of land on the coast that one would observe from the sea in antiquity as one sailed from east to west, until passing well beyond the mouth of the Axius "). He thus weakens his previous statement: " --- that Therme gave its name to the gulf --- probably indicates that it was the most important city on the Thermaic Gulf proper." On the whole, we are inclined to retain the equation of Therme with Serme.

[124] It was Makedonian pressure that drove the Bottiaians from the shores of the Thermaic Gulf to Olynthos, where Artabazos found them in possession in 480; Herodotos, VIII, 127.

[125] Thucydides, V, 18, 5 (T134): τὰς δὲ πόλεις φερούσας τὸν φόρον τὸν ἐπ' Ἀριστείδου αὐτονόμους εἶναι. --- εἰσὶ δὲ Ἄργιλος, Στάγιρος, Ἄκανθος, Σκῶλος, Ὄλυνθος, Σπάρτωλος. His Σκῶλος is the Στῶλος of the tribute lists; cf. the variation Μιλτώριοι, Μιλκώριοι. For the identification see West, A. J. P., LVIII (1937), pp. 157-166.

[126] Wade-Gery, Hesperia, XIV (1945), note 12 on p. 218: " the phrase appears to cover both " the assessment of Thucydides, I, 96, 2 " and all developments or revisions of it down to 450."

[127] The reading XᴾP in List 1, IV, 22 we believe to have been the stonecutter's error for HᴾP; see above, pp. 5-6. Argilos is absent from the full Thrakian panels of 435/4 and 432/1.

would unquestionably have been thought a hardship; rather, the Athenians committed themselves to avoid the strikingly high assessments of war-time after the death of Perikles.[128] The contrast, which, as Gomme notes,[129] becomes a commonplace in later authors, is between the exorbitant demands of the demagogues and the just determinations of Aristeides. It may be that the assessment of Aristeides was held to prevail, in general, even down to the outbreak of the Archidamian war.[130]

The clause may, on the other hand, be interpreted quite strictly to show that the six towns were to pay their original tributes. Argilos would then return to the 1½ talents which she had once been assessed. We must recall that the marked decrease was occasioned by the founding of Amphipolis, which, at the time of the peace, was still held by Sparta. We cannot tell what dispositions, in relation to Argilos, Athens planned to make in Amphipolis. Territorial adjustments could have justified an assessment of 1½ talents, which, furthermore, could have been a decrease from the figure in 425/4.

A less restricted interpretation, however, need not invalidate the conclusion that the six cities who were to pay the tribute of Aristeides' time were original members of the Confederacy. Justice to original members would mean a return to the tribute of Aristeides' time (i. e., a reasonable tribute, like that assessed upon them by Aristeides); justice to later recruits would mean a return to a scale like that of Aristeides (κατὰ τὴν Ἀριστείδου τάξιν), in accordance with which they had been assessed at the time of their entry into the Confederacy (although not by Aristeides personally).

The record of Akanthos, one of the six cities, merits further investigation. It was used as a base by the ill-fated fleet of Dareios which was wrecked off Mt. Athos and later by Xerxes during his march into Greece.[131] The city was looked upon with favour by Xerxes, who seemed to find the Akanthians willing helpers in building the canal and eager for the war.[132] Since Dareios' stated purpose in invading Greece was to attack Athens and Eretria,[133] the later zeal of the Akanthians for the campaign of Xerxes might suggest that they were not anxious to become allies of Athens as early as 478/7.

On the other hand, Akanthos had more than its full share of the burden which the Persian army imposed in 480 wherever it went[134] and disillusionment must have

---

[128] Argilos was assessed in A9 but the amount is lost.

[129] *Commentary*, I, note 1 on p. 274.

[130] Additions to the Confederacy between 477 and 450 had increased the total assessment by perhaps as much as 100 talents before an effort was made to return approximately to the original total of Aristeides; see below, note 42 on p. 243, and above, pp. 57-58.

[131] Herodotos, VI, 44, 2; VII, 116.

[132] Herodotos, VII, 116: --- ξεινίην τε ὁ Ξέρξης τοῖσι Ἀκανθίοισι προεῖπε καὶ ἐδωρήσατό σφεας ἐσθῆτι Μηδικῇ ἐπαίνεέ τε, ὁρέων αὐτοὺς προθύμους ἐόντας ἐς τὸν πόλεμον καὶ τὸ ὄρυγμα † ἀκούων †.

[133] Herodotos, VI, 43, 4.

[134] Herodotos, VII, 118-120.

come easily, especially after the Persian defeat. Furthermore the Chalkidic area in general had suffered at the hands of the Persians.[135] After the Persian defeat these cities, we imagine, lost no time in joining the Greek alliance.[136] Among them was Akanthos, which, in the early years of the Confederacy, furnished ships rather than money, as we shall urge.[137] Her record does not militate against the restricted interpretation of " the tribute of Aristeides' time " (τὸν φόρον τὸν ἐπ' Ἀριστείδου) which we prefer.

The original Thrakian panel, then, comprised the Chalkidic peninsula, base and prongs; Aineia was the western limit, while to the east Argilos was the Greek bastion until the fall of Eion. The islands of Thasos and Samothrake in the northern Aegean and Skiathos, Ikos, and Peparethos [138] north of Euboia were early adherents. These, to our mind, were the members:

Aige (Pallene)	Olophyxos (Athos)	Skabala
Aineia	Olynthos	Skapsa
Akanthos	Peparethos (island)	Skiathos (island)
Aphytis (Pallene)	Pharbelos	Skione (Pallene)
Argilos	Phegetos	Spartolos
Assera	Polichne	Stageira
Dion (Athos)	Poteidaia (Pallene)	Stolos
Ikos (island)	Samothrake (island)	Thasos (island)
Mekyberna	Sane (Athos)	Therambe (Pallene)
Mende (Pallene)	Sermylia (Sithonia)	Thyssos (Athos)
Neapolis (Μενδαίων, Pallene)	Singos (Sithonia)	Torone (Sithonia)[139]

AKTE, EUXINE, DISTRICT UNKNOWN

The remaining cities of the Empire will not detain us long. The Aktaian panel (*A. T. L.*, I, p. 459) may be dismissed at once, for no Aktaian city was assessed before

---

[135] In 479 the Bottiaians defending Olynthos were massacred by Artabazos; Herodotos, VIII, 127.

[136] Poteidaia and the rest of Pallene revolted from Persia after Salamis: οἱ γὰρ Ποτειδαιῆται — — — ἐκ τοῦ φανεροῦ ἀπέστασαν ἀπὸ τῶν βαρβάρων· ὡς δὲ καὶ ὧλλοι οἱ τὴν Παλλήνην ἔχοντες (Herodotos, VIII, 126, 3). For Olynthos and the Bottiaians see note 135 above.

[137] See below, pp. 267-268. It is significant that Akanthos does not appear in the quota lists until List 5 (450/49); cf. above, p. 197.

[138] The evidence for Peparethian participation against Persia by sea is positive; see *I. G.*, I², 523, where the notes cite a Peparethian dedication at Delphi made from Persian spoils (the Peparethians captured two Karian ships).

[139] The towns of Pallene are guaranteed by Herodotos, VIII, 126, 3; Poteidaia was on the Serpent Column. Othoros, which does not appear until List 7, and Chedrolos, whose first appearance is in List 5, probably paid earlier through neighbours; see above, note 110, and pp. 61-63. Nesselhauf, *Klio*, Beiheft XXX, p. 36, thinks that Skiathos may have belonged to Chalkis before 446 and so not have paid tribute until 446/5. We believe that our restoration in 5, III, 40 (450/49)

the revolt of Mytilene in 428/7.[140] Similarly, no city from the Euxine was assessed before 425/4 (A9) and the names printed in *A. T. L.*, I, p. 460 do not enter the discussion of original membership [criterion (B)]. The location of Eurymachitai, a name which is found only in 7, III, 16 and 8, II, 46, is unknown. We have (in the Gazetteer, *s. v., A. T. L.*, I, p. 487) suggested eastern Thrace or the interior of Karia; but we now believe the Hellespont more likely (see the note in *A. T. L.*, II, pp. 85-86). We can safely eliminate it from early or regular membership in the Confederacy according to criterion (C).

If the principles of this survey are correct, the Confederacy, in the beginning, was primarily an organization of the Greek cities of the Aegean islands and the coast. The Persians had been driven from these areas and the inhabitants, especially in Ionia and the eastern islands, were glad to avail themselves of Athenian and allied protection against Persia and to participate in the ravaging of Persian lands. The extremities of the Confederacy in the first year were Aineia in the northwest, Byzantion in the Propontis, Siphnos in the southwest, and Rhodes in the southeast.[141]

---

is sound in spite of early Euboian connections; cf. Steph. Byz., *s. v.* Σκίαθος· νῆσος Εὐβοίας, and [Skymnos], αὐτὰς ἁπάσας Χαλκιδεῖς συνῴκισαν (line 586, with reference to Skiathos and other islands).

[140] Thucydides, III, 50, 3 (T128): παρέλαβον δὲ καὶ τὰ ἐν τῇ ἠπείρῳ πολίσματα οἱ Ἀθηναῖοι ὅσων Μυτιληναῖοι ἐκράτουν, καὶ ὑπήκουον ὕστερον Ἀθηναίων. Cf. D22. The Aktaian cities fall under criterion (C); their separate assessment was a form of apotaxis.

[141] There remain only those fragmentary entries in the quota lists and assessments which we have been unable to restore. These represent either known names, in forms or combinations which we have not recognized, or unknown towns; the first will have been treated in this chapter; the second, by criterion (C), would be unlikely candidates for membership in 478/7. We feel reasonably confident that our roster of the Empire (*A. T. L.*, I, pp. 457-460) includes all regular members.

CHAPTER IV

THE FIRST CONGRESS AT DELOS

Even as Pausanias received his summons to return home, in the summer of 478, the allies were approaching the Athenians with the plea that they assume the hegemony. That the allies had not changed their minds and that their agitation had not been caused solely by their hatred of Pausanias is shown by the cool reception which they accorded Dorkis, his successor. During the interval between Spartan commanders Aristeides must have been recognized as the ranking officer and it was with him primarily that plans for the new order were discussed. The departure of Dorkis, whether or not he remained until the end of the season, signified that their decision had been made and that any further united effort against the Persians would rest upon Athenian leadership and would demand a new organ for the formulation of policy.[1]

The Spartan proposal of 479 at the congress of Samos to transplant the people of mainland Ionia on the ground that their lands could not be effectively defended no doubt rankled with the Ionians. They had not forgotten that it was the Athenians who had resisted that proposal. The alternative was to continue the war, and to continue it largely by sea; Athens had the largest fleet (not all of it, at the moment, under Aristeides' command), and the energy and enterprise to use it. A naval war required money; Sparta was hardly likely to devise anything better than the present irregular and arbitrary levies, but Athens no doubt could. Besides a change of leadership, the new task demanded a complete change of organization. When Dorkis departed, the last link which bound them to the old Hellenic League was cut; the plans which culminated in the synod on Delos marked, for the allies and for Athens, a fresh start. The naval arm of the Hellenic League was no more.

The details of the procedure that followed the departure of Dorkis are not reported. We can scarcely be wrong in believing that Aristeides now became commander-in-chief, representing the hegemonic power, and that plans were laid for the meeting of organization at Delos, to which all Hellenes (and perhaps non-Hellenes) who sought permanent protection from Persia as well as revenge were to be invited. The fleet moved from Byzantion on its journey to Delos, but swift triremes, we imagine, preceded it, carrying invitations to the coastal areas of the Aegean world which were no longer under Persian duress. It was now very late in the season, perhaps the beginning of winter, 478 B. C.

Not long afterwards, the delegates gathered at Delos. States which had already

[1] Thucydides, I, 94-95.

contributed to the fleet were no doubt represented by their naval commanders; from others, representatives, perhaps probouloi, had come, in response to the invitation. We need not suppose that all of those whom we have listed as original members were actually represented at the conference; some joined the Confederacy during the winter of 478/7, in time to be included in the first assessment of contributions, but not in time to participate in the first deliberations. Nevertheless, it must have been a sizable number of delegates that sat down to debate the future of the naval alliance and the problems which the venture raised. In the chair was Aristeides the Athenian.[2]

Among the items on the agenda needing clarification was the purpose of the Confederacy. The old League had first been organized in 481/0 by Sparta to defeat the invader, and after the victory of Plataia the invader was defeated well and truly; the war had been fought.[3] But now the Greeks of Asia were to be liberated and their liberty maintained, and further, Persia was to be made to pay: " the programme was to obtain satisfaction for their losses by spoiling the King's land." [4] This programme required that resources, navies and money, be organized. The necessity for some such programme had been shown by the failure of the revolt of 499 and was to be shown again by the difficulty of keeping Kypros permanently out of Persian hands. It was the Athenian programme of active war which attracted states to the congress at Delos.

But although this was the immediate programme, it was not the end; the Confederacy was to be permanent. The allies knew that the war with Persia would some day come to an end; their statesmen were farsighted enough, in 478/7, to realize that the end of the war would not bring them safety for ever. Greek resources must continue to be integrated; when the Athenian power was weakened and the Confederacy shattered, early in the Dekeleian War, this was the prelude to the reincorporation of the Asiatic Greeks in the Persian satrapies. The clarity of vision which the exalted days of 479 and 478 brought to the allies was soon blurred by the strains of campaigning; only Athens remembered the bright prospects of 478/7. And Athens, it could be charged, had most to gain.

What was to be the Confederacy's permanent function, when the war was over? To answer this question we naturally turn to the Congress Decree (D12), to the plan which Perikles offered for the consideration of Greece just after peace had been made with Persia.[5] As Plutarch (*Pericles*, 17, 1) reports the proposals, the states were to

---

[2] This is a safe deduction from the prominence of Aristeides in the negotiations; Plutarch, *Aristides*, 23, 4 (T94c); 24 (T94); Aristotle, Ἀθ. Πολ., 23, 4-5 (T39). The latest work on the constitution of the Confederacy is by Larsen, " The Constitution and Original Purpose of the Delian League," *Harv. Stud. Cl. Phil.*, LI (1940), pp. 175-213. We do not argue points which he has established nor do we, as a practice, make individual references to his conclusions.

[3] T68a: [τ]ο[ίδε τὸν] πόλεμον [ἐ]πολ[έ]μεον.

[4] Thucydides, I, 96, 1 (T109): πρόσχημα γὰρ ἦν ἀμύνεσθαι ὧν ἔπαθον δῃοῦντας τὴν βασιλέως χώραν.

[5] The Greek text is: ὁ Περικλῆς — — — γράφει ψήφισμα, πάντας Ἕλληνας — — — εἰς σύλλογον πέμπειν — — — τοὺς βουλευσομένους περὶ τῶν Ἑλληνικῶν ἱερῶν, ἃ κατέπρησαν οἱ βάρβαροι, καὶ τῶν θυσιῶν, ἃς ὀφείλουσιν

discuss (1) the Hellenic sanctuaries destroyed by the barbarians, (2) the sacrifices owed to the gods on behalf of Hellas, and (3) the policing of the seas, security and peace for travellers in normal times. In such terms Perikles tried to persuade the slightly disillusioned second generation that there were still functions for an organized Greek nation (and still good pretexts for organizing its finances), in peace as much as in war. To the Greeks at Delos, deeply conscious of their nationhood and delighted with their newly found champion, such questions hardly required an answer. A Greek nation was being formed, permanent, as nations naturally believe themselves to be; its immediate business was a war of liberation, and in the long future peace would undoubtedly have its victories no less renowned.

The hegemon of the Confederacy was to be Athens, not for the duration of the specific war (as Sparta had been in the Hellenic League in 481), but rather (as Sparta was in the Peloponnesian League) for as long as the Confederacy should last. This is shown by the fact that the oath to share friendships and enmities, which was to endure till the iron floated,[6] was sworn bilaterally between Athens (or Aristeides) of the one party and the Ionians of the other. The hegemon may be defined as the executive power: the executive, not the sovereign. Policy was to be framed by the common synods[7] of the allies; Athens, or her generals, executed that policy. Her executive function included administration: Thucydides speaks of her management of affairs,[8] the first assessment was entrusted to an Athenian, and the funds were the responsibility of Athenians, the hellenotamiai. The executive member had an equal vote with the other allies, but her special responsibilities and her greater prestige made her *prima inter pares*, even at the beginning. Later she encroached, as an able and ambitious executive will often do.[9]

At first, Athens had only the executive power, while the powers of making policy

ὑπὲρ τῆς Ἑλλάδος εὐξάμενοι τοῖς θεοῖς ὅτε πρὸς τοὺς βαρβάρους ἐμάχοντο, καὶ τῆς θαλάττης, ὅπως πλέωσι πάντες ἀδεῶς καὶ τὴν εἰρήνην ἄγωσιν.

[6] Aristotle, Ἀθ. Πολ., 23, 5 (T39): ὥστε τὸν αὐτὸν ἐχθρὸν εἶναι καὶ φίλον, ἐφ᾽ οἷς καὶ τοὺς μύδρους ἐν τῷ πελάγει καθεῖσαν. We do not know the reasons which led Hampl (*Staatsverträge*, p. 123, note 1, and pp. 124-125, note 2) to think that an oath of this type cannot have been sworn in 477. For the bilateral nature of the oath cf. Thucydides, III, 10, 6 (T122).

[7] Thucydides, I, 97, 1 (T109): κοιναὶ ξύνοδοι.

[8] *Loc. cit.*: διαχείρισις πραγμάτων.

[9] Aristotle, Ἀθ. Πολ., 23, 5 (T39), says that Aristeides swore the oaths with " the Ionians " (τοῖς Ἴωσι), and this might be understood as referring to the Greeks of the mainland (*i. e.*, Ἰωνικὸς φόρος). But we prefer not to restrict the term, for many Ionians lived outside Ionia proper, in Thrace and the Hellespont, for example. So we take " the Ionians " as a rough designation for " the allies, mainly Ionians." The actual Ionians surely took the lead. They were in the majority at Delos, and it was the Ionians who had been especially provoked by Pausanias; further, Delos was the pan-Ionian sanctuary. The Ionians were the prime movers in offering the hegemony to Athens. See also Thucydides, VI, 76, 3 (T137a): ἡγεμόνες γὰρ γενόμενοι ἑκόντων τῶν τε Ἰώνων καὶ ὅσοι ἀπὸ σφῶν ἦσαν ξύμμαχοι ---.

rested with the Delian synod.[10] How long these synods continued to meet, and what were the limits of their competence, are questions that we have discussed above (pp. 138-141). Our information is extremely meagre but it is certain that the synods had totally disappeared some while before 432 B. C. The original members swore to have friends and enemies in common for ever,[11] so that secession from the Confederacy was a breach of oath; but oaths are in fact sometimes broken and in 470 Naxos seceded. We do not know what provision, if any, the original charter[12] had made for this contingency. Athens dealt with it as Lincoln dealt with it in 1861, by making war.[13] Naxos surrendered and in the settlement lost her charter rights: " she was subjected contrary to the charter." [14] Thucydides remarks that this formed a precedent, and that as time went on this loss of charter rights, this " subjection," became common. The fundamental charter right was autonomy, the contrary of " subjection," and when the Thirty Years' Peace was made in 446 the process had gone so far that the right to autonomy had become exceptional.[15]

Autonomy was breached in various ways, e. g., by dictating " regulations " (ξυγγραφαί, cf. D10 and D11), or by installing garrisons and commanders (phrourarchs). Autonomy was (after the Naxian precedent) forfeited by revolt; the main causes of revolt were defaulting in the required contribution of ships or money, and absence from military duty. These contributions and this military duty were evidently the chief allied obligations, and the Athenians were meticulous in exacting them.[16] In a rather similar passage the Syracusan Hermokrates names among the pretexts which Athens found for subjecting her allies, besides absence from military duty, the

[10] But Athens must have had some control even here; see above, p. 141, where we suggest that the Athenian members presided in the synods and had some sort of probouleutic authority.

[11] " Until the iron swam "; Aristotle, 'Αθ. Πολ., 23, 5 (T39); cf. Herodotos, I, 165, 3.

[12] This charter, by ordinary Greek usage, would be contained in, or else annexed to, the oaths taken by the contracting parties. The oath thus corresponds to the modern signature. The whole document, including the oath formula, was perhaps engraved at Delos. Aristotle's brief reference is not of course intended as a full account; what he reports is the normal basic formula of alliance (cf. Thucydides, I, 44, 1; III, 70, 6; 75, 1) with the addition that the alliance was perpetual (see note 11 above). The charter required, e. g., that all members be autonomous (Thucydides, I, 98, 4 [T109]) and probably that the money be kept in Delos (Plutarch, Aristides, 25, 3 [T94]).

[13] The war was most probably voted in the synod; Thucydides, III, 10, 5 (T122) and 11, 4 (T123).

[14] Thucydides, I, 98, 4 (T109): παρὰ τὸ καθεστηκὸς ἐδουλώθη. For the meaning of ἐδουλώθη, " suffered douleia," see above, pp. 155-157.

[15] Thucydides, I, 144, 2 (autonomy not the rule in the Thirty Years' Peace); I, 67, 2 (exceptionally covenanted for Aigina).

[16] Thucydides, I, 99, 1 (T109); the difference between νεῶν ἔκδειαι (defaulting in the contribution of ships) and λιποστράτιον (absence from military duty) is not clearly defined. A city might build and man its tale of ships but fail to send them to some campaign (no doubt Egypt was a special strain; see below, pp. 253-254); or contributors in money might have some military duties (see I. G., I², 45, 13-17 [T78c]). See further below, pp. 248-249.

offense of making war on one another.[17] He is evidently referring in the first place to the well-known case of Samos, who made war on Miletos and, when Athens required her to keep the peace, revolted.[18] This requirement was natural in the circumstances,[19] and Samos was obligated by the charter to have the same friends as Athens, but so literal an interpretation of the normal oath of alliance seems to have been unusual,[20] and Hermokrates' words do not entitle us to suppose either that the obligation was more explicit in the Delian Confederacy than elsewhere, or that Athens had always been as peremptory as she was in 440 B. C.

Athens too undertook certain responsibilities. As the hegemonic power she provided leadership in the field, she presided at the synod, and she no doubt played the major rôle in the determining of policy and the mapping of strategy. Further, she contributed ships and men, just as the other allies supplied ships or money. This Athenian quota of ships, financed by the Athenian treasury, remained for many years standard, and it was not until sometime after the assumption of Empire by Athens (*i. e.*, after the Thirty Years' Peace) that this Athenian core (apart from ships launched by Athens to replace those of allies who had commuted to money) was transferred to imperial funds.[21]

If the Confederacy was to resume the war with Persia, it had to be financed. The venture was essentially coöperative and, since there were members who could not provide ships, it followed that they must contribute money. The matter was delicate, however, for Themistokles had aroused intense hostility by his exactions in 480.[22] What was needed was a regular system, and for this, fortunately, the precedent had been supplied by Persia. So the allied representatives adopted, initially, a system of contributions (φόροι), the amount in each case to be determined by the executive power. The executive power was Athens; more specifically, it was Aristeides, who had won the confidence of the allies. His task was, on the basis of an examination of territories and revenues, to make an assessment according to each member's ability to contribute.[23] That the total assessment, a rough draft of which may have been

---

[17] Thucydides, VI, 76, 3 (T137a).

[18] Plutarch, *Pericles*, 24, 1: Περικλῆς ψηφίζεται τὸν εἰς Σάμον πλοῦν, αἰτίαν ποιησάμενος κατ᾽ αὐτῶν ὅτι τὸν πρὸς Μιλησίους κελευόμενοι διαλύσασθαι πόλεμον οὐχ ὑπήκουον.

[19] See below, p. 307.

[20] In the Peloponnesian League the practice was to forbid war within the League only when the League as a whole was at war; Larsen, *Cl. Phil.*, XXVIII (1933), pp. 270-276, especially pp. 274-275 (with note 53); *Harv. Stud. Cl. Phil.*, LI (1940), p. 188 with note 4. Hermokrates had been prepared to concede a similar right in the Sicilian League which he advocated in 425: πολεμήσομέν τε, οἶμαι, ὅταν ξυμβῇ, καὶ ξυγχωρησόμεθά γε πάλιν – – –· τοὺς δὲ ἀλλοφύλους ἐπελθόντας ἀθρόοι αἰεί, ἢν σωφρονῶμεν, ἀμυνούμεθα (Thucydides, IV, 64, 3-4).

[21] See further above, p. 89.

[22] See above, note 15 on p. 189.

[23] Plutarch, *Aristides*, 24, 1 (T94): κατ᾽ ἀξίαν ἑκάστῳ καὶ δύναμιν. For the Persian precedent and the work of Aristeides see below, pp. 234-239, 275 with note 6.

drawn up on Delos before the synod adjourned, was in the first place in terms of cash is implied, we believe, by Thucydides' words: "the Athenians detailed those cities which should provide cash and those which should provide ships."[24] This division of the allies was probably not made until after the conference at Delos and was in all likelihood carried out later at Athens, on the recommendation of Aristeides.

The delegation instituted a permanent financial board, charged with the administration of the funds.[25] These were the hellenotamiai, and once more the activation was to come from Athens, where these officials were to be appointed. The assessor was to be Athenian, the division of contributions into ships and cash was entrusted to Athens, and the "treasurers of the Hellenes" were to be Athenians.[26] Truly, the responsibilities, and therefore the power, of the hegemon were great. These hellenotamiai would of course serve on Delos, where the funds were to be deposited.

Aristotle's report makes it evident that the oaths were sworn by Aristeides (i. e., Athens) on the one hand and the allies on the other.[27] This enhanced the prestige and the de facto superiority of Athens. The form of the oaths, the throwing of the iron into the sea, proves conclusively that the alliance was envisaged as permanent. Even if Persia was the immediate foe, she was not the permanent one; the oaths were framed in more general terms, binding the participants to have the same friends and enemies for ever. This indicates that the Hellenes looked beyond the immediate war. An eventual peace with Persia would not void the oaths, and secession, unilateral denunciation of the treaties, would be contrary to the agreements.

The oaths make no mention of phoros, but we have not the whole formula. Was this phoros considered permanent? Our answer is negative; the alliance was permanent, the phoros might reasonably have been expected to cease with the signing of peace with Persia. When Thucydides writes, "for it was their intention to avenge their losses" (πρόσχημα γὰρ ἦν ἀμύνεσθαι ὧν ἔπαθον), he is explaining his preceding sentence: "the Athenians made certain arrangements for contributions against the barbarian" (– – – παρέχειν – – – πρὸς τὸν βάρβαρον – – –). The assessment of Aristeides was "against the barbarian," for the immediate aim of the Confederacy was vengeance. The more distant aim was "to have the same enemies and friends." That

---

[24] I, 96, 1 (T109): ἔταξαν ἅς τε ἔδει παρέχειν τῶν πόλεων χρήματα πρὸς τὸν βάρβαρον καὶ ἃς ναῦς. See further below, pp. 236-237.

[25] Thucydides, I, 96, 2: καὶ Ἑλληνοταμίαι τότε πρῶτον Ἀθηναίοις κατέστη ἀρχή, οἳ ἐδέχοντο τὸν φόρον.

[26] Walker, C. A. H., V, p. 46, on the ground that the ἀρχαί of the hellenotamiai in the quota lists are dated from 454, believes that these officials must have been Delian in the early period or that the office was not constituted until the removal of the treasury to Athens. But the boards of hellenotamiai are dated from the first ἀρχή in which quota was paid to Athena, not from the year of their institution; 454 began an era. So in the records of the Parthenon the Boule is dated from the year in which the project was begun; see, e. g., I. G., I², 352, lines 3-4, where the fourteenth Boule dates the account to 434/3 B. C. No one argues that the Boule was created in 447/6.

[27] Ἀθ. Πολ., 23, 5 (T39); cf. Plutarch, Aristides, 25, 1 (T94), where Aristeides swears ὑπὲρ τῶν Ἀθηναίων.

many, perhaps a majority, of the allies took it for granted that payment of phoros ended with the cessation of hostilities explains, in a large part, the many partial payments of List 5 (450/49), for the Peace of Kallias was about to be signed as the tribute fell due. Athens very soon cancelled the tribute for the following year (449/8), a step which probably reflects Confederate expectations.[28]

The oaths also support our belief that the Confederacy of Delos was a completely new organization and not just a reworking of the naval arm of the old Hellenic League. Sparta's withdrawal from naval activity was definite; no less definite was the determination of the allies to begin afresh. The naval arm of the Hellenic League ceased in fact to exist. If the Delian Confederacy was organized, as Larsen says,[29] to act for the Hellenic League in the conduct of the naval war, it is difficult to explain satisfactorily the comprehensiveness of the agenda at Delos and the necessity of the oaths at all. It was no doubt comforting and convenient that the Spartans were so willing to withdraw, but the consent of Sparta was scarcely vital and Sparta surely did not regard the Delian commanders as acting for her. The Spartans looked upon the Athenians as " competent to lead " (ἱκανοὺς ἐξηγεῖσθαι, i. e., Sparta could retire and not be accused of leaving her fellow Greeks without competent leadership) and as " amenable to them at that moment " (σφίσιν ἐν τῷ τότε παρόντι ἐπιτηδείους, i. e., the Athenians, who would inherit a position of power, were not hostile to Sparta).[30] The Spartans viewed their retirement into the Peloponnese as above criticism and safe.

This is not to say that the Hellenic League was ever formally dissolved. When the helots revolted the Lakedaimonians summoned to their assistance, among other allies, the Athenians. The summons must have been by virtue of the alliance of 481/0 against the Mede (ἐπὶ τῷ Μήδῳ). In other words, the Athenians (and others) recognized their alliance with Sparta as still binding.[31] After they had been dismissed, they abandoned the alliance which had been made against the Mede (τὴν γενομένην ἐπὶ τῷ Μήδῳ ξυμμαχίαν).[32] There are other references later in the century but these do not present the alliance as an active entity; rather, they cry back for the most part to the union which had once existed. This is particularly true of passages concerning the Plataians, for whom the alliance against Persia (winter, 481/0), their loyalty to the Greek cause, and the special privileges guaranteed to them after the battle of Plataia made effective talking points. The Plataian appeal is essentially pathetic.[33]

[28] On the permanence of the Confederacy as against the temporary assessment of phoros see Wade-Gery, *Hesperia*, XIV (1945), p. 217, note 11. For the moratorium see below, pp. 277-281.

[29] *Harv. Stud. Cl. Phil.*, LI (1940), p. 184.

[30] Thucydides, I, 95, 7.

[31] The Athenian response was made at the insistence of the pro-Lakonian Kimon; no doubt others (*e. g.*, Plataia) followed the lead of Athens. For Kimon's Spartan sympathies, Plutarch, *Cimon*, 15, 3-4; 16, 1-4 and 8-10. For his influence on policy, 16, 9 (over the opposition of Ephialtes).

[32] Thucydides, I, 102, 4.

[33] In Thucydides, III, 58, 1 the Plataians, in their appeal to the Spartans, mention " the gods

The Hellenic League, then, although not formally dissolved, ceased to function as a unit in Greek international politics. It was replaced by the Confederacy of Delos, which inherited its specific policy, war against the Persian, and its name, " the Hellenes " (οἱ Ἕλληνες); [34] to this extent the Confederacy was a continuation of the League. There was no abrupt deterioration of relations with Sparta until Athens denounced the alliance against the Mede, i. e., that of 481/0, which had not contemplated permanence. [35] The Confederacy represented a thorough reorganization independent of Sparta, a revitalized policy, an expansion of membership, and new oaths; to this extent it was new. It was also a sovereign body, although the very limitations placed upon the members in respect to secession and interstate warfare infringed upon complete individual sovereignty, which was not compatible with the ideals of the organization.

The Confederacy of Delos had the opportunity to learn from its predecessors, notably from the Peloponnesian League. [36] There is a natural similarity between the two organizations. Each was organized on a permanent basis; in each the most powerful state (in its own sphere) was recognized as hegemon among autonomous allies. Whereas Athens in the Confederacy held one vote in a single body, Sparta enjoyed a half share in determining the policies of the Peloponnesian League through the separate functioning of her ekklesia as an organ of the League. Both the League and the Confederacy were formed as offensive and defensive alliances; the Spartans tolerated wars between members, the Confederacy, strictly, did not. Separate wars

who *once* (i. e., on the day it was made) witnessed our alliance " (θεῶν ἕνεκα τῶν ξυμμαχικῶν ποτὲ γενομένων); in 59, 2 they cite " the oaths which your fathers swore " (ὅρκους οὓς οἱ πατέρες ὑμῶν ὤμοσαν); in 63, 2 the Thebans, in their reply, point out that the Plataians could always have joined them (i. e., the Thebans and Peloponnesians), for " the Lakedaimonian alliance had already been made against the Mede " (τῆς τῶν Λακεδαιμονίων τῶνδε ἤδη ἐπὶ τῷ Μήδῳ ξυμμαχίας γεγενημένης. The tense of the participle, in conjunction with ἤδη, is instructive). In 64, 2-3 the Thebans say that the Plataians chose the Athenians, so " do not plead the compact that was sworn *then*, and *now* expect salvation by virtue of it; for you abandoned it " (μὴ προφέρετε τὴν τότε γενομένην ξυνωμοσίαν ὡς χρὴ ἀπ' αὐτῆς νῦν σῴζεσθαι. ἀπελίπετε·γὰρ αὐτήν ---). Here the compact (ξυνωμοσία) is not the alliance (ξυμμαχία), but rather the special honours paid to the Plataians after the battle in 479. The passages cite an alliance (or compact) of long ago; they do not suggest an existing one. The speech of the Plataians in II, 71 has nothing to do with an alliance, only with the special honours. For the Plataian position see above, pp. 101-104 with the notes.

[34] The name hellenotamiai is the best example; but see also above, note 12 on p. 97.

[35] When the Thasians revolted (465/4) they appealed for help to Sparta, who (κρύφα τῶν Ἀθηναίων) promised to send it. The appeal was based, probably, not upon a previous alliance ἐπὶ τῷ Μήδῳ, but on the fact that Sparta had once before aided Thasos by expelling her tyrant; Plutarch, *Moralia*, 859d. It was natural for a state which had revolted from Athens to turn to Sparta. Ephialtes no doubt used this example of Spartan hostility in opposing Kimon's proposal to aid the Spartans against the helots; see note 31 above.

[36] The genesis and constitution of the Peloponnesian League have been studied in three papers by Larsen: *Cl. Phil.*, XXVII (1932), pp. 136-150; XXVIII (1933), pp. 257-276; XXIX (1934), pp. 1-19. In using his conclusions we make no separate references.

with outsiders were carried on by members of the Peloponnesian League; that the Delian synod controlled the foreign policy of its members suggests that this was not the case in the Confederacy.

In time of war the members of the Peloponnesian League supplied levies in men, sometimes in money.[37] When the war ended, these contributions ended too. Here the Delian Confederacy marked an advance; the institution of hellenotamiai indicates that the allies contemplated a permanent war fund from the beginning. Some would contribute ships, some money; in time of peace or only mild campaigning the contribution of ships (and therefore men) would bring little strain, but the payment of cash never varied. In this way the burdens would be equalized, for the hazards of war could be very costly to those who participated directly. The advance is an advance in system and efficiency, and was meant as an equitable safeguard against the needs of the future. We have suggested that the allies assumed that with the signing of peace with Persia the payment of phoros automatically stopped. Whether they thought of this in 478/7, and, if so, whether they thought their material contributions would come to an end, are other questions. It looks, from the outcome, as though they had not studied these eventualities in their details; in fact, this is the likely answer.

The Confederacy of Delos had a specific enemy in mind, and if he was not named in the oaths, at least the members were assessed against him; we have speculated concerning the ambition to achieve a genuine peace in the Aegean. The Peloponnesian League named no particular foe; its intention was to produce stability in the Peloponnesos. Our discussion of the two organizations, of course, has been in terms of the original constitution and its intent. The actual practice of the two hegemons, which departed at times from strict constitutionality, and the charges mutually levelled are not relevant to the enquiry.

The ratification of the constitution of the Confederacy was no doubt embodied in the exchange of oaths; either the delegates consulted their respective governments first, or they had been given power to act. The general outline of the proposals must have been known before the synod began its sessions on Delos. The arrangements were probably completed late in 478. All that remained to be done had been entrusted to Athens. Aristeides had to draw up his assessment; the Athenians had to establish a board of hellenotamiai, a duty which required approval and action at Athens.

Thus the winter of 478/7 was consumed in the establishing of the machinery. By the spring of 477 the ambitious Confederacy was in being and ready to meet its responsibilities.

---

[37] For money instead of men, based on a *per capita* assessment, Xenophon, *Hell.*, V, 2, 21-22; VI, 2, 16; cf. Wade-Gery, *Hesperia*, XIV (1945), p. 217, note 11.

CHAPTER V

THE ASSESSMENT OF 478/7 B. C.

The invitations despatched to the prospective members of the Confederacy as the allied fleet, under the command of Aristeides, left Byzantion in the late summer of 478 undoubtedly mentioned, at least in a general way, the agenda proposed for the meeting at Delos. Prominent on the agenda was the question of finance. This meant that the delegates who conferred at the first meeting on Delos had been instructed by their governments and could debate in terms of figures.

At Delos Aristeides (representing Athens) was given the responsibility of drawing up the first taxis ($\tau\acute{\alpha}\xi\iota\varsigma$), which for years afterwards bore his name. We can assume that he discussed his draft in a series of conferences with the allied representatives and that agreement was easily reached with most of them. It was a time of great enthusiasm and the cities, who had entered the Confederacy freely, expected to bear a just share of the costs. And, to anticipate, we may be sure that in this first year collection just about matched assessment.

The drafting of the assessment was in itself not a difficult task. Plutarch tells us that the allies entrusted to Aristeides the responsibility of inspecting their lands and revenues to determine what was a proper assessment.[1] But such an inspection had already been made, as a passage from Herodotos (VI, 42, 1-2) proves. Artaphernes, after the Ionian revolt, made certain agreements among the Ionians. Then " he surveyed their lands by parasangs (the name applied to 30 stades by the Persians) and on this basis he assessed tributes on each of them; these tributes have continued to hold valid on the same scale from this time right down into my own day, just as they were assessed by Artaphernes." [2] Herodotos and Plutarch here report a single operation, an assessment based upon resources, which was made originally by the Persians and, we believe, taken over by Aristeides and Athens. It is entirely probable that a similar system had been employed by the Persians in other Greek lands subject to their rule, i. e., in the Hellespont, Aiolis, and Karia.[3]

---

[1] *Aristides*, 24, 1 (T94): προσέταξαν αὐτῷ χώραν τε καὶ προσόδους ἐπισκεψάμενον ὁρίσαι τὸ κατ' ἀξίαν ἑκάστῳ καὶ δύναμιν.

[2] VI, 42, 2 (T66d): καὶ τὰς χώρας σφέων μετρήσας κατὰ παρασάγγας, τοὺς καλέουσι οἱ Πέρσαι τὰ τριήκοντα στάδια, κατὰ δὴ τούτους μετρήσας φόρους ἔταξε ἑκάστοισι, οἳ κατὰ χώρην διατελέουσι ἔχοντες ἐκ τούτου τοῦ χρόνου αἰεὶ ἔτι καὶ ἐς ἐμὲ ὡς ἐτάχθησαν ἐξ Ἀρταφρένεος. For further comment on this passage, and its significance for the Peace of Kallias, see below, p. 275 with note 6.

[3] Kathleen M. T. Atkinson, in *The London Times Literary Supplement* (June 30, 1945), p. 307, proposed that Thucydides' 460 talents were based upon Persian assessments of Ionians and others. This is close to the view which we adopt. Cf. also Gomme, *The London Times Literary Supplement* (July 28, 1945), p. 355; *Commentary*, I, pp. 279-280; McGregor, *A. J. P.*, LXVII (1946), p. 271, note 6.

If this is a reasonable view, then Aristeides' work had in a large measure been done for him; personal examination of the resources of individual states was not needed, except in the case of those who were inclined to dispute the drafted figures or whose proposals Aristeides and the others questioned. But if we believe that morale was high and participation was willing, then Aristeides had few visits to make and he consumed little time in making them.

For the assessment itself, which had been drawn up in cash, Aristeides was answerable to the Delian synod, although he had probably been given power to act and was not obliged to report back to Delos immediately. The synod had adjourned but we may suppose that Aristeides did deposit in the temple on Delos a copy of his first assessment, the first document of the Confederacy as a functioning organization.

The total assessment reached about 460 talents. We do not suppose that this was the figure aimed at on the basis of need; rather, we think that the cities bound themselves to contribute according to their ability to pay (κατὰ δύναμιν) and that the stipulated sums added up to 460 talents.[4] When Aristeides conferred with allied representatives the subject of ships was undoubtedly raised. Aristeides himself knew which cities could man ships, just as his familiarity with the Aegean world gave him a good idea of the comparative wealth and strength of the Greek communities. So, when he finally returned to Athens, he knew precisely to which members of the Confederacy the obligation to furnish ships ought to be assigned; this had undoubtedly been agreed on by the members.

The official division of the allies by ships and cash, however, had been assigned by the Delian synod to Athens and Aristeides could only make recommendations to the Boule and the Demos. His recommendations, we may be sure, were adopted in the voting with little or no change. That this mandate should have been given to Athens is quite natural. She was the hegemonic power and much of the administration would be bound to fall upon her. As the hegemonic power she commanded at sea; thus the state, and the generals, had to know from whom to expect ships and could claim a primary right to stipulate which cities should contribute to the allied fleet under her command. When the campaigning season opened, it was the Athenians

---

[4] The evidence of the later assessments proves that the total was achieved by the addition of individual items. The assessment of the islands in 425/4, for example, was 163 talents, 410½ drachmai (A9, I, 101: [ΗΡΔΑΤΤΤΗΗΗΗΔΙΙΙ]); the figure is restored by the addition of the separate items, each a round number except Keria, which makes a round number in the total impossible. The sum could never have been chosen arbitrarily for subsequent division among the Insular cities. The same may be said of the Hellespontine assessed total of 95 talents, 5400+ drachmai in 421 B.C. (A10, IV, 13: [ᵛᵛ]ΡΔΔΔΔΡΡΗΗΗΗ − −). So it was with the Aristeidean taxis. The total was of minor concern, but, as it chanced, came close enough to 460 talents for the figure to enter the literary tradition. Nesselhauf (Klio, Beiheft XXX, p. 111) follows Diodoros (XI, 47, 2 [T53]), whose distribution (διαμερισμός) of the total among the cities is no more than an ancient guess about the relationship of the total to the component parts, and is inferior to the evidence of A9 and A10. The view is combatted by Schaefer, Hermes, LXXIV (1939), pp. 225-229.

who notified the various contingents of the place of assembly and of the immediate naval plans, although in the formulation of long-range policy and strategy the synod of the allies might exercise a theoretical sovereignty.

The other administrative task which demanded action at Athens was the institution of the hellenotamiai. It is likely that arrangements for their establishment were carried out at once, for their duties at Delos would begin as soon as the phoroi started to come in.[5]

Thucydides' first mention of the division between ships and money lies in a famous statement (I, 96, 1 [T109]): οἱ Ἀθηναῖοι – – – ἔταξαν ἅς τε ἔδει παρέχειν τῶν πόλεων χρήματα πρὸς τὸν βάρβαρον καὶ ἃς ναῦς. This has been variously translated. Some insist that the meaning is, the Athenians " settled which cities were to furnish money and which ships ";[6] others, clinging to the technical meaning of τάττειν (" to assess "),[7] render it, " the Athenians assessed the contributions both of the states that were to provide money and of those that were to provide ships."[8] When the verb means " to assess," usage in a simple sentence demands an accusative of the thing and a dative of the person,[9] which we do not have;[10] instead, we have what is most simply taken as an accusative of the person. When the verb means " to detail," or " to appoint," it requires an accusative of the person, followed by an infinitive. This is precisely the usage in our passage and we therefore follow Gomme in believing that the unencumbered approach is to take the verb ἔταξαν with its accusative object: " the Athenians appointed which cities were to furnish money against the barbarian and which ships."[11] This, then, was not the assessment, which had already been made and filed by Aristeides, and ἔταξαν does not mean " assessed." The assessment was carried out by Aristeides, as the representative of Athens to be sure, who owed his responsibility direct to the synod of the allies; it was an earlier piece of business, when all commitments of the allies were still reckoned in terms of that universal common denominator, cash. So, when Thucydides says that the first tribute assessed was 460 talents,[12] we may take him literally at his word. The division into categories followed long enough after the assessment to allow, on the basis of Aristeides' copy of the taxis, a determination of who should accept one obligation (money) and who the

---

[5] Cf. Thucydides, I, 96, 2 (T109): καὶ Ἑλληνοταμίαι τότε πρῶτον Ἀθηναίοις κατέστη ἀρχή, οἳ ἐδέχοντο τὸν φόρον.

[6] E. g., Gomme, Commentary, I, p. 272.

[7] Liddell-Scott-Jones, Lexicon, s. v. τάσσω, III, 3.

[8] E. g., E. C. Marchant, Thucydides Book I (London, Macmillan, 1937), p. 232.

[9] See, e. g., A9, line 58: [κατὰ τάδε ἔτα]χσεν τὸμ φό[ρον τἐ]σι πόλεσιν hε βολ[ἐ]; cf. [Andokides], IV, 11 (T8) and Thucydides, I, 19 (T104).

[10] But either accusative or dative may be omitted. Cf., e. g., List 25, III, 54: ταῖσδ[ε ἔτ]αχσαν hοι τάκται, and D3, line 6: εἴτε φόρον δοκεῖ τάττεν.

[11] Liddell-Scott-Jones, Lexicon, s. v. τάσσω, II, 2. The Athenians decided which were to be in each category.

[12] I, 96, 2 (T109): ἦν δ' ὁ πρῶτος φόρος ταχθεὶς τετρακόσια τάλαντα καὶ ἑξήκοντα.

other (ships). Later, Thucydides himself tells us that ships had their monetary equivalent, and naturally the converse must have been true.[13] The duty of making the division, we propose, had been assigned to the state of Athens (not to Aristeides the representative) and no report was owed to the synod.[14] So the assessment as such is clearly removed in time and place from the final division into ships and money. On Delos it had been a cash assessment.

The contributions of those members who paid money remained stable, year in and year out; the burden never varied. The citizens of such states could remain at home and did not face the hazards of naval campaigning. They paid for and received protection.

Far different was the lot of those who furnished ships to the allied fleet. They not only supplied the ships, they manned and maintained them.[15] Further, the crews faced the rigours and casualties of war. Their losses in men alone in a given year might be severe; in another year their burdens might be light. Participants in a campaign were likely to capture considerable booty, which was probably divided among the allies with the squadron, including Athens. Sometimes this booty was very rich, as is attested by Plutarch's account of Kimon's spoils.[16] No doubt some effort had been made to equate the liabilities of those paying money (which did not vary) and those contributing ships (whose losses and gains varied a great deal). Yet the naval allies tired of service and, " in order not to be away from home, accepted assessment in cash instead of their ships." [17] The payment of phoros came to be looked upon as preferable.

Athens herself contributed the largest naval contingent to the fleet; this, in effect, was her assessment on the basis of her resources ($\kappa\alpha\tau\grave{\alpha}$ $\delta\acute{\upsilon}\nu\alpha\mu\iota\nu$). This she manned and maintained. In addition, she shouldered the responsibilities of the hegemon, she

---

[13] I, 99, 3 (T109): χρήματα ἐτάξαντο ἀντὶ τῶν νεῶν τὸ ἱκνούμενον ἀνάλωμα φέρειν.

[14] The distinction would be difficult to prove. But we note that, according to Thucydides, it was the Athenians who, by virtue of their newly-won hegemony, decided who should supply money and who ships: παραλαβόντες δὲ οἱ Ἀθηναῖοι τὴν ἡγεμονίαν ---. Conceivably, Aristeides and οἱ Ἀθηναῖοι, whom he represented, could be used interchangeably of the first assessment.

[15] Thucydides (I, 99, 1 [T109]) gives as the causes of revolt failure to supply tribute, failure to supply ships, and failure to serve (λιποστράτιον εἴ τῳ ἐγένετο). We take λιποστράτιον to mean a refusal by allied contingents (i. e., allied ships manned by allies) to join the fleet, or, having done so, to follow the orders of the hegemon; see further below, pp. 248-249 with notes 16, 17, and cf. F. B. Marsh, *Modern Problems in the Ancient World* (Austin, Texas, 1943), pp. 36-37. Maintenance is a logical conjecture; we note that, in the Athenian alliance with Argos, Mantineia, and Elis, troops serving outside their own territory are to be maintained by their governments for a limited period (Thucydides, V, 47, 5-6).

[16] For the booty after the capture of Byzantion and Sestos, *Cimon*, 9 (where, clearly, the allies participate with the Athenians in the fruits of victory); for the Eurymedon, *Cimon*, 13, 5-7.

[17] Thucydides, I, 99, 3 (T109): ἵνα μὴ ἀπ' οἴκου ὦσι, χρήματα ἐτάξαντο ἀντὶ τῶν νεῶν. See further below, pp. 246-248.

supplied the commanders, and she accepted most of the administrative detail without which the organization could scarcely function effectively. Her share was a full one.

The expenses of campaigning, then, were borne by the participants, including Athens, and often these must have been more than covered by the booty won. The money contributed annually was deposited in the temple on Delos as a Confederate reserve fund, to be employed in emergency. Little, if any, was used for current expenses. This is proved by the fact that by 450/49 there had accumulated 5000 talents in the tribute fund,[18] now housed at Athens. This can only be explained by a deposit of very nearly 200 talents a year on Delos.

The expenses of the allied contingents in the fleet did not fall upon Athens, nor upon the contributors of money. Later, as more and more allies commuted from ships to money, Athenian expenses did not increase although her navy and the sailors who manned it did. Athens used the new money to finance her own additions to the fleet, and her consequent domination at sea led to a complete change in the nature of the Confederacy. At the beginning, however, the burdens of Athens, the allies supplying ships, and the allies paying money were meant to be equalized.

We believe that every effort must have been made to complete the assessment by the spring of 477, when the allies must have hoped to begin the naval and military tasks discussed at the conference on Delos. Some, however, would extend the time consumed by Aristeides in his work of assessment and would thus delay the operations of the allies as a newly organized Confederacy. Cavaignac, for example, would date the first synod at Delos as late as spring, 476.[19] But Cavaignac would differentiate between the first phoroi (πρῶτοι φόροι) of Aristotle[20] (individual phoroi assessed by Aristeides in, presumably, 478/7) and the first tribute assessed (ὁ πρῶτος φόρος ταχθείς) of Thucydides[21] (the sum total of the assessment, after several years of work by Aristeides); he would lay upon Aristeides years of visits to the cities of the Confederacy, he would send him to Rhodes on the evidence of Timokreon's poem,[22] and to the Pontos to continue his assessment.[23] Finally, Cavaignac believes that the assessment in ships was made first, and the cash levied upon the remainder; this we have already disputed.

We maintain, however, that the evidence does not justify a change in our reconstruction. When Aristotle writes of Aristeides, " and so it was he who laid the assess-

---

[18] D13, 5-8: [ἐπ' Εὐ]θυδήμο[υ] Περικλέους γνώμη[ν] εἰσ[ηγησαμένου 'Αθηναίους κινεῖν] τά ἐν δη-μοσί⟨ω⟩ι ἀποκείμενα τάλαν[τα τὰ ἐκ τῶν φόρων συνηγμένα] πεντακισχείλια κατὰ τὴν 'Αριστεί[δου τάξιν].

[19] Études, pp. 37 (with note 5), 42-43.

[20] 'Αθ. Πολ., 23, 5 (T39).

[21] I, 96, 2 (T109).

[22] Plutarch, Themistocles, 21, 4 (T97d): ἐγὼ δ' 'Αριστείδαν ἐπαινέω ἄνδρ' ἱερᾶν ἀπ' 'Αθανᾶν ἐλθεῖν ἕνα λῷστον. Aristeides no doubt passed by Rhodes on his way to and from Kypros in 478.

[23] " On public business " (πράξεων ἕνεκα δημοσίων), says Plutarch, Aristides, 26, 1.

ment of their tributes upon the cities – – – in the archonship of Timosthenes," [24] he is thinking in terms of individual assessments to be sure, but no less in terms of the completion of a task. " The cities " (ταῖς πόλεσι) means " the cities of the Confederacy," not " some of the cities." Thucydides, on the other hand, writes collectively of the first assessment of tribute (ὁ πρῶτος φόρος ταχθείς). But in meaning there is no essential difference between the phoroi of Aristotle and the phoros of Thucydides. Further, it is at least implied in Aristotle that the assessment and the swearing of the oaths took place in the archonship of Timosthenes, 478/7. Aristeides completed his assessment within this year. His visit to Rhodes, along with Pausanias, we have already placed in 478.[25] He may have traveled to the Black Sea on business of state towards the end of his life; but that it was not on the business of the assessment is convincingly proved by the fact that no Pontic cities were assessed until 425/4, when they appear in A9.[26] We hold to the thesis developed at the beginning of this chapter.[27]

We are now ready to consider the cash value of the assessment of 478/7 B.C. On the principle that the original members continued to pay, down to the middle of the century at least, the tribute of Aristeides' day (τὸν φόρον τὸν ἐπ' Ἀριστείδου) and new members on the scale of Aristeides' assessment (κατὰ τὴν Ἀριστείδου τάξιν),[28] we shall start with the assessment of 454 B.C., whose gross value we have computed at 498 talents, 1390 drachmai,[29] and subtract from this the figures included for the states which made no contribution in cash when the Confederacy was formed. They may have been furnishing ships, or they may not yet, in 478/7, have joined the Confederacy at all.

Our study of the collection of 454[30] will show that in our opinion fourteen states[31] were even then supplying ships rather than money, representing an assessment of 67 talents, 2200 drachmai. We are left with a net assessment of 430 talents, 5190 drachmai. But between 478/7 and 454 we know of two islands, Thasos and Naxos,[32]

[24] T39: διὸ καὶ τοὺς φόρους οὗτος ἦν ὁ τάξας ταῖς πόλεσι τοὺς πρώτους – – – ἐπὶ Τιμοσθένους ἄρχοντος.

[25] See above, p. 191 with note 26.

[26] It might be argued that Thrace could not have been assessed until after the capture of Eion (476/5); but most of Thrace west of Eion, and the two islands of Thasos and Samothrake, were already in the Confederacy, and this comprised the bulk of the later Thrakian panel.

[27] Aristeides was strategos, not taktes, and so the question of the duration of his office does not arise. The taktai were instituted later at Athens.

[28] For the interpretation of these phrases see above, pp. 221-222.

[29] For the assessment of 454 see Chapter II in Part I above (pp. 19-28); for the total see p. 28. It is to this chapter that reference should be made for the assessments of individual states.

[30] Chapter VII below (pp. 265-274).

[31] Akanthos, Andros, Chalkis, Eretria, Hestiaia, Iasos, Keos, Kythnos, Paros, Poteidaia, Seriphos, Siphnos, Styra, Tenos. See below, pp. 267-268.

[32] For Thasos see Thucydides, I, 101, 3 (T110): Θάσιοι δὲ τρίτῳ ἔτει πολιορκούμενοι ὡμολόγησαν Ἀθηναίοις τεῖχός τε καθελόντες καὶ ναῦς παραδόντες, χρήματά τε ὅσα ἔδει ἀποδοῦναι αὐτίκα ταξάμενοι καὶ τὸ λοιπὸν φέρειν, τήν τε ἤπειρον καὶ τὸ μέταλλον ἀφέντες. Naxos was an original member of the Confederacy

which converted from ships to money, and there must have been many more, besides Chios, Lesbos, and Samos,[33] who originally contracted to supply ships. The removal of Thasos and Naxos from the list reduces the total of the early cash assessment to 418 talents, 5190 drachmai.

After this deduction we proceed to remove from the assessed roster of 478/7 those cities which were not yet members of the Confederacy but which we reckoned in our initial calculations for 454:[34]

		Talents	Drachmai			Talents	Drachmai
1.	Ἀβδηρῖται	15	——	77.	Καύνιοι	——	3000
6.	Αἰγινῆται	30	——	78.	Κεβρήνιοι	3	——
8.	Αἴνιοι	12	——	81.	Κελένδερις	1	——
10.	Αἰσώνιοι	——	1500	84.	Κιλλαρῆς	——	1000
13.	Ἀλινδῆς	1	3000	85.	Κινδυῆς	1	——
19.	Ἀρκέσσεια	——	1000	87.	Κλαυνδῆς	1	——
20.	Ἁρπαγιανοί	——	300	89.	Κοδαπῆς	——	1000
22.	Ἄσπενδος	(amount unknown)		91.	Κρυῆς	——	2000
25.	Ἀστυπαλαιῆς	2	——	92.	Κυδαιῆς	——	400
30.	Βεργαῖοι	——	3000	95.	Κυλλάνδιοι	2	——
31.	Βηρύσιοι	——	1000	97.	Κυρβισσῆς	——	2000
32.	Βολβαιῆς	——	1000	106.	Λύκιοι		
34.	Γαλήψιοι	1	3000	183.	Τελεμήσσιοι	12	——
36.	Γεντίνιοι	——	500	109.	Μαρωνῖται	1	3000
45.	Δίκαια παρ' Ἄβδηρα	——	3000	113.	Μυδονῆς	——	1500
46.	Δικαιοπολῖται	4	——	116.	Μυλασῆς	1	——
48.	Δῶρος	(amount unknown)		119.	Μυσοί	——	2000
51.	Ἐρινῆς	——	4000	120.	Ναξιᾶται	——	1000
54.	Εὐρυμαχῖται	——	1000	122.	Ναρισβαρῆς	——	1000
57.	Θασθαρῆς	——	500	124.	Νεάπολις παρ' Ἀντισάραν	——	1000
61.	Θύδονος	——	1000	128.	Ὀθώριοι	——	500
65.	Ἰδυμῆς	1	890	133.	Οὐλαιῆς	——	1000
70.	Καρβασυανδῆς	——	1000	134.	Οὐρανιῆται	——	1000
71.	Κᾶρες ὧν Τύμνης ἄρχει	——	3000	137.	Παργασῆς	——	1000
73.	Καρπάθιοι	——	1000	140.	Παρπαριῶται	——	1000
75.	Καρύστιοι	7	3000	141.	Πασανδῆς	——	3000
76.	Κασωλαβῆς	——	2500	142.	Πεδιῆς ἐν Λίνδῳ	——	2000

(Thucydides, I, 98, 4 [T109]), had her name on the Serpent Column (T68a), and furnished four ships at Salamis (Herodotos, VIII, 46, 3).

[33] Otherwise what Thucydides says in I, 99, 3 (T109) is difficult to interpret: οἱ πλείους αὐτῶν, ἵνα μὴ ἀπ' οἴκου ὦσι, χρήματα ἐτάξαντο ἀντὶ τῶν νεῶν τὸ ἱκνούμενον ἀνάλωμα φέρειν. See also the account of the change from ships to money in Plutarch, Cimon, 11 (T95). The two passages are discussed at length on pp. 244-252 below.

[34] The reader should refer to Part III, Chapter III, " The Original Membership of the Confederacy " (pp. 194-224 above), and to the tabulation of the assessment of 454 on pp. 20-28 above, whose serial numbers we employ.

	Talents	Drachmai			Talents	Drachmai
147. Πηδασῆς	2	——	191. Ὑβλισσῆς		—	1000
149. Πλαδασῆς	—	2000	192. Ὑμισσῆς		—	1200
150. Πολιχναῖοι Κᾶρες	—	1000	193. Ὑρωμῆς		—	2500
158. Σ/―――	(amount unknown)		195. Φασηλῖται		6	——
159. Σαμβακτύς	1	——	199. Χαλκητορῆς		—	2000
163. Σερμαῖοι	—	500	202. Χεδρώλιοι		—	500
168. Σίλοι	—	1500	205. Χῖοι Κᾶρες		—	2000
172. Σκάψιοι	1	——	206. [.]σσυρι―――		—	1000
177. Στρεψαῖοι	1	——	207. [..⁵...]ῆται		—	4000
182. Ταρβανῆς	—	1000	208. An unknown name		1	——
187. Τηλάνδριοι	1	——				

These further deductions reduce the cash assessment in the first year by 121 talents, 5790 drachmai and the revised amount now stands at 296 talents, 5400 drachmai. The incompatibility of this figure with the known assessment of Aristeides in 478/7 makes it clear that the entire burden of the 460 talents cannot have fallen on those who did not furnish ships. But if the first assessment was computed in cash, inclusive of ships, the figure is intelligible. For our own calculation we must add the following items:

		Talents	Drachmai
Thasos [35]	ships	30	——
Naxos	ships	9	——
Samos, Chios, Lesbos [36]	ships	90	——
Others [37]	ships	67	2200
Others	cash	296	5400
Total assessment	ships and cash	493	1600

The fact that this total overshoots the 460 talents of Thucydides indicates that we have included too much territory in the Confederacy at the beginning. We have argued that no garrisons held out in Ionia and the Hellespont, and we may still be right; we have perhaps been too generous in admitting at once to the Confederacy all cities which in our opinion had freed themselves from Persia. It is not impossible that one or two sizable communities,[38] which we thought it best to include, remained in the beginning outside the Confederacy, for reasons which we cannot now discern.

[35] When Thasos controlled her territory on the mainland, with its mine, she paid the maximum tribute of 30 talents (cf. List 11, III, 15).

[36] We assess each island with what we conceive to have been the maximum figure.

[37] See above, p. 239.

[38] In our study of the original membership we admitted the following with reservations: Alopekonnesos, Karene (assessment unknown), Kolophon, Limnai (assessed with Χερρονησῖται), Maiandros, Palaiperkote, Pyrnos, Syangela. To these we might add Astakos, Daskyleion, and Kios,

The list of cities which, we think, were still furnishing ships in 454 B. C.[39] is for the most part of island names, with no city from the Hellespont, only Iasos from Karia, and Akanthos and Poteidaia from Thrace. It is, in fact, a remarkably short list, and no name in it rates more than 6 talents of tribute except Paros. Going back to the beginning of the Confederacy we have added Thasos and Naxos, and of course there were Samos, Chios, and Lesbos which never changed from ships to money at all.

But if we want a total of as much as 296 talents, 5400 drachmai in cash in 478/7 we must make some very remarkable assumptions. We must assume that no city from the Hellespont furnished ships. Where then were Abydos, Kalchedon, Kyzikos, Lampsakos, Perinthos, Selymbria, and Tenedos, to say nothing of Byzantion? Where also are the great cities of Karia? It would be surprising if only Iasos from this area supplied ships, and not Halikarnassos, Knidos, Kos, Termera, and the prosperous states of Rhodes, Lindos, Ialysos, and Kameiros. The same question can be asked in Ionia. Samos, Chios, and Lesbos we know; but some at least of Erythrai, Klazomenai, Miletos, Teos, and Phokaia may have contributed directly to the fleet.[40]

The cash value of the cities just named is 137 talents, 4000 drachmai and to suppose that this money was represented in ships would reduce the cash assessment to about 160 talents. This we do not urge, nor do we imply that all important cities furnished ships at the beginning. The fact is that precise information is lacking and we can do little more than speculate about the details. But the general scheme seems quite clear, and if we were to conjecture that in 478/7 the assessment of 460 talents was about evenly divided between ships and money we should probably not be far wrong. Furthermore, the text of Thucydides (I, 98, 4 - 99, 3 [T109]), followed by Plutarch (*Cimon*, 11 [T95]), demands that we allow for commutation from ships to money by many states between 478/7 and 454/3, *i. e.*, that a good many contributed ships in the beginning.

The alternatives are to claim (a) that the cash figure may still be raised to 460 talents by placing heavier assessments on those who paid in money, and (b) that considerable territory not assessable in 454 was assessed in cash in 478/7. The objections to (a) are twofold. First, it puts the cash burden on those least able to bear it, doubling or trebling the tribute of small places; it thus makes impossible any reasonable explanation of the universal testimony that everyone thought of the first assessment as a kind of Golden Age which he remembered nostalgically when the later increases began. Second, it is incompatible with what we believe to be the correct

because of their rather isolated positions, Didymoteichitai (inland, in the Odrysian sphere), Kyzikos (see p. 24 above), Doric Nisyros, and Tyrodiza (in the Odrysian sphere). If we make these deductions our figure is lowered to 474 talents, 5600 drachmai. To reach a total of about 460 talents we have only to suppose that a city like, say, Perinthos lagged. Thucydides' 460, of course, is a round number; the precise amount could have been a few talents more or less.

[39] See note 31 above.
[40] For Miletos and Erythrai see below, pp. 252-258.

interpretation of the phrase " according to the assessment of Aristeides " (κατὰ τὴν Ἀριστείδου τάξιν) and its validity down to about 450.[41] The objection to (b) is that the extent of Empire broadened, rather than diminished, between 477 and 454.[42] There is no evidence, and there should be very good evidence indeed, to justify adding something like 230 talents (at least) of new money to the original assessment from cities not named in the tribute lists.

We conclude, therefore, that the assessment of 478/7 demanded contributions in ships from a good number of cities whom we cannot identify with precision. We shall return to the argument in more detail in the next chapter.

[41] See above, pp. 221-223 with note 126.

[42] The assessment of 454, in ships and money, may be reckoned at rather less than 600 talents; see above, pp. 28 and (for Samos, Chios, and Lesbos) 241 with note 36.

CHAPTER VI

THE GROWTH OF EMPIRE

Thucydides, after his description of the unsuccessful revolt of Naxos,[1] remarks that Naxos was the first allied city to be " subjected contrary to the law of the Confederacy," but that her fate was later shared by others as occasion offered.[2] " Subjection " was not Athens' deliberate policy; rather, it came about because, in Athenian eyes, certain of the allies failed to live up to the terms of the Delian constitution. For the Athenians, says Thucydides, by way of explanation, were meticulous in their management.[3]

Thucydides does not give the specific reason for the revolt of Naxos, but his account of it and its result leads him to an analysis of the causes of revolt and the change in the nature of the Confederacy (I, 99).[4] It is this chapter which proves conclusively that many of the members must, at the beginning, have been providing ships rather than money. The chapter would be difficult to understand if the only example of revolt caused by failure to supply ships is Naxos,[5] or if the only states that found themselves helpless after conversion to cash were the fourteen who were still supplying ships in 454/3,[6] only six of which are known to have revolted. The narrative of Plutarch (*Cimon*, 11)[7] is no more intelligible under these conditions.

---

[1] I, 98, 4. We catalogue I, 96-99 as T109.

[2] Παρὰ τὸ καθεστηκὸς ἐδουλώθη, ἔπειτα δὲ καὶ τῶν ἄλλων ὡς ἑκάστῃ ξυνέβη.

[3] I, 99, 1: οἱ γὰρ Ἀθηναῖοι ἀκριβῶς ἔπρασσον. Gomme translates (*Commentary*, I, p. 283): ' were very exacting in their management of the League '; --- ' insisted on the last drachma and every ship, properly equipped.'

[4] " Of all the causes of revolt the greatest were failure to pay the financial levies and to supply ships, and failure to serve, as happened in some cases. For the Athenians were exacting in their behaviour and were offensive in applying pressure to men who were not accustomed and indeed not willing to endure hardship. In one way or another the Athenians no longer ruled with their former popularity; they participated in campaigns on an unequal basis and it was easy for them to coerce those who rebelled. The allies themselves were responsible for these developments. For because of this reluctance of theirs to participate in the expeditions, the majority of the cases in question, in order not to be away from home, had accepted an assessment in cash as their appropriate future contribution in place of their ships; thus the Athenians' naval strength was gradually increasing from the funds which the allies contributed, while the latter, whenever they revolted, found themselves unequipped and without fighting experience."

[5] We do not know that this was the cause of the Naxian secession.

[6] See below, pp. 267-268, and above, p. 239. The states were Akanthos, Andros, Chalkis, Eretria, Hestiaia, Iasos, Keos, Kythnos, Paros, Poteidaia, Seriphos, Siphnos, Styra, Tenos. Those who revolted were Eretria, Styra, Chalkis, and Hestiaia in 446 (revolt of Euboia), Poteidaia in 432, Akanthos in 424.

[7] " The allies regularly made their financial payments, but did not provide men and ships as they had been assessed to do, for they soon grew weary of the expeditions and, in no way wanting

Plutarch's story is in all essentials the same as Thucydides', except that it is centred around the virtues of Kimon. All that he says about the development of the Confederacy can be read with less elaboration in Thucydides.

THUCYDIDES	PLUTARCH
αἰτίαι δὲ ἄλλαι τε ἦσαν τῶν ἀπο-στάσεων καὶ μέγισται αἱ τῶν φόρων καὶ νεῶν ἔκδειαι καὶ λιποστράτιον εἴ τῳ ἐγένετο·	ἐπεὶ δ᾽ οἱ σύμμαχοι τοὺς φόρους μὲν ἐτέλουν, ἄνδρας δὲ καὶ ναῦς ὡς ἐτάχθησαν οὐ παρεῖχον, ἀλλ᾽ ἀπα-γορεύοντες ἤδη πρὸς τὰς στρατείας, καὶ πολέμου μὲν οὐδὲν δεόμενοι, γεωργεῖν δὲ καὶ ζῆν καθ᾽ ἡσυχίαν ἐπιθυμοῦντες, ἀπηλλαγμένων τῶν βαρβάρων καὶ μὴ διοχλούντων, οὔτε τὰς ναῦς ἐπλήρουν οὔτ᾽ ἄνδρας ἀπέστελλον, οἱ μὲν ἄλλοι στρατη-γοὶ τῶν Ἀθηναίων προσηνάγκαζον αὐτοὺς ταῦτα ποιεῖν, καὶ τοὺς ἐλλεί-ποντας ὑπάγοντες δίκαις καὶ κο-λάζοντες ἐπαχθῆ τὴν ἀρχὴν καὶ λυπηρὰν ἐποίουν, Κίμων δὲ τὴν ἐναν-τίαν ὁδὸν ἐν τῇ στρατηγίᾳ πορευό-μενος βίαν μὲν οὐδενὶ τῶν Ἑλλήνων προσῆγε,
οἱ γὰρ Ἀθηναῖοι ἀκριβῶς ἔπρασ-σον καὶ λυπηροὶ ἦσαν οὐκ εἰωθόσιν οὐδὲ βουλομένοις ταλαιπωρεῖν προσ-άγοντες τὰς ἀνάγκας. ἦσαν δέ πως καὶ ἄλλως οἱ Ἀθηναῖοι οὐκέτι ὁμοίως ἐν ἡδονῇ ἄρχοντες, καὶ οὔτε ξυνεστράτευον ἀπὸ τοῦ ἴσου ῥᾴδιόν τε προσάγεσθαι ἦν αὐτοῖς τοὺς ἀφι-σταμένους. ὧν αὐτοὶ αἴτιοι ἐγένοντο οἱ ξύμμαχοι· διὰ γὰρ τὴν ἀπόκνησιν ταύτην τῶν στρατειῶν οἱ πλείους αὐτῶν, ἵνα μὴ ἀπ᾽ οἴκου ὦσι, χρή-	χρήματα δὲ λαμβάνων παρὰ τῶν οὐ βουλομένων στρατεύεσθαι καὶ ναῦς κενάς, ἐκείνους εἴα δελεαζομένους τῇ

war, they yearned to till their soil and live at leisure. They were freed of the barbarians, who did not press them, and they neither manned their ships nor sent contingents of men. The other Athenian generals tried to compel them to do this, and by prosecuting and punishing defaulters made the Empire burdensome and offensive. Kimon, on the other hand, took the opposite course during his term as general, and did not bring compulsion to bear upon a single Hellene; instead, accepting money and empty hulls from those who were unwilling to serve, he allowed them, ensnared with the bait of their own leisure, to spend their time on domestic affairs and, in their self-indulgent folly, to become farmers and unwarlike businessmen instead of warriors. Large numbers of the Athenians, however, he embarked on their ships in relays and exposed to the hardships of the expeditions, and in a short time, with the wages obtained in cash from the allies, he made the Athenians the absolute rulers of the very men who supplied the money." We catalogue this passage as T95.

THUCYDIDES	PLUTARCH
ματα ἐτάξαντο ἀντὶ τῶν νεῶν τὸ ἱκνούμενον ἀνάλωμα φέρειν, καὶ τοῖς μὲν Ἀθηναίοις ηὔξετο τὸ ναυτικὸν ἀπὸ τῆς δαπάνης ἣν ἐκεῖνοι ξυμφέροιεν, αὐτοὶ δέ, ὁπότε ἀποσταῖεν, ἀπαράσκευοι καὶ ἄπειροι ἐς τὸν πόλεμον καθίσταντο.	σχολῇ περὶ τὰ οἰκεῖα διατρίβειν, γεωργοὺς καὶ χρηματιστὰς ἀπολέμους ἐκ πολεμικῶν ὑπὸ τρυφῆς καὶ ἀνοίας γινομένους, τῶν δ' Ἀθηναίων ἀνὰ μέρος πολλοὺς ἐμβιβάζων καὶ διαπονῶν ταῖς στρατείαις, ἐν ὀλίγῳ χρόνῳ τοῖς παρὰ τῶν συμμάχων μισθοῖς καὶ χρήμασι δεσπότας αὐτῶν τῶν διδόντων ἐποίησε.

Apart from his remarks about Kimon, Plutarch's account shows some distortions, some suppressions,[8] and some accretions.[9] It is quite evident, however, that Plutarch (or his source) kept close to Thucydides and has clearly understood his original to say that the many allies who accepted assessment in cash instead of ships had not made this choice in the beginning, but had supplied ships, found it irksome, and willingly converted to cash.

The crucial statement in Thucydides is: οἱ πλείους αὐτῶν – – – χρήματα ἐτάξαντο ἀντὶ τῶν νεῶν τὸ ἱκνούμενον ἀνάλωμα φέρειν (" the majority of the cases in question – – – had accepted an assessment in cash as their appropriate future contribution in place of their ships "). It must be said that the whole tenor of Thucydides' chapter supports Plutarch's interpretation rather than that of Gomme, who refers χρήματα ἐτάξαντο to the time of the first assessment.[10] It will be worth while to devote some attention to the chapter as a whole before returning to the clause under discussion.

The chapter, we repeat, is a commentary, occasioned by the reduction of Naxos (ca. 470), on the causes of defection among the allies. The most important of these are failure to pay phoros, failure to supply ships, and failure to participate in campaigns (λιποστράτιον). Yet strictly, and with due respect for Thucydidean brachylogy, these were not in themselves causes; they became causes only after the Athenians had brought pressure upon defaulters. Failure to contribute according to the pact (κατὰ τὸ καθεστηκός, we may say) resulted in compulsion by the Athenians (προσάγοντες

[8] E. g., that failure to pay tribute led to revolt. This item in Thucydides militates against Plutarch's thesis that the phoros was more bearable than furnishing ships and so was welcomed by the allies.

[9] E. g., that the allies provided empty ships. This may be Plutarch's conjecture, in which case we should need to suppose no other source than Thucydides for the chapter. On the other hand, Plutarch may have found the item in his " naval " source, which he certainly employs in his next chapter (Cimon, 12, 2) in describing the changes which Kimon made in naval construction.

[10] Commentary, I, p. 283: " ' had assessed themselves to contribute money rather than ships,' at the beginning, when they had the choice." This rendering is challenged by McGregor, A. J. P., LXVII (1946), pp. 270-271.

τὰς ἀνάγκας), which in turn provoked revolt. The allies were not accustomed to the rigours of constant campaigning nor were they minded to accept them (οὐκ εἰωθόσιν οὐδὲ βουλομένοις ταλαιπωρεῖν); the Athenians, however, insisted (ἀκριβῶς ἔπρασσον καὶ λυπηροὶ ἦσαν). Consequently, the Athenians, in one way and another, ceased to enjoy their former popularity (ἦσαν δέ πως καὶ ἄλλως — — — οὐκέτι ὁμοίως ἐν ἡδονῇ ἄρχοντες).[11] Revolt followed. From the next clauses in Thucydides we may draw the conclusion that failure to supply ships and men had been remedied by conversion to cash, for now the Athenians no longer campaigned upon an equal footing with their allies (καὶ οὔτε ξυνεστράτευον ἀπὸ τοῦ ἴσου),[12] and besides, they found it easy to suppress revolt (ῥᾴδιόν τε προσάγεσθαι ἦν αὐτοῖς τοὺς ἀφισταμένους), i. e., the allies had already ceased to maintain their ships and men in fighting trim, as Thucydides goes on to explain. The allies, he says, had themselves to blame for their inequality and for the futility of their revolts. For because of this reluctance of theirs to go on campaigns (διὰ γὰρ τὴν ἀπόκνησιν ταύτην τῶν στρατειῶν), the majority of them, in order not to be away from home, had accepted an assessment in cash instead of their ships (χρήματα ἐτάξαντο ἀντὶ τῶν νεῶν). The vital word in the first parenthesis is ταύτην: " this reluctance of which I have been speaking," i. e., a reluctance, born of harsh experience, which manifested itself in failure to supply ships (νεῶν ἔκδειαι) and, sometimes, in failure to serve (λιποστράτιον). The presence of the article in the phrases τῶν στρατειῶν and τῶν νεῶν corroborates this: it was not that the allies had originally chosen money instead of ships because they wished to avoid campaigns; rather, they later preferred to contribute money instead of *their* ships (which they had been using) because *the* Confederate campaigns (in which they had already participated) had proved irksome and kept them from home. If " they had accepted an assessment in cash " (χρήματα ἐτάξαντο) referred back to the original division of 478/7, we should expect " instead of ships " (ἀντὶ νεῶν), without the article;[13] the presence of the article suggests that those cities had previously been in the category of the allies who accepted assessment in ships (ξύμμαχοι ναῦς ταξάμενοι) and we must understand that here is a statement not of original choice, but of change of status. The usage of the article with στρατειῶν is not decisive of itself, but cumulative with ταύτην and τῶν νεῶν.[14]

So, continues Thucydides, Athenian naval power was steadily increasing (καὶ τοῖς μὲν Ἀθηναίοις ηὔξετο τὸ ναυτικόν; note the imperfect), thanks to the funds con-

---

[11] Cf. I, 96, 1, where the Athenians assume hegemony of willing allies: παραλαβόντες δὲ οἱ Ἀθηναῖοι τὴν ἡγεμονίαν τούτῳ τῷ τρόπῳ ἑκόντων τῶν ξυμμάχων.

[12] I. e., Athenian naval preponderance increased, the inevitable outcome of allied naval withdrawals.

[13] Cf. I, 96, 1: ἅς τε ἔδει παρέχειν χρήματα — — — καὶ ἃς ναῦς.

[14] It would be possible to urge that τῶν στρατειῶν in 478/7 would refer to the anticipated campaigns and that the reluctance was anticipatory; but ταύτην with ἀπόκνησιν is a strong argument against this interpretation.

tributed by the allies (who converted from ships to cash) ; as for the allies, when they revolted, they were unequipped to fight (ἀπαράσκευοι) and their experience in war was not fresh (ἄπειροι ἐς τὸν πόλεμον καθίσταντο) ; these weaknesses we have anticipated above.

The context proves that, when Thucydides says " the majority of them had accepted assessment " (οἱ πλείους αὐτῶν – – – ἐτάξαντο), he means not " a majority of the allies," but " a majority of the allies who tried to secede." The sequence which Thucydides envisaged should now be clear: (1) the Confederates undertook campaigns as planned, some participating under Athenian leadership, some contributing cash to the treasury; (2) some of the allies found the hardships too much and either failed to supply ships or withdrew them (at the same time a waning of enthusiasm caused others to default in their cash obligations) ; (3) the Athenians insisted that the allies adhere to their commitments; (4) the defaulters in cash paid up, under compulsion, many (or a majority) of the naval allies converted from ships to money, also under virtual compulsion; (5) the extra cash enabled Athens to put more ships to sea and made the fleet predominantly Athenian; (6) Athenian discipline and naval superiority detracted from Athens' popularity; (7) revolts followed; (8) the revolts failed because the majority of the rebels, having before this converted to cash, had lost their fighting edge and were unprepared.

We are now ready to return to the sentence which prompted this digression: διὰ γὰρ τὴν ἀπόκνησιν ταύτην τῶν στρατειῶν οἱ πλείους αὐτῶν, ἵνα μὴ ἀπ' οἴκου ὦσι, χρήματα ἐτάξαντο ἀντὶ τῶν νεῶν τὸ ἱκνούμενον ἀνάλωμα φέρειν. We have proved, we think, that this has no reference to the original assessment of 478/7,[15] and we render it as follows, bearing in mind that it is part of a commentary on revolts: " For because of this reluctance (which I have mentioned) to participate in the Confederacy's expeditions (in which they had been sharing), the majority of those who (later) revolted had accepted an assessment in cash as their appropriate future contribution in place of their ships (which they had been furnishing from the beginning)." This is precisely how Plutarch understood the passage.

When he cites defaulting in money and ships Thucydides is subdividing a single failure: defaulting in the assessed contributions. The allies grew lax in paying their monetary obligations, and they ceased to build or to commission enough ships. Failure to serve on expeditions (λιποστράτιον), on the other hand, is a more general and comprehensive term. Obviously, it embraces an original refusal to serve and is equivalent to the failure to supply ships; it may also mean " desertion," and so would refer to occasions on which allied contingents refused during a campaign to follow the Athenian lead.[16]

[15] Still less does it imply self-assessment; Gomme's translation (note 10 above) shows that our difference with him over the meaning of τάττω persists; see our discussion above, pp. 83-85.

[16] In Thucydides, VI, 76, 3 (T137a) Hermokrates says that the Athenians used " failure to

At the beginning, we think, the allies were not expected to supply troops apart from ships' crews; yet later it looks as though they did so, for there were allies at Tanagra.[17] But the context in I, 99 puts the emphasis upon naval operations and the allies' preference to stay at home; so we take it that here the only men involved are the crews of allied ships and that refusal to serve (λιποστράτιον) applies to naval desertion specifically. The continuous campaigning of the 'seventies, 'sixties, and 'fifties proved too much for allied endurance; for Athens it built an empire.

As late as 454 there remained (apart from Samos, Chios, and Lesbos, who never commuted) fourteen cities contributing ships rather than money, ostensibly to the Confederacy's operations, in fact, we should perhaps say, to Athens.[18] It was not until about 450 that Athens began the final move that was to change their obligations to cash; it was completed by the end of Period II, the last conversion being that of Poteidaia. West[19] combined the evidence of the Serpent Column and of the quota lists to identify the majority of the fourteen as charter members of the Confederacy who had supplied ships from the beginning; their persistence he ascribed to the fact that they had fought against the Persians in the earliest battles and so enjoyed a certain prestige. Their ultimate conversion he thought was the work of Kimon after his return from ostracism.

This view has much to commend it, although, if Plutarch's story (*Cimon*, 11) is derived chiefly from Thucydides (as we think), we must discount Plutarch's contrast between the gentle Kimon and his harsh predecessors, and the change described by Thucydides (as a gradual change) and Plutarch (who wishes to give Kimon credit) should be placed in the years after the revolt of Naxos down to about 450, or even later, rather than credited specifically to Kimon after his return from ostracism.[20] Nesselhauf sees in the absence of the Insular names from the early quota lists signs

serve " (λιποστρατίαν) and wars within the Confederacy as pretexts for reducing the allies. Here the meaning is very general and includes every form of defaulting: failure to supply ships and desertion in the field. Cf. Herodotos, V, 27, 2.

[17] Thucydides' " other allies " (τῶν ἄλλων ξυμμάχων) in I, 107, 5 could refer to allies who were not members of the Confederacy; but Pausanias (V, 10, 4) saw at Olympia a dedication set up by the Lakedaimonians and their allies for the victory at Tanagra over Argives, Athenians, and Ionians. Cf. Meiggs, *J. H. S.*, LXIII (1943), p. 22 with note 6; Gomme, *Commentary*, I, pp. 283 and 315. The Madytioi, Byzantioi and perhaps Kebrenioi of *I. G.*, I², 928 were fighting with the Athenians in Hellespontine territory virtually in self-defense (465); for discussion of this casualty list see above, pp. 108-110. It may be that in Period II certain Hellespontines (*e. g.*, Perinthos) provided men in lieu of tribute; see above, pp. 60-61 with note 61.

[18] For the cities see above, note 6.

[19] *Am. Hist. Rev.*, XXXV (1929-1930), pp. 267-275. Perhaps Poteidaia was the only remaining naval ally after the assessment of 450.

[20] See also Gomme, *Commentary*, I, pp. 285-286. Nesselhauf's criticism (*Klio*, Beiheft XXX, p. 4, note 1) of West betrays a misunderstanding of Thucydides, who in I, 99 is not confining himself to campaigns between 478 and 467 but rather describing a process that continued for some years, perhaps as far as the revolt of Samos (440); the chapter is a commentary on revolts.

of disaffection occasioned by the Egyptian defeat and the removal of the treasury to Athens.[21] This, however, we do not believe; for one thing, the islanders absent from the first three or four lists are so many that Nesselhauf's explanation would demand widespread disaffection under Athens' very eyes, in the home district. This suggests the most likely explanation of the islanders' absence from the early quota lists. They were still furnishing ships, as we have argued, and that they continued to do so for so long was natural enough because of their proximity to Peiraieus and the resulting ease of administrative arrangements for naval service.[22]

The conversion to cash by all the remaining naval allies except Samos, Chios, and Lesbos began about 454 and was completed by the end of Period II (perhaps, except for Poteidaia, at the Panathenaia of 450). The change was very likely a part of the general reorganization of the Empire after the removal of the treasury from Delos to Athens; Kimon, during his last campaign, may well have encouraged the islanders to convert from ships to cash. Meiggs[23] and Gomme[24] find it difficult to accept any large-scale commutation in 450, because it would have reduced the size of Kimon's fleet just when strength was needed for the Kyprian campaign. The assumption is that allied ships were decommissioned or destroyed or allowed to remain idle; Athens would have required time to build replacements and train crews.

Yet we need not think that, when a city substituted cash for ships, the vessels lay idle or were decommissioned. Probably Athens acquired part of them by purchase, thus increasing the strength of the Confederate fleet which she commanded. Occasionally, warships were confiscated from rebels; this, we know, is what happened to Thasos and it may have been the fate of Naxos.[25] Furthermore, Athens herself was surely building during these years of ambitious expansion. Thus the cessation of allied naval contribution did not decrease the size of the fleet; Athens provided more ships and the extra tribute paid for them.[26]

[21] *Klio*, Beiheft XXX, pp. 11-13; followed by Meiggs, *J. H. S.*, LXIII (1943), p. 31.

[22] Cf. Wade-Gery, *Hesperia*, XIV (1945), pp. 219-220 with note 16.

[23] *Loc. cit.*

[24] *Commentary*, I, p. 286.

[25] The case is not certain. Her " subjection " (δουλεία) consisted of infringement upon her autonomy, probably the installation of a garrison. Her name is on the Serpent Column and does not appear in the quota records until List 5; in this she is like West's charter members who did not convert to cash until about 450, and so she may have continued to supply ships after her revolt. But this we doubt; it is more likely that Athens saw to it that, if she did not lose her weapons of war (her ships) outright, at least the opportunity to use them was taken from her by the substitution of cash for ships as her contribution to the Confederacy. The absence of Naxos from Period I would then have to be interpreted as the accident of survival. We have included Naxos in our reconstruction of the quota list of 454/3; see below, p. 272, no. 95.

[26] Plutarch's statement that allies provided empty hulls (ναῦς κενάς), whether it is his conjecture or not (see above, note 9), is in fact right. Kimon, in planning his change in naval construction (Plutarch, *Cimon*, 12, 2), would naturally encourage the allies to commute, for this would increase the homogeneity of his fleet.

The change in the system of contribution was welcomed by the allies and by Athens. The allies were enabled to stay at home, to avoid the perils of war, and to shift all naval responsibility to Athens. Thucydides' emphasis upon allied weariness of war and consequent eagerness to remain at home (I, 99) must be reconciled with a remark made by the Korinthians at the second congress in Lakedaimon before the Peloponnesian War (I, 121, 3) and the reply to it spoken by Perikles later at Athens (I, 143, 1). The Korinthians say: " We shall fit out our armies from our private resources and from the moneys at Delphi and Olympia. A loan from them, after all, will enable us to seduce Athens' foreign sailors with the promise of greater pay. For Athenian power is mercenary rather than national." [27] Perikles' answer is: " Even if they should tamper with the moneys at Olympia or Delphi and try to seduce the foreigners among our sailors with offers of greater pay, that would be disastrous only if we ourselves and our metics could not embark and prove a match for them." [28]

The two passages prove that in 432 B. C. an appreciable percentage of the crews cf Athenian ships was mercenary. The mercenaries came from the tributary states.[29] We deduce that, after the naval allies turned to cash contributions, many of their sailors, individually, missed the excitement of campaigns and enlisted as rowers in the Athenian fleet. This was not done officially by the allied state, nor did Athens demand this service; [30] the enlistments were voluntary. But the Athenians could, when and if necessary, man their own fleet and they were not dependent on hired hands to surpass their enemies at sea. " But as things are this is always true," continues Perikles, " and, most important of all, we have among our own citizens steersmen and other personnel in greater numbers and of better quality than all the rest of Hellas combined." [31] The Athenians as a whole had maintained their naval skill, perhaps by

---

[27] Ἀπὸ τῆς ὑπαρχούσης τε ἑκάστοις οὐσίας ἐξαρτυσόμεθα καὶ ἀπὸ τῶν ἐν Δελφοῖς καὶ Ὀλυμπίᾳ χρημάτων· δάνεισμα γὰρ ποιησάμενοι ὑπολαβεῖν οἷοί τ' ἐσμὲν μισθῷ μείζονι τοὺς ξένους αὐτῶν ναυβάτας. ὠνητὴ γὰρ ἡ Ἀθηναίων δύναμις μᾶλλον ἢ οἰκεία.

[28] Εἴ τε καὶ κινήσαντες τῶν Ὀλυμπίασιν ἢ Δελφοῖς χρημάτων μισθῷ μείζονι πειρῷντο ἡμῶν ὑπαλαβεῖν τοὺς ξένους τῶν ναυτῶν, μὴ ὄντων μὲν ἡμῶν ἀντιπάλων ἐσβάντων αὐτῶν τε καὶ τῶν μετοίκων δεινὸν ἂν ἦν.

[29] This is shown by Perikles' words a sentence later (I, 143, 2) : " and in addition to the danger involved, not one of our foreign sailors would choose to become an exile from his native country " (καὶ ἐπὶ τῷ κινδύνῳ οὐδεὶς ἂν δέξαιτο τῶν ξένων τήν τε αὐτοῦ φεύγειν). The sailors would be choosing exile, in effect, because they came from cities of the Empire. We follow Gomme in reading αὐτοῦ as against the αὑτοῦ of the mss.; see his note, Commentary, I, p. 461. Note too the distinction between ξένοι and μέτοικοι. Isokrates knew that Athens employed mercenaries and, typically, exaggerated the fact in his castigation of the Empire, saying that the triremes were manned by the sweepings of Hellas; see, e. g., VIII, 79 (T79b) : συναγαγόντες ἐξ ἁπάσης τῆς Ἑλλάδος τοὺς ἀργοτάτους καὶ τοὺς ἁπασῶν τῶν πονηριῶν μετέχοντας.

[30] I. e., it is not to be used to interpret λιποστράτιον.

[31] Νῦν δὲ τόδε τε ὑπάρχει, καί, ὅπερ κράτιστον, κυβερνήτας ἔχομεν πολίτας καὶ τὴν ἄλλην ὑπηρεσίαν πλείους καὶ ἀμείνους ἢ ἅπασα ἡ ἄλλη Ἑλλάς. We take ὑπηρεσία to be citizens, who were not open to Peloponnesian seduction (as were the ξένοι, potentially) ; cf. Gomme's note, Commentary, I, pp. 460-461.

what was in effect a system of service in relays;[32] the allies had not (their citizens who chose to serve in Athenian ships do not enter the question) and so were unprepared (ἀπαράσκευοι, they had sold most of their ships to Athens, the rest were not in fighting condition) and unskilled (ἄπειροι, they had abandoned naval service).

The commutation from ships to money brought advantages to Athens, notably the opportunity to construct a more homogeneous fleet under a single command, a fleet that could be more easily assembled, trained, and manoeuvred. Previously, allied contingents had joined the Confederate fleet as units with their own officers; they of course recognized Athens (through her generals) as commander-in-chief, but a provincial loyalty no doubt existed. Ease of assembly was obtained when most of the naval allies far from Peiraieus ceased to send ships; homogeneity was the next goal and it was reached soon after 450.[33] Further, the increase in the numbers of ships that came to be launched by Athens herself (whether she built them or purchased hulls from allies or confiscated ships from rebels) meant an enormous increase in Athenian opportunities for employment; the navy was essentially a citizen arm, even if foreigners are later found in Athenian ships.[34]

In I, 99 Thucydides has thus given the story of the slow development of the Confederacy, with the accompanying changes from ships to phoros, as a commentary on his analysis of revolt. This analysis takes its theme from Naxos, the first city to suffer subjection after revolt, and finds its most striking illustration later in the suppression of the revolt of Euboia (446), some four years after its most important cities had commuted their obligations from ships to money. But there had been disloyalty in the interim and these instances may shed some light on the causes of revolt as listed by Thucydides.

Not much more than a decade had passed before Erythrai and Miletos were in revolt. The evidence comes from the quota lists. In Period I the name Erythraioi does not appear, but in Lists 1 and 2 Boutheia makes payments, only the second of which, the quota on 3 talents, is preserved. In Period II the Erythraian syntely as a whole (Erythrai, Boutheia, Pteleon, Sidousa, Elaiousa, Polichna) makes syntelic payments of 9 talents. Later, when separate amounts are credited to each city, although the names are entered in a group, Boutheia's tribute is 1000 drachmai. Clearly the payment of 3 talents by Boutheia in Lists [1] and 2 represents the loyal Erythraians (and the dependencies) for whom Boutheia is acting as a syntelic centre. Erythrai proper was disaffected.

[32] Cf. Plutarch, *Cimon*, 11, 2: τῶν δ' Ἀθηναίων ἀνὰ μέρος πολλοὺς ἐμβιβάζων. See also the remarks of [Xenophon], Ἀθ. Πολ., I, 19-20: the Athenians learn as civilians how to row and steer a ship, and naval technique in general.

[33] See above, note 26.

[34] The case is well put by F. B. Marsh, " Unemployment and Imperialism," in *Modern Problems in the Ancient World* (Austin, Texas, 1943), pp. 29-55, especially p. 47.

The record of Miletos is similar. In List 1 the only Milesians entered are from Leros (paying 3 talents) and Teichioussa, places which are demonstrably Milesian dependencies and which do not appear again until List 28 when with Miletos they form a single group.[35] It is not until List 3 (452/1) that Milesians are recorded without qualification, and are therefore presumably from the city of Miletos itself. We infer that before this time Miletos was in revolt and that the loyal Milesians had fled to Leros and Teichioussa.[36]

Inasmuch as neither Erythrai nor Miletos was among the loyal members of the Confederacy in 454/3 we must seek the occasion for their secession at a somewhat earlier date. With our analysis of Thucydides, I, 99 in mind we turn at once to the expeditions which began in 460, first against Kypros and then against Egypt; these must have aggravated acutely allies who were reluctant to participate in campaigns away from home. Allies were with the fleet at Kypros and presumably in this first year they went also with the Athenians to Egypt.[37] So far as Erythrai and Miletos are concerned, this campaign offers all the conditions which Thucydides says were preliminary to revolt. No formal proof can be produced, but we suggest that Erythrai and Miletos had been furnishing ships down to 460 and that they then objected to the participation required of them in a campaign so far away as Memphis in Egypt. Perhaps they refused to send ships or their squadrons were under strength;[38] perhaps their contingents, already with the fleet, refused to follow Athenian commanders to Egypt.[39] Whatever the details, the Athenians will have brought compulsion to bear, probably forcing Erythrai and Miletos to pay henceforth in cash; subsequently the two cities revolted. Probably the western satraps gave all the encouragement that they could and supported with money this damage to the Athenian cause. That the Persians were alive to their opportunities about this time is shown by Megabazos' attempt to

[35] See the Register, s. v. Μιλήσιοι.

[36] Compare the conduct of the loyal Kolophonians who in 430 fled to Notion when Kolophon was taken by the Persians; Thucydides, III, 34, 1-2 [T127] (cf. the Register, s. v. Κολοφώνιοι and Νοτιῆς, for the effect on tribute payment). For Erythrai and Miletos see Meiggs, J. H. S., LXIII (1943), pp. 25-27.

[37] Thucydides, I, 104, 2: οἱ δέ (ἔτυχον γὰρ ἐς Κύπρον στρατευόμενοι ναυσὶ διακοσίαις αὐτῶν τε καὶ τῶν ξυμμάχων) ἦλθον ἀπολιπόντες τὴν Κύπρον, καὶ ἀναπλεύσαντες ἀπὸ θαλάσσης ἐς τὸν Νεῖλον ---. Among the allies were the Samians, who are attested by an epigram found in the Heraion on Samos in 1932 and published by Peek (Klio, XXXII [1939], pp. 289-306) with the following text:

[τοδ'] ἔργο πολλοὶ τάρα [μάρτ]υρε[ς, εὖτ' ἐπὶ Νείλωι]
[Μέμ]φιος ἀμφ' ἐρατῆς νηυσὶν ἔθηκ[ε μάχην]
[θο]ῦρος Ἄρης Μήδων τε καὶ Ἑλλήν[ων, Σάμιοι δὲ]
[νῆ]ας Φοινίκων πέντε τε καὶ δ[έχ' ἕλον].

A fifth, very fragmentary, line names the particular Samian hero commemorated, Hegesagoras.

[38] In so far as Thucydides, in I, 99, 1, makes a distinction between the specific νεῶν ἔκδειαι and the more comprehensive λιποστράτιον, this was the former.

[39] This, if we make the distinction, was λιποστράτιον.

negotiate by bribery at Sparta an invasion of Attica in the spring of 456; [40] this is all part of a single policy directed at forcing Athenian withdrawal from Egypt by fomenting trouble in the Aegean. [41]

Our belief that Erythrai and Miletos revolted during this decade, based primarily upon the evidence of the quota lists, [42] is confirmed by the epigraphical survival of the regulations which followed their return to allegiance. Our text of the Erythrai decree we have printed in *A. T. L.*, II as D10, Regulations for Erythrai; for Miletos see *A. T. L.*, II, D11, Regulations for Miletos.

The significant features of D10 (Erythrai) are that the document can be dated by the archon Lysikrates precisely to 453/2 and that it embodies the recommendations of the syngrapheis which returned Erythrai to good standing in the Confederacy. [43] In the quota list of 453/2 the loyal Erythraians are still represented by Boutheia, whose position in List 2 (X, 5) indicates that the payment was booked rather late in the year. We may therefore date the recovery of Erythrai near the end of the archonship of Lysikrates, possibly towards midsummer of 452 B. C.

The decree provides for close Athenian control of Erythrai, in which democracy is now established. The new democratic Council is to be instituted by Athenian episkopoi and by the Athenian phrourarchos. The former are civil officials, the latter would command the Athenian garrison, [44] although he clearly has some political authority. The installation of the Athenian garrison in the city should probably be read in conjunction with the clause in the Council's oath against harbouring fugitives to the Persians [45] and with the penalty of death invoked against those who would betray the city to the tyrants. The deduction to be made is that during Erythrai's defection, which had been encouraged by the satraps, Persia had supported tyrants in the city, that her recovery forced the pro-Persians and the tyrants and their sympathizers to flee, and that the Athenian garrison was intended as a protection for the city against

[40] Thucydides, I, 109, 2; cf. Meiggs, *J. H. S.*, LXIII (1943), p. 22. For the date see above, p. 171.

[41] Megabazos was to bribe the Spartans into activity which would compel Athenian withdrawal from Egypt (ὅπως --- ἀπ᾽ Αἰγύπτου ἀπαγάγοι ᾽Αθηναίους). The pro-Persian activities of Arthmios in the Peloponnese (Demosthenes, IX, 42) may also belong in the same context; see above, note 42 on p. 171. We place the revolts, with Persian stimulation, before Persian successes in Egypt, and we look upon them as illustrations of the consequences of refusal to send ships (νεῶν ἔκδειαι) and refusal to serve (λιποστράτιον). Meiggs (*J. H. S.*, LXIII [1943], pp. 22-23) seems to feel that Athenian defeat in Egypt and the threat of a Persian fleet in the Aegean encouraged the revolts.

[42] *I. e.*, Boutheia (but not Erythrai) and Leros and Teichioussa (but not Miletos, or Latmos or Myous) paid in 454/3. Erythrai and Miletos, however, though in revolt, probably stood in the assessment list of 454.

[43] For these improvements in the text see the commentary on D10 in *A. T. L.*, II. Cf. also D11, line 1: [Μι]λεσί[οις χσυγ]γρ[αφαί]; procedure was probably standard in such cases.

[44] D10, 38-39: καταστε̑σαι [δὲ τὸν φρόρα]ρχον τὸν ᾽Αθεναίον [τὲν δέοσαν] φυλακέν ---.

[45] D10, 25-27: [οὐδέ ποτε] τὸν φ[υγά]δον [κατ]αδέχσομαι οὐδ[ὲ] ℏένα --- [τὸν ἐς] Μέδος φευγό[ντο]ν ---.

the Persians fully as much as, if not rather than, an imperialistic measure. We note that both the Council and Demos in Erythrai swear loyalty not only to Athens but to the allies of Athens, and that Erythraian exiles are to be banned from all Confederate territory.[46] The oath shows that Athens had not yet openly acknowledged the transformation of Confederacy into Empire; the excommunication reveals her actual power and status.

The garrison of the decree and the measures which contemplate the Persians and the tyrants as enemies may fairly be taken to corroborate the conjectures which we have already made in seeking the events which led to the revolt of Erythrai. Our picture is in sharper focus and we may reconstruct with greater sureness. Erythrai, tired of campaigning, converted to money and subsequently revolted, provoked by Athenian conduct and aided by Persian encouragement. The revolt was accompanied by political upheaval in which a pro-Persian tyrant was established. The recovery of the city by Athens caused the flight of the tyrant and his followers, who were Persian sympathizers. Athens created a democratic constitution under the supervision of her episkopoi and phrourarchos, and left a garrison in the city as a safety measure. Her control over Erythrai was firm but not autocratic.[47]

The Regulations for Erythrai give us good reason to believe that there was considerable Persian activity on the coast of Asia Minor in the 'fifties. The belief is strengthened by Athenian Regulations for Miletos (450/49), to which we shall come shortly, and by the Athenian decree of 451/0 (*I. G.*, I², 32) praising Sigeion, to whom protection is guaranteed against any enemy " on the mainland " of Asia, *i. e.*, in the satrap's service.[48]

The appearance of the Milesians in List 3, without the qualification that would refer them to Leros or Teichioussa, shows that by 452/1 Miletos had been recovered by Athens. The beginning of this recovery, however, may be reflected in List 2 (453/2), where Latmos appears in the closing lines (X, 3). Miletos, Latmos, and Myous appear frequently together in the early quota lists [49] and this, coupled with their geographical positions, suggests that the fate of Miletos was shared by its two

---

[46] D10, 30-31: ἐ[ὰ]ν δ[ὲ φεύγεν] γνοσθεῖ φευγέτο ℎάπασαν τὲν Ἀθεναίον χσυνμαχί[δα].

[47] Erythrai retained, apparently, her judicial autonomy (D10, 29-32); the right to banish or to recall is controlled by Athens (D10, 25-29). For epigraphical notes on the fragments of the decree see Meritt, *Hesperia*, XV (1946), pp. 246-248; for an analysis of the terms see Meiggs, *J. H. S.*, LXIII (1943), pp. 23-25, with epigraphical notes on pp. 33-34.

[48] Lines 13-16, as published by Meritt, *Hesperia*, V (1936), pp. 360-362.

[49] 3, II, 28-30; 5, V, 18-20; 8, I, 108-110. It is probable that [Μυέσσιοι] and [Μιλέσιοι] should be restored in 4, II, 17-18, immediately below Λ[άτμιοι]. The three are absent from List 7 but we now think that they stood together in the body of List 8 discharging their arrears, as well as in I, 108-110, where the payment, we suspect, is current; see above, pp. 35-36, 49. In 9, V, 7-8 we have [Μυ]έσσιοι and [Λ]άτμιοι, and in 25 Μυέσσιοι; [Μιλέσιοι] perhaps belongs in line 6. *S. E. G.*, V, 9 printed line 7 as [Μι]λέσιοι, a reading which we have discarded on epigraphical grounds; see the note on fragment 94, *A. T. L.*, I, p. 46.

less powerful neighbours. Myous and Latmos, indeed, may have been in revolt in 454/3 along with Miletos; if so, Latmos was recovered in time to pay its tribute late in 453/2, Myous and Miletos later, probably in the same campaigning season that witnessed the restoration of Erythrai. We have therefore included Myous and Latmos among the defaulters in 454/3.[50]

The Athenian decree which brought Miletos back into the Confederacy in 452 has not been preserved. The regulations of D11 are subsequent to the initial reconciliation; they do not contain the oath of allegiance as we find it in, for example, the decree concerning Erythrai (D10). The brief references to oaths in lines 73-74 are obviously not to be placed in the same category as the formal oaths of imperial fealty.

The Regulations for Miletos of D11 have preserved for us the record of subsequent intervention by Athens in the internal and external affairs of Miletos.[51] The decree, in the form of syngraphai (cf. D10), is securely dated to 450/49 by the archon Euthynos. It does not establish a democratic constitution in Miletos but it does provide for the appointment of five Athenians who are to collaborate in government with the local Milesian magistrates.[52] Athenian control seems rather more severe than in Erythrai, for penalties are provided against those who fail to respect Athenian decrees [53] and certain cases, at least, are to be heard in Athenian courts.[54] Miletos, like Erythrai, is to have a garrison [55] and it looks as if Miletos is to supply military and naval assistance.[56]

Again, the garrison should be connected with the Persian threat, and the parallel with Erythrai leads us directly to a local Milesian inscription [57] in which certain families and their descendants are outlawed for ever. The crime must have been a form of treason, " in all probability," as Tod says, " an attempt (whether temporarily successful or not) to establish a tyranny at Miletus." The inscription has been dated about 450. We now associate it with Persian connivance in the revolt of Miletos and the institution of a pro-Persian tyranny in the city. Recovery by Athens led to the banishing of the tyrants and their sympathizers, and the Milesian inscription belongs probably in 452, about the time when the Athenians reincorporated Miletos in the Confederacy through a decree (perhaps syngraphai) which is now lost. During this decade the policy of the Persian satraps conforms to a recognizable pattern.

[50] Se below, p. 269.

[51] For analysis of the decree and of the contemporary history of Miletos see Meiggs, *J. H. S.*, LXIII (1943), pp. 25-27.

[52] D11, 4-7; cf. 64: ℎοι πέντε ℎοι ἄρχοντες.

[53] The text is fragmentary but this is implied by lines 28-30, 53-54.

[54] Lines 30-35, especially 33-34: [ℎαι δ]ὲ δίκαι 'Αθένεσι ὄντον — — —. The following lines concern the dates, courts, and dikastai.

[55] Lines 77, 87.

[56] Lines 10-15.

[57] Tod, *Greek Hist. Inscr.*, I², no. 35, commentary on pp. 67-68.

Athenian support of the Milesian oligarchs, noted by [Xenophon],[58] may belong to the restoration, for the government of Miletos in D11 is clearly not democracy. Meiggs believes that absence of Miletos from List 7 (448/7) indicates the stasis that followed, and he posits a new settlement in which democracy on the Athenian model was imposed. We, however, do not interpret Milesian absence from List 7 in this way; rather, we see it as part of the widespread indecision which resulted from the Peace of Kallias. Then many of the states believed that the tribute should be cancelled. As a matter of fact, we think that Miletos (with her neighbours Latmos and Myous, and several others) made two full payments in 447/6, one for the current year and one to erase her default of the previous year.[59] The paying of past tribute obligations was not, so far as we know, demanded by Athens of towns that had revolted; payment of arrears may imply reluctance, but it does not mean revolt.

One more inference may be drawn to support our proposal that Athenian military installations in Asia Minor were directed against the Persians and were not measures concerning imperial discipline. Miletos and Erythrai, which revolted and were recovered before the Peace of Kallias, accepted garrisons; Kolophon, whose recovery followed the peace, did not.[60] There is no evidence, in fact, epigraphic or from Thucydides, which mentions or implies garrisons in Asia Minor after the peace. We therefore conclude that the demilitarization clause in the peace banned Athenian garrisons in Asia; this was a reciprocal concession to Persia, and it meant a change in Athenian practice. The garrisons had been aimed at Persia and any such installation in the future would be interpreted by Persia as an act of aggression.[61]

This is not to say that the Athenians abandoned their concern for the safety of Asia Minor. But other means had to be found and the Athenians solved the problem by a system of colonies shortly after the signing of the peace. One of these, we think, was despatched to Erythrai; there were others.[62]

We have examined the revolts of Erythrai and Miletos, and we have seen that they conform to Thucydides' analysis in I, 99.[63] We have noted also that they led to Athenian infringement of the autonomy of these allies. The first revolt had been that of Naxos; " this was the first allied city to be subjected contrary to the established

[58] III, 11: τοῦτο δὲ ὅτε Μιλησίων εἵλοντο τοὺς βελτίστους, ἐντὸς ὀλίγου χρόνου ἀποστάντες τὸν δῆμον κατέκοψαν.

[59] See above, pp. 35-36, 49; Miletos, Latmos, and Myous are members of the late-paying " southeastern group."

[60] For the revolt of Kolophon see D15 and below, pp. 282-283.

[61] For the terms of the Peace of Kallias see Wade-Gery, Harv. Stud. Cl. Phil., Suppl. Vol. I (1940), pp. 132-143; cf. below, p. 284 with note 40.

[62] I. G., I², 396: τὲς ἀποι[κίας] τὲς ἐς Ἐρ[υθράς]. The colony replaces the δέουσα φυλακή (see above, note 44). For the restoration and for the other colonies see below, pp. 282-284.

[63] For similar revolts in Euboia see below, pp. 294-295.

covenant."[64] Later there were others, whom Thucydides does not name specifically.[65] Erythrai and Miletos were among them and in each case Thucydides might have written, " she was subjected contrary to the established covenant." But by this time the terms of the original constitution, so far as Athens was concerned, had ceased to obtain.

The revolt of Thasos, in 465, did not spring from desertion, or from failure to supply ships, as Thasos had been doing from the first years of the Confederacy. According to Thucydides,[66] the issue concerned Thasian holdings on the mainland: " somewhat later the Thasians revolted from Athens, in disagreement concerning the trading-stations, on the coast of Thrace opposite, and the mine which they owned."[67] The Athenians under Kimon[68] promptly beat the Thasians at sea and landed on the island. At about the same time 10,000 Athenian and allied colonists were settled at Ennea Hodoi: " having about the same time despatched 10,000 Athenian and allied colonists to the Strymon with the intention of establishing a settlement at what was then called Ennea Hodoi, but is now Amphipolis, they gained control of Ennea Hodoi, which the Edonians were holding, but, after advancing into the interior of Thrace, they were destroyed at Drabeskos."[69]

We do not doubt Thucydides' statement that Athenian interest in the rich Thasian peraia provoked the revolt. In this year (465) the Athenians, with allies at least from the Hellespont, had been fighting in the Chersonese as part of the operations directed against Doriskos. The project at Ennea Hodoi was probably conceived as part of the over-all strategy to secure Thrace and would serve too as a bastion against Makedonia. The colony was to be a true Confederate venture, as Thucydides says,[70] and it would take time to assemble the colonists. So news of the plan would have reached Thasos before the colonists were ready to set out for Thrace. It was no doubt the anticipated colony which especially alarmed the Thasians and was the immediate cause of the revolt. To this development the Athenians' answer was twofold: naval and military action, and the despatching of the colonists, who were now ready, to Ennea Hodoi.[71]

---

[64] Thucydides, I, 98, 4: πρώτη τε αὕτη πόλις ξυμμαχὶς παρὰ τὸ καθεστηκὸς ἐδουλώθη.

[65] Ἔπειτα δὲ καὶ τῶν ἄλλων ὡς ἑκάστῃ ξυνέβη.

[66] I, 100, 2. The date was 465 B. C.; see above, pp. 175-176 with notes 57, 58.

[67] Χρόνῳ δὲ ὕστερον ξυνέβη Θασίους αὐτῶν ἀποστῆναι, διενεχθέντας περὶ τῶν ἐν τῇ ἀντιπέρας Θράκῃ ἐμπορίων καὶ τοῦ μετάλλου ἃ ἐνέμοντο.

[68] Plutarch, Cimon, 14, 1-2 (T95f).

[69] Ἐπὶ δὲ Στρυμόνα πέμψαντες μυρίους οἰκήτορας αὐτῶν καὶ τῶν ξυμμάχων ὑπὸ τοὺς αὐτοὺς χρόνους ὡς οἰκιοῦντες τὰς τότε καλουμένας Ἐννέα ὁδούς, νῦν δὲ Ἀμφίπολιν, τῶν μὲν Ἐννέα ὁδῶν αὐτοὶ ἐκράτησαν, ἃς εἶχον Ἠδωνοί, προελθόντες δὲ τῆς Θράκης ἐς μεσόγειαν διεφθάρησαν ἐν Δραβησκῷ --- (Thucydides, I, 100, 3). We date the disaster at Drabeskos in the early winter of 465/4; see above, pp. 108-110, 175-176 with notes 57, 58.

[70] Αὐτῶν καὶ τῶν ξυμμάχων. Cf. IV, 102, 2 and our discussion above, pp. 106-108.

[71] That the colony was at once sent to Thrace shows that it was not devised as a strategic reply to the revolt, for allied participation prevented rapid execution of the project. Rather, at the time of the Thasian outbreak, the colonists were still gathering in Peiraieus and could be hurried off.

The colonists were not far behind the fleet and made their landing at about the same time [72] as the Thasian defeat at sea.

The Confederate colony proceeded under Athenian convoy. The Athenians send out the colonists,[73] intending to settle (οἰκιοῦντες) them in Ennea Hodoi, of which they (αὐτοί, the Athenians) obtain control against the Edonians who have been in possession. Thucydides' text, if it be sound (and we see no cause to doubt this), reveals that the Athenians supplied the military protection and did the fighting. Though the colonists included allies as well as Athenians, it was the Athenian escort which drove out the Edonians, and it was the Athenian force, too, which proceeded ambitiously inland and came to grief at Drabeskos.[74] The effect upon the colony must have been disastrous; in any event, whatever the fate of the colonists, the undertaking was abandoned.[75]

The Thasians, under siege, eventually surrendered (τρίτῳ ἔτει, 463/2) and came to terms with the Athenians. Their punishment was harsh; they had to take down their walls, give up their ships, along with their peraia and its mine, pay an indemnity, and accept assessment in cash for the future.[76]

That Thasian possessions on the mainland (and on the island) were rich we know from Herodotos (VI, 46-47), whose evidence is corroborated by the quota lists. In Periods I and II the tribute of Thasos is 3 talents, with Period III it becomes 30 talents. This increase we interpret as evidence that Thasos regained at least part of her former territories, perhaps by the terms of the peace of 446/5 B. C.[77] We therefore conjecture that the original assessment of Thasos, which she discharged in ships, was 30 talents; the difference between Thasos with her peraia and Thasos deprived of its revenues is the difference between 30 talents and 3.

It may be that the confiscation of the Thasian ships constituted a precedent. Thucydides says that Naxos was " subjected " (ἐδουλώθη) and this is sometimes taken to mean the confiscation of her ships; we cannot say decisively. But the subjugation of Thasos is the first occasion on which we are specifically told that the Athenians took an ally's ships.

So far we have been concerned with the steady growth of Empire as described by Thucydides and accelerated by revolts among the allies. The process was also affected by the aggressive campaigns undertaken by the Athenians and their allies together, particularly during the Egyptian campaign of the 'fifties, when, according

---

[72] Ὑπὸ τοὺς αὐτοὺς χρόνους. The navy no doubt cleared passage for the colonists.

[73] See above, pp. 106-108, where we analyse this passage.

[74] The contrast (τῶν μὲν — — — ἐκράτησαν, — — — προελθόντες δέ — — —) is between the original success and the ultimate failure (Gomme, Commentary, I, p. 296), as our interpretation brings out.

[75] For the casualty list (I. G., I², 928) which has sometimes been connected with the defeat at Drabeskos see above, pp. 108-110. We believe that this association is correct.

[76] Thucydides, I, 101, 3 (T110): Θάσιοι δὲ τρίτῳ ἔτει πολιορκούμενοι ὡμολόγησαν Ἀθηναίοις τεῖχός τε καθελόντες καὶ ναῦς παραδόντες, χρήματά τε ὅσα ἔδει ἀποδοῦναι αὐτίκα ταξάμενοι καὶ τὸ λοιπὸν φέρειν, τήν τε ἤπειρον καὶ τὸ μέταλλον ἀφέντες.

[77] See below, pp. 301-302.

to Diodoros, the Empire reached its greatest extent. Diodoros gives the maximum under the archonship of Sosistratos (455/4), in which he sets Perikles' voyage through the Gulf of Korinth (it belongs in 454/3) and Tolmides' activity in Boiotia, which we place in the summer of 454.[78] The assessment of 454/3, then, the first which was beyond all question wholly Athenian, might be considered a sort of public proclamation of the extent of Empire.

After the battle of the Eurymedon the eastern outpost of the Confederacy was Phaselis. The new advance began with the revolt of Egypt from Persia (winter, 461/0); the invitation from Inaros to participate in the war against Persia in the spring of 460 found an Athenian and allied fleet already campaigning against Kypros.[79] The allies had enjoyed sufficient success, apparently, to leave Kypros safely behind them; their departure (ἀπολιπόντες τὴν Κύπρον) need not mean that they abandoned Kypros without garrisons, as Pausanias had probably done in 478.[80]

For six years the Athenians were involved in Egypt[81] and during this time the maintenance of secure lines of supply was of cardinal importance. East of Phaselis the map of the Athenian Empire shows Ityra, Perge, Sillyon, Aspendos, Kelenderis, and Doros in Phoinike. These cities, with the exception of Doros, make their sole appearance in the tribute records in A9. The only excuse for their appearance in the assessment list of 425 was that they had at some time been held by Athens, had been

[78] Diodoros, XI, 85: ἐπ' ἄρχοντος δ' Ἀθήνησι Σωσιστράτου Ῥωμαῖοι μὲν ὑπάτους κατέστησαν Πούπλιον Οὐαλέριον Ποπλικόλαν καὶ Γάιον Κλώδιον Ῥήγιλλον. ἐπὶ δὲ τούτων Τολμίδης μὲν περὶ τὴν Βοιωτίαν διέτριβεν, Ἀθηναῖοι δὲ Περικλέα τὸν Ξανθίππου, τῶν ἀγαθῶν ἀνδρῶν, στρατηγὸν κατέστησαν, καὶ δόντες αὐτῷ τριήρεις πεντήκοντα καὶ χιλίους ὁπλίτας ἐξέπεμψαν ἐπὶ τὴν Πελοπόννησον. οὗτος δὲ τῆς Πελοποννήσου πολλὴν ἐπόρθησεν, εἰς δὲ τὴν Ἀκαρνανίαν διαβὰς πλὴν Οἰνιαδῶν ἁπάσας τὰς πόλεις προσηγάγετο. οἱ μὲν οὖν Ἀθηναῖοι κατὰ τοῦτον τὸν ἐνιαυτὸν πλείστων πόλεων ἦρξαν, ἐπ' ἀνδρείᾳ δὲ καὶ στρατηγίᾳ μεγάλην δόξαν κατεκτήσαντο. The clause πλείστων πόλεων ἦρξαν (possibly taken from Krateros) must refer to the Athenian Empire, not to alliances or influence as far west as Sicily, as De Sanctis thinks; *Storia dei Greci*, II, pp. 123-124. For the chronology of this decade see above, pp. 165-175, 177-178.

[79] Thucydides, I, 104, 1-2: Ἰνάρως δὲ — — — Ἀθηναίους ἐπηγάγετο. οἱ δέ (ἔτυχον γὰρ ἐς Κύπρον στρατευόμενοι ναυσὶ διακοσίαις αὑτῶν τε καὶ τῶν ξυμμάχων) ἦλθον ἀπολιπόντες τὴν Κύπρον — — —. It would be natural to understand the words ἐς Κύπρον στρατευόμενοι as meaning that the campaign was in progress, as Crawley takes them, not that the allies were just beginning operations. But Thucydides uses (I, 112, 2) almost the same words of the resumption of activity against Kypros ten years later, after the Five Years' Truce: καὶ Ἑλληνικοῦ μὲν πολέμου ἔσχον οἱ Ἀθηναῖοι, ἐς δὲ Κύπρον ἐστρατεύοντο ναυσὶ διακοσίαις αὑτῶν τε καὶ τῶν ξυμμάχων Κίμωνος στρατηγοῦντος. Here the natural meaning seems to be that after the truce the allies made a campaign against Kypros (as Crawley renders it). We believe that the meaning in each passage is the same, that we are to see the allies in the midst of their campaigns, and that the second passage is "episodic" and can be expressed, very freely, as follows: "The Athenians broke off Hellenic war, and we next find them, with 200 ships of their own and their allies, under the command of Kimon, campaigning in Kyprian waters." This suits the tense of ἐστρατεύοντο.

[80] Actual fighting on Kypros in 460, the first year of the Egyptian campaign, is proved by *I. G.*, I², 929 (the Erechtheid casualty list), which we date to 460; see above, pp. 174-175.

[81] Thucydides, I, 110, 1: οὕτω μὲν τὰ τῶν Ἑλλήνων πράγματα ἐφθάρη ἐξ ἔτη πολεμήσαντα.

assessed, and perhaps (but not certainly) had paid tribute.[82] Since Phaselis became once more the eastern outpost of Empire by the Peace of Kallias, we should seek that time before 450/49. We find it most naturally in the years of the Egyptian campaign, when we should expect the way-stations to be in Athenian hands. The assumption is removed from the realm of pure conjecture by the record of Palestinian Doros, a town which is even more remote. Krateros has cited Doros and Phaselis from an assessment which can be no other than that of 454/3. Our reconstruction of the assessment of 454/3, therefore, includes Doros (which is attested), Aspendos, and Kelenderis; we believe that the remaining names cited from this area (plus Milyai and probably others) were produced for A9 by apotaxis.[83] There is no evidence in the quota lists that a single one of these cities responded to the assessment of 454; if they ever paid tribute, then, it was between 459 and 454. After that, the final defeat in Egypt (summer, 454) effectively removed them from Athenian reach. For four years Athens abandoned the eastern Mediterranean.

The main Athenian base during the Egyptian campaign was Kypros, whose fortunes fluctuated considerably between Pausanias' victories in 478 and the Peace of Kallias in 450/49. The Persians reconquered the island in the 'seventies and by the time of the battle of the Eurymedon (469) were using it as a naval base.[84] Now (460), less than ten years later, parts of it must have been in Athenian hands, and remained under Athenian domination until the general withdrawal after the defeat in Egypt. The absence of Kyprian cities from List 1 (454/3) is therefore not surprising. It is more significant that no city of Kypros appears in the long, although incomplete, Ionic-Karic panel of A9. Our belief is that Kypros never paid tribute to Athens, and perhaps indeed was never assessed, even though it was for a time under Athenian control. It was the keystone of security along the route from Athens to Egypt and we suspect that it was an Athenian base which was not incorporated in the Confederacy.

In 450 the Athenians were back again and part at least of the island was recovered.[85] This latest attempt, three years or more after the dismal season of 454, is reported by Thucydides (I, 112, 2-4).[86] Though Kimon died, the Athenian offensive had a measure of success,[87] but again we find no reflection of this in the quota lists and we conjecture that Kypros was not assessed in 450.[88] So the evidence of the

---

[82] It has been remarked many times that the assessment of 425 contained the names of cities from whom there was no reasonable anticipation of exacting payment.

[83] See the note on Ἰτύρα, p. 23 above.

[84] Diodoros, XI, 60, 5; Plutarch, *Cimon*, 12, 5.

[85] We do not know that Kypros was lost in 454 or that the Persians returned to the island; we believe, however, that this is what happened.

[86] See above, note 79.

[87] Diodoros, XII, 3, 3, says that the Athenians took Kition and Marion.

[88] We are convinced that no Kyprian city stood in List 5.

tribute records is uniform, although not conclusive, for a city could be assessed and fail to pay (e. g., Doros, as we think). With the Peace of Kallias Athens relinquished her claims to territories east of Phaselis and Kypros reverted to Persia.[89]

The absence of cities east of Phaselis from the quota lists of Period I may be taken to mark the probable spheres of influence of the Persian and Athenian fleets after 454 B. C. This was the year in which the treasury of the Confederacy was moved from Delos to Athens; it has become almost traditional to remark that the transfer was carried out, at the suggestion of the Samians, because of the fear that the money might fall into the hands of the Persians. The only authority for Samian sponsorship of the idea is Plutarch, who (drawing probably from Theophrastos)[90] says that when the proposal was made during debate Aristeides called it unjust but advantageous.[91] Since, by 454, Aristeides had long been dead, the passage is suspect. Nevertheless, it may be historical as a whole, in which case it must be referred to some earlier occasion, when the Samian proposal was not adopted. On the other hand, the story may be historical in part, in which case the comment of Aristeides must be eliminated. We are inclined to adopt the second, as the more economical alternative. There is nothing inherently improbable in the proposal coming from the Samians during the 'fifties, when their loyalty to Athens was firm.[92]

The motive of fear of the Persians has also been given considerable emphasis. Once again Plutarch supplies the ancient testimony, in his description of the attacks

[89] See also Gomme, *Commentary*, I, p. 331.

[90] The context of Plutarch, *Aristides*, 25, 3 (see below, note 91) points to Theophrastos, for Plutarch has just (25, 2) cited him as saying (φησι) that Aristeides was just, but recognized the expediency of injustice in national policy; the anecdote about the Samian proposal is a specific illustration of the general statement. In 25, 3 the text of Lindskog and Ziegler reads φασιν, although there is manuscript authority for φησιν, which is adopted by Perrin (Loeb), Dundas (see below, note 92), and, apparently, by Gomme (see below, note 92). We should expect φησιν, and it may well be right.

[91] *Aristides*, 25, 3 (T94): καὶ γὰρ τὰ χρήματά φασιν ἐκ Δήλου βουλευομένων Ἀθήναζε κομίσαι παρὰ τὰς συνθήκας [καὶ] Σαμίων εἰσηγουμένων εἰπεῖν ἐκεῖνον (sc. Aristeides), ὡς οὐ δίκαιον μὲν συμφέρον δὲ τοῦτ' ἐστί. If the passage is historical, the debate (βουλευομένων) perhaps suggests the synod of the Confederacy; if, further, the Samian recommendation belongs in 454, we may have here some ground for believing that the allies actually met on Delos as late as 454. The synods would then have been superseded by the Panathenaic meetings.

[92] Samians fought in Egypt (see above, note 37) and are surely included in the allies of 460 (Thucydides, I, 104, 2) and 450 (Thucydides, I, 112, 2); in the latter passage, indeed, they and the Lesbians and Chians may be the only allies (most of the remaining naval allies had perhaps commuted to cash in 450). Dundas, *Cl. Rev.*, XLVII (1933), p. 62, accepts Plutarch's story but dates it early (which is possible), regarding Samian friendship in 454 as improbable (which we think is a false view); Gomme, *Commentary*, I, note 2 on pp. 370-371, says that there is "no evidence" for Samian sponsorship of the transfer (this is an obvious exaggeration), "though it is not at all unlikely in itself" (with which we agree). With Aristeides' advice we may compare the similar tale in Plutarch, *Themistocles*, 20, 2. Most scholars are prepared to eliminate the anecdote about Themistokles in Aristotle, Ἀθ. Πολ., 25, 3-4; but it is a rash sort of criticism to condemn all information which carries such anachronisms.

on Perikles: " his detractors clamoured that the Demos had lost its reputation and was spoken of ill for having moved the common treasury of the Hellenes from Delos to Athens, and that Perikles had destroyed the most respectable motive it could present to its critics, namely, that it had transferred the moneys from the island in fear of the barbarians and was watching over them in a safe place." [93] So security was given to the allies as the reason for the transfer and Perikles had stultified that reason.

The question arises, was this fear justified? There is no evidence of withdrawal of Athenian forces west of Phaselis [94] and the disaster in Egypt was not a crushing blow to the Athenian navy or to its prestige, although the losses in men and material were serious enough. The Persian victory was essentially a victory in land fighting. Megabyxos made his way to Memphis and Prosopitis by land ($\kappa\alpha\tau\grave{\alpha}$ $\gamma\hat{\eta}\nu$), and his initial triumph at Memphis was by land. His final assault on the besieged island of Prosopitis was made on foot, after he had drained the water from a canal and left the Greek ships on dry land. When the Athenians had their ships and could not be reached by land they were invincible. Even the later calamity which befell the relieving squadron came from the Persian infantry, when the Athenians (who knew nothing of what had happened) put in to shore at the Mendesian promontory. True, Phoinikian ships helped in the defeat, but the battle was a land battle begun when the Athenian ships were beached. [95] The treasury at Delos was in the heart of the Aegean and invulnerable to Persian attack. So serious fear about the treasury ought not to have been the deciding motive for the transfer. [96]

But this is wisdom after the event and tells us nothing of Athenian and allied feelings at the time. It is true that the navy had not been defeated at sea, and the morale of the crews was probably as high as it had ever been; it is equally true that the Egyptian expedition had ended in a disaster that must have had repercussions in the Aegean. It is therefore quite likely that there were, among the Athenians and allies, those who took the pessimistic view and, in anticipation of Persian attack, sincerely advocated the removal of the treasury to Athens as a precautionary measure. This pessimism, or fear, was probably not justified; none the less, it could have existed.

At the same time there were Athenians who saw that the removal of the treasury

[93] *Pericles*, 12, 1 (T96): βοῶντες ὡς ὁ μὲν δῆμος ἀδοξεῖ καὶ κακῶς ἀκούει τὰ κοινὰ τῶν Ἑλλήνων χρήματα πρὸς αὑτὸν ἐκ Δήλου μεταγαγών, ἣ δ' ἔνεστιν αὐτῷ πρὸς τοὺς ἐγκαλοῦντας εὐπρεπεστάτη τῶν προφάσεων, δείσαντα τοὺς βαρβάρους ἐκεῖθεν ἀνελέσθαι καὶ φυλάττειν ἐν ὀχυρῷ τὰ κοινά, ταύτην ἀνῄρηκε Περικλῆς.

[94] Phaselis paid tribute in the spring of 453; List 1, IV, 24. She would scarcely have done so while the war lasted if she was beyond Athenian naval power. The Peace of Kallias, by which Phaselis remained in the Athenian Empire, laid down a neutral, or demilitarized, zone between Phaselis and Kyaneai; Wade-Gery, *Harv. Stud. Cl. Phil.*, Suppl. Vol. I (1940), pp. 134-143, especially 142-143.

[95] Thucydides, I, 109-110.

[96] We question Wallace's view that the Athenians were worried about the threat of Persian sea-power to Delos even before the Egyptian disaster; *T.A.P.A.*, LXVII (1936), pp. 252-260. De Sanctis held a somewhat similar opinion; *Atthis*[2], p. 486.

was to the advantage of an imperialistic Athens and who recognized in the current misgivings of others a fair-sounding pretext for the move. There is no doubt that in 454 Athens was powerful enough to do with the treasury of the Confederacy as she pleased. The fiction of the Confederacy had already worn very thin. In fact, at that very time Athens was busy suppressing disaffection in Miletos and Erythrai. So the transfer merely stresses the reality of Athenian sovereignty. To the cautious the Egyptian disaster was ominous and dictated safeguards; to the imperialists, it provided an excuse.[97] But Plutarch's " most respectable motive " (εὐπρεπεστάτη τῶν προφάσεων) was real enough and that the Samians made the actual proposal is entirely credible.

Between 477 and 450 Athenian domination of the Confederacy had steadily become more apparent, even though the Confederacy continued to be recognized. Athens did not publicly acknowledge her Empire (ἀρχή), which existed in fact. The Peace of Kallias brought matters to a head and compelled Athens to take the overt steps (e. g., D7, D13, D14) which completed the transformation of a Confederacy into an Empire. In this sense the change from Confederacy to Empire can be placed in the years between the Peace of Kallias (450/49), which brought the specific task of the Confederacy to an end, and the Thirty Years' Peace (446/5), in which Sparta recognized the Athenian Empire.

---

[97] It may be, indeed, a significant fact that the pan-Ionic centre of the Confederacy, even as the repository of the funds, was abandoned while Athens was putting down by force rebellions in two of the Ionic cities.

CHAPTER VII

THE COLLECTION OF 454/3 B.C.

By a computation similar to that which we have made for the assessment of 454 Gomme achieved a total of 493 talents, from about 200 cities.[1] He gives the number of places on the stone for the quota lists of Period I as 141, 163, 147, and 157. Our own count, from the texts of *A. T. L.*, II, gives 140, 162, 145,[2] and 157. The high years are obviously 2 and 4, but these are also the years when cities on the outskirts of the Confederacy, mostly in Karia, evidently paid under compulsion from the presence of the Athenian navy.

The problem of how to reconcile a panel of assessment of over 200 names with a list of about 140 of those who actually paid is troublesome, but not impossible of solution. It is a more serious matter to reconcile the high value of the assessment with low returns in terms of money, and this cannot be done, in our judgment, without granting that a considerable number of cities were still furnishing ships and not cash. Gomme has sought another way out of the difficulty. He suggests that some cities paid their tribute directly to generals in the field and that in these cases no quota was paid to Athena and so no record made in the quota lists.[3] But this cannot be, because it is precisely for those years in which the fleet was active that the greater, not the lesser, number of names appears in the lists. The generals in fact did report what they received and the record of quota was duly entered. When the lists become more explicit this obligation of the generals to report what they took can be documented with specific examples. In 448/7 Abdera paid only 14 talents of its assessed tribute to Athens (7, II, 27) and in the following year the generals reported the amount of 1 talent which had been brought from Abdera to them at Eion, their naval base; its quota was duly recorded (8, I, 105): ἐς ['E]ιόνα haβδερῖ:. The entries ἐς Τένεδον in 8, II, 108-109 mean that contributions had been made to an officer at Tenedos. Later, special rubrics were established for the quotas of cities that had paid their tribute to magistracies (ἀρχαῖς) or an armed force (στρατιᾶι) in the field.[4] The

---

[1] *Commentary*, I, p. 275. For our computations see above, pp. 19-28; we reckoned 208 names, and an assessment of 498 talents, 1390 drachmai.

[2] Or 146, if two names were entered in 3, II, 2-4.

[3] *Commentary*, I, pp. 275-278. Cary, *Cl. Rev.*, LX (1946), p. 29, notes Gomme's view with approval: "Gomme makes a capital point in suggesting that payments of tribute were sometimes made directly to Athenian strategi in the field, in which case they might not figure at all in the accounts of the Hellenotamiae. If this is correct, the bottom will have been knocked out of some recent calculations of the allies' tribute."

[4] See *A. T. L.*, I, pp. 449 and 453-454, under captions I, VIII, IX, and XI; cf. McGregor, *A. J. P.*, LXVII (1946), p. 271.

occasional presence in the quota lists of unassessed cities (πόλεις ἄτακτοι) shows that the generals officially deposited at Athens even unassessed money that they had collected, and that the quota from it was regularly recorded. The quota was given to the Goddess from all such exactions made in the field, whether the money came from an assessed ally or not.

So the discrepancy between the assessment list of 208 names and the quota list of 140 names in 454/3 still remains. But it would have been much less had all the payments of 454/3 come in promptly. The names of the first column of List 2, all payments which were due the previous year, must be subtracted from the total of 208 before a better idea can be won of the efficiency of collection in this period. We also subtract their tribute, not as paid, but as assessed, before trying to reach the total actually collected in the previous year. This involves a tentative restoration of the first nine names in column I of List 2 (now no longer preserved),[5] and will give us a total of seventeen cities to be subtracted, along with their assessed tributes, from the figures with which we started. The assessed evaluation of the seventeen is 6 talents, 290 drachmai; we are left with 191 names and 492 talents, 1100 drachmai.

Miletos and Erythrai are known to have been in revolt in 454/3, and payments were made for Miletos only by the loyal allies at Leros and Teichioussa, and for Erythrai through the syntely at Boutheia. Thus the assessments amounted, for all practical purposes, not to 10 and 9 talents, but to 5 and 3 talents respectively. The total cash assessment is thus reduced to 481 talents, 1100 drachmai, although the names for List 1 are increased to 192.

Fortunately 454/3 is one of the years when it is known within limits what the total collection in money was. The summary of receipts for the year, inscribed in the *Postscript* on the right lateral face of the First Stele, gives the total of silver as [. .]XXHHḤΔΔ[- - -] for the quota; the amount of gold, in staters, might be as little as 56 or as much as 96. The figure for silver is restored in *A. T. L.*, I, p. 129, as [ᚼX]XXHHḤΔΔ[- - -], giving a total silver quota of 33,320+ drachmai and representing a tribute of 333 talents. The Kyzikene staters,[6] tariffed at 24 drachmai a stater, amount to as little as 13½ or as much as 23½ talents (the figures are approximate); the grand total is *ca.* 346½ or 356½ talents. The sum is too low and the calculation on which it was made,[7] based in large measure on an analogy with List 7, must now be revised in the light of our study of the first assessment period and of

---

[5] We have argued the case above, pp. 7-9. The names come from the last column of List 4 and are: Σ/. - - -, ᾿Αλινδῆς, [.]σσυρι - -, Χαλκετορῆς, Κυδαιὲς, ἡυβλισῆς, Κιλλαρῆς, Θύδονος, Σίλοι; they are all Karic.

[6] In *A. T. L.*, I, we printed [ḥεχσέκοντ]ạ ḥὲχ[ς: ḥέκται τέτταρες], but in *A. T. L.*, II, we have refrained from restoration. Schwahn, in P. W., *R. E., s. v. φόροι*, pp. 636-637, argues for a tariff of 27 : 1, which is not satisfactory; he does not know Woodward's article, *J. H. S.*, XXXIV (1914), pp. 276-292.

[7] Meritt, *D. A. T.*, pp. 61-65.

List 1 in particular. One higher restoration is possible for the quota of silver: [ᛒT]XXHHḤΔΔ[– – –], which gives a tribute of 383 talents of silver and a total in gold and silver of 396-406 talents. The known total is sure within very narrow limits, and, if we use as an estimate 400 talents, we cannot be far wrong.[8]

This discrepancy between an assessment in cash of *ca.* 481 talents and an actual collection (even after a special effort to cull in reluctant outlying districts) of only 400 talents is a cause for grave concern. As Gomme rightly says,[9] " It is difficult to believe (in view of the much greater regularity in later years) that this was due simply to inefficiency of one sort or another, and that Athens expected to get a much larger tribute than she ever, at this time, succeeded in getting." Gomme is worried about the numbers of names as well as the amount of money. Relatively, the money is a serious matter, whereas the number of names counts for less. We have just removed from the original panel of 208 a list of seventeen names with a loss in tribute of only about 6 talents. In names alone, the discrepancy between the available space for 140 and the revised panel of 192 could be reduced markedly, whereas the loss in cash would be slight. Much depends on what the names were. Nevertheless, we cannot tolerate too great a discrepancy between the names assessed and the names from whom collection was made, for the good reason that defaulting by too many cities would have had a deleterious effect upon discipline. Inefficiency is shown if collection falls far below assessment; it is also shown if easily accessible cities fail to pay and are not coerced. We should expect the defaulters to be distant (*e. g.*, in Karia), or to be involved in secessionist movements (*e. g.*, Erythrai, Miletos, Latmos, Myous).[10] But Athens lost no time in bringing the disaffected to heel, and we take the Karic names mentioned above (note 5) to indicate the presence of a fleet in Karian waters in the summer of 453. This fleet was not despatched for the express purpose of collecting tribute from recalcitrants, it is true, for to send a squadron so far for so little might have been considered inefficient, even though the disciplinary effects were good. There were fewer names in List 3 than in List 2, but the tribute may not have been much less, and it was apparently not worth the effort to do anything immediate about the income from small and distant defaulters. But there must be an explanation for the great discrepancy between assessment and collection. Herein lies the proof that some relatively important cities were still furnishing ships when the assessment of 454 was drafted and the tribute of 454/3 was paid.

The following, in our judgment, may still have been furnishing ships in 454: Andros, Chalkis, Eretria, Hestiaia, Keos, Kythnos, Poteidaia, Seriphos, Siphnos,

---

[8] This is just what the restoration of staters in *A. T. L.*, I ([στατέρ]ες Κυ[ζικενοὶ: h̥εχσέκοντ]α h̥ὲχ[ς: h̥έκται τέτταρες]) would give.

[9] *Commentary*, I, p. 277.

[10] See above, pp. 252-256.

Styra, Tenos.[11] Akanthos, Iasos, Paros. The cash equivalent of the ships which these cities furnished has been reckoned as 67 talents, 2200 drachmai; so the expected cash for 454 now amounts to 413 talents, 4900 drachmai.[12] The number of names for the quota list is simultaneously reduced from 192 to 178.

The discrepancy in names is still great, but we may note that for the first period there is no direct evidence that any of the following cities were separately assessed: Arkesseia, Chedrolos, Euromos, Eurymachitai, Harpagion, Kalynda (Κλαυνδῆς), Karpathos, Mylasa, Othoros, Pargasa, Pedies, Pladasa, Serme, Sigeion, Skiathos, Tymnes (Κᾶρες ὧν Τύμνης ἄρχει).[13] The probabilities strongly favour including Mylasa, Sigeion, and Skiathos in the assessment, but for the other names the explanation of absence may be either (a) that they paid through neighbouring cities, or (b) that they came into the Empire only after 450. Our belief is that the thirteen available cities from this list of sixteen belong largely in category (a); for example, Pedies probably paid through Lindos. But some names from the Karic mainland may have belonged in group (b); for example, Tymnes may have given formal adherence to the Confederacy only after Kimon's last expedition. Perhaps Kasolaba, which was assessed in the first period, continued to pay under the name Tymnes or Kares (Κᾶρες ὧν Τύμνης ἄρχει) after 450.[14] These thirteen cities, removed from the assessment list, reduce the number of names in the panel to 165 and the cash assessment to 410 talents, 1600 drachmai.

In our judgment a discrepancy between the possible number of names (165) and the actual number (140) is not cause for undue anxiety. Even if we discount the likelihood that some states may have paid with neighbours as a temporary expedient, the total of 25 defaulters is not large.[15] The conditions of collection and of organization that we find in the fourth period were not present in the first, where the lists themselves testify to much greater irregularity. For the most part, absentees in 454/3

[11] These are West's charter members of the Confederacy; *Am. Hist. Rev.*, XXXV (1929-1930), pp. 267-275, and see above, p. 197 with note 18. Naxos, which had long since been reduced, is omitted; we may assume that by her subjugation (douleia) she had lost her option and become tributary (see above, pp. 156-157, 250 with note 25). Keos, Seriphos, and Andros pay in List 4, but there is no reason why commutation from ships to money should not have occurred during an assessment period. See also above, pp. 249-250.

[12] 481 talents, 1100 drachmai (p. 266) minus 67 talents, 2200 drachmai = 413 talents, 4900 drachmai.

[13] Naxos does not appear in Period I; if she had been tributary since her reduction she must have been assessed in 454, and her absence from the lists of Period I is ascribable to the accident of survival. Her status after the revolt is perhaps debatable.

[14] Κασωλαβῆς is in Periods I and II, Κᾶρες in Periods III and IV; cf. the Gazetteer, *s. vv.*, pp. 499 and 495, in *A. T. L.*, I. They may come from a single site; for the mention of both in A9 cf. the doublet Ὑρωμῆς, Κυρωμῆς (in the Register, *s. v.* Ὑρωμῆς).

[15] The number will be in fact 26 if Δαυνιοτειχῖται is to be restored in two lines, as we think it should be; the number of names in the quota list is in this way decreased to 139.

were probably small (except possibly in Lykia) and remote. Without claiming that the following table gives the actual defaulters, we have drawn it up to show, concretely, what our ideas of possible absentees are.

ABSENTEES FROM THE QUOTA LIST OF 454/3

1. Ἀζειοί	—	400	14. Μυλασῆς	1	—
2. Ἄσπενδος [16]		?	15. Παισηνοί	—	1000
3. Ἀστυρηνοὶ Μυσοί [17]	—	500	16. Παρπαριῶται [18]	—	1000
4. Δῶρος [16]		?	17. Πολιχναῖοι Κᾶρες	—	1000
5. Θασθαρῆς [18]	—	500	18. Πύρνιοι	—	1000
6. Καρηναῖοι		?	19. Σιγειῆς	—	1000
7. Καρυανδῆς	—	1000	20. Σκαψαῖοι	—	1000
8. Κελένδερις [16]	1	—	21. Σκιάθιοι	—	1000
9. Κοδαπῆς	—	1000	22. Τηλάνδριοι	1	—
10. Λάτμιοι [19]	1	—	23. Τυρόδιζα	—	1000
11. Τελεμήσσιοι	} 12	—	24. Ὑμισσῆς	—	1200
12. καὶ Λύκιοι			25. Φηγήτιοι	—	1600
13. Μυήσσιοι [19]	1	3000	26. One unknown [20]	1	—

The total assessment of these 26 absentees is 20 talents, 5200 drachmai. So the assessed tributaries of List 1 are now reduced to 139, whose estimated cash obligation is 389 talents, 2400 drachmai. In addition there were fourteen cities still furnishing ships (besides Lesbos, Chios, and Samos), to the value of 67 talents, 2200 drachmai.

In order to make quite clear what we conceive the list of the year 454/3 to have been, we give the names that may have belonged to it in alphabetical order, except that all other members of a syntely follow at once upon that member whose name comes first. The amounts of quota frequently indicate that the payments were partial or irregular. Where the known quota indicates such a payment, we add the assessed amount in parentheses after the name; where the quota is restored, it is for a regular payment.

[16] See above, p. 23.

[17] Astyra may have been a genuine absentee; or did she pay with Gargara?

[18] Thasthara and Parpariotai lie near Maiandros and Mydones, both of whom are in List 1. They may have paid with one or the other; if they were included originally with Maiandros they might have been held on separately by Athens in 451/0 (when they make their first appearance) after Maiandros had been temporarily lost. Maiandros was close to Magnesia, subject to Persian influence, and a very uncertain ally.

[19] Latmos and Myous may have been in revolt along with Miletos in 454/3 B.C.; see above, pp. 255-256.

[20] This is no. 208 in the list on p. 28 above.

The Quota List of 454/3

1.	haβ[δερî]ται (15 T.)	XHHℙΔΔΔΓΙΙ	12	5120
2.	['Αβυδενοί] (4 T.)	HHHHΔΔΔΓϜΙΙΙΙ	4	2260
3.	['Αθêναι Διάδες]	[ΔΔΔϜϜΙΙ]	—	2000
4.	[Αἰγάντιοι]	[ℙ]	—	3000
5.	[Α]ἰγινêται	XXX	30	——
6.	[Αἰνιᾶται]	[HHH]	3	——
7.	[Αἴνιοι]	XHH	12	——
8.	Αἰραîοι	HHH	3	——
9.	[Αἴσον]	[ΔΔΓ]	—	1500
10.	halικαρ νασσêς	HℙΔΓϜΙΙΙΙ	1	4000
11.	['Αλοπεκοννέσιοι]	[H]	1	——
12.	'Αργίλιοι	⟨H⟩ℙ	1	3000
13.	['Αρισβαîοι]	[HH]	2	——
14.	'Αρτακενο[ί]	[ΔΔΔϜϜΙΙ]	—	2000
15.	'Ολύνθ[ιοι]			
16.	Σκαβλαîο[ι] ⟩ (2 T. 5400 Dr.)	H[HℙΔΓ]ϜΙΙΙΙ	2	4000
17.	['Ασ]σερîται			
18.	'Αστακενοί	Hℙ	1	3000
19.	['Αστυπαλαιês]	[HH]	2	——
20.	Αὐλιᾶται Κâρες	ΓϜϜ[ϜΙΙ]	—	500
21.	['Αφυταîοι]	[HHH]	3	——
22.	[Βαργυλιês]	[ΔΓϜΙΙΙΙ]	—	1000
23.	[Βεργαîοι]	[ℙ]	—	3000
24.	Βερ[ύ]σιοι hυπὸ τêι Ἴδει	ΔΓϜΙΙΙΙ	—	1000
25.	Βουθειês (for Erythrai)	[HHH]	3	——
26.	[Βυζάντιοι]	[Xℙ]	15	——
27.	Γαλέφσιοι	Hℙ	1	3000
28.	[Γαργαρês]	[ℙΔΔΓ]	—	4500
29.	[Γεντίνιοι]	[ΓϜϜΙΙ]	—	500
30.	[Γρυνειês]	[ΔΓϜΙΙΙΙ]	—	1000
31.	[Γρυνχês]	[ΔΓϜΙΙΙΙ]	—	1000
32.	[Δαρδανês]	[Hℙ]	1	3000
33.	[Δ]ασκύλειον [ἐν] Προποντίδι	ΓϜϜΙΙ	—	500
34.	[Δαυνιοτει] [χîται]	[ΔΓϜΙΙΙΙ]	—	1000

35.	Διδυμοτει χῖται	ΔΓϜΙΙΙΙ	—	1000
36.	[Διês] (Ins.)	[ΔΓϜΙΙΙΙ]	—	1000
37.	[Σαναῖοι]			
38.	['Ολο]φύχσ[ιοι]	[ΗΗ]ΔΔΔϜϜϜΙ	2	2000
39.	[Διês] (Th.)			
40.	Δίκ[αια] πα[ρ᾽ ῎Αβδερα]	[Ⴥ]	—	3000
41.	Δ[ικ]αιοπο λῖτα[ι]	ḤΗΗΗ	4	——
42.	Διοσερῖται	ΔΓϜΙΙΙΙ	—	1000
43.	['Ελαιῖτ]αι	[ΔΓϜΙΙ]ΙΙ	—	1000
44.	['Εφέσιο]ι	ႶΗΗ[Ⴥ]	7	3000
45.	῎Εσσιοι	Η	1	——
46.	Θάσιοι	ΗΗΗ	3	——
47.	[Θερμαῖοι] ἐ[ν ᾽Ικάροι]	[Ⴥ]	—	3000
48.	Σ[κιοναῖοι καὶ]			
49.	Θ[ραμβαῖοι]	[ႶΗ]	6	——
50.	Θ[ύσσιοι]	[ႶΔΓϜΙΙΙΙ]	—	4000
51.	᾽Ιᾶται	Η	1	——
52.	['Ιελύσιοι]	[Χ]	10	——
53.	[῎Ικιοι]	[ΔΔΓ]	—	1500
54.	[Καλύδνιοι]	[ΗႶ]	1	3000
55.	[Καμερês]	ႶΗΗΗΗ	9	——
56.	Καρβασνανδês	[ΔΓϜΙΙΙΙ]	—	1000
57.	[Καρύστιοι]	[ႶΗΗႶ]	7	3000
58.	Κασολ[αβês]	[ΔΔΔΔϜΙΙΙΙ]	—	2500
59.	[Καύνιοι]	[Ⴥ]	—	3000
60.	Κεβρένιοι	ΗΗΗ	3	——
61.	Κεδριêται	[Ⴥ]	—	3000
62.	Κεράμιοι	[ΗႶ]	1	3000
63.	Κια[ν]οί	Δ[ΓϜΙΙΙΙ]	—	1000
64.	[Κινδυês]	[Η]	1	——
65.	Κλαζομέν[ιοι]	[ΗႶ]	1	3000
66.	[Κνίδιοι]	[ΗΗΗ]	3	——
67.	[Κολοφόν]ιοι	ΗΗΗ	3	——
68.	[Κρυês]	[ΔΔ]ΔϜϜΙ	—	2000
69.	[Κυζικενοί]	[ႶΗΗΗΗ]	9	——
70.	Κυλλάνδι[οι]	[ΗΗ]	2	——

71.	[Κυμαῖοι]	[ΧΗΗ]	12	——
72.	Κυρβισσός	ΔΔΔⱵⱵⱵΙΙ	—	2000
73.	[Κôιοι]	[Ͱ]	5	——
74.	Λαμπόνεια	ΔΓͰΙΙΙ[Ι]	—	1000
75.	[Λαμφσακενοί]	[ΧΗΗ]	12	——
76.	[Λεβέδιοι]	[ΗΗΗ]	3	——
77.	[Λέμνιοι]	[ͰΗΗΗΗ]	9	——
78.	[Λί]νδιοι	ͰΗΗΗΔΔΔΔΓ·	} 9	——
79.	Λινδίον Οἰᾶται	Ͱ·Γ		
80.	[Μαδνασ]ês	ΗΗ·	2	——
81.	Μαιάνδριοι	ͰΔΓͰΙΙΙΙ	—	4000
82.	[Μαρ]ονῖται	ΗͰ·	1	3000
83.	[Μενδαῖοι]	[ͰΗΗΗ]	8	——
84.	Μεκυπερ[να]ῖοι			
85.	Στόλιοι	(2 T. 2000 Dr.)	ΗΗΔ[Δ]ΔͰΙΙ	2	1880
86.	Π[ολ]ιχνῖται			
87.	Μιλέσιοι [ἐ]χς Λέρο		ΗΗΗ	3	——
88.	[Μι]λέσιοι [ἐκ Τ]ειχιόσσε[ς]	(for Miletos)	[ΗΗ]	2	——
89.	Μυδ[ο]νês	[ΔΔΓ]	—	1500
90.	[Μυκόνιοι]	[ΗͰ·]	1	3000
91.	[Μύνδιοι]	[ΓͰͰΙΙ]	—	500
92.	[Μυριναῖοι] (Ion.)	[Η]	1	——
93.	Μυσοί	ΔΔΔͰ[ͰͰΙΙ]	—	2000
94.	[Ναχσιâ]ται	Δ[ΓͰΙΙΙΙ]	—	1000
95.	[Νάχσιοι]	[ͰΗΗΗΗ]	9	——
96.	Ναρ[ι]σ[βαρês]	[ΔΓͰΙΙΙΙ]	—	1000
97.	Νεάνδρεια	ΔΔΔͰͰ[ΙΙ]	—	2000
98.	Νεάπολις [ἐ]ν [Θ]ράικει	ΔΓ[ͰΙΙΙΙ]	—	1000
99.	Νεοπολῖται	Ͱ·	—	3000
100.	[Νισύριοι]	[ΗͰ·]	1	3000
101.	Νοτ[ι]ês	ΔΔΔͰͰΙΙ	—	2000
102.	[Οἰ]ναῖοι ἐν Ἰκάροι	ΗΔΔΔͰͰΙΙ	1	2000
103.	[Παλαιπερκόσιοι]	[ΓͰͰΙΙ]	—	500
104.	Παριανοί	Η	1	——
105.	[Πασανδês]	[Ͱ·]	—	3000
106.	[Πελειâται]	[Ͱ·ΔΓͰΙΙΙΙ]	—	4000

107.	[Πεπαρέθιο]ι	ΗΗΗ	3	——
108.	[Περίνθιοι]	[Χ]	10	——
109.	[Περκόσιοι]	[ΔΓΗΙΙΙΙ]	—	1000
110.	[Πεδασῆς]	[ΗΗ]	2	——
111.	Πι[ταναῖοι]	[ΔΓΗΙΙΙΙ]	—	1000
112.	[Πριανῆς]	[Η]	1	——
113.	[Πριαπῆς]	[ΓΗΗΙΙ]	—	500
114.	[Προκοννέσιοι]	[ΗΗΗ]	3	——
115.	['Ρεναιῆς]	[ΔΓΗΙΙΙΙ]	—	1000
116.	[Σαμβακτ]ύς (1 Τ.)	ΗΓΗΙΙΙΙ	1	400
117.	[Σαμοθρᾶικες]	[ΓͰΗ]	6	——
118.	Σερμυλ[ιῆς] (6 Τ.)	ΓͰΗΗΓͰΔΔͰͰ	7	4320
119.	[Σελυμβριανοί]	[ΓͰΗ]	6	——
120.	Σίνγιοι (4 Τ.)	ΗΗ[...]ͰͰΙΙ	3	500 (?)
121.	[Σκάφσιοι]	[Η]	1	——
122.	Σπαρτόλιοι	ΗΗ	2	——
123.	[Σταγιρῖτ]αι	[Δ]Γ[Ͱ]ΙΙΙΙ	—	1000
124.	Στρεφσαῖοι	Η	1	——
125.	Πίκρες Συαν[γελεύς]	[ͰͰ]	—	3000
126.	[Σύριοι]	[ΔΔΓ]	—	1500
127.	[Τενέδιοι]	[ΗΗΗΗΓͰͰ]	4	3000
128.	Τερμερῆς	ΗΗͰͰ	2	3000
129.	[Τέιοι]	[ΓͰΗ]	6	——
130.	Το[ροναῖοι]	[ΧΗΗ]	12	——
131.	[Φαρβέ]λ[ι]ο[ι]	[ΔΓͰ]ΙΙΙΙ	—	1000
132.	Φασελῖται	ΓͰΗ	6	——
133.	[Φοκαιῆς]	[ΗΗΗ]	3	——
134.	[Χαλκεᾶται]	[ͰͰ]	—	3000
135.	[Χαλχεδόνιοι]	[ΓͰΗΗͰͰ]	7	3000
136.	[Χερρονέσιοι]	[ΗΗΗ]	3	——
137.	[Χερρονεσ]ῖται	ΧΓͰΗΗΗ	18	——
138.	Χῖοι Κ[ᾶ]ρ[ες]	[ΔΔΔͰͰͰΙΙ]	—	2000
139.	[..⁵...]ῆται (Ι, 28)	ͰͰΔ[ΓͰΙΙΙΙ]	—	4000

It may also be shown that such a list is not physically incompatible with the broken entries preserved on the epigraphical monument of 454/3. We can restore, for example, names from the above list where the broken entries appear on the stone and then fill out at random the completely blank lacunae with the rest of the available names:

I, 5: [B]ε[ργαῖοι: ⅋]   II, 16: Κα[λύδνιοι: ΗⅢ]
I, 17: [Χερρονέ]σ[ιοι: ΗΗΗ]   II, 17: Πε[ρίνθιοι: Χ]
I, 18: [Βυζάντι]ο[ι: ΧⅢ]   II, 18: [Π]ε[δασῆς: ΗΗ]
I, 19: [Τενέδιο]ι[: ΗΗΗΗⅢ]   II, 19: [Κ]α[ρύστιοι: ⅢΗΗⅢ]
I, 21: ['Αφυταῖ]οι: Η[ΗΗ]   III, 12: [Πελειᾶται: ⅢΔΓⱵ]ΙΙΙΙ
I, 24: [Γεντίνι]οι: ΓⱵ[ⱵⱵΙΙ]   III, 13: [Σαμοθρᾷκες:] ⅢΗ
I, 27: [Κνίδι]οι: Η[ΗΗ]   III, 14: [Μύνδιοι]: ΓⱵⱵΙΙ
II, 11: Π[ριανῆς: Η]   III, 15: [Προκοννέσιοι:] Η[ΗΗ]
II, 12: Κ[αύνιοι: ⅋]

The space available for 139 names in the year 454/3 thus permits a collection of 388 talents, 1480 drachmai. This comes so near the total that may be restored in the *Postscript* of the first list that we believe it must be substantially correct.[21] It is more difficult to deal with Lists 2, 3, and 4, for there is no control over the total for any of these years, as there is for List 1. Inasmuch as the first column of List 2 has already been largely usurped for purposes of calculating the delayed payments due, but not received, in List 1,[22] the second list itself will be relatively short, like List 3. The number of names rises again in List 4. In all these years approximately the same total sum of 400 talents can be restored, and probably should be. There may have been (apart from discipline) little profit in sending out ships to collect tribute in 453/2 and 452/1 from numerous small states that counted for very little. Had some city that really mattered failed to pay its assessment, except possibly in Lykia or beyond, the Athenians might well have succeeded in making the collection.

[21] There are doubtless adjustments that can and should be made, for some of our figures are approximations. We have made no attempt to restore any quotas in staters. Perhaps this should be done, *par excellence*, for Kyzikos; but it is probable that the individual quotas, no matter how the tribute was paid, were recorded in drachmai.

[22] See above, pp. 7-9, 266.

CHAPTER VIII

THE PEACE OF KALLIAS

The second assessment period began with an almost normal collection of tribute in 450/49,[1] but Kimon was dead and plans for concluding the war with Persia were already in the making. The actual treaty was negotiated by Kallias, son of Hipponikos, of Alopeke[2] in the spring of 449, and the resultant peace has come to bear his name. The date and terms of this peace have been made the subject of a special study by Wade-Gery,[3] which is the basis for our own discussion here.[4] We have one substantial change to make in the definition of the terms: we accept Cary's interpretation of Herodotos (VI, 42, 2 [T66d]) and Isokrates (IV, 120 [T80d]) and so avoid the need to believe that the Greek cities of Asia Minor paid tribute simultaneously both to Athens and to Persia.[5] The words of Herodotos are to this effect: "Artaphernes fixed each city's payment, and these payments still continue to be on their old scale, as they were assessed by Artaphernes, down to my time." We understand this passage to mean that the cities kept the same scale of assessment when they became members of the Delian Confederacy that they had earlier when subject to Persia, and it reveals the pattern (already in operation) which Aristeides adopted when he undertook to draw up the panel of the first assessment.[6] As for Isokrates, when he says that the Athenians by the Peace of Kallias were able to dictate some of the tributes which the king should receive, one may believe that the reference is to Greek cities taxable by Persia who were not members of the Confederacy, like the two Magnesias and the cities of Kypros, and that Athens was able through her power and influence to interfere in the affairs of the King sufficiently to restrict his powers of taxation over Greeks within his own realm. This is the contrast which Isokrates wished to emphasize with the shameful Peace of Antalkidas.

There is, however, something to add about the record of the peace. Wade-Gery

---

[1] See above, p. 58.

[2] The deme of Kallias has been known only since 1936; cf. Meritt, *Hesperia*, V (1936), p. 410.

[3] Wade-Gery, *Harv. Stud. Cl. Phil.*, Suppl. Vol. I (1940), pp. 121-156.

[4] See also Cary, *Cl. Quart.*, XXXIX (1945), pp. 87-91.

[5] The conflict over liability to tribute evidenced by Thucydides, VIII, 5, 5 comes late in the war (after 413?), and is testimony rather to the collapse of the peace than to the terms of the peace itself (cf. Cary, *op. cit.*, p. 89).

[6] The Greek of Herodotos is: φόρους ἔταξε ἑκάστοισι, οἳ κατὰ χώρην διατελέουσι ἔχοντες ἐκ τούτου τοῦ χρόνου αἰεὶ ἔτι καὶ ἐς ἐμὲ ὡς ἐτάχθησαν ἐξ Ἀρταφρένεος. The antecedent of οἵ is no doubt φόρους, not ἑκάστοισι, and ἔχοντες is therefore intransitive. Powell, *Lexicon, s. v.* ἔχω, B2c, cites this passage as an example of the intransitive use of ἔχω with a prepositional phrase; *s. v.* χώρη (*sub finem*), he collects examples of κατὰ χώρην in the sense of *in statu quo ante*, "valid" (*e. g.*, IV, 201, 2). This passage, and Plutarch, *Aristides*, 24, 1 (T94), are discussed above, pp. 234-235.

suggested as one of many possible hypotheses (*op. cit.*, p. 127) that the original treaty with Artaxerxes, inscribed in 449, was given a new headline inscribed *in rasura* in 423, the headline alone being in Ionic script, and that this Ionic heading may have been the excuse which led Theopompos to refer to the treaty as a treaty with Dareios and to describe it as a forgery. The examples cited to illustrate the renewal of treaties by erasure of the headline only and provision of a new date and heading were the treaties with Rhegion and Leontinoi (*I. G.*, I², 51, 52),[7] originally covenanted near the middle of the century and renewed in 433 B. C. We now maintain that these treaties with Rhegion and Leontinoi are more than an illustrative example. They have added value as being themselves treaties made by Kallias, like the peace with Persia, and, having been made for all time, they were renewed with no alteration in the terms and were not even reëngraved on a new stele; in each case the heading was erased and the new date substituted. The name of the orator remained the same.

It has always been thought difficult to explain who this Kallias was who sponsored the treaties with Rhegion and Leontinoi. Usually he has been identified with Kallias, the son of Kalliades, who moved the financial decrees (D1 and D2) of 434, and who lost his life in battle before Poteidaia in 432 (Kirchner, *P. A.*, no. 7827). But we now distinguish between Kallias the Treaty-Maker and Kallias the Financier. The Treaty-Maker was Kallias, son of Hipponikos, of Alopeke (Καλλίας Ἱππονίκου Ἀλωπεκῆθεν), husband of Kimon's sister Elpinike, author of the peace with Persia which bore his name, at about the same time author of the treaties with Rhegion and Leontinoi, proxenos of the Lakedaimonians, and in 446/5 ambassador to Sparta to conclude the terms of the Thirty Years' Peace (Kirchner, *P. A.*, no. 7825; cf. note 2 above).

It is not known who was the author of the renewal of the treaties with Rhegion and Leontinoi. His only motion before the Council was that the old heading of date be expunged and in its place be written the names of the new ambassadors and the new date. The important observation is that the words which follow the orator's name, after " Kallias moved " (Καλλίας εἶπε), are the words of the original sponsor, not the renewer, and hence that Kallias is the man who made the original motion. He is thus dated *ca.* 448[8] and his identification with Kallias the Treaty-Maker rendered virtually certain.[9] It has already been suggested that the reason for leaving

---

[7] See the texts and discussion of date by Meritt, *Cl. Quart.*, XL (1946), pp. 85-91.

[8] Cf. Meritt, *Cl. Quart.*, XL (1946), pp. 88-90.

[9] The technical considerations about the erasures in *I. G.*, I², 51 and 52 are as follows: all lines involving change were erased. Thus, Kallias' name in *I. G.*, I², 52, line 15, was erased and reinscribed because the last letter in the name of the epistates began the line. This letter was not sigma and hence could not be kept as part of the name Τιμόχσενος. Moreover, the need for crowding 15 lines where only 14 existed before (cf. Meritt, *Cl. Quart.*, XL [1946], p. 85) may have influenced the stonecutter who hoped to gain a better distribution by erasing the last line and not trying to patch its broken beginning, which would have had to be erased in any case and left uninscribed.

the texts of the treaties with Rhegion and Leontinoi undisturbed, and merely changing the preambles when they were reaffirmed, was that both treaties were made in perpetuity (ἐς ἀίδιον, ἀίδιοι); [10] they both stood on their monuments of stone, unchanged, to be cherished and observed for ever.

The same was true of the peace with Persia. The fact that Kallias' terms of 449 were reaffirmed in 423 does not affect their perpetual validity. Rather, the reference which Andokides (III, 29) makes to the terms of the peace of 423 (when his uncle, Epilykos, was ambassador) shows that here too Kallias had made a covenant in perpetuity.[11] It was Kallias' peace in 449 with Artaxerxes; it remained Kallias' peace in 423 when it was renewed with Dareios Ochos. Theopompos thought it a forgery because he did not trouble to read beyond the Ionic letters of the reinscribed heading, but this, at least, he copied faithfully. The Ionic letters belonged to the time of Dareios, not Artaxerxes.

We therefore submit that the reinscribing of the heading is sufficiently well established to be accepted as fact. It explains not only the curious and obscure assertions of Theopompos, but also (since the terms of 423 were merely a renewal of those of 449) the otherwise remarkable silence of Thucydides about the mission of Epilykos.[12] The peace of Kallias was ratified in the early spring of 449 B. C.; it was a covenant in perpetuity between Athens and her allies on the one hand and the King of Persia on the other; and its terms were inscribed on stone at Athens from the beginning.

The news of the peace brought with it the end of the payment of phoros by the Athenian allies.[13] A year intervened between the final collection "against the barbarian" (Thucydides, I, 96, 1 [T109])[14] and the renewed payments which Athens attempted to justify even in time of peace. While Kimon lived, even during his ostracism, the war against Persia was waged vigorously. Perikles' rise to power in

In I. G., I², 51, line 9, the last two letters of the name Καλλίας remained on the stone, even after the erasure, to begin the line.

[10] Meritt, Cl. Quart., XL (1946), p. 90.

[11] Σπονδὰς ποιησάμενοι καὶ συνθέμενοι φιλίαν εἰς τὸν ἅπαντα χρόνον. The phrase εἰς τὸν ἅπαντα χρόνον belongs to the orator Andokides; Kallias probably wrote ἀίδιοι or ἐς ἀίδιον in his own chancery style. It should be well noted, and the treaties with Leontinoi and Rhegion prove it, that the Greeks saw no inconsistency in renewing a treaty that had been made originally " for all time." Hence we discount the weight of Gomme's argument from Andokides that the treaty of 423 cannot have been a renewal of that of 449. We believe that it could in normal practice have been, and actually was, such a renewal (cf. Gomme, A. J. P., LXV [1944], p. 333, note 36).

[12] See, for example, Wade-Gery, Harv. Stud. Cl. Phil., Suppl. Vol. I (1940), pp. 127-132; Gomme, A. J. P., LXV (1944), p. 331.

[13] It did not end the alliance between the cities and Athens, which was in perpetuity (Aristotle, Ἀθ. Πολ., 23, 5 [T39]); cf. Wade-Gery, Harv. Stud. Cl. Phil., Suppl. Vol. I (1940), p. 150; see also above, pp. 230-231.

[14] See Wade-Gery, Harv. Stud. Cl. Phil., Suppl. Vol. I (1940), pp. 150-151; Hesperia, XIV (1945), pp. 212-229.

the late 'sixties led to Kimon's eclipse and ostracism, and the war against Peloponnese during the 'fifties (on which no doubt some of the money paid " against the barbarian " was spent) was full of dangerous precedent. But so long as Kimon lived, the original justification of the tribute was not publicly questioned. We do not hear that the status of the allies was a matter of controversy between the two men; and when Kimon went to Kypros in 450, he could reasonably look forward to many years of activity against Persia. When he fell ill and died, Perikles broke abruptly with his traditions; the war was suddenly ended, the allies found they had lost a friend and got a master. For a short time Perikles (whether sincerely or not is hard to say) sought a settlement by consent; the Congress Decree (D12) and the hesitation in claiming tribute in time of peace are the symptoms. When Sparta refused to trust him, he changed his tone; the symptoms are the Papyrus Decree (D13), the Decree of Klearchos (D14), and the Decree of Kleinias (D7). The cause of the allies devolved on Kimon's political heir, his brother-in-law Thoukydides. He had nothing like Kimon's prestige, and against him Perikles forced, successfully, the issue which he had not ventured to force whilst Kimon lived.[15]

In *A. T. L.*, I, we stated our belief that no tribute was collected in 449/8.[16] Meritt has since expressed doubt that the absence of a quota list in that year necessarily implied failure to collect tribute,[17] and this scepticism was reaffirmed by Hill and Meritt in 1944.[18] But there is no good way to justify the absence of record if, in fact, any tribute was received, and we are now once more in agreement that since there is no quota list there must have been no collection. We go further, and argue that if there was no collection it must have been because Athens willed it so. To put the case in extreme terms, we may claim that some few states might have paid almost by accident, and surely even a modest show of compulsion would have produced some return. The logical conclusion must be that Athens expected no tribute and that the allies generally knew that this was the fact. No doubt there had been a spontaneous reaction to the news of the peace, in which the allies expressed their conviction that tribute was no longer needed. This attitude of the allies was natural and intelligible.

[15] We repeat, more or less verbatim, the words of Wade-Gery, *Hesperia*, XIV (1945), pp. 228-229.

[16] Pp. 133 and 175, with references to Wade-Gery, *B. S. A.*, XXXIII (published in 1935), p. 112 and Meritt, *D. A. T.*, pp. 65 and 69. The statement has been challenged: cf. Dow, *A. J. A.*, XLV (1941), p. 642; Gomme, *Cl. Rev.*, LIV (1940), pp. 65-67. We do not need to reopen the debate which favoured (abortively) a date 447/6 for the year of the missing, or sensationally short, quota list: cf. Dow, *Cl. Phil.*, XXXVII (1942), p. 384; XXXVIII (1943), pp. 20-27; Meritt, *Cl. Phil.*, XXXVIII (1943), pp. 223-239; Accame, *Riv. di Fil.*, LXVI (1938), pp. 411-415; LXIX (1941), pp. 154-155; Gomme, *Cl. Rev.*, LIV (1940), p. 66, note 1 (in the second column); Wade-Gery, *Hesperia*, XIV (1945), pp. 212-215.

[17] *The Greek Political Experience*, p. 53. See also Gomme, *Cl. Rev.*, LIV (1940), p. 67.

[18] Hill and Meritt, *Hesperia*, XIII (1944), p. 9.

The evidence is that Athens consented and that in the brief hiatus between Confederacy and Empire no collection of tribute was made.

This was the critical time of the call to the Panhellenic Congress. The problem before the Greek cities of the Confederacy was not only one of readjusting their lives to freedom from the obligations of furnishing ships and money against the Persian; it was also one of how to dispose of the grand total of 5000 talents which belonged to the Confederacy and which now could not be spent on the purpose for which it had been collected. So Perikles proposed, in effect, that the Greek cities, whether in Europe or in Asia, small and large alike, should send deputies to a council at Athens. Plutarch, who tells of the decree (D12), does not say (*Pericles*, 17) that the invitation was limited to those who had fought the barbarian, though they were naturally the most concerned. The council was to discuss:

(a) the Greek sanctuaries which the barbarians burned (περὶ τῶν Ἑλληνικῶν ἱερῶν, ἃ κατέπρησαν οἱ βάρβαροι),

(b) the sacrifices which they owed for the vows made to the gods on Greece's behalf when they were fighting against the barbarians (καὶ τῶν θυσιῶν, ἃς ὀφείλουσιν ὑπὲρ τῆς Ἑλλάδος εὐξάμενοι τοῖς θεοῖς ὅτε πρὸς τοὺς βαρβάρους ἐμάχοντο),

(c) and the sea, how all men might sail it in safety and keep the peace (καὶ τῆς θαλάττης, ὅπως πλέωσι πάντες ἀδεῶς καὶ τὴν εἰρήνην ἄγωσιν).[19]

The participants were primarily (b) those who had fought against the Persians, but the call was sent to the membership of the old Hellenic League [20] and to the new allies of Athens in central Greece [21] as well as to the Delian Confederacy. With 5000 talents to spend, the discussion was to turn on three main issues: the rebuilding of the shrines burned by the Persians, the sacrifices which they had pledged to the gods, and the patrolling of the sea. Perikles was here hoping to gain by consent what he later had to take by force.[22] We suggest that the heralds who carried the call to the

[19] Wade-Gery sees in the words καὶ τὴν εἰρήνην ἄγωσιν a quotation from the decree and hence a contemporary reference to the peace (cf. *Harv. Stud. Cl. Phil.*, Suppl. Vol. I [1940], p. 150, note 2).

[20] The heralds reached every city named on the Serpent Column, except possibly Leukas. We think it most probable that Leukas was also invited, in spite of the language of Plutarch (*Pericles*, 17): ἐκ δὲ ταύτης (i. e., Peloponnesos) διὰ Λοκρῶν ἐπὶ τὴν πρόσοικον ἤπειρον ἕως Ἀκαρνανίας καὶ Ἀμβρακίας ἀπεστάλησαν.

[21] Heralds were sent to Boiotia, Phokis, Oitaia, the Maliac Gulf, Achaia Phthiotis, and Thessaly. Many of these places had medized during the Persian Wars (Herodotos, VII, 132), but they were all allies of Athens in 449. For the Boiotians and Phokians see Thucydides, I, 108, 3 and 111, 1 (the Opountian Lokrians also were conquered by Athens in 458 B. C.); the Thessalians had been allies since 461 (Thucydides, I, 102, 4); and soon after the battle of Oinophyta the Athenians had contracted an alliance with all members of the Delphic Amphiktyony, which included the states around the Maliac Gulf (cf. *I. G.*, I², 26 as restored in *S. E. G.*, X, 18; Meritt, *A. J. P.*, LXIX [1948], pp. 312-314). Athenian interference in the civil war at Pharsalos in 454 B. C. (Thucydides, I, 111, 1) may have caused a temporary break in relations with Thessaly.

[22] Wade-Gery, *Hesperia*, XIV (1945), p. 229.

Congress carried also the financial report of ample money in the reserves to pay the expenses of the first two items on the agenda and, temporarily at least, the third. It was a delicate bit of diplomacy, for even a sum so large as 5000 talents could not pay for rebuilding all the ruined temples, and the patrolling of the sea would be a continuous drain which in time would require a replenishing of the revenues. But these were items for the agenda, and Perikles could make the invitation more immediately attractive by announcing also to the allies a moratorium in the collection of tribute. It is our belief that this is what he did, and that he did it at this time.[23] It is our belief, further, that the moratorium as announced was indefinite and that the continued payment of phoros to support the fleet was a proposition which Perikles expected to lay before the council. We do not know when, or on what scale, he thought the payment of tribute might be resumed. The invitation to all the former enemies of Persia and to the allied members of the Delphic Amphiktyony implies that Perikles had in mind a broader taxable base than the membership of the Delian Confederacy, and doubtless Sparta's realization of what this manoeuvre implied was one of her reasons for outright and summary rejection of the whole plan. Under the circumstances this was perhaps the best that the Spartans could do, for the invitation to the Congress had put them in an embarrassing situation. If they attended the meeting, they would be asked to vote " yes " or " no " on the issue of Athenian leadership in matters of religion, and quite probably asked to authorize contributions even from the Peloponnese for the support of the Athenian fleet. It may have been Perikles' wish to force this issue and so put upon the Spartans the odium of refusing to coöperate " for the welfare of Greece " and of failing to meet their obligations to the gods. But the political effect of the plan must have been considerable even though the Congress was never held. It emphasized to all the world the claim of Athens to play the dominant rôle in the religious leadership of Greece,[24] and its failure gave Athens the excuse for considering the reconstruction of her own temples, at least, out of funds collected against the barbarian, as part of an imperial plan which had fallen short of a more nearly perfect consummation through no fault of hers.[25] The attack by the Spartans on Delphi in 449 seems to have been occasioned by their anxiety about the way that Athens was using the Amphiktyony for her own political purposes and by their desire to counter this menacing development. The outbreak of the Sacred War, we believe, was one of the immediate consequences of the Congress Decree.

[23] At the same time insisting on the payment of all arrears, to bring the record properly to a close. Second payments in List 5 (see above, pp. 30-36) are to be explained by this insistence.

[24] As it was later emphasized in the Eleusinian decree, I. G., I², 76 (Tod, Greek Hist. Inscr., I², no. 74). Cf. Ehrenberg, A. J. P., LXIX (1948), p. 163: " the proposal of a Panhellenic congress – – – had implied political imperialism upheld by religious leadership." The political effect of the call to the Congress has been well stressed by Nesselhauf, Klio, Beiheft XXX, pp. 31-33.

[25] See Busolt, Gr. Gesch., III, 1, pp. 444-449; Bernadotte Perrin, Plutarch's Cimon and Pericles (New York, 1910), pp. 237-238.

The peace must be dated soon after the Dionysiac festival of 449, for the tribute of 450/49 was paid in the normal way, and no proclamation of a moratorium could have gone out before that time. But that talk of peace was in the air is reflected by the many partial payments of List 5. Then the invitation to the Panhellenic Congress followed almost immediately after the Peace. This too belongs early in the spring or summer of 449, for Perikles could not have proposed the Papyrus Decree (D13) until Sparta's refusal to come to the Congress had frustrated that plan and shown that there could be no common consent to the continued support of the Athenian navy with allied (and other) money.

The Papyrus Decree was passed toward midsummer, but still in the archon-year 450/49. By the terms of it Perikles appropriated 5000 talents from the funds of the Confederacy to the Treasury of Athena. Athens, at any rate, would rebuild her own temples.[26] The precise sum of 5000 talents was undoubtedly named in the decree which Perikles moved, just as the precise sum of 3000 talents was later named in one of the decrees of Kallias (D1) as a gift to Athena. Yet it would have been extraordinary had this grant in 449 represented exactly the accumulation which had come to the chest of the hellenotamiai since the beginning of the Confederacy. Perikles no doubt planned to pay the current expenses of the fleet in 449/8 out of reserve, and he must have budgeted this item when he announced the moratorium on tribute payments for that year. There must have been more, but not much more, in the reserve besides, for Perikles was by now evidently depending upon an early renewal of tribute payments.[27] We believe that the reserve was completely exhausted by the current expenses of the Empire and by a payment of 200 talents to Athena in 448. The grant of 5000 talents in 449 was probably transferred at the time of the Panathenaia, just as we believe the first of the later annual payments of 200 talents to have been made at the Panathenaia of 448.[28]

The Monetary Decree (D14, the Decree of Klearchos) and the Kleinias Decree (D7) completed the subjugation of the allies again to the will of Athens.[29] List 7 shows that tribute was collected in 448/7, and List 8 of 447/6 reflects for the first time the strict application of the procedure for tribute collection laid down in D7.[30]

[26] Wade-Gery, *Harv. Stud. Cl. Phil.*, Suppl. Vol. I (1940), pp. 150-151.

[27] Most probably the decision to end the moratorium and renew the payments of tribute in 448/7 was part of the Papyrus Decree.

[28] See below, pp. 327-328.

[29] E. S. G. Robinson's essay, " The Athenian Currency Decree and the Coinages of the Allies," *Hesperia*, Supplement VIII (1949), pp. 324-340, shows that the ban on coinage was immediately and generally effective, but that the provisions of D14 were difficult to enforce and that the attempt was at last tacitly abandoned. For the history of the Empire it is important that the study of the mints shows " a sudden and practically universal stoppage during the forties." We assign D14 to the year of the moratorium, which would have been an ideal time for changing the currency. It is perhaps an indication of the correctness of this early date that we find the 3000 talents of D1 described as Athenian currency (νομίσματος ἡμεδαποῦ).

[30] Reimposition of tribute was enacted by vote of the Demos (Wade-Gery, *Hesperia*, XIV

To this same year (447/6) belongs the decree concerning the Kolophonians (D15),[31] whose recalcitrance about belonging to the Empire and paying tribute had evidently claimed the particular attention of the Athenians. Their name is absent from the quota lists from 450/49 to 447/6 inclusive, and we assume that they did not pay tribute in these years. At any rate List 7 can be restored almost completely with small opportunity for Kolophon to appear in any of the remaining lacunae. List 8 repeats List 7, with an appendix of late bookings and arrears, and Kolophon is again absent. And in List 5 we explain the absence by assuming that no payment was made before the Dionysia and that Kolophon did not respond to the call for payment of arrears when Athens declared the moratorium shortly thereafter. Kolophon was not on the coast, and so was less amenable to Athenian discipline than the cities that were, and in 431/0 it deserted the Confederacy and went over to Persia. Thucydides (III, 34, 1 [T127]) reports the civil dissension, and the betrayal to Itamanes. In 447/6 the Athenians dealt with Kolophon by establishing colonists there. The oikistai named in lines 40-41 of D15 were undoubtedly the Athenian colonizers, like the Athenians who " colonized " Notion in 428/7.[32] Whether they colonized Kolophon with settlers from elsewhere in Asia Minor on whose loyalty they could depend, as Notion was later colonized with loyal Kolophonians, is not stated in the text of the inscription. But " colonists " are named (line 22: [οἰκέτ]ορες), and it may well be that some of them were Athenian. Apparently this colony occupied a certain amount of Kolophonian territory, for the new tribute assessed in 446 was only 1½ instead of the earlier 3 talents. This reduction was the natural consequence of using the land for the benefit of the colony, and as a phenomenon can be attested by reductions in amount of tribute affecting other allies who are known to have had colonies or klerouchies settled upon them. The reduction of the assessment of Argilos which followed the settlement of the Athenian colony at Amphipolis in 437/6 is a notable example.

But the colony to Kolophon affected not only Kolophon. It affected also its neighbours Lebedos and Dios Hieron. The quota lists give the necessary evidence: the tribute of Lebedos was reduced in 446 from 3 talents to 1; and the tribute of Dios Hieron, which had been 1000 drachmai in 447/6, was remitted entirely in the third assessment period and reimposed as only 500 drachmai in 443. The Athenian colony undoubtedly encroached very considerably on the territory of Lebedos, and on that of Dios Hieron, as well as on that of Kolophon, though Kolophon apparently was the

[1945], p. 226) after the failure of the Congress (cf. note 27 above). The collection of 448/7 seems low (Meritt, D. A. T., p. 85), but this is almost certainly to be explained by the fact that there were no reserves in this year: the generals in the field had to make advance collections, which were reported to the hellenotamiai only in the subsequent year. See the discussion of Period II above, pp. 29-63, especially 59-61.

[31] See the text in A. T. L., II, pp. 68-69.

[32] Thucydides, III, 34, 4 (T127): καὶ ὕστερον Ἀθηναῖοι οἰκιστὰς πέμψαντες κατὰ τοὺς ἑαυτῶν νόμους κατῴκισαν τὸ Νότιον, ξυναγαγόντες πάντας ἐκ τῶν πόλεων, εἴ πού τις ἦν Κολοφωνίων.

only one of the three cities that had been in revolt. The record of the Kolophonian
oath in accepting the Athenian terms has been preserved in lines 42-55; in lines 25-26
are the stipulations about adjustments to be made in Kolophon and Dios Hieron, as
we believe, on the occasion of the founding of the colony. Inasmuch as Lebedos also
was affected, that name too should be included in the text, the critical lines being 25
and 26 (perhaps also line 13).[33] The division of lines at this point in the inscription
is uncertain because the stone is broken on all sides, but the probable length of line
(non-stoichedon) comes to about forty letters. This is the same as the width of stone
established by one of the later significant lines (46), where Kolbe (*Hermes*, LXXIII
[1938], pp. 256-259) has undoubtedly given the correct restoration:

[λ]όγοι οὔτ᾽ ἔργ[οι οὔτ᾽ αὐτὸς ἐγὸ οὔτ᾽ ἄλλοι πείσομαι].

Kolbe's latest date is 448/7 or 447/6; in *Phil. Woch.*, XLVI (1926), p. 1157, he had
suggested a date *ca.* 450.

It was Hondius' opinion, rejected by Klaffenbach, that the two larger fragments
of this text were, in fact, parts of one inscription.[34] The only objection has been the
difference in lettering between the two pieces. But, as Hondius noted, the character
of the lettering changes within a fragment; so he again assigns both fragments to
one number in *S. E. G.*, III, 3. The probability of their belonging together is enhanced
by the fact that the length of line seems to be the same, and by the propriety of
assuming (in the light of the tribute lists) that the decree about Kolophon [and
Lebedos] and Dios Hieron was directly connected with the colony mentioned in the
Kolophonian oath. Another piece (E. M. 2376), identified by Wade-Gery some years
ago, belongs to the top of the same stele, and has been included in our publication
of the text.

For the establishment of an Athenian colony at (or near) Kolophon this inscription gives ample evidence, and the effects of the settlement have made themselves
evident in the changed tribute not only of Kolophon, but of Lebedos and Dios Hieron
as well. It is at least a possible explanation, though by no means the only one, of the
reduced tributes of some other cities to assume that colonies under Athenian auspices
were settled near them, for an Athenian policy of control through colonization is now
attested.[35] The assumption has been made even of a colony, an apoikia in the technical
sense of the term, to Eretria, based on the evidence of a dedication which has been

[33] [τὸ] δὲ ἀργύριον ὀφε[λόντον Κολοφόνιοι καὶ Λεβέδιο]ι καὶ Διοσιρῖται κ[— — — — — — — — — —].

[34] Hondius, *N. I. A.*, pp. 7-21, with photographs in Plates II and III; Klaffenbach, *Gnomon*,
II (1926), pp. 708-709, in a review of Hondius' book. Cf. *S. E. G.*, III, 3. Schaefer, *Hermes*,
LXXI (1936), pp. 129-150, uses these inscriptions in his discussions of the history of the
Confederacy.

[35] Loeschcke, *de tit. aliquot att.*, p. 22, note 1, used the evidence of the quota lists and of D15
to prove a colony at Kolophon. Busolt, *Gr. Gesch.*, III, 1, p. 418 with note, mistakenly interpreted
Loeschcke's colony as a klerouchy, which it certainly was not, and then denied its existence because
he thought it would have been a violation of the terms of the Peace of Kallias. See below, note 40.

restored in *I. G.*, I², 396 to read as follows: τῆς ἀποι[κίας] τῆς ἐς Ἐρ[έτριαν]. It is usually stated that the date is after the suppression of the Euboian revolt in 446, but the only colony in Euboia for which there is any evidence is that to Hestiaia.[36] No mention of a colony appears in either the Chalkidic or Eretrian oath sworn after the terms of the capitulation, and indeed we hold that the Athenians resident in Chalkis after 446 were called aliens (ξένοι), at least by the Chalkidians.[37] So the restoration ἐς Ἐρ[έτριαν] is to be rejected.[38] On the other hand, the lowered quotas of Erythrai and of its neighbour Hairai justify the assumption that there was a colony in the southern part of the Erythraian peninsula and recommend the restoration ἐς Ἐρ[υ-θράς].[39] This colony was contemporaneous with that to Kolophon, and must have been part of the Athenian plan for keeping in order the coast of Asia Minor.[40] We already know that the plan was operative elsewhere as well as in Ionia.

Colonies and klerouchies, in their relation to the control which Athens exercised over the Empire, have been often discussed, most recently, and from our point of view most profitably, by Nesselhauf,[41] Ehrenberg,[42] and Gomme.[43] One result of these investigations has been to show that the settlements named by Plutarch, *Pericles*, 11 (T96), should all be dated in the period between the death of Kimon and the

---

[36] Thucydides, I, 114, 3; had there been an Athenian colony at Eretria, surely it would have appeared in Thucydides, VII, 57, 2 (T143), where the inference is that Hestiaia was the only colony in Euboia.

[37] Cf. D16 and D17 in *A. T. L.*, II, especially D17, line 53.

[38] Nesselhauf, *Klio*, Beiheft XXX, p. 136, rejects the restoration ἐς Ἐρ[έτριαν] because he thinks that the establishment of an ἀποικία implies the dissolution of the city (as such) to which the new colony is sent; hence, since Eretria continued on, there could have been no ἀποικία there. But Kolophon after 447/6 continued on, and the οἰκισταί and οἰκήτορες are proof enough that the Athenians established a colony. Fischer's suggestion (*de Atheniensium sociis*, p. 29) ἐς Ἐρ[εσον], associating the dedication with Lesbos in 427, is vitiated by the fact that the Athenians sent klerouchs, not a colony, to Lesbos.

[39] Loeschcke, *de tit. aliquot att.*, p. 22, note 1, had suggested a colony to Erythrai, which Busolt, *Gr. Gesch.*, III, 1, p. 418 with note, rather summarily dismissed as an untenable thesis. The idea has since been tentatively revived by Hampl, *Klio*, XXXII (1939), p. 37: " Es wäre aber denkbar, dass in der Inschrift Ἐρ[ύθρας] stand."

[40] There is no basis for the opinion, sometimes expressed, that the establishment of Athenian colonies on the mainland of Asia was forbidden by the Peace of Kallias (cf., *e. g.*, Busolt, *Gr. Gesch.*, III, 1, p. 418; Gomme, *Commentary*, I, p. 376). Military occupation was forbidden, and it is a noteworthy fact that no φρούραρχοι or φρουροί of the Athenians are named in Asia Minor after the Peace of Kallias, although they are present both in D10 of 453/2 (Erythrai) and D11 of 450/49 (Miletos); see above, pp. 142-144.

[41] *Klio*, Beiheft XXX, pp. 120-140.

[42] *Aspects of the Ancient World*, pp. 116-143. This essay, under the title " Zur älteren athenischen Kolonisation," was prepared for *Eunomia*, I (1939), pp. 11-32. We have not seen the periodical; cf. Ehrenberg, *Aspects of the Ancient World*, p. 63, note 1, and Gomme, *Commentary*, I, p. 375, note 3.

[43] *Commentary*, I, pp. 373-380.

ostracism of Thoukydides.[44] Plutarch uses without distinction the words for " klerouchs " and " colonists " in describing the thousand settlers who went to the Chersonese, and because of this an element of doubt arises as well about those who went to
Naxos and Andros.[45] But however much the later writers may have confused these
terms, there was in fact a sharp distinction in meaning between them, and there is
never any evidence of confusion either in Thucydides or in the Attic inscriptions of
the fifth century.[46] We take it as certain that apoikoi (ἄποικοι) and epoikoi (ἔποικοι)
are the same, differing only in meaning as do our own words " emigrant " and " immi-
grant," and reflecting merely the point of view from which the writer envisaged the
process of colonization: either from the mother city or to the new location. The settlement of apoikoi or epoikoi constituted an apoikia (ἀποικία), which by the act of
settlement became a new city-state, with its own citizenship and its own *ius soli*.
A settlement of klerouchoi (κληροῦχοι) was called, in the abstract, a klerouchia
(κληρουχία), but it created no new city-state, and the klerouchoi themselves retained
Athenian citizenship and the *ius soli* of Athenians. Although the Athenian apoikos
(*e. g.*, to Amphipolis) remained an Athenian by blood, there was no *ius sanguinis*
which kept him politically an Athenian, and indeed he had no Athenian political rights.
The Athenian klerouchos, on the other hand (*e. g.*, to Lesbos), was an Athenian by
blood, but he kept enrollment in his deme and had political rights and duties like those
of the Athenian who lived in Athens.[47] It will be axiomatic that klerouchs did not

[44] Busolt, *Gr. Gesch.*, III, 1, note 1 on pp. 412-413, quotes Sauppe's observation that Plutarch
names the foundations in the chronological order of their settlement (cf. *Abh. Gött.*, XIII [1866-
1867], p. 25). The quota records for Andros, Naxos, and the Chersonese do not support this suggestion. Gomme's dates (*op. cit.*, p. 380) place Andros in 450, Naxos before 447, and the Chersonese between 449 and 446.

[45] *Pericles*, 11, 5-6 (T96) : πρὸς δὲ τούτοις χιλίους μὲν ἔστειλεν εἰς Χερρόνησον κληρούχους, εἰς δὲ
Νάξον πεντακοσίους, εἰς δ' Ἄνδρον ⟨τοὺς⟩ ἡμίσεις τούτων, εἰς δὲ Θρᾴκην χιλίους Βισάλταις συνοικήσοντας,
ἄλλους δ' εἰς Ἰταλίαν ἀνοικιζομένης Συβάρεως, ἣν Θουρίους προσηγόρευσαν. καὶ ταῦτ' ἔπραττεν ἀποκουφίζων
μὲν ἀργοῦ καὶ διὰ σχολὴν πολυπράγμονος ὄχλου τὴν πόλιν, ἐπανορθούμενος δὲ τὰς ἀπορίας τοῦ δήμου, φόβον
δὲ καὶ φρουρὰν τοῦ μὴ νεωτερίζειν τι παρακατοικίζων τοῖς συμμάχοις. *Pericles*, 19, 1 (T97a) : τῶν δὲ στρατη-
γιῶν ἠγαπήθη μὲν ἡ περὶ Χερρόνησον αὐτοῦ μάλιστα, σωτήριος γενομένη τοῖς αὐτόθι κατοικοῦσι τῶν Ἑλλήνων·
οὐ γὰρ μόνον ἐποίκους Ἀθηναίων χιλίους κομίσας ἔρρωσεν εὐανδρίᾳ τὰς πόλεις .... Plutarch (*Pericles*, 34, 2)
also thought of the Athenians sent to Aigina as klerouchs; Thucydides (II, 27, 1 and VIII, 69, 3)
called them ἔποικοι.

[46] The distinction is made in *I. G.*, I², 140, lines 8-9, where both types of settlement are named:
[ταῖ]ς ἀποικίαις καὶ κλεροχία[ις]. See also *I. G.*, I², 274, line 178: [- - - - -]ι κλεροῦχοι ἀνέθεσ[αν - -].
We must challenge Ehrenberg's statement (*Aspects of the Ancient World*, p. 131) that " even in
Thucydides, the expressions for the colonists themselves (ἄποικοι, ἔποικοι, κληροῦχοι) are sometimes
confused, although their original meanings were evident."

[47] Berve, *Miltiades*, p. 53, insisted upon the precision with which Thucydides in VII, 57, 2
(T143) called the Hestiaians ἄποικοι. We hold the insistence entirely justifiable, and do not find
(as does Gomme, *Commentary*, I, p. 375, note 3) that " the word was often loosely used," certainly
not in *I. G.*, I², 45. It is much to be regretted that Walker, in *C. A. H.*, V, pp. 96-97, speaks
indiscriminately of Eion, Skyros, Lemnos, Imbros, the Chersonese, Brea, Hestiaia, Poteidaia,
Lesbos, Aigina, and Melos all as klerouchies.

pay tribute to Athens. Athenian colonies sent out after the organization of the Confederacy were not assessed either, and though they became separate city-states there is no evidence that they ever paid, or were expected to pay, tribute; earlier Athenian settlements which were already in existence as separate city-states when the assessment of Aristeides was made were enrolled along with their neighbours.

The prolific Athenian colonization, ascribed to Perikles by Plutarch, and (as noted above) to be dated between 450 and 443, had as its reasons " lightening the city of its mob of lazy and idle busybodies, rectifying the embarrassments of the poorer people, and giving the allies for neighbours an imposing garrison which should prevent rebellion." [48] We have already seen that the last purpose motivated the establishment of colonies near Kolophon and Erythrai, and the amendment in the Brea inscription makes it evident that the colony there was intended in part at least as a relief to the poor.[49] Isokrates later stressed the element of protection afforded in thinly held districts; [50] this guarantee of security, Plutarch assures us, was most particularly welcome to the Chersonese.[51]

In the early years of the Confederacy, the Athenians enslaved Eion and then enslaved the Dolopians on Skyros and themselves settled the island.[52] These cities never paid tribute. But the Athenian settlers on Skyros gave to that island a population which placed it in the same category with Lemnos and Imbros. The Athenians who went there in 476/5 paid no tribute, for they were, in fact, Athenians, and there was evidently no appropriate date at which to bring up later the question of their non-Athenian statehood, even if the Athenians at home had wished to do so. Early in the fourth century, the islands of Lemnos, Imbros, and Skyros had been recovered by Konon,[53] and in the Peace of Antalkidas these three islands were recognized as peculiarly Athenian.[54]

Klerouchs are reported to have been sent to Euboia under Tolmides,[55] as well as

[48] Translation of *Pericles*, 11, 5, by Bernadotte Perrin in *The Loeb Classical Library*.

[49] *I. G.*, I², 45, lines 39-42: ἐς δὲ [Β]ρέαν ἐχ θετὸν καὶ ζε[υ]γιτὸν ἰέναι τὸς ἀπο[ί]κος. Cf. Busolt, *Gr. Gesch.*, III, 1, p. 411, note 7. It is generally accepted that the settlement at Brea is the same as that among the Bisaltai mentioned by Plutarch (*Pericles*, 11, 5). For the text of the inscription see now *S. E. G.*, X, 34 and the commentary by Tod, *Greek Hist. Inscr.*, I², no. 44 (pp. 88-90, 261), who gives the date *ca.* 445 B. C. Our preference is for a date in 447/6, before rather than after the commencement of regular and continuous payment of tribute by Argilos. See the Register (*A. T. L.*, I, p. 232, *s. v.* Ἀργίλιοι) and above, pp. 60-61.

[50] Isokrates, IV, 107 (T80c): ὑπὲρ ὧν προσήκει τοὺς εὖ φρονοῦντας μεγάλην χάριν ἔχειν πολὺ μᾶλλον ἢ τὰς κληρουχίας ἡμῖν ὀνειδίζειν, ἃς ἡμεῖς εἰς τὰς ἐρημουμένας τῶν πόλεων φυλακῆς ἕνεκα τῶν χωρίων ἀλλ' οὐ διὰ πλεονεξίαν ἐξεπέμπομεν.

[51] *Pericles*, 19, 1 (T97a): see above, note 45.

[52] Thucydides, I, 98, 2 (T109).

[53] Xenophon, *Hell.*, IV, 8, 15.

[54] Xenophon, *Hell.*, V, 1, 31: τὰς δὲ ἄλλας Ἑλληνίδας πόλεις καὶ μικρὰς καὶ μεγάλας αὐτονόμους ἀφεῖναι πλὴν Λήμνου καὶ Ἴμβρου καὶ Σκύρου· ταύτας δὲ ὥσπερ τὸ ἀρχαῖον εἶναι Ἀθηναίων.

[55] Diodoros, XI, 88, 3: μετὰ δὲ ταῦτα ἐλθὼν (Perikles) εἰς Χερρόνησον χιλίοις τῶν πολιτῶν κατεκλη-

to Naxos,[56] and if these klerouchs were indeed led by him the settlements must have antedated his death at Koroneia early in 446. It is not possible to say with certainty that the klerouchy at Naxos resulted in a reduction in tribute because the first quota for Naxos does not appear on the stone until 448/7 (the figure is restored for 450/49). Nesselhauf has argued that some klerouchies were founded without bringing with them the compensation of reduced tribute,[57] and he claims Naxos as an example to prove this point. The record of Naxos can now be documented more fully than was possible in 1933, and the late assessments show a tribute of 7 talents or more (cf. Lists 38 and 39). The figure may have been exactly 7 or it may have been as much as 9; in any case it may be taken as approximately the Aristeidean sum,[58] and it gives a clue to the figure possibly to be restored, as a minimum, earlier than 450 B. C. So the decrease in the tribute with the settling of the klerouchs, which Busolt claimed and which Nesselhauf denied, though it may have been on a minor scale, may equally well have been from 9 to 6⅔ talents. All that we can surely say about the date is that it must be earlier than the spring of 447, but we regard the probable time of the change in tribute to be the same as that for Andros and, consequently, we hold that the present restoration of the quota in 5, IV, 35 is correct.

The tribute of Andros was reduced in 450 from 12 to 6 talents, and the reduction is almost certainly to be associated with the settlement of the klerouchy.[59]

The colony at Brea has left nothing but its name; yet we know more about its organization than we do of any of the others because of the preserved epigraphical record.[60] It was Tod's view that the colony, like that unhappily settled at Ennea Hodoi, might have been destroyed.[61] Cavaignac and Nesselhauf have thought that it may have been absorbed by Amphipolis when the latter was successfully founded on the site of Ennea Hodoi in 437/6.[62] Like Amphipolis, Brea was near Argilos, for we have identified Brea with Plutarch's colony to the Bisaltai, and Argilos was in

ρούχησε τὴν χώραν. ἅμα δὲ τούτοις πραττομένοις Τολμίδης ὁ ἕτερος στρατηγὸς εἰς τὴν Εὔβοιαν παρελθὼν ἄλλοις χιλίοις πολίταις * * * τὴν τῶν Ναξίων γῆν διένειμε. Pausanias, I, 27, 5: ὕστερον δὲ ὡς ἐπανῆλθεν (Tolmides) ἐς ᾿Αθήνας, ἐσήγαγε μὲν ἐς Εὔβοιαν καὶ Νάξον ᾿Αθηναίων κληρούχους. Cf. also Andokides, III, 9 (T6) and Aischines, II, 175 (T3, in A. T. L., I).

[56] See note 45 above.

[57] Klio, Beiheft XXX, note 1 on pp. 30-31. He also argues, and he is surely right, that every lowering of tribute does not imply a klerouchy.

[58] See below, pp. 347-353.

[59] See above, note 45; cf. also Gomme, Commentary, I, p. 374. Nesselhauf, op. cit., p. 30, note 1, thought that some explanation other than the klerouchy might be found for the change, but with this good and sufficient explanation at hand it seems unjustifiable to neglect it and unnecessary to seek another.

[60] See above, note 49.

[61] Greek Hist. Inscr., I², p. 89.

[62] Cavaignac, Histoire de l'antiquité, II, p. 97 with note 4; Nesselhauf, Klio, Beiheft XXX, p. 133.

Bisaltia.[63] The normal tribute of Argilos seems to have been 1½ talents before 446 and we associate the decrease in the tribute of Argilos directly with the colony.[64] The soldiers who were to go out to the colony will have been those who were returning from the campaign in Euboia.[65] Nine years later the colony at Amphipolis was founded, and the tribute of Argilos was again reduced.[66]

In 446, also, after the suppression of the revolt of Euboia, the Hestiaians were expelled and the Athenians themselves took possession of the land. These settlers were called colonists (ἄποικοι, not κληροῦχοι), and Hestiaia became an Athenian colony.[67] A number of other settlements need not detain us long: (1) a colony was founded at Astakos about 435/4;[68] (2) Aigina was settled by Athenians in the summer of 431, and became an Athenian colony (for the new settlers were called

[63] Herodotos, VII, 115, 1: αὔτη (Argilos) δὲ καὶ ἡ κατύπερθε ταύτης καλέεται Βισαλτίη. Cf. Nessel-hauf, op. cit., p. 131. The lexicographers do no more than put Brea in Thrace: (1) Hesychios, s. v. Βρέα· Κρατῖνος (frag. 395 Kock) μέμνηται τῆς εἰς Βρέαν ἀποικίας. ἔστι δὲ πόλις Θρᾴκης, εἰς ἣν Ἀθηναῖοι ἀποικίαν ἐξέπεμπον (cf. Kock, I, p. 121). Busolt (Gr. Gesch., III, 1, p. 417, note 1; cf. Gomme, Commentary, I, p. 374, note 1) conjectures that the play in which Kratinos named Brea was the Θρᾷτται. Gomme, Commentary, I, p. 374, reminds us that the suggestion has been made to read Κρατερός for Κρατῖνος, in which case the reference belongs to the former's collection of Attic decrees and probably goes back to I. G., I², 45. (2) Stephanos, s. v. Βρέα· πόλις [Θρᾴκης], εἰς ἣν ἀποικίαν ἐστείλαντο Ἀθηναῖοι. τὸ ἐθνικὸν ἔδει Βρεάτης. ἔστι δὲ Βρεαῖος παρὰ Θεοπόμπῳ εἰκοστῷ τρίτῳ (frag. 145 Jacoby [no. 115]).

[64] Epigraphically, this date is sound. The rho's with tails in I. G., I², 45 require a date as early as may be when the sigma with four bars was also used.

[65] I. G., I², 45, lines 26-29: hόσοι δ' ἂν γράφσοντα[ι ἐποικέσεν τὸ]ν στρατιοτôν, ἐπειδὰν hέκοσ[ι Ἀθέναζε, τριά]κοντα ἐμερôν ἐμ Βρέαι ἔναι ἐπ[οικέσοντας]. Busolt, Gr. Gesch., III, 1, note 1 on pp. 417-418, was right about this, but was misled to a date after 443 because of his misconception about the organiza-tion of a " Thrakian district."

[66] Like Brea, Amphipolis was an apoikia. Cf. Thucydides, IV, 102, 1: Ἀμφίπολιν τὴν ἐπὶ Στρυμόνι ποταμῷ Ἀθηναίων ἀποικίαν. See above, pp. 5-6.

[67] Thucydides, I, 114, 3: Ἑστιαῖας δὲ ἐξοικίσαντες αὐτοὶ τὴν γῆν ἔσχον; VII, 57, 2 (T143): Ἑστιαῆς οἱ ἐν Εὐβοίᾳ Ἑστίαιαν οἰκοῦντες ἄποικοι ὄντες ξυνεστράτευσαν. Cf. Plutarch, Pericles, 23, 4: Χαλκιδέων μὲν τοὺς ἱπποβότας λεγομένους πλούτῳ καὶ δόξῃ διαφέροντας ἐξέβαλεν, Ἑστιεῖς δὲ πάντας ἀναστήσας ἐκ τῆς χώρας Ἀθηναίους κατῴκισε, μόνοις τούτοις ἀπαραιτήτως χρησάμενος; Diodoros, XII, 7: τὴν μὲν πόλιν τῶν Ἑστιαιῶν ἑλὼν κατὰ κράτος ἐξῴκισε τοὺς Ἑστιαεῖς ἐκ τῆς πατρίδος, τὰς δ' ἄλλας καταπληξάμενος ἠνάγκασε πάλιν πειθαρχεῖν Ἀθηναίοις; schol. Aristophanes, Clouds, 213 (T33): Περικλέους δὲ στρατηγοῦντος κατα-στρέψασθαι αὐτοὺς πᾶσάν φησι Φιλόχορος· καὶ τὴν μὲν ἄλλην ἐπὶ ὁμολογίᾳ κατασταθῆναι, Ἑστιαιέων δὲ ἀποικισθέντων αὐτοὺς τὴν χώραν ἔχειν. Most recently Westlake alludes, mistakenly, to Hestiaia as a klerouchy; Cl. Rev., LXII (1948), p. 4, note 2.

[68] Strabo, XII, 4, 2. See A. T. L., I, pp. 238 and 471-472; II, p. 79; Meiggs, Eng. Hist. Rev., LV (1940), p. 105. The date is from Diodoros (XII, 34, 5) and has only approximate value. Having described the revolt and siege of Poteidaia, Diodoros continues: ἅμα δὲ τούτοις πραττομένοις ἔκτισαν οἱ Ἀθηναῖοι πόλιν ἐν τῇ Προποντίδι τὴν ὀνομαζομένην Λέτανον. For the correction of Λέτανον to Ἀστακόν see A. T. L., I, p. 472, note 1. Astakos paid no tribute after the founding of the colony; in 450 its tribute had been markedly reduced from 9000 to 1000 drachmai, for which we have no explanation. The reduction might be explained if the colony was founded ca. 450, perhaps in connection with Perikles' expedition to the Pontos (see above, pp. 114-117).

epoikoi); [69] (3) epoikoi were sent to colonize Poteidaia in 429; [70] (4) Lesbos was divided into allotments in 427 and klerouchs were sent to the island; [71] (5) Athenian colonizers reorganized the Kolophonians in Notion in 428/7; [72] (6) the Plataians who had been given Athenian citizenship were resettled at Skione in 421/0; [73] (7) five hundred apoikoi were sent to Melos in 416/5. [74]

There was, of course, no further tribute from Aigina, Hestiaia, Poteidaia, and Skione. Melos, though assessed, had never paid. The Athenians on Lesbos were not a colony, but a klerouchy. The scant remnant of loyal Kolophonians appears with its token tribute in List 27, as does also what was left of Notion. So far as we have observed, when the Athenians took complete possession tribute ceased; when they settled a colony near by, tribute was lowered. A klerouchy always implied the continued existence of the original city-state to whose territory it was sent; a colony might be sent to land either partially or wholly dispossessed. In the strict sense there was no new land: Brea and Amphipolis impinged on Argilos; presumably Astakos impinged on the Persians; Hellespontine Neapolis must have included some non-Athenian inhabitants who paid tribute under the name Νεάπολις ἀπ᾿ Ἀθηνῶν (see above, p. 205 with note 51).

The Chersonese, Lemnos, and Imbros are problems which must be considered together, for the first Athenian settlements there antedated the Persian Wars, as did the Athenian settlement at Sigeion, which we shall not treat further at this time. [75] No doubt they were all charter members of the Confederacy and all were given their first assessments by Aristeides. We hold that Imbros was originally grouped with the Chersonese. It appears separately in the quota lists first in 447/6 (8, II, 112), and subsequently became a regular member of the Island panel. The settlement in the

---

[69] Thucydides, II, 27, 1: ἀνέστησαν δὲ καὶ Αἰγινήτας τῷ αὐτῷ θέρει τούτῳ ἐξ Αἰγίνης Ἀθηναῖοι, αὐτούς τε καὶ παῖδας καὶ γυναῖκας, ἐπικαλέσαντες οὐχ ἥκιστα τοῦ πολέμου σφίσιν αἰτίους εἶναι· καὶ τὴν Αἴγιναν ἀσφαλέστερον ἐφαίνετο τῇ Πελοποννήσῳ ἐπικειμένην αὐτῶν πέμψαντας ἐποίκους ἔχειν. καὶ ἐξέπεμψαν ὕστερον οὐ πολλῷ ἐς αὐτὴν τοὺς οἰκήτορας; VII, 57, 2 (T143): αὐτοῖς τῇ αὐτῇ φωνῇ καὶ νομίμοις ἔτι χρώμενοι Λήμνιοι καὶ Ἴμβριοι καὶ Αἰγινῆται, οἳ τότε Αἴγιναν εἶχον; VIII, 69, 3: Αἰγινητῶν τῶν ἐποίκων, οὓς Ἀθηναῖοι ἔπεμψαν οἰκήσοντας.

[70] I. G., I², 397: ἐποίκον ἐς Ποτείδαιαν; D21, line 9: [τ]οῖς ἐποίκοι[ς] τ[οῖς] ἐμ Ποτειδαία[ι]; Thucydides, II, 70, 4: ὕστερον ἐποίκους ἔπεμψαν.

[71] D22; Thucydides, III, 50, 2 (T128): ὕστερον δὲ φόρον μὲν οὐκ ἔταξαν Λεσβίοις, κλήρους δὲ ποιήσαντες τῆς γῆς πλὴν τῆς Μηθυμναίων τρισχιλίους τριακοσίους μὲν τοῖς θεοῖς ἱεροὺς ἐξεῖλον, ἐπὶ δὲ τοὺς ἄλλους σφῶν αὐτῶν κληρούχους τοὺς λαχόντας ἀπέπεμψαν.

[72] Thucydides, III, 34, 4 (T127): καὶ ὕστερον Ἀθηναῖοι οἰκιστὰς πέμψαντες κατὰ τοὺς ἑαυτῶν νόμους κατῴκισαν τὸ Νότιον, ξυναγαγόντες πάντας ἐκ τῶν πόλεων, εἴ πού τις ἦν Κολοφωνίων.

[73] Thucydides, V, 32, 1: Σκιωναίους μὲν Ἀθηναῖοι ἐκπολιορκήσαντες ἀπέκτειναν τοὺς ἡβῶντας, παῖδας δὲ καὶ γυναῖκας ἠνδραπόδισαν, καὶ τὴν γῆν Πλαταιεῦσιν ἔδοσαν νέμεσθαι.

[74] Thucydides, V, 116, 4: τὸ δὲ χωρίον αὐτοὶ ᾤκισαν, ἀποίκους ὕστερον πεντακοσίους πέμψαντες.

[75] Colonized in the late seventh century by Phrynon (Ehrenberg, Aspects of the Ancient World, p. 117), as was also Elaious in the Chersonese; [Skymnos], 707-708, where we read Φρύνων for the Φορβοων of the ms. (Müller, G. G. M., I, p. 224, who adopts Φόρβας).

Chersonese, which came after the Persian wars, and which caused the marked lowering of the tribute of the Chersonese from 18 to *ca.* 2 talents, has been dated in 447/6.[76] It is mentioned not only by Plutarch, who reports it twice, once as a klerouchy and once as a colony,[77] but also by Diodoros, Andokides, and Aischines.[78] There is a possible epigraphical reference to it in *I. G.*, I², 375. Andokides (and Aischines) imply that the settlement was a colony, for, having named the Chersonese, Naxos, and Euboia, Andokides says: " to recount the other colonies, one by one, would be a long story " (τάς τε ἄλλας ἀποικίας καθ᾽ ἕκαστον διηγεῖσθαι μακρὸς ἂν εἴη λόγος), and Aischines has the variation: " we despatched a great many colonies in these years " (πλείστας δ᾽ ἀποικίας ἐν τοῖς χρόνοις τούτοις ἀπεστείλαμεν). For lack of evidence we shall have to confess that we do not know with certainty in which of the two categories these new Cherronesitai belong; we suspect that they were klerouchs. For the question of tribute it makes no difference, for they paid nothing themselves and their arrival, whether as colonists or klerouchs, reduced the payment of the Cherronesitai already there.

There is more evidence about Lemnos and Imbros, which were first settled by Athenians between 510 and 495 B. C.[79] Our belief is that Aristeides assessed Imbros along with the Chersonese, but Lemnos was assessed on its own, and makes an appearance in the quota list of 452/1 as Lemnioi with a quota which represents 9 talents of tribute.[80] The tribute of Lemnos after 450/49 was paid by Hephaistia (3 T.) and Myrina (1½ T.) separately, and was thus just half what it had been before. Imbros began in 447/6 to pay in its own name a tribute of 1 talent.[81] These early Lemnians were unquestionably Athenian by blood, many of them (the older ones) also by birth, and yet as Lemnians they had formed a city-state which gave them political independence. Had they been Athenian citizens in 477 they could not have been separately assessed.

The inscriptions make an important contribution to this question of Lemnian citizenship. There has been found at Hephaistia on Lemnos a list of names, which must be dated *ca.* 500 B. C., arranged according to the Athenian phylai of the reforms of Kleisthenes. The principal face of the stone reads as follows:[82]

---

[76] See above, p. 59.

[77] See above, note 45.

[78] See above, note 55, and T3 (in *A. T. L.*, I) and T6.

[79] Gomme, *Commentary*, I, p. 375, note 1, with a reference to Berve, *Miltiades*, pp. 49-50, who favours a date between 510 and 505 B. C.

[80] It is very probable that a quota of 900 drachmai should be restored with the name ['Εφαισσ]τιἐς in 2, V, 14, representing a tribute of 9 talents also in 453/2. The phenomenon of one city paying for the area is similar to the interchange of Σπαρτώλιοι and Βοττιαῖοι in the third assessment period. See Gomme's enquiry in *Commentary*, I, p. 375, note 2.

[81] Cf. above, pp. 45-46, 51, 59.

[82] Picard and Reinach, *B. C. H.*, XXXVI (1912), pp. 329-338, with photographs, apparently made from squeezes, of all three faces; cf. *I. G.*, I², 948, note.

$$[\mathrm{E}]\dot{v}\theta\acute{v}\mu\alpha\chi o[\varsigma]$$
$$\hbar\iota\pi\pi o\theta o\nu\tau\acute{\iota}\varsigma$$
$$\text{'}A\nu\pi\nu\kappa\acute{\iota}\delta\epsilon\varsigma$$
$$[\Delta\acute{o}?]\rho\kappa o\nu$$
5 $$[K\alpha\lambda\lambda\iota?]\kappa\rho\acute{\alpha}\tau\epsilon\varsigma$$
$$[\ldots^{7}\ldots]\mu o\varsigma$$

Two similar inscriptions, from the second half of the fifth century (*I. G.*, I², 947 and 948), have been found in Athens. It is assumed that they are lists of warriors fallen in battle, but the salient fact is that names of Lemnians, arranged by Attic phylai, were inscribed on stone both in Lemnos and in Athens. Berve explains all three lists as belonging to citizens of the Lemnian state, not citizens of Athens, who have yet brought with them from Athens the nomenclature of the Attic phylai. The inscription on Lemnos is not evidence (argues Berve) of an Athenian klerouchy.[83] Ehrenberg takes vigorous exception to this view, claiming for the men in all three texts full Athenian citizenship and developing the idea of a municipal klerouchy for Lemnos in which the concepts of klerouchy and city-state tend to merge.[84] This vague and undefined concept does not explain the reduction in tribute for Lemnos in 450 B. C., nor does it account for the language in which Thucydides described the Lemnians in VII, 57, 2.[85] Thucydides knew the word for klerouchs as well as the word for colonists, and he could have used either one or the other if it had been applicable.

The following is our translation of the Thucydidean text: " The Athenians themselves, as Ionians, went of their own free will against the Syracusans, who were Dorians, as did also—enjoying still the same language and customs with them [86]—the Lemnians and Imbrians, and the Aiginetans who at that time held Aigina; and in addition the Hestiaians who inhabited Hestiaia in Euboia, being colonists, joined the expedition." [87] Thucydides here names only the Hestiaians as colonists,[88] though else-

[83] Berve, *Miltiades*, pp. 51-53. Commenting on the texts at Athens, he remarks: " Wurden doch auch sonst in Athen die Namen gefallener Bundesgenossen aufgezeichnet."

[84] Ehrenberg, *Aspects of the Ancient World*, pp. 129-137: " Legal thinking, especially in public law, was frequently not very clear and definite " (p. 133).

[85] T143: 'Αθηναῖοι μὲν αὐτοὶ Ἴωνες ἐπὶ Δωριᾶς Συρακοσίους ἑκόντες ἦλθον, καὶ αὐτοῖς τῇ αὐτῇ φωνῇ καὶ νομίμοις ἔτι χρώμενοι Λήμνιοι καὶ Ἴμβριοι καὶ Αἰγινῆται, οἳ τότε Αἴγιναν εἶχον, καὶ ἔτι Ἑστιαῆς οἱ ἐν Εὐβοίᾳ Ἑστίαιαν οἰκοῦντες ἄποικοι ὄντες ξυνεστράτευσαν.

[86] As Classen correctly remarked (*Thukydides*, VII² [1884], p. 99), " τῇ αὐτῇ umfasst auch νομίμοις und regiert αὐτοῖς."

[87] The aorist ξυνεστράτευσαν (" joined the expedition ") is to be contrasted with ξυνεστράτευον in the next sentence (" took part in the expedition "). Classen translated ξυνεστράτευσαν as " hatten sich angeschlossen." Clearly αὐτοῖς, in the phrase αὐτοῖς τῇ αὐτῇ φωνῇ, depends upon αὐτῇ and not upon the remote verb ξυνεστράτευσαν at the end of the sentence. The verb for which Λήμνιοι and Ἴμβριοι, and probably Αἰγινῆται, are still the subject is ἦλθον. So we place our semicolon before καὶ ἔτι, which introduces the Hestiaians.

[88] Smith's translation in *The Loeb Classical Library* edition is in this detail incorrect. Ehrenberg's

where he calls the Aiginetans epoikoi (VIII, 69, 3). Nor does Thucydides say that the Hestiaians enjoyed still the same language and customs with the Athenians. He explains sufficiently their participation by saying that they were colonists. We hold that, strictly speaking, the phrase " enjoying still the same language and customs with them " (αὐτοῖς τῇ αὐτῇ φωνῇ καὶ νομίμοις ἔτι χρώμενοι) should not be associated even with the Aiginetans. They were a recent colony, and " still " (ἔτι), if applied to Aigina, emphasizes unduly a state of affairs that one might have been expected to take for granted, even more so than for Hestiaia. Those who still enjoyed the same language and customs as the Athenians, and who came from city-states which had been independent long enough to make this continued fact worth notice, were the Lemnians and Imbrians. Yet they could not be described either as apoikoi or as klerouchoi. In point of fact, we believe that both were true: that the pre-Persian Athenian settlers who paid tribute were organized into their own civic communities of Hephaistia and Myrina, and that the settlers who came in 450 to Lemnos and perhaps (though not necessarily) somewhat later to Imbros were Athenian klerouchs who remained such within the strict meaning of that word and who consequently did not pay tribute. When tribute was to be paid, a vague definition of citizenship was impracticable; each individual Lemnian must have known whether he was a Lemnian citizen (πολίτης) or an Athenian klerouch (κληροῦχος). Presumably the inscriptions should be divided into the same two categories, according to the place of their discovery. Those named in the Athenian texts were klerouchs, and even if there had been no reduction in tribute in 450 these documents would have been the logical clue to the existence of such a klerouchy at some time in the fifth century; the reduction in tribute is principally useful in providing the date.[89] The Lemnian text names Lemnians, not Athenian klerouchs. One can accept all Ehrenberg's objections to the idea of the Kleisthenian phyle as " a kinship group," and yet hold that the Lemnians who were

translation is correct about the colonists (*op. cit.*, p. 134) but not for the complete sentence structure, and we believe that some of his difficulty in interpretation is due to the fundamental misunderstanding discussed above.

[89] Nesselhauf, *Klio*, Beiheft XXX, note 3 on pp. 127-128, could find no evidence for a klerouchy on Lemnos at this time. One ought to mention, though not as proof, the Lemnian Athena of Pheidias, which has often been associated with the klerouchy (Pausanias, I, 28, 2): δύο δὲ ἄλλα ἐστὶν ἀναθήματα, Περικλῆς ὁ Ξανθίππου, καὶ τῶν ἔργων τῶν Φειδίου θέας μάλιστα ἄξιον, Ἀθηνᾶς ἄγαλμα ἀπὸ τῶν ἀναθέντων καλουμένης Λημνίας (see G. M. A. Richter, *The Sculpture and Sculptors of the Greeks* [New Haven and London, 1929], pp. 170-171). Gomme, *Commentary*, I, p. 375, notes Busolt's view that the reduction in tribute implies a further settlement (*Gr. Gesch.*, III, 1, p. 414), but he thinks the reduction " may have been due to other causes than a new cleruchy, especially as the cities had been settled from Athens itself only two generations earlier and were doubtless more than willing members of the League." We believe that these klerouchies to the Chersonese and to Lemnos imply no wavering there in loyalty to Athens. They were the new blood which Perikles contributed to districts already by sentiment and tradition, as well as blood, strongly Athenian in sympathies. They were the new infusion to which Plutarch referred as stocking " the cities anew with vigorous manhood " (*Pericles*, 19, 1 [T97a]).

Athenian in blood but not in citizenship used the names of the Attic phylai. What else but imitation of this sort can the " customs " (νομίμοις) of Thucydides mean? When Athenian oikistai refounded Notion in 428/7 (see note 72 above) they did so with their own institutions as models (κατὰ τοὺς ἑαυτῶν νόμους). We do not know that this means organization into phylai with Attic names, but in Lemnos at least the close copying of the Athenian pattern seems not at all surprising. In all three inscriptions the Lemnians were called Lemnians, irrespective of their citizenship, because of where they lived. This has nothing to do with the *ius soli*; in simple terms, the people who lived on Lemnos were Lemnians.[90]

When Thucydides undertook to write the catalogue of Athenian forces at Syracuse he divided them into (1) Athenians and those closely bound by speech and customs, and (2) all others. The first group contains the apoikoi and the epoikoi.[91] It also contains the hybrid Lemnians and Imbrians, part descendants of early colonists and part klerouchoi. Had all the Lemnians and Imbrians been klerouchs there would have been no need to name them.[92] Other klerouchs are not named, but must be inferred under their proper classification as Athenians (Ἀθηναῖοι). The Cherronesitai ought surely to have been named, like the Lemnians and Imbrians, if they had been in Sicily. But they had their own task to perform at home in protecting the Chersonese against Thrakian raids from the north, and indeed, while the Lemnians and Imbrians appear again and again as a kind of mobile unit at the disposal of Athenian generals,[93] the Cherronesitai are not associated with them, but must be thought of as a unit of the Home Guard, as it were, doing a less spectacular but none the less useful service to the Empire.[94] There is less expectation of finding in Sicily

[90] Gomme, *Commentary*, I, p. 375, note 3, has given the correct clue to this in a reference to Thucydides, III, 19, 2. The Samian refugees at Anaia were called Ἀναῖται, though clearly they did not regard themselves as other than Samian in citizenship.

[91] Hestiaia and Aigina.

[92] Lemnians and Imbrians helped the Athenians at Lesbos (Thucydides, III, 5, 1): οὗτοι δὲ (Μηθυμναῖοι) τοῖς Ἀθηναίοις ἐβεβοηθήκεσαν, καὶ Ἴμβριοι καὶ Λήμνιοι καὶ τῶν ἄλλων ὀλίγοι τινὲς ξυμμάχων; Kleon boasted that he would use at Pylos no new soldiers from the city (Thucydides, IV, 28, 4), but only a few outsiders, including Λημνίους δὲ καὶ Ἰμβρίους τοὺς παρόντας; a Lemnian and Imbrian contingent fought at Amphipolis (Thucydides, V, 8, 2): Λημνίων καὶ Ἰμβρίων τὸ κράτιστον; and, of course, Lemnians and Imbrians were in Sicily (Thucydides, VII, 57, 2). Cf. also D18, line 4, for another reference to Lemnos, in 439 B. C.

[93] Kleon's boast before his departure for Pylos would be difficult, though perhaps not impossible, to comprehend if the Lemnians and Imbrians were all Athenian citizens, still enrolled in Attic demes. Kleon promised that he would take no one from the city, but only Lemnians and Imbrians who were present and the peltasts who had come from Ainos and 400 bowmen from elsewhere, and with the soldiers at Pylos either slay or bring back the Lakedaimonians alive within twenty days. The contrast is marked in the sequence: λαβὼν ἐκ μὲν τῆς πόλεως οὐδένα, Λημνίους δὲ καὶ Ἰμβρίους τοὺς παρόντας. But Thucydides may have in mind here principally the place of official residence. See above with note 90.

[94] This was the service which made the new settlers of 447 so welcome in the Chersonese; Plutarch, *Pericles*, 19, 1 (T97a).

soldiers from the colonies at Poteidaia, Melos, and Skione, but klerouchs from Andros, Naxos, Lesbos, and Euboia may have been present. We should like to emphasize the propriety of Lesbian participation, especially since the Methymnaioi were there with their ships, and of Euboian participation, especially since the colonists from Hestiaia gave their aid. These Lesbian and Euboian klerouchs, however, are not named, nor indeed, since they were Athenians, is there any special reason why they should have been.[95]

The klerouchs in Euboia must have been settled principally at Chalkis and Eretria. These cities had been among the last to commute their service with ships to payments of phoros. We have argued above that the date for this change was the assessment of 450. Almost at once came the peace with Persia, and the Euboian cities found that after the moratorium they were to be permanently burdened with a tribute which even one year more of patience would have made wholly unnecessary. Actually, Chalkis and Eretria paid this tribute in 448/7; both names appear in List 7, the former with a tribute of 5 talents and the latter with a tribute which we now believe should be restored as 6 talents.[96] General unrest prevailed in Euboia, and Euboian exiles joined with exiles from Boiotia in maintaining resistance to the Athenians from Orchomenos and Chaironeia. The campaign of Tolmides early in 446 aimed to crush this resistance and he was successful at least in capturing Chaironeia and in temporarily establishing a guard. We believe that the klerouchs on Euboia were settled there by Tolmides as part of the strategy of this campaign, and that they were intended partly to prevent communication through Chalkis between disaffected elements on the island and exiles in Boiotia. Tolmides died at Koroneia in the spring or early summer of 446; so we date his klerouchies in the winter of 447/6 or in the early spring of 446. We have restored the pre-klerouchy payments in List 8 for Chalkis and Eretria, since it is quite possible that the tribute was paid before the klerouchs arrived. They were in any case established before the Euboian revolt, and in the event proved helpless against the successful attack of the Euboian exiles from Orchomenos and the uprisings at home, although no doubt they helped Perikles in his ultimate reconquest. The terms which Athens made with Eretria and Chalkis after the revolt had been crushed were part of a different and wholly new negotiation in which Tolmides, now dead, had no part. Thucydides calls the capitulation a ὁμολογία,

---

[95] Gomme, *Commentary*, I, p. 344, has confused κληροῦχοι and ἄποικοι when he argues *ex silentio* for the withdrawal of Tolmides' klerouchy and, by inference, denies a second klerouchy after 446. It is incorrect to speak of klerouchs in Aigina and Hestiaia. Nesselhauf, *Klio*, Beiheft XXX, pp. 133-136, uses the same *argumentum ex silentio*, without allowing for the difference between ἀποικία and κληρουχία, but he avoids calling Hestiaia by its wrong name.

[96] Reading the figure in 7, IV, 11 as [Γ]H. This is slightly higher than the Γ of Chalkis, but presumably Eretria was the wealthier state. The assessments of Eretria and Chalkis in A9 were 15 and 10 talents, respectively. We believe that the two cities paid in 450/49 and that the names probably belong in 5, IV, 36-37; see above, note 7 on p. 31.

and we have in D16 and D17 the terms of the oaths exchanged between both states and Athens. Both agreed to pay whatever tribute they might persuade the Athenians, and we find in the lists that each city paid in fact 3 talents. The reduction is not great, when we consider that the new settlement was larger and required much more land than Tolmides' 1000 klerouchs had needed. Other measures which seemed good to the Athenians were adopted for the policing of the island.

To this settlement after the suppression of the revolt we assign the reference which Aelian makes (T1) to dividing among the klerouchs the so-called " Hippo-botos " land (Ἱππόβοτον χώραν) into 2000 kleroi, which we hold to be part of the same condition of the peace of which Plutarch speaks, with evident reference to the same land (*Pericles*, 23, 4): " Perikles expelled the wealthiest and noblest Chal-kidians, the so-called Hippobotai." [97] The reference in both cases is to the settlement in 446. It has been argued at length by Nesselhauf that the passage from Aelian does not mean a klerouchy but the establishment of a public domain, and he claims that there is no other evidence for a klerouchy after 446.[98] There is at least the evidence of the Ravennas scholion (T33) on the *Clouds* of Aristophanes (213) that a klerouchy was established after the suppression of the revolt, that is, different from the klerouchy of Tolmides,[99] and we prefer to see in Thucydides, VIII, 95 an indi-cation that there were klerouchs in the Eretrian plain rather than that there were none.[100] There is also a passage in Lysias' speech in defense of the ancestral con-stitution which virtually demands our acceptance of the klerouchy.[101] The Athenians legalized marriage with Euboians in order to gain manpower, and the compelling interpretation is that the klerouchs in Chalkis and Eretria were to marry Euboian women in order to produce sons to add to the roll of Athenian citizens. This dis-pensation cannot apply, surely, to Hestiaia, for the Hestiaians were colonists (ἄποικοι) only and no longer Athenians themselves. Real Athenians must be meant, and who

---

[97] Χαλκιδέων μὲν τοὺς ἱπποβότας λεγομένους πλούτῳ καὶ δόξῃ διαφέροντας ἐξέβαλεν. Plutarch goes on to relate the dispossession of Hestiaia in the same year (446) ; cf. above, note 67.

[98] *Klio*, Beiheft XXX, pp. 133-140, and especially p. 136: " Die literarische Überlieferung kennt eine Kleruchie in Chalkis nach 446 nicht."

[99] Ὑπὸ γὰρ ἡμῶν παρετάθη: εἰς φόρον ἐξετάθη, πλείονα φόρον παρέχουσα. δηλοῖ δὲ καὶ τὸ ἡπλῶσθαι. ἐκληρούχησαν δὲ αὐτὴν Ἀθηναῖοι, κρατήσαντες αὐτῆς.

[100] After the Athenian ships were defeated, Thucydides says (VIII, 95, 6), καὶ ὅσοι μὲν αὐτῶν πρὸς τὴν πόλιν τῶν Ἐρετριῶν ὡς φιλίαν καταφεύγουσι, χαλεπώτατα ἔπραξαν φονευόμενοι ὑπ' αὐτῶν· οἱ δὲ ἐς τὸ τείχισμα τὸ ἐν τῇ Ἐρετρίᾳ, ὃ εἶχον αὐτοί, περιγίγνονται καὶ ὅσαι ἐς Χαλκίδα ἀφικνοῦνται τῶν νεῶν. Nessel-hauf translates ἐς τὸ τείχισμα as " in die Burg," which it surely was not, and so has missed the fact that the Athenians had their own walled compound separate from the city proper. Whether neigh-bouring klerouchs as well as military personnel lived within the compound we do not know. But the existence of a fortified stockade in the plain seems to us to argue for rather than against the klerouchs.

[101] Lysias, XXXIV, 3 (T88a): ἡγοῦμαι ταύτην μόνην σωτηρίαν εἶναι τῇ πόλει, ἅπασιν Ἀθηναίοις τῆς πολιτείας μετεῖναι, ἐπεὶ ὅτε καὶ τὰ τείχη καὶ τὰς ναῦς καὶ [τὰ] χρήματα καὶ συμμάχους ἐκτησάμεθα, οὐχ ὅπως Ἀθηναῖόν τινα ἀπώσομεν διενοούμεθα, ἀλλὰ καὶ Εὐβοεῦσιν ἐπιγαμίαν ἐποιούμεθα.

could they be, in sufficient numbers to make the plan effective, if not the klerouchs whose existence Nesselhauf denies?

The source of the misunderstanding has been mainly the passage from Aelian, which in the texts reads as follows (*Varia Historia*, VI, 1) : " After conquering the Chalkidians the Athenians divided their so-called ' Hippobotos ' land among klerouchs, making 2000 kleroi; and they made reservations for Athena in the place called Lelanton and the remainder they let out at rentals at the rates shown in the stelai which stood against the Royal Stoa and contained the accounts of these rentals." [102] Nesselhauf makes a good argument that the land (exclusive of sacred reservations) cannot have been both leased out by the state and given to klerouchs, but he has reconciled the paradox by making the wrong correction. One of the stelai mentioned in Aelian's notice has been preserved, showing rentals of temple property in Chalkis and Eretria and elsewhere (including Hestiaia), and proving that these rentals were inscribed on stelai and set up to public view at Athens.[103] Aelian's text says that all the other property was rented, and, by implication, that the temene were excluded. Of the stelai of these other rentals, which must have been many times as numerous, if this is what happened, no single fragment has been preserved. In other words, Aelian has said, according to the traditional text, precisely the wrong thing. The stelai displayed before the Stoa Basileios carried in fact the rentals of the sacred property; there were no other stelai for the other property, for that had gone to the Athenian klerouchs. There can be no doubt that this is what Aelian intended to say with " they divided it among klerouchs " (κατεκληρούχησαν), and this is right; the words that are wrong are " the remainder " (τὴν δὲ λοιπήν).[104] One can even conjecture what the feasible emendation in the text must be to make it consistent with itself and with the epigraphical record: for τὴν δὲ λοιπήν read τὸ δὲ λοιπόν (" for the future "). This does not give a smooth text, and there may have been some other change either by Aelian or his copyist, but we hold that the idea behind the emendation is sound and epigraphically attested. The Athenians divided the land among their klerouchs, set aside precincts for Athena, and rented these thereafter according to the testimony of the stelai.

In the still unpublished fragments of poletai records found in the Agora at Athens there is described a property of Oionias, son of Oionochares, of Atene, situated " in the Lelantine plain " (ἐλ Λελάντο[ι πεδίοι]).[105] Possibly he was one of the klerouchs. He was condemned, along with Alkibiades and others, for profaning the Mysteries, but as a klerouch he had every right to be in Athens in 415 preparing

---

[102] T1 : ’Αθηναῖοι κρατήσαντες Χαλκιδέων κατεκληρούχησαν αὐτῶν τὴν γῆν ἐς δισχιλίους κλήρους, τὴν Ἱππόβοτον καλουμένην χώραν, τεμένη δὲ ἀνῆκαν τῇ Ἀθηνᾷ ἐν τῷ Ληλάντῳ ὀνομαζομένῳ τόπῳ, τὴν δὲ λοιπὴν ἐμίσθωσαν κατὰ τὰς στήλας τὰς πρὸς τῇ βασιλείῳ στοᾷ ἑστηκυίας, αἵπερ οὖν τὰ τῶν μισθώσεων ὑπομνήματα εἶχον.

[103] I. G., I², 376 plus *Hesperia*, XII (1943), pp. 28-33, where Raubitschek suggests tentatively (p. 32) that one of the items refers to a precinct ἐν Ἄνδ[ροι], possibly to be connected with the klerouchy established there in 450 B. C.

[104] Gomme, *Commentary*, I, p. 344, note 1, gives a very fair statement of the dilemma.

[105] Raubitschek, *Hesperia*, XII (1943), p. 31, note 65.

to do his duty with the army if in fact he had been called upon to serve in the expedition to Sicily.

But the clearest reference to Athenian klerouchs in Chalkis is in the text of D17, lines 52-57.[106] The terms of agreement between Athens and Chalkis after the suppression of the revolt of 446 stipulated that foreigners in Chalkis should pay their taxes to Chalkis " just as do also the Chalkidians," but exemptions were made for those who lived there and paid their taxes to Athens and for any to whom the Athenians had given immunity. No group of non-Athenians could be so described; these must have been the klerouchs.[107] Obviously the Chalkidians had addressed an enquiry to the Athenians asking in diplomatic language how, for purposes of taxation, they were to look upon the strangers within their land. The Athenians gave a polite, but harsh, answer. The fact of the enquiry shows that the problem was new, and agrees with the date of the klerouchy in 446 B. C.

The revolt of Euboia was the last in that long series which Thucydides describes as beginning with Naxos, and each, because in the development of the Empire payments of money had been substituted for ships, easier for the Athenians to suppress than the one preceding. The revolt of Euboia had marked also the most serious threat to the reimposition of tribute after the Peace of Kallias and to the reëstablishment of discipline in the Empire under the terms of the Decree of Klearchos and the Decree of Kleinias. The next significant revolt after Euboia was that of Samos, but with Samos it was a question neither of changed status within the Empire nor of payment of tribute. Other causes were in play, which had no connection with the sweeping reorganizations of the second assessment period. The revolt and suppression of Euboia were the last manifestations of the old and recurrent tragedy in which the allied cities one by one had found that they were indeed not free but completely at the mercy of the Athenians. Although Athens had lost the land empire in Central Greece over which she had held uneasy dominion since 458, she had consolidated the Empire of her maritime allies into which she had transformed the Delian Confederacy. Both the renunciation and the new imperialism were officially confirmed in the Thirty Years' Peace which was ratified with Sparta in the winter of 446/5.

We append here a chronological chart of imperial affairs from the transfer of the treasury to Athens (454) to the Thirty Years' Peace (446/5). We do not cite all the literary evidence in the right-hand column but we refer the reader to the argument in this chapter and in Chapter III of Part I, " The Texts of the Second Assessment Period." The references, unless otherwise specified, are to the quota lists.

---

[106] See *A. T. L.*, II, pp. 71-72.

[107] Nesselhauf, *Klio*, Beiheft XXX, p. 138, note 2, writes " Auch die im Chalkisdekret genannten ξένοι in Chalkis können keine athenischen Kleruchen sein, wie man mit Recht allgemein annimmt." He gives a reference to Lehmann-Haupt, *Klio*, XVI (1920), pp. 193-196 [Nesselhauf says pp. 396 ff.], whose views on these ξένοι are indeed strange. The situation of the Chalkidian klerouchs is similar to that of the klerouchs in Salamis (*I. G.*, I², 1) ; see Wade-Gery, *Cl. Quart.*, XL (1946), pp. 101-104.

CHRONOLOGICAL TABLE

454 summer	Transfer of the treasury from Delos to Athens	List 1
454/3	Erythrai and Miletos (and Latmos and Myous) in revolt	Absence from List 1
453 spring	Payment of tribute in Athens	List 1
	Boutheia the centre for loyal Erythraians	1, V, 19
	Milesians in Leros and Teichioussa loyal	1, VI, 19-22
453 summer	Fleet in Karic waters, collects arrears	2, I
452 spring	Payment of tribute	List 2
452 late spring	Boutheia remains loyal, but pays late	2, X, 5
	Latmos recovered and pays late	2, X, 3
452 early summer	Erythrai recovered; Athenian Regulations for Erythrai	D10
452 summer	Miletos (and Myous) recovered	3, II, 28-30
451 spring	Return of Kimon	Thuc. I, 112, 1
451 spring	Payment of tribute	List 3
451 summer	Five Years' Truce	Thuc. I, 112, 1
451/0	Sigeion threatened	*I. G.*, I², 32 + *Hesperia*, V (1936), pp. 360-362
450 spring	Payment of tribute	List 4
450 spring	Kimon's campaign to Kypros; tribute collected from Karic cities	Thuc. I, 112, 2 4, V
450 late spring	60 ships sail to Egypt	Thuc. I, 112, 3
450 summer	Death of Kimon	Thuc. I, 112, 4
450 midsummer	Panathenaia; reassessment; commutations from ships to money	[A2]; Insular payments in Period II
450 summer	Victories in Kypros	Thuc. I, 112, 4
450 summer	Klerouchy to Naxos ([lowering of tribute])	Paus. I, 27, 5; Plut. *Pericles*, 11, 5
450 summer	Klerouchy to Andros (lowering of tribute)	Plut. *Pericles*, 11, 5; 5, IV, 22
450 autumn	Return of fleet from Kypros and Egypt	Thuc. I, 112, 4
450 autumn	Klerouchy to Lemnos (lowering of tribute)	5, IV, 40-41
450/49	Trouble in Kolophon	Absence from Period II
450/49	Regulations for Miletos	D11
450/49 winter	Fighting in Thrace	Thrakian absences from Period II (*e. g.*, Argilos)

449 winter	Negotiations for peace with Persia	
449 spring	Payment of tribute; many partial payments	List 5 5, I-IV
449 spring	Peace of Kallias	
449 late spring	Congress Decree, which declares tribute moratorium, requires completion of current dues	D12
449 late spring	Late payments of tribute	5, V
449 late spring	Failure of Congress	
449 early summer	Papyrus Decree, which reimposes tribute beginning in 448/7	D13
449 summer	Sacred War: Spartan attack	Thuc. I, 112, 5
449 midsummer	Panathenaic payment of 5000 T. to Athena	D13
449/8	Decree of Klearchos	D14
448 spring	Tribute moratorium	No List 6
448/7	Fighting in the Chersonese and in Thrace	Plut. *Pericles*, 19, 1; Hel. and Th. absences from List 7
448/7 winter	Officer at Eion receives 1 T. from Abdera	8, I, 105
448/7 winter	Officer at Tenedos receives money from Hel. cities	Partial payments in List 7 (balances)
447 spring	Decree of Kleinias	D7
447 spring	Payment of tribute resumed; many partial payments, some through recalcitrance, some through payments in the field	List 7
447 early summer	Application of D7	7, IV, 31-39
447 summer	Sacred War: Athenian reprisal	Thuc. I, 112, 5
447/6 winter	Berge recovered by force based at Eion	8, I, 93
447/6 winter	Fighting in the Chersonese, money raised	Partial payments in List 8
447/6	Klerouchies to Imbros and the Chersonese; Chersonese syntely breaks up (lowering of tributes)	8, I, 91, 97, 100; 8, II, 112
447/6	Colony to Brea	*I. G.*, I², 45 + *Hesperia*, XIV (1945), pp. 86-87
447/6	Klerouchies to Chalkis and Eretria, led by Tolmides	Diod. XI, 88, 3; Paus. I, 27, 5
446 spring	Payment of tribute	List 8
	Strict application of D7	List 8, appendix

446 spring	Battle of Chaironeia	Thuc. I, 113, 1
446 spring	Battle of Koroneia	Thuc. I, 113, 2
446	Treaty with Kolophon	D15
446	Colony to Kolophon (lowering of tributes)	D15; 9, I, 10 (Kolophon), 13 (Lebedos); absence of Dioseritai from Period III
446	Colony to Erythrai (lowering of tributes)	*I. G.*, I², 396 11, II, 27; 9, I, 12 (Hairai)
446 early summer	Revolt of Euboia	Thuc. I, 114, 1
446 summer	Revolt of Megara	Thuc. I, 114, 1
446 summer	Spartan invasion of Attica	Thuc. I, 114, 2
446 midsummer	Panathenaia; reassessment	[A3]
446/5	Reduction of Euboia	Thuc. I, 114, 3
446/5	Colony to Hestiaia	Thuc. I, 114, 3; disappearance from quota lists
446/5	Treaty with Eretria	D16
446/5	Treaty with Chalkis	D17
446/5	Additional klerouchs to Chalkis [and Eretria] (lowering of tributes)	T1 (Aelian); T33 (schol. Aristoph.); D17; Period IV (absence from Period III)
446/5 autumn or winter	Thirty Years' Peace	Thuc. I, 115, 1

CHAPTER IX

THE THIRTY YEARS' PEACE

1. To the End of the Samian War

The Thirty Years' Peace was in its fourteenth year when the Spartan ekklesia, in the late summer or the autumn of 432 (Thucydides, I, 87, 6),[1] voted that Athens had broken its terms, and in its fifteenth when the Thebans attacked Plataia, at the beginning of the spring of 431 (Thucydides, II, 2, 1). It was therefore sworn in the autumn or winter, 446/5. The embarrassing moment when Athens had had to face not only the loss of Megara and the revolt of Euboia, but also an invasion of Attica by the Peloponnesian army, had passed. The Spartan king had taken the Peloponnesians home and Athens had been able to deal with Euboia at her leisure. There can be little doubt that Sparta's failure to press her advantage had saved Athens from a very serious situation. If Perikles had had to stay and defend Attica, he might well have lost Euboia;[2] and the remoter consequences can hardly be calculated. The Spartan king was thought to have been bribed, and he and his principal adviser both had to leave Sparta.[3] But the critical moment was past, no recriminations could recapture it, and perhaps the more responsible Spartans did not regret this. At all events, when the peace negotiations began Euboia was safely in Athens' hands and the maritime empire was secure.[4] The assessment of 446 was also no doubt completed

---

[1] The exact date of this decision is notoriously uncertain; Gomme gives an impartial statement in his note on I, 125, 2 (*Commentary*, I, pp. 420-425). If the numeral ἔκτῳ be retained in Thucydides, II, 2, 1, then the decision can hardly have been taken before November, 432, and Wade-Gery has argued that this is feasible (*J. H. S.*, LIII [1933], pp. 135-136). Gomme, chiefly because of Thucydides' words in I, 125, 2, would correct ἔκτῳ to δεκάτῳ and place the decision in August. The peace was sworn, then, later than August or else later than November in 446. Since it followed " not long after " (οὐ πολλῷ ὕστερον, I, 115, 1) the Athenian subjection of Euboia, later than November seems rather late, but not perhaps impossible since there was much to discuss.

[2] Thucydides says (I, 114) that Perikles had taken his army to Euboia when he was recalled by the news from Megara and the threatened invasion. The Spartan king, however, did not advance beyond Eleusis and Thria (cf. II, 21, 1), and Perikles was able to return and complete the conquest of Euboia.

[3] Thucydides, II, 21, 1; V, 16, 3; Strabo, VI, 1, 14; Plutarch, *Pericles*, 22-23.

[4] The importance to Athens of Euboia scarcely needs stating; see Thucydides, VIII, 96, and D17, lines 76-79. With Central Greece lost, the Euripos became the frontier between peninsular Greece and the maritime empire. In *I. G.*, I², 40, lines 19-24 (very soon after the Thirty Years' Peace), Athens regulated the sea route between Chalkis and Oropos, with no land alternative; from Chalkis to Hestiaia alternative routes were possible, by sea or land. We offer several new readings in the text and, quite tentatively, suggest restorations with a stoichedon line of 36 letters:

ἐ[ὰν δέ τις πορθμεύει ἐκ Χ]
[α]λκίδος ἐς Ὀροπὸν πρ[αττέσθο δύο ὀβολό· ἐὰν δ]
ἐ τις ἐχς Ὀροπô ἐ[ς] heσ[τίαιαν ἒ ἐχς Ἐστιαίας ἐ]

301

before the negotiations opened; its generally moderate scale, and such things as the return of mainland possessions to Thasos, were probably accomplished facts when the Athenians' envoys went to Sparta.[5]

Athens had already lost Boiotia and Megara, and her whole policy in Central Greece had collapsed, including the Amphiktyonic alliance.[6] She had, further, to give up her acquisitions in the Peloponnese. These things touched Sparta nearly; she could not tolerate Athenian holdings in the Peloponnese, and it was also vital to her that she should control the Megarid, since this gave her land communication with Boiotia[7] and (perhaps more important) a frontier from which Attica could be easily invaded.[8]

ς Ὀροπὸν πορθμεύει πρ[αττέσθο δραχμέν· ἐὰν δ]
ἐ τις ἐκ Χαλκίδος ἐς ℎε[στίαιαν πέμπει πραττ]
[ἐ]σθο τέτταρας ὀβολός.

On the significance of Euboia see Westlake, *Cl. Rev.*, LXII (1948), pp. 2-5, with a reference to the inscription in note 2 on p. 4. After 411 Chalkis changed the picture totally by bridging the Euripos (Diodoros, XIII, 47, 3-5). Just before the crisis, Tolmides' klerouchs were no doubt intended to cut the communication between Euboia and Boiotia (see above, p. 294); perhaps they also served to cover Perikles' first landing, his evacuation, and his second landing, in 446 (Thucydides, I, 114; and for the difficulty of such operations, IV, 10).

[5] Diodoros, XII, 7, names these negotiators as Kallias and Chares; see above, p. 276. That they went to Sparta may perhaps be inferred from Andokides, III, 6. We assume that the assessment was completed at the Panathenaia (*i. e.*, in August). Whether this was the Panathenaia at which Phrynis won his first victory (schol. Aristophanes, *Clouds*, 971, ἐπὶ Καλλι⟨μάχ⟩ου?) we need not seek to determine, but even if it was it can hardly have been the Panathenaia for which Perikles introduced his Panathenaic decree and himself served as athlothetes (see below, note 32). The earlier date for the Spartan decision in 432 is also August (see note 1 above), and Thucydides says that the peace was then still in its fourteenth year (I, 87, 6). This does not quite formally exclude the possibility that the peace was sworn before the Panathenaia but it makes it unlikely; and unless we change Thucydides' ἕκτῳ in II, 2, 1, it completely excludes it. Our own belief (without prejudice to the date of the Spartan decision in 432) is that the assessment was in August, 446, and preceded the final settlements with Euboia and Chalkis, the Euboian tributes being reserved for individual consideration (D16, lines 11-12, D17, lines 26-27), and that both of these operations preceded the negotiations with Sparta.

[6] *I. G.*, I², 26 as restored in *S. E. G.*, X, 18; see Meritt, *A. J. P.*, LXIX (1948), pp. 312-314, and above, note 21 on p. 279. Athens' Amphiktyonic policy may be traced from the original oath against the medizers in 479 (Herodotos, VII, 132; see above, p. 105), through Themistokles' resistance to the medizers' expulsion (Plutarch, *Themistocles*, 20, 3-4, perhaps in 478) and the Skyros episode (Plutarch, *Cimon*, 8, 4, and *Theseus*, 36, 1, in 476/5), to the alliance of 458 (*S. E. G.*, X, 18) and the noticeable Amphiktyonic tinge in the phraseology of the Congress Decree of 449 (D12; note the names Ἴωνας, Δωριεῖς, Βοιωτίαν, Φωκίδα, Λοκρῶν, Οἰταίους καὶ τὸν Μαλιέα κόλπον, Φθιώτας Ἀχαιούς, Θεσσαλούς). The Spartan action at Delphi in the same year was no doubt directed against this policy (see above, p. 280). Athens' rejoinder in 447 (see above, pp. 178-179 with note 65) will have become ineffective after the loss of Boiotia; Thucydides, I, 118, 3; II, 54, 4; III, 92 and 101, 1. An echo of all this may be detected in the tribal name Amphiktyonis at Thouria; Diodoros, XII, 11, 3 (cf. Ehrenberg, *A. J. P.*, LXIX [1948], pp. 157-159).

[7] This is why the prospect of an Athenian recovery of the Megarid seemed dangerous to the Thebans; Thucydides, IV, 72, 1: οὐκ ἀλλοτρίου ὄντος τοῦ κινδύνου.

[8] Contrast the situation in 458; Thucydides, I, 107, 3: δύσοδός τε γὰρ ἡ Γερανεία καὶ ἐφρουρεῖτο αἰεὶ ὑπὸ Ἀθηναίων.

But this was enough for Spartan realists. Athens was now amenable to pressure. To disable her seriously would produce a radical change in the equilibrium of Greece, and any such change was unwelcome to the lethargy or caution which the helot system bred in Sparta. It is hard to doubt that the ring of revolts which faced Athens in 446 had been concerted (cf. especially Thucydides, I, 113, 2) and that Sparta had promised her support; but Euboia was not the first nor the last to be disappointed in the hope that such support would be sustained and effective.[9]

Sparta, then, left the Athenians free to deal with Euboia, and the rest of the Empire, as they thought fit. An exception was made of Aigina, which Athens had conquered in the course of the foregoing war; it was expressly stipulated that Aigina should be " autonomous." [10] We may conceive this clause as phrased like part of a clause in the Peace of Nikias, about certain cities which Sparta handed over to Athens in 421; [11] Aigina was to continue to pay her tribute and so long as she did was to be autonomous. Aigina had made a partial payment in 449, and probably none at all in 477 and 446 (see above, pp. 38-39 and 57-58), and had no doubt been counting on Spartan support for this attitude. We imagine the arrears were not demanded.[12] But she paid with regularity henceforth, and thus (tacitly or perhaps even explicitly?) Sparta conceded to Athens the right to continue the collection of tribute, though the Persian war was ended.

In 432, when Athens had in some way violated Aigina's autonomy, Sparta first demanded that it be respected and then followed this up with a more general demand that autonomy be granted to the whole alliance.[13] Perikles replied (I, 144, 2) : " We shall allow autonomy to the cities, if we were allowing them autonomy when we made the peace." He contends, evidently, that while the peace had stipulated autonomy for Aigina it had not done so for the cities in general. He can hardly be wrong about the fact. The process which Thucydides calls douleia (or doulosis), " subjection," [14] had

---

[9] Cf. Thucydides, V, 111, 1 (the Athenians answer the Melian suggestion of Spartan support) : οὐδ' ἀπὸ μιᾶς πώποτε πολιορκίας Ἀθηναῖοι δι' ἄλλων φόβον ἀπεχώρησαν.

[10] The Aiginetans complain in 432: οὐκ εἶναι αὐτόνομοι κατὰ τὰς σπονδάς (Thucydides, I, 67, 2; cf. I, 139, 1 and 140, 3). The grievance was probably recent, i. e., Athens had lately established a garrison or the like; see below, p. 320.

[11] Thucydides, V, 18, 5 (T134) : τὰς δὲ πόλεις φερούσας τὸν φόρον τὸν ἐπ' Ἀριστείδου αὐτονόμους εἶναι. For Aigina it would be τὸν ὑπάρχοντα φόρον, or the like. The further stipulations may also perhaps have applied to Aigina : the cities are not to join the Spartan alliance at all, nor the Athenian except voluntarily, and so long as they pay the tribute (ἀποδιδόντων τὸν φόρον) they are not to be molested.

[12] That is, for 448/7 and 447/6. No doubt the complement for 450/49 had been extracted.

[13] Thucydides, I, 140, 3: οἱ δὲ τελευταῖοι οἵδε ἥκοντες καὶ τοὺς Ἕλληνας προαγορεύουσιν αὐτονόμους ἀφιέναι. " The Hellenes " here, as often, means the members of Athens' Confederacy or Empire; see above, note 12 on p. 97.

[14] Δουλεία or δούλωσις: " subjection " rather than " enslavement," which is andrapodismos (ἀνδραποδισμός). Eion, for example, had been enslaved but Naxos subjected (I, 98, 1 and 4 [T109]). See the discussion, pp. 155-157.

begun with Naxos in 470 and had gone on steadily, culminating with Chalkis and Eretria in 446 (see above, p. 297), and although their reduction was the last thing Athens had accomplished before starting to negotiate the peace, Sparta had made no protest or had at least not stipulated that the subject cities should have their autonomy restored. Sparta, indeed, had in the Thirty Years' Peace tacitly recognized the fact of the Athenian Empire.

The peace divided Greece into two grand alliances. Cities already affiliated to one or the other might not change sides.[15] Argos belonged to neither and sometimes felt her possible isolation to be alarming.[16] She had made her own Thirty Years' Peace with Sparta in 451, about the same time as Kimon's Five Years' Truce between Sparta and Athens (Thucydides, V, 14, 4 and 28, 2), but does not seem to have felt easy about it. Rather more than a year later, when Kallias was negotiating with the Persians, Argive envoys also arrived to ascertain how the credit of Argos stood at Sousa (Herodotos, VII, 151), and now, about four years later again, Argos sought to be admitted as a third party to this Thirty Years' Peace between Sparta and Athens. This could not please Sparta, who did not wish her treaties with these two formidable ex-enemies to expire together; it was provided therefore that Argos' existing treaty with Sparta should stand, and that she might enter into any treaty or alliance she chose with Athens.[17] Nothing came of this, for Athens was in no position to intrigue in the Peloponnese or anywhere in the Greek peninsula; and the Peace of Kallias had limited her activity in Asia Minor. Two fields were open to her energies, the west and the north.

In the west, Athens had held Naupaktos since 461, and the peace did not require her to surrender her interest there. Tolmides in 457 and Perikles in 454 had attempted to consolidate Athenian influence in the Korinthian Gulf. In 458/7 Athens made a treaty with Egesta in Sicily,[18] and sometime probably between 450 and 446 Kallias

---

[15] The Kerkyran who seeks to persuade Athens to accept the Kerkyran alliance says (I, 35, 1): λύσετε δὲ οὐδὲ τὰς Λακεδαιμονίων σπονδὰς δεχόμενοι ἡμᾶς μηδετέρων ὄντας ξυμμάχους· εἴρηται γὰρ ἐν αὐταῖς, τῶν Ἑλληνίδων πόλεων ἥτις μηδαμοῦ ξυμμαχεῖ, ἐξεῖναι παρ' ὁποτέρους ἂν ἀρέσκηται ἐλθεῖν. Cf. I, 40, 2 (the Korinthian reply): εἴρηται ἐν ταῖς σπονδαῖς ἐξεῖναι παρ' ὁποτέρους τις βούλεται τῶν ἀγράφων πόλεων ἐλθεῖν. The treaty, then, included lists of the allies of each party, and these allies were bound not to change sides. This clause probably explains an apparent contradiction between Perikles and the Megarians. Perikles (I, 144, 2) says that the peace did not forbid his exclusion of Megara from market and harbours any more than it forbade the Spartan practice of xenelasia, and he can hardly be wrong on the fact. But the Megarians had complained that their exclusion *was* contrary to the peace (I, 67, 4: εἴργεσθαι — — — παρὰ τὰς σπονδάς). Perikles speaks of the letter, the Megarians of the spirit; the exclusion was an attempt to entice Megara out of the Spartan alliance into the Athenian.

[16] Cf. Thucydides, V, 40, 1: ἔδεισαν μὴ μονωθῶσι. This was in 420, but the problem was constantly recurring.

[17] Pausanias, V, 23, 4; cf. Thucydides, V, 40, 2.

[18] *I. G.*, I², 19, as republished by Woodhead, *Hesperia*, XVII (1948), pp. 58-59; cf. *S. E. G.*, X, 7. Woodhead follows Raubitschek in reading the archon's name as [há]βρον instead of ['Αρίστ]ον.

the Treaty-Maker arranged " perpetual " alliances with Rhegion and with Leontinoi (see above, pp. 276-277 with note 9). The Athenian support of New Sybaris, of which we have evidence in coins which antedate the founding of Thouria, no doubt also belongs to the period before the crisis of 446.[19] Most of this activity was nullified by that crisis, which deprived Athens of her port at Pegai and of all her influence on the shores of the Korinthian Gulf except at Naupaktos. Kallias' two treaties, although " perpetual," are deemed to require renewal in 433. Only in the region of Sybaris have we evidence that the activity was maintained, by the founding under Athenian auspices of the Panhellenic colony at Thouria, in 443/2,[20] and this foundation was of a kind which could not make Korinth uneasy. On the whole, between 446 and 433, Athens treated Korinth's western pretentions with respect.

In the north Athens had a free hand, and could act as champion of Greeks against the Thrakians. In 447 she had undertaken two operations against Thrace, in the Chersonese and on the Strymon.[21] The former led, that same year, to the consolidation of the Thrakian Chersonese and the establishment of Athenian klerouchs (or colonists?), and Plutarch tells us that this action was welcomed by the Greeks who lived there and who had been unable to hold their own against the Thrakians (*Pericles*, 19, 1 [T97a]). The quota lists of Period II suggest that the situation had been similar at the Strymon mouth. Argilos is probably absent throughout the period (*i. e.*, 450-446) and this no doubt indicates trouble. There is an officer at Eion (on the Strymon) who receives part of the local tribute, as the officer at Tenedos (near the Chersonese) does; these are, we may be sure, both military commanders, and the tribute which they receive is for expenses of their campaigns.[22] The outcome of the

---

[19] The coins are those in Head, *Hist. Num.*[2], p. 85 (" *circ.* B. C. 443," but the date depends on the historical interpretation). See *J. H. S.*, LII (1932), p. 217, note 49, where Wade-Gery writes " probably in 446-5 "; it now seems to us more likely that the project was conceived before the crisis of 446. Cf. Ehrenberg, *A. J. P.*, LXIX (1948), pp. 149-170.

[20] See Wade-Gery, *J. H. S.*, LII (1932), pp. 215-219, whose view needs certain modifications. The idea of " relentless pressure " on Korinth requires that the treaties with Rhegion and Leontinoi be dated after 446 (p. 216, note 43) and that the Akarnanian alliance be dated before Sybota (Wade-Gery himself argues against this latter, p. 216, note 45); for New Sybaris see note 19 above. The likeness between the Panhellenic Congress Decree and the Panhellenic Thouria is closer than he allows; see, *e. g.*, note 6 above. We think, then, that between 446 and 433 Athens avoided overt provocation of Korinth, and that the project at Thouria looked to something like the same supporting opinion as the Congress Decree had done. In the main, however, we agree that the plan for Thouria was strongly coloured by the opposition to Perikles, which (as in Plutarch, *Pericles*, 12, 1 [T96]) took an εὐπρεπὴς πρόφασις at its face value and countered Perikles' real intention.

[21] See above, pp. 59-61.

[22] See above, pp. 59-61. We believe that not only the talent from Abdera which is expressly stated to have been paid to an officer was so paid, but also the balance of the partial payments of, *e. g.*, Thasos and Galepsos. Akanthos seems to be completely absent from Lists 7 and 8 and perhaps supplied troops.

Strymon campaign was, no doubt, the colony at Brea. This is barely mentioned in our literary evidence, but the second half of the decree which authorized the foundation is extant on marble,[23] and we believe that it is rightly attributed to the year 447/6.[24] Nothing is heard of the colony later and it was perhaps incorporated in the more ambitious colony of Amphipolis,[25] in 437/6. The defense of Brea was provided for in certain Regulations, syngraphai (ξυγγραφαί), which had been laid down for the " cities Thraceward " shortly before the despatch of the colony (T78c);[26] those cities were charged to defend the colony if it was attacked.

The programme of colonies, to Asia Minor[27] as well as to Thrace, was part of the consolidation of Athens' imperial status, that position which Perikles and his imitator Kleon called her " despotism " (τυραννὶς ἀρχή).[28] Though this was a source of pride to some,[29] it encountered lively opposition in Athens, which was more or less silenced by the ostracism of Perikles' rival, Thoukydides the son of Melesias, in 443 B. C.[30] The main issue had been Perikles' building programme and the expenditure on it of the Akropolis fund which was comprised mostly of accumulated tribute.[31] The ostracism freed Perikles' hands, and he planned to make of the Great Panathenaia of 442 a demonstration that Athens was the centre of the civilized world; his " Panathenaic Decree " devoted special attention to the musical programme, and he himself served as athlothetes (Master of Ceremonies).[32] It was perhaps with a view to keeping this celebration clear of business that the assessment which was due in 442 was advanced to 443, the summer immediately following the ostracism. The first two quota lists of this assessment period, Lists 12 and 13, are exceptionally well preserved. They are very methodical (showing for the first time a formal grouping into tribute districts) but are not in any way exorbitant. It has been suggested that Marathesion was now first included and that this was an affront to Samos; this is

[23] Tod, *Greek Hist. Inscr.*, I², no. 44. It is no doubt the same as the settlement of 1000 men which, Plutarch says (*Pericles*, 11, 5 [T96]), Perikles sent to settle among the Bisaltai. Hesychios, *s. v.* Βρέα, quotes Kratinos as mentioning the colony to Brea. This quotation could be from his *Thrakian Women* of probably 442, but it is not impossible that Κρατῖνος is an error for Κρατερός, and, if so, Krateros will have quoted the decree; see above, notes 49 and 63 on pp. 286 and 288.

[24] For the date and for further discussion of the colony see above, pp. 286-288 with note 49.

[25] *I. e.*, it was one of the σύνεγγυς φρούρια of Diodoros, XII, 32, 3. Its fate is not recorded among the Strymonian calamities in schol. *Aischines*, II, 34 (quoted above, p. 170).

[26] See above, pp. 146-147.

[27] See above, pp. 282-284.

[28] Thucydides, II, 63, 2; III, 37, 2.

[29] Perikles says, to all: τῷ τιμωμένῳ ἀπὸ τοῦ ἄρχειν, ὧπερ ἅπαντες ἀγάλλεσθε (II, 63, 1; cf. 64, 3, where Athens' title to glory is, Ἑλλήνων τε ὅτι Ἕλληνες πλείστων δὴ ἤρξαμεν).

[30] Wade-Gery, *J. H. S.*, LII (1932), p. 206.

[31] See below, pp. 337-341.

[32] Plutarch, *Pericles*, 13, 11; the quotation in 13, 10 from Kratinos' *Thrakian Women* probably determines the date. It is inconceivable that Perikles could have found the leisure for this in 446 (see note 5 above).

very possible, although such an interpretation is not inevitable.[33] Whether or no, in the Samian War which broke out very soon after, the Samian rebels appear to have seized and held both Marathesion and Priene.[34]

The demilitarizing of Ionia (cf. especially Thucydides, III, 33, 2) required that internal peace be maintained in the Empire. When therefore in 441 war broke out between Samos and Miletos, the Samians, who were winning, were called to order by Athens. Not only had Samos not been demilitarized, she was one of the three allies who had kept their fleets in commission; indeed, she was perhaps the one whose energies most nearly matched Athens' own.[35] At the instance of certain Samian democrats the Athenians established democracy in Samos, posted a garrison in the island, and, taking 100 hostages, deposited them with the new klerouchs in Lemnos. This was high-handed behaviour and provoked a crisis which endangered Athens' whole position. Both Persia and Sparta were tempted to denounce their treaties, but neither actually did so; Samos had to face Athens virtually single-handed, supported only by Byzantion, and the issue was now only a matter of time. Samos submitted after a nine months' siege, early in 439, and the treaty was sworn soon after midsummer. She did not become tributary, but she lost her fleet and had to pay a heavy indemnity of 1300 talents in 26 annual payments of 50 talents.[36] Athens remained at peace with both Sparta and Persia. The Athenian garrison in Samos was captured early in the war and handed over to the satrap of Sardis, who may have been prepared to contend that such troops constituted a breach of treaty. Presumably, when

---

[33] Nesselhauf, *Klio*, Beiheft XXX, p. 48 with note 4. Marathesion does not actually appear before List 13; the restoration of the name in List 12 is virtually certain, and it is possible that it stood in Lists 9-11 also. We have suggested (above, p. 22) that, like Isinda and Pygela, it had until then paid through Ephesos, but it is quite conceivable that it had been Samian (see Strabo, XIV, 1, 20, quoted in the Gazetteer, *s. v.* Πυγελῆς).

[34] Marathesion and Priene are both absent from the full panel in List 15, *i. e.*, during the siege of Samos.

[35] Samos seems to have participated with enthusiasm in the Eurymedon and Egyptian campaigns; see the monuments to Maiandrios (Peek, *Harv. Stud. Cl. Phil.*, Suppl. Vol. I [1940], p. 120) and Hegesagoras (above, note 37 on p. 253). The absence of comparable monuments in other allied cities may be partly an accident of excavation. In Thucydides, VI, 76, 3 (T137a) Hermokrates names the two main charges which Athens brought against her allies as λιποστρατία and ἐπ' ἀλλήλους στρατεύειν, which may be roughly paraphrased as " too little energy or too much "; Samos is the chief example of the second.

[36] For the terms of her oath see D18, lines 15-21; for the financial settlement see below, pp. 334-335. The primary narrative of the Samian War is in Thucydides, I, 115-117; the *casus belli* was the claims of Miletos and Samos to Priene. The primary documents are the statement of expenses of the war (*I. G.*, I², 293 = Tod, *Greek Hist. Inscr.*, I², no. 50; both are superseded by Meritt's text in *A. J. P.*, LV [1934], pp. 365-366) and the treaty made after Samos' surrender (D18). The projected Peloponnesian support is recorded in Thucydides, I, 40, 5 and 41, 2, where the Korinthian speaker claims that Korinth was decisive in preventing it. No doubt Megara had wished to support Byzantion.

Persia decided not to break with the Athenians these troops were returned to Athens.[37]

The Samian War no doubt strengthened Perikles' position. Coming on top of the ostracism of Thoukydides it virtually silenced opposition. But Perikles was unquestionably aware that goodwill is an important asset, and the crisis had shown weakness as well as strength in Athens' position. Her treaties had proved just strong enough to prevent the Persian-Spartan-Ionian coalition,[38] but only just; there had been little margin of goodwill. The weakness of the peace with Persia was that Athens was no longer the protector of Greece against the Asiatic barbarian; instead, Persia could now champion Greeks against Athens.[39] The barbarians of Europe remained, and the enterprises of the next few years are directed to them. Perikles' expedition into the Euxine Sea perhaps belongs here, although we are inclined to place it considerably earlier.[40] More certain is the founding of Amphipolis in Thrace, in 437/6.

2. AMPHIPOLIS

In the year 437/6 Athens at last achieved the foundation of a colony at the spot where the Strymon could be bridged; the founder was Hagnon (Theramenes' father)[41] and the new city was named Amphipolis. It was evidently meant to be an important city with large territory and population; it may have absorbed the earlier colony at Brea, and the reduction in the tribute of Argilos[42] suggests that much Argilian territory was incorporated. The Athenian element was comparatively small, the majority were Greeks from the neighbouring cities.[43] The foundation was resented by Argilos,[44]

---

[37] See above, note 15 on p. 143. The peace had named the King's boundaries (T80d), and the contention that Samos lay within the demilitarized zone could hardly have been upheld; but it might have been advanced.

[38] This was eventually to prove fatal; Thucydides, II, 65, 12.

[39] A few small Karian communities are dropped in 440/39 and more in the assessment of 438 (altogether about forty), when the Karic and Ionic districts are once more, and permanently, combined into one; see above, pp. 212-213 with note 79.

[40] Plutarch, *Pericles*, 20, 1-2 (T97b); see above, pp. 114-117.

[41] The founder of Amphipolis was Hagnon son of Nikias; Thucydides, IV, 102, 3. Theramenes and his father Hagnon were of the deme Steiria; schol. Aristophanes, *Frogs*, 541. The identity of these two Hagnons was always likely and a papyrus of Kratinos' *Ploutoi* now shows that Nikias' son was indeed a Steirian; D. L. Page, *Greek Literary Papyri*, I (*The Loeb Classical Library*, London and Cambridge, Mass., 1942), no. 38, lines 29-38 (p. 200).

[42] Argilos paid 1 talent in 438/7, the same as she had paid ever since 446/5. After that her record is sketchy; she pays 1000 drachmai in 433/2, 430/29, and 429/8, and is absent from the full Thrakian panel in 435/4 and 432/1.

[43] Thucydides, IV, 106, 1: βραχὺ μὲν Ἀθηναίων ἐμπολιτεῦον, τὸ δὲ πλέον ξύμμεικτον. Cf. IV, 103, 3-4: Ἀργιλίων τε ἐν αὐτῇ οἰκήτορες ––– καὶ ἄλλοι and τοὺς ἐμπολιτεύοντας σφῶν ἐκεῖ (Argilians). See also Diodoros, XII, 32, 3: συνῴκισαν Ἀμφίπολιν, καὶ τῶν οἰκητόρων οὓς μὲν ἐκ τῶν πολιτῶν κατέλεξαν, οὓς δ' ἐκ τῶν σύνεγγυς φρουρίων. The word συνοικίσας is used also by schol. Aischines, II, 34.

[44] Thucydides, IV, 103, 4: οἱ Ἀργίλιοι, ἐγγύς τε προσοικοῦντες καὶ ἀεί ποτε τοῖς Ἀθηναίοις ὄντες ὕποπτοι καὶ ἐπιβουλεύοντες τῷ χωρίῳ. The word ὕποπτοι has perhaps an active sense, "they were

but in general it was no doubt welcome to the Greek cities to have this position so strongly held against the Thrakians. For Athens, Amphipolis was of use in many ways. It commanded the only crossing of the Strymon and so all lateral communication along the Thrakian coast; particularly, it prevented any Greeks of the peninsula from approaching the Hellespont by land (Thucydides, IV, 108, 1). It was one of Athens' most important sources of ship-timber (IV, 108, 1; cf. Herodotos, V, 23, 2). It was also, Thucydides says, a source of revenue to Athens, though we do not know exactly how.[45] But above all, its prestige value was enormous, and its loss some twelve years later was correspondingly fatal.

Thucydides speaks of the site of Amphipolis as Thrakian, and specifically Edonian, and gives the name Thrace to the country immediately east of the city.[46] On the west, however, the Makedonian kingdom had for some time past extended to the lower Strymon.[47] The colony thus lay on the frontier between the two peoples and was no doubt intended as a focus of Athenian influence on both kingdoms. Thucydides seems to have thought the Thrakian power the more formidable,[48] and we may therefore begin with the Odrysians, their dominant race.

The Odrysian homeland was in the Bulgarian plain, not far from the Black Sea; Dareios passed through the Odrysian country on his way to the Danube.[49] Teres,

suspicious of the Athenian element " (cf. I, 90, 2), but the converse was no doubt true. For the irregularity of Argilos' tribute payments see note 42 above and the Register, s. v. 'Αργίλιοι.

[45] Thucydides, IV, 108, 1: ἡ πόλις αὐτοῖς ἦν ὠφέλιμος ξύλων τε ναυπηγησίμων πομπῇ καὶ χρημάτων προσόδῳ. Amphipolis never paid tribute, and, as a colony, was an independent city, in alliance with Athens. The alliance and the state of war combine to justify the presence of a strategos with troops (IV, 104, 4 and 106, 2), and Amphipolis may have made voluntary contributions to the cost of war, as the Athenians had done (Thucydides, III, 19 [T125]). But the reference (in IV, 108, 1) may be to mining property which was Athenian domain, and from the rental on which considerable revenue came in to the public treasury. Thucydides is known to have held a concession (μετάλλων ἐργασίας, IV, 105, 1) in this area.

[46] I, 100, 3; IV, 102, 3; 105, 1; cf. 107, 3 (Myrkinos is Ἠδωνικὴ πόλις). The Odrysians' power, however, perhaps did not here extend west of the Nestos river though further north they reached the upper Strymon (II, 97, 1-2).

[47] Thucydides, II, 99, 3-4: Alexandros I and his ancestors conquered Mygdonia between Axios and Strymon (an unusually wide extension for Mygdonia); II, 99, 6: these early Makedonians conquered, and their descendants still hold, Anthemous and Grestonia and Bisaltia. Bisaltia appears to be on the right bank of the lower Strymon, from Argilos (Herodotos, VII, 115, 1) up to Berge and Herakleia (Strabo, VII, frag. 36 Loeb, who says, however, that the Strymon divides, διαιρεῖ or διαρρεῖ, the Bisaltian land; so this passage cannot be used to fix Berge to the right bank of the river). In 479 its king was still a Thrakian (Herodotos, VIII, 116, 1).

[48] II, 97, 5: " Of all the kingdoms between the Adriatic and Black Sea, the Thrakian was the wealthiest and most prosperous, though in military power and size of army it came a long way second to the Skythian." Makedon could not offer resistance to the Thrakian invasion (II, 100, 1 and 101, 1).

[49] Herodotos, IV, 92; cf. Strabo, VII, frag. 47 Loeb: the Bessoi who live on the middle Hebros are neighbours of the Odrysai.

who founded their power, was allied with the Skythians (Thucydides, II, 29, 2; Herodotos, IV, 80, 1). His son Sitalkes ruled from Abdera to the Danube and from Byzantion to the Strymon (Thucydides, II, 97, 1-2). We do not know when either of these began to reign; the next king, Seuthes, succeeded his uncle Sitalkes in 424.[50] Some little while before the end of the century, the Odrysian fortunes declined,[51] but Seuthes at first ruled over his uncle's whole kingdom, and raised the tribute to its highest figure, namely, gold and silver tribute to the value of 400 talents annually, and as much again in gifts of gold and silver.[52] This came from " his whole non-Greek kingdom and from the Greek cities "; Thucydides unfortunately does not say how much from each. That tribute was taken from Greek cities of the Athenian Empire is indicated by a reference to the " hereditary tribute " ($[τὸμ φό]ρον τὸμ πάτριον$) due to the Odrysian kings from the Greek cities of the Chersonese, in a treaty of 357 B. C. between Athens and Thrace.[53] Tribute which was " hereditary " for the Odrysian kings in 357 no doubt went back to the great days of Sitalkes and Seuthes, and what applied to the Chersonese should a fortiori apply to the coastal cities on the coasts between Abdera and Byzantion. We believe that a clause in this same treaty provides that these coastal cities must, in 357, make payments both to Thrace and to Athens.[54] In Figure 4 (p. 312) we present the record of these cities between 454 and 425, and the fluctuations of payment are very remarkable; no doubt these fluctuations are partly due to counterclaims which the Odrysian king was making. We have not tried to interpret these fluctuations in detail, but we observe that the startling downward plunges of Ainos and Selymbria, and the no less startling increase of Maroneia, are probably later than the founding of Amphipolis.[55] Thucydides tells us (II, 29, 1)

---

[50] Thucydides, IV, 101, 5. Teres' reign belongs perhaps to the second, and Sitalkes' to the third quarter of the century. Did Teres take part in the battle of Drabeskos ($διεφθάρησαν --- ὑπὸ τῶν Θρᾳκῶν ξυμπάντων$, in 465; Thucydides, I, 100, 3)?

[51] Xenophon, Anab., VII, 2, 32: $ἐπεὶ τὰ Ὀδρυσῶν πράγματα ἐνόσησεν$ (evidently while the younger Seuthes was still a child).

[52] Thucydides, II, 97, 3; the gifts of textiles and the like are additional to both these items.

[53] I. G., II², 126 (Tod, Greek Hist. Inscr., II, no. 151). We print lines 4-16 as T78d. For $[τὸμ φό]ρον τὸμ πάτριον$ see line 15. The agreement is that, so long as the Greek cities of the Chersonese (lines 13-14: $ἐ[ν Χερρονήσωι]$) pay their dues both to the kings and to Athens, they shall be autonomous; cf. Thucydides, V, 18, 5 (T134) and Xenophon, Hell., III, 4, 25.

[54] This clause (lines 4-13) provides that, if certain cities do not pay their dues to the kings, Athens shall see that they do; and similarly the kings, if the cities do not pay their dues to Athens. The editors suppose that these are not Greek cities (cf. Cloché, Rev. de Phil., XLVI [1922], p. 8, note 1: " Il s'agit ici de villes thraces, par opposition aux villes grecques signalées plus loin "); accordingly their restoration mentions phoros as due to Athens. In our text (T78d) we have replaced this phoros by syntaxis (line 8), and have supposed that one of the stelai in question in line 5 is the stele of Aristoteles (I. G., II², 43 [Tod, Greek Hist. Inscr., II, no. 123]); the cities in question will then be probably Abdera, Dikaia, Maroneia, Samothrake (for her peraia), Ainos, Perinthos, Selymbria, Byzantion (see the list in Tod, op. cit., pp. 68-69). What is special for the Chersonese cities is that, having paid their double dues, they shall be autonomous.

[55] The evidence for Period V, especially for 438/7 and 437/6 (and for 436/5 in the Helles-

that Sitalkes made a marriage alliance with Nymphodoros of Abdera; that down to 431 B. C. this alliance was hostile to Athens; but that in 431 Nymphodoros was made an Athenian proxenos and arranged an alliance between Athens and Sitalkes. We may perhaps see symptoms of this: Abdera's payments drop in the course of Period VI, and since Nymphodoros was then still hostile to Athens this may mean that Abdera was drawing away from Athens and towards Sitalkes. The alliance with Sitalkes is probably reflected in the assessment of 430, in which the assessments of the cities of the south coast are all very low indeed.[56] Athens seems to have compensated herself on the east coast, where she was bound to appear in force[57] and was consequently prepared to be less conciliatory.

In Figure 4 we have given figures (of tribute, not of quota) for Periods I-VII and IX; for Period VIII there is no evidence. For the full statement of evidence we must, as always, refer to the Register; here we give for the most part the presumed tribute assessed, and the dates are therefore in general the dates of assessment years. For Period V, however, we give the payments as known from the best record preserved for most of these cities, that of 435/4; on the southern coast we also tabulate the payments for the year 432/1, which has a complete Thrakian panel. The extra data for Periods IV and V on the southern coast will explain themselves. Period IX is from A9. Figures in brackets depend on restoration; empty brackets indicate that the city is known to have paid but the amount is lost. The figures are talents except where drachmai are specified.

As it turned out, Thrace was less important than Makedon. The alliance with Sitalkes seems to have lasted till his death in 424, but little came of his great invasion of Makedon in 429 (Thucydides, II, 95-101). It was not his pro-Athenian son Sadokos[58] who succeeded him, but Seuthes his nephew, who had allied himself by marriage with Perdikkas (Thucydides, II, 101, 5-6; IV, 101, 5). Athens sought and probably won his friendship.[59] But the sensational increases in the assessments of the south coast in A9, just before Sitalkes' death, perhaps indicate that Athens was no longer much concerned for Thrakian friendship; and even in the very moderate

pont), is so poor that we are uncertain whether the figures of 435/4 ought to be presumed or not for the assessment of 438.

[56] And so, presumably, they were to pay substantial sums to Sitalkes; οὐ γὰρ ἦν πρᾶξαι οὐδὲν μὴ διδόντα δῶρα, says Thucydides (II, 97, 4), who is no doubt speaking as an individual. Compare the advice of Herakleides of Maroneia in Xenophon, *Anab.*, VII, 3, 16-17.

[57] The Hellespontophylakes appear first in D4 (36-40), in 426; but levies are made by military commanders on Hellespontine tribute from the beginning of Period VII (25, III, 42-53; 26, I, 11-21; 27, lines 36-39).

[58] Thucydides, II, 67, 2; Aristophanes, *Acharnians*, 141-150 (just before Sitalkes' death). Sadokos was responsible for the arrest of Aristeus and his fellow envoys in 430; Thucydides, II, 67, 2 and Herodotos, VII, 137.

[59] King Philip in [Demosthenes], XII, 9 (implying that Seuthes murdered Sitalkes); cf. Xenophon, *Anab.*, VII, 2, 31 (the younger Seuthes' testimonial to Athens).

EASTERN COAST OF THRACE

	Period I (454)	Period II (450)	Period III (446)	Period IV (443)	Period V (435/4)	Period VI (434)	Period VII (430)	Period IX (425)
Byzantion	[15]	15	[ ]	15 T. 4300 Dr.	[ ]	18 T. 1800 Dr.	30	[ ]
Selymbria	[6]	6	[ ]	5	900 Dr.	900 Dr.	9	[ ]
Daunioteichitai	[1000 Dr.]	1000 Dr.	1000 Dr.	1000 Dr.	[1000 Dr.]	1000 Dr.	2 T. 4000 Dr.	[ ]
Totals	21 +	21 +	[21?]	21-	[18?]	19-	42-	?

SOUTHERN COAST OF THRACE

	Period I (454)	Period II (450)	Period III (446)	Period IV (443)	Period V (435/4)	Period V (436/5)	Period VI (434)	Period VI (432/1)	Period VII (430)	Period IX (425)
Ainos	12	12	10	10	abs.	4	[abs.]	abs.	abs.	20
Samothrake	6	6	6	6 (440/39) 4	6		[6]	6	2	15
Maroneia	1 T. 3000 Dr.	1 T. 3000 Dr.	1 T. 3000 Dr.	1 T. 3000 Dr. (442/39) [ ] (442/1) [15]	10		10	abs.	3	21 +
Dikaia	3000 Dr.	3000 Dr.	2000 Dr.	abs.	[3000 Dr.]		[3000 Dr.]	[3000 Dr.] 3000 Dr.	abs.	} 75
Abdera	15	15	15	abs.	15		15	10	10	
Totals	35	35	33-	17 +	31 +	35 +	31 +	16 +	15	131 +
GRAND TOTALS	56 +	56 +	54?	38	49?	53?	50	35	57-	200?

Fig. 4: The tribute of cities on the eastern and southern coasts of Thrace. Cities which show no significant variations are not included.

A10, more tribute is assessed on two towns of the Samothrakian peraia (Drys and Zone) than Samothrake had paid in 430 for herself and her peraia together.

Amphipolis' other neighbour was Makedon, and on Athens' relations with Makedon the foundation of Amphipolis had effects of great consequence. We have seen (note 47 above) that Alexandros I had conquered Bisaltia, up to the west bank of the Strymon. One of the charges brought against Kimon in 463 was that he had taken bribes from Alexandros, and the grievance was probably that he had let the king start exploiting the silver mines on the middle Strymon.[60] Amphipolis, had the venture worked out, would have prevented further encroachment, and perhaps one of the early fruits of the foundation was Athens' alliance with Perdikkas, son of Alexandros. Extensive remains survive of a treaty between Athens and Perdikkas, which is probably to be dated to this occasion.[61] The alliance did not last long. In the

[60] The charge, Plutarch, *Cimon*, 14, 3. King Alexandros' silver mines at Dysoron, Herodotos, V, 17, 2 (revenue of one talent a day). His coinage, Head, *Hist. Num.*[2], pp. 219-220, and Gaebler, *Münzen von Makedonia*, II, Plate XXVIII. Edson, *Cl. Phil.*, XLII (1947), p. 95, note 56, notes that his early coins " are direct copies of late archaic Bisaltic pieces."

[61] There was certainly an alliance between Athens and Perdikkas sometime before 433 (Thucydides, I, 57, 2: ἐπεπολέμωτο [in 433] ξύμμαχος πρότερον καὶ φίλος ὤν). We hold that this has been in part preserved in *I. G.*, I[2], 71, an inscription which has been traditionally and, we believe, incorrectly dated in 423/2. Part of the text is now published again in *S. E. G.*, X, 86, where the date 423/2 is still maintained. As the text has been reconstructed in *S. E. G.*, X, with a length of line of 68 letters, there is no room in lines 52-54 for the name of Perdikkas' brother Philip (Φίλιππος Ἀλεχσάνδρο). This might be taken as indicating that Philip had died, and so as favouring a " late " (*i. e.*, 423/2) as against an " early " date (*ca.* 436) for the inscription. But the length of line is certainly greater than 68 letters; the space of seven letters thus allowed is clearly insufficient for the name and patronymic in lines 53-54, where, in fact, the final omicron of the patronymic is still preserved: [...⁶...]o (cf. *I. G.*, I[2], 71, line 79). We accept a standard line of 100 letters (suggested by Edson) and restore lines 47-53 as follows:

47 [ἔδοχσεν τêι βολêι καὶ τôι] δέμοι· Αἰαντὶ[s ἐπρυτάνευε, γνόμε] στρατεγôν· ἄρχεν τὲν [φιλίαν καὶ
τὲν χσυμμαχίαν ταύτεν αὐτίκα μ]

48 [άλα· hυπάρχεν δὲ χρêσιν ἐμ]πορίον Ἀρραβ[αίοι καὶ τοῖς χσυμ]μάχοις hέπερ ἂν καὶ Περδ[ίκκαι
καὶ τοῖς χσυμμάχοις· περὶ δὲ τούτον]

49 [γνόμεν ἐχσενεγκέτο hε βο]λὲ Ἀρραβαίοι [καὶ τοῖς χσυμμάχ]οις· ποιέτο δὲ καὶ Ἀρραβ[αῖος πρὸς
Περδίκκαν χσυμμαχίαν καθάπερ Ἀ]

50 [θεναῖοι κελεύοσιν, καὶ hό]ταν φίλος γίγ[νεται Ἀρραβαῖο]s ποιêν καὶ Ἀρραβαίοι φιλ[ίαν καὶ
χσυμμαχίαν· τὸ δὲ φσέφισμα τόδε τὸ]

51 [ν γραμματέα τὸν τês βολês π]ροσγράφσαι [πρὸς τὸ πρότερ]ον φσέφισμα.   vacat

52 [ὄμνυον ἄρχο]ντες Μακεδ[όνο]ν· Περδίκκαs [Ἀλεχσάνδρο,] Ἀλκέτες Ἀλεχσάνδρο, Ἀρχέλαs Π[ερ-
δίκκο, Φίλιππος Ἀλεχσάνδρο, Ἀμύντας Φ]

53 [ιλίππο], Μενέλαος Ἀλεχσά[νδρ]ο, Ἀγέλαος Ἀ[λκέτο ---].

The length of line of 100 letters is determined by the desirability of allowing the second decree to commence at the left edge of the stele ([ἔδοχσεν τêι βολêι καὶ τôι] δέμοι) and by the desirability of allowing the rubric for the Makedonian princes who swore the oath ([ὄμνυον ἄρχο]ντες Μακεδ[όνο]ν) also to commence at the left margin. The position of the fragments with reference to the left margin is thus determined, and the necessary restorations at the end of line 50 define the length of line. Technically, the treaty with Perdikkas (as with Arrhabaios) was one of φιλία καὶ ξυμμαχία (cf.

late summer of 433, when Korinth after the battle of Sybota wished to make trouble for Athens, she found Perdikkas ready to help. " Perdikkas had become hostile to Athens," says Thucydides (I, 57, 2-3), " though before that he had been her friend and ally. The alienation was due to the alliance which Athens had made with his brother Philip, and with Derdas; these two were making common cause against Perdikkas." So began the long and unhappy encounter between Athens and Makedon, to be decided finally, just under a century after the founding of Amphipolis, on the field of Chaironeia.

Symptoms of the quarrel may probably be found in the quota lists of Period VI, representing the assessment of 434, and in the references to that same assessment in the first Methone decree (D3, lines 8-9 and 31: τοῖς προτέροις Παναθεναίοις). There are many doubtful or controversial factors in this enquiry, and it will be necessary both to look closely at Thucydides' narrative and to take a general survey of Perdikkas' position. It will be convenient to begin with Thucydides' narrative of the events of 432 (I, 56-62). The problems of exact chronology need not detain us; the main bulk of the events recorded certainly falls within the year 432. We cannot avoid the problems of geography, which are due to three main factors: first the text of Thucydides (should ἐπιστρέψαντες in I, 61, 4 be corrected to ἐπὶ Στρέψαν?), next the question of identity of certain Athenian tributaries (Strepsaioi, Sermaioi), and third the uncertainty of the physical facts (was Beroia close to the sea in antiquity?). All these elements of uncertainty contribute to the difficulty of understanding Thu-

Thucydides, I, 57, 2, as quoted above), and the secretary of the Council, as restored, was the proper officer to look to the inscribing of it. The lower right corner of the stele, containing the concluding lines of the list of Makedonian princes (among them [Παυ]σανίας Μαχέτο of the house of Elimiotis), has on its reverse a drafting along the margin which covers a width of about eight letter-spaces. This fact led Davis (A. J. A., XXX [1926], p. 187) to reject the fragment altogether and to assign it, along with I. G., I², 71b₁ (I. G., I, 43), to a different stele. As Davis remarked, " This drafting, then, according to my restoration, should appear also on fragments a and g; and it does not." But Davis was using the width of 68 letter-spaces for the stele, and he believed that this lower right corner fell almost directly beneath his fragment g. With a line of 100 letters there is no difficulty; the marginal drafting on the reverse passes comfortably by the preserved upper portions of the stone. There is one final test of width to be applied: the names of the Makedonian princes in lines 52-53 must match it, whatever it may be assumed to be on the basis of any other evidence. And the names must be chosen, not from the lesser houses, but from the immediate family of Perdikkas himself. The fact that the names of his brother Philip and his nephew Amyntas exactly fill out the 100 spaces otherwise required gives a strong presumption that these names are indeed a proper supplement and that the length of line of 100 letters is correct. Amyntas was high in the favour of Athens (Thucydides, II, 100, 3), and those who have dated this inscription in 423/2 have had to assume that by that time he was not mentioned because he, as well as his father Philip, was dead (Geyer, in P. W., R. E., s. v. Perdikkas [2], p. 600). But they have no restoration for the end of line 52. In 436 Philip and Amyntas were both alive, and the restoration of their names is in conformity with this early date. One should note also that I. G., I², 71 is much more suitable to the original treaty of 436 than to the patching up of differences which Athens had with Perdikkas near the close of the Archidamian War.

cydides' narrative. We therefore begin by advising the reader of our opinion on these points. We believe that in I, 61, 4 ἐπιστρέψαντες must be corrected to ἐπὶ Στρέψαν, and consequently that the Strepsaioi are spoken of in this passage; we believe that the Sermaioi are the people of Therme, and consequently that the Sermaioi are spoken of in I, 61, 2; we believe that the Thermaic Gulf has been greatly reduced in size since antiquity by the alluvial deposits of the Haliakmon and Axios (Vistritza and Vardar) and consequently that in the fifth century B. C. the Haliakmon mouth was a comparatively short distance north of Beroia.[62]

In 432, the Athenians were projecting a campaign against Perdikkas, in support of the two rebels Philip and Derdas. Perdikkas was therefore eager to add to Athens' embarrassments, and encouraged the revolt of Poteidaia and of other cities in and near Chalkidike. Athens consequently had two military objectives in the north, Perdikkas being one, her revolted allies the other. Athens was in the act of sending Archestratos with a force against the former, when she got wind of the projected revolts and ordered him to proceed against the latter also (I, 57, 6), so that " the fleet meant for the Makedonian front was sailing likewise against Poteidaia " (I, 58, 1). Archestratos on arrival found that Poteidaia and other cities had already revolted, and, judging that his force was not large enough to cope simultaneously with both objectives, he decided to concentrate on Makedonia, his original objective (I, 59, 2). Later, Athens sent reinforcements under Kallias, naming as his objectives the revolted allies (I, 61, 1). Kallias first joined Archestratos on the Makedonian front (I, 61, 2) but soon, judging that Poteidaia was more urgent, came to terms with Perdikkas (I, 61, 3); the whole force was now concentrated on Poteidaia (I, 61, 4-62, 6). This distinction between the two " fronts " or " objectives " is perhaps also indicated in I. G., I², 296, which contains the accounts of military expenditure in the year 432/1.[63]

---

[62] The most controversial of these three theses is the identity of Serme and Therme; see above, note 123 on pp. 220-221. The Haliakmon river runs in a steep bed down to Beroia (Verria) and below Beroia through an alluvial plain, making a sharp turn to the south. Herodotos says that in his day it formed a common estuary with the Lydias which came from the north (VII, 127, 1; for further discussion see Oberhummer, s. vv. Lydias and Pella [3], in P. W., R. E.). For Pluygers' correction ἐπὶ Στρέψαν in Thucydides, I, 61, 4, Gomme's note (Commentary, I, pp. 215-218), impartial and inconclusive as it is, makes clear that the great desideratum of the passage is that the χωρίον mentioned in the next line be specified, and Pluygers' correction meets this desideratum. Gomme's difficulties about Beroia are perhaps partly due to the sense which he gives to the words ἀπανίστανται ἐκ τῆς Μακεδονίας in I, 61, 3. We understand these words as meaning " they abandon their campaign in Makedonia "; cf. I, 139, 1 and 140, 3 (Ποτειδαίας ἀπανίστασθαι); II, 70, 1 (in the active); VII, 48, 2 and 49, 1 (where it is similarly used of " abandoning the siege " of Syracuse); I, 105, 3 (ἀνίστασθαι in the same sense [desistere]). They say nothing about the direction in which the Athenians should march. Unless they shipped their whole force by sea, they would be bound to go to Beroia.

[63] The latest complete text is in Meritt, A. F. D., pp. 80-83; see also S. E. G., X, 223. Lines 2-28 record the payments for northern campaigns: the first payment is certainly [ἐς Μακ]εδονίαν (line 5); the next few are restored as [ἐς Μακεδονίαν καὶ Ποτείδαιαν] or ἐς [Ποτείδαιαν καὶ Μακεδονίαν]

We may call these Objective A (Perdikkas or Makedonia) and Objective B (Poteidaia and the other allies in revolt, τὰ ξυναφεστῶτα χωρία in I, 59, 2). When Archestratos decides to abandon Objective B, his first action appears to be the successful siege of Therme (I, 61, 2); when Kallias decides to abandon Objective A, his first action appears to be an unsuccessful assault on Strepsa (I, 61, 4). It might be claimed that the first of these actions proves that Therme was not an Athenian ally, the second that Strepsa was not in Makedonia.[64] This seems over-logical. Because Archestratos judged that Objective B was beyond his powers, this did not mean that he bound himself to touch no town that had once been Athenian; in a military sense it is clear that Therme belonged to Objective A in a way that Poteidaia did not. In the second case, Kallias had indeed bound himself by truce not to touch Objective A, so that Strepsa was surely not " in Makedonia " in a political sense.[65] But this does not mean that it cannot have been on the northern shore of the Thermaic Gulf.

We come now to the general survey of Perdikkas' position. The seat of the Makedonian kingdom was at Aigai (or Edessa) at the north end of Mt. Bermios, a northern outlier of the Olympos massif, and the next most important centre was perhaps Beroia at the south end of Bermios. The large alluvial plain which now stretches eastward of Bermios towards Salonika is of recent formation; in antiquity the Thermaic Gulf reached further west (see note 62 above). The northwestern shore of this gulf, between the Axios and Haliakmon mouths, was called Bottiaiis, south and east of the Haliakmon was what Herodotos calls Makedonis.[66] These shores of the gulf were early conquered by the Makedonian kings, who expelled the native Thrakians (Thucydides, II, 99, 3). By the time of Perdikkas, Makedonian conquests

(lines 6-7, 11, 13, 15, 17, 19); the last two as [ἐς Ποτείδαιαν] (line 23) and ἐς Ποτε[ίδαιαν] (line 25). A great deal of this, however, is restored, and its close interpretation involves the problem of chronology.

[64] Gomme, *Commentary*, I, p. 214; various things, including " the fact that the capture of Therme by Archestratos is expressly part of the campaign against Macedonia and not of that against the revolted cities, weigh heavily against the identification " of Therme with Sermaioi. In the Gazetteer, *s. v.* Στρεψαῖοι, we noted that, while most of the ancient lexica describe Strepsa as πόλις Θρᾳκης (this is from Hellanikos; the Ionian geographers regarded Thrace as stretching very far west), Stephanos has πόλις Μακεδονίας, and we suggested that this meant that some commentator on Aischines, II, 27 had read ἐπὶ Στρέψαν in Thucydides. Gomme, *Commentary*, I, p. 217, note 5, objects that " after ἀπανίστανται ἐκ τῆς Μακεδονίας, it [*i. e.*, πόλις Μακεδονίας] cannot be based on the reading ἐπὶ Στρέψαν." This is not precisely the contention to which we refer in the text above; but the distinction between what is politically and what is geographically in Makedonia applies to both contentions equally.

[65] That is to say, Archestratos' decision was wholly military, Kallias' was partly diplomatic.

[66] Thucydides, II, 99, 3, uses the form Bottia; for Bottiaiis and Makedonis see Herodotos, VII, 127, 1. How far this Makedonis extended is not clear: it may be just the old coast between Beroia and Methone (cf. Thucydides, VI, 7, 3: Μεθώνην τὴν ὅμορον Μακεδονίᾳ). Edson, *Cl. Phil.*, XLII (1947), p. 92, note 36, understands it as more or less equivalent to Pieria, *i. e.*, as far as the northern approaches of Tempe.

had extended eastward to the Strymon (see note 47 above) and southward to the approaches to Tempe and the southern bend of the Haliakmon, in fact, to the Thessalian borders.[67] Perdikkas' father Alexandros had been a patron of Pindar, and he was himself on terms of close friendship with the Thessalian magnates.[68] The cavalry was the only important military arm.[69] Besides the king, there were many local rulers; in Perdikkas' reign we hear of his brother Philip ruling in northern Makedonia, Arrhabaios in Lynkestis, and Derdas probably in Elimiotis,[70] all three of whom are in rebellion.

Makedonia was thus the hinterland of the whole western half of the Thrakian district of Athens' Confederacy, including the Thermaic Gulf and past Chalkidike up to the Strymon River. We use the term Thermaic Gulf for all the coasts north of Tempe in the west and Poteidaia in the east; by the "inner gulf" we mean all inside Methone and Aineia.[71] The heart of the country was at the northwestern end of the inner gulf; the coastal approaches are, from the south Pieria (from Tempe to Methone), from the east Anthemous (the east coast of the inner gulf), Mygdonia, and Bottiaiis (the north coast of the inner gulf; we put the division conventionally at the Axios River). All of these may be called Makedonian home waters. Between Aineia and Poteidaia is what we shall call the Bottic coast or Bottike.[72] From Poteidaia round the three peninsulas to Stageira is Chalkidike. Chalkidike is separated from Makedonian territory by the considerable mountain range which we conven-

[67] Dion and Herakleion, on the coast just north of Tempe; Edson, op. cit., p. 97. For Elimiotis, in the southern bend of the Haliakmon, Thucydides, II, 99, 2.

[68] Pindar, frag. 106 Bowra (cf. Herodotos, V, 22). For Perdikkas and Thessaly see Thucydides, IV, 78, 2 and 132, 2. For a hostile Thessalian view of his son Archelaos see [Herodes], περὶ πολιτείας.

[69] See, e. g., Thucydides, II, 100, 5; IV, 124, 1 and 126, 3. How far the infantry had been yet organized on a Greek model (Lynkestian hoplites in IV, 124, 3) is a debated point; see F. W. Walbank, *Philip V of Macedon* (Cambridge University Press, 1940), p. 1, note 5.

[70] For Philip's ἀρχή see Thucydides, II, 100, 3; for Arrhabaios IV, 79, 2 (βασιλεύς, cf. II, 99, 2); for Derdas I, 57, 3 and 59, 2. The only indication Thucydides gives of Derdas' territory is the word ἄνωθεν in I, 59, 2. For Derdas' connection with Elimiotis see Kaerst, s. v. Derdas, and Oberhummer, s. v. Elimeia (1), in P. W., R. E.; Berve, *Das Alexanderreich*, II, p. 440. He probably is of the same family as the notorious Harpalos, and as the Machaitas of Plutarch, *Mor.*, 178f; [Παυ]ϲανίας Μαχέτο in *I. G.*, I², 71, line 93 is probably (as Droysen suggested, *Gesch. d. Hellenismus*², I, 1, p. 87, note 1) the same as the Pausanias in Thucydides, I, 61, 4, and perhaps Derdas' brother (either brother or son, says the scholiast).

[71] For the greater extension in antiquity of this inner gulf see note 62 above.

[72] This Bottike must be distinguished from Bottiaiis or Bottia (see note 66 above). The Bottiaioi had been expelled by early Makedonian kings from Bottia into Bottike; Thucydides, II, 99, 3. Herodotos calls this Bottic coast Κροσσαίη (VII, 123, 2) and A10 speaks of [Πόλε]ϲ [Κροσ- σί]δος. Thucydides' Κρουσίς (II, 79, 4) is no doubt the same. Mygdonia began at the Axios and stretched east to the Strymon, according to Thucydides, II, 99, 4; more conservatively, he brings Mygdonia to Lake Bolbe (I, 58, 2) and so, no doubt, to Bormiskos (IV, 103, 1).

tionally name Kissos.[73] From the seaward end of Kissos to the Strymon we are back in what is, geographically, Makedonia: first the eastern coast of Mygdonia (see note 72 above) and then Bisaltia up to the Strymon (see note 47 above).

How far did Athens abstain from including cities on these coasts in her Confederacy? In Chalkidike (that is, from Poteidaia to Stageira) she did not abstain at all. But Chalkidike was not and had never been Makedonian; it was a peninsula, whose base was clearly divided from Makedonian territory by the Kissos range, except at the western end.[74] In Bisaltia Argilos was a fairly regular tributary to Athens and inland Berge less regular. Athens was of course always strongly posted on the Strymon, where Eion was a naval station (Thucydides, IV, 108, 1). It was not till A9 and A10 (425 and 421) that Bormiskos, at the outflow of Lake Bolbe, was assessed. There are, however, a number of cities,[75] whose position is unknown, which may have lain north of the Kissos range.

We come now to the Thermaic Gulf. The certain tributaries are not in the inner gulf. Dikaia (Ἐρετριῶν), after an assessment of 4 talents in Period I, pays 1 talent from Period II to the end of Period VII. The exact site of Dikaia is unknown, but it is close to the promontory of Cape Aineia which bounds the inner gulf. Aineia pays a tribute of 3 talents, quite steadily, throughout Periods I to VI. Strepsa pays 1 talent through the same period, and we believe that the reasons which led us to place it on the northern shore of the inner gulf are valid.[76] More dubious is our equation of Sermaioi with Therme, which we nevertheless retain.[77] Serme pays an insignificant amount compared with Strepsa, and if Strepsa be in Mygdonia (as we believe) there is no *a priori* reason why Serme should not also be. Nor, *a priori*, do we see any reason why Haison should not be located in Pieria, on the battlefield of

[73] We now use this name for the whole southern watershed of the Bolbe district; see Oberhummer, *s. v.* Kissos (2), in P. W., *R. E.*, and Edson, *op. cit.*, p. 89. Strictly, it is perhaps only the western part. Our interpretation of Lykophron, *Alexandra*, 1236-1237, in the Gazetteer, *s. v.* Αἰνειᾶται (*A. T. L.*, I, p. 465), criticized by Edson (*loc. cit.*), was incorrect.

[74] At the western end, between Anthemous and Bottike, the division was less clear. Anthemous was traditionally Makedonian; Herodotos, V, 94, 1; Thucydides, II, 99, 6; Demosthenes, VI, 20 (ἧς πάντες οἱ πρότερον Μακεδονίας βασιλεῖς ἀντεποιοῦντο).

[75] Especially the group Miltoros, Othoros, Pharbelos, Chedrolos. For their records (rather irregular) see above, pp. 61-63 and 80-88. If not in the Bolbe region they are perhaps to be placed in Bottike; they surely belong on one or other of the debatable Makedonian frontiers.

[76] See the Gazetteer, *s. v.* Στρεψαῖοι, in *A. T. L.*, I, pp. 550-551, and above, note 122 on p. 220. Edson, *Cl. Phil.*, XLII (1947), p. 105, note 125, asserts that Thucydides, I, 61, 4 cannot be used for the location of Strepsa, referring to Gomme, *Commentary*, I, pp. 215-218. We believe that ἐπὶ Στρέψαν is the true reading in that passage (see note 62 above); if so, its evidence must of course be considered.

[77] See above, note 123 on pp. 220-221. We note Herodotos' statement (VII, 128, 1) that the mountains of east Thessaly are visible from Therme.

Pydna.[78] Haison pays a small tribute and its strategic possibilities were evidently not exploited.

Therme and Haison, in fact, if we have rightly identified them, will be unexploited potentialities. That Athens did not yet advance into the Thermaic Gulf was, we believe, less out of deference to the king of Makedon than because it was a recess and lay off the main lines of traffic.[79] The true relative strengths of Athens and Makedon were perhaps seriously misconceived in the fifth century, but there can be no question that Athens was regarded, down to and after the founding of Amphipolis, as the vastly stronger power; the language of D3, which to readers of Demosthenes sounds ridiculous, will not have seemed ridiculous to contemporaries.[80]

In 434, Athens evidently felt prepared to exploit her position and to humiliate Perdikkas. It was probably then that she made alliance with the rebel princes Philip and Derdas; it was then, we believe, that she received Methone into her Confederacy, with a tribute of 3 talents. Perdikkas was expected not to move troops through Methone's territory without permission, and this was a serious matter if the rebel Derdas was operating in the south.[81] Already in 435/4, tribute had been collected from Berge north of Amphipolis and from the " Miltoros group," whether this be in Bisaltia or Bottike (see note 75 above). These were all assessed in 434, and at the same time Athens raised her demands in Bottike. From Spartolos, the capital of Bottike, she now took tribute of 3 talents, 500 drachmai instead of 2 talents, and small sums from Bottic cities not hitherto assessed (500 drachmai from Aioleion, 1000 from Pleume, 3000 from the five cities of the west coast, the cities of Krousis [πόλεις Κροσσίδος]). The total effect of this was approximately to double the tribute of Bottike, and very much to tighten Athens' hold on this stretch of the Thermaic Gulf between Poteidaia and Aineia. It is now, too, that Sinos is first assessed, for 1500 drachmai, a further reinforcement of Athens' position, probably in Bottike.[82]

Athens had seriously miscalculated her position, and Perdikkas was able to retaliate strongly. The battle of Sybota in September, 433, moved Korinth on to his side, and in 432 Korinth and Perdikkas together intrigued with disastrous results among Athens' northern allies.

---

[78] See the discussion above, pp. 218-220. We have no specific site in view, but (if anywhere near the battlefield) it will be a few miles south of Pydna and it will certainly be near the best road from central Makedonia southwards.

[79] We may compare the relatively empty area on the Thrakian coast between the Chersonese and Perinthos, or on the Asiatic coast between Kyzikos and Kalchedon. In appraising the latter we have to remember that the satrap's seat was quite close to Kyzikos (see the Gazetteer, s. v. Δασκύλειον ἐν Προποντίδι, in A. T. L., I, p. 480).

[80] D3, lines 27-29: " The envoys shall tell Perdikkas that if the troops at Poteidaia praise him he will earn Athenian regard."

[81] For the movement of troops see D3, lines 22-23. For Derdas in the south see note 70 above; Elimiotis is in the southern bend of the Haliakmon.

[82] See A. T. L., II, s. v. Σίνος, p. 87.

3. THE BREAKDOWN OF THE PEACE

The financial decrees of Kallias (D1 and D2) belong to the winter of 434/3. They came at the time they did because a fresh financial settlement was required with the expiration of the 15 years (449/8–435/4) which the Papyrus Decree (D13) had envisaged; but the instruction to collect the treasures of the temples of Attica into the Akropolis of Athens, and the general tone of economy, probably imply that Athens was facing the likelihood of war and making provision against a possible invasion.[83] It was only a few months later that the crisis over Kerkyra arose, virtually offering a choice between peace and war; Athens, by accepting Kerkyra's alliance, chose war. For just over twelve years Athens had abstained from affronting Korinth and had reaped the benefit in the Samian War (above, pp. 305 with note 20 and 307-308 with note 36). That phase was now ended.

It was probably Athens' reply to Kerkyra which led the western cities, Rhegion and Leontinoi, to seek for the revival of their treaties, which had been sworn some 15 years back as " perpetual," but had then been brought into desuetude by the Thirty Years' Peace. Since the Athenians were no longer concerned to reassure Korinth, they might be useful allies against Syracuse. Another consequence was the Akarnanian alliance. After the battle of Sybota in September, 433, Korinth and Kerkyra began to manoeuvre for position in the Ambrakiot Gulf, and Ambrakiots (Ambrakia was a loyal Korinthian colony) seized the town of Argos at the east end of the Gulf. These Argives, and their Akarnanian allies, appealed to Athens, who sent Phormion with 30 ships probably early in 432; he recovered Argos, sold the Ambrakiots as slaves, and concluded an alliance between Athens and Akarnania.[84]

In the spring of 432 Aigina made a payment of 9 or 14 talents instead of her usual 30 (22, I, 88). If the Thirty Years' Peace had protected Aigina in the way we have supposed (in note 11 above, namely, that she should be autonomous while paying a specified tribute), this partial payment exposed her perhaps to the action which Athens now took. We are not told exactly what this action was, only that later in the year Aigina complained privately at Sparta that her autonomy was being violated. Possibly Athens installed a garrison; strategic control of Aigina was vital in case of war.[85] Perikles' decree against Megara, similarly, had no doubt a strategic motive,

---

[83] See below, pp. 326-334.

[84] Thucydides, II, 68, 6-8. For the date see Wade-Gery, *J. H. S.*, LII (1932), p. 216, note 45. The strongest argument (not there mentioned) is that if such a decisive Athenian appearance against Korinth's allies in the west, and especially the selling into slavery of the Ambrakiots, had happened before 433, the Kerkyra crisis loses its critical quality; the careful argumentation of both parties in Thucydides, I, 32-43 and the circumspect behaviour of Korinthians and Athenians in I, 53 become meaningless.

[85] Accordingly, in 431, when war was certain, Athens took the more thorough step of colonizing the island; Thucydides, II, 27.

namely, the desire for a defensible frontier,[86] and belongs likewise to 432.[87] The pressure on Megara, though maintained until 424 (Thucydides, II, 31 and IV, 66-74), failed of its objective; Athens never acquired her strategic frontier, Attica always lay open to invasion, Peloponnese and Boiotia always retained their land communications. Here, then, in the skirmishing of 432, Athens was less successful than in Akarnania; but her outstanding failure was in the north, where Korinth won an ample revenge.

In the north, Poteidaia was a loyal Korinthian colony, but had been tributary to Athens since 446/5. Before that, we imagine, she had been a ship-providing ally. We hear of no trouble, even during the First Peloponnesian War, though there is possibly an allusion to such trouble in the *Eumenides* of Aischylos, played in 458, soon after the outbreak of that war.[88] But in 434 Athens raised Poteidaia's tribute from 6 talents to 15; it is indeed possible that this increase began in 436/5.[89] After the breach with Korinth (probably in the winter of 433/2) Athens ordered the Poteidaians to pull down their walls and break off their connection with Korinth. Poteidaia refused.

[86] See above, notes 7, 8, 15. Gomme, *Commentary*, I, p. 448: " possession of the Megarid meant for Athens comparative security from Peloponnesian invasions " (quoting Thucydides, I, 107, 3).

[87] For the date of Perikles' decree (Aristophanes, *Acharnians*, 530-534; Plutarch, *Pericles*, 30, 2-3, cf. 8, 7; [Lysias], VI, 10 and 54) see Gomme, *Commentary*, I, pp. 447-448 (with references to Busolt, Bonner, Miltner, and Adcock). It is possible that there had been some action against Megara at the time of the Samian War (Gomme, *loc. cit.*) but Perikles' decree no doubt belongs to 432. Gomme writes (p. 466) of " the mutual suspicions caused by the Megarian question " as having been mentioned in the Korinthian's speech in 433; but is not this ὑπάρχουσα πρότερον διὰ Μεγαρέας ὑποψία (I, 42, 2) a polite synonym for what Thucydides calls in his own person τὸ σφοδρὸν μῖσος (I, 103, 4)? There is a real parallel, as the Korinthian here implies, between the action which Athens took in 461/0 regarding Megara and the action which she now has a chance of declining to take regarding Kerkyra.

[88] Thucydides (I, 103, 4) dates the " intense hatred " of Korinth for Athens to the winter of 461/0. Aischylos in the *Eumenides* alludes clearly to the war, especially in the curse which Orestes lays upon any Peloponnesian army which marches against Attica; lines 762-774, especially 767-771 (for Orestes' relation to the Peloponnesian League see Herodotos, I, 67-68 and VII, 159). An allusion to the campaign in Egypt is often detected in lines 292-295 (T5). Such allusions are not uncommon (cf. Euripides, *Electra*, 1347-1348); in the *Eumenides* the allusion probably requires the deletion of line 293, but the words φίλοις ἀρήγουσα in 295 very strongly point to it. If lines 292-295 do refer to the fighting in Egypt, then very possibly lines 295-296,

εἴτε Φλεγραίαν πλάκα
θρασὺς ταγοῦχος ὡς ἀνὴρ ἐπισκοπεῖ,

will refer to some sort of trouble in Pallene, and this would surely mean Poteidaia. It is not impossible that Poteidaia remained recalcitrant till Kimon made his Five Years' Truce in 451.

[89] Or even with the assessment of 438. See above, pp. 64-65, for the suggestion that in 435/4 the quotas of Poteidaia and Skione have been mistakenly inverted by the stonecutter. If so, Poteidaia paid 15 talents in 435/4 and probably in 436/5, where the figure is lost. No list is extant for 437/6, and List 17 (438/7) is blank for the Thrakian district (cf. note 55 above). But here, as in the case of Berge and the " Miltoros group," we are more inclined to associate the change with the founding of Amphipolis than with the assessment of 438. For our immediate purpose we must note that, whether or not we presume the figures have been inverted, there was a surprising increase in tribute somewhere in Pallene at some time in Period V.

With active support from both Perdikkas and Korinth she revolted and prepared for siege; and many others of Athens' northern allies joined her. Perdikkas encouraged them to concentrate. He gave them land in his own territory of Mygdonia, round Lake Bolbe; with this compensation, he invited them to leave their coastal sites and make their political centre at Olynthos.[90]

This was all in 432; we can see the results in List 23 (432/1), which has the Thrakian panel complete. The absentees include Argilos, Assera, Mekyberna, Olynthos, Phegetos, Poteidaia, Sermylia, Singos, Skabala, Skapsa, Spartolos, Stolos, Strepsa. The rubrics are not quite complete, but certainly most of the " Miltoros group " is absent, and Aioleion, Gale, Kleonai, Pleume; perhaps also Piloros, Pistasos, and the cities of Krousis. This was the situation which called for the action described by Thucydides (I, 57, 6; 59; 61). We have already analysed this narrative in our geographical enquiry (above, pp. 313-319); we may now resume it, with our geographical conclusions.

Athens' original plan for the season's campaign had been to encourage the civil war in Makedonia by helping the rebel princes. Perdikkas' counter-action created a second front, and the Athenian commanders were at first uncertain which to attack. Archestratos decided to concentrate on Makedonia; he captured Therme, and consequently the Sermaioi are found paying their tribute next spring (23, II, 57).[91] No doubt he thought it vital to give Methone support; Methone too pays next spring (23, II, 67), the only time when she is known[92] to have paid her tribute in full. But his decision enabled Korinth to get reinforcements into Poteidaia, and, when Kallias superseded him, the decision was reversed. Kallias abandoned the Makedonian campaign and conveyed his forces to Poteidaia.

He was accompanied by 600 cavalry provided by Philip and Pausanias (Thucydides, I, 61, 4). Philip was one of the two rebel princes, and Pausanias was very probably brother to the second rebel, Derdas.[93] The pay for these 600 is recorded as a charge on the Athenians from the 14th day of (probably) Prytany VIII, 432/1, that is, the end of February, 431 (I. G., I², 296, lines 19-21, as in Meritt, A. F. D., pp. 80-81). Exactly what this means is uncertain,[94] but it certainly does not mean that this Makedonian cavalry did not join the Athenians until February, 431. It can hardly be doubted that they had collaborated in the sieges of Therme and Pydna.

---

[90] Thucydides, I, 56-58.

[91] This sequence, the capture of Therme and the immediate payment by the Sermaioi, perhaps strengthens our case for the identification of Therme and Serme; see above, note 123 on pp. 220-221.

[92] The case is not quite certain; see above, pp. 133-137.

[93] I. e., he is the [Παυ]σανίας Μαχέτο of I. G., I², 71, line 93; see note 70 above.

[94] It may be that Athens had paid all along, but only now records it as a special item, or it may be that for some reason Philip and Pausanias began in February to ask for the pay; cf. the shifting arrangement between Perdikkas and Brasidas (Thucydides, IV, 83, 6).

If so, Kallias must almost certainly have moved from Pydna to Poteidaia by land;[95] this would mean marching westward to Beroia (note 62 above) and then around the north shore of the gulf. On their march the Athenians attempted to storm Strepsa, but failed. From Strepsa to Gigonos they advanced by easy stages, arriving at Gigonos on the third day. If they marched ten miles a day, Strepsa must have been well inside the inner gulf; Aischines' account of an invasion of Makedonia in which " Anthemous and Therme and Strepsa " are captured (in that order?) suggests that it was on the north coast.[96]

The siege of Poteidaia lasted over two years and cost over 2000 talents.[97] This diversion of money and energy perhaps did nearly as much as the great plague to upset Perikles' calculations and falsify his hopes of victory. The position in Chalkidike was never restored; instead, Brasidas exploited Sparta's advantage. Sparta was indeed prepared to sacrifice these allies in the Peace of Nikias, but by then they were able to look after themselves. We conclude this chapter with a brief survey of Athens' further relations with Perdikkas.

The second alliance between Athens and Perdikkas was the " forced alliance " of 432. This saved Pydna for Perdikkas and for the Athenians assured the safe march of their forces from Pydna to Poteidaia. It did no more; the rebels were not disarmed, Perdikkas did not recover Therme or Methone,[98] and at the battle of Poteidaia late in 432 Perdikkas fought against the Athenians. In 431 Nymphodoros reconciled him to Athens; he recovered Therme[99] and helped Athens against Chalkidike (II, 29, 6). This third alliance lasted nominally till 424; the failure of the Spartan invasion of Akarnania in 429, to which Perdikkas had sent a contingent (II, 80, 7), warned him not to break openly with Athens. But his hostility was hardly veiled, and three loyal Athenian allies who were near to his country, Methone, Dikaia, and Haison, evidently suffered severely and in compensation their tribute was reduced to a merely nominal figure.[100] We hear of several embassies from Athens to Makedon between 430 and 425 in D3 and D4. The great Thrakian invasion of 429 with its

[95] Gomme, *Commentary*, I, p. 217: " they went by sea the shortest way to Chalkidike, landing probably near or at the town of Aineia which had not revolted." The cavalry would make this impossible. Gomme's view is perhaps due to his understanding of ἀπανίστανται in I, 61, 3, for which see note 62 above. The march was certainly slow (I, 61, 5, κατ' ὀλίγον δὲ προϊόντες) and Gomme rightly observes that κατήπειγεν in 61, 3 does not contradict this; the decision to march on Poteidaia could not be delayed, but there was no need to arrive with tired troops.

[96] Aischines, II, 27. The only alternative to the inner gulf is that Strepsa was the most important town on the Bottic coast, and that the stages from Strepsa to Gigonos were of five miles or less a day.

[97] Thucydides, II, 70, 2 (T120), says 2000 talents; Isokrates, XV, 113 (T82b), gives 2400.

[98] Thucydides, I, 61, 4, speaks of the rebel princes' cavalry. Therme was restored later (II, 29, 6); the Methone decrees (D3-D6) run from 430 to 423.

[99] Consequently the Sermaioi probably pay no tribute till 421.

[100] See D3 and the ἀπαρχήν rubric (*A. T. L.*, I, p. 450).

evident Athenian backing proved useless as a threat and must have forfeited his good-will. In 425, however, Athens felt secure; the Thrakian panel in A9 is very poorly preserved, but we may note three phenomena.

First, the three cities Singos, Mekyberna, and Gale are assessed for 10 drachmai each. These cities are evidently those which Thoudippos had in view in the clause which grants leniency to cities whose land has become incapable of paying (A9, lines 21-22). These are the peoples who had accepted Perdikkas' offer in 432 and pulled down their own cities and migrated inland (Thucydides, I, 58, 2); the tribute of 10 drachmai is levied on the remnant which had stayed behind. The peoples of these cities are ordered, in the Peace of Nikias, to return to their cities and then pay the Aristeidean tribute.[101] They probably did not obey, since in A10 the same low assessment is repeated (A10, V, 22-24) and in the winter of 421/0 Mekyberna was captured by the rebels (Thucydides, V, 39, 1).

Second, new tributaries are added in Makedonian territory: Bormiskos (on the east coast of Mygdonia) is assessed 1000 drachmai, Trailos (Tragilos, inland in Bisaltia) 1 talent, Herakleion (in Pieria) 1000 drachmai. In spite of Brasidas' successes in 424 and 423, all these are found again in A10 (421).[102] The strategic importance of Herakleion is explained by Edson.[103] " The fortress rests on a steep bluff, which falls away abruptly to the sea. It completely dominates the important route from the Vale of Tempe into Pieria along the coast. Both to the north and to the south of the citadel are open beaches on which triremes could land. An Athenian seizure of Herakleion by a *coup de main* would have been perfectly feasible. The possession of Herakleion would enable the Athenians to control the more important of the two chief routes from Macedonia south into Thessaly." Herakleion was added to the Athenian Confederacy whilst Athens and Perdikkas were in nominal alliance, but the alliance was so nominal that such a *coup de main* is not out of the question. We observe, however, that Herakleion was assessed in 425, and in 424 Brasidas was able to get from Thessaly to Dion (just north of Herakleion) apparently without fighting; on the other hand, his force was too large simply to have escaped notice.[104] It looks as if the Athenians did not fortify Herakleion; it, like Haison earlier, was an unexploited potentiality. The only attempt to exploit such positions of which we can be sure is at Methone in 430 (D3, lines 22-23).

Third, there is perhaps a tendency for Athens to compensate herself for the many

---

[101] Thucydides, V, 18, 5-6 (T134); for the corrections in this text see above, pp. 90-91.

[102] A9, IV, 108-113; A10, V, 21-26. The six names comprise the two categories discussed in the text: (1) Singos, Mekyberna, Gale, and (2) Herakleion, Trailos, and Bormiskos. It must be noted that the names in A9 are all restored from the identical sequence in A10; the figures alone are extant in A9 but are sufficiently remarkable to justify the restorations.

[103] *Cl. Phil.*, XLII (1947), p. 97.

[104] Thucydides, IV, 78, 6.

defections by taking increased tribute from the loyal cities. The only clear example of this is at Torone,[105] whose tribute rises from 6 talents to 12 in 430, and is increased again to 15 or more in 425 (A9, III, 160). This is not comparable to the huge increases further east (especially at Abdera, as shown in Figure 4 on p. 312), but it no doubt helped to prepare the way for Brasidas in the following year.

This third alliance between Perdikkas and Athens was openly broken when Brasidas appeared in the north in 424. Perdikkas was not an easy man to deal with, and that Athens' difficulties with him were not wholly her fault is shown by Brasidas' troubles. Perdikkas was concerned to use Brasidas' magnificent troops for the purpose of coercing the rebel Arrhabaios. The first campaign Brasidas settled by parley (Thucydides, IV, 83); on the second Perdikkas and Brasidas openly quarrelled, and henceforth Perdikkas began intriguing once more with Athens (IV, 128, 5 and 132, 1). The fourth alliance was made in 423 and Perdikkas' first action as ally was to use his influence in Thessaly to stop Brasidas' reinforcements (IV, 132). In 422 Kleon called on him for troops (V, 6, 2), and this fourth alliance lasted till 417. In the winter of 418/7 Argos made alliance with Sparta and Perdikkas was invited to join (V, 80, 2; cf. 79, 2 and 4). Moved (it is said) by his presumed Argive descent, Perdikkas agreed, and in 417 refused help to Nikias in an attempt on Amphipolis; accordingly, in the winter of 417/6 the Athenians subjected him to blockade (V, 83, 4), and a year later (winter 416/5) an invasion of Makedonia, in conjunction with Makedonian exiles, was launched from Methone. The Greeks of Chalkidike stayed neutral (VI, 7, 3-4). This apparently brought Perdikkas to terms, for at the very end of his life, in 414, we find him supporting the Athenian Euetion in an attack on Amphipolis (VII, 9); this is the fifth alliance between Perdikkas and Athens.

In the next year Perdikkas died and Athens' power was broken in Sicily. Archelaos, Perdikkas' son, is stated by the author of the περὶ πολιτείας (19) to have remained neutral, but there is evidence that he and Athens collaborated a certain amount. Athens was no longer dangerous, and Athenians were useful to Archelaos for his policy of Hellenization. It is interesting to find among his earliest Athenian friends Theramenes, the son of the founder of Amphipolis, who helped him recover Pydna in 410. Archelaos' chief service to Athens was to supply her with timber for naval construction.[106]

---

[105] We have no figures in A9 for Akanthos, Mende, Sermylia, Skione. Skione, like Torone, was raised in 430. For Skione's figure in 435/4 (20, VI, 6) see above, pp. 64-65.

[106] I. G., I², 105; Tod, Greek Hist. Inscr., I², no. 91; Meritt, Capps Studies, pp. 246-252 (improved text on pp. 249-250). This is the Attic decree in honor of Archelaos, moved (perhaps by Alkibiades) in 407 B.C. For Theramenes at Pydna see Diodoros, XIII, 49, 1-2. For Andokides' services in obtaining timber from Archelaos see Andokides, II, 11; cf. above, p. 136.

CHAPTER X

THE RESERVE FUND TO 421 B. C.

I

The two financial decrees of Kallias (D1 and D2) are now known to have been passed by the Athenian Demos on the same day.[1] There have been those who held that D2 was earlier than D1, but the traditional opinion for many years was that D1 must have been the earlier because (*inter alia*) a sum which is named without specification of its amount in D1 (lines 4-7) for the payment of debts to the gods appears in D2 (lines 22-23) as fixed definitely at 200 talents. A third decree, even, has been assumed, intervening between D1 and D2, in which the Demos is supposed to have set the figure at 200 talents.

Such views are no longer tenable. Kallias, the orator, must have drafted both decrees in their probouleumatic form with full knowledge when he composed the one of what was contained in the other. It follows from this that Kallias knew (in D1) that the money which had been voted for payment to the gods from a fund described as " the sum now in the chest of the hellenotamiai and the other moneys of the same fund, including the proceeds of the dekate when it is farmed out "[2] amounted to 200 talents, and also that the 200 talents (in D2) voted for payment to the Other Gods were made up from the fund described in D1.[3]

The funds voted for repayment (ἐς ἀπόδοσιν) in D1, line 5, and in D2, line 22, were in fact identical, and the vote alluded to in D1 must have been the same as the vote alluded to in D2. It is of importance to note that this vote must have preceded, in point of time, both the preserved decrees of Kallias.

Inasmuch as the hellenotamiai, and they alone, are named as the paymasters of the repayment (ἀπόδοσις) in D2, line 21, it follows that they controlled the sums described in D1, lines 6-7, as the source of the payments, including the tithe (dekate).

---

[1] Wade-Gery, *J. H. S.*, LI (1931), pp. 58-62. For general background on the financial history of Athens see principally Meyer, *Forschungen*, II, pp. 88-148 (the results of this study are utilized in Meyer's *Gesch. d. Alterthums*); Cavaignac, *Études*; Beloch, *Gr. Gesch.*, II, 2², pp. 324-371. The brief chapter in Glotz-Cohen, *Histoire grecque*, II, pp. 367-393, has little to offer.

[2] Lines 6-7: τά τε παρὰ τοῖς ἑλλενοταμίαις ὄντα νῦν καὶ τἄλλα ἅ ἐστι τούτον [τὸ]ν χρεμάτον, καὶ τὰ ἐκ τῆς δεκάτες ἐπειδὰν πραθέι.

[3] Kallias, even within D1, must have known of a fixed limit, else his provision (lines 30-32) that the " balance " should be used for the walls and shipyards would have known no bounds: ἐπειδὰν δὲ ἀποδεδομένα ἐι τοῖς θεοῖς [τὰ χρ]έματα, ἐς τὸ νεόριον καὶ τὰ τείχε τοῖς περιῶσι χρέσθαι χρέμασ[ιν ---]. Kahrstedt, *Gött. gel. Anz.*, 1939, pp. 411-412, thought of D2 as earlier than D1, with the fund described in D1 as a kind of supplement or amplification of that in D2.

This is the first tangible evidence for the fact that the hellenotamiai had at their disposal, at least as early as 434, funds other than the phoros.[4]

Furthermore, since the completion of the transfer of 3000 talents to Athena was made the condition for putting into effect the decree authorizing 200 talents, already voted, to be used for the Other Gods, it follows that the 3000 talents must have come also from this source. At the time when the vote for repayment was taken Athena had already been given prior claim against the hellenotamiai in the amount of the 3000 talents. The question arises immediately, when, before 434, or in what period of years down to 434, the hellenotamiai could have had a surplus that ran so high. They were without funds in midsummer of 449, for the most probable interpretation of the decree of Perikles in that year (the Papyrus Decree, D13) is that the Athenians transferred to Athena 5000 talents lying in the old treasury of the Confederacy for use on their newly projected scheme of public building,[5] leaving only enough in the reserve to cover the current expenses of 449/8.[6] In 441/0 also the hellenotamiai apparently had no available funds, for in those years Athena Polias alone paid the entire cost of the Samian War.[7] Evidently the hellenotamiai had accumulated no disposable reserve between 448 and 440 to enable them to make a payment toward the war against Samos, and likewise no disposable reserve between 440 and 434 to make possible a liquidation of the debt to the Other Gods before that time.

This means that from 448 to 434 the hellenotamiai had no reserves, though the evidence of D13 is that between 477 and 449 they had built up reserves of 5000 talents. The explanation of this seeming paradox lies in the decrees of Kallias: from 448 the estimated reserves, at the rate of 200 talents a year, were being contributed systematically to the chest of the treasurers of Athena. Hence this third decree, which manifests itself in both the decrees of Kallias, must be dated earlier than 448. The first 3000 talents were to go to Athena, and when that amount had been put on the

---

[4] This problem has been much discussed. See Nesselhauf, *Klio*, Beiheft XXX, pp. 117-120, with references to Ravà, Busolt, Beloch, and West. See also below, p. 334.

[5] [−− ἐπ' Εὐ]θυδήμο[υ] Περικλέους γνώμη[ν] εἰσ[ηγησαμένου 'Αθηναίους κινεῖν] τὰ ἐν δημοσί⟨ω⟩ι ἀπο-κείμενα τάλαν[τα τὰ ἐκ τῶν φόρων συνηγμένα] πεντακισχείλια κατὰ τὴν 'Αριστεί[δου τάξιν]. See above, p. 281.

[6] See above, p. 281.

[7] *I. G.*, I², 293; cf. Meritt, *A. F. D.*, pp. 42-48, and *A. J. P.*, LV (1934), pp. 365-366; see note 12 below. The cost of the Samian War was 1276 + talents. Cavaignac, *Études*, p. 95, suggested that an initial payment of 200 talents was exacted, and in this way he attempted to explain the figure 200 given by Diodoros (XII, 28, 3 [T56]) as the cost of the war. Our preference is to regard the figure διακοσίων in Diodoros as a corruption of χιλίων καὶ διακοσίων (cf. Beloch, *Gr. Gesch.*, II, 2², p. 337). Cavaignac (*loc. cit.*) thought the subsequent annuities were of 80 talents, and he thus sought to utilize Diodoros, XII, 27. There is no justification for this, but Cavaignac observed quite rightly that Samos was not free of its obligation before 426 (cf. D8, lines 21-24). Neither was she free before 414, and a smaller annual payment, which we have estimated at 50 talents, must be assumed (see below, pp. 334-335).

Akropolis (there is no mention here of paying a debt; the money is a grant)[8] an additional 200 talents, evidently the surplus of the next following year, was to be used for the Other Gods. It is an economical interpretation of the evidence to assume that this decree is, in fact, the Papyrus Decree (D13), moved by Perikles in 449, in which the initial grant of 5000 talents was voted out of past reserves. But this was only one of the financial clauses, dealing with the past; presumably the 5000 talents were to be given to Athena on her birthday, only a short time hence, at the Panathenaia of 449. The second clause provided that thereafter a sum of 200 talents should be taken up to the Akropolis at every succeeding Panathenaic festival until an additional total of 3000 talents had been reached. After this, the accumulating 200 talents were to be used to pay debts to the Other Gods.[9]

This rate of pay seems to have been determined on the basis of past experience. If, in the approximately twenty-five years that had intervened between 477 and 449, a surplus of more than 5000 talents had been gathered, the budgeting could be done on the basis of an annual surplus income of 200 talents. At any rate, this was the scale set and evidently adhered to down through the 'forties and 'thirties (for 15 years) until the gift of 3000 talents to Athena had been consummated. The year 434/3 was to see the final payment of 200 talents made to the Other Gods.

The Athenians were careful to protect this annual grant of 200 talents to Athena out of the money which was derived from the tribute. We have included in *A. T. L.*, II a decree from the mid 'thirties about the building of a springhouse, because its last lines specify not only the use of current tribute but also give the restriction to which this use was liable (D19). The family of Perikles, in a magnanimous gesture, had evidently offered to bear the expense of the building, but the Athenian state voted to decline the offer with thanks, and to meet the cost out of the phoros, " when the accustomed amount had been given to the Goddess." [10] It is not enough to suppose that this refers to the aparche alone, for the payment of the aparche (barely more than 6 talents) could hardly have jeopardized the building programme or have been jeopardized by it.[11] The text becomes intelligible when one understands that the " accustomed amount " ($\tau\grave{a}$ $\nu o\mu\iota\zeta\acute{o}\mu\epsilon\nu a$) must mean not only the sixtieth, but also the annual grant of 200 talents a year voted in 449 and payable down to 434. The present tense of the verb ($[\lambda a\mu]\beta\acute{a}\nu\epsilon\iota$) implies that the building operation would be in progress at least more than one year, and that the restriction must hold for more than one year. This adds weight to the determination already made that the grant of 200 talents was recurrent down through the period preceding 434.

---

[8] Meyer, *Forschungen*, II, pp. 104-106, conceives an annual grant of 300 talents a year. Beloch's argument (*Gr. Gesch.*, II, 2², p. 346) that the 3000 talents were in repayment of a debt is not convincing.

[9] The payment in 448 must have been made from the balance of the surplus. See above, p. 281.

[10] Lines 15-16: [$\grave{\epsilon}\pi\epsilon\iota\delta\grave{a}\nu$ $\mathring{\eta}$ $\theta\epsilon\grave{o}s$ $\grave{\epsilon}\chi s$ $a\mathring{v}\tau\acute{o}\nu$ $\lambda a\mu$]$\beta\acute{a}\nu\epsilon\iota$ $\tau\grave{a}$ $\nu o\mu\iota\zeta\acute{o}\mu\epsilon\nu a$.

[11] See Meritt, *D. A. T.*, pp. 18-19; Accame, *Riv. di Fil.*, LXVI (1938), pp. 409-410.

Now it becomes clear why the payments made by the treasurers of Athena for the Samian War were not regarded as loans. Inasmuch as the estimated available surplus was being drained away each year from the chest of the hellenotamiai to fund a grant to Athena, there was no expectation that the hellenotamiai would have to pay for emergency wars, like Samos, Euboia, and (?) Kerkyra. Samos and Euboia were affairs *par excellence* for the Empire, and the fact that Athena paid for them without considering the payments loans proves first that the hellenotamiai had no money and second that they had given their surplus which might have kept them in funds to Athena. Athena bore the burden in emergencies, and she did so because it was the price she had to pay for receiving this annual donation of 200 talents from the hellenotamiai.

With Kerkyra the affair was different. The hellenotamiai still had no money, for during the year 434/3 they had deposited 200 talents with the treasurers of the Goddess (over and above normal operating costs) and any balance from the 200 talents, if there was one, had been used on the walls and shipyards. But presumably there was to be no grant to Athena, or to the Other Gods, in 433/2. The hellenotamiai were expected to pay for all the wars of the Empire, emergency fighting as well as routine patrolling, and any contribution from Athena or the Other Gods after 433 would count as a loan.

It is a striking confirmation of the relationship between the sacred funds and the imperial funds as outlined above that the records of state borrowings from the sacred treasuries do in fact begin in 433.[12]

It is also a confirmation of the idea of routine expenditures, over and above the annual grant to Athena, to find in the building accounts of the Propylaia specific references to them. Several of the items of receipts which came in to the overseers of the building must be interpreted anew. The texts appear in *I. G.*, I², 365, 366, and 367 as follows:

I. G., I², 365, lines 13-16 (435/4 B. C.)

```
------ας τês με[γ]άλ[ες]
[παρὰ hελλενοτ]αμιôν ἀπὸ σ[τρατ]ιâς
[τιμὲ ...ʼ....]τεο: παρὰ Δεμ[ο]χάρος
.........¹²..... ασίππο Φλυέος.
```

---

[12] Cavaignac, *Études*, p. 92, conceives that the imperial funds had been merged with the funds of Athena at least as early as 440. He is quite right in his observation that the Samian War ought to have been financed by the hellenotamiai if they had had the funds for it in their reserve. They had no reserve, because in each year they gave Athena 200 talents and spent the rest. But this does not mean that the imperial funds were merged with the sacred funds. The borrowings of *I. G.*, I², 324, among other things, prove the contrary; see below, pp. 341-344, and also Beloch, *Gr. Gesch.*, II, 2², pp. 329 and 332, where the fact that Athena paid for the Samian War and the expedition to Kerkyra is taken as evidence that there was no imperial reserve in the time of Perikles.

I. G., I², 366, lines 16-17 (434/3 B. C.)

[παρὰ ℎελλενοταμιον ἀ]πὸ στρατιᾶς τι[μέ]

— — — — — — — σίππο 'Αγρυλέθε[ν]

I. G., I², 367, lines 4-5 (433/2 B. C.)

παρὰ ℎελλε[νοταμιον — —]

μεταρχεν — —

Woodward made the very acute observation that these entries are of the same type and that they complement each other in restoration. If the first line of all is read [ἀπὸ τες στρατι]ᾶς τες με[τ]ὰ Γ — — —,[13] a formula is established by which a campaign, or expedition, is described as " the one with so-and-so," presumably giving the name of a general. In the line in question the name of the general may be restored as Γ[λαύκονος], which is not too long to be accommodated in the space before the right edge of the stone and the beginning of a new rubric. Nor is there any reason to believe that Glaukon was not general in 435/4; he is known to have been general in 439/8 and again in 433/2, both times with Perikles.[14] There is now some indication that Glaukon was with Perikles again in the generalship in 435/4.

The next item, also from 435/4, may be restored in part with the same formula and with the name of another general: ἀπὸ σ[τρατ]ιᾶς: [τες μετὰ Προ]τέο.[15] So far Proteas has made his first appearance as a general in 433/2 (*I. G.*, I², 295),[16] but there is no reason why he may not have served also two years earlier. He represents the phyle of Kekropis (VII) and alternates with Xenophon, who served both before him (439/8) and after him (430/29).

The item which appears in *I. G.*, I², 366 must now be read [ἀ]πὸ στρατιᾶς τ⟨έ⟩[ς μετὰ ..^ca.6.. παρὰ .^ca.4.]σίππο 'Αγρυλέθε[ν]. The name of the general is lost.[17]

---

[13] " From the army with G — — —." The sloping stroke of the last letter, still preserved and visible on squeeze and photograph, belongs almost certainly to an Attic gamma. It is not shown in the majuscule copy in *I. G.*, I, Suppl., p. 77, no. 331*d*; Hiller, in *I. G.*, I², 365, interprets it as a doubtful lambda. See also note 18 below.

[14] Cf. Meritt, *A. F. D.*, p. 49 (439/8), and *I. G.*, I², 295 (433/2). See Ehrenberg, *A. J. P.*, LXVI (1945), pp. 130 and 133.

[15] " From the army with Proteas."

[16] See Ehrenberg, *A. J. P.*, LXVI (1945), p. 133. The tribal affiliation of Proteas is erroneously shown (on pp. 133 and 134) for 432/1 and 431/0 as VI; the numeral should be VII.

[17] The letter at the end of line 16 looks like iota, rather than epsilon (*i. e.*, Attic eta). Hence we suggest that by error either ΤΙϹ or ΤΗϹ was cut instead of ΤΕϹ. Dinsmoor assures us (by letter) that his reading of the stone left no doubt that the final letter is iota, and he confirms a judgment which he published in *A. J. A.*, XVII (1913), p. 397: " ἀ or λι]ΓΟϹΤΡΑΤΙΑϹΓ, Kirchhoff; the last letter, Γ, is certainly to be read ΤΙ, and I can only suggest that the somewhat inappropriate word τιμέ was written here by mistake; it does not appear in the similar entry in Column II." Bannier's attempt to explain τι[μέ] as necessary to the text (*B. ph. Woch.*, XXXV [1915], p. 543) is quite unconvincing: " Mir scheint aber τι als Rest von τιμή ganz richtig und die Fassung des

In *I. G.*, I², 367, the reading should be παρὰ ℎελλε[νοταμιõν ἀπὸ στρατιᾶς τε͂ς] μετ' Ἀρχενα[ύτο — — — — — — —].¹⁸ At last there is an explanation, in keeping with the formula, for the enigmatic letters μεταρχεν. After the nu the stone shows part of the left bar of the letter alpha. The name of this general is so far unknown, but there is room for him in the list of generals of 433/2. It will have been observed that these receipts of money came once directly from the army (*I. G.*, I², 365, line 13), presumably having been handed over by Glaukon to the overseers. But the usual procedure was for the general to hand back his unspent funds to the hellenotamiai and for the hellenotamiai—one or more delegated members of the college, at least— to transfer the money to the overseers. The opening words παρὰ ℎελλενοταμιõν connote this normal procedure; the concluding words (παρά with names and demotics) designate the individuals who managed the transaction.

Thus the records show the names of two of the board of hellenotamiai in 435/4 (παρὰ Δεμ[ο]χάρος [—*ca.* ¹⁰———]ασίππο Φλυέος) and one member in 434/3 ([παρὰ —*ca.* ⁴—]σίππο Ἀγρυλε͂θε[ν]). These are new names, but they do not conflict with those already known from the two years in question.¹⁹

Perhaps most important of all is the new evidence for four routine expeditions, financed from the funds of the Empire, about which there is no information, at least no direct information, in the literary or the epigraphic tradition. Here we see the normal business of managing an empire, and this is the service for which the hellenotamiai paid out of imperial funds. There are no records of any accounting for these funds. They amounted to the annual revenue of the hellenotamiai (φόρος and other) after the commitments of 200 talents had been set aside in 435/4 and 434/3, possibly to the entire revenue in 433/2. Moreover, it is now clear that the balances left on hand from these grants to the generals did not revert to form an imperial surplus.²⁰

Satzes tadellos zu sein. Ich verstehe unter dem Posten eine Summe, welche von den Hellenotamien der Baukommission aus dem Erlös eines Verkaufs an Demochares oder -ippos überwiesen worden ist. Eine genauere Bezeichnung dieses Objektes, von welchem noch ἀπὸ στρατιᾶς τιμὴ ...έου (-είου) übrig ist, kann ich allerdings nicht geben." The word τιμέ has here been injected into the text of *I. G.*, I², 365 (as well as 366) where, as Dinsmoor noted, it does not appear, and where it does not belong. Possibly the error is to be explained by assuming that the stonecutter wrote τιᾶς twice at the end of *I. G.*, I², 366, line 16, but we have preferred to look upon the iota as an unfinished E. Such instances are on record, as, for example, in A9, II, 149 (Π⟨ε⟩δ⟨α⟩σε͂ς) and in D3, line 26 (διαφ⟨έ⟩ρονται).

¹⁸ " From the hellenotamiai, from the army with Archenautes." The three revised texts have been printed by us in *A. T. L.*, II as T72d, T72e, and T72f. For the sake of alignment at the left we now believe that line 13 of T72d should be read as [ἀπὸ τε͂ς στρατι]ᾶς τε͂ς με[τ]ὰ Γ[λαύκονος].

¹⁹ Cf. *A. T. L.*, I, p. 568; II, p. 125.

²⁰ The alternative to the assumption that the hellenotamiai gave Athena 200 talents a year from 449 to 435 and then spent the surplus (cf. above, pp. 327-329) is the assumption that they spent whatever they needed to spend on the Empire and then gave Athena the balance (cf. Meritt, *The Greek Political Experience*, p. 56). If balances, and not a fixed sum, had been given to Athena, one

They were utilized on the buildings of Athens (the Propylaia) just as the surplus from the 200 talents committed to the Other Gods in 434/3 was so used (walls and shipyards).

In every year the authorities could find many ways of using these apparent surpluses, and it must be recognized that there was a policy of so doing. For the hellenotamiai, this meant of course that from 448 to 433 they spent all they received and never, in any year, had any reserve. There is no evidence that a decision was again taken in 433 to make annual grants to the Goddess, and the financial history of the Peloponnesian War is best explained if no such grants are assumed. Thucydides (II, 13) gives the state of Athenian public finance in 431, but the critical year is 433. Then the hellenotamiai ceased to give money to Athena and the Other Gods; funds paid out by Athena and the Other Gods began to count as loans when used for purposes of war. If the hellenotamiai accumulated a reserve in 433/2 it was probably small; they could hardly have accumulated anything after the outbreak of the war with Poteidaia and Makedonia in 432. It follows, therefore, that the reserve funds which Thucydides describes as available in 431 belonged mostly to the sacred treasuries, very little to the hellenotamiai. But this reserve fund is only one of the resources which Perikles mentioned to cheer the Athenians in 431. He named others, the entire roster being as follows, with the items in the following order: [21]

1. An annual revenue of 600 talents a year, by and large, of tribute from the allies, not counting other revenue.

2. A reserve of 5700 talents of minted silver.

3. Public and private dedications, sacred paraphernalia, the Persian spoils, and such like: not less than 500 talents.

4. No little wealth from the other sanctuaries.

5. The gold from the statue (40 talents of refined gold).

It has been thought by some [22] that the borrowings from the Other Gods during

would expect to find these grants from the hellenotamiai to the overseers of the Propylaia passing through the hands of the treasurers of Athena.

[21] Thucydides, II, 13, 3-5 (T117): θαρσεῖν τε ἐκέλευε προσιόντων μὲν ἑξακοσίων ταλάντων ὡς ἐπὶ τὸ πολὺ φόρου κατ᾽ ἐνιαυτὸν ἀπὸ τῶν ξυμμάχων τῇ πόλει ἄνευ τῆς ἄλλης προσόδου, ὑπαρχόντων δὲ ἐν τῇ ἀκροπόλει αἰεί ποτε ἀργυρίου ἐπισήμου ἑξακισχιλίων ταλάντων (τὰ γὰρ πλεῖστα τριακοσίων ἀποδέοντα περιεγένετο, ἀφ᾽ ὧν ἔς τε τὰ προπύλαια τῆς ἀκροπόλεως καὶ τἆλλα οἰκοδομήματα καὶ ἐς Ποτείδαιαν ἐπανηλώθη), χωρὶς δὲ χρυσίου ἀσήμου καὶ ἀργυρίου ἔν τε ἀναθήμασιν ἰδίοις καὶ δημοσίοις καὶ ὅσα ἱερὰ σκεύη περί τε τὰς πομπὰς καὶ τοὺς ἀγῶνας καὶ σκῦλα Μηδικὰ καὶ εἴ τι τοιουτότροπον, οὐκ ἐλάσσονος [ἦν] ἢ πεντακοσίων ταλάντων. ἔτι δὲ καὶ τὰ ἐκ τῶν ἄλλων ἱερῶν προσετίθει χρήματα οὐκ ὀλίγα, οἷς χρήσεσθαι αὐτούς, καὶ ἢν πάνυ ἐξείργωνται πάντων, καὶ αὐτῆς τῆς θεοῦ τοῖς περικειμένοις χρυσίοις· ἀπέφαινε δ᾽ ἔχον τὸ ἄγαλμα τεσσαράκοντα τάλαντα σταθμὸν χρυσίου ἀπέφθου, καὶ περιαιρετὸν εἶναι ἅπαν. χρησαμένους τε ἐπὶ σωτηρίᾳ ἔφη χρῆναι μὴ ἐλάσσω ἀντικαταστῆσαι πάλιν. The text of this passage is discussed on pp. 118-132 above.

[22] E. g., West, T. A. P. A., LXI (1930), p. 219, note 6.

the Archidamian War (cf. *I. G.*, I², 324) came out of item 4.²³ This cannot be. If Thucydides is taken at his word the total of item 2 must include the sacred treasure of Athena Polias, Athena Nike, Hermes Propylaios, the Other Gods, and the hellenotamiai. Incidentally, this passage proves that the hellenotamiai kept their money on the Akropolis (which is likely in any case), or that they had no money (which is possible, but in the strict sense unlikely).²⁴ Item 4 refers to places like Rhamnous and Eleusis which did not join with the combined Other Gods (ἄλλοι θεοί) in 434. So " the wealth from the other sanctuaries " (τὰ ἐκ τῶν ἄλλων ἱερῶν) means not what had been brought in already from the other sanctuaries, but what Perikles expected might be got from them in the future. This is proved by the order of enumeration, for the item is lower down than (3) in value, though we know from *I. G.*, I², 324 that the Other Gods possessed coined money of about 766 talents which could be borrowed between 433 and 426. The item is also lower than (3) in the scale of availability, but if it had been ready-to-hand coin on the Akropolis it must have rated above dedications, sacred utensils, and Persian spoils. Hence it is clear that " the wealth from the other sanctuaries " (τὰ ἐκ τῶν ἄλλων ἱερῶν) did not include the money of the Other Gods.

The value of the gold from the statue of Athena, at the current ratio of gold to silver (14: 1),²⁵ was 560 talents, but this was named as a rock-bottom reserve only, in case all other sources were exhausted.

Perikles gave the annual war revenue as 600 talents, and he implied that the " other revenue " (ἄλλη πρόσοδος) was not available for war purposes. This other revenue was doubtless sacred money used for games, festivals, and the like, and profane money too used for internal purposes. In all it must have amounted to 400 talents a year, for Xenophon (*Anabasis*, VII, 1, 27 [T156]) says that in 431 the total revenues of Athens yearly were 1000 talents. The testimony of these authors is reconciled by evaluating the " other revenue " in this way, and since Perikles wished to encourage his hearers by naming to them all the available resources for war he should have included this figure—if indeed it could be accounted a war asset—and not have left it as an exception.

The available 600 talents were described by Thucydides as tribute, though he

---

²³ See Cavaignac, *Études*, p. 111: " Quant aux autres divinités, Périclès dit seulement qu'il y a dans leurs temples des richesses qui ne sont pas négligeables: visiblement les inventaires prescrits par Kallias ne sont pas encore achevés. Le trésor constitué en vertu du même décret s'ajoutait à ces ressources dispersées."

²⁴ Cf. Deinarchos, I, 37 (T46): Ἀριστείδην καὶ Θεμιστοκλέα, τοὺς ὀρθώσαντας τὰ τείχη τῆς πόλεως καὶ τοὺς φόρους εἰς ἀκρόπολιν ἀνενεγκόντας παρ' ἑκόντων καὶ βουλομένων τῶν Ἑλλήνων – – –. This is rhetorical, and inexact, for neither Aristeides nor Themistokles put any tribute on the Akropolis. Yet Deinarchos evidently thought of it as lying there.

²⁵ Cf. *I. G.*, I², 352 = Tod, *Greek Hist. Inscr.*, I², no. 52.

apparently used the word here in its broader sense of money from overseas.[26] Strictly speaking, the actual amount of tribute received in the nearest year (433/2) for which there is good evidence was about 388 talents.[27] So this leaves other income of the hellenotamiai, and also sacred income available for war, to add up to the remaining 212 talents.[28] It will appear later that the sacred revenue may be estimated at approximately 80 talents a year; hence the extra funds coming to the hellenotamiai, over and above the phoros, were about 132 talents a year. The well-known lines of D1 may now be understood more specifically than was indicated in the translation above (p. 326): τά τε παρὰ τοῖς ἑλλενοταμίαις ὄντα νῦν (tribute and other imperial funds on hand) καὶ τᾶλλα ἅ ἐστι τούτον [τὸ]ν χρεμάτον (more tribute still to come and other imperial funds) καὶ τὰ ἐκ τῆς δεκάτες (not forgetting the 10% tax).[29]

Much of the annual war income of the gods must have been composed of the repayments to Athena of the money she spent on Samos.[30] The repayments which must be inferred from Byzantion (I. G., I², 293) were less and must have been repaid sooner. Byzantion returned to the status of a tribute-paying member of the Empire. Samos never paid tribute,[31] but there is considerable evidence for the repayment of her indemnity and for the fact that the money was paid to Athena.[32]

The text of D8, lines 21-25, shows that Thera and Samos were both still paying their instalments in 426/5. Thera will be discussed at length later; the important fact now is that this evidence shows the Samian indemnity not to have been liquidated before 433;[33] and other evidence carries the date well below 426/5. An item in the records of the logistai for 423/2 gives the source of one of the loans made by Athena

---

[26] See above, p. 132.

[27] Cf. Tod, *Greek Hist. Inscr.*, I², p. 56; Meritt, *A. J. P.*, LV (1934), p. 286. Our computation from the texts in *A. T. L.*, II yields substantially the same figure.

[28] Nesselhauf, *Klio*, Beiheft XXX, pp. 117-120, determines a total of only 140 talents, for he uses (erroneously) the theoretical Aristeidean figure of 460 as the total for tribute instead of the actual annual receipts, though even these (p. 108) he gets too high. Schwahn, in P. W., R. E., s. v. φόροι, p. 630, reckoned a total of 180 talents.

[29] Nesselhauf, *op. cit.*, p. 120, errs in thinking the δεκάτη problematic and in believing that its proceeds ought not to be classed with receipts from the Empire: "--- die Einnahmen aus der sehr problematischen δεκάτη konnten nicht gut als Einkünfte von den Bundesgenossen bezeichnet werden." The authority of the hellenotamiai in stewarding these funds is clear from the context; cf. above, pp. 326-327.

[30] Thucydides, I, 117, 3 (T113): χρήματα τὰ ἀναλωθέντα ταξάμενοι κατὰ χρόνους ἀποδοῦναι.

[31] Cf. Kolbe, *Sitzungsber. Ak. Berlin*, 1930, p. 340, note 1; Ferguson, *Treasurers*, p. 35, note 1; Meritt, *D. A. T.*, pp. 35-36. See note 36 below.

[32] So also Beloch, *Gr. Gesch.*, II, 2², p. 334.

[33] Schwahn, in P. W., R. E., s. v. φόροι, p. 629, in the midst of much confused speculation, recognized this fact. Ferguson, *Treasurers*, p. 155 (cf. p. 35, note 1), thought that by 434/3 "the Samians had already made good the sums borrowed from Athena in 441/39 B. C." The fact that the debt of the Athenian state to Athena was squared in 433 does not mean that the debt of the Samians to Athena had been squared. Nor are the records of *I. G.*, I², 324 concerned with borrowings or debts from abroad.

to the Athenian state as " from the Samians " ([παρὰ] Σαμ[ίον]).[34] Not only does this show the indemnity still being paid; it makes it clear that the repayment was to the Goddess Athena and that it was her money, to lend out at interest if she wished. A reference to borrowings from Athena in 418/7 again gives Samos as the source from which the money was derived: " the annual income from Samos " (τô ἐχσ[άμο κατὰ τὸν ἐνιαυτὸν ἐ]πελθόντος).[35] Finally, an inscription of 414/3 again refers to these receipts from Samos; the reading [παρὰ Σα]μίον (" from the Samians ") occurs in one of the items of borrowing from Athena in that year.[36] If the annual payments were commenced in 439/8, as undoubtedly they were, the payment in 414/3 was the twenty-sixth in the series and, at the rate of 50 talents a year, should have liquidated the obligation imposed by the peace of 439.[37] Samos was given autonomy by Athens in 412,[38] and hence the ἀνομολογήματα of I. G., I², 304 have no connection with the repayment of the debt.[39] These " acknowledgments " merely show that Samos was being used as a branch bank for Athena in 410/09, and incidentally that imperial funds were credited directly to Athena, probably according to the terms of the decree D9.

For the analysis of income from the allies that Perikles reported in 431, the evidence now points to his having included in his calculation an annual revenue of 50 talents accruing to the sacred funds of Athena from the Samian indemnity. We do not know for sure how much else accrued to Athena, and except as the question concerns the amounts available for borrowing during the Archidamian War it does not much matter. The sum of *ca.* 212 talents annually, over and above the tribute, could be spent from overseas income on the war, and it is a matter of less importance how the sum should be divided between funds on which the state could draw with or without paying interest, that is, how much belonged to the chest of the hellenotamiai and how much was sacred treasure. But we have found with a high degree of probability that the 50 talents annually from Samos belonged to Athena. Her income, without counting these 50 talents, was estimated by Beloch as *ca.* 25-30 talents.[40]

[34] Cf. the text of *I. G.*, I², 324 as published in Meritt, *A. F. D.*, p. 139, line 42; see also West, *T. A. P. A.*, LXI (1930), pp. 219-220, note 8.

[35] *I. G.*, I², 302. See the text in Meritt, *A. F. D.*, p. 160, lines 18-19. For the orthography see Tod, *A. J. P.*, LXVII (1946), p. 333.

[36] *I. G.*, I², 297. See the text in Meritt, *A. F. D.*, p. 89, line 16. Thucydides (VII, 57, 4 [T143]) reckons the Samians as ὑπήκοοι καὶ φόρου ὑποτελεῖς in 415 B. C. This can only refer to the indemnity, and it betrays on the part of Thucydides a latitude in the use of the word φόρος which permits it to cover any income from one of the allies. See the discussion of Thucydides, II, 13, 3 (T117), on pp. 131-132 above.

[37] See note 7 above.

[38] Thucydides, VIII, 21.

[39] Cf. Meritt, *A. F. D.*, pp. 95, line 20 (τὰ ἐχσάμο ἀνομολογέθε), and 96, lines 34-35 (τὰ ἐχσάμο ἀνομολογέσα[ντο hοι σύ]μμαχ[οι ⋮ το]ῖς στρατεγοῖς ἐς Σάμοι).

[40] *Gr. Gesch.*, II, 2², p. 326. Ferguson, *Treasurers*, pp. 153-154, thinks Beloch's estimate too

Adding the 50 talents from Samos we have estimated at 80 talents the sacred funds included in Perikles' report of 600 talents a year at the outbreak of the war.[41]

The status of Thera was somewhat like that of Samos.[42] Having been forced into the Empire between 431 and 430 she paid tribute (which Samos did not), and she was compelled also to pay in instalments the amount expended by Athens in her own subjugation. The provisions of D8, lines 21-25, apply equally to Thera and Samos about the time and method of the payment of these instalments. But whereas the payments from Samos went to the treasurers of Athena, those from Thera can only have gone to the chest of the hellenotamiai. Samos had been conquered before, and Thera after, the critical date 433. Whatever indemnity may have been exacted from Euboia, suppressed in 446, could have gone only to Athena. Euboia is not mentioned in D8, and it is quite probable that the Euboian indemnity, smaller than that of Samos, had been paid by 426. But it may have entered into Perikles' estimate of revenue in 431. At any rate Athenian revenue from confiscated property on Euboia must have continued to come in as long as Athens held the island.

The suggestion has already been made that these " moneys owed " which are mentioned in D8 may be the same as " the debts on the panels " of D3.[43] But the debts on the panels were doubtless mostly arrears of tribute, caused largely (in 430/29) by default upon the revolt of Chalkidike, Poteidaia, and Bottike. This gives point to the exception to be made for Methone if any general decree should be passed about the debts.[44] And since Methone's debt is thus classified with arrears of tribute we learn that these obligations were paid to the chest called the demosion (τὸ δεμόσιον in D3, line 10). This is the name of the chest in which the 5000 talents collected from the tribute lay in 449 (D13). It was the public chest, into which fines were paid.[45] That it was, in fact, the name applied over-all to the profane moneys as distinct

---

low, and observes that even the Other Gods had about 700 talents in coined money in 433. Rather more than that had, indeed, been borrowed from them by the state by 429 (see below, pp. 342-343 with notes 79, 82, 90) ; but evidently less than 200 talents had been borrowed, and not repaid, before 433 (D2), and one can hardly compare the two treasures in such a way as to estimate from one the probable income of the other.

[41] Cavaignac, *Études*, p. 72, estimated the revenues of Athena in this period at not much less than 100 talents. Again, on p. 103 he writes: " Il ne faut donc pas supposer ces revenus, dans la période qui suit la conquête de Samos, trop inférieurs à 100 talents." Cf. also pp. 114-115: " Les revenus d'Athèna peuvent être évalués à 100 talents environ." Francotte, *Finances*, p. 174, dates the commencement of the yearly income of 600 talents after the Samian War: " Je propose l'époque qui suit la guerre de Samos, comme étant celle où s'affirme le plus énergiquement l'hégémonie d'Athènes." This is undoubtedly correct, but Francotte (*op. cit.*, p. 176) did not include the Samian indemnity in the receipts, as Perikles must have done.

[42] Cf. Meritt, *D. A. T.*, pp. 36-38.

[43] See above, pp. 15-16.

[44] D3, lines 13-16: καὶ ἐὰν [κοινὸν] φσέφισμά τι περὶ τôν ὀφειλεμάτον τôν ἐν τê[ισι σανί]σι γίγνεται μεδὲν προσ͞εκέτο Μεθοναίο[ις ἐὰμ μὲ χ]ορὶς γίγνεται φσέφισμα περὶ Μεθοναίον.

[45] Cf. *I. G.*, I², 1, lines 5-7: ἀποτί[νεν ---] ἐς δεμόσιο[ν].

from the sacred moneys is further proved by the well-known formula of confiscation:
" He shall be disfranchised and his money shall become state property ($\delta\eta\mu\dot{o}\sigma\iota\alpha$) and
the Goddess shall take a tenth." [46] So the money in this chest was counted as public
funds belonging to the Athenian state. From the oath of the Chalkis decree (446/5)
one learns that the tribute was Athenian property,[47] and in D8, lines 39-40 (426/5),
" the money of the Athenians " is almost certainly made to include—whatever else
it included—the tribute from the allies. There was no " Imperial Treasury," therefore, distinct from the " State Treasury " of the Athenian people. The evidence
carries this identity of state funds and imperial funds back to 449, and it is most
probable that the moneys of the Confederacy came to be " Athenian " moneys when
the funds were moved from Delos in 454. But the separate identity of the sacred
funds of the Goddess continued, as is proved by the formalities of transfers and
borrowings, down to the end of the war.[48]

II

In his study of the financial administration of Perikles Stevenson came to the
conclusion that before the transfer of the funds from Delos there was no reserve in
the public treasury of Athens.[49] When the funds of the Confederacy were placed on
the Akropolis there was created a very considerable reserve, but in 449 this was
transferred to the Goddess and not reëstablished. It is more difficult to be precise
about the reserve that may have been available in 449 in the treasury of Athena before
any bequests had been made to her from imperial funds, but it is certain that it could
not have been large. We have reckoned annual income of sacred money at about 80
talents after the increment from Samos; it must be reckoned as 30 talents before that,
and presumably at an even lower figure before the commencement of whatever income
Athena received from Euboia after the suppression of the revolt. If one strikes an
average of 25 talents a year from 480 down to 450 the total accumulation could be
only 750 talents. Furthermore, this must be counted the total reserve, for any accumulation that may have existed earlier than 480 was undoubtedly wiped out when the
Persians sacked Athens.[50]

[46] Ἄτιμος ἔστω καὶ τὰ χρήματα αὐτοῦ δημόσια ἔστω καὶ τῆς θεοῦ τὸ ἐπιδέκατον (vel. sim.).

[47] I. G., I², 39 (D17), line 26: τὸν φόρον ℎυποτελô Ἀθεναίοισιν.

[48] See note 12 above. For the rôle of the kolakretai see below, pp. 359-365.

[49] J. H. S., XLIV (1924), pp. 1-9, especially p. 1: " The sums which they [the kolakretai]
administered must have been considerable, but there is no reason to think that they accumulated
any reserve, or that the Athenian people consented to pay heavier taxes than were necessary to meet
current expenditure. Just as the Romans abolished direct taxation after the conquest of Macedonia,
so the Athenians during the period of their ἀρχή paid only indirect taxes, nor is there any evidence
that an εἰσφορά was actually imposed before the crisis of the year 428. Any savings were made at
the expense of the allies and not of the Athenian δῆμος."

[50] See Cavaignac, Études, pp. v and 31-32 (refuting Meyer, Gesch. d. Alterthums, III, p. 475).
See also Beloch, Gr. Gesch., II, 2², pp. 325-326. The treasure evidently was not taken to Salamis,

We have now reached at least an approximate estimate of the state of the reserves in 449 to compare with the very definite report of Thucydides (II, 13, 3 [T117]) in 431. The available cash balance was almost the same in both years. In 449 the total figure was 5750 talents, composed of the known 5000 talents from the Confederacy and an estimated 750 talents accumulated by the Goddess; in 431 the total figure was 5700, all in the reserve fund of Athena and the Other Gods.[51] There is no time between these dates at which an accumulation of 9700 talents is conceivably possible, and one must reject as a false text the alleged statement in Thucydides (II, 13, 3) that this impossibly high figure was ever reached. The statement of Thucydides that the total sum in the reserve kept an average balance down through the years of 6000 talents is completely justified: " There has been for some years an average balance on the Akropolis of 6000 talents in minted silver." [52]

Between 449/8 and 432/1 the yield from the tribute was as follows:

449/8	———		(moratorium)
448/7	———	ca. 360 T.[53]	
447/6	———	364 T.[54]	
446-443	———	1125 T.	(ca. 375 × 3)[55]
443-431	———	4656 T.	(ca. 388 × 12)[56]

$$\overline{}$$

6505 T.

for Herodotos (VIII, 51) relates that the treasurers of the Goddess remained on the Akropolis where they were slain by the Persians. Beloch reckons the annual income of Athena at ca. 15 talents maximum from 478 to 454 (25 years yielding 375 talents) and ca. 23 talents maximum after the beginning of the ἀπαρχή from the tribute (the 4 years from 453 down to 450 yielding 92 talents). His maximum figure is thus ca. 467 talents, not much more than half ours.

[51] For the inclusion of the Other Gods see pp. 332-333 above. These figures are remarkably close to those of Meyer, Gesch. d. Alterthums, IV, pp. 33-38, who gives 6000 talents as the sum on the Akropolis in 448 and 6600 as the sum available in 434/3.

[52] T117: ὑπαρχόντων δὲ ἐν τῇ ἀκροπόλει αἰεί ποτε ἀργυρίου ἐπισήμου ἑξακισχιλίων ταλάντων. See the discussion of this text above, pp. 118-132.

[53] The collection of this year was about 360 T. (see above, pp. 52-57). This assumes the completion of arrears. Without these arrears, which were recorded in the later lines of List 8, Meritt (D. A. T., p. 85) estimated the collection at 280 T.

[54] A probable figure of 363 T. 4940 Dr. has been determined from the study of the lists of Period II (see above, pp. 29-61, especially 52-57).

[55] The average is taken from I. G., I², 342, from which the exact amount of the tribute for 444/3 may be determined as 376 talents, 4550 drachmai. See Tod, Greek Hist. Inscr., I², p. 56; Meritt, D. A. T., p. 96. Nesselhauf, Klio, Beiheft XXX, pp. 112-114, thought the actual collection after 446 was not far behind the assessment. He estimated collection at ca. 400 talents (too high), and thought that the assessment must have been lower than 460 talents (which is surely true). He writes (p. 114): " Durch die Schatzung vom Jahre 446 wurde der Phoros um rund 90 Tal. herabgesetzt, von denen nur etwa 30 Tal. durch Neueinnahmen ausgeglichen wurden, d. h. es trat im ganzen ein Effektivverlust von rund 60 Tal. ein." But Nesselhauf thought this lag was only temporary.

[56] The average is taken from the figure for 433/2. See above, p. 334 with note 27. Cf. Meritt, D. A. T., p. 96, and A. J. P., LV (1934), p. 287.

Although Lists 12 and 13 (443/2 and 442/1) may be restored almost in their entirety, the total tribute collected cannot be estimated within 30 talents because of uncertainty about Thasos.[57] It may be noted here that the collection of tribute in 430/29 and in 429/8 was probably about the same as in 433/2. The total for the Hellespont was increased after 430 from *ca.* 74 talents to *ca.* 98 talents (List 25), but the total for Thrace had been diminished from *ca.* 123 talents to *ca.* 87½ talents (List 25). The dropping of Aigina was the principal, though not the only, change in the Island panel; 25 names appeared in List 26 (I, 18-19, II, 46-47, and III, 7-28) as against 24 in List 22 (I, 72-94, and II, 94-95); there were three new names (Diakrioi in Euboia, Thera, Nisyros)—and hence two absentees (one of them of course being Aigina)—but no individual changes in quota. The three new names account for an additional tribute of 5 talents, 2000 drachmai, but this does not compensate for the absence of Aigina. Evidence for the Ionic-Karic panel is incomplete.

In the period preceding 431 there was available income from other sources of *ca.* 212 talents a year back to the founding of Amphipolis;[58] before Amphipolis this annual revenue may have been as low as 137 talents; before the beginning of the Samian indemnity it was probably about 87 and before the suppression of Euboia perhaps it was no more than 82.[59] So the other income from 449 to 431 amounted to $3 \times 82 = 246$ T. before 446, $7 \times 87 = 609$ T. between Euboia and Samos, $2 \times 137 = 274$ T. between Samos and Amphipolis, and $6 \times 212 = 1272$ T. after Amphipolis: total, 2401 talents. Together with the tribute this adds up to 8906 talents.

There was also, during the interval from 449 to 431, at least one rather large non-recurring additional item. The treasure of the Other Gods was assembled on the Akropolis in 434/3. Inasmuch as *ca.* 766 talents were borrowed from this source early in the Archidamian War, it may be reasonable to add *ca.* 750 talents as the

[57] Cf. Tod, *Greek Hist. Inscr.*, I², p. 56. In *A.T.L.*, I (p. 282) we took it as certain that Thasos did not pay tribute in 443/2, and we restored [Σερμαιῆς] rather than [Θάσιοι] in 12, III, 33, basing our preference on the order of names in List 13. The absence of Thasos from List 12 seemed reasonable also to Nesselhauf (*Klio*, Beiheft XXX, p. 100, note 2), and Gomme's criticism (*Commentary*, I, pp. 276-277, note 3) has recently brought from McGregor (*A.J.P.*, LXVII [1946], p. 273) a restatement of our reasons for the choice. See *A.T.L.*, II, p. 5.

[58] See above, p. 309 with note 45, for the association between Amphipolis and the state revenues. The Athenian revenue which Thucydides names (IV, 108, 1) in connection with Amphipolis was obviously important and may have amounted to *ca.* 70 or 75 talents a year.

[59] For the Samian indemnity see above, pp. 334-335. The fact that certain temple properties were reserved and rented in Euboia after 446 is known from *I. G.*, I², 376 + *Hesperia*, XII (1943), pp. 28-29. Further, Aelian, *Varia Historia*, VI, 1 (T1), says of Chalkis: Ἀθηναῖοι κρατήσαντες Χαλκιδέων κατεκληρούχησαν αὐτῶν τὴν γῆν ἐς δισχιλίους κλήρους, τὴν Ἱππόβοτον καλουμένην χώραν, τεμένη δὲ ἀνῆκαν τῇ Ἀθηνᾷ ἐν τῷ Ληλάντῳ ὀνομαζομένῳ τόπῳ, τὸ δὲ λοιπὸν ἐμίσθωσαν κατὰ τὰς στήλας τὰς πρὸς τῇ βασιλείῳ στοᾷ ἑστηκυίας, αἵπερ οὖν τὰ τῶν μισθώσεων ὑπομνήματα εἶχον. τοὺς δὲ αἰχμαλώτους ἔδησαν, καὶ οὐδὲ ἐνταῦθα ἔσβεσαν τὸν κατὰ Χαλκιδέων θυμόν. If the analogy of Lesbos can be taken as in any sense applicable, these rentals mentioned by Aelian may have amounted to 5 or 10 talents a year. For the emendation τὸ δὲ λοιπόν see above, pp. 295-296.

aggregate accumulated before the war. It would be only a guess to name the annual income of the Other Gods between 431 and 422, and no account has been taken of it in the table on pp. 342-344 below. We believe that the element of error thus admitted is not large: perhaps as much as 100 talents or so. But before 431 the money of the Other Gods must be reckoned in, and added to the total of the money of the Goddess and of the money of the treasury of State. The grand total thus becomes 9656 talents.

Since the reserve on the Akropolis in 431 was about the same as the reserve on the Akropolis in 449, these 9656 talents must all have been spent in the intervening 18 years. Many of the expenses are known. The routine cost of empire was whatever remained of the tribute from 448 to 431 and of the other imperial income after 200 talents had been laid aside each year from 448 to 434 (15 payments) for Athena, and after 200 talents (one payment) had been given to the Other Gods in 434/3. It will be, therefore, the total tribute of 6505 — 3200 (16 × 200) = 3305 talents, plus that part of the additional income of 2401 talents which did not go into the sacred treasure (2401 — 925 = 1476 T.).[60] The total routine expense amounts to 4781 talents, or rather less than half the grand total. So Athena spent the balance: about 4875 talents. Of this Samos and Byzantion cost 1400 talents, but one reckons only 1276 because Byzantion had probably repaid its debt to Athena, and the amount was not counted above toward her income.[61] Nor, for the same reason, should the expense of reducing Euboia be taken into account on the debit side of the ledger. But the land campaigns in Boiotia and Phokis in the 40's and the expedition to Kerkyra are deductible items. The expense of Kerkyra was 76 talents (*I. G.*, I², 295; cf. Meritt, *A. F. D.*, p. 69). The land campaigns may have cost more, and we suggest a combined total of *ca.* 200 talents. Thus we reckon Athena's extraordinary war expenses at about 1476 talents down to the autumn of 433. This leaves 3399 talents for Poteidaia in 432/1 and for the Periklean building programme. We shall see cause to estimate Poteidaia at *ca.* 400 talents down to the time of Perikles' speech; so the building programme receives *ca.* 2999 talents. If we wish to use a round sum we may say that Athena contributed 3000 talents to the Parthenon, the Gold and Ivory Statue, and the Propylaia, between 449 and 431.

The expenses of the buildings, however, came not only from the money of the reserve. Money came to the Parthenon, for example, from the xenodikai (ξενοδίκαι, in *I. G.*, I², 342, line 38; *I. G.*, I², 343, line 89),[62] from the mines at Laureion (*I. G.*, I², 347, line 15; *I. G.*, I², 348, line 60), from individuals (*I. G.*, I², 348, lines 65-66),

[60] For the sacred money see above, pp. 333-339. The sacred funds, not at the disposal of the hellenotamiai, are to be estimated at 25 talents a year from 449 to 446 (75 T.), at 30 talents from 446 to 439 (210 T.), and at 80 talents a year from 439 to 431 (640 T.), a total of 925 talents.

[61] For the figure cf. Meritt, *A. F. D.*, p. 47; *A. J. P.*, LV (1934), pp. 365-366.

[62] Cf. Cavaignac, *Études*, p. lxvii, who connects this with the ξενίας δίκαι, active at just this time; Philochoros, frag. 90 Müller. See Körte, *Hermes*, LXVIII (1933), pp. 238-242.

from the baths (*I. G.*, I², 343, lines 83-84), from the trieropoioi (*I. G.*, I², 342, line 40),[63] and from the teichopoioi (*I. G.*, I², 343, line 90).[64]

Similarly, in the case of the Propylaia, it is evident (*I. G.*, I², 363-367) that receipts came to the overseers not only from the reserve fund but also from rentals of property, private individuals, the mines at Laureion, and even from generals in the field who had surplus money to dispose of when their routine missions were over.[65]

If we count these additional sources which can only be estimated by conjecture the cost of the Periklean building programme on the Akropolis, as financed from the reserve chest and other sources, probably came to be well over 3000 talents, perhaps 3500 talents or more.[66] There was other building too, like the springhouse (D19) which the Athenians decided to charge against the imperial treasury, and like the Hephaisteion, which must have been paid for largely out of profits on the exchange of foreign money sanctioned in the decree of Klearchos (D14, especially §5). It makes no difference in the present calculations how great a part of these profits passed first through the treasury of Athena and Hephaistos.

III

One can construct an analytical table to show the records of borrowings and interest over the period of eleven years comprised in the accounts of *I. G.*, I², 324, by beginning with the known fact that 5700 talents were in the reserve when Perikles made his speech at the beginning of the war and by using other evidence of borrowings in the epigraphical record and the evidence already set forth for the regular income to the sacred treasury both before and after 431. The process is in part empirical, but the various items of income, loans, and interest are so delicately adjusted that a table which utilizes the known evidence and does not lead at some point to a demonstrable absurdity must reflect approximately the actual course of the financial record.

In the following table the rates of interest are those used in *I. G.*, I², 324, and

---

[63] This payment of 15 talents toward the Parthenon probably was the balance left in the hands of the trieropoioi after they had completed an order for triremes; cf. Dinsmoor, *A. J. A.*, XVII (1913), p. 78, and XXV (1921), p. 243. It was not a true primary source, for the money had already been paid out once as routine cost of the Empire. But it should be added to the rest in estimating the cost of the building.

[64] This item shows that the long wall was finished in 443/2 and that the balance which the teichopoioi had in hand was spent on the Parthenon. The amount of the balance is not recorded. See Dinsmoor, *locc. citt.* Kallikrates was at the head of the epistatai of the walls, just as he was of the work on the Parthenon. Like the money from the trieropoioi this item was first allocated to the cost of the Empire (cf. Meyer, *Forschungen*, II, pp. 100, note 3, and 104).

[65] See above, pp. 329-332. This was money first allocated to the maintenance of the Empire.

[66] The cost of the Athena Parthenos was 847 talents. Cf. Dinsmoor, Ἀρχ. Ἐφ., 1937, II, pp. 507-511; see also *I. G.*, I², 354-362 and Meritt, *A. F. D.*, pp. 30-41.

the fundamental premise is adopted that the total loan of a year was made in the middle of the year, unless specific dates are known or unless correlation with military operations makes an earlier or later relative date desirable. It is also assumed that after 433/2, at least, there was never any money which the hellenotamiai were free to add to the sacred treasures.

Date	Reserve	Income	Loans	Interest
433 summer	6021 [67]	280 [68]	76 [69]	4½ [70]
432 summer	6020 [71]	80 [72]	1145 [73]	32 [74]
431 summer	3955 [75]	85 [76]	1370 [77]	116 [78]
430 summer	2670	85	1300 [79]	213½ [80]

[67] This is scaled to give the Thucydidean figure in 432/1.

[68] During the year the income to the sacred treasury was 80 talents, and the hellenotamiai probably had their usual surplus of 200 talents, which they either kept or gave to Athena. In any case it was an increment to the reserve. In this year also there were items of expense other than loans. Work was still in progress in a small way on the Parthenon (I. G., I², 353; receipts by the overseers had amounted to about 5 talents in the previous year) and presumably a very considerable activity was being continued on the as yet unfinished Propylaia (an estimated 200 talents). So net income will amount only to 75 talents, and this calculation affects the amount tabulated for the reserve in 432. As noted above, we do not attempt to make allowance in this table for the annual income to the Other Gods. The amounts are quite uncertain, and our belief is that the error involved in the omission is not large.

[69] I. G., I², 295.

[70] In the years from 433 to 427 inclusive interest is reckoned at one drachma a day a talent. Cf. West, T. A. P. A., LXI (1930), p. 236.

[71] See note 68 above.

[72] This represents the annual income to the sacred treasure.

[73] The loans (I. G., I², 296) were probably divided over the year so that ca. 400 talents should be dated before the speech of Perikles and ca. 745 talents afterwards. We assume that at the time of the speech there were 5700 talents on the Akropolis. During this year the untouchable reserve of 1000 talents was set aside (Thucydides, II, 24 [D20]), and this figure also must be deducted from the standard reserve in 431.

[74] The interest includes 4½ talents on previous loans and 27½ talents (estimated) on current loans. The figure 27½ is used instead of the arithmetical mean of 35 for the year, because the heavy loans came late. Cf. I. G., I², 296.

[75] See note 73 above.

[76] This figure is higher than last year's by 5 talents, estimated as the possible increment to Athena after the dispossession of Aigina (cf. Thucydides, II, 27).

[77] See Meritt, A. F. D., pp. 84-86; Ferguson, Treasurers, p. 158, note 1.

[78] This figure comprises 74½ talents interest on previous loans and 41½ talents on current loans.

[79] This probably includes a loan from Athena Nike of about 22½ talents; see Meritt, Cl. Quart., XL (1946), pp. 63-64. It may also include a loan of some 400 talents from the Other Gods; see note 90 below.

[80] This figure comprises interest of 158½ talents on previous loans and 55 talents on current loans. This estimate of 55 is more than the arithmetical mean of 39½ because the heavy loans were probably made early in the year.

429 summer	1455	90 [81]	600 [82]	255 [83]
428 summer	945 [84]	90 [85]	200	280 [86]
427 summer	835	100 [87]	100	289 [88]
426 summer	835 [89]	100	261 [90]	—— [91]
425 summer	674	110 [92]	130	——

[81] The revenues may have been increased after the capture and colonization of Poteidaia (Thucydides, II, 70, 4).

[82] This figure may include a loan of some 366 talents from the Other Gods; see note 90 below.

[83] This figure comprises interest on previous loans of 237 talents, and on current loans of 18 talents.

[84] Facing the siege of Lesbos the Athenians, needing additional funds ($\pi\rho\sigma\delta\epsilon\acute{o}\mu\epsilon\nu o\iota$ $\delta\grave{\epsilon}$ —— $\chi\rho\eta\mu\acute{a}\tau\omega\nu$), levied an $\epsilon\grave{\iota}\sigma\phi o\rho\acute{a}$ of 200 talents, and sent out money-collecting ships (Thucydides, III, 19 [T125]). They also raised the tribute (cf. Meritt, *A. F. D.*, p. 19; *A. T. L.*, I, p. 197), and thus brought expenses better in line with income. But the amount of available cash on the Akropolis in 428 may have been less than the 945 talents here suggested if the Golden Nikai mentioned in D2 were five in number and made between 431 and 428. Seven Golden Nikai were melted down in 406/5 (Ferguson, *Treasurers*, note 2 on pp. 122-123), each weighing about 2 talents (*op. cit.*, pp. 91 [with note 2] -92), and one was left. Two had been made in 426/5 (*I. G.*, I², 368; cf. 369), so six may have been in mind in 434. Three at any rate were considered, because the plural—not the dual—was used in D2. With a gold ratio of 14 to 1 each Nike was worth intrinsically 28 talents and may have cost as much as 40. Five of them would have cost the available reserve 200 talents. It is the opinion of D. B. Thompson (*Hesperia*, XIII [1944], pp. 173-209) that three may have been made earlier than 425 (*op. cit.*, pp. 205-206) and that those of D2 may commemorate Samos. The relative value of the cost of the gold to the cost of the total work has been taken here from the accounts of the Parthenos, the total cost of which was 847 + talents, with gold of 40 talents (= 560 talents of silver); cf. Dinsmoor's edition of *I. G.*, I², 354 in ᾿Αρχ. ᾿Εφ., 1937, II, pp. 507-511. The spending of 10 talents a year on the Akropolis (D2) may also have depleted the reserve by as much as 30 talents after 431, but there is no evidence that any work was done between the outbreak of the war and 428/7 B. C.

[85] The increased quota from the tribute should be added to this figure, but we have left the approximation at 90 talents because of uncertainties about the increments from Aigina and Poteidaia.

[86] This figure includes 274 talents of interest on previous loans and 6 talents on current loans.

[87] There is now an additional income of 10 talents from Lesbos (Thucydides, III, 50, 2 [T128]).

[88] This figure comprises 286 talents of interest on previous loans and 3 talents on current loans.

[89] No reduction is here made for the two golden Nikai of *I. G.*, I², 368, for they were made from the spoils of war and not from original reserve.

[90] The sums now come from the detailed accounts of the logistai, *I. G.*, I², 324. Down to this point (but not including the 261 talents of 426/5) the total loans have been 4791 talents (cf. Tod, *Greek Hist. Inscr.*, I², no. 64, lines 99-100, 103-105, 107-108, 110-111). Down to this same point the total accumulated interest was 1190 talents. The figure is not attested epigraphically, but depends on the calculations in this table. The total interest for Athena Polias, Athena Nike, (and Hermes), in "the seven years" amounted to 1053 talents [Tod, *op. cit.*, no. 64, line 117 minus lines 101 and 108 = 1249 — (195 + 1) = 1053]. Hence interest for the Other Gods in the seven years is estimated at 137 talents (1190 — 1053). If principal of 400 talents had been borrowed early in 430/29 (cf. note 79 above) the interest might have been 92 talents; if principal of 366 talents had been borrowed late in 429/8 (cf. note 82 above) the interest might have been 45 talents. It is known that the borrowings from the Other Gods amounted to 766 talents (Tod, *op. cit.*, no. 64, lines 103-105), and the interest amount of 137 talents is thus achieved.

[91] From this point the rate of interest is 1 drachma *per diem* for 5 talents. The amounts appear in *I. G.*, I², 324 and are no longer a necessary part of our own calculation.

[92] The quota from the tribute added to the income in this year because of the higher assessment of A9.

424 summer	654	105 [93]	163	——
423 summer	596	105	257	——
422 summer	444 [94]	——	——	——

IV

The *Wasps* of Aristophanes was produced in 422, and together with the assessment decree of 425 it gives the best evidence for the state of the treasury near the end of the Archidamian War. In lines 656-660 (T38a) the sources of Athenian revenue are described in considerable detail (the speaker is Bdelykleon):

" And not with pebbles precisely ranged, but roughly thus on your fingers count
The tribute paid by the subject States, and just consider its whole amount;
And then, in addition to this, compute the many taxes and one-per-cents,
The fees and the fines, and the silver mines, the markets and harbours and sales
     and rents.
If you take the total result of the lot, 'twill reach two thousand talents or near." [95]

The total income was upwards of 2000 talents, and of all the items the phoros from the Empire was first and most important. That the income must have been more than 1500 talents is shown by the lines immediately following:

" And next put down the Justices' pay, and reckon the sums they receive a year:
Six thousand Justices, count them through, there dwell no more in the land as yet,
One hundred and fifty talents a year I think you will find is all they get.
(Ph.) Then not one tithe of our income goes to furnish forth the Justices' pay?
(Bd.) No, certainly not. (Ph.) And what becomes of all the rest of the revenue,
     pray? " [96]

[93] It is assumed here that the loss of Amphipolis and its territory occasioned a reduction of income, though in the early years of the city (from 437 B. C.) we added no corresponding increase to the sacred treasury.

[94] In this year the treasury was almost depleted, the sum still available being considerably less than was required for one year of war, and the balance growing progressively smaller. This final entry brings the record down to the approximate time of the assessment of 422/1 (A10). Meyer, *Forschungen*, II, p. 130, estimated that only 700 talents were left in the treasury in 421.

[95] The translation is by Rogers:

καὶ πρῶτον μὲν λόγισαι φαύλως, μὴ ψήφοις, ἀλλ' ἀπὸ χειρός,
τὸν φόρον ἡμῖν ἀπὸ τῶν πόλεων συλλήβδην τὸν προσιόντα·
κᾆξω τούτου τὰ τέλη χωρὶς καὶ τὰς πολλὰς ἑκατοστάς,
πρυτανεῖα, μέταλλ', ἀγοράς, λιμένας, μισθώσεις, δημιόπρατα·
τούτων πλήρωμα τάλαντ' ἐγγὺς δισχίλια γίγνεται ἡμῖν.

[96]
Ἀπὸ τούτου νυν κατάθες μισθὸν τοῖσι δικασταῖς ἐνιαυτοῦ
ἐξ χιλιάσιν, — κοὔπω πλείους ἐν τῇ χώρᾳ κατένασθεν, —
γίγνεται ἡμῖν ἑκατὸν δήπου καὶ πεντήκοντα τάλαντα.
Φι.   οὐδ' ἡ δεκάτη τῶν προσιόντων ἡμῖν ἆρ' ἐγίγνεθ' ὁ μισθός;
Βδ.   μὰ Δί' οὐ μέντοι.
Φι.   καὶ ποῖ τρέπεται δὴ 'πειτα τὰ χρήματα τἄλλα;

One notes that 150 talents a year is possible for the jurymen,[97] and since they complain that they receive less than one tenth of the income, a minimum figure of 1500 talents is indicated. West suggested that one might strike a balance between the 1500 and the 2000 and say provisionally that the revenues were, on the average, 1750 talents a year.[98]

This total in 422 must be compared with that of 1000 talents given by Xenophon for 431 [99] and with the statement of Thucydides (II, 13, 3 [T117]) that in 431 the annual revenue from overseas was approximately 600 talents. The computations in the preceding pages have classified this as 388 talents of tribute and 212 talents from other sources.[100] The annual domestic revenue (Xenophon minus Thucydides) thus amounted to 400 talents at the beginning of the war and there is little reason to believe that it had changed much in the course of ten years. Hence the imperial revenue in 422 was approximately 1350 talents. But revenue from overseas other than tribute had also been increased. Possibly Aigina and Poteidaia added 100 talents,[101] and it is known that Lesbos added 100 talents (Thucydides, III, 50, 2 [T128]). The income of 1350 talents from the Empire, therefore, in 422 included 412 talents that were over and above the tribute; hence the tribute alone was 938 talents. This figure differs from that of 675 achieved by West (op. cit., p. 225), but West assumed the continuation of eisphora even in 422, and did not have at his disposal the now known total of 1460 talents for the assessment of 425. There is every reason to believe that the eisphora had been abandoned in 425; indeed, one purpose of the new assessment must have been to make a direct tax unnecessary. A total collection in tribute of 938 talents, realized in actual cash, seems low against an assessment of 1460 talents, but one must never forget that many cities in the assessment list are known never to have paid tribute at all, including Melos and probably many of the Pontic cities, that many were included for their propaganda value, like the cities beyond Phaselis, long after they had ceased to belong to the Athenian Empire, and that large areas of Thrace were in revolt.[102]

If one feels, even so, that the discrepancy between 938 talents of collection and 1460 talents of assessment is unduly great, it is possible to move the estimate of 1750 talents a year as the total of all revenues closer to the maximum of 2000 named by Aristophanes, and by so much to reduce the gap between the assessment and collection of the tribute. Probably the actual collection amounted to approximately 1000 talents in a normal year during the assessment period following 425 B. C.

[97] It is immaterial here that such a theoretical maximum was higher than any actual figure.

[98] T. A. P. A., LXI (1930), p. 224.

[99] Anabasis, VII, 1, 27 (T156).

[100] See above, pp. 333-334.

[101] 5 talents each to the Goddess (cf. notes 76 and 81 above) and perhaps 45 talents each to the State.

[102] To name only the larger cities, the rebels in 422 included Akanthos, Argilos, Olynthos, Skione, Spartolos, Stageira, Stolos.

CHAPTER XI

THE PEACE OF NIKIAS

The blessings of the Peace of Nikias were described to Athenians of a generation later in the opening paragraphs of Andokides' speech urging peace with Sparta. Confused and inaccurate though he was in recounting the historical events of the Fifty Years,[1] Andokides was speaking of events of his own lifetime when he came to 421 B. C., and one expects from him a more nearly accurate record than he gave of the earlier part of the century. Two of his statements touch upon the question of the tribute: " I think all of you know this, that thanks to this peace we deposited 7000 talents of coined money on the Akropolis, we acquired more than 300 ships, and more than 1200 talents of tribute came in annually – – –."[2]

The fund of 7000 talents has been held difficult to explain,[3] and one may well question where Andokides found precisely this figure. But the answer almost certainly is that this was the amount due to the gods for borrowing from the sacred treasures down to the end of the Archidamian War and that when the Peace of Nikias had been ratified provision had been made for paying the debt. This implies a decree authorizing the repayment, and we assume that such a decree existed, known to everyone, naming the total of 7000 talents. Whether the 7000 talents were ever actually put on the Akropolis (Andokides says they were) is another matter. The fact of importance is that the Athenians, after the Peace of Nikias, undertook to pay back to Athena and to the Other Gods the money that they had borrowed from them.[4] Andokides knew the decree, and this is all that his text implies.

The money that Athens owed to her gods at the end of the fiscal (conciliar) year in 422 is known, or can be learned, from the accounts of the logistai, *I. G.*, I², 324.[5]

---

[1] See K. J. Maidment's edition of the *Minor Attic Orators*, I (*The Loeb Classical Library*, 1941), p. 495.

[2] III, 8-9 (T6): οἶμαι δ' ὑμᾶς ἅπαντας εἰδέναι τοῦτο, ὅτι διὰ ταύτην τὴν εἰρήνην ἑπτακισχίλια μὲν τάλαντα νομίσματος εἰς τὴν ἀκρόπολιν ἀνηνέγκαμεν, ναῦς δὲ πλείους ἢ τριακοσίας ἐκτησάμεθα, καὶ φόρος προσῄει κατ' ἐνιαυτὸν πλέον ἢ διακόσια καὶ χίλια τάλαντα – – –. Andokides knew that he was speaking to citizens who, with him, were contemporaries of the event and in a position to know the facts. It is of less significance (though important) for the truth of the statements that Aischines later (II, 175 [T3]) used them almost word for word. See the text in *A. T. L.*, I, p. 571; there is a misprint in *A. T. L.*, II, p. 88.

[3] Maidment, *op. cit.*, p. 505: " The mention of a reserve of 7000 talents is suspicious. Athens did, it is true, recover remarkably from the effects of the Archidamian War during the period between 421 and the Sicilian Expedition of 415. But Andocides is here talking of the years 421-419 only. He may be basing his figures on the financial reserve of Athens before the Archidamian War."

[4] This was denied by Ferguson, *Treasurers*, p. 161, but he had no way of explaining Andokides.

[5] The numbering of the lines here follows that of Meritt, *A. F. D.*, pp. 136-143. For the text

The total of the borrowings amounted to 5599 T. 4900 Dr.[6] In addition to the principal, there was also the accumulated interest of 1424 T. 1925⅚ Dr.[7] The grand total of the debt was 7024 T. 825⅚ Dr.; at least this is an amount which is approximately correct (only one item in the reckoning of the interest being subject to rough approximation) and the decree to repay it gave Andokides his figure.

To find the source of Andokides' other figure of an annual revenue from the tribute of more than 1200 talents it is necessary to review the political events of the year 422/1 and the history of the peace. The story, in its relation to the tribute, has been lucidly and convincingly told by West, and one needs only to reread what he has written,[8] and make the necessary corrections for the changes in our knowledge of the epigraphical evidence since 1925. The participation of the allies in the blessings of the peace was heralded by Aristophanes in his comedy, the *Peace*, which was produced at the Great Dionysia of 421; the peace itself was ratified soon after the Dionysia.[9] The assessment of tribute, which had been introduced at the previous Panathenaia,[10] and which had been postponed because the scale of payments would depend on the outcome of the negotiations for peace, was finally embodied in a decree (presumably later than Elaphebolion) which did in fact give the allies the relief promised by Aristophanes. It was an assessment on a pre-war scale, and the individual amounts of tribute were returned, wherever feasible, to the Aristeidean level. There were many adjustments, of course, because of changed conditions between 477 and 421, and there were many new names, but the scale has been accurately defined in the terms of the peace itself. The covenant between Athens and Sparta guaranteed to Argilos, Stageira, Akanthos, Stolos, Olynthos, and Spartolos their autonomy as long as they paid to Athens the tribute they had paid in Aristeides' day.[11] The allies who came to Athens to pay their own tribute at the time of the Dionysia must have known of this provision in the terms of the peace, and, as West observed, the question of the hour must have

---

see also Oguse, *B. C. H.*, LIX (1935), pp. 416-420; Broneer, *Hesperia*, IV (1935), pp. 158-159; Tod, *Greek Hist. Inscr.*, I², no. 64; Pritchett and Neugebauer, *Calendars of Athens*, pp. 95-105; Meritt, *Cl. Quart.*, XL (1946), pp. 60-64.

[6] Cf. Meritt, *Cl. Quart.*, XL (1946), p. 61.

[7] The component figures are:

    a) Total interest for Athena Nike and Athena Polias (lines 117-118) of 1249 T. 3385⅚₁₂ Dr. (cf. Meritt, *Cl. Quart.*, XL [1946], p. 64).

    b) Interest for the Other Gods from 433 to 426 of 137 T. (cf. above, note 90 on p. 343).

    c) Interest for the Other Gods for 426 to 422, on earlier loans (line 105), of 37 T. 2338⅚₁₂ Dr.

    d) Interest for the Other Gods for 422 B. C., on current loans (line 97), of 2202 Dr.

[8] West, *A. J. A.*, XXIX (1925), pp. 135-151.

[9] Thucydides, V, 19, 1: Ἐλαφηβολιῶνος μηνὸς ἕκτῃ φθίνοντος.

[10] This must have been true, for the penalties laid down in A9 were severe if the prytaneis in office at the Great Panathenaia of 422 failed to set in motion the machinery of assessment at that time.

[11] Thucydides, V, 18, 5 (T134).

been whether the loyal allies were to fare worse than the unrepentant rebels. Sparta had succeeded in stipulating that these six cities should pay the phoros of Aristeides' day (ὁ ἐπ' Ἀριστείδου φόρος), much as Athens in 449 had protected some Greek cities subject to Persia from harsh taxation after the Peace of Kallias by settling with Artaxerxes what sums they were to pay.[12] So far as the covenants of peace were concerned both Persia in 449 and Athens in 421 could tax the rest of their Empires as they saw fit, but in fact Athens could not generally grant to her friends less than she gave her enemies. On the other hand, Sparta could hold out for a good bargain for the six cities of the Peace of Nikias, because they were physically in her possession. Along with Aristeidean tribute, she claimed for them, and won, autonomy, which we take to mean freedom from political interference through resident Athenian archontes or episkopoi or garrisons. No concessions of this sort could have been made at large in the Empire, and one is entitled to believe that the Aristeidean assessment, precisely stipulated, was also a notable concession. For her friends, Athens could make necessary individual adjustments in matters of tribute; for Athens' late enemies (Argilos, Stageira, Akanthos, Stolos, Olynthos, and Spartolos), Sparta evidently saw the danger of these " adjustments " and avoided all debate by specifying exactly the Aristeidean figure in these six individual cases.[13] The tribute generally after 421 may be said to have been determined on the scale of Aristeides' assessment (κατὰ τὴν Ἀριστείδου τάξιν), and undoubtedly many of the figures were the same as they had been in 478/7. For her six proteges Sparta insisted that this be so.

Only Akanthos was large enough to make much difference to the Athenian board of assessors. Presumably it could have paid 5 talents a year after 421 (cf. List 5, III, 34), whereas its regular tribute before the Archidamian War had been 3 talents. Similarly Argilos would have paid 1½ talents (1, IV, 22), Olynthos and Spartolos 2 talents each, Stolos possibly 1 talent (we do not know), and Stageira its invariable and relatively insignificant tribute of 1000 drachmai.

The following list of cities whose tribute after 421 is known will show the Aristeidean character of the assessment of that year:

	Before 425	425	421	418
Ἀθηνῖται	2000 Dr.	1 T.		4000 Dr.
Αἰολῖται	500 Dr.		500 Dr.	
Ἄνδριοι	12 T. > 6 T.	15 T.		7 T.
Ἄντανδρος		15 T.	8 T.	
Αὐλιᾶται	500 Dr.			500 Dr.
Βρικινδάριοι			1 T.	
Γαλαῖοι	800 Dr. < 3000 Dr.	10 Dr.	10 Dr.	
Γρυγχῆς	1000 Dr.	2000 Dr.		1000 Dr.

[12] See above, p. 275.

[13] It is one of the ironies of fate that in no single instance do we know what the figure was.

	Before 425	425	421	418
Δαυνιοτειχῖται	1000 Dr. < 2 T. 4000 Dr.		2 T.	
Διακρῆς ἀπὸ Χαλκιδέων	800 Dr.	2000 Dr.		3000 Dr.
Διάκριοι ἐν 'Ρόδῳ			2 T.	2 T.
Διοσερῖται	1000 Dr. > 500 Dr.		500 Dr.	500 Dr.
'Ηφαιστιῆς	6 T. > 3 T.	4 T.	2 T.	
Θάσιοι	3 T. < 30 T.	60 T.	[409 B. C.]	30 T.
'Ιασῆς	1 T.		3 T.	3 T.
'Ιᾶται	1 T. > 3000 Dr.	1 T.		3000 Dr.
'Ιηλύσιοι	10 T. > 6 T. < 10 T.		5 T.	
"Ιμβριοι	1 T.	1 T.	1 T.	
'Ισίνδιοι	1000 Dr.			1000 Dr.
Καμειρῆς	9 T. > 6 T.			10 T.
Καρπάθιοι	1000 Dr.			1500 Dr.
Καρυανδῆς	1000 Dr. > 500 Dr.	1000 Dr.		1000 Dr.
Καρύστιοι	7½ T. > 5 T.	5 T.		5 T.
Κάσιοι	1000 Dr.			1000 Dr.
Κεῖοι	4 T. > 3 T.	10 T.		6 T.
Κλαζομένιοι	1½ T. < 6 T.			15 T.
Κλεωναί	500 Dr.		100 Dr.	
Κολοφώνιοι	3 T. > 1½ T. < 3 T. > 500 Dr.		500 Dr.	500 Dr.
Κύθνιοι	3 T.	6 T.		6 T.
Λίνδιοι	9 T. < 10 T. > 6 T. < 10 T.		15 T.	15 T.
Μαδύτιοι	500 Dr. < 2000 Dr.		2000 Dr.	
Μηκυβερναῖοι	1 T. > 4000 Dr. < 1 T.	10 Dr.	10 Dr.	
Μιλήσιοι	5 T. < 10 T. > 5 T.		10 T.	10 T.
Μυκόνιοι	1½ T. > 1 T.	2 T.		1 T.
Μύνδιοι	500 Dr.	1000 Dr.	1000 Dr.	
Μυριναῖοι ἐν Λήμνῳ	3 T. > 1½ T.	(see Hephaisties)	500 Dr.	
Νάξιοι	9 T. > 6⅔ T.	15 T.		9 T.
Νοτιῆς	2000 Dr. > 100 Dr.	100 Dr.	2000 Dr.	2000 Dr.
'Οθώριοι	500 Dr. < 700 Dr. > 500 Dr.		1000 Dr.	
Πάριοι	16 T. 1200 Dr. < 18 T.	30 T.		18 T.
Πεδιῆς	2000 Dr. > 100 Dr. < 5000 Dr.		1 T.	
Πίστασος	500 Dr.		500 Dr.	
'Ρηναιῆς	1000 Dr. > 300 Dr.	1000 Dr.		500 Dr.
Σάριοι	300 Dr.			200 Dr.
Σαρταῖοι	1500 Dr.		100 Dr.	
Σερίφιοι	2 T. > 1 T.	[2 T.]		1+ T.
Σερμαῖοι	500 Dr.		500 Dr.	
Σικινῆται		1000 Dr.		500 Dr.
Σῖνος	1500 Dr.		800 Dr.	
Τράϊλος		1 T.	1 T.	
Φαρβήλιοι	1000 Dr. > 500 Dr.		500 Dr.	
Φασηλῖται	6 T. > 3 T. < 6 T.			6 T.
Φολεγάνδριοι		2000 Dr.		1000 Dr.
Χαλκειᾶται	3000 Dr. > 2000 Dr.	2000+ Dr.		2000 Dr.

One observes first from a study of the table the absence of any increase in the assessment of 418.[14] There are seven instances in which the payments of the assessment period following 421 can be compared with the payments of the assessment period following 418, and in all of them the preserved amounts are exactly the same. The smaller amounts are not particularly significant, for small amounts seldom change much in any case, but we do regard it as important that Iasos, Lindos, and Miletos remain the same. They all show changes from their pre-war figure and they are all relatively high. There have been many hypotheses about the increase, or absence of increase, in the scale of tribute after 418,[15] the most forcefully stated argument for a notable increase being that of West in 1926.[16] West attempted to explain the confused references of Plutarch and the orators in the light of epigraphical texts, but the texts at that time had not been correctly assigned. There was no "doubling" or "trebling" of the tribute in 418 (or 417). The authority for this doubling, and trebling, is Plutarch's *Aristides*: "The allies of the Athenians sang the praises of the tribute of Aristeides' time, calling it a sort of blessing for Hellas, especially as it was soon doubled and then tripled."[17] Plutarch knew of the Thucydidean figure of 600 talents in II, 13, 3 (T117), for he quotes it, though he does not understand it. This misunderstanding is both intelligible and excusable, for Thucydides did not use the word in its technical sense and Plutarch did not have the quota lists (as we have them) to make this clear. Then Plutarch proceeds to say that the demagogues, after Perikles' death, little by little pushed the total up to 1300 talents. Once again Plutarch could have corrected his maximum if he had had (as we have) the text of A9. We know that the total was more than 1460 talents in 425/4. But Plutarch was not using the epigraphical evidence. This figure comes from Andokides, whose record is set forth above, and from Aischines who copied him (T3 and T6). They speak of "more than 1200 talents" (πλέον ἢ διακόσια καὶ χίλια [or χίλια καὶ διακόσια] τάλαντα), which becomes in Plutarch's story "1300 talents" (χιλίων τριακοσίων ταλάντων).[18]

It was a thesis of West that Alkibiades doubled the tribute, the evidence being the oration against Alkibiades falsely attributed to Andokides: "First he persuaded you to lay upon the cities a revised assessment of the tribute which was assessed most justly of all by Aristeides, and having been selected chairman of a board of ten to

---

[14] Beloch, *Gr. Gesch.*, II, 2², pp. 342-344, denied an increase at this time, for he thought there could be no justification for it in time of peace.

[15] Or after 417, as the date has sometimes been assumed.

[16] *T. A. P. A.*, LVII (1926), pp. 60-70.

[17] 24, 3 (T94) : --- οἱ σύμμαχοι τῶν ᾿Αθηναίων τὸν ἐπ᾿ ᾿Αριστείδου φόρον εὐποτμίαν τινὰ τῆς ῾Ελλάδος ὀνομάζοντες ὕμνουν, καὶ μάλιστα μετ᾿ οὐ πολὺν χρόνον διπλασιασθέντος, εἶτ᾿ αὖθις τριπλασιασθέντος.

[18] Cf. West, *T. A. P. A.*, LVII (1926), p. 61. After discovering (with Meritt) that the greater total of 1460 was valid in 425 (A9), West would have been the first to retract his maximum attribution of 1300 to 417 if he had lived to do so.

perform this task he practically doubled the tribute of each of the allies." [19] Rightly judging Alkibiades to have been too young to have any rôle of influence in the assessment of 425, West suggested 417 as the logical time for Alkibiades to have persuaded the Athenians, and himself to have served as an assessor (taktes).[20] He thus found support for assuming an increase of tribute in 417. But the evidence contradicts all this. There was no change in or near 417. Moreover, the increase in the tribute came first early in the war [21] and then reached its maximum in 425. The odium of the assessment of 425 belonged to Kleon, not to Alkibiades, and the whole rhetorical story, inconsistent with the facts, is nothing but a fabric of the imagination. The author was a fair antiquarian, however, and perhaps his reference to Alkibiades as himself the tenth assessor (δέκατος αὐτός) shows that he knew the board of taktai to have been composed of ten men, one from each phyle. It can hardly be taken as evidence for the nature of the board, for [Andokides] may have fashioned it from his general fund of knowledge concerning Athenian constitutional antiquities: reasonable speculation, without tangible support. About Alkibiades he must have been simply wrong.[22]

The evidence about the Insular tribute is much more nearly complete now than it was before the discovery by Welter of the fragments of List 39. We can now compare (see the table on pp. 348-349) the pre-war tribute, the tribute of 425, and the post-421 tribute of 16 cities: Andros, Athenai Diades, Diakres (Euboia), Grynche, Hephaistia, Imbros, Ios, Karystos, Keos, Kythnos, Mykonos, Myrina (Lemnos), Naxos, Paros, Rhenaia, and Seriphos. Before the war they paid 68 T. 4800 Dr. if one takes the high figures or 48 T. 3300 Dr. if one takes the low figures; in 425 they paid 92 T. 5000 Dr.; and after 421 they paid about 58 T. Clearly, in the Island district the Aristeidean figure had been in all its essentials restored.

There is also evidence about the Hellespont, though it is more difficult to interpret. Meritt's dating of our present List 33 in 418/7 was in agreement with his belief that the high quotas of the Hellespontine panel were not inconsistent with a hypothetically high general assessment in 418, but it now appears that there is no other evidence whatever for a change of the magnitude thus suggested between the assessments of 422/1 and 418/7. Reference to the table above will show not only that the seven quotas that can be compared between 421 and 418 are identical, but that (except for

---

[19] [Andokides], IV, 11 (T8): πρῶτον μὲν οὖν πείσας (Alkibiades) ὑμᾶς τὸν φόρον ταῖς πόλεσιν ἐξ ἀρχῆς τάξαι τὸν ὑπ' Ἀριστείδου πάντων δικαιότατα τεταγμένον, αἱρεθεὶς ἐπὶ τούτῳ δέκατος αὐτὸς μάλιστα διπλάσιον αὐτὸν ἑκάστοις τῶν συμμάχων ἐποίησεν – – –.

[20] Cf. T. A. P. A., LVII (1926), pp. 64-70.

[21] There was an increase of unknown magnitude in 428.

[22] His error was copied by Aelius Aristeides, XLVI, 149 (T22; cf. the scholion, T23). West cites the attempts that have been made to salvage the credibility (or partial credibility) of [Andokides] (op. cit., p. 63, note 12). Kolbe has since written of Alkibiades as τάκτης in 425 (Sitzungsber. Ak. Berlin, 1930, pp. 352-354) and in this he has been followed by Raubitschek, Hesperia, XII (1943), pp. 32-33 (vix recte).

Klazomenai) the quotas for the years after 418 are low even elsewhere than in the islands, which we have just passed in review: Auliatai, Chalke, Isinda, and Phaselis pay what they paid before the war; the slight quota of Saros was still further reduced. In these surroundings the high quotas of List 33 are quite out of place, and we leave the text, as we had originally assigned it, in 422/1 B. C. The only difference in the prescript is that Prepis can now no longer be the first secretary of the Council (cf. List 34). But though the Hellespontine quotas of List 33 reflect only the high assessment of 425, there is preserved (fortunately) a significant part of the figure for the Hellespontine total in A10.[23] The damage at the end of the figure is of little significance, for no change in restoration could there involve more than a few drachmai. But at the beginning two spaces have been broken away, both or neither or only the second of which may have been inscribed. Epigraphically, the restoration can be [HH] ⲢΔΔΔΔⲢⲢHHHĤ [– –] (ca. 296 T.) or [ᵛ H] ⲢΔΔΔΔⲢⲢHHHĤ [– –] (ca. 196 T.) or [ᵛᵛ] ⲢΔΔΔΔⲢⲢHHHĤ [– –] (ca. 96 T.).[24] Of these three, the Aristeidean character of the assessment of 421 clearly favours the last, and we have so restored the figure in our text of A10. In general, information about the Hellespontine district is good. The complete panels in the fourth assessment period, when the collection of tribute was systematic and thorough, indicate actual payments of ca. 77 talents a year,[25] and in the first years of the war this total was raised to ca. 98 talents (List 25).[26] There was an increase again with the assessment of 428. At least, List 27 indicates a possible total of 15 talents for Lampsakos instead of an earlier 12, and shows a number of new names whose tribute must have swelled the composite total. Then in 425 came the grand maximum of 250 to 300 talents (A9). This achievement must have required very considerable increases all along the line, some of which are reflected in the quotas of List 33. The return to an Aristeidean figure in 421 meant not only that the total was ca. 96 talents (rather than 196 talents), but in individual cases like Byzantion and Lampsakos the figures must have been reduced to their pre-war level. The increase which the assessment of 96 talents in 421 shows over the pre-war collection of ca. 77 talents is almost certainly to be explained for the greater part by the addition of new names, for some of which the assessment list itself gives evidence.

We take it, therefore, that the low assessment on the Aristeidean scale (κατὰ τὴν Ἀριστείδου τάξιν) can be demonstrated in 421 for the districts of the Islands and

---

[23] See the comments by West, A. J. A., XXIX (1925), p. 149.

[24] Meiggs, Eng. Hist. Rev., LV (1940), p. 105, thought the restoration of a total of ca. 196 talents the most probable, because of the analogy of A9 in which the total for the Hellespontine district was indented from the margin by one letter-space; cf. A. T. L., I, p. 115, Fig. 164.

[25] Tod, Greek Hist. Inscr., I², p. 56, gives the total for 443/2 as 77 T. 880 Dr., with which we agree.

[26] The amount is 95 T. 3640 Dr. in counted tribute, with some allowance for a small lacuna in the text; see above, pp. 70, 339.

of the Hellespont. There is no real evidence for Thrace, and the evidence from Ionia and Karia does not militate against it: Klazomenai is the notable increase, and the cities on Rhodes show adjustments that in part counterbalance one another. The tribute from the Euxine was, of course, an outright addition to the Aristeidean total.

But although the hope and expectation of lowered assessments were in everyone's mind at the Dionysia of 421, it was, after all, the date of tax collection and the old rates were still in force. Indeed, the old rates were undoubtedly reaffirmed at the Panathenaia of 422 when Kleon was still the guiding spirit of the Athenian democracy. Talk of lower rates came only after his death, and the death of Brasidas, and the progress of negotiations for peace. Just as in 449 the allies paid their tribute for 450/49 though peace with Persia was in sight, and paid late instalments to bring the record down to date even after Perikles had declared the moratorium for 449/8, so in 421 the allies paid Kleon's tribute at the Dionysia (List 33) even though within a few weeks they were certain of peace and of a lowering of the scale so that they might in the following year pay the tribute of Aristeides.

Andokides connects an annual payment of more than 1200 talents with the Peace of Nikias. This can have been the payment at (and after) the Dionysia of 421. It is an impossibly high figure for either of the two following years of which he speaks, and we have seen that there was no increase of tribute in the assessment of 418/7 over that of 422/1 to justify the reference of his figures to a later year. Payments after the Dionysia are included, for the text of D8 shows that substantial sums, not strictly tribute,[27] were normally collected later, and these are almost surely to be reckoned in Andokides' figure.[28]

We have before us, therefore, the plan of the Athenians to repay the gods for their loans made during the Archidamian War. The decree which authorized the repayment named the figure of 7000 talents and was passed after the Peace of Nikias in the spring of 421. The amount of the debt stood at 7000 talents in midsummer, 422. If we wished to have these figures match exactly, with no rough edges, we might assume that there were no loans from the sacred treasure between summer of 422 and spring of 421. Yet this is hardly likely. Kleon's campaign to Thrace fell in late summer of 422, and though normal revenues of the Empire may have been used largely in financing it there may also have been borrowings. But if the borrowings were on the relatively minor scale of the preceding four years,[29] and if the decree was passed soon after the peace (as we believe to have been the case) and before the

---

[27] Like the indemnities from Samos and Thera; see above, pp. 334-336.

[28] Even for 421 an actual collection of φόρος, in the strict sense of that word, cannot have reached as high as 1200 talents. We assume that Andokides here uses φόρος in the sense of Thucydides, II, 13, 3 (T117) and VII, 57, 4 (T143) to mean any revenue from the allies; see above, pp. 131-132, 333-334, and note 36 on p. 335.

[29] See the table on pp. 342-344 above.

routine expenditure of 100 talents to the generals,[30] the addition to the borrowed total may have amounted to less than 100 talents. The Athenians, in any case, could (and doubtless did) start at once to liquidate the debt.

There are no records of money paid out by the treasurers of Athena for expenses of state between 422 and 418. There are, however, records for the years from 418 to 414 and from 414 to 410.[31] Since the arrangement at this time seems to be by Panathenaic quadrennia, most probably there were payments also between 422 and 418, recorded on a stone now lost.

But what shall one say of these payments by the treasurers of Athena for purposes of state at a time when the state is making repayment to Athena of loans already borrowed? Why pay back money, if it merely has to be borrowed again?

In the interval between the Peace of Kallias and the Decrees of Kallias, the Athenian state made an initial grant of 5000 talents to Athena and then gave each year a sum of 200 talents, managing to pay for the routine of the Empire out of the balance of imperial income. In return for this donation and these annual gifts Athena agreed to finance exceptional undertakings that fell within the orbit of imperial business. In this way, for example, Athena paid the cost of the Samian War. It was not a loan to the state, and Athena eventually got back her money (in instalments), but the heading of the account began with the words "the Athenians spent" (Ἀθεναῖοι ἀνέλοσαν, I. G., I², 293), just as do the accounts in 418/7. Were these accounts in 418/7, perhaps, gifts and not loans? Such an arrangement would be financial nonsense, and we believe it incredible. The state could not repay a debt if it so depleted its reserves that the business of Empire could only be carried on by getting other money (or the same money) back from the creditor as a gift. Or if it could, it would be an exceedingly bad bargain for Athena.

Rather, the payments of I. G., I², 302 must count as loans to the state, and since the financial decree of 421 authorized Athens to pay off her indebtedness to the Goddess as well (supposedly) as to keep up the peace-time establishment of the Empire, Athens must have been using all her annual resources from the allies for these two purposes, and then finding that from time to time she needed money that had to be borrowed back. This is intelligible. The peace-time establishment in the years between 437 and 433 was financed from the annual income of 600 talents (Thucydides, II, 13, 3 [T117]) after 200 talents had been donated to Athena and 80 talents more, which belonged to her in any case, had been put into her treasury.[32] So the routine cost of Empire was about 320 talents a year. We assume that it was approximately the same after 421 B. C., when the income from the tribute may have yielded an actual 500 talents a year (on the Aristeidean scale, but including many

---

[30] In this year there may have been no such loan.

[31] I. G., I², 302, and 297, 298. Cf. Meritt, A. F. D., pp. 160-163 and 88-93.

[32] The indemnity from Samos, and other sacred money.

new cities, those in the Euxine among them) and other revenues probably amounted to 412 talents:[33] a total of 912 talents. Of this total figure *ca.* 105 talents belonged to the Goddess under any circumstances;[34] so the amount available for the dual purposes of the decree of 421 was *ca.* 807 talents (912 — 105 = 807). All these figures are approximations, but it cannot be far wrong to claim that with 320 to spend each year on routine there would be about 500 talents a year that could be used to fund the debt. This was the normal amount after the assessment of 422/1 had taken effect. But the tribute collection of 422/1 itself had been on the old scale, and we believe that a larger initial amount could have been paid at the Panathenaia of 421. The revenue from the Empire in 422/1 consisted of the tribute (φόρος), which we have estimated (above, p. 345) at *ca.* 938 talents, and of other funds, which we have found to be *ca.* 307 talents.[35] The actual imperial revenue in 422/1, therefore, was *ca.* 1245 talents. In consideration of the fact that many sums budgeted for the year in connection with possible campaigning in the spring were probably not spent, it seems to us likely that the current expenses for 421/0 could have been provided out of a hypothetical unexpended balance from the budget of 422/1 and, let us say, 245 talents from the current income of 422/1. In fine, the Athenians were in a position in 421 to make an initial payment against the sacred debt of 1000 talents. It is our belief that the same procedure was followed in 421 that had been followed in 449. The decree of 421 specified the repayment of the debt to the gods with an initial instalment (all that was available) of 1000 talents from the year's receipts of 1245 talents, this first payment to be made at the Panathenaia of 421, and then with succeeding annual instalments of 500 talents out of current income so long as might be necessary to expunge the debt.[36] It allocated the balance of annual imperial income to purposes of running the Empire. From this decree, his one source of information, we believe that Andokides derived not only his figure of 7000 talents for the debt but also his figure of " more than 1200 " talents for the annual income.[37]

As was the case between 449 and 433, the hellenotamiai had no balance in their chest at the end of any year, and the sacred funds had to be called upon for payments that the imperial balance could not manage in its budget. After 421 there was one vital difference: before 433 these payments by Athena had not been loans; after 421, when the state was trying to pay back its debt of the Archidamian War, these payments by Athena were loans, and each one of them served only to swell the total of the debt to be repaid and postpone the date of final liquidation. Without any new loans it would have taken twelve years to pay off 7000 talents under the plan adopted.

---

[33] See above, p. 345.

[34] See above, pp. 342-344 with the notes.

[35] 412 — 105 = 307.

[36] The first grant had been 5000 talents in 449 and 200 talents a year thereafter.

[37] It is a matter of small moment that he called the total income φόρος.

Obviously, when Andokides said that the Peace of Nikias enabled the Athenians to put 7000 talents on the Akropolis he was confusing intention with performance. Before the twelve years had passed Athens was bankrupt and had been compelled to devise a new plan for funding the debt (D9). Within the first eight years she had squandered all available money in the Sicilian expedition and in 412 she had had recourse to the iron reserve.[38]

There are two corollaries which follow from the establishment of the financial structure outlined above for the period after 421.

1. Every expense of the Empire beyond the budgeted routine will appear in the records of borrowing from the sacred treasure.

2. If the income in any year falls below the amount necessary to pay for both routine expense and the funding of the debt, part of the routine expense will have to be met by further borrowing and will therefore appear in the records of borrowing from the sacred treasure.

An example to illustrate this second corollary is the payment made on Prytany VIII, 2 in the year 415/4 to a general in Ephesos.[39] This general was apparently on patrol duty, attempting to hold the loyalty of a wavering state. He may possibly have been giving aid to the rebel Amorges, although this would have been in violation of the terms of the Peace of Kallias. But, in any case, the payment to him was small. His payment, that to the general in the Thermaic Gulf, and the two for the soldiers at Melos, amounted in all to only *ca.* 28 talents. We take it that the general in Thrace was also on patrol; the soldiers in Melos were obviously an occupying garrison, and, had the revenues of the Empire not already begun to diminish, these items, or surely the first two of them, would have come out of current income without recourse to borrowing.

The outstanding example of a non-routine expenditure, of course, is that for the Sicilian expedition. The figures are not preserved for 416/5, but this must have been the year of the heaviest outlay.[40] In 415/4 a further loan of 300 talents was carried

---

[38] In *I. G.*, I², 302, lines 66-68 (as quoted by Meritt, *A. F. D.*, p. 163), there is a payment made by the treasurers of the sacred moneys of Athena which is specifically called a loan: ἑλλενο-ταμίαις καὶ παρέδροις ἐδανείσα[μεν ......15......] Ἀριστοκράτει Εὐονυμεῖ καὶ χουνάρχοσι ΓΤΤΤ οὗτοι δὲ ἔδοσαν ἀθλοθέταις ἐς Παναθέναια Ἀμέμπτο[ι ....11.... καὶ] χουνάρχοσι ἐπὶ τὲς Ἐρεχθείδος δευτέρας πρυτανευόσες εἰκοστεῖ ἡεμέραι τὲς πρυτανείας. It might seem that by implication the other payments, introduced with παρέδομεν or παρέδοσαν, were not loans. This is not a correct inference, and yet there does seem to be a distinction in the use of the word ἐδανείσαμεν. We believe it to be this: that whereas all the other loans were of a type normally added to the state debt, the loan to the athlothetai for the Panathenaia was symptomatic of a new obligation. More and more Athens was charging her public obligations to the allies (see below, pp. 364-365).

[39] *I. G.*, I², 302 (cf. the text in Meritt, *A. F. D.*, p. 163, lines 77-79); cf. also Meritt, *Hesperia*, V (1936), p. 382.

[40] Thucydides (VI, 31, 5) says that if one counted up all the expense of the great armada that sailed in 415 and of the provision that went with it πολλὰ ἂν τάλαντα ηὑρέθη ἐκ τῆς πόλεως τὰ πάντα

to the army in Sicily;[41] then a loan of 120 talents was made in the winter of 414/3,[42] and a final (or near-final) grant of money was taken by Demosthenes early in 413.[43] The Athenians collected what money they could in Sicily, but from Athens itself borrowed money only was used to finance the expedition. If *I. G.*, I², 302 and 297 were entire, we should have the complete record of the Athenian expenditures.[44]

Other campaigns beyond the normal routine are described by Thucydides for the interval between summer of 418 and spring of 415, and they all have their counterparts in the financial records of borrowed money in *I. G.*, I², 302.[45] As noted above, there is no epigraphical control for the period from 422 to 418. Granted that Athena received 1000 talents in 421, and 500 each year thereafter down to 414 (seven payments), the technical repayment on her debt would have amounted to 4500 talents. On her own, Athena collected in the eight years in question *ca.* 840 talents,[46] and in 422 she presumably had left in her treasury *ca.* 444 talents. So the total available fund against which borrowings could be made down through the year 414/3 was *ca.* 5784 talents. Against this were borrowed at least 3420 talents for Sicily,[47] all the money that was used at Melos, and the other non-routine expenditures of the years

ἐξαγόμενα. The epigraphical record mentions 3000 talents (*I. G.*, I², 99, line 28: [τὸν ταλάντον τὸν τ]ρισχιλίον), and it is known that Egesta contributed 60 talents of unminted silver (Thucydides, VI, 8, 1).

[41] Thucydides, VI, 94, 4, confirmed by the epigraphical record in Meritt, *A. F. D.*, p. 163, lines 73-76. For the date of the payment see Meritt, *A. J. A.*, XXXIV (1930), p. 151.

[42] Thucydides, VII, 16, 2 (confirmed epigraphically in Meritt, *A. F. D.*, p. 88, lines 6-11).

[43] Cf. Meritt, *A. F. D.*, p. 89, lines 11-13, possibly also 13-15. The departure of Demosthenes is described in Thucydides, VII, 26, 1.

[44] Ferguson, *Treasurers*, p. 160, reached quite the contrary conclusion.

[45] Alkibiades visited Argos with twenty ships in the spring of 416 B. C. and removed Spartan sympathizers to exile on the islands. Thucydides next tells of the opening of the campaign against Melos (V, 84, 1), for which the first payment was made in the prytany of Aiantis (Meritt, *A. F. D.*, p. 161, lines 29-30). In this same prytany Athens and Argos entered into an alliance for fifty years (Meritt, *Hesperia*, XIV [1945], pp. 122-127), which they had already had in mind since the previous summer, but which was now consummated apparently on Alkibiades' return. This is the alliance which justified Argive participation in the Athenian venture to Sicily (Thucydides, VII, 57, 9: οὐ τῆς ξυμμαχίας ἕνεκα μᾶλλον ἢ τῆς Λακεδαιμονίων τε ἔχθρας καὶ τῆς παραυτίκα ἕκαστοι ἰδίας ὠφελίας). One of the terms of the alliance was that money from the tribute should be used to help the Argives in their war against Sparta (T75): χρέμασι δὲ hόπος ἂν ['Αργεῖοι χρõνται hικανοῖς ἐχσελ]ὲν ἐ[κ τ]õ φόρο μ[ὲ ἔλαττον ἒ .....¹² .....] τάλαντα ἐς τὸν πόλε[μον κατ' ἐνιαυτὸν hέκαστον ---]. In *Hesperia*, XIV (1945), p. 124 (cf. p. 126) Meritt restored the figure as τετταράκοντα. This seems rather high, and πέντε καὶ δέκα would be better, we believe, especially since this was obviously to be considered as a routine expense (ἐκ τõ φόρο) and not as anything significant enough to be borrowed from the treasurers of Athena. There is no trace of this payment in the borrowings for 417/6 (Meritt, *A. F. D.*, p. 161, lines 24-35), nor should one expect any reference in this or in succeeding years. The payment to Rhinon (*op. cit.*, lines 26-28) was evidently connected with the blockade of Makedonia (Thucydides, V, 83, 4).

[46] See above, pp. 342-344, 355, for the annual rate.

[47] 3000 + 300 + 120. But the amount was surely more, because the final payment to Demosthenes in 413 is not here included.

between 422/1 and 414/3. It is evident that in 414 the reserve fund in the treasury of Athena and in the treasury of the Other Gods must have been once more reduced to the low figure of 422. Again Athens needed money, and it was at this point in her history that the five per cent tax was instituted instead of the phoros. Thucydides gives the reason: " They thought that more revenue would thus come in to them. For their expenses were not the same as before but had increased proportionately with the increased scale of the war, while their revenues had dwindled." [48]

There is no evidence whether the hope for thus raising greater revenue was realized, even temporarily; but we do know that the crisis of 412 (precipitated by the revolt of Chios) seemed to justify the use of the iron reserve (Thucydides, VIII, 15, 1 [D25]), and that in 411 all financial resources were exhausted (Thucydides, VIII, 76, 6 [T151a]).[49]

---

[48] VII, 28, 4 (D24): πλείω νομίζοντες ἂν σφίσι χρήματα οὕτω προσιέναι. αἱ μὲν γὰρ δαπάναι οὐχ ὁμοίως καὶ πρίν, ἀλλὰ πολλῷ μείζους καθέστασαν, ὅσῳ καὶ μείζων ὁ πόλεμος ἦν· αἱ δὲ πρόσοδοι ἀπώλλυντο.

[49] Cf. Ferguson, *Treasurers*, p. 164.

CHAPTER XII

THE FINAL YEARS

The political revolution in 411 came in the midst of the financial crisis, and before the year was out the character and function of the board of hellenotamiai had been changed. Their number, down to 411, had always been ten. Except for the extraordinary years of organization in 443/2 and 442/1 when there was a supernumerary secretary (the same Satyros of Leukonoe for both years) this board of ten had the services of a single secretary. Between 439/8 and 430/29 he was chosen from the phylai in the reverse of their official order, but there is no other evidence of a secretary-cycle for the hellenotamiai.[1] In the constitution drafted by Theramenes and put into effect, in part at least, with the regime of the Five Thousand provision was made for a board of twenty hellenotamiai. The evidence for the innovation is in Aristotle's *Constitution of the Athenians*, where, among officers to be chosen from the Council by election, the treasurers and hellenotamiai appear as follows: " ten treasurers of the sacred moneys of Athena and the Other Gods, and twenty hellenotamiai, who shall steward the imperial revenues and all the other profane moneys." [2] In the expenses of state for 410/09 it is possible to demonstrate that there were, in fact, two hellenotamiai from each of the phylai Akamantis and Aiantis and hence, with two from each phyle, a total board of twenty,[3] and from the records of state expense for 407/6 and the audited accounts of 424/3 it is also possible to prove that the term of office of the hellenotamiai was the Panathenaic year, before as well as after the reform of 411.[4]

But the function of the board had changed. It continued to receive and keep the record of tribute from the allies. It continued to receive and dispense other money which came from overseas, for there is no reason to believe that items like the tithe (δεκάτη) of 434 were removed from the jurisdiction of the hellenotamiai either at this time or earlier.[5] Down to 411 there can be little question, we believe, that the hellenotamiai had had charge of the phoros in its larger sense of " revenue from the

---

[1] Meritt, *A. F. D.*, pp. 4-5; cf. *A. T. L.*, I, pp. 567-568, and II, p. 125.

[2] 30, 2 (T41): ταμίας τῶν ἱερῶν χρημάτων τῇ θε[ῷ] καὶ τοῖς ἄλλοις θεοῖς δέκα, καὶ ἑλληνοταμίας καὶ τῶν ἄλλων ὁσίων χρημάτων ἁπάντων εἴκοσιν οἳ διαχειριοῦσιν. See Ferguson, *Treasurers*, p. 3 with note 1.

[3] Meritt, *A. F. D.*, pp. 98-103.

[4] The reading in *I. G.*, I², 324, lines 26-28, is: hελλενοταμίαις hένοις Δ[. . . . . . .¹⁴. . . . . . | . .⁵. . . καὶ χσυνάρχοσιν καὶ νέοις] Χαροπίδει Σκα[μβ]ονίδει καὶ χσυνάρχοσιν [ἐπὶ τῆς hιπποθον|τίδος πρυτανείας πρότες πρυταν]ευόσες hέκτει καὶ εἰκοστῆι τῆς πρυτανεί[ας – – –]. Cf. *A. T. L.*, I, p. 569; Meritt, *Ath. Cal.*, p. 19. For 407/6 see the text of *I. G.*, I², 304B in Meritt, *A. F. D.*, pp. 119-122, and the commentary on the term of office of the hellenotamiai, *op. cit.*, pp. 98, 103, 126, 128.

[5] See above, pp. 326-327, 334.

allies," so far as this pertained to state income as distinct from sacred treasure, and as Andokides used the word in his oration *On the Peace* (III, 9 [T6]).[6] Now, by the conditions of the reform in 411, the hellenotamiai assumed responsibility for stewarding all the profane moneys of the state, while the treasurers of Athena and the treasurers of the Other Gods kept the sacred funds.[7] In this sharp distinction between the sacred and profane chests, the kolakretai, who from time immemorial had been the treasurers of the Athenian state, were eliminated.[8] Before the removal of the money of the Confederacy from Delos to Athens in 454 the division between the sacred and profane treasuries had been clear: the treasurers of the gods managed the sacred funds, and the moneys of the state (the δημόσια χρήματα) were disbursed on order by the kolakretai. They were a financial board that changed, during the fifth century, at least, with the changing prytanies of the Council, and their orders to make payment came from the Council or from the Council and Demos.[9]

The lexicographers define the kolakretai as having charge of jurors' pay,[10] but they refer also to payments of money " for the gods," and the scholiast on the *Birds* of Aristophanes, 1541 (T32a), is even more specific, for he not only gives these generalities but adds that they paid the expenses of the theoroi who went to Delphi.[11] The payment of 50 drachmai a year to the priestess of Athena Nike, attested in *I. G.*, I², 25 (424/3; cf. *S. E. G.*, X, 85), comes convincingly under the head of religious expenses (τὰ εἰς θεοὺς ἀναλώματα [or ἀναλισκόμενα]), but it does not make necessary the belief that the kolakretai used sacred money. Payment of the salary of the priestess by the kolakretai shows rather that secular money was used; the kolakretai, as ordered, drew on the funds which were available to them. In the absence

---

[6] See above, p. 353 with note 28.

[7] The proposal to amalgamate the two boards (Aristotle, ᾽Αθ. Πολ., 30, 2, quoted in note 2 above) was not implemented at this time; Ferguson, *Treasurers*, pp. 4-7.

[8] Stevenson, *J. H. S.*, XLIV (1924), p. 1 with note 2; Ferguson, *Treasurers*, pp. 3-4.

[9] The reading in Meritt, *Hesperia*, X (1941), p. 323, lines 26-28, is: καὶ δõναι Ποταμοδόροι πεντακοσίας δ[ραχμὰς τ]ὸς κολακρέτ[α]s τὸς ἐπὶ τẽς ᾽Ακαμαντίδος ἐν τ[ẽι αὐτẽι] ἐμέραι. Wilhelm's text of *I. G.*, I², 166, lines 1-3, has [τὸ] δὲ ἀργ[ύριον δõναι τὸς κ]ολακρέτα[s τὸς ἐπὶ τẽς Αἰ]γεῖδος (*Attische Urkunden*, IV, p. 62; cf. Meritt, *Hesperia*, X [1941], p. 332). The board is defined by the prytany with which it served; its responsibility to the Council in the first instance is clear in both decrees, and ultimately to the Demos in the decree which honours Potamodoros, because the Demos amended the instructions of the Council and gave new orders to the kolakretai (lines 41-44, in Meritt, *Hesperia*, X [1941], p. 323). Wilhelm (*op. cit.*, pp. 63-65) has a complete discussion of the term of tenure and concludes that these designations are not irreconcilable with the definition by month in *I. G.*, I², 25, lines 8-9, τὸς κωλακρ[έτας] οἳ ἂν κωλακρετῶσι τõ Θ[αργηλιõ]νος μηνός, as he (differing from Tod, *Greek Hist. Inscr.*, I², pp. 178-179, and others) interprets the text.

[10] Hesychios, *s. v.* κωλακρέται· ἀργυρικοὶ ταμίαι, οὓς τινες οἴονται μόνου τοῦ δικαστικοῦ προΐστασθαι. Suidas, *s. v.* κωλακρέται· οἱ ταμίαι τοῦ δικαστικοῦ μισθοῦ καὶ τῶν εἰς θεοὺς ἀναλωμάτων.

[11] The scholiast quotes Aristophanes the grammarian as saying that the kolakretai were ταμίαι τοῦ δικαστικοῦ μισθοῦ and adds that they also had charge of τὰ εἰς θεοὺς ἀναλισκόμενα. Androtion (frag. 4 Müller) says: τοῖς δὲ ἰοῦσι Πυθῶδε θεωροῖς τοὺς κωλακρέτας διδόναι ἐκ τῶν ναυκληρικῶν ἐφόδιον ἀργύρια, καὶ εἰς ἄλλο ὅ τι ἂν δέῃ ἀναλῶσαι.

of evidence to the contrary we believe that this was the public chest, or state treasury, commonly known as the demosion (τὸ δημόσιον) and specifically referred to in those words in the Papyrus Decree moved by Perikles in 449 (D13).[12] This was the chest into which the money of the Confederacy was put when it was brought to Athens in 454; so the " public " treasury, from 454 down to 411, had two boards that enjoyed the privilege of drawing upon it. Had it not been for the general supervision which the Council exercised over the expenditures of the state, this might have led to the confusion which Kahrstedt postulated for a later date, and which he thought intolerable, protesting that no fund can have two chiefs simultaneously.[13] The fact is that the existence of two paymasters from one fund can be demonstrated for the later date, and that here in the fifth century a combination thus known to have been possible seems to have developed when both the kolakretai and the hellenotamiai paid from the demosion. It helped save confusion that the Council was ultimately in control, and that the functions seldom, if ever, overlapped. The hellenotamiai were concerned with the affairs of the Confederacy, the kolakretai with the internal requirements and contingent expenses of the Athenian state. Some exceptions to the rule were doubtless permissible, since all receipts, whether destined ultimately for the kolakretai or the hellenotamiai as custodial boards, passed through the hands of the apodektai under the supervision of the Council, and it was always possible for the Council directly to authorize payment by the apodektai to any executive board. We believe, for example, that in 407/6 the apodektai were thus ordered to give money to the generals for immediate transfer to the naupegoi, though the normal routine would have been for the hellenotamiai to keep the record, making the transfer to the trieropoioi who in turn dealt with the contracting naupegoi.[14]

At times the kolakretai must have had considerable money. They paid for the statue of Athena Promachos,[15] which was dedicated after the Persian Wars,[16] and to defray the cost of which perhaps some of the booty from the Eurymedon was contributed.[17] And yet, as Stevenson observed,[18] there is no reason to think that they

[12] The source ἐκ δεμοσίο is restored by Meritt, in *Hesperia*, X (1941), p. 323, line 43, but cannot, of course, be counted here as evidence.

[13] Kahrstedt, *Untersuchungen*, p. 14: " Kein Etatsposten kann zwei konkurrierende Chefs haben." For the problem see Pritchett, *Hesperia*, X (1941), pp. 271-272.

[14] Cf. *I. G.*, I², 105 and the text and discussion by Meritt in *Capps Studies*, pp. 246-252. In the instance here under consideration the trieropoioi were to assume final responsibility (as was proper) and repay the temporary loan made to the generals.

[15] *I. G.*, I², 338; Meritt, *Hesperia*, V (1936), pp. 362-380; Raubitschek, *Hesperia*, XII (1943), pp. 12-17.

[16] Testimonia are collected by Jahn and Michaelis, *Arx*, pp. 76-78.

[17] This booty was very great (Plutarch, *Cimon*, 13, 5-7), and Pausanias says (X, 15, 4) that the Athenians dedicated from it at Delphi a bronze palm tree and on it a gold-plated statue of Athena.

[18] *J. H. S.*, XLIV (1924), p. 1; cf. above, p. 337 with note 49.

accumulated any reserve. But they must have handled the normal routine of receipts and expenses of the state, so far as these were not in the hands of the hellenotamiai: their duties were mainly domestic, those of the hellenotamiai imperial. Their income was probably even more diversified than the catalogue which Aristophanes gives in the *Wasps* (422 B. C.), exclusive of the tribute (his main item):

> " And then, in addition to this, compute the many taxes and one-per-cents,
> The fees and the fines, and the silver mines, the markets and harbours and
> sales and rents." [19]

Their expenditure was whatever the Council and Demos wished to make it. They disbursed the dikastic pay (δικαστικὸς μισθός, see above), sometimes the cost of erecting stelai (*e. g.*, A9, lines 25-26), the pay of heralds even for the purpose of proclaiming an assessment of tribute (A9, lines 50-51),[20] the pay of theoroi to Delphi (see above), the pay of certain hieropoioi (*I. G.*, I², 84, line 23), the cost of grants to distinguished visitors (*e. g.*, *I. G.*, I², 70 in Meritt, *Hesperia*, X [1941], p. 323, lines 27-30 and 41-44), the expense of the robe for the ancient statue (ἀρχαῖον ἕδος) of Athena (*I. G.*, I², 80, lines 7-9), and the cost of an offering to Bendis (*S. E. G.*, X, 64).

How the kolakretai contributed to the early campaign expenses of the Athenians is not clear. Even if the Spartans paid a large part of the expense of Kimon's expedition to Ithome, the effort will have cost Athens something, and it is difficult to see how she can have expected so early in the history of the Confederacy to transfer funds from Delos, stored there for use against the Persians, in order to pay for a punitive expedition against the Messenians in western Peloponnesos. Kypros and Egypt in 460 were obviously affairs of the Confederacy, as was the siege of Aigina, which capitulated in the spring of 457 and thenceforth paid tribute. Tolmides used the ships from Aigina for his renowned periplous of the Peloponnesos, and possibly thus diverted funds and effort that should have been reserved to the Confederates on an Athenian venture which was not theirs.[21] We are not informed of the source of the revenue used in the other western campaigns or in the land campaigns to the north, but one can justify the hypothetical use of money from the demosion controlled by the kolakretai before 454, whereas it is hard to make a case for the use of the funds of the hellenotamiai while they were still on Delos and when none of the new land

---

[19] 658-659 (T38a):

κἄξω τούτου τὰ τέλη χωρὶς καὶ τὰς πολλὰς ἑκατοστάς,
πρυτανεῖα, μέταλλ', ἀγοράς, λιμένας, μισθώσεις, δημιόπρατα.

The translation is Rogers'.

[20] The restoration is not beyond question.

[21] Wade-Gery, *Hesperia*, XIV (1945), p. 228, suggested that some of the money collected πρὸς τὸν βάρβαρον was no doubt spent against the Peloponnesos in the 'fifties. Tolmides has as good a claim as any other to this doubtful honour.

allies became members of the Confederacy. We conceive that some confusion in the funds, to the advantage of Athens, was easier after 454, and that after 449 Athens could use any part of the demosion for any purpose she pleased.

So the kolakretai, who had been an important board in Athens down to 454, lost some of their importance at that time when the demosion was swollen by the addition of the funds from Delos and the hellenotamiai became the dominant paymasters; they lost still more of their former prestige in 449, but continued to carry on as paymasters of the Council down to the reform of 411. At that date, under the constitution of the Five Thousand, the hellenotamiai absorbed and exercised all their functions that could not more appropriately be given to the treasurers of the sacred funds.

There is too little evidence to show how the management of state funds was controlled during the regime of the Four Hundred. The one payment of which there is epigraphical record was made late in Hekatombaion of 411 by the treasurers of the Goddess to the hellenotamiai from the funds of Athena Polias and Athena Nike.[22] The amount involved was between 27 and 28 talents, and can perhaps be explained satisfactorily as intended for use in combatting the threat offered by Euboia (Thucydides, VIII, 95). It is possible to believe that, fundamentally, the terms of the decree of 421 about repayment of the debt were still valid: the hellenotamiai were (at least in theory) making their deposits to the Goddess and the Goddess was lending them some of the money back for extraordinary expenditures and possible deficits in running expense. The payment of this money in 411 comes under the head of extraordinary expenditures.

When complete democracy was restored to Athens in 410,[23] there was again a financial as well as political reorganization. Tribute was assessed (A13), as of old, at the Panathenaia, instead of the five per cent tax which had been substituted in 414, and in the third prytany of the year 410/09 a decree was passed which again called for the payment to Athena of the moneys owed to her and for the accumulation on the Akropolis of a reserve fund. It was a gesture which followed the tradition of 421 and which was meant to achieve the glorious results of 449. But Athens was weak, and the debt was great. The whole scale of receipts and expenditures must have been more modest than it had been before the Sicilian expedition, and now at last the hellenotamiai were also charged with some (at least) of the duties of the old kolakretai. The reflection of these new, and straitened, circumstances is seen in the accounts of state borrowings for 410/09 (*I. G.*, I², 304A), the record of which has been preserved almost in its entirety.[24] All the loans for the year were made from

---

[22] *I. G.*, I², 298; cf. the text in Meritt, *A. F. D.*, p. 93.

[23] For the time see Meritt, *A. F. D.*, pp. 106-115.

[24] See the text in Meritt, *A. F. D.*, pp. 94-96.

current income, none from reserve, and it is logical to deduce from this a confirmation of our belief that no reserve had as yet been created.[25]

The items which the Athenians " spent " in 410/09 are obviously not all listed in the inscription. There is no reference to pay for the dikasts, for example, the continuance of which after 410 is proved by a reference in the *Frogs* of Aristophanes (lines 1463-1466) :

> AIS.   When they shall count the enemy's soil their own,
> And theirs the enemy's: when they know that ships
> Are their true wealth, their so-called wealth delusion.
> DI.   Aye, but the justices suck that down, you know.[26]

This is one fairly heavy expenditure which had been the charge of the kolakretai and which appears not to have been transferred to the hellenotamiai. The hellenotamiai, after 411, set up stelai [27] and apparently paid for crowns for distinguished persons,[28] but these had been only rather minor obligations of the kolakretai. The big obligation of the kolakretai had been the payment of the dikasts. When pay for all except military services to the Athenian state was abolished in 411 (Thucydides, VIII, 65, 3 and 67, 3) and when the Council of the Five Hundred was itself suspended, the kolakretai too were abolished. They had been paymasters of the prytanies which no longer existed in the old sense of that term,[29] and moreover they had under the Five Thousand no work to do. But the jurors' pay was again revived after the restoration of democracy—as presumably other non-military pay as well. The logical conclusion must be that the reconstituted tribal prytanies had their reconstituted paymasters, the kolakretai, again available to take care of it. We know of no evidence to the contrary, and this interpretation conforms admirably to the fact that the hellenotamiai, who continued to perform some of the former functions of the kolakretai, had nothing to do with jurors' pay.[30]

The distinctions between charges that could or could not be paid from imperial funds were not always clear in these last years of the Empire. Evidently the Athenians had persuaded themselves that the expense of the Panathenaia was properly

----

[25] See Ferguson, *Treasurers*, pp. 29-35; Meritt, *A. F. D.*, p. 63.

[26]   ΑΙΣ.   τὴν γῆν ὅταν νομίσωσι τὴν τῶν πολεμίων
          εἶναι σφετέραν, τὴν δὲ σφετέραν τῶν πολεμίων,
          πόρον δὲ τὰς ναῦς, ἀπορίαν δὲ τὸν πόρον.
     ΔΙ.   εὖ, πλήν γ' ὁ δικαστὴς αὐτὰ καταπίνει μόνος.

The translation is Rogers'. Cf. also the scholion on line 140: δυ' ὀβολὼ μισθὸν λαβών· οὐχ ὡς τοῦτο λαμβάνοντος, ἀλλὰ πρὸς τὸν δικαστικὸν μισθόν, ὅτι δύο ὀβολῶν ἦν.

[27] *E. g., I. G.*, I², 110, lines 34-36, and 115, lines 4-9; *I. G.*, II², 1 (lines 39-40).

[28] *I. G.*, I², 110, lines 10-12.

[29] See Meritt, *A. F. D.*, pp. 105-106.

[30] Ferguson, *Treasurers*, p. 136, note 1, writes: " It is indeed odd that we do not know by whom or from what fund the δικαστικὸς μισθός was paid after 411 B. C."

chargeable against the Empire. The treasurers of the Goddess loaned the money to the athlothetai in 415/4 and again in 410/09 and 406/5.[31] In 410/09 they also paid the hieropoioi for the sacrifice. The diobelia was evidently reckoned as an imperial expense; at any rate money for it was loaned to the hellenotamiai, though one might have expected logically that it should come from the kolakretai. But Kleophon, the author of the dole, apparently planned to have this largess come from the allies rather than from domestic revenue.[32] The other expenses named in *I. G.*, I², 304A are more easily explained as imperial business. The grain for the cavalry reminds one of the similar item in the record of state expenses for 432/1 (*I. G.*, I², 296, lines 27-28), while payments to the archon at Pylos and to the generals in Eretria and Samos perhaps need no further comment.

The payments at Eretria and Samos prove that all imperial revenue was credited to Athena. One has the choice of assuming (a) that the hellenotamiai made an annual grant to the Goddess from their income and then covered routine expenses from what was left,[33] or (b) that the hellenotamiai paid their current expenses and then gave to Athena their balance, or (c) that the hellenotamiai gave all their income to Athena and borrowed back what was needed to finance the Empire. In our judgment the borrowing of small amounts of petty cash, as documented for both 410/09 and 407/6 (*I. G.*, I², 304A and B), is incompatible with schemes (a) and (b). So also is the booking of a credit in the sixth prytany of 410/09 for the general Eukleides at Eretria.[34] In this transaction the hellenotamiai handled no money, only a voucher of credit (ἀνομολόγημα). It authorized Eukleides to use the odd sum of 3740 drachmai 1¼ obols, but Eukleides presumably was to find the actual money himself. The odd amount of the figure leads us to believe that Eukleides had already found and used the money and that the ἀνομολόγημα was nothing more than an *ex post facto* record of what the treasurers of Athena were writing down as a loan. Under scheme (c) this is an intelligible procedure. The general at Eretria had dutifully reported money collected in the field, which the treasurers of Athena were entitled to claim by virtue of the general provision of D9 that all imperial money should go to fund the debt, expenses made from such funds being made only as additional loans. The case is similar with the ἀνομολογήματα from Samos. On the 30th day of the sixth prytany a total of 57 talents 1000 drachmai was " credited " to the hellenotamias Anaitios and his paredros, and on the 36th day of the ninth prytany a variety of sums, totaling *ca.* 39 or 40 talents, were assigned to generals and trierarchs at Samos from sums " credited " at Samos by the allies. Money from the allies, which did not

---

[31] See above, note 38 on p. 356. Cf. also *I. G.*, I², 304A (lines 5-7) ; *I. G.*, I², 305 (line 8).

[32] For the diobelia see Ferguson, *Treasurers*, pp. 39 with note 1, 81, 83-84, and note 1 on p. 136.

[33] This was the practice before the Archidamian War and after the Peace of Nikias.

[34] Lines 16-18: ℎενδεκάτει τῆς πρυτανείας ℎελλενοταμίαις παρεδόθε Προχσένοι 'Αφιδναίοι καὶ συνάρχοσιν στρατεγοῖ ἐχς 'Ερετρίας ⋮ Εὐκλείδει ἀνομολόγεμα ⋮ XXXℾHHΔΔΔΔΙϹ.

come to Athens, was used in the field but nevertheless credited as loans from the Goddess. As Ferguson observed, the first such loans at Samos may have been used to help fit out the expedition of Thrasyllos to Ionia.[35] It cannot be argued that the money was not used by Thrasyllos because his name does not appear in the inscription, nor indeed does the absence of any mention of Alkibiades and his colleagues prove that the hellenotamiai failed to credit to Athena all the money they received.[36] Alkibiades was notorious for helping himself, and the unhappy fact, after 411, must have been that generals in the field more and more collected money and lived off the land, perhaps only casually or irregularly informing the treasurers of Athena that such items ought to be carried on their books as loans.

Some reserve was accumulated in 410/09. The record of *I. G.*, I², 301 proves that the treasurers of the sacred funds were lending money in 409/8, partly from their own annual revenue and partly from what they had received from their predecessors.[37] There were payments from this reserve even in 406/5 [38] but soon Athens had exhausted not only her silver, but her gold, and finally resorted even to a debased currency.[39] The dole at the end of the war was made in kind and not in currency,[40] and at the last, with her money gone, her allies disaffected, and her fleet lost at Aigospotamoi, the Empire of Athens came to an end.

[35] *Treasurers*, pp. 39-40.

[36] Cf. Ferguson, *loc. cit.*

[37] Incidentally, the appearance of the Thasian phoros in *I. G.*, I², 301 (if our interpretation is correct) proves that the inscription cannot be dated earlier than 410, when tribute was again assessed after the break between 414 and 410. We regard the date of the inscription in 409/8 as certain, in the light of Ferguson's demonstration, *Treasurers*, pp. 16-37, and reject the scepticism of Accame, *Riv. di Fil.*, LXIII (1935), p. 398. Cf. Meritt, *A. F. D.*, pp. 60-62.

[38] Cf. *I. G.*, I², 305, line 13.

[39] On the gold currency and the debased bronze see Head, *Hist. Num.²*, p. 373. The exhaustion of Athena's reserves, including even the melting down of dedications, is shown by the barren record of the last of the inventories of the Pronaos, *I. G.*, I², 255 (cf. Ferguson and Dinsmoor, *A. J. A.*, XXXVII [1933], pp. 52-57).

[40] *I. G.*, II², 1686. Cf. Meritt, *Hesperia*, XI (1942), pp. 275-278; Ferguson, *Treasurers*, pp. 77-84.